Dodge Dakota Pick-up Automotive Repair Manual

**by Brian Styve
and John H Haynes**
Member of the Guild of Motoring Writers

Models covered:
Dodge Dakota models
1987 through 1993

(8V2 – 1668)

ABCDE
FGHIJ
KLM

Haynes Publishing Group
Sparkford Nr Yeovil
Somerset BA22 7JJ England

Haynes North America, Inc
861 Lawrence Drive
Newbury Park
California 91320 USA

Acknowledgements

We are grateful to the Chrysler Corporation for assistance with technical information, certain illustrations and vehicle photos. The Champion Spark Plug Company supplied the illustrations of various spark plug conditions. Technical writers who contributed to this project include Larry Warren and Ken Freund.

© Haynes Publishing Group 1990, 1993

A book in the **Haynes Automotive Repair Manual Series**

Printed in the USA

ISBN 1 56392 079 4

Library of Congress Catalog Card Number 93-78148

Contents

1989 Dodge Dakota

About this manual

Its purpose

The purpose of this manual is to help you get the best value from your vehicle. It can do so in several ways. It can help you decide what work must be done, even if you choose to have it done by a dealer service department or a repair shop; it provides information and procedures for routine maintenance and servicing; and it offers diagnostic and repair procedures to follow when trouble occurs.

We hope you use the manual to tackle the work yourself. For many simpler jobs, doing it yourself may be quicker than arranging an appointment to get the vehicle into a shop and making the trips to leave it and pick it up. More importantly, a lot of money can be saved by avoiding the expense the shop must pass on to you to cover its labor and overhead costs. An added benefit is the sense of satisfaction and accomplishment that you feel after doing the job yourself.

Using the manual

The manual is divided into Chapters. Each Chapter is divided into numbered Sections, which are headed in bold type between horizontal lines. Each Section consists of consecutively numbered paragraphs.

At the beginning of each numbered section you will be referred to any illustrations which apply to the procedures in that section. The reference numbers used in illustration captions pinpoint the pertinent Section and the Step within that section. That is, illustration 3.2 means the illustration refers to Section 3 and Step (or paragraph) 2 within that Section.

Procedures, once described in the text, are not normally repeated. When it's necessary to refer to another Chapter, the reference will be given as Chapter and Section number. Cross references given without use of the word "Chapter" apply to Sections and/or paragraphs in the same Chapter. For example, "see Section 8" means in the same Chapter.

References to the left or right side of the vehicle assume you are sitting in the driver's seat, facing forward.

Even though we have prepared this manual with extreme care, neither the publisher nor the author can accept responsibility for any errors in, or omissions from, the information given.

NOTE

A **Note** provides information necessary to properly complete a procedure or information which will make the procedure easier to understand.

CAUTION

A **Caution** provides a special procedure or special steps which must be taken while completing the procedure where the **Caution** is found. Not heeding a **Caution** can result in damage to the assembly being worked on.

WARNING

A **Warning** provides a special procedure or special steps which must be taken while completing the procedure where the **Warning** is found. Not heeding a **Warning** can result in personal injury.

Introduction to the Dodge Dakota

Dodge Dakota models are available in short and long-bed pick-up body styles. All models are two-door and some have an extended cab. In 1989, a convertible option became available.

The inline four-cylinder, V6 and V8 engines used in these models are equipped with either a carburetor or fuel injection. The engine drives the rear wheels through either a five-speed manual or three or four-speed automatic transmission via a driveshaft and solid rear axle. A transfer case and driveshaft are used to drive the front driveaxles on 4WD models.

The suspension is independent at the front. On 2WD models, coil springs are used at the front. On 4WD models, torsion bars are used instead of coil springs. The solid rear axle is suspended by leaf springs on all models. Conventional shock absorbers are used at both the front and rear.

Steering on 2WD models is rack and pinion; the steering gear is mounted to the front crossmember, underneath the engine. On 4WD models, a recirculating ball steering box, mounted to the left of the engine, is connected to the steering arms through a series of rods. Power assist is optional on most models.

The brakes are disc at the front and drums at the rear, with power assist standard. Some models are equipped with a rear-wheel Antilock Braking System (ABS).

Vehicle identification numbers

Modifications are a continuing and unpublicized process in vehicle manufacturing. Since spare parts manuals and lists are compiled on a numerical basis, the individual vehicle numbers are essential to correctly identify the component required.

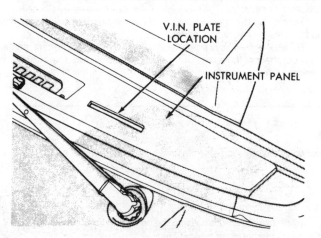

The Vehicle Identification Number (VIN) is visible through the driver's side of the windshield

Vehicle Identification Number (VIN)

This very important identification number is stamped on a plate attached to the left side of the dashboard just inside the windshield on the driver's side of the vehicle **(see illustration)**. The VIN also appears on the Vehicle Certificate of Title and Registration. It contains information such as where and when the vehicle was manufactured, the model year and the body style.

Equipment identification plate

This plate is located on the front of the inside of the hood **(see illustration)**. It contains information on the vehicle model, wheelbase, order number and all production or special equipment installed.

Body code plate

This metal plate is riveted to the floorpan on the passenger's side of the vehicle **(see illustration)**. It contains valuable information concerning the production of the vehicle as well as information about the way in which the vehicle is equipped. This plate is especially useful for matching the color and type of paint during repair work.

Safety Certification label

The Safety Certification label is affixed to the left front door pillar. The plate contains the name of the manufacturer, the month and year of production, the Gross Vehicle Weight Rating (GVWR) and the certification statement.

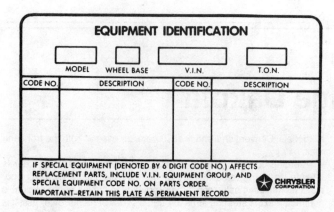

The equipment identification plate is located at the front of the inside of the hood

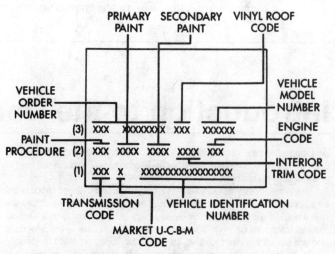

The body code plate is riveted to the floorpan on the passenger's side of the vehicle

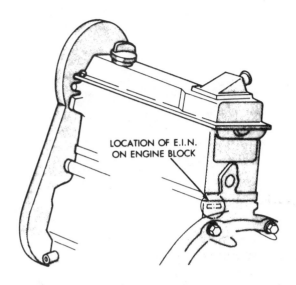

On 2.2 liter engines, the identification number is at the rear of the engine block

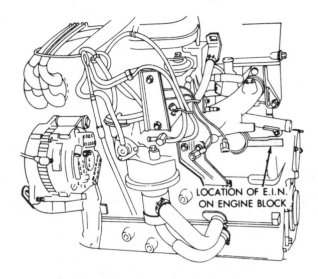

The engine identification number on 2.5 liter engines is on the left side of the block

Engine identification number

The engine ID number on the 2.2 liter engine is stamped into the rear of the block, just above the bellhousing **(see illustration)**. On the 2.5 liter engine, it's on the left side of the block **(see illustration)**. On the V6 and V8 engine, the number is on the front of the left cylinder bank, just below the cylinder head.

Engine serial number

In addition to the engine identification number, a serial number, which is required when buying replacement parts, is used on 2.2 and 2.5 liter engines. On 2.2 liter engines, the number is directly below the engine identification number. On 2.5 liter engines, the number is on the left rear side of the block, adjacent to the exhaust manifold stud.

Transmission identification number

The ID number on manual transmissions is located on a tag attached to the left side of the case **(see illustration)**. On automatic transmissions, the number is stamped into the transmission case.

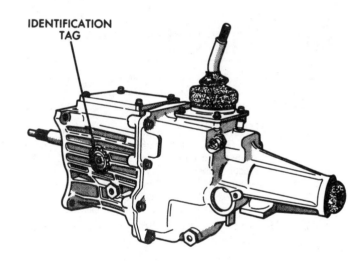

On manual transmissions, the identification number is on a tag attached to the left side of the case

Buying parts

Replacement parts are available from many sources, which generally fall into one of two categories – authorized dealer parts departments and independent retail auto parts stores. Our advice concerning these parts is as follows:

Retail auto parts stores: Good auto parts stores will stock frequently needed components which wear out relatively fast, such as clutch components, exhaust systems, brake parts, tune-up parts, etc. These stores often supply new or reconditioned parts on an exchange basis, which can save a considerable amount of money. Discount auto parts stores are often very good places to buy materials and parts needed for general vehicle maintenance such as oil, grease, filters, spark plugs, belts, touch-up paint, bulbs, etc. They also usually sell tools and general accessories, have convenient hours, charge lower prices and can often be found not far from home.

Authorized dealer parts department: This is the best source for parts which are unique to the vehicle and not generally available elsewhere (such as major engine parts, transmission parts, trim pieces, etc.).

Warranty information: If the vehicle is still covered under warranty, be sure that any replacement parts purchased – regardless of the source – do not invalidate the warranty!

To be sure of obtaining the correct parts, have engine and chassis numbers available and, if possible, take the old parts along for positive identification.

Maintenance techniques, tools and working facilities

Maintenance techniques

There are a number of techniques involved in maintenance and repair that will be referred to throughout this manual. Application of these techniques will enable the home mechanic to be more efficient, better organized and capable of performing the various tasks properly, which will ensure that the repair job is thorough and complete.

Fasteners

Fasteners are nuts, bolts, studs and screws used to hold two or more parts together. There are a few things to keep in mind when working with fasteners. Almost all of them use a locking device of some type, either a lockwasher, locknut, locking tab or thread adhesive. All threaded fasteners should be clean and straight, with undamaged threads and undamaged corners on the hex head where the wrench fits. Develop the habit of replacing all damaged nuts and bolts with new ones. Special locknuts with nylon or fiber inserts can only be used once. If they are removed, they lose their locking ability and must be replaced with new ones.

Rusted nuts and bolts should be treated with a penetrating fluid to ease removal and prevent breakage. Some mechanics use turpentine in a spout-type oil can, which works quite well. After applying the rust penetrant, let it work for a few minutes before trying to loosen the nut or bolt. Badly rusted fasteners may have to be chiseled or sawed off or removed with a special nut breaker, available at tool stores.

If a bolt or stud breaks off in an assembly, it can be drilled and removed with a special tool commonly available for this purpose. Most automotive machine shops can perform this task, as well as other repair procedures, such as the repair of threaded holes that have been stripped out.

Flat washers and lockwashers, when removed from an assembly, should always be replaced exactly as removed. Replace any damaged washers with new ones. Never use a lockwasher on any soft metal surface (such as aluminum), thin sheet metal or plastic.

Fastener sizes

For a number of reasons, automobile manufacturers are making wider and wider use of metric fasteners. Therefore, it is important to be able to tell the difference between standard (sometimes called U.S. or SAE) and metric hardware, since they cannot be interchanged.

All bolts, whether standard or metric, are sized according to diameter, thread pitch and length. For example, a standard 1/2 – 13 x 1 bolt is 1/2 inch in diameter, has 13 threads per inch and is 1 inch long. An M12 – 1.75 x 25 metric bolt is 12 mm in diameter, has a thread pitch of 1.75 mm (the distance between threads) and is 25 mm long. The two bolts are nearly identical, and easily confused, but they are not interchangeable.

In addition to the differences in diameter, thread pitch and length, metric and standard bolts can also be distinguished by examining the bolt heads. To begin with, the distance across the flats on a standard bolt head is measured in inches, while the same dimension on a metric bolt is sized in millimeters (the same is true for nuts). As a result, a standard wrench should not be used on a metric bolt and a metric wrench should not be used on a standard bolt. Also, most standard bolts have slashes radiating out from the center of the head to denote the grade or strength of the bolt, which is an indication of the amount of torque that can be applied to it. The greater the number of slashes, the greater the strength of the bolt. Grades 0 through 5 are commonly used on automobiles. Metric bolts have a property class (grade) number, rather than a slash, molded into their heads to indicate bolt strength. In this case, the higher the number, the stronger the bolt. Property class numbers 8.8, 9.8 and 10.9 are commonly used on automobiles.

Strength markings can also be used to distinguish standard hex nuts from metric hex nuts. Many standard nuts have dots stamped into one side, while metric nuts are marked with a number. The greater the number of dots, or the higher the number, the greater the strength of the nut.

Metric studs are also marked on their ends according to property class (grade). Larger studs are numbered (the same as metric bolts), while smaller studs carry a geometric code to denote grade.

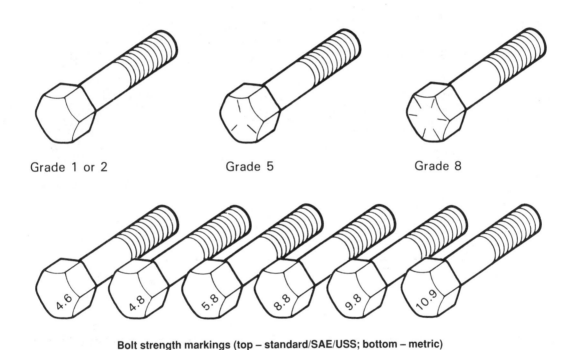

Grade 1 or 2   Grade 5   Grade 8

Bolt strength markings (top – standard/SAE/USS; bottom – metric)

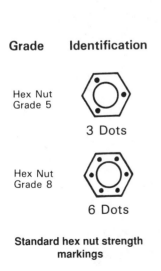

Standard hex nut strength markings

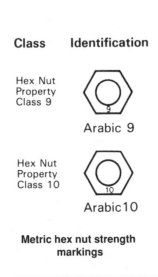

Metric hex nut strength markings

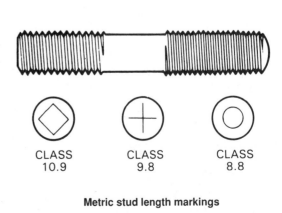

Metric stud length markings

It should be noted that many fasteners, especially Grades 0 through 2, have no distinguishing marks on them. When such is the case, the only way to determine whether it is standard or metric is to measure the thread pitch or compare it to a known fastener of the same size.

Standard fasteners are often referred to as SAE, as opposed to metric. However, it should be noted that SAE technically refers to a non-metric *fine thread* fastener only. Coarse thread non-metric fasteners are referred to as USS sizes.

Since fasteners of the same size (both standard and metric) may have different strength ratings, be sure to reinstall any bolts, studs or nuts removed from your vehicle in their original locations. Also, when replacing a fastener with a new one, make sure that the new one has a strength rating equal to or greater than the original.

Tightening sequences and procedures

Most threaded fasteners should be tightened to a specific torque value (torque is the twisting force applied to a threaded component such as a nut or bolt). Overtightening the fastener can weaken it and cause it to break, while undertightening can cause it to eventually come loose. Bolts, screws and studs, depending on the material they are made of and their thread diameters, have specific torque values, many of which are noted in the Specifications at the beginning of each Chapter. Be sure to follow the torque recommendations closely. For fasteners not assigned a specific torque, a general torque value chart is presented here as a guide. These torque values are for dry (unlubricated) fasteners threaded into steel or cast iron (not aluminum). As was previously mentioned, the size and grade of a fastener determine the amount of torque that can safely be

Metric thread sizes	Ft-lbs	Nm
M-6	6 to 9	9 to 12
M-8	14 to 21	19 to 28
M-10	28 to 40	38 to 54
M-12	50 to 71	68 to 96
M-14	80 to 140	109 to 154

Pipe thread sizes		
1/8	5 to 8	7 to 10
1/4	12 to 18	17 to 24
3/8	22 to 33	30 to 44
1/2	25 to 35	34 to 47

U.S. thread sizes		
1/4 – 20	6 to 9	9 to 12
5/16 – 18	12 to 18	17 to 24
5/16 – 24	14 to 20	19 to 27
3/8 – 16	22 to 32	30 to 43
3/8 – 24	27 to 38	37 to 51
7/16 – 14	40 to 55	55 to 74
7/16 – 20	40 to 60	55 to 81
1/2 – 13	55 to 80	75 to 108

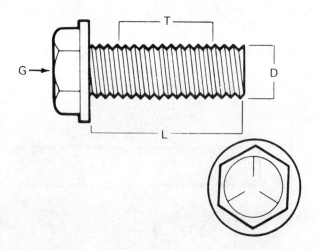

Standard (SAE and USS) bolt dimensions/grade marks

G   Grade marks (bolt length)
L   Length (in inches)
T   Thread pitch (number of threads per inch)
D   Nominal diameter (in inches)

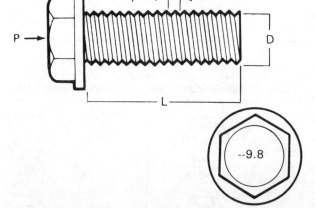

Metric bolt dimensions/grade marks

P   Property class (bolt strength)
L   Length (in millimeters)
T   Thread pitch (distance between threads in millimeters)
D   Diameter

applied to it. The figures listed here are approximate for Grade 2 and Grade 3 fasteners. Higher grades can tolerate higher torque values.

Fasteners laid out in a pattern, such as cylinder head bolts, oil pan bolts, differential cover bolts, etc., must be loosened or tightened in sequence to avoid warping the component. This sequence will normally be shown in the appropriate Chapter. If a specific pattern is not given, the following procedures can be used to prevent warping.

Initially, the bolts or nuts should be assembled finger-tight only. Next, they should be tightened one full turn each, in a criss-cross or diagonal pattern. After each one has been tightened one full turn, return to the first one and tighten them all one-half turn, following the same pattern. Finally, tighten each of them one-quarter turn at a time until each fastener has been tightened to the proper torque. To loosen and remove the fasteners, the procedure would be reversed.

Component disassembly

Component disassembly should be done with care and purpose to help ensure that the parts go back together properly. Always keep track of the sequence in which parts are removed. Make note of special characteristics or marks on parts that can be installed more than one way, such as a grooved thrust washer on a shaft. It is a good idea to lay the disassembled parts out on a clean surface in the order that they were removed. It may also be helpful to make sketches or take instant photos of components before removal.

When removing fasteners from a component, keep track of their locations. Sometimes threading a bolt back in a part, or putting the washers and nut back on a stud, can prevent mix-ups later. If nuts and bolts cannot be returned to their original locations, they should be kept in a compartmented box or a series of small boxes. A cupcake or muffin tin is ideal for this purpose, since each cavity can hold the bolts and nuts from a particular area (i.e. oil pan bolts, valve cover bolts, engine mount bolts, etc.). A pan of this type is especially helpful when working on assemblies with very small parts, such as the carburetor, alternator, valve train or interior dash and trim pieces. The cavities can be marked with paint or tape to identify the contents.

Whenever wiring looms, harnesses or connectors are separated, it is a good idea to identify the two halves with numbered pieces of masking tape so they can be easily reconnected.

Gasket sealing surfaces

Throughout any vehicle, gaskets are used to seal the mating surfaces between two parts and keep lubricants, fluids, vacuum or pressure contained in an assembly.

Many times these gaskets are coated with a liquid or paste-type gasket sealing compound before assembly. Age, heat and pressure can sometimes cause the two parts to stick together so tightly that they are very difficult to separate. Often, the assembly can be loosened by striking it with a soft-face hammer near the mating surfaces. A regular hammer can be used if a block of wood is placed between the hammer and the part. Do not hammer on cast parts or parts that could be easily damaged. With any particularly stubborn part, always recheck to make sure that every fastener has been removed.

Avoid using a screwdriver or bar to pry apart an assembly, as they can easily mar the gasket sealing surfaces of the parts, which must remain smooth. If prying is absolutely necessary, use an old broom handle, but keep in mind that extra clean up will be necessary if the wood splinters.

After the parts are separated, the old gasket must be carefully scraped off and the gasket surfaces cleaned. Stubborn gasket material can be soaked with rust penetrant or treated with a special chemical to soften it so it can be easily scraped off. A scraper can be fashioned from a piece of copper tubing by flattening and sharpening one end. Copper is recommended because it is usually softer than the surfaces to be scraped, which reduces the chance of gouging the part. Some gaskets can be removed with a wire brush, but regardless of the method used, the mating surfaces must be left clean and smooth. If for some reason the gasket surface is gouged, then a gasket sealer thick enough to fill scratches will have to be used during reassembly of the components. For most applications, a non-drying (or semi-drying) gasket sealer should be used.

Hose removal tips

Warning: *If the vehicle is equipped with air conditioning, do not disconnect any of the A/C hoses without first having the system depressurized by a dealer service department or a service station.*

Hose removal precautions closely parallel gasket removal precautions. Avoid scratching or gouging the surface that the hose mates against or the connection may leak. This is especially true for radiator hoses. Because of various chemical reactions, the rubber in hoses can bond itself to the metal spigot that the hose fits over. To remove a hose, first loosen the hose clamps that secure it to the spigot. Then, with slip-joint pliers, grab the hose at the clamp and rotate it around the spigot. Work it back and forth until it is completely free, then pull it off. Silicone or other lubricants will ease removal if they can be applied between the hose and the outside of the spigot. Apply the same lubricant to the inside of the hose and the outside of the spigot to simplify installation.

As a last resort (and if the hose is to be replaced with a new one anyway), the rubber can be slit with a knife and the hose peeled from the spigot. If this must be done, be careful that the metal connection is not damaged.

If a hose clamp is broken or damaged, do not reuse it. Wire-type clamps usually weaken with age, so it is a good idea to replace them with screw-type clamps whenever a hose is removed.

Tools

A selection of good tools is a basic requirement for anyone who plans to maintain and repair his or her own vehicle. For the owner who has few tools, the initial investment might seem high, but when compared to the spiraling costs of professional auto maintenance and repair, it is a wise one.

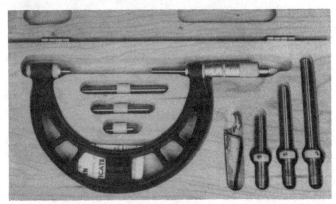

Micrometer set

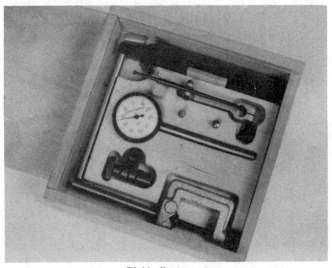

Dial indicator set

Dial caliper

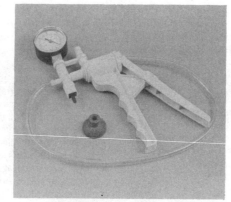

Hand-operated vacuum pump

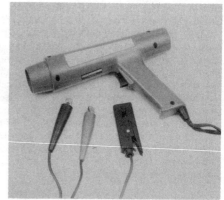

Timing light

Compression gauge with spark plug hole adapter

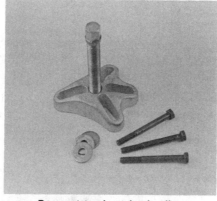

Damper/steering wheel puller

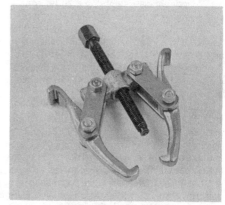

General purpose puller

Hydraulic lifter removal tool

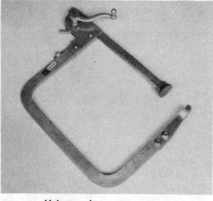

Valve spring compressor

Valve spring compressor

Ridge reamer

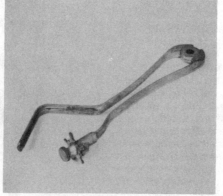

Piston ring groove cleaning tool

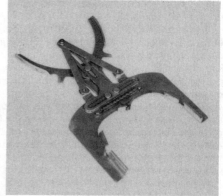

Ring removal/installation tool

Ring compressor

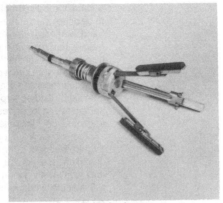

Cylinder hone

Brake hold-down spring tool

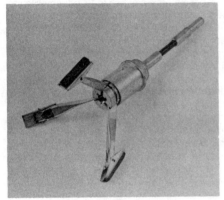

Brake cylinder hone

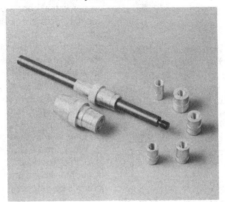

Clutch plate alignment tool

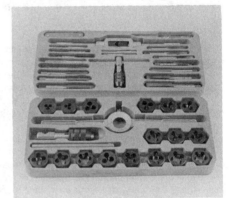

Tap and die set

To help the owner decide which tools are needed to perform the tasks detailed in this manual, the following tool lists are offered: *Maintenance and minor repair, Repair/overhaul* and *Special.*

The newcomer to practical mechanics should start off with the maintenance and minor repair tool kit, which is adequate for the simpler jobs performed on a vehicle. Then, as confidence and experience grow, the owner can tackle more difficult tasks, buying additional tools as they are needed. Eventually the basic kit will be expanded into the repair and overhaul tool set. Over a period of time, the experienced do-it-yourselfer will assemble a tool set complete enough for most repair and overhaul procedures and will add tools from the special category when it is felt that the expense is justified by the frequency of use.

Maintenance and minor repair tool kit

The tools in this list should be considered the minimum required for performance of routine maintenance, servicing and minor repair work. We recommend the purchase of combination wrenches (box-end and open-end combined in one wrench). While more expensive than open end wrenches, they offer the advantages of both types of wrench.

Combination wrench set (1/4-inch to 1 inch or 6 mm to 19 mm)
Adjustable wrench, 8 inch
Spark plug wrench with rubber insert
Spark plug gap adjusting tool
Feeler gauge set
Brake bleeder wrench
Standard screwdriver (5/16-inch x 6 inch)
Phillips screwdriver (No. 2 x 6 inch)
Combination pliers – 6 inch
Hacksaw and assortment of blades
Tire pressure gauge
Grease gun
Oil can
Fine emery cloth
Wire brush

Battery post and cable cleaning tool
Oil filter wrench
Funnel (medium size)
Safety goggles
Jackstands(2)
Drain pan

Note: *If basic tune-ups are going to be part of routine maintenance, it will be necessary to purchase a good quality stroboscopic timing light and combination tachometer/dwell meter. Although they are included in the list of special tools, it is mentioned here because they are absolutely necessary for tuning most vehicles properly.*

Repair and overhaul tool set

These tools are essential for anyone who plans to perform major repairs and are in addition to those in the maintenance and minor repair tool kit. Included is a comprehensive set of sockets which, though expensive, are invaluable because of their versatility, especially when various extensions and drives are available. We recommend the 1/2-inch drive over the 3/8-inch drive. Although the larger drive is bulky and more expensive, it has the capacity of accepting a very wide range of large sockets. Ideally, however, the mechanic should have a 3/8-inch drive set and a 1/2-inch drive set.

Socket set(s)
Reversible ratchet
Extension – 10 inch
Universal joint
Torque wrench (same size drive as sockets)
Ball peen hammer – 8 ounce
Soft-face hammer (plastic/rubber)
Standard screwdriver (1/4-inch x 6 inch)
Standard screwdriver (stubby – 5/16-inch)
Phillips screwdriver (No. 3 x 8 inch)
Phillips screwdriver (stubby – No. 2)

Pliers – vise grip
Pliers – lineman's
Pliers – needle nose
Pliers – snap-ring (internal and external)
Cold chisel – 1/2-inch
Scribe
Scraper (made from flattened copper tubing)
Centerpunch
Pin punches (1/16, 1/8, 3/16-inch)
Steel rule/straightedge – 12 inch
Allen wrench set (1/8 to 3/8-inch or 4 mm to 10 mm)
A selection of files
Wire brush (large)
Jackstands (second set)
Jack (scissor or hydraulic type)

Note: *Another tool which is often useful is an electric drill with a chuck capacity of 3/8-inch and a set of good quality drill bits.*

Special tools

The tools in this list include those which are not used regularly, are expensive to buy, or which need to be used in accordance with their manufacturer's instructions. Unless these tools will be used frequently, it is not very economical to purchase many of them. A consideration would be to split the cost and use between yourself and a friend or friends. In addition, most of these tools can be obtained from a tool rental shop on a temporary basis.

This list primarily contains only those tools and instruments widely available to the public, and not those special tools produced by the vehicle manufacturer for distribution to dealer service departments. Occasionally, references to the manufacturer's special tools are included in the text of this manual. Generally, an alternative method of doing the job without the special tool is offered. However, sometimes there is no alternative to their use. Where this is the case, and the tool cannot be purchased or borrowed, the work should be turned over to the dealer service department or an automotive repair shop.

Valve spring compressor
Piston ring groove cleaning tool
Piston ring compressor
Piston ring installation tool
Cylinder compression gauge
Cylinder ridge reamer
Cylinder surfacing hone
Cylinder bore gauge
Micrometers and/or dial calipers
Hydraulic lifter removal tool
Balljoint separator
Universal-type puller
Impact screwdriver
Dial indicator set
Stroboscopic timing light (inductive pick-up)
Hand operated vacuum/pressure pump
Tachometer/dwell meter
Universal electrical multimeter
Cable hoist
Brake spring removal and installation tools
Floor jack

Buying tools

For the do-it-yourselfer who is just starting to get involved in vehicle maintenance and repair, there are a number of options available when purchasing tools. If maintenance and minor repair is the extent of the work to be done, the purchase of individual tools is satisfactory. If, on the other hand, extensive work is planned, it would be a good idea to purchase a modest tool set from one of the large retail chain stores. A set can usually be bought at a substantial savings over the individual tool prices, and they often come with a tool box. As additional tools are needed, add–on sets, individual tools and a larger tool box can be purchased to expand the tool selection. Building a tool set gradually allows the cost of the tools to be spread over a longer period of time and gives the mechanic the freedom to choose only those tools that will actually be used.

Tool stores will often be the only source of some of the special tools that are needed, but regardless of where tools are bought, try to avoid cheap ones, especially when buying screwdrivers and sockets, because they won't last very long. The expense involved in replacing cheap tools will eventually be greater than the initial cost of quality tools.

Care and maintenance of tools

Good tools are expensive, so it makes sense to treat them with respect. Keep them clean and in usable condition and store them properly when not in use. Always wipe off any dirt, grease or metal chips before putting them away. Never leave tools lying around in the work area. Upon completion of a job, always check closely under the hood for tools that may have been left there so they won't get lost during a test drive.

Some tools, such as screwdrivers, pliers, wrenches and sockets, can be hung on a panel mounted on the garage or workshop wall, while others should be kept in a tool box or tray. Measuring instruments, gauges, meters, etc. must be carefully stored where they cannot be damaged by weather or impact from other tools.

When tools are used with care and stored properly, they will last a very long time. Even with the best of care, though, tools will wear out if used frequently. When a tool is damaged or worn out, replace it. Subsequent jobs will be safer and more enjoyable if you do.

Working facilities

Not to be overlooked when discussing tools is the workshop. If anything more than routine maintenance is to be carried out, some sort of suitable work area is essential.

It is understood, and appreciated, that many home mechanics do not have a good workshop or garage available, and end up removing an engine or doing major repairs outside. It is recommended, however, that the overhaul or repair be completed under the cover of a roof.

A clean, flat workbench or table of comfortable working height is an absolute necessity. The workbench should be equipped with a vise that has a jaw opening of at least four inches.

As mentioned previously, some clean, dry storage space is also required for tools, as well as the lubricants, fluids, cleaning solvents, etc. which soon become necessary.

Sometimes waste oil and fluids, drained from the engine or cooling system during normal maintenance or repairs, present a disposal problem. To avoid pouring them on the ground or into a sewage system, pour the used fluids into large containers, seal them with caps and take them to an authorized disposal site or recycling center. Plastic jugs, such as old antifreeze containers, are ideal for this purpose.

Always keep a supply of old newspapers and clean rags available. Old towels are excellent for mopping up spills. Many mechanics use rolls of paper towels for most work because they are readily available and disposable. To help keep the area under the vehicle clean, a large cardboard box can be cut open and flattened to protect the garage or shop floor.

Whenever working over a painted surface, such as when leaning over a fender to service something under the hood, always cover it with an old blanket or bedspread to protect the finish. Vinyl covered pads, made especially for this purpose, are available at auto parts stores.

Booster battery (jump) starting

Observe these precautions when using a booster battery to start a vehicle:

a) Before connecting the booster battery, make sure the ignition switch is in the Off position.
b) Turn off the lights, heater and other electrical loads.
c) Your eyes should be shielded. Safety goggles are a good idea.
d) Make sure the booster battery is the same voltage as the dead one in the vehicle.
e) The two vehicles MUST NOT TOUCH each other!
f) Make sure the transmission is in Neutral (manual) or Park (automatic).
g) If the booster battery is not a maintenance-free type, remove the vent caps and lay a cloth over the vent holes.

Connect the red jumper cable to the positive (+) terminals of each battery.

Connect one end of the black jumper cable to the negative (–) terminal of the booster battery. The other end of this cable should be connected to a good ground on the vehicle to be started, such as a bolt or bracket on the engine block **(see illustration)**. Make sure the cable will not come into contact with the fan, drivebelts or other moving parts of the engine.

Start the engine using the booster battery, then, with the engine running at idle speed, disconnect the jumper cables in the reverse order of connection.

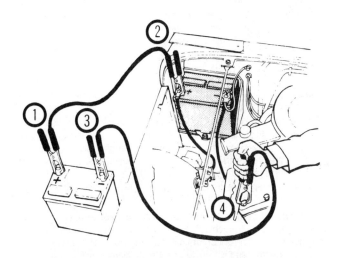

Make the booster battery cable connections in the numerical order shown (note that the negative cable of the booster battery is NOT attached to the negative terminal of the dead battery)

Automotive chemicals and lubricants

A number of automotive chemicals and lubricants are available for use during vehicle maintenance and repair. They include a wide variety of products ranging from cleaning solvents and degreasers to lubricants and protective sprays for rubber, plastic and vinyl.

Cleaners

Carburetor cleaner and choke cleaner is a strong solvent for gum, varnish and carbon. Most carburetor cleaners leave a dry-type lubricant film which will not harden or gum up. Because of this film it is not recommended for use on electrical components.

Brake system cleaner is used to remove grease and brake fluid from the brake system, where clean surfaces are absolutely necessary. It leaves no residue and often eliminates brake squeal caused by contaminants.

Electrical cleaner removes oxidation, corrosion and carbon deposits from electrical contacts, restoring full current flow. It can also be used to clean spark plugs, carburetor jets, voltage regulators and other parts where an oil-free surface is desired.

Demoisturants remove water and moisture from electrical components such as alternators, voltage regulators, electrical connectors and fuse blocks. They are non-conductive, non-corrosive and non-flammable.

Degreasers are heavy-duty solvents used to remove grease from the outside of the engine and from chassis components. They can be sprayed or brushed on and, depending on the type, are rinsed off either with water or solvent.

Lubricants

Motor oil is the lubricant formulated for use in engines. It normally contains a wide variety of additives to prevent corrosion and reduce foaming and wear. Motor oil comes in various weights (viscosity ratings) from 5 to 80. The recommended weight of the oil depends on the season, temperature and the demands on the engine. Light oil is used in cold climates and under light load conditions. Heavy oil is used in hot climates and where high loads are encountered. Multi-viscosity oils are designed to have characteristics of both light and heavy oils and are available in a number of weights from 5W-20 to 20W-50.

Gear oil is designed to be used in differentials, manual transmissions and other areas where high-temperature lubrication is required.

Chassis and wheel bearing grease is a heavy grease used where increased loads and friction are encountered, such as for wheel bearings, balljoints, tie-rod ends and universal joints.

High-temperature wheel bearing grease is designed to withstand the extreme temperatures encountered by wheel bearings in disc brake equipped vehicles. It usually contains molybdenum disulfide (moly), which is a dry-type lubricant.

White grease is a heavy grease for metal-to-metal applications where water is a problem. White grease stays soft under both low and high temperatures (usually from −100 to +190-degrees F), and will not wash off or dilute in the presence of water.

Assembly lube is a special extreme pressure lubricant, usually containing moly, used to lubricate high-load parts (such as main and rod bearings and cam lobes) for initial start-up of a new engine. The assembly lube lubricates the parts without being squeezed out or washed away until the engine oiling system begins to function.

Silicone lubricants are used to protect rubber, plastic, vinyl and nylon parts.

Graphite lubricants are used where oils cannot be used due to contamination problems, such as in locks. The dry graphite will lubricate metal parts while remaining uncontaminated by dirt, water, oil or acids. It is electrically conductive and will not foul electrical contacts in locks such as the ignition switch.

Moly penetrants loosen and lubricate frozen, rusted and corroded fasteners and prevent future rusting or freezing.

Heat-sink grease is a special electrically non-conductive grease that is used for mounting electronic ignition modules where it is essential that heat is transferred away from the module.

Sealants

RTV sealant is one of the most widely used gasket compounds. Made from silicone, RTV is air curing, it seals, bonds, waterproofs, fills surface irregularities, remains flexible, doesn't shrink, is relatively easy to remove, and is used as a supplementary sealer with almost all low and medium temperature gaskets.

Anaerobic sealant is much like RTV in that it can be used either to seal gaskets or to form gaskets by itself. It remains flexible, is solvent resistant and fills surface imperfections. The difference between an anaerobic sealant and an RTV-type sealant is in the curing. RTV cures when exposed to air, while an anaerobic sealant cures only in the absence of air. This means that an anaerobic sealant cures only after the assembly of parts, sealing them together.

Thread and pipe sealant is used for sealing hydraulic and pneumatic fittings and vacuum lines. It is usually made from a teflon compound, and comes in a spray, a paint-on liquid and as a wrap-around tape.

Chemicals

Anti-seize compound prevents seizing, galling, cold welding, rust and corrosion in fasteners. High-temperature anti-seize, usually made with copper and graphite lubricants, is used for exhaust system and exhaust manifold bolts.

Anaerobic locking compounds are used to keep fasteners from vibrating or working loose and cure only after installation, in the absence of air. Medium strength locking compound is used for small nuts, bolts and screws that may be removed later. High-strength locking compound is for large nuts, bolts and studs which aren't removed on a regular basis.

Oil additives range from viscosity index improvers to chemical treatments that claim to reduce internal engine friction. It should be noted that most oil manufacturers caution against using additives with their oils.

Gas additives perform several functions, depending on their chemical makeup. They usually contain solvents that help dissolve gum and varnish that build up on carburetor, fuel injection and intake parts. They also serve to break down carbon deposits that form on the inside surfaces of the combustion chambers. Some additives contain upper cylinder lubricants for valves and piston rings, and others contain chemicals to remove condensation from the gas tank.

Miscellaneous

Brake fluid is specially formulated hydraulic fluid that can withstand the heat and pressure encountered in brake systems. Care must be taken so this fluid does not come in contact with painted surfaces or plastics. An opened container should always be resealed to prevent contamination by water or dirt.

Weatherstrip adhesive is used to bond weatherstripping around doors, windows and trunk lids. It is sometimes used to attach trim pieces.

Undercoating is a petroleum-based, tar-like substance that is designed to protect metal surfaces on the underside of the vehicle from corrosion. It also acts as a sound-deadening agent by insulating the bottom of the vehicle.

Waxes and polishes are used to help protect painted and plated surfaces from the weather. Different types of paint may require the use of different types of wax and polish. Some polishes utilize a chemical or abrasive cleaner to help remove the top layer of oxidized (dull) paint on older vehicles. In recent years many non-wax polishes that contain a wide variety of chemicals such as polymers and silicones have been introduced. These non-wax polishes are usually easier to apply and last longer than conventional waxes and polishes.

Safety first!

Regardless of how enthusiastic you may be about getting on with the job at hand, take the time to ensure that your safety is not jeopardized. A moment's lack of attention can result in an accident, as can failure to observe certain simple safety precautions. The possibility of an accident will always exist, and the following points should not be considered a comprehensive list of all dangers. Rather, they are intended to make you aware of the risks and to encourage a safety conscious approach to all work you carry out on your vehicle.

Essential DOs and DON'Ts

DON'T rely on a jack when working under the vehicle. Always use approved jackstands to support the weight of the vehicle and place them under the recommended lift or support points.

DON'T attempt to loosen extremely tight fasteners (i.e. wheel lug nuts) while the vehicle is on a jack – it may fall.

DON'T start the engine without first making sure that the transmission is in Neutral (or Park where applicable) and the parking brake is set.

DON'T remove the radiator cap from a hot cooling system – let it cool or cover it with a cloth and release the pressure gradually.

DON'T attempt to drain the engine oil until you are sure it has cooled to the point that it will not burn you.

DON'T touch any part of the engine or exhaust system until it has cooled sufficiently to avoid burns.

DON'T siphon toxic liquids such as gasoline, antifreeze and brake fluid by mouth, or allow them to remain on your skin.

DON'T inhale brake lining dust – it is potentially hazardous (see Asbestos below)

DON'T allow spilled oil or grease to remain on the floor – wipe it up before someone slips on it.

DON'T use loose fitting wrenches or other tools which may slip and cause injury.

DON'T push on wrenches when loosening or tightening nuts or bolts. Always try to pull the wrench toward you. If the situation calls for pushing the wrench away, push with an open hand to avoid scraped knuckles if the wrench should slip.

DON'T attempt to lift a heavy component alone – get someone to help you.

DON'T rush or take unsafe shortcuts to finish a job.

DON'T allow children or animals in or around the vehicle while you are working on it.

DO wear eye protection when using power tools such as a drill, sander, bench grinder, etc. and when working under a vehicle.

DO keep loose clothing and long hair well out of the way of moving parts.

DO make sure that any hoist used has a safe working load rating adequate for the job.

DO get someone to check on you periodically when working alone on a vehicle.

DO carry out work in a logical sequence and make sure that everything is correctly assembled and tightened.

DO keep chemicals and fluids tightly capped and out of the reach of children and pets.

DO remember that your vehicle's safety affects that of yourself and others. If in doubt on any point, get professional advice.

Asbestos

Certain friction, insulating, sealing, and other products – such as brake linings, brake bands, clutch linings, torque converters, gaskets, etc. – contain asbestos. *Extreme care must be taken to avoid inhalation of dust from such products since it is hazardous to health.* If in doubt, assume that they *do* contain asbestos.

Fire

Remember at all times that gasoline is highly flammable. Never smoke or have any kind of open flame around when working on a vehicle. But the risk does not end there. A spark caused by an electrical short circuit, by two metal surfaces contacting each other, or even by static electricity built up in your body under certain conditions, can ignite gasoline vapors, which in a confined space are highly explosive. Do not, under any circumstances, use gasoline for cleaning parts. Use an approved safety solvent.

Always disconnect the battery ground (–) cable *at the battery* before working on any part of the fuel system or electrical system. Never risk spilling fuel on a hot engine or exhaust component.

It is strongly recommended that a fire extinguisher suitable for use on fuel and electrical fires be kept handy in the garage or workshop at all times. Never try to extinguish a fuel or electrical fire with water.

Fumes

Certain fumes are highly toxic and can quickly cause unconsciousness and even death if inhaled to any extent. Gasoline vapor falls into this category, as do the vapors from some cleaning solvents. Any draining or pouring of such volatile fluids should be done in a well ventilated area.

When using cleaning fluids and solvents, read the instructions on the container carefully. Never use materials from unmarked containers.

Never run the engine in an enclosed space, such as a garage. Exhaust fumes contain carbon monoxide, which is extremely poisonous. If you need to run the engine, always do so in the open air, or at least have the rear of the vehicle outside the work area.

If you are fortunate enough to have the use of an inspection pit, never drain or pour gasoline and never run the engine while the vehicle is over the pit. The fumes, being heavier than air, will concentrate in the pit with possibly lethal results.

The battery

Never create a spark or allow a bare light bulb near a battery. They normally give off a certain amount of hydrogen gas, which is highly explosive.

Always disconnect the battery ground (–) cable *at the battery* before working on the fuel or electrical systems.

If possible, loosen the filler caps or cover when charging the battery from an external source (this does not apply to sealed or maintenancefree batteries). Do not charge at an excessive rate or the battery may burst.

Take care when adding water to a non maintenance–free battery and when carrying a battery. The electrolyte, even when diluted, is very corrosive and should not be allowed to contact clothing or skin.

Always wear eye protection when cleaning the battery to prevent the caustic deposits from entering your eyes.

Household current

When using an electric power tool, inspection light, etc., which operates on household current, always make sure that the tool is correctly connected to its plug and that, where necessary, it is properly grounded. Do not use such items in damp conditions and, again, do not create a spark or apply excessive heat in the vicinity of fuel or fuel vapor.

Secondary ignition system voltage

A severe electric shock can result from touching certain parts of the ignition system (such as the spark plug wires) when the engine is running or being cranked, particularly if components are damp or the insulation is defective. In the case of an electronic ignition system, the secondary system voltage is much higher and could prove fatal.

Conversion factors

Length (distance)

Inches (in)	X	25.4	= Millimetres (mm)	X 0.0394	= Inches (in)
Feet (ft)	X	0.305	= Metres (m)	X 3.281	= Feet (ft)
Miles	X	1.609	= Kilometres (km)	X 0.621	= Miles

Volume (capacity)

Cubic inches (cu in; in³)	X	16.387	= Cubic centimetres (cc; cm³)	X 0.061	= Cubic inches (cu in; in³)
Imperial pints (Imp pt)	X	0.568	= Litres (l)	X 1.76	= Imperial pints (Imp pt)
Imperial quarts (Imp qt)	X	1.137	= Litres (l)	X 0.88	= Imperial quarts (Imp qt)
Imperial quarts (Imp qt)	X	1.201	= US quarts (US qt)	X 0.833	= Imperial quarts (Imp qt)
US quarts (US qt)	X	0.946	= Litres (l)	X 1.057	= US quarts (US qt)
Imperial gallons (Imp gal)	X	4.546	= Litres (l)	X 0.22	= Imperial gallons (Imp gal)
Imperial gallons (Imp gal)	X	1.201	= US gallons (US gal)	X 0.833	= Imperial gallons (Imp gal)
US gallons (US gal)	X	3.785	= Litres (l)	X 0.264	= US gallons (US gal)

Mass (weight)

Ounces (oz)	X	28.35	= Grams (g)	X 0.035	= Ounces (oz)
Pounds (lb)	X	0.454	= Kilograms (kg)	X 2.205	= Pounds (lb)

Force

Ounces-force (ozf; oz)	X	0.278	= Newtons (N)	X 3.6	= Ounces-force (ozf; oz)
Pounds-force (lbf; lb)	X	4.448	= Newtons (N)	X 0.225	= Pounds-force (lbf; lb)
Newtons (N)	X	0.1	= Kilograms-force (kgf; kg)	X 9.81	= Newtons (N)

Pressure

Pounds-force per square inch (psi; lbf/in²; lb/in²)	X	0.070	= Kilograms-force per square centimetre (kgf/cm²; kg/cm²)	X 14.223	= Pounds-force per square inch (psi; lbf/in²; lb/in²)
Pounds-force per square inch (psi; lbf/in²; lb/in²)	X	0.068	= Atmospheres (atm)	X 14.696	= Pounds-force per square inch (psi; lbf/in²; lb/in²)
Pounds-force per square inch (psi; lbf/in²; lb/in²)	X	0.069	= Bars	X 14.5	= Pounds-force per square inch (psi; lbf/in²; lb/in²)
Pounds-force per square inch (psi; lbf/in²; lb/in²)	X	6.895	= Kilopascals (kPa)	X 0.145	= Pounds-force per square inch (psi; lbf/in²; lb/in²)
Kilopascals (kPa)	X	0.01	= Kilograms-force per square centimetre (kgf/cm²; kg/cm²)	X 98.1	= Kilopascals (kPa)

Torque (moment of force)

Pounds-force inches (lbf in; lb in)	X	1.152	= Kilograms-force centimetre (kgf cm; kg cm)	X 0.868	= Pounds-force inches (lbf in; lb in)
Pounds-force inches (lbf in; lb in)	X	0.113	= Newton metres (Nm)	X 8.85	= Pounds-force inches (lbf in; lb in)
Pounds-force inches (lbf in; lb in)	X	0.083	= Pounds-force feet (lbf ft; lb ft)	X 12	= Pounds-force inches (lbf in; lb in)
Pounds-force feet (lbf ft; lb ft)	X	0.138	= Kilograms-force metres (kgf m; kg m)	X 7.233	= Pounds-force feet (lbf ft; lb ft)
Pounds-force feet (lbf ft; lb ft)	X	1.356	= Newton metres (Nm)	X 0.738	= Pounds-force feet (lbf ft; lb ft)
Newton metres (Nm)	X	0.102	= Kilograms-force metres (kgf m; kg m)	X 9.804	= Newton metres (Nm)

Power

Horsepower (hp)	X	745.7	= Watts (W)	X 0.0013	= Horsepower (hp)

Velocity (speed)

Miles per hour (miles/hr; mph)	X	1.609	= Kilometres per hour (km/hr; kph)	X 0.621	= Miles per hour (miles/hr; mph)

Fuel consumption*

Miles per gallon, Imperial (mpg)	X	0.354	= Kilometres per litre (km/l)	X 2.825	= Miles per gallon, Imperial (mpg)
Miles per gallon, US (mpg)	X	0.425	= Kilometres per litre (km/l)	X 2.352	= Miles per gallon, US (mpg)

Temperature

Degrees Fahrenheit = (°C x 1.8) + 32   Degrees Celsius (Degrees Centigrade; °C) = (°F - 32) x 0.56

*It is common practice to convert from miles per gallon (mpg) to litres/100 kilometres (l/100km),
where mpg (Imperial) x l/100 km = 282 and mpg (US) x l/100 km = 235

Jacking and towing

FRONT JACK REPLACEMENT   **REAR JACK REPLACEMENT**

To raise a front wheel, place the jack under the jackpad on the frame, behind the wheel; to raise a rear wheel, place the jack under the axle, close to the shock mount

Jacking

The jack supplied with the vehicle should only be used for raising the vehicle when changing a tire or placing jackstands under the frame. **Warning:** *Never work under the vehicle or start the engine while this jack is being used as the only means of support.*

The vehicle should be on level ground with the hazard flashers on, the wheels blocked, the parking brake applied and the transmission in Park (automatic) or Reverse (manual). If a tire is being changed, loosen the lug

nuts one-half turn and leave them in place until the wheel is raise ground.

Place the jack under the vehicle suspension in the indicated **(see illustration).** Operate the jack with a slow, smooth motion wheel is raised off the ground. Remove the lug nuts, pull off the w stall the spare and thread the lug nuts back on with the bevelled si ing in. Tighten them snugly, but wait until the vehicle is lowered t them completely. Note that some spare tires are designed for te use only – don't exceed the recommended speed, mileage or othe tions accompanying the spare.

Lower the vehicle, remove the jack and tighten the nuts (if l or removed) in a criss-cross pattern.

Towing

As a general rule, vehicles can be towed with all four wheel ground for 15 miles or less at speeds below 30 mph. If the vehic be towed further, the driveshaft(s) must be removed (see Chapt

Equipment specifically designed for towing should be used an be attached to the main structural members of the vehicle, not the or brackets.

Safety is a major consideration when towing and all applicab and local laws must be obeyed. A safety chain must be used for a (in addition to the tow bar).

While towing, the parking brake should be released and the tr sion and (if equipped) transfer case must be in Neutral. On 4WD be sure drive to the front wheels has been disengaged. The steeri be unlocked (ignition switch in the Off position). Remember tha steering and power brakes will not work with the engine off.

Troubleshooting

Contents

This Section provides an easy reference guide to the more common problems that may occur during the operation of your vehicle. Various symptoms and their probable causes are grouped under headings denoting components or systems, such as Engine, Cooling system, etc. They also refer to the Chapter and/or Section that deals with the problem.

Remember that successful troubleshooting isn't a mysterious 'black art' practiced only by professional mechanics, it's simply the result of knowledge combined with an intelligent, systematic approach to a problem. Always use a process of elimination starting with the simplest solution and working through to the most complex – and never overlook the obvious. Anyone can run the gas tank dry or leave the lights on overnight, so don't assume that you're exempt from such oversights.

Finally, always establish a clear idea why a problem has occurred and take steps to ensure that it doesn't happen again. If the electrical system fails because of a poor connection, check all other connections in the system to make sure they don't fail as well. If a particular fuse continues to blow, find out why – don't just go on replacing fuses. Remember, failure of a small component can often be indicative of potential failure or incorrect functioning of a more important component or system.

Engine and performance

1   Engine will not rotate when attempting to start

1   Battery terminal connections loose or corroded. Check the cable terminals at the battery; tighten cable clamp and/or clean off corrosion as necessary (see Chapter 1).
2   Battery discharged or faulty. If the cable ends are clean and tight on the battery posts, turn the key to the On position and switch on the headlights or windshield wipers. If they won't run, the battery is discharged.
3   Automatic transmission not engaged in park (P) or Neutral (N).
4   Broken, loose or disconnected wires in the starting circuit. Inspect all wires and connectors at the battery, starter solenoid and ignition switch (on steering column).
5   Starter motor pinion jammed in flywheel ring gear. If manual transmission, place transmission in gear and rock the vehicle to manually turn the engine. Remove starter (Chapter 5) and inspect pinion and flywheel (Chapter 2) at earliest convenience.
6   Starter solenoid faulty (Chapter 5).
7   Starter motor faulty (Chapter 5).
8   Ignition switch faulty (Chapter 12).
9   Engine seized. Try to turn the crankshaft with a large socket and breaker bar on the pulley bolt.

2   Engine rotates but will not start

1   Fuel tank empty.
2   Battery discharged (engine rotates slowly). Check the operation of electrical components as described in previous Section.
3   Battery terminal connections loose or corroded. See previous Section.
4   Fuel not reaching carburetor or fuel injector. Check for clogged fuel filter or lines and defective fuel pump. Also make sure the tank vent lines aren't clogged (Chapter 4).
5   Choke not operating properly (Chapter 1).
6   Faulty distributor components. Check the cap and rotor (Chapter 1).
7   Low cylinder compression. Check as described in Chapter 2.
8   Water in fuel. Drain tank and fill with new fuel.
9   Defective ignition coil (Chapter 5).
10   Dirty or clogged carburetor jets or fuel injector. Carburetor out of adjustment. Check the float level (Chapter 4).
11   Wet or damaged ignition components (Chapters 1 and 5).
12   Worn, faulty or incorrectly gapped spark plugs (Chapter 1).

13   Broken, loose or disconnected wires in the starting circuit (see previous Section).
14   Loose distributor (changing ignition timing). Turn the distributor body as necessary to start the engine, then adjust the ignition timing as soon as possible (Chapter 1).
15   Broken, loose or disconnected wires at the ignition coil or faulty coil (Chapter 5).
16   Timing belt or chain failure or wear affecting valve timing (Chapter 2).

3   Starter motor operates without turning engine

1   Starter pinion sticking. Remove the starter (Chapter 5) and inspect.
2   Starter pinion or flywheel/driveplate teeth worn or broken. Remove the inspection cover and inspect.

4   Engine hard to start when cold

1   Battery discharged or low. Check as described in Chapter 1.
2   Fuel not reaching the carburetor or fuel injectors. Check the fuel filter, lines and fuel pump (Chapters 1 and 4).
3   Choke inoperative (Chapters 1 and 4).
4   Defective spark plugs (Chapter 1).

5   Engine hard to start when hot

1   Air filter dirty (Chapter 1).
2   Fuel not reaching carburetor or fuel injectors (see Section 4). Check for a vapor lock situation, brought about by clogged fuel tank vent lines.
3   Bad engine ground connection.
4   Choke sticking (Chapter 1).
5   Defective pick-up coil in distributor (Chapter 5).
6   Float level too high (Chapter 4).

6   Starter motor noisy or engages roughly

1   Pinion or flywheel/driveplate teeth worn or broken. Remove the inspection cover on the left side of the engine and inspect.
2   Starter motor mounting bolts loose or missing.

7   Engine starts but stops immediately

1   Loose or damaged wire harness connections at distributor, coil or alternator.
2   Intake manifold vacuum leaks. Make sure all mounting bolts/nuts are tight and all vacuum hoses connected to the manifold are attached properly and in good condition.
3   Insufficient fuel flow (see Chapter 4).

8   Engine 'lopes' while idling or idles erratically

1   Vacuum leaks. Check mounting bolts at the intake manifold for tightness. Make sure that all vacuum hoses are connected and in good condition. Use a stethoscope or a length of fuel hose held against your ear to listen for vacuum leaks while the engine is running. A hissing sound will be heard. A soapy water solution will also detect leaks. Check the intake manifold gasket surfaces.
2   Leaking EGR valve or plugged PCV valve (see Chapters 1 and 6).
3   Air filter clogged (Chapter 1).
4   Fuel pump not delivering sufficient fuel (Chapter 4).
5   Leaking head gasket. Perform a cylinder compression check (Chapter 2).
6   Timing belt or chain worn (Chapter 2).

7   Camshaft lobes worn (Chapter 2).
8   Valves burned or otherwise leaking (Chapter 2).
9   Ignition timing out of adjustment (Chapter 1).
10 Ignition system not operating properly (Chapters 1 and 5).
11 Thermostatic air cleaner not operating properly (Chapter 1).
12 Choke not operating properly (Chapters 1 and 4).
13 Dirty or clogged injectors. Carburetor dirty, clogged or out of adjustment. Check the float level (Chapter 4).
14 Idle speed out of adjustment (Chapter 4).

9   Engine misses at idle speed

1   Spark plugs faulty or not gapped properly (Chapter 1).
2   Faulty spark plug wires (Chapter 1).
3   Wet or damaged distributor components (Chapter 1).
4   Short circuits in ignition, coil or spark plug wires.
5   Sticking or faulty emissions systems (see Chapter 6).
6   Clogged fuel filter and/or foreign matter in fuel. Remove the fuel filter (Chapter 1) and inspect.
7   Vacuum leaks at intake manifold or hose connections. Check as described in Section 8.
8   Incorrect idle speed (Chapter 4) or idle mixture (Chapter 4).
9   Incorrect ignition timing (Chapter 1).
10 Low or uneven cylinder compression. Check as described in Chapter 2.
11 Choke not operating properly (Chapter 1).
12 Clogged or dirty fuel injectors (Chapter 4).

10   Excessively high idle speed

1   Sticking throttle linkage (Chapter 4).
2   Choke opened excessively at idle (Chapter 4).
3   Idle speed incorrectly adjusted (Chapter 4).

11   Battery will not hold a charge

1   Alternator drivebelt defective or not adjusted properly (Chapter 1).
2   Battery cables loose or corroded (Chapter 1).
3   Alternator not charging properly (Chapter 5).
4   Loose, broken or faulty wires in the charging circuit (Chapter 5).
5   Short circuit causing a continuous drain on the battery.
6   Battery defective internally.

12   Alternator light stays on

1   Fault in alternator or charging circuit (Chapter 5).
2   Alternator drivebelt defective or not properly adjusted (Chapter 1).

13   Alternator light fails to come on when key is turned on

1   Faulty bulb (Chapter 12).
2   Defective alternator (Chapter 5).
3   Fault in the printed circuit, dash wiring or bulb holder (Chapter 12).

14   Engine misses throughout driving speed range

1   Fuel filter clogged and/or impurities in the fuel system. Check fuel filter (Chapter 1) or clean system (Chapter 4).
2   Faulty or incorrectly gapped spark plugs (Chapter 1).
3   Incorrect ignition timing (Chapter 1).

4   Cracked distributor cap, disconnected distributor wires or damaged distributor components (Chapter 1).
5   Defective spark plug wires (Chapter 1).
6   Emissions system components faulty (Chapter 6).
7   Low or uneven cylinder compression pressures. Check as described in Chapter 2.
8   Weak or faulty ignition coil (Chapter 5).
9   Weak or faulty ignition system (Chapter 5).
10 Vacuum leaks at intake manifold or vacuum hoses (see Section 8).
11 Dirty or clogged carburetor or fuel injector (Chapter 4).
12 Leaky EGR valve (Chapter 6).
13 Carburetor out of adjustment (Chapter 4).
14 Idle speed out of adjustment (Chapter 4).

15   Hesitation or stumble during acceleration

1   Ignition timing incorrect (Chapter 1).
2   Ignition system not operating properly (Chapter 5).
3   Dirty or clogged carburetor or fuel injector (Chapter 4).
4   Low fuel pressure. Check for proper operation of the fuel pump and for restrictions in the fuel filter and lines (Chapter 4).
5   Carburetor out of adjustment (Chapter 4).

16   Engine stalls

1   Idle speed incorrect (Chapter 4).
2   Fuel filter clogged and/or water and impurities in the fuel system (Chapter 1).
3   Choke not operating properly (Chapter 1).
4   Damaged or wet distributor cap and wires.
5   Emissions system components faulty (Chapter 6).
6   Faulty or incorrectly gapped spark plugs (Chapter 1). Also check the spark plug wires (Chapter 1).
7   Vacuum leak at the carburetor, intake manifold or vacuum hoses. Check as described in Section 8.

17   Engine lacks power

1   Incorrect ignition timing (Chapter 1).
2   Excessive play in distributor shaft. At the same time check for faulty distributor cap, wires, etc. (Chapter 1).
3   Faulty or incorrectly gapped spark plugs (Chapter 1).
4   Air filter dirty (Chapter 1).
5   Faulty ignition coil (Chapter 5).
6   Brakes binding (Chapters 1 and 10).
7   Automatic transmission fluid level incorrect, causing slippage (Chapter 1).
8   Clutch slipping (Chapter 8).
9   Fuel filter clogged and/or impurities in the fuel system (Chapters 1 and 4).
10 EGR system not functioning properly (Chapter 6).
11 Use of sub-standard fuel. Fill tank with proper octane fuel.
12 Low or uneven cylinder compression pressures. Check as described in Chapter 2.
13 Air leak at carburetor or intake manifold (check as described in Section 8).
14 Dirty or clogged carburetor jets or malfunctioning choke (Chapters 1 and 4).

18   Engine backfires

1   EGR system not functioning properly (Chapter 6).
2   Ignition timing incorrect (Chapter 1).
3   Thermostatic air cleaner system not operating properly (Chapter 6).

4   Vacuum leak (refer to Section 8).
5   Damaged valve springs or sticking valves (Chapter 2).
6   Intake air leak (see Section 8).
7   Carburetor float level out of adjustment (Chapter 4).

19   Engine surges while holding accelerator steady

1   Intake air leak (see Section 8).
2   Fuel pump not working properly (Chapter 4).

20   Pinging or knocking engine sounds when engine is under load

1   Incorrect grade of fuel. Fill tank with fuel of the proper octane rating.
2   Ignition timing incorrect (Chapter 1).
3   Carbon build-up in combustion chambers. Remove cylinder head(s) and clean combustion chambers (Chapter 2).
4   Incorrect spark plugs (Chapter 1).

21   Engine diesels (continues to run) after being turned of

1   Idle speed too high (Chapter 4).
2   Ignition timing incorrect (Chapter 1).
3   Incorrect spark plug heat range (Chapter 1).
4   Intake air leak (see Section 8).
5   Carbon build-up in combustion chambers. Remove the cylinder head(s) and clean the combustion chambers (Chapter 2).
6   Valves sticking (Chapter 2).
7   EGR system not operating properly (Chapter 6).
8   Fuel shut-off system not operating properly (Chapter 6).
9   Check for causes of overheating (Section 27).

22   Low oil pressure

1   Improper grade of oil.
2   Oil pump worn or damaged (Chapter 2).
3   Engine overheating (refer to Section 27).
4   Clogged oil filter (Chapter 1).
5   Clogged oil strainer (Chapter 2).
6   Oil pressure gauge not working properly (Chapter 2).

23   Excessive oil consumption

1   Loose oil drain plug.
2   Loose bolts or damaged oil pan gasket (Chapter 2).
3   Loose bolts or damaged front cover gasket (Chapter 2).
4   Front or rear crankshaft oil seal leaking (Chapter 2).
5   Loose bolts or damaged rocker arm cover gasket (Chapter 2).
6   Loose oil filter (Chapter 1).
7   Loose or damaged oil pressure switch (Chapter 2).
8   Pistons and cylinders excessively worn (Chapter 2).
9   Piston rings not installed correctly on pistons (Chapter 2).
10   Worn or damaged piston rings (Chapter 2).
11   Intake and/or exhaust valve oil seals worn or damaged (Chapter 2).
12   Worn valve stems.
13   Worn or damaged valves/guides (Chapter 2).

24   Excessive fuel consumption

1   Dirty or clogged air filter element (Chapter 1).
2   Incorrect ignition timing (Chapter 1).

3   Incorrect idle speed (Chapter 4).
4   Low tire pressure or incorrect tire size (Chapter 10).
5   Fuel leakage. Check all connections, lines and components in the fuel system (Chapter 4).
6   Choke not operating properly (Chapter 1).
7   Dirty or clogged carburetor jets or fuel injectors (Chapter 4).

25   Fuel odor

1   Fuel leakage. Check all connections, lines and components in the fuel system (Chapter 4).
2   Fuel tank overfilled. Fill only to automatic shut-off.
3   Charcoal canister filter in Evaporative Emissions Control system clogged (Chapter 1).
4   Vapor leaks from Evaporative Emissions Control system lines (Chapter 6).

26   Miscellaneous engine noises

1   A strong dull noise that becomes more rapid as the engine accelerates indicates worn or damaged crankshaft bearings or an unevenly worn crankshaft. To pinpoint the trouble spot, remove the spark plug wire from one plug at a time and crank the engine over. If the noise stops, the cylinder with the removed plug wire indicates the problem area. Replace the bearing and/or service or replace the crankshaft (Chapter 2).
2   A similar (yet slightly higher pitched) noise to the crankshaft knocking described in the previous paragraph, that becomes more rapid as the engine accelerates, indicates worn or damaged connecting rod bearings (Chapter 2). The procedure for locating the problem cylinder is the same as described in Paragraph 1.
3   An overlapping metallic noise that increases in intensity as the engine speed increases, yet diminishes as the engine warms up indicates abnormal piston and cylinder wear (Chapter 2). To locate the problem cylinder, use the procedure described in Paragraph 1.
4   A rapid clicking noise that becomes faster as the engine accelerates indicates a worn piston pin or piston pin hole. This sound will happen each time the piston hits the highest and lowest points in the stroke (Chapter 2). The procedure for locating the problem piston is described in Paragraph 1.
5   A metallic clicking noise coming from the water pump indicates worn or damaged water pump bearings or pump. Replace the water pump with a new one (Chapter 3).
6   A rapid tapping sound or clicking sound that becomes faster as the engine speed increases indicates "valve tapping." This can be identified by holding one end of a section of hose to your ear and placing the other end at different spots along the valve cover. The point where the sound is loudest indicates the problem valve. If the pushrod and rocker arm components are in good shape, you likely have a collapsed valve lifter. Changing the engine oil and adding a high viscosity oil treatment will sometimes cure a stuck lifter problem. If the problem persists, the lifters, pushrods and rocker arms must be removed for inspection (see Chapter 2).
7   A steady metallic rattling or rapping sound coming from the area of the timing chain cover indicates a worn, damaged or out-of-adjustment timing chain. Service or replace the chain and related components (Chapter 2).

Cooling system

27   Overheating

1   Insufficient coolant in system (Chapter 1).
2   Drivebelt defective or not adjusted properly (Chapter 1).
3   Radiator core blocked or radiator grille dirty and restricted (Chapter 3).
4   Thermostat faulty (Chapter 3).

5   Fan not functioning properly (Chapter 3).
6   Radiator cap not maintaining proper pressure. Have cap pressure tested by gas station or repair shop.
7   Ignition timing incorrect (Chapter 1).
8   Defective water pump (Chapter 3).
9   Improper grade of engine oil.
10 Inaccurate temperature gauge (Chapter 12).

28   Overcooling

1   Thermostat faulty (Chapter 3).
2   Inaccurate temperature gauge (Chapter 12).

29   External coolant leakage

1   Deteriorated or damaged hoses. Loose clamps at hose connections (Chapter 1).
2   Water pump seals defective. If this is the case, water will drip from the weep hole in the water pump body (Chapter 3).
3   Leakage from radiator core or header tank. This will require the radiator to be professionally repaired (see Chapter 3 for removal procedures).
4   Engine drain plugs or water jacket freeze plugs leaking (see Chapters 1 and 2).
5   Leak from coolant temperature switch (Chapter 3).
6   Leak from damaged gaskets or small cracks (Chapter 2).
7   Damaged head gasket. This can be verified by checking the condition of the engine oil as noted in Section 30.

30   Internal coolant leakage

Note: *Internal coolant leaks can usually be detected by examining the oil. Check the dipstick and inside the rocker arm cover for water deposits and an oil consistency like that of a milkshake.*
1   Leaking cylinder head gasket. Have the system pressure tested or remove the cylinder head (Chapter 2) and inspect.
2   Cracked cylinder bore or cylinder head. Dismantle engine and inspect (Chapter 2).
3   Loose cylinder head bolts (tighten as described in Chapter 2).

31   Abnormal coolant loss

1   Overfilling system (Chapter 1).
2   Coolant boiling away due to overheating (see causes in Section 27).
3   Internal or external leakage (see Sections 29 and 30).
4   Faulty radiator cap. Have the cap pressure tested.
5   Cooling system being pressurized by engine compression. This could be due to a cracked head or block or leaking head gasket(s).

32   Poor coolant circulation

1   Inoperative water pump. A quick test is to pinch the top radiator hose closed with your hand while the engine is idling, then release it. You should feel a surge of coolant if the pump is working properly (Chapter 3).
2   Restriction in cooling system. Drain, flush and refill the system (Chapter 1). If necessary, remove the radiator (Chapter 3) and have it reverse flushed or professionally cleaned.
3   Loose water pump drivebelt (Chapter 1).
4   Thermostat sticking (Chapter 3).
5   Insufficient coolant (Chapter 1).

33   Corrosion

1   Excessive impurities in the water. Soft, clean water is recommended. Distilled or rainwater is satisfactory.
2   Insufficient antifreeze solution (refer to Chapter 1 for the proper ratio of water to antifreeze).
3   Infrequent flushing and draining of system. Regular flushing of the cooling system should be carried out at the specified intervals as described in (Chapter 1).

Clutch

Note: *All clutch related service information is located in Chapter 8, unless otherwise noted.*

34   Fails to release (pedal pressed to the floor – shift lever does not move freely in and out of Reverse)

1   Clutch contaminated with oil. Remove clutch plate and inspect.
2   Clutch plate warped, distorted or otherwise damaged.
3   Diaphragm spring fatigued. Remove clutch cover/pressure plate assembly and inspect.
4   Leakage of fluid from clutch hydraulic system. Inspect master cylinder, operating cylinder and connecting lines.
5   Air in clutch hydraulic system. Bleed the system.
6   Insufficient pedal stroke. Check and adjust as necessary.
7   Piston seal in operating cylinder deformed or damaged.
8   Lack of grease on pilot bearing.

35   Clutch slips (engine speed increases with no increase in vehicle speed)

1   Worn or oil soaked clutch plate.
2   Clutch plate not broken in. It may take 30 or 40 normal starts for a new clutch to seat.
3   Diaphragm spring weak or damaged. Remove clutch cover/pressure plate assembly and inspect.
4   Flywheel warped (Chapter 2).
5   Debris in master cylinder preventing the piston from returning to its normal position.
6   Clutch hydraulic line damaged.

36   Grabbing (chattering) as clutch is engaged

1   Oil on clutch plate. Remove and inspect. Repair any leaks.
2   Worn or loose engine or transmission mounts. They may move slightly when clutch is released. Inspect mounts and bolts.
3   Worn splines on transmission input shaft. Remove clutch components and inspect.
4   Warped pressure plate or flywheel. Remove clutch components and inspect.
5   Diaphragm spring fatigued. Remove clutch cover/pressure plate assembly and inspect.
6   Clutch linings hardened or warped.
7   Clutch lining rivets loose.

37   Squeal or rumble with clutch engaged (pedal released)

1   Improper pedal adjustment. Adjust pedal free play.

2   Release bearing binding on transmission shaft. Remove clutch components and check bearing. Remove any burrs or other damage on the shaft.
3   Pilot bearing worn or damaged.
4   Clutch rivets loose.
5   Clutch plate cracked.
6   Fatigued clutch plate torsion springs. Replace clutch plate.

38   Squeal or rumble with clutch disengaged (pedal depressed)

1   Worn or damaged release bearing.
2   Worn or broken pressure plate diaphragm fingers.

39   Clutch pedal stays on floor when disengaged

Binding linkage or release bearing. Inspect linkage or remove clutch components as necessary.

Manual transmission

Note: *All manual transmission service information is located in Chapter 7, unless otherwise noted.*

40   Noisy in Neutral with engine running

1   Input shaft bearing worn.
2   Damaged main drive gear bearing.
3   Insufficient transmission lubricant (see Chapter 1).
4   Transmission lubricant in poor condition. Drain and fill with proper grade lubricant. Check old lubricant for water and debris (Chapter 1).
5   Noise can be caused by variations in engine torque. Change the idle speed and see if noise disappears.

41   Noisy in all gears

1   Any of the above causes, and/or:
2   Worn or damaged output gear bearings or shaft.

42   Noisy in one particular gear

1   Worn, damaged or chipped gear teeth.
2   Worn or damaged synchronizer.

43   Slips out of gear

1   Transmission loose on clutch housing.
2   Stiff shift lever seal.
3   Shift linkage binding.
4   Broken or loose input gear bearing retainer.
5   Dirt between clutch lever and engine housing.
6   Worn linkage.
7   Damaged or worn check balls, fork rod ball grooves or check springs.
8   Worn mainshaft or countershaft bearings.
9   Loose engine mounts (Chapter 2).
10   Excessive gear end play.
11   Worn synchronizers.

44   Oil leaks

1   Excessive amount of lubricant in transmission (see Chapter 1 for correct checking procedures). Drain lubricant as required.
2   Rear oil seal or speedometer oil seal damaged.
3   To pinpoint a leak, first remove all built-up dirt and grime from the transmission. Degreasing agents and/or steam cleaning will achieve this. With the underside clean, drive the vehicle at low speeds so the air flow will not blow the leak far from its source. Raise the vehicle and determine where the leak is located.

45   Difficulty engaging gears

1   Clutch not releasing completely.
2   Loose or damaged shift linkage. Make a thorough inspection, replacing parts as necessary.
3   Insufficient transmission lubricant (Chapter 1).
4   Transmission lubricant in poor condition. Drain and fill with proper grade lubricant. Check lubricant for water and debris (Chapter 1).
5   Worn or damaged striking rod.
6   Sticking or jamming gears.

46   Noise occurs while shifting gears

1   Check for proper operation of the clutch (Chapter 8).
2   Faulty synchronizer assemblies. Measure baulk ring-to-gear clearance. Also, check for wear or damage to baulk rings or any parts of the synchromesh assemblies.

Automatic transmission

Note: *Due to the complexity of the automatic transmission, it's difficult for the home mechanic to properly diagnose and service. For problems other than the following, the vehicle should be taken to a reputable mechanic.*

47   Fluid leakage

1   Automatic transmission fluid is a deep red color, and fluid leaks should not be confused with engine oil which can easily be blown by air flow to the transmission.
2   To pinpoint a leak, first remove all built-up dirt and grime from the transmission. Degreasing agents and/or steam cleaning will achieve this. With the underside clean, drive the vehicle at low speeds so the air flow will not blow the leak far from its source. Raise the vehicle and determine where the leak is located. Common areas of leakage are:
   a) Fluid pan: tighten mounting bolts and/or replace pan gasket as necessary (Chapter 1).
   b) Rear extension: tighten bolts and/or replace oil seal as necessary.
   c) Filler pipe: replace the rubber oil seal where pipe enters transmission case.
   d) Transmission oil lines: tighten fittings where lines enter transmission case and/or replace lines.
   e) Vent pipe: transmission overfilled and/or water in fluid (see checking procedures, Chapter 1).
   f) Speedometer connector: replace the O-ring where speedometer cable enters transmission case.

48   General shift mechanism problems

Chapter 7 deals with checking and adjusting the shift linkage on automatic transmissions. Common problems which may be caused by out of

adjustment linkage are:
   a) Engine starting in gears other than P (park) or N (Neutral).
   b) Indicator pointing to a gear other than the one actually engaged.
   c) Vehicle moves with transmission in P (Park) position.

49   Transmission will not downshift with the accelerator pedal pressed to the floor

Chapter 7 deals with adjusting the TV linkage to enable the transmission to downshift properly.

50   Engine will start in gears other than Park or Neutral

Chapter 7 deals with adjusting the Neutral start switch installed on automatic transmissions.

51   Transmission slips, shifts rough, is noisy or has no drive in forward or Reverse gears

1   There are many probable causes for the above problems, but the home mechanic should concern himself only with one possibility; fluid level.
2   Before taking the vehicle to a shop, check the fluid level and condition as described in Chapter 1. Add fluid, if necessary, or change the fluid and filter if needed. If problems persist, have a professional diagnose the transmission.

Driveshaft

Note: *Refer to Chapter 8, unless otherwise specified, for service information.*

52   Leaks at front of driveshaft

Defective transmission or transfer case seal. See Chapter 7 for replacement procedure. As this is done, check the splined yoke for burrs or roughness that could damage the new seal. Remove burrs with a fine file or whetstone.

53   Knock or clunk when transmission is under initial load (just after transmission is put into gear)

1   Loose or disconnected rear suspension components. Check all mounting bolts and bushings (Chapters 7 and 10).
2   Loose driveshaft bolts. Inspect all bolts and nuts and tighten them securely.
3   Worn or damaged universal joint bearings (Chapter 8).
4   Worn sleeve yoke and mainshaft spline.

54   Metallic grating sound consistent with vehicle speed

Pronounced wear in the universal joint bearings. Replace U-joints or driveshafts, as necessary.

55   Vibration

Note: *Before blaming the driveshaft, make sure the tires are perfectly balanced and perform the following test.*

1   Install a tachometer inside the vehicle to monitor engine speed as the vehicle is driven. Drive the vehicle and note the engine speed at which the vibration (roughness) is most pronounced. Now shift the transmission to a different gear and bring the engine speed to the same point.
2   If the vibration occurs at the same engine speed (rpm) regardless of which gear the transmission is in, the driveshaft is NOT at fault since the driveshaft speed varies.
3   If the vibration decreases or is eliminated when the transmission is in a different gear at the same engine speed, refer to the following probable causes.
4   Bent or dented driveshaft. Inspect and replace as necessary.
5   Undercoating or built-up dirt, etc. on the driveshaft. Clean the shaft thoroughly.
6   Worn universal joint bearings. Replace the U-joints or driveshaft as necessary.
7   Driveshaft and/or companion flange out of balance. Check for missing weights on the shaft. Remove driveshaft and reinstall 180-degrees from original position, then recheck. Have the driveshaft balanced if problem persists.
8   Loose driveshaft mounting bolts/nuts.
9   Defective center bearing, if so equipped.
10   Worn transmission rear bushing (Chapter 7).

56   Scraping noise

Make sure the dust cover on the sleeve yoke isn't rubbing on the transmission extension housing.

57   Whining or whistling noise

Defective center bearing, if so equipped.

Axle(s) and differential(s)

Note: *For differential servicing information, refer to Chapter 8, unless otherwise specified.*

58   Noise – same when in drive as when vehicle is coasting

1   Road noise. No corrective action available.
2   Tire noise. Inspect tires and check tire pressures (Chapter 1).
3   Front wheel bearings loose, worn or damaged (Chapter 1).
4   Insufficient differential oil (Chapter 1).
5   Defective differential.

59   Knocking sound when starting or shifting gears

Defective or incorrectly adjusted differential.

60   Noise when turning

Defective differential.

61   Vibration

See probable causes under Driveshaft. Proceed under the guidelines listed for the driveshaft. If the problem persists, check the rear wheel bearings by raising the rear of the vehicle and spinning the wheels by hand. Listen for evidence of rough (noisy) bearings. Remove and inspect (Chapter 8).

62 Oil leaks

1 Pinion oil seal damaged (Chapter 8).
2 Axleshaft oil seals damaged (Chapter 8).
3 Differential cover leaking. Tighten mounting bolts or replace the gasket as required.
4 Loose filler or drain plug on differential (Chapter 1).
5 Clogged or damaged breather on differential.

Transfer case (4WD models)
Note: *Refer to Chapter 7 for service and repair information.*

63 Gear jumping out of mesh

1 Incorrect control lever freeplay (Chapter 7C).
2 Interference between the control lever and the console.
3 Play or fatigue in the transfer case mounts.
4 Internal wear or incorrect adjustments.

64 Difficult shifting

1 Lack of oil.
2 Internal wear, damage or incorrect adjustment.

65 Noise

1 Lack of oil in transfer case.
2 Noise in 4H and 4L, but not in 2H indicates cause is in the front differential or front axle.
3 Noise in 2H, 4H and 4L indicates cause is in rear differential or rear axle.
4 Noise in 2H and 4H but not in 4L, or in 4L only, indicates internal wear or damage in transfer case.

Brakes
Note: *Before assuming a brake problem exists, make sure the tires are in good condition and inflated properly, the front end alignment is correct and the vehicle is not loaded with weight in an unequal manner. All service procedures for the brakes are included in Chapter 9, unless otherwise noted.*

66 Vehicle pulls to one side during braking

1 Defective, damaged or oil contaminated brake pad on one side. Inspect as described in Chapter 1. Refer to Chapter 9 if replacement is required.
2 Excessive wear of brake pad material or disc on one side. Inspect and repair as necessary.
3 Loose or disconnected front suspension components. Inspect and tighten all bolts securely (Chapters 1 and 10).
4 Defective caliper assembly. Remove caliper and inspect for stuck piston or damage.
5 Brake pad to rotor adjustment needed. Inspect automatic adjusting mechanism for proper operation.
6 Scored or out of round rotor.
7 Loose caliper mounting bolts.
8 Incorrect wheel bearing adjustment.

67 Noise (high-pitched squeal)

1 Front brake pads worn out. This noise comes from the wear sensor rubbing against the disc. Replace pads with new ones immediately!
2 Glazed or contaminated pads.
3 Dirty or scored rotor.
4 Bent support plate.

68 Excessive brake pedal travel

1 Partial brake system failure. Inspect entire system (Chapter 1) and correct as required.
2 Insufficient fluid in master cylinder. Check (Chapter 1) and add fluid – bleed system if necessary.
3 Air in system. Bleed system.
4 Excessive lateral rotor play.
5 Brakes out of adjustment. Check the operation of the automatic adjusters.
6 Defective proportioning valve. Replace valve and bleed system.

69 Brake pedal feels spongy when depressed

1 Air in brake lines. Bleed the brake system.
2 Deteriorated rubber brake hoses. Inspect all system hoses and lines. Replace parts as necessary.
3 Master cylinder mounting nuts loose. Inspect master cylinder bolts (nuts) and tighten them securely.
4 Master cylinder faulty.
5 Incorrect shoe or pad clearance.
6 Defective check valve. Replace valve and bleed system.
7 Clogged reservoir cap vent hole.
8 Deformed rubber brake lines.
9 Soft or swollen caliper seals.
10 Poor quality brake fluid. Bleed entire system and fill with new approved fluid.

70 Excessive effort required to stop vehicle

1 Power brake booster not operating properly.
2 Excessively worn linings or pads. Check and replace if necessary.
3 One or more caliper pistons seized or sticking. Inspect and rebuild as required.
4 Brake pads or linings contaminated with oil or grease. Inspect and replace as required.
5 New pads or linings installed and not yet seated. It'll take a while for the new material to seat against the rotor or drum.
6 Worn or damaged master cylinder or caliper assemblies. Check particularly for frozen pistons.
7 Also see causes listed under Section 69.

71 Pedal travels to the floor with little resistance

Little or no fluid in the master cylinder reservoir caused by leaking caliper piston(s) or loose, damaged or disconnected brake lines. Inspect entire system and repair as necessary.

72 Brake pedal pulsates during brake application

1 Wheel bearings damaged, worn or out of adjustment (Chapter 1).
2 Caliper not sliding properly due to improper installation or obstructions. Remove and inspect.
3 Rotor not within specifications. Remove the rotor and check for excessive lateral runout and parallelism. Have the rotors resurfaced or re-

place them with new ones. Also make sure that all rotors are the same thickness.
4   Out of round rear brake drums. Remove the drums and have them turned or replace them with new ones.

73   Brakes drag (indicated by sluggish engine performance or wheels being very hot after driving)

1   Output rod adjustment incorrect at the brake pedal.
2   Obstructed master cylinder compensator. Disassemble master cylinder and clean.
3   Master cylinder piston seized in bore. Overhaul master cylinder.
4   Caliper assembly in need of overhaul.
5   Brake pads or shoes worn out.
6   Piston cups in master cylinder or caliper assembly deformed. Overhaul master cylinder.
7   Rotor not within specifications (Section 72).
8   Parking brake assembly will not release.
9   Clogged brake lines.
10   Wheel bearings out of adjustment (Chapter 1).
11   Brake pedal height improperly adjusted.
12   Wheel cylinder needs overhaul.
13   Improper shoe to drum clearance. Adjust as necessary.

74   Rear brakes lock up under light brake application

1   Tire pressures too high.
2   Tires excessively worn (Chapter 1).
3   Defective power brake booster.

75   Rear brakes lock up under heavy brake application

1   Tire pressures too high.
2   Tires excessively worn (Chapter 1).
3   Front brake pads contaminated with oil, mud or water. Clean or replace the pads.
4   Front brake pads excessively worn.
5   Defective master cylinder or caliper assembly.

Suspension and steering

Note: *All service procedures for the suspension and steering systems are included in Chapter 10, unless otherwise noted.*

76   Vehicle pulls to one side

1   Tire pressures uneven (Chapter 1).
2   Defective tire (Chapter 1).
3   Excessive wear in suspension or steering components (Chapter 1).
4   Front end alignment incorrect.
5   Front brakes dragging. Inspect as described in Section 73.
6   Wheel bearings improperly adjusted (Chapter 1).
7   Wheel lug nuts loose.

77   Shimmy, shake or vibration

1   Tire or wheel out of balance or out of round. Have them balanced on the vehicle.
2   Loose, worn or out of adjustment wheel bearings (Chapter 1).
3   Shock absorbers and/or suspension components worn or damaged (see Chapter 10).

78   Excessive pitching and/or rolling around corners or during braking

1   Defective shock absorbers. Replace as a set.
2   Broken or weak leaf springs and/or suspension components.
3   Worn or damaged stabilizer bar or bushings.

79   Wandering or general instability

1   Improper tire pressures.
2   Incorrect front end alignment.
3   Worn or damaged steering linkage or suspension components.
4   Improperly adjusted steering gear.
5   Out-of-balance wheels.
6   Loose wheel lug nuts.
7   Worn rear shock absorbers.
8   Fatigued or damaged rear leaf springs.

80   Excessively stiff steering

1   Lack of fluid in the power steering fluid reservoir, where appropriate (Chapter 1).
2   Incorrect tire pressures (Chapter 1).
3   Lack of lubrication at balljoints (Chapter 1).
4   Front end out of alignment.
5   Steering gear out of adjustment or lacking lubrication.
6   Improperly adjusted wheel bearings.
7   Worn or damaged steering gear.
8   Interference of steering column with turn signal switch.
9   Low tire pressures.
10   Worn or damaged balljoints.
11   Worn or damaged steering linkage.
12   See also Section 79.

81   Excessive play in steering

1   Loose wheel bearings (Chapter 1).
2   Excessive wear in suspension bushings (Chapter 1).
3   Steering gear improperly adjusted.
4   Incorrect front end alignment.
5   Steering gear mounting bolts loose.
6   Worn steering linkage.

82   Lack of power assistance

1   Steering pump drivebelt faulty or not adjusted properly (Chapter 1).
2   Fluid level low (Chapter 1).
3   Hoses or pipes restricting the flow. Inspect and replace parts as necessary.
4   Air in power steering system. Bleed system.
5   Defective power steering pump.

83   Steering wheel fails to return to straight-ahead position

1   Incorrect front end alignment.
2   Tire pressures low.
3   Steering gears improperly engaged.
4   Steering column out of alignment.
5   Worn or damaged balljoint.
6   Worn or damaged steering linkage.

7 Improperly lubricated idler arm.
8 Insufficient oil in steering gear.
9 Lack of fluid in power steering pump.

10 Worn or damaged rear shock absorber mounting bushing.
11 Incorrect rear axle endplay.
12 See also causes of noises at the rear axle and driveshaft.

84 Steering effort not the same in both directions (power system)

1 Leaks in steering gear.
2 Clogged fluid passage in steering gear.

85 Noisy power steering pump

1 Insufficient oil in pump.
2 Clogged hoses or oil filter in pump.
3 Loose pulley.
4 Improperly adjusted drivebelt (Chapter 1).
5 Defective pump.

86 Miscellaneous noises

1 Improper tire pressures.
2 Insufficiently lubricated balljoint or steering linkage.
3 Loose or worn steering gear, steering linkage or suspension components.
4 Defective shock absorber.
5 Defective wheel bearing.
6 Worn or damaged suspension bushings.
7 Damaged leaf spring.
8 Loose wheel lug nuts.
9 Worn or damaged rear axleshaft spline.

87 Excessive tire wear (not specific to one area)

1 Incorrect tire pressures.
2 Tires out of balance. Have them balanced on the vehicle.
3 Wheels damaged. Inspect and replace as necessary.
4 Suspension or steering components worn (Chapter 1).

88 Excessive tire wear on outside edge

1 Incorrect tire pressure.
2 Excessive speed in turns.
3 Front end alignment incorrect (excessive toe-in).

89 Excessive tire wear on inside edge

1 Incorrect tire pressure.
2 Front end alignment incorrect (toe-out).
3 Loose or damaged steering components (Chapter 1).

90 Tire tread worn in one place

1 Tires out of balance. Have them balanced on the vehicle.
2 Damaged or buckled wheel. Inspect and replace if necessary.
3 Defective tire.

Chapter 1   Tune-up and routine maintenance

Contents

1

Specifications

Recommended lubricants and fluids

Engine oil type	API grade SF or SF/CC multigrade and fuel efficient oil
Engine oil viscosity	See accompanying chart
Automatic transmission fluid type	Dexron II automatic transmission fluid
Manual transmission lubricant type	SAE 10W30 SG or SG/CD multigrade engine oil
Transfer case lubricant type	Dexron II automatic transmission fluid
Differential lubricant type	SAE 80W-90 GL-5 gear lubricant
Limited slip differential	Add Chrysler Friction Modifier No. 4318060 to the specified lubricant
Brake fluid type	DOT 3 brake fluid
Clutch fluid type	DOT 3 brake fluid
Power steering fluid	Chrysler power steering fluid or equivalent
Manual steering gear lubricant type (2WD models) . . .	SAE 90 GL-5 hypoid gear lubricant
Chassis grease type	MOPAR lubricant 43801062 or equivalent
Front wheel bearing grease	MOPAR lubricant 43801064 or equivalent

Capacities

Engine oil (with filter change – approximate)	4 qts
Cooling system (approximate)	
Four-cylinder engine	9.8 qts
V6 and V8 engine	14 qts
Automatic transmission (approximate)	4 qts (when draining pan and replacing filter only)
Manual transmission	2 qts
Transfer case	2 pts

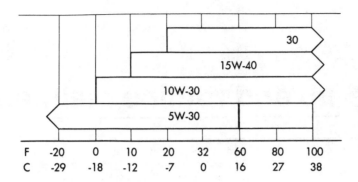

Engine oil viscosity chart

For best fuel economy and cold starting, select the lowest SAE viscosity grade oil for the expected temperature range

Ignition system

Spark plug type
    Through 1991 (all engines) .... Champion no. RN12YC
    1992 and later
        Four–cylinder engine .... Champion no. RN12YC
        V6 and V8 engines .... Champion no. RC12YC
    Spark plug gap (all engines, all years) .... 0.035 in
Ignition timing .... Refer to the *Vehicle Emissions Control Information* label
                                         in the engine compartment

Firing order
    Four-cylinder engine 1-3-4-2
    V6 engine 1-6-5-4-3-2
    V8 engine 1-8-4-3-6-5-7-2

Brakes

Disc brake pad lining thickness (minimum) 5/16-in
Drum brake shoe lining thickness (minimum) 1/16-in

Torque specifications   **Ft-lbs**

Automatic transmission pan bolts 12
Carburetor/throttle body mounting nuts/bolts 8
Differential cover bolts .... 10 to 20
EGR valve bolts 17
Spark plugs
    V6 and V8 engine 30
    Four-cylinder engine 25
Engine oil drain plug 20
Oxygen sensor 20
Wheel lug nuts 85

1   Introduction

This Chapter is designed to help the home mechanic maintain the Dodge Dakota with the goals of maximum performance, economy, safety and reliability in mind.

Included is a master maintenance schedule (page 1-6), followed by procedures dealing specifically with each item on the schedule. Visual checks, adjustments, component replacement and other helpful items are included. Refer to the accompanying illustrations of the engine compartment and the underside of the vehicle for the locations of various components.

Servicing your vehicle in accordance with the mileage/time maintenance schedule and the step-by-step procedures will result in a planned maintenance program that should produce a long and reliable service life. Keep in mind that it's a comprehensive plan, so maintaining some items but not others at the specified intervals will not produce the same results.

As you service your vehicle, you will discover that many of the procedures can – and should – be grouped together because of the nature of the particular procedure you're performing or because of the close proximity of two otherwise unrelated components to one another.

For example, if the vehicle is raised for chassis lubrication, you should inspect the exhaust, suspension, steering and fuel systems while you're under the vehicle. When you're rotating the tires, it makes good sense to check the brakes since the wheels are already removed. Finally, let's suppose you have to borrow or rent a torque wrench. Even if you only need it to tighten the spark plugs, you might as well check the torque of as many critical fasteners as time allows.

The first step in this maintenance program is to prepare yourself before the actual work begins. Read through all the procedures you're planning to do, then gather up all the parts and tools needed. If it looks like you might run into problems during a particular job, seek advice from a mechanic or an experienced do-it-yourselfer.

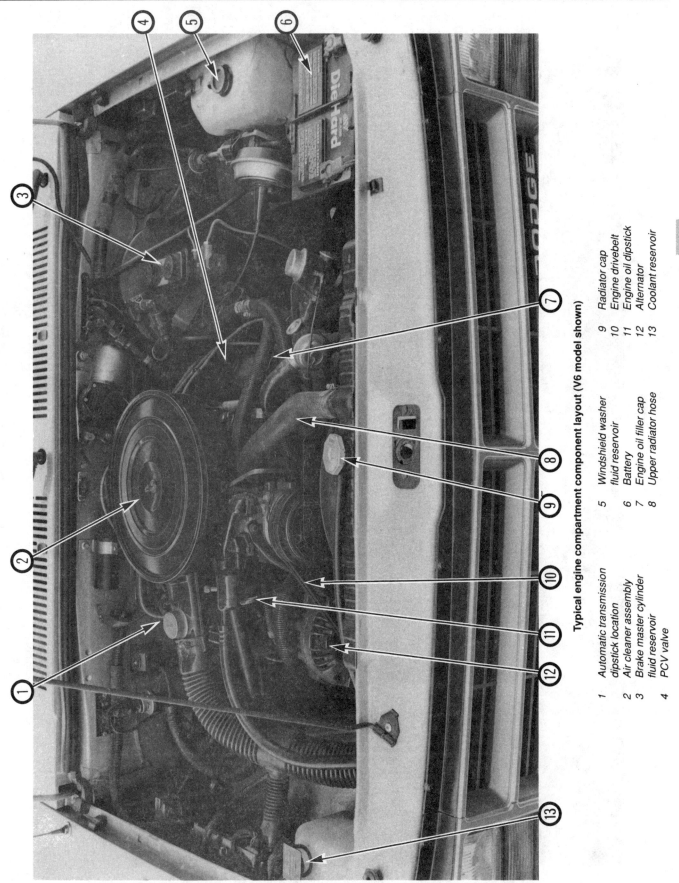

Typical engine compartment component layout (V6 model shown)

1   Automatic transmission
    dipstick location
2   Air cleaner assembly
3   Brake master cylinder
    fluid reservoir
4   PCV valve

5   Windshield washer
    fluid reservoir
6   Battery
7   Engine oil filler cap
8   Upper radiator hose

9   Radiator cap
10 Engine drivebelt
11 Engine oil dipstick
12 Alternator
13 Coolant reservoir

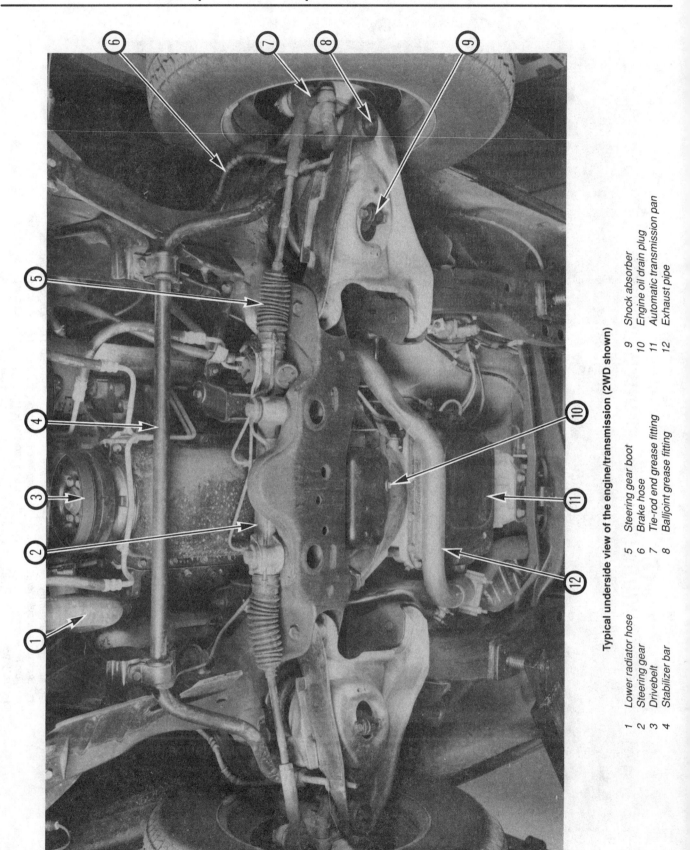

Typical underside view of the engine/transmission (2WD shown)

1   Lower radiator hose
2   Steering gear
3   Drivebelt
4   Stabilizer bar
5   Steering gear boot
6   Brake hose
7   Tie-rod end grease fitting
8   Balljoint grease fitting
9   Shock absorber
10 Engine oil drain plug
11 Automatic transmission pan
12 Exhaust pipe

Typical rear underside component layout

1 Rear axle/differential
2 Brake hydraulic line
3 Shock absorber
4 Parking brake cable

5 Muffler
6 Driveshaft U-joint
7 Fuel tank
8 Leaf spring

1

2 Dodge Dakota Maintenance schedule

The following maintenance intervals are based on the assumption the vehicle owner will be doing the maintenance or service work, as opposed to having a dealer service department do the work. Although the time/mileage intervals are loosely based on factory recommendations, most have been shortened to ensure, for example, that such items as lubricants and fluids are checked/changed at intervals that promote maximum engine/driveline service life. Also, subject to the preference of the individual owner interested in keeping the vehicle in peak condition at all times, and with the vehicle's ultimate resale in mind, many of the maintenance procedures may be performed more often than recommended in the following schedule. We encourage such owner initiative.

When the vehicle is new it should be serviced initially by a factory authorized dealer service department to protect the factory warranty. In many cases the initial maintenance check is done at no cost to the owner (check with your dealer service department for additional information).

Every 250 miles or weekly, whichever comes first

Check the engine oil level (Section 4)
Check the engine coolant level (Section 4)
Check the windshield washer fluid level (Section 4)
Check the brake and clutch fluid levels (Section 4)
Check the tires and tire pressures (Section 5)

Every 3000 miles or 3 months, whichever comes first

All items listed above, plus . . .
Check the automatic transmission fluid level (Section 6)
Check the power steering fluid level (Section 7)
Check and service the battery (Section 8)
Check the cooling system (Section 9)
Inspect and replace, if necessary, all underhood hoses (Section 10)
Inspect and replace, if necessary, the windshield wiper blades (Section 11)
Change the engine oil and filter (Section 12)
Inspect the suspension and steering components (Section 13)
Inspect the exhaust system (Section 14)
Check the hydraulic clutch (Section 15)
Check the manual transmission lubricant (Section 16)
Check the transfer case lubricant level (4WD models only) (Section 17)
Check the differential lubricant level (Section 18)

Every 7500 miles or 6 months, whichever comes first

All items listed above, plus . . .
Rotate the tires (Section 19)
Check the brakes (Section 20)
Inspect the fuel system (Section 21)
Check the carburetor/throttle body mounting bolt/nut torque (Section 22)
Check the throttle linkage (Section 23)
Check the engine drivebelt (Section 24)
Check the seatbelts (Section 25)
Check the starter safety switch (Section 26)
Lubricate the chassis components (Section 28)

Every 30,000 miles or 24 months, whichever comes first

All items listed above, plus . . .
Change the automatic transmission fluid (Section 29)**
Replace the air filter (Section 27)
Change the manual transmission lubricant (Section 30)
Change the transfer case lubricant (4WD models only) (Section 31)
Change the differential lubricant (Section 32)
Check and repack the front wheel bearings (2WD models only) (Section 33)*
Service the cooling system (drain, flush and refill) (Section 34)
Check the Positive Crankcase Ventilation (PCV) system (Section 35)
Check the evaporative emissions control system (Section 36)
Check the Exhaust Gas Recirculation (EGR) system (V6 engines only) (Section 37)
Check the thermostatically-controlled air cleaner (Section 38)
Check the crankcase inlet filter (V6 engines only) (Section 39)
Replace the fuel filter (Section 40)
Check and clean, if necessary, the exhaust manifold heat control valve (V6 engines only) (Section 41)
Clean the carburetor choke shaft (Section 42)
Replace the spark plugs (Section 43)
Inspect the spark plug wires, distributor cap and rotor Section 44)
Check and adjust, if necessary, the ignition timing (Section 45)

Every 52,500 miles or 36 months, whichever comes first

All items listed above, plus . . .
Replace the oxygen sensor (Section 46)
Replace the EGR valve and clean the passages (1987 through 1989 V6 models) (Section 47)

Every 60,000 miles or 40 months, whichever comes first

All items listed above, plus . . .
Replace the EGR valve and clean the passages (1990 V6 models) (Section 47)

* This item is affected by "severe" operating conditions as described below. If the vehicle is operated under severe conditions, perform all maintenance indicated with an asterisk (*) at 3000 mile/three-month intervals. Severe conditions exist if you mainly operate the vehicle . . .
in dusty areas
towing a trailer
idling for extended periods and/or driving at low speeds
when outside temperatures remain below freezing and most trips are less than four miles long
** If operated under one or more of the following conditions, change the automatic transmission fluid every 15,000 miles:
in heavy city traffic where the outside temperature regularly reaches 90-degrees F or higher
in hilly or mountainous terrain
frequent trailer pulling

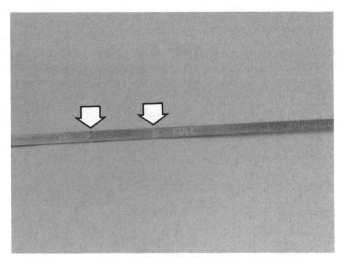

4.4   The engine oil level must be maintained between the marks at all times – it takes one quart of oil to raise the level from the ADD mark to the FULL mark

4.6   Oil is added to the engine after unscrewing the cap from the valve cover (V6 engine shown)

3   Tune-up general information

The term tune-up is used in this manual to represent a combination of individual operations rather than one specific procedure.

If, from the time the vehicle is new, the routine maintenance schedule is followed closely and frequent checks are made of fluid levels and high wear items, as suggested throughout this manual, the engine will be kept in relatively good running condition and the need for additional work will be minimized.

More likely than not, however, there will be times when the engine is running poorly due to lack of regular maintenance. This is even more likely if a used vehicle, which has not received regular and frequent maintenance checks, is purchased. In such cases, an engine tune-up will be needed outside of the regular routine maintenance intervals.

The first step in any tune-up or diagnostic procedure to help correct a poor running engine is a cylinder compression check. A compression check (see Chapter 2, Part B) will help determine the condition of internal engine components and should be used as a guide for tune-up and repair procedures. If, for instance, the compression check indicates serious internal engine wear, a conventional tune-up won't improve the performance of the engine and would be a waste of time and money. Because of its importance, the compression check should be done by someone with the right equipment and the knowledge to use it properly.

The following procedures are those most often needed to bring a generally poor running engine back into a proper state of tune.

Minor tune-up

Check all engine related fluids (Section 4)
Clean, inspect and test the battery (Section 8)
Check the cooling system (Section 9)
Check all underhood hoses (Section 10)
Check the air filter (Section 27)
Check and adjust the drivebelts (Section 24)
Check the PCV valve (Section 35)
Replace the spark plugs (Section 43)
Inspect the spark plug and coil wires (Section 44)
Inspect the distributor cap and rotor (Section 44)
Check and adjust the ignition timing (Section 45)

Major tune-up

All items listed under Minor tune-up, plus . . .
Check the fuel system (Section 21)
Replace the air filter (Section 40)
Check the EGR system (Section 37)
Replace the spark plug wires (Section 44)

Replace the distributor cap and rotor (Section 44)
Check the ignition system (Chapter 5)
Check the charging system (Chapter 5)

4   Fluid level checks

Note: *The following are fluid level checks to be done on a 250 mile or weekly basis. Additional fluid level checks can be found in specific maintenance procedures which follow. Regardless of intervals, be alert to fluid leaks under the vehicle which would indicate a fault to be corrected immediately.*

1   Fluids are an essential part of the lubrication, cooling, brake, clutch and windshield washer systems. Because the fluids gradually become depleted and/or contaminated during normal operation of the vehicle, they must be periodically replenished. See Recommended lubricants and fluids at the beginning of this Chapter before adding fluid to any of the following components. **Note:** *The vehicle must be on level ground when fluid levels are checked.*

Engine oil

Refer to illustrations 4.4 and 4.6

2   The engine oil level is checked with a dipstick that extends through a tube and into the oil pan at the bottom of the engine.
3   The oil level should be checked before the vehicle has been driven, or about 15 minutes after the engine has been shut off. If the oil is checked immediately after driving the vehicle, some of the oil will remain in the upper engine components, resulting in an inaccurate reading on the dipstick.
4   Pull the dipstick out of the tube and wipe all the oil from the end with a clean rag or paper towel. Insert the clean dipstick all the way back into the tube, then pull it out again. Note the oil at the end of the dipstick. Add oil as necessary to keep the level between the ADD and FULL marks on the dipstick **(see illustration)**.
5   Do not overfill the engine by adding too much oil since this may result in oil fouled spark plugs, oil leaks or oil seal failures.
6   Oil is added to the engine after unscrewing a cap from the valve cover **(see illustration)**. A funnel may help to reduce spills.
7   Checking the oil level is an important preventive maintenance step. A consistently low oil level indicates oil leakage through damaged seals, defective gaskets or past worn rings or valve guides. If the oil looks milky or has water droplets in it, the cylinder head gasket(s) may be blown or the head(s) or block may be cracked. The engine should be checked immediately. The condition of the oil should also be checked. Whenever you check the oil level, slide your thumb and index finger up the dipstick before wiping off the oil. If you see small dirt or metal particles clinging to the dipstick, the oil should be changed (Section 12).

4.8   Be aware of the engine temperature when checking the coolant level

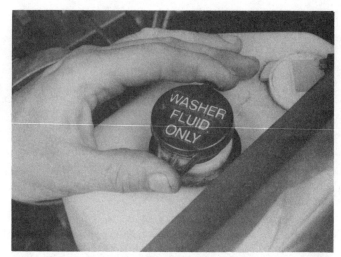

4.14   The windshield washer fluid level can be checked visually through the translucent plastic reservoir – do not overfill it

Engine coolant

Refer to illustration 4.8

Warning: *Do not allow antifreeze to come in contact with your skin or painted surfaces of the vehicle. Flush contaminated areas immediately with plenty of water. Don't store new coolant or leave old coolant lying around where it's accessible to children or pets – they're attracted by its sweet taste. Ingestion of even a small amount of coolant can be fatal! Wipe up garage floor and drip pan coolant spills immediately. Keep antifreeze containers covered and repair leaks in the cooling system as soon as they are noted.*

8   All vehicles covered by this manual are equipped with a pressurized coolant recovery system. A white plastic coolant reservoir located in the engine compartment is connected by a hose to the radiator filler neck **(see illustration)**. If the engine overheats, coolant escapes through a valve in the radiator cap and travels through the hose into the reservoir. As the engine cools, the coolant is automatically drawn back into the cooling system to maintain the correct level. **Warning:** *Do not remove the radiator cap to check the coolant level when the engine is warm.*

9   The coolant level in the reservoir should be checked regularly. The level in the reservoir varies with the temperature of the engine. When the engine is cold, the coolant level should be at or slightly above the MIN mark on the reservoir. Once the engine has warmed up, the level should

be at or near the MAX mark. If it isn't, allow the engine to cool, then remove the cap from the reservoir and add a 50/50 mixture of ethylene glycol-based antifreeze and water.

10   Drive the vehicle and recheck the coolant level. If only a small amount of coolant is required to bring the system up to the proper level, water can be used. However, repeated additions of water will dilute the antifreeze and water solution. In order to maintain the proper ratio of antifreeze and water, always top up the coolant level with the correct mixture. An empty plastic milk jug or bleach bottle makes an excellent container for mixing coolant. Do not use rust inhibitors or additives.

11   If the coolant level drops consistently, there may be a leak in the system. Inspect the radiator, hoses, filler cap, drain plugs and water pump (see Section 9). If no leaks are noted, have the radiator cap pressure tested by a service station.

12   If you have to remove the radiator cap, wait until the engine has cooled, then wrap a thick cloth around the cap and turn it to the first stop. If coolant or steam escapes, let the engine cool down longer, then remove the cap.

13   Check the condition of the coolant as well. It should be relatively clear. If it's brown or rust colored, the system should be drained, flushed and re-filled. Even if the coolant appears to be normal, the corrosion inhibitors wear out, so it must be replaced at the specified intervals.

4.19   The brake fluid level is easily checked after unscrewing the cap – the level should be even with the ring at the base of the filler neck

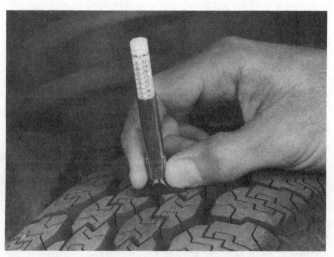

5.2   A tire tread depth indicator should be used to monitor tire wear – they're available at auto parts stores and service stations and cost very little

Windshield washer fluid

Refer to illustration 4.14

14   Fluid for the windshield washer system is located in a plastic reservoir in the engine compartment **(see illustration)**.

15   In milder climates, plain water can be used in the reservoir, but it should be kept no more than 2/3 full to allow for expansion if the water freezes. In colder climates, use windshield washer system antifreeze, available at any auto parts store, to lower the freezing point of the fluid. Mix the antifreeze with water in accordance with the manufacturer's directions on the container. **Caution:** *Don't use cooling system antifreeze – it will damage the vehicle's paint.*

16   To help prevent icing in cold weather, warm the windshield with the defroster before using the washer.

Battery electrolyte

17   All vehicles with which this manual is concerned are equipped with a battery which is permanently sealed (except for vent holes) and has no filler caps. Water doesn't have to be added to these batteries at any time. If a maintenance-type battery is installed, the caps on the top of the battery should be removed periodically to check for a low water level. This check is most critical during the warm summer months.

Brake and clutch fluid

Refer to illustration 4.19

18   The brake master cylinder is mounted on the front of the power booster unit in the engine compartment. The clutch cylinder used on manual transmission-equipped vehicles is mounted adjacent to it on the firewall.

19   The fluid inside can be checked after removing the cap **(see illustration)**. Be sure to wipe the top of the reservoir cover with a clean rag to prevent contamination of the brake and/or clutch system before removing the cover.

20   When adding fluid, pour it carefully into the reservoir to avoid spilling it on surrounding painted surfaces. Be sure the specified fluid is used, since mixing different types of brake fluid can cause damage to the system. See Recommended lubricants and fluids at the front of this Chapter or your owner's manual. **Warning:** *Brake fluid can harm your eyes and damage painted surfaces, so use extreme caution when handling or pouring it. Do not use brake fluid that has been standing open or is more than one year old. Brake fluid absorbs moisture from the air. Excess moisture can cause a dangerous loss of brake performance.*

21   At this time the fluid and master cylinder can be inspected for contamination. The system should be drained and refilled if deposits, dirt particles or water droplets are seen in the fluid.

22   After filling the reservoir to the proper level, make sure the cover is on tight to prevent fluid leakage.

23   The brake fluid level in the master cylinder will drop slightly as the pads and the brake shoes at each wheel wear down during normal operation. If the master cylinder requires repeated additions to keep it at the proper level, it's an indication of leakage in the brake system, which should be corrected immediately. Check all brake lines and connections (see Section 20 for more information).

24   If, upon checking the master cylinder fluid level, you discover one or both reservoirs empty or nearly empty, the brake system should be bled (Chapter 9).

5   Tire and tire pressure checks

Refer to illustrations 5.2, 5.3, 5.4a, 5.4b and 5.8

1   Periodic inspection of the tires may spare you the inconvenience of being stranded with a flat tire. It can also provide you with vital information regarding possible problems in the steering and suspension systems before major damage occurs.

2   The original tires on this vehicle are equipped with 1/2-inch wear bands that will appear when tread depth reaches 1/16-inch, but they don't appear until the tires are worn out. Tread wear can be monitored with a simple, inexpensive device known as a tread depth indicator **(see illustration)**.

3   Note any abnormal tread wear **(see illustration)**. Tread pattern irregularities such as cupping, flat spots and more wear on one side than the other are indications of front end alignment and/or balance problems. If any of these conditions are noted, take the vehicle to a tire shop or service station to correct the problem.

Condition	Probable cause	Corrective action	Condition	Probable cause	Corrective action
Shoulder wear	• Underinflation (both sides wear) • Incorrect wheel camber (one side wear) • Hard cornering • Lack of rotation	• Measure and adjust pressure. • Repair or replace axle and suspension parts. • Reduce speed. • Rotate tires.	Feathered edge Toe wear	• Incorrect toe	• Adjust toe-in.
Center wear	• Overinflation • Lack of rotation	• Measure and adjust pressure. • Rotate tires.	Uneven wear	• Incorrect camber or caster • Malfunctioning suspension • Unbalanced wheel • Out-of-round brake drum • Lack of rotation	• Repair or replace axle and suspension parts. • Repair or replace suspension parts. • Balance or replace. • Turn or replace. • Rotate tires.

5.3   This chart will help you determine the condition of the tires, the probable cause(s) of abnormal wear and the corrective action necessary

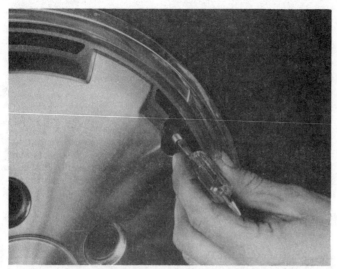

5.4a   If a tire loses air on a steady basis, check the valve core first to make sure it's snug (special inexpensive wrenches are commonly available at auto parts stores)

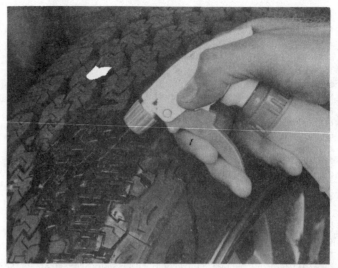

5.4b   If the valve core is tight, raise the corner of the vehicle with the low tire and spray a soapy water solution onto the tread as the tire is turned – slow leaks will cause small bubbles to appear

4   Look closely for cuts, punctures and embedded nails or tacks. Sometimes a tire will hold air pressure for a short time or leak down very slowly after a nail has embedded itself in the tread. If a slow leak persists, check the valve stem core to make sure it's tight **(see illustration)**. Examine the tread for an object that may have embedded itself in the tire or for a "plug" that may have begun to leak (radial tire punctures are repaired with a plug that's installed in a puncture). If a puncture is suspected, it can be easily verified by spraying a solution of soapy water onto the puncture area **(see illustration)**. The soapy solution will bubble if there's a leak. Unless the puncture is unusually large, a tire shop or service station can usually repair the tire.

5   Carefully inspect the inner sidewall of each tire for evidence of brake fluid leakage. If you see any, inspect the brakes immediately.

6   Correct air pressure adds miles to the lifespan of the tires, improves mileage and enhances overall ride quality. Tire pressure cannot be accurately estimated by looking at a tire, especially if it's a radial. A tire pressure gauge is essential. Keep an accurate gauge in the vehicle. The pressure gauges attached to the nozzles of air hoses at gas stations are often inaccurate.

7   Always check tire pressure when the tires are cold. Cold, in this case, means the vehicle has not been driven over a mile in the three hours preceding a tire pressure check. A pressure rise of four to eight pounds is not uncommon once the tires are warm.

8   Unscrew the valve cap protruding from the wheel or hubcap and push the gauge firmly onto the valve stem **(see illustration)**. Note the reading on the gauge and compare the figure to the recommended tire pressure shown on the placard on the driver's side door pillar. Be sure to reinstall the valve cap to keep dirt and moisture out of the valve stem mechanism. Check all four tires and, if necessary, add enough air to bring them up to the recommended pressure.

9   Don't forget to keep the spare tire inflated to the specified pressure (refer to your owner's manual or the tire sidewall).

---

6   Automatic transmission fluid level check

Refer to illustrations 6.3 and 6.6

1   The automatic transmission fluid level should be carefully maintained. Low fluid level can lead to slipping or loss of drive, while overfilling can cause foaming and loss of fluid. Some models are equipped with an electronic automatic transmission fluid level sensor; the transmission fluid level should be checked as described below whenever the sensor light is on.

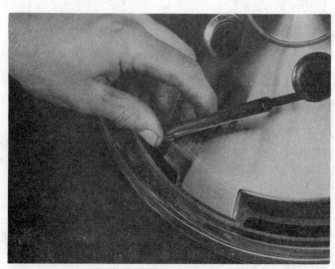

5.8   To extend the life of the tires, check the air pressure at least once a week with an accurate gauge (don't forget the spare!)

6.3   The automatic transmission dipstick is located at the rear of the engine compartment

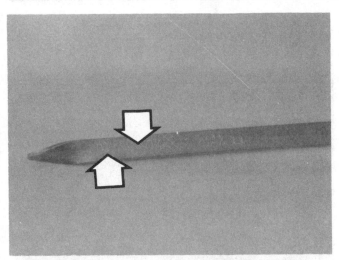

6.6 When checking the automatic transmission fluid level, be sure to note the fluid temperature – when it's warm, it should be between the two dimples (arrows); when it's hot, it should be in the crosshatched area, near the MAX line

7.2 The power steering fluid reservoir is located near the front of the engine – turn the cap counterclockwise to remove it

2   With the parking brake set, start the engine, then move the shift lever through all the gear ranges, ending in Neutral. The fluid level must be checked with the vehicle level and the engine running at idle. **Note:** *Incorrect fluid level readings will result if the vehicle has just been driven at high speeds for an extended period, in hot weather in city traffic, or if it has been pulling a trailer. If any of these conditions apply, wait until the fluid has cooled (about 30 minutes).*

3   With the transmission at normal operating temperature, remove the dipstick from the filler tube. The dipstick is located at the rear of the engine compartment on the passenger's side **(see illustration)**.

4   Carefully touch the fluid at the end of the dipstick to determine if it's warm or hot. Wipe the fluid from the dipstick with a clean rag and push it back into the filler tube until the cap seats.

5   Pull the dipstick out again and note the fluid level.

6   If the fluid felt warm, the level should be between the two dimples **(see illustration)**. If it felt hot, the level should be in the crosshatched area, near the MAX line. If additional fluid is required, add it directly into the tube using a funnel. It takes about one pint to raise the level from the bottom of the crosshatched area to the MAX line with a hot transmission, so add the fluid a little at a time and keep checking the level until it's correct.

7   The condition of the fluid should also be checked along with the level. If the fluid at the end of the dipstick is a dark reddish-brown color, or if it smells burned, it should be changed. If you are in doubt about the condi-tion of the fluid, purchase some new fluid and compare the two for color and smell.

---

7   Power steering fluid level check

Refer to illustrations 7.2, 7.6a and 7.6b

1   Unlike manual steering, the power steering system relies on fluid which may, over a period of time, require replenishing.

2   The fluid reservoir for the power steering pump is located on the pump body at the front of the engine **(see illustration)**.

3   For the check, the front wheels should be pointed straight ahead and the engine should be off.

4   Use a clean rag to wipe off the reservoir cap and the area around the cap. This will help prevent any foreign matter from entering the reservoir during the check.

5   Twist off the cap and check the temperature of the fluid at the end of the dipstick with your finger.

6   Wipe off the fluid with a clean rag, reinsert the dipstick, then withdraw it and read the fluid level. The fluid should be at the proper level, depending on whether it was checked hot or cold **(see illustrations)**. Never allow the fluid level to drop below the lower mark on the dipstick.

7.6a The power steering fluid dipstick has marks on both sides so the fluid level can be checked when hot . . .

7.6b . . . or cold

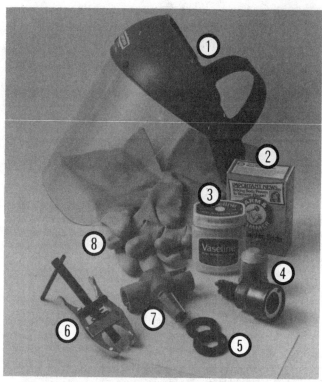

8.1   Tools and materials required for battery maintenance

1   *Face shield/safety goggles* – *When removing corrosion with a brush, the acidic particles can easily fly up into your eyes*
2   *Baking soda* – *A solution of baking soda and water can be used to neutralize corrosion*
3   *Petroleum jelly* – *A layer of this on the battery posts will help prevent corrosion*
4   *Battery post/cable cleaner* – *This wire brush cleaning tool will remove all traces of corrosion from the battery posts and cable clamps*
5   *Treated felt washers* – *Placing one of these on each post, directly under the cable clamps, will help prevent corrosion*
6   *Puller* – *Sometimes the cable clamps are very difficult to pull off the posts, even after the nut/bolt has been completely loosened. This tool pulls the clamp straight up and off the post without damage.*
7   *Battery post/cable cleaner* – *Here is another cleaning tool which is a slightly different version of number 4 above, but it does the same thing*
8   *Rubber gloves* – *Another safety item to consider when servicing the battery; remember that's acid inside the battery!*

7   If additional fluid is required, pour the specified type directly into the reservoir, using a funnel to prevent spills.
8   If the reservoir requires frequent fluid additions, all power steering hoses, hose connections and the power steering pump should be carefully checked for leaks.

8   Battery check and maintenance

Refer to illustrations 8.1, 8.7a, 8.7b, 8.7c and 8.7d
Warning: *Certain precautions must be followed when checking and serv-icing the battery. Hydrogen gas, which is highly flammable, is always pres-ent in the battery cells, so don't smoke and keep open flames and sparks away from the battery. The electrolyte inside the battery is actually dilute sulfuric acid, which will cause injury if splashed on your skin or in your*

8.7a   Battery terminal corrosion usually appears as light, fluffy powder

8.7b   Removing a cable from the battery post with a wrench – sometimes a special battery pliers is required for this procedure if corrosion has caused deterioration of the nut hex (always remove the ground cable first and hook it up last!)

eyes. It will also ruin clothes and painted surfaces. When removing the battery cables, always detach the negative cable first and hook it up last!
1   Battery maintenance is an important procedure which will help ensure that you are not stranded because of a dead battery. Several tools are re-quired for this procedure **(see illustration)**.
2   When checking/servicing the battery, always turn the engine and all accessories off.
3   A sealed (sometimes called maintenance-free), battery is standard equipment on these vehicles. The cell caps cannot be removed, no elec-trolyte checks are required and water cannot be added to the cells. How-ever, if a maintenance-type aftermarket battery has been installed, the following maintenance procedure can be used.
4   Remove the caps and check the electrolyte level in each of the battery cells. It must be above the plates. There's usually a split-ring indicator in each cell to indicate the correct level. If the level is low, add distilled water only, then reinstall the cell caps. **Caution:** *Overfilling the cells may cause electrolyte to spill over during periods of heavy charging, causing corro-sion and damage to nearby components.*

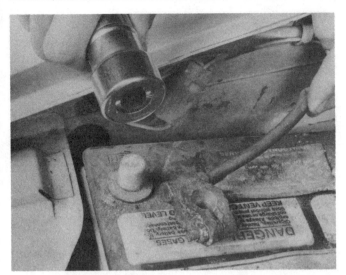

8.7c   Regardless of the type of tool used to clean the battery posts, a clean, shiny surface should be the result

8.7d   When cleaning the cable clamps, all corrosion must be removed (the inside of the cable is tapered to match the taper on the post, so don't remove too much material)

5   The external condition of the battery should be checked periodically. Look for damage such as a cracked case.

6   Check the tightness of the battery cable bolts/nuts to ensure good electrical connections. Inspect the entire length of each cable, looking for cracked or abraded insulation and frayed conductors.

7   If corrosion (visible as white, fluffy deposits) is evident, remove the cables from the terminals, clean them and reinstall them (see illustrations). Corrosion can be kept to a minimum by applying a layer of petroleum jelly or grease to the bolt threads.

8   Make sure the battery carrier is in good condition and the hold-down clamp is tight. If the battery is removed (see Chapter 5 for the removal and installation procedure), make sure that no parts remain in the bottom of the carrier when it's reinstalled. When reinstalling the hold-down clamp, don't overtighten the bolt.

9   Corrosion on the carrier, battery case and surrounding areas can be removed with a solution of water and baking soda. Apply the mixture with a small brush, let it work, then rinse it off with plenty of clean water.

10   Any metal parts of the vehicle damaged by corrosion should be coated with a zinc-based primer, then painted.

11   Additional information on the battery, charging and jump starting can be found in the front of this manual and Chapter 5.

9   Cooling system check

Refer to illustration 9.4

1   Many major engine failures can be attributed to a faulty cooling system. If the vehicle is equipped with an automatic transmission, the cooling system also cools the transmission fluid and thus plays an important role in prolonging transmission life.

2   The cooling system should be checked with the engine cold. Do this before the vehicle is driven for the day or after it has been shut off for at least three hours.

3   Remove the radiator cap by turning it to the left until it reaches a stop. If you hear a hissing sound (indicating there is still pressure in the system), wait until this stops. Now press down on the cap with the palm of your hand and continue turning to the left until the cap can be removed. Thoroughly clean the cap, inside and out, with clean water. Also clean the filler neck on the radiator. All traces of corrosion should be removed. The coolant inside the radiator should be relatively transparent. If it is rust colored, the system should be drained and refilled (Section 34). If the coolant level is not up to the top, add additional antifreeze/coolant mixture (see Section 4).

4   Carefully check the large upper and lower radiator hoses along with the smaller diameter heater hoses which run from the engine to the fire-

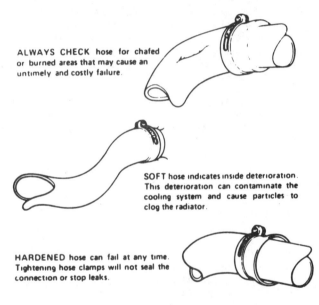

ALWAYS CHECK hose for chafed or burned areas that may cause an untimely and costly failure.

SOFT hose indicates inside deterioration. This deterioration can contaminate the cooling system and cause particles to clog the radiator.

HARDENED hose can fail at any time. Tightening hose clamps will not seal the connection or stop leaks.

SWOLLEN hose or oil soaked ends indicate danger and possible failure from oil or grease contamination. Squeeze the hose to locate cracks and breaks that cause leaks.

9.4   Hoses, like drivebelts, have a habit of failing at the worst possible time – to prevent the inconvenience of a blown radiator or heater hose, inspect them carefully as shown here

wall. Inspect each hose along its entire length, replacing any hose which is cracked, swollen or shows signs of deterioration. Cracks may become more apparent if the hose is squeezed (see illustration). Regardless of condition, it's a good idea to replace hoses with new ones every two years.

10.1   Air conditioning hoses are identified by the metal tubes used at connections (arrow) – DO NOT disconnect or accidently damage the air conditioning hoses (the system is under high pressure)

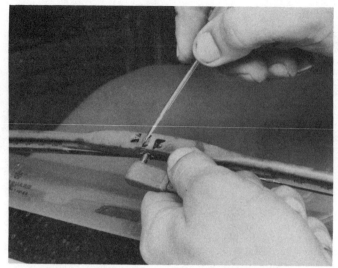

11.6   Use a small screwdriver to pry the release lever up

5   Make sure all hose connections are tight. A leak in the cooling system will usually show up as white or rust colored deposits on the areas adjoining the leak. If wire-type clamps are used at the ends of the hoses, it may be a good idea to replace them with more secure screw-type clamps.
6   Use compressed air or a soft brush to remove bugs, leaves, etc. from the front of the radiator or air conditioning condenser. Be careful not to damage the delicate cooling fins or cut yourself on them.
7   Every other inspection, or at the first indication of cooling system problems, have the cap and system pressure tested. If you don't have a pressure tester, most gas stations and repair shops will do this for a minimal charge.

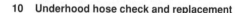

10   Underhood hose check and replacement

Refer to illustration 10.1

General

1   **Caution:** *Replacement of air conditioning hoses must be left to a dealer service department or air conditioning shop that has the equipment to depressurize the system safely. Never remove air conditioning components or hoses (see illustration) until the system has been depressurized.*
2   High temperatures in the engine compartment can cause the deterioration of the rubber and plastic hoses used for engine, accessory and emission systems operation. Periodic inspection should be made for cracks, loose clamps, material hardening and leaks. Information specific to the cooling system hoses can be found in Section 9.
3   Some, but not all, hoses are secured to the fittings with clamps. Where clamps are used, check to be sure they haven't lost their tension, allowing the hose to leak. If clamps aren't used, make sure the hose has not expanded and/or hardened where it slips over the fitting, allowing it to leak.

Vacuum hoses

4   It's quite common for vacuum hoses, especially those in the emissions system, to be color coded or identified by colored stripes molded into them. Various systems require hoses with different wall thicknesses, collapse resistance and temperature resistance. When replacing hoses, be sure the new ones are made of the same material.
5   Often the only effective way to check a hose is to remove it completely from the vehicle. If more than one hose is removed, be sure to label the hoses and fittings to ensure correct installation.

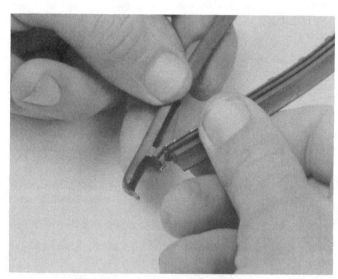

11.7   Squeeze the tabs on the end of the blade, pull the end out of the bridge claw, then slide the element out of the blade

6   When checking vacuum hoses, be sure to include any plastic T-fittings in the check. Inspect the fittings for cracks and the hose where it fits over the fitting for distortion, which could cause leakage.
7   A small piece of vacuum hose (1/4-inch inside diameter) can be used as a stethoscope to detect vacuum leaks. Hold one end of the hose to your ear and probe around vacuum hoses and fittings, listening for the "hissing" sound characteristic of a vacuum leak. **Warning:** *When probing with the vacuum hose stethoscope, be very careful not to come into contact with moving engine components such as the drivebelt, cooling fan, etc.*

Fuel hose

Warning: *There are certain precautions which must be taken when inspecting or servicing fuel system components. Work in a well ventilated area and do not allow open flames (cigarettes, appliance pilot lights, etc.) or bare light bulbs near the work area. Mop up any spills immediately and do not store fuel soaked rags where they could ignite. On fuel-injected models, the fuel system is under high pressure, so if any fuel lines are to be disconnected, the pressure in the system must be relieved first (see Chapter 4 for more information).*

12   If a section of metal fuel line must be replaced, only seamless steel tubing should be used, since copper and aluminum tubing don't have the strength necessary to withstand normal engine vibration.

13   Check the metal brake lines where they enter the master cylinder and brake proportioning unit (if used) for cracks in the lines or loose fittings. Any sign of brake fluid leakage calls for an immediate thorough inspection of the brake system.

---

11   Wiper blade inspection and replacement

Refer to illustrations 11.6 and 11.7

1   The windshield wiper and blade assembly should be inspected periodically for damage, loose components and cracked or worn blade elements.

2   Road film can build up on the wiper blades and affect their efficiency, so they should be washed regularly with a mild detergent solution.

3   The action of the wiping mechanism can loosen the bolts, nuts and fasteners, so they should be checked and tightened, as necessary, at the same time the wiper blades are checked.

4   If the wiper blade elements (sometimes called inserts) are cracked, worn or warped, they should be replaced with new ones.

5   Pull the wiper blade/arm assembly away from the glass.

6   Insert a small screwdriver into the release slot, pry up to detach the blade assembly and slide it off the wiper arm and over the retaining stud **(see illustration)**.

7   Squeeze the tabs on the end, pull the blade out of the bridge claw, then slide the element out of the blade assembly bridge **(see illustration)**.

8   Compare the new element with the old for length, design, etc.

9   Slide the new element into place. It will automatically lock at the correct location.

10   Reinstall the blade assembly on the arm, wet the windshield and check for proper operation.

---

12   Engine oil and filter change

Refer to illustrations 12.3, 12.9, 12.14 and 12.18

1   Frequent oil changes are the most important preventive maintenance procedures that can be done by the home mechanic. As engine oil ages, it becomes diluted and contaminated, which leads to premature engine wear.

2   Although some sources recommend oil filter changes every other oil change, we feel that the minimal cost of an oil filter and the relative ease with which it is installed dictate that a new filter be installed every time the oil is changed.

3   Gather together all necessary tools and materials before beginning this procedure **(see illustration)**.

4   You should have plenty of clean rags and newspapers handy to mop up any spills. Access to the under side of the vehicle may be improved if the vehicle can be lifted on a hoist, driven onto ramps or supported by jackstands. **Warning:** *Do not work under a vehicle which is supported only by a bumper, hydraulic or scissors-type jack.*

5   If this is your first oil change, get under the vehicle and familiarize yourself with the locations of the oil drain plug and the oil filter. The engine and exhaust components will be warm during the actual work, so note how they are situated to avoid touching them when working under the vehicle.

6   Warm the engine to normal operating temperature. If the new oil or any tools are needed, use this warm-up time to gather everything necessary for the job. The correct type of oil for your application can be found in Recommended lubricants and fluids at the beginning of this Chapter.

7   With the engine oil warm (warm engine oil will drain better and more built-up sludge will be removed with it), raise and support the vehicle. Make sure it's safely supported!

8   Move all necessary tools, rags and newspapers under the vehicle. Set the drain pan under the drain plug. Keep in mind that the oil will initially flow from the pan with some force; position the pan accordingly.

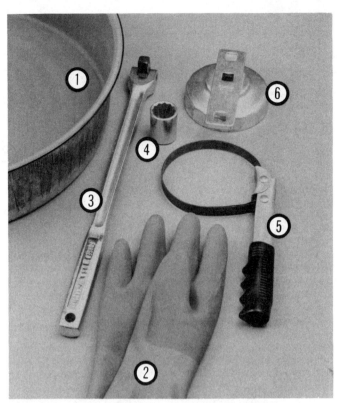

12.3   These tools are required when changing the engine oil and filter

1 **Drain pan** – *It should be fairly shallow in depth, but wide to prevent spills*
2 **Rubber gloves** – *When removing the drain plug and filter, you will get oil on your hands (the gloves will prevent burns)*
3 **Breaker bar** – *Sometimes the oil drain plug is tight and a long breaker bar is needed to loosen it*
4 **Socket** – *To be used with the breaker bar or a ratchet (must be the correct size to fit the drain plug – 6-point preferred)*
5 **Filter wrench** – *This is a metal band-type wrench, which requires clearance around the filter to be effective*
6 **Filter wrench** – *This type fits on the bottom of the filter and can be turned with a ratchet or breaker bar (different size wrenches are available for different types of filters)*

8   Check all rubber fuel lines for deterioration and chafing. Check especially for cracks in areas where the hose bends and just before fittings, such as where a hose attaches to the fuel filter.

9   High quality fuel line, usually identified by the word Fluroelastomer printed on the hose, should be used for fuel line replacement. Never, under any circumstances, use unreinforced vacuum line, clear plastic tubing or water hose for fuel lines.

10   Spring-type clamps are commonly used on fuel lines. These clamps often lose their tension over a period of time, and can be "sprung" during removal. Replace all spring-type clamps with screw clamps whenever a hose is replaced.

Metal lines

11   Sections of metal line are often used for fuel line between the fuel pump and carburetor or fuel injection unit. Check carefully to be sure the line has not been bent or crimped and that cracks have not started in the line.

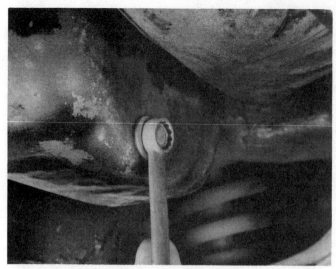

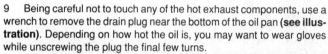

12.9   The oil drain plug is located at the bottom of the pan and should be removed with a socket or box-end wrench – DO NOT use an open-end wrench (the corners on the hex can be easily rounded off)

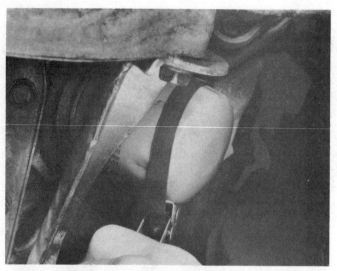

12.14   Use a strap-type oil filter wrench to loosen the filter – if access makes removal difficult, other types of filter wrenches are available

9   Being careful not to touch any of the hot exhaust components, use a wrench to remove the drain plug near the bottom of the oil pan **(see illustration)**. Depending on how hot the oil is, you may want to wear gloves while unscrewing the plug the final few turns.

10   Allow the old oil to drain into the pan. It may be necessary to move the pan as the oil flow slows to a trickle.

11   After all the oil has drained, wipe off the drain plug with a clean rag. Small metal particles may cling to the plug and would immediately contaminate the new oil.

12   Clean the area around the drain plug opening and reinstall the plug. Tighten the plug securely with the wrench. If a torque wrench is available, use it to tighten the plug to the torque listed in this Chapter's Specifications.

13   Move the drain pan into position under the oil filter.

14   Use the filter wrench to loosen the oil filter **(see illustration)**. Chain or metal band filter wrenches may distort the filter canister, but it doesn't matter since the filter will be discarded anyway.

15   Completely unscrew the old filter. Be careful; it's full of oil. Empty the oil inside the filter into the drain pan.

16   Compare the old filter with the new one to make sure they're the same type.

17   Use a clean rag to remove all oil, dirt and sludge from the area where the oil filter mounts to the engine. Check the old filter to make sure the rubber gasket isn't stuck to the engine. If the gasket is stuck to the engine (use a flashlight if necessary), remove it.

18   Apply a light coat of clean oil to the rubber gasket on the new oil filter **(see illustration)**.

19   Attach the new filter to the engine, following the tightening directions printed on the filter canister or packing box. Most filter manufacturers recommend against using a filter wrench due to the possibility of overtightening and damage to the seal.

20   Remove all tools, rags, etc. from under the vehicle, being careful not to spill the oil in the drain pan, then lower the vehicle.

21   Move to the engine compartment and locate the oil filler cap.

22   Pour the fresh oil through the filler opening. A funnel may be helpful.

23   Pour four quarts of fresh oil into the engine. Wait a few minutes to allow the oil to drain into the pan, then check the level on the oil dipstick (see Section 4 if necessary). If the oil level is above the ADD mark, start the engine and allow the new oil to circulate.

24   Run the engine for only about a minute and then shut it off. Immediately look under the vehicle and check for leaks at the oil pan drain plug and around the oil filter. If either is leaking, tighten with a bit more force.

25   With the new oil circulated and the filter now completely full, recheck the level on the dipstick and add more oil as necessary.

12.18   Lubricate the gasket with clean oil before installing the filter on the engine

26   During the first few trips after an oil change, make it a point to check frequently for leaks and proper oil level.

27   The old oil drained from the engine cannot be reused in its present state and should be disposed of. Oil reclamation centers, auto repair shops and gas stations will normally accept the oil, which can be refined and used again. After the oil has cooled it can be drained into a container (capped plastic jugs, topped bottles, milk cartons, etc.) for transport to one of these disposal sites. Don't dispose of the oil by pouring it on the ground or down a drain!

---

13   Suspension and steering check

Refer to illustration 13.4

1   Indications of a fault in these systems are excessive play in the steering wheel before the front wheels react, excessive sway around corners, body movement over rough roads or binding at some point as the steering wheel is turned.

2   Raise the front of the vehicle periodically and visually check the suspension and steering components for wear. Because of the work to be done, make sure the vehicle cannot fall from the stands.

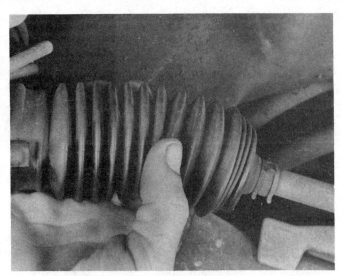

13.4   Push on the steering gear boots to check for cracks or leaking grease

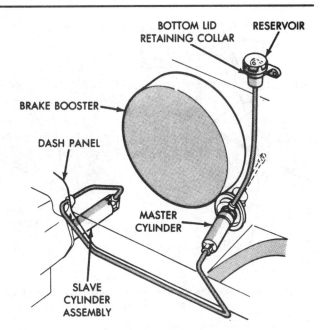

15.1   A typical clutch hydraulic system

3   Check the wheel bearings. Do this by spinning the front wheels. Listen for any abnormal noises and watch to make sure the wheel spins true (doesn't wobble). Grab the top and bottom of the tire and pull in-and-out on it. Notice any movement which would indicate a loose wheel bearing assembly. If the bearings are suspect, refer to Section 33 and Chapter 10 for more information.

4   From under the vehicle check for loose bolts, broken or disconnected parts and deteriorated rubber bushings on all suspension and steering components. Look for fluid leaking from the steering assembly. Check the power steering hoses and connections for leaks. On 2WD models, check the steering gear boots for cracks or leaks **(see illustration)**.

5   Have an assistant turn the steering wheel from side-to-side and check the steering components for free movement, chafing and binding. If the steering doesn't react with the movement of the steering wheel, try to determine where the slack is located.

6   Check the driveaxle boots on 4WD models. The driveaxle boots are very important because they prevent dirt, water and foreign material from entering and damaging the constant velocity joints. Oil and grease can cause the boot material to deteriorate prematurely, so it's a good idea to wash the boots with soap and water. Inspect the boots for tears and cracks as well as loose clamps. If there is any evidence of cracks or leaking lubricant, they must be replaced as described in Chapter 8.

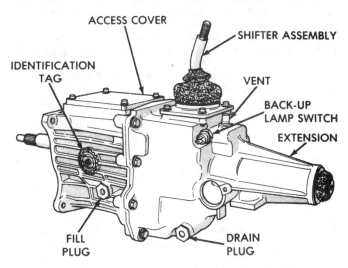

16.1   Typical manual transmission component locations

---

14   Exhaust system check

1   With the engine cold (at least three hours after the vehicle has been driven), check the complete exhaust system from the manifold to the end of the tailpipe. Be careful around the catalytic converter, which may be hot even after three hours. The inspection should be done with the vehicle on a hoist to permit unrestricted access. If a hoist isn't available, raise the vehicle and support it securely on jackstands.

2   Check the exhaust pipes and connections for signs of leakage and/or corrosion indicating a potential failure. Make sure that all brackets and hangers are in good condition and tight.

3   Inspect the underside of the body for holes, corrosion, open seams, etc. which may allow exhaust gasses to enter the passenger compartment. Seal all body openings with silicone sealant or body putty.

4   Rattles and other noises can often be traced to the exhaust system, especially the hangers, mounts and heat shields. Try to move the pipes, mufflers and catalytic converter. If the components can come in contact with the body or suspension parts, secure the exhaust system with new brackets and hangers.

---

15   Hydraulic clutch check

Refer to illustration 15.1

1   Check all hoses for cracks and distortion **(see illustration)**.

2   Check the clutch master cylinder and slave cylinder for loose mounting screws and leaks.

3   Check for smooth operation of the clutch pedal with no binding, looseness or sponginess.

4   Replace any damaged or leaking components. Bleed the system if the pedal is spongy, the pushrod travel is not sufficient, or the slave cylinder, master cylinder or any lines were disconnected (see Chapter 8).

---

16   Manual transmission lubricant level check

Refer to illustration 16.1

1   The manual transmission has a fill plug which must be removed to check the lubricant level **(see illustration)**. If the vehicle is raised to gain

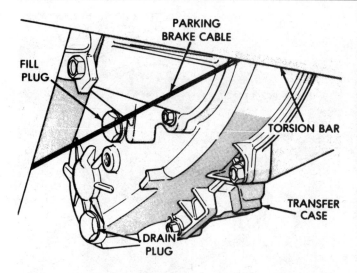

17.1   Locations of the transfer case drain and fill plugs (4WD models only)

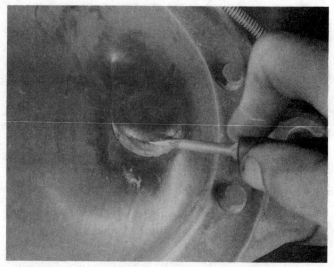

18.2   Use a small screwdriver to pry the rubber fill plug out

access to the plug, be sure to support it safely on jackstands – DO NOT crawl under a vehicle which is supported only by a jack! Be sure the vehicle is level or the check may be inaccurate.

2   Remove the plug from the transmission and use your little finger to reach inside the housing to feel the lubricant level. The level should be at or near the bottom of the plug hole.

3   If it isn't, add the recommended lubricant through the plug hole with a syringe or squeeze bottle.

4   Install and tighten the plug and check for leaks after the first few miles of driving.

17   Transfer case lubricant level check (4WD models only)

Refer to illustration 17.1

1   The transfer case lubricant is checked by removing the fill plug located in the side of the case **(see illustration)**. Be sure the vehicle is level or the check may be inaccurate.

2   After removing the plug, reach inside the hole with your little finger. The lubricant level should be just at the bottom of the hole. If it isn't, add the recommended lubricant through the hole with a syringe or squeeze bottle.

18   Differential lubricant level check

Refer to illustrations 18.2 and 18.3

1   The rear (and front on 4WD models) differential has a rubber filler plug which must be removed to check the lubricant level. If the vehicle is raised to gain access to the plug, be sure to support it safely on jackstands – DO NOT crawl under the vehicle when it's supported only by the jack. Be sure the vehicle is level or the check may not be accurate.

2   Use a small screwdriver to pry the plug from the filler hole in the differential cover **(see illustration)**.

3   The lubricant level should be at the bottom of the filler hole **(see illustration)**. If not, use a syringe to add the recommended lubricant until it just starts to run out of the opening. On some models a tag is located in the area of the plug which gives information regarding lubricant type, particularly on models equipped with a limited slip differential.

4   Press the plug securely into the filler hole.

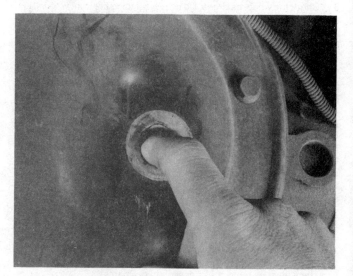

18.3   Use your finger as a dipstick to check the lubricant level

19   Tire rotation

Refer to illustration 19.2

1   The tires should be rotated at the specified intervals and whenever uneven wear is noticed.

2   Refer to the accompanying illustration for the preferred tire rotation pattern.

3   Refer to the information in Jacking and towing at the front of this manual for the proper procedures to follow when raising the vehicle and changing a tire. If the brakes are to be checked, don't apply the parking brake as stated. Make sure the tires are blocked to prevent the vehicle from rolling as it's raised.

4   Preferably, the entire vehicle should be raised at the same time. This can be done on a hoist or by jacking up each corner and then lowering the vehicle onto jackstands placed under the frame rails. Always use four jackstands and make sure the vehicle is safely supported.

5   After rotation, check and adjust the tire pressures as necessary and be sure to check the lug nut tightness.

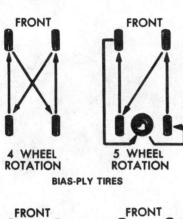

20.5   The front disc brake pads can be checked easily by looking through the inspection window in each caliper

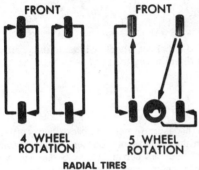

19.2   Tire rotation diagram

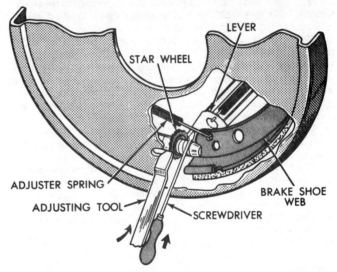

20.11   Use a thin screwdriver to push the lever away, then use an adjusting tool or another screwdriver to back off the star wheel

20   Brake check

Note: *For detailed photographs of the brake system, refer to Chapter 9.*
Warning: *Brake system dust may contain asbestos, which is hazardous to your health. DO NOT blow it out with compressed air, inhale it or use gasoline or solvents to remove it. Use brake system cleaner or denatured alcohol only.*

1   In addition to the specified intervals, the brakes should be inspected every time the wheels are removed or whenever a defect is suspected.
2   To check the brakes, raise the vehicle and place it securely on jackstands. Remove the wheels (see Jacking and towing at the front of the manual, if necessary).

Disc brakes

Refer to illustration 20.5

3   Disc brakes are used on the front wheels. Extensive rotor damage can occur if the pads are not replaced when needed.
4   The disc brake calipers, which contain the pads, are visible with the wheels removed. There is an outer pad and an inner pad in each caliper. All pads should be inspected.
5   Each caliper has a "window" to inspect the pads. Check the thickness of the pad lining by looking into the caliper at each end and down through the inspection window at the top of the housing **(see illustration)**. If the pad material has worn to about 5/16-inch or less, the pads should be replaced.
6   If you're unsure about the exact thickness of the remaining lining material, remove the pads for further inspection or replacement (refer to Chapter 9).
7   Before installing the wheels, check for leakage and/or damage (cracks, splitting, etc.) around the brake hose connections. Replace the hose or fittings as necessary, referring to Chapter 9.

8   Check the condition of the rotor. Look for score marks, deep scratches and burned spots. If these conditions exist, the hub/rotor assembly should be removed for servicing (Section 33).

Drum brakes

Refer to illustrations 20.11, 20.13 and 20.15

9   On rear brakes, remove the drum by pulling it off the axle and brake assembly. If this proves difficult, make sure the parking brake is released, then squirt penetrating oil around the center hub areas. Allow the oil to soak in and try to pull the drum off again.
10   If the drum still cannot be pulled off, the parking brake lever will have to be lifted slightly off its stop. This is done by first removing the small plug from the backing plate.
11   With the plug removed, insert a thin screwdriver and lift the adjusting lever off the starwheel, then use an adjusting tool or screwdriver to back off the star wheel several turns **(see illustration)**. This will move the brake shoes away from the drum. If the drum still won't pull off, tap around its inner circumference with a soft-face hammer.
12   With the drum removed, do not touch any brake dust (see the Warning at the beginning of this Section).

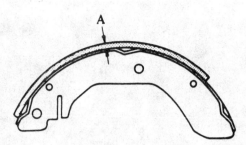

20.13   If the lining is bonded to the brake shoe, measure the lining thickness from the outer surface to the metal shoe, as shown here; if the lining is riveted to the shoe, measure from the lining outer surface to the rivet head

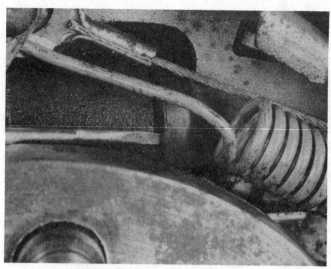

20.15   To check for wheel cylinder leakage, use a small screwdriver to pry the boot away from the cylinder

13   Note the thickness of the lining material on both the front and rear brake shoes. If the material has worn away to within 1/16-inch of the recessed rivets or metal backing, the shoes should be replaced **(see illustration)**. The shoes should also be replaced if they're cracked, glazed (shiny surface) or contaminated with brake fluid.

14   Make sure that all the brake assembly springs are connected and in good condition.

15   Check the brake components for any signs of fluid leakage. Carefully pry back the rubber cups on the wheel cylinders located at the top of the brake shoes **(see illustration)**. Any leakage is an indication that the wheel cylinders should be overhauled immediately (Chapter 9). Also check brake hoses and connections for signs of leakage.

16   Wipe the inside of the drum with a clean rag and brake cleaner or denatured alcohol. Again, be careful not to breathe the dangerous asbestos dust.

17   Check the inside of the drum for cracks, score marks, deep scratches and hard spots, which will appear as small discolorations. If these imperfections cannot be removed with fine emery cloth, the drum must be taken to a machine shop equipped to turn the drums.

18   If after the inspection process all parts are in good working condition, reinstall the brake drum.

19   Install the wheels and lower the vehicle.

Parking brake

20   The parking brake operates from a foot pedal and locks the rear brake system. The easiest, and perhaps most obvious method of periodically checking the operation of the parking brake assembly is to stop the vehicle on a steep hill with the parking brake set and the transmission in Neutral. If the parking brake cannot prevent the vehicle from rolling, adjust it (see Chapter 9).

21   Fuel system check

Warning: *Gasoline is extremely flammable, so take extra precautions when working on any part of the fuel system. Don't smoke or allow open flames or bare light bulbs in or near the work area, and don't work in a garage where a natural gas-type appliance (such as a water heater or clothes dryer) with a pilot light is present. If you spill fuel on your skin, rinse it off immediately with soap and water. Have a Class B fire extinguisher on hand. On fuel-injected models, no components should be disconnected until the fuel pressure has been relieved (see Chapter 4).*

1   On most models the main fuel tank is located under the left side of the vehicle.

2   The fuel system is most easily checked with the vehicle raised on a hoist so the components underneath the vehicle are readily visible and accessible.

3   If the smell of gasoline is noticed while driving or after the vehicle has been in the sun, the system should be thoroughly inspected immediately.

4   Remove the gas tank cap and check for damage, corrosion and an unbroken sealing imprint on the gasket. Replace the cap with a new one if necessary.

5   With the vehicle raised, check the fuel tank and filler neck for punctures, cracks and other damage. The connection between the filler neck and the tank is especially critical. Sometimes a rubber filler neck will leak due to loose clamps or deteriorated rubber, problems a home mechanic can usually rectify. **Warning:** *Do not, under any circumstances, try to repair a fuel tank yourself (except rubber components). A welding torch or any open flame can easily cause the fuel vapors to explode if the proper precautions are not taken!*

6   Carefully check all rubber hoses and metal lines leading away from the fuel tank. Look for loose connections, deteriorated hoses, crimped lines and other damage. Follow the lines to the front of the vehicle, carefully inspecting them all the way. Repair or replace damaged sections as necessary.

7   If a fuel odor is still evident after the inspection, refer to Section 36.

22   Carburetor/throttle body mounting bolt/nut torque check

Refer to illustrations 22.4a and 22.4b

1   The carburetor or throttle body is attached to the top of the intake manifold by several bolts or nuts. These fasteners can sometimes work loose from vibration and temperature changes during normal engine operation and cause a vacuum leak.

2   If you suspect that a vacuum leak exists at the bottom of the carburetor or throttle body, obtain a length of hose. Start the engine and place one end of the hose next to your ear as you probe around the base with the other end. You will hear a hissing sound if a leak exists (be careful of hot or moving engine components).

3   Remove the air cleaner assembly (see Chapter 4), tagging each hose to be disconnected with a piece of numbered tape to make reassembly easier.

4   Locate the mounting bolts at the base of the carburetor or top of the throttle body. Decide what special tools or adapters will be necessary, if any, to tighten the fasteners **(see illustrations)**.

22.4a   The carburetor mounting nuts (arrows – there are four nuts) located at the base of the carburetor

22.4b   The four mounting bolts on fuel-injected models are accessible after removing the air cleaner (typical)

5   Tighten the bolts or nuts to the torque listed in this Chapter's specifications. Don't overtighten them, as the threads could strip.
6   If, after the bolts are properly tightened, a vacuum leak still exists, the carburetor or throttle body must be removed and a new gasket installed. See Chapter 4 for more information.
7   After tightening the fasteners, reinstall the air cleaner and return all hoses to their original positions.

23   Throttle linkage inspection

Refer to illustration 23.1

1   Inspect the throttle linkage for damage and missing parts and for binding and interference when the accelerator pedal is depressed **(see illustration)**.
2   Lubricate the various linkage pivot points with chassis grease. Do not lubricate carburetor or throttle body linkage balljoint type pivots, throttle control cables or transmission control cables.

24   Drivebelt check, adjustment and replacement

Refer to illustrations 24.3, 24.4, 24.6 and 24.13

1   The drivebelts, or V-belts as they are often called, are located at the front of the engine and play an important role in the overall operation of the vehicle and its components. Due to their function and material make-up, the belts are prone to failure after a period of time and should be inspected and adjusted periodically to prevent major engine damage.
2   The number of belts used on a particular vehicle depends on the accessories installed. Drivebelts are used to turn the alternator, power steering pump, water pump and air-conditioning compressor. Depending on the pulley arrangement, more than one of these components may be driven by a single belt. Some later models are equipped with a single serpentine belt that drives all the engine components.
3   With the engine off, open the hood and locate the various belts at the front of the engine. Using your fingers (and a flashlight, if necessary), move along the belts checking for cracks and separation of the belt plies. Also check for fraying and glazing, which gives the belt a shiny appearance **(see illustration)**. Both sides of each belt should be inspected, which means you will have to twist the belt to check the underside.

23.1   Check the throttle linkage and springs for damage and binding

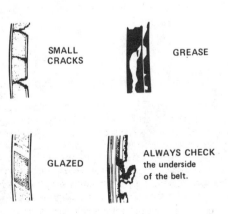

SMALL CRACKS

GREASE

GLAZED

ALWAYS CHECK
the underside
of the belt.

24.3   Here are some of the more common problems associated with drivebelts (check the belts very carefully to prevent an untimely breakdown)

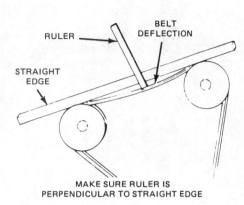

24.4   Measuring drivebelt deflection with a straightedge and ruler

4   The tension of each V-belt is checked by pushing on the belt at a distance halfway between the pulleys. Push firmly with your thumb and see how much the belt moves (deflects) **(see illustration)**. A rule of thumb is that if the distance from pulley center-to-pulley center is between 7 and 11 inches, the belt should deflect 1/4-inch. If the belt travels between pulleys spaced 12 to 16 inches apart, the belt should deflect 1/2-inch. **Note:** *On serpentine belts, the belt tension is controlled by a tensioner and the belt does not require periodic adjustment.*

5   If it is necessary to adjust the belt tension, either to make the belt tighter or looser, it is done by moving the belt-driven accessory on the bracket.

6   For each component there will be an adjusting bolt and a pivot bolt. Both bolts must be loosened slightly to enable you to move the component **(see illustration)**.

7   After the two bolts have been loosened, move the component away from the engine to tighten the belt or toward the engine to loosen the belt. Hold the accessory in position and check the belt tension. If it is correct, tighten the two bolts until just snug, then recheck the tension. If the tension is all right, tighten the bolts.

8   To adjust the alternator drivebelt on some later models, loosen the pivot bolt and locknut, then turn the adjusting bolt to tension the belt. After the belt is tensioned, tighten the pivot bolt and locknut.

9   It will often be necessary to use some sort of prybar to move the accessory while the belt is adjusted. If this must be done to gain the proper

leverage, be very careful not to damage the component being moved or the part being pried against.

10   To replace a belt, follow the above procedures for drivebelt adjustment but slip the belt off the pulleys and remove it. Since belts tend to wear out more or less at the same time, it's a good idea to replace all of them at the same time. Mark each belt and the corresponding pulley grooves so the replacement belts can be installed properly.

11   Take the old belts with you when purchasing new ones in order to make a direct comparison for length, width and design.

12   Adjust the belts as described earlier in this Section.

13   When replacing a serpentine drivebelt (used on some later models), loosen the bolt on the idler and rotate it out of the way to release the belt tension **(see illustration)**. Make sure the new belt is routed correctly (refer to the label in the engine compartment). Also, the belt must completely engage the grooves in the pulleys.

25   Seatbelt check

1   Check the seatbelts, buckles, latch plates and guide loops for any obvious damage or signs of wear.

2   Make sure the seatbelt reminder light comes on when the key is turned on.

3   The seatbelts are designed to lock up during a sudden stop or impact, yet allow free movement during normal driving. The retractors should hold the belt against your chest while driving and rewind the belt when the buckle is unlatched.

4   If any of the above checks reveal problems with the seatbelt system, replace parts as necessary.

26   Neutral start switch check (models with automatic transmission)

Warning: *During the following checks there is a chance the vehicle could lunge forward, possibly causing damage or injuries. Allow plenty of room around the vehicle, apply the parking brake firmly and hold down the regular brake pedal during the checks.*

1   The neutral start switch prevents the engine from being cranked unless the gear selector is in Park or Neutral.

2   Try to start the vehicle in each gear. The engine should crank only in Park or Neutral. If it cranks in any other gear, the neutral start switch is faulty or in need of adjustment (see Chapter 7 Part B).

3   Make sure the steering column lock allows the key to go into the Lock position only when the shift lever is in Park.

4   The ignition key should come out only in the Lock position.

24.6   With the pivot bolt and adjusting bolt (arrow) loose, pivot the alternator up to increase the drivebelt tension, then tighten the pivot and adjusting bolts

24.13   Loosen the bolt on the serpentine belt idler (arrow) and move the idler to release the belt tension

27.4a   Remove the wingnut, release the clips (if equipped), then lift off the cover and pull out the filter element (V6 model shown, V8 similar)

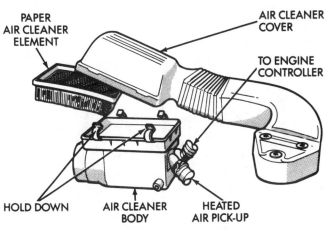

27.4b   Four-cylinder engine air cleaner details

1

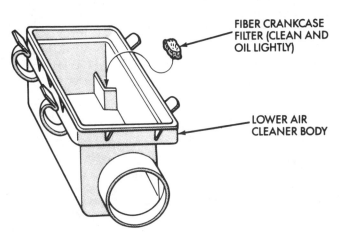

27.5   Clean and oil the crankcase filter (some four-cylinder models)

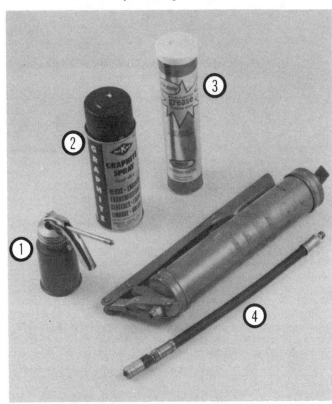

28.1   Materials required for chassis and body lubrication

1   **Engine oil** – *Light engine oil in a can like this can be used for door and hood hinges*
2   **Graphite spray** – *Used to lubricate lock cylinders*
3   **Grease** – *Grease, in a variety of types and weights, is available for use in a grease gun. Check the Specifications for your requirements.*
4   **Grease gun** – *A common grease gun, shown here with a detachable hose and nozzle, is needed for chassis lubrication. After use, clean it thoroughly!*

27   Air filter replacement

Refer to illustrations 27.4a, 27.4b and 27.5

1   At the specified intervals, the air filter element should be replaced with a new one.
2   The filter is located on top of, or adjacent to, the carburetor or throttle body and is replaced by unscrewing the wing nut from the top of the filter housing and/or disengaging the clips and lifting off the cover.
3   While the top plate is off, be careful not to drop anything down into the carburetor/throttle body or air cleaner assembly.
4   Lift the air filter element out of the housing **(see illustrations)** and wipe out the inside of the air cleaner housing with a clean rag.
5   Some four-cylinder models have a fiber crankcase filter located in the air cleaner housing which should be washed in solvent, oiled and reinstalled whenever the air filter element is replaced **(see illustration)**.
6   Place the new filter element in the air cleaner housing. Make sure it seats properly in the bottom of the housing.
7   Installation is the reverse of removal.

28   Chassis lubrication

Refer to illustrations 28.1, 28.2a, 28.2b, 28.8a and 28.8b

1   Refer to Recommended lubricants and fluids at the front of this Chapter to obtain the necessary grease, etc. You'll also need a grease gun **(see illustration)**. Occasionally plugs will be installed rather than grease fittings. If so, grease fittings will have to be purchased and installed.

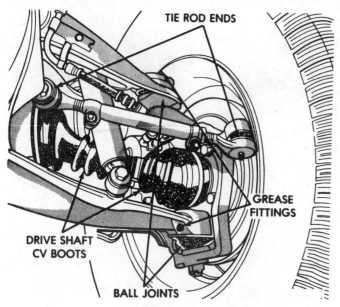

28.2a   Front suspension lubrication points (4WD shown, 2WD similar)

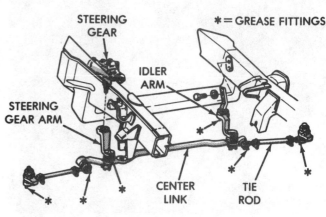

28.2b   4WD steering linkage lubrication points

2   Look under the vehicle and locate the grease fittings **(see illustrations)**.
3   For easier access under the vehicle, raise it with a jack and place jack-stands under the frame. Make sure it's safely supported by the stands. If the wheels are to be removed at this interval for tire rotation or brake inspection, loosen the lug nuts slightly while the vehicle is still on the ground.
4   Before beginning, force a little grease out of the nozzle to remove any dirt from the end of the gun. Wipe the nozzle clean with a rag.
5   With the grease gun and plenty of clean rags, crawl under the vehicle and begin lubricating the components.
6   Wipe one of the grease fitting nipples clean and push the nozzle firmly over it. Pump the gun until the component is completely lubricated. On balljoints, stop pumping when the rubber seal is firm to the touch. Do not pump too much grease into the fitting as it could rupture the seal. For all other suspension and steering components, continue pumping grease into the fitting until it oozes out of the joint between the two components. If it escapes around the grease gun nozzle, the nipple is clogged or the nozzle is not completely seated on the fitting. Resecure the gun nozzle to the fitting and try again. If necessary, replace the fitting with a new one.

7   Wipe the excess grease from the components and the grease fitting. Repeat the procedure for the remaining fittings.
8   On 4WD models, lubricate the front and rear driveshafts (propeller shafts) **(see illustrations)**.
9   Also clean and lubricate the parking brake cable, along with the cable guides and levers. This can be done by smearing some of the chassis grease onto the cable and its related parts with your fingers.

29   Automatic transmission fluid and filter change

Refer to illustrations 29.6, 29.9, 29.11a and 29.11b
1   At the specified intervals, the transmission fluid should be drained and replaced. Since the fluid will remain hot long after driving, perform this procedure only after the engine has cooled down completely. The manufacturer also recommends adjusting the transmission bands at this time since this procedure requires removing the fluid pan (see Chapter 7B).
2   Before beginning work, purchase the specified transmission fluid (see Recommended lubricants and fluids at the front of this Chapter) and a new filter.

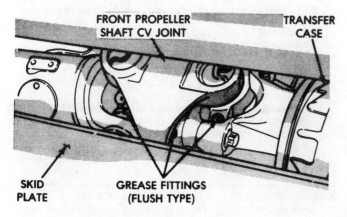

28.8a   4WD front driveshaft grease points

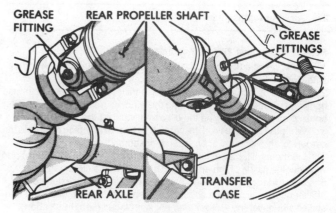

28.8b   4WD rear driveshaft (propeller shaft) grease fitting locations

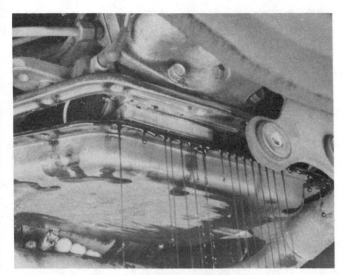

29.6   With the front bolts in place but loose, pull the rear of the pan down to drain the fluid

29.9   Use a Phillips screwdriver to remove the filter screws

3   Other tools necessary for this job include a floor jack, jackstands to support the vehicle in a raised position, a drain pan capable of holding at least eight pints, newspapers and clean rags.
4   Raise the vehicle and support it securely on jackstands.
5   Place the drain pan underneath the transmission pan. Remove the rear and side pan mounting bolts, but only loosen the front pan bolts approximately four turns.
6   Carefully pry the transmission pan loose with a screwdriver, allowing the fluid to drain **(see illustration)**.
7   Remove the remaining bolts, pan and gasket. Carefully clean the gasket surface of the transmission to remove all traces of the old gasket and sealant.
8   Drain the fluid from the transmission pan, clean it with solvent and dry it with compressed air, if available.
9   Remove the filter from the valve body inside the transmission **(see illustration)**. Use a gasket scraper to remove any traces of old gasket material that remain on the valve body. **Note:** *Be very careful not to gouge the delicate aluminum gasket surface on the valve body.*
10   Install a new gasket and filter. On many replacement filters, the gasket is attached to the filter to simplify installation.

11   Make sure the gasket surface on the transmission pan is clean, then install a new gasket on the pan **(see illustration)**. Put the pan in place against the transmission and, working around the pan, tighten each bolt a little at a time until the final torque figure is reached **(see illustration)**.
12   Lower the vehicle and add approximately seven pints of the specified type of automatic transmission fluid through the filler tube (see Section 6).
13   With the transmission in Park and the parking brake set, run the engine at a fast idle, but don't race it.
14   Move the gear selector through each range and back to Park. Check the fluid level. It will probably be low. Add enough fluid to bring the level between the two dimples on the dipstick.
15   Check under the vehicle for leaks during the first few trips. Check the fluid level again when the transmission is hot (see Section 6)

---

30   Manual transmission lubricant change

1   Raise the vehicle and support it securely on jackstands.
2   Move a drain pan, rags, newspapers and wrenches under the transmission.

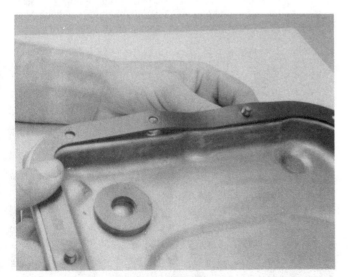

29.11a   Place a new gasket in position on the pan and install two bolts to hold it in place – some gaskets, like the one shown here, have two holes slightly smaller than the others so the bolts can grip the gasket securely

29.11b   Hold the pan in place and install all of the bolts finger tight before tightening them fully

32.4a   Remove the bolts from the lower edge of the cover,. . .

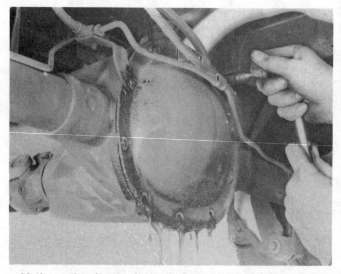

32.4b   . . .then loosen the top bolts and let the lubricant drain

3   Remove the transmission drain plug at the bottom of the case **(see illustration 16.1)** and allow the lubricant to drain into the pan.
4   After the lubricant has drained completely, reinstall the plug and tighten it securely.
5   Remove the fill plug from the side of the transmission case. Using a hand pump, syringe or funnel, fill the transmission with the specified lubricant until it begins to leak out through the hole. Reinstall the fill plug and tighten it securely.
6   Lower the vehicle.
7   Drive the vehicle for a short distance, then check the drain and fill plugs for leakage.

5   Remove the fill plug from the side of the transfer case. Using a hand pump, syringe or funnel, fill the transfer case with the specified lubricant until it begins to leak out through the hole. Reinstall the fill plug and tighten it securely.
6   Lower the vehicle.
7   Drive the vehicle for a short distance, then check the drain and fill plugs for leakage.

31   Transfer case lubricant change (4WD models only)

1   Raise the vehicle and support it securely on jackstands.
2   Move a drain pan, rags, newspapers and wrenches under the transmission.
3   Remove the transfer case drain plug at the bottom of the case **(see illustration 17.1)** and allow the lubricant to drain into the pan.
4   After the lubricant has drained completely, reinstall the plug and tighten it securely.

32   Differential lubricant change

Refer to illustrations 32.4a, 32.4b, 32.4c and 32.6
1   On these models it's necessary to remove the cover plate on the differential housing to drain the differential lubricant. As an alternative, a hand suction pump can be used to remove the differential lubricant through the filler hole. If a suction pump isn't available, or the gasket is leaking, be sure to obtain a new gasket at the same time the gear lubricant is purchased.
2   Raise the vehicle and support it securely on jackstands. Move a drain pan, rags, newspapers and wrenches under the vehicle.
3   Remove the fill plug from the differential (Section 18). If a suction pump is being used, insert the flexible hose. Work the hose down to the bottom of the differential housing and pump the lubricant out.

32.4c   After the lubricant has drained, remove the cover

32.6   Carefully scrape the old gasket material off to ensure a leak-free seal

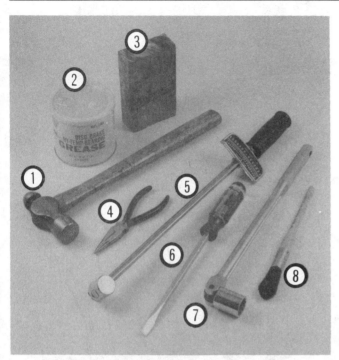

33.1   Tools and materials needed for front wheel bearing maintenance

1 **Hammer** – *A common hammer will do just fine*
2 **Grease** – *High-temperature grease which is formulated specially for front wheel bearings should be used*
3 **Wood block** – *If you have a scrap piece of 2x4, it can be used to drive the new seal into the hub*
4 **Needle-nose pliers** – *Used to straighten and remove the cotter pin in the spindle*
5 **Torque wrench** – *This is very important in this procedure; if the bearing is too tight, the wheel won't turn freely – if it's too loose, the wheel will "wobble" on the spindle. Either way, it could mean extensive damage.*
6 **Screwdriver** – *Used to remove the seal from the hub (a long screwdriver would be preferred)*
7 **Socket/breaker bar** – *Needed to loosen the nut on the spindle if it's extremely tight*
8 **Brush** – *Together with some clean solvent, this will be used to remove old grease from the hub and spindle*

4   If the differential is being drained by removing the cover plate, remove the bolts on the lower half of the plate (**see illustration**). Loosen the bolts on the upper half and use them to keep the cover loosely attached (**see illustration**). Allow the oil to drain into the pan, then completely remove the cover (**see illustration**).
5   Using a lint-free rag, clean the inside of the cover and the accessible areas of the differential housing. As this is done, check for chipped gears and metal particles in the lubricant, indicating that the differential should be more thoroughly inspected and/or repaired.
6   Thoroughly clean the gasket mating surfaces of the differential housing and the cover plate. Use a gasket scraper or putty knife to remove all traces of the old gasket (**see illustration**).
7   Apply a thin layer of RTV sealant to the cover flange, then press a new gasket into position on the cover. Make sure the bolt holes align properly.
8   Place the cover on the differential housing and install the bolts. Tighten the bolts securely.
9   Use a hand pump, syringe or funnel to fill the differential housing with the specified lubricant until it's level with the bottom of the plug hole.
10   Install the filler plug and tighten it securely.

33   Front wheel bearing check, repack and adjustment (2WD models only)

Refer to illustrations 33.1, 33.6, 33.7, 33.8, 33.11 and 33.15
1   In most cases the front wheel bearings will not need servicing until the brake pads are changed. However, the bearings should be checked whenever the front of the vehicle is raised for any reason. Several items, including a torque wrench and special grease, are required for this procedure (**see illustration**).
2   With the vehicle securely supported on jackstands, spin each wheel and check for noise, rolling resistance and freeplay.
3   Grasp the top of each tire with one hand and the bottom with the other. Move the wheel in-and-out on the spindle. If there's any noticeable movement, the bearings should be checked and then repacked with grease or replaced if necessary.
4   Remove the wheel.
5   Fabricate a wood block (1-1/16 inch by 1/2-inch by 2-inches long) which can be slid between the brake pads to keep them separated. Remove the brake caliper (see Chapter 9) and hang it out of the way on a piece of wire.
6   Pry the dust cap out of the hub using a screwdriver or hammer and chisel (**see illustration**).
7   Straighten the bent ends of the cotter pin, then pull the cotter pin out of the nut lock (**see illustration**). Discard the cotter pin and use a new one during reassembly.

33.6   Dislodge the dust cap by working around the outer circumference with a hammer and chisel

33.7   Remove the cotter pin and discard it – use a new one when the hub is reinstalled

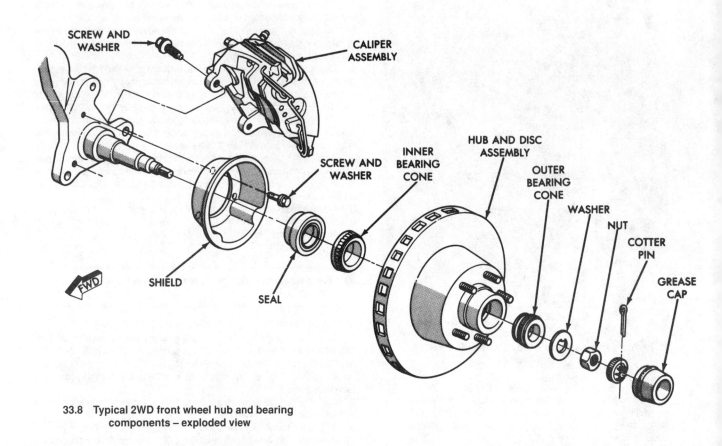

33.8   Typical 2WD front wheel hub and bearing components – exploded view

8   Remove the nut lock, nut and washer from the end of the spindle (see illustration).
9   Pull the hub/disc assembly out slightly, then push it back into its original position. This should force the outer bearing off the spindle enough so it can be removed.
10   Pull the hub/disc assembly off the spindle.
11   Use a screwdriver to pry the seal out of the rear of the hub (see illustration). As this is done, note how the seal is installed.
12   Remove the inner wheel bearing from the hub.
13   Use solvent to remove all traces of the old grease from the bearings, hub and spindle. A small brush may prove helpful; however make sure no bristles from the brush embed themselves inside the bearing rollers. Allow the parts to air dry.
14   Carefully inspect the bearings for cracks, heat discoloration, worn rollers, etc. Check the bearing races inside the hub for wear and damage. If the bearing races are defective, the hubs should be taken to a machine shop with the facilities to remove the old races and press new ones in. Note that the bearings and races come as matched sets and old bearings should never be installed on new races.
15   Use high-temperature front wheel bearing grease to pack the bearings. Work the grease completely into the bearings, forcing it between the rollers, cone and cage from the back side (see illustration).

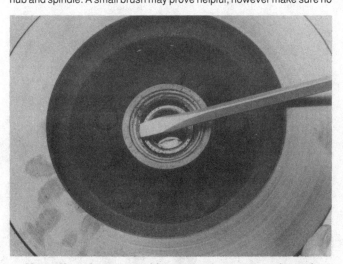

33.11   Use a large screwdriver to pry the grease seal out of the rear of the hub

33.15   Work the grease into each bearing until it's full

34.3   The drain fitting is located at the lower corner of the radiator (V6 model shown)

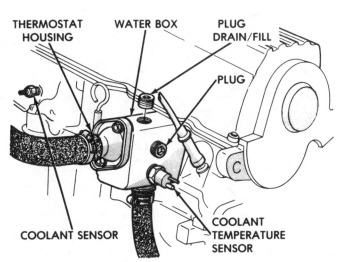

34.4   Details of the thermostat housing water box used on four-cylinder models

16   Apply a thin coat of grease to the spindle at the outer bearing seat, inner bearing seat, shoulder and seal seat.
17   Put a small quantity of grease inboard of each bearing race inside the hub. Using your finger, form a dam at these points to provide extra grease availability and to keep thinned grease from flowing out of the bearing.
18   Place the grease-packed inner bearing into the rear of the hub and put a little more grease outboard of the bearing.
19   Place a new seal over the inner bearing and tap the seal evenly into place with a hammer and blunt punch until it's flush with the hub.
20   Carefully place the hub assembly onto the spindle and push the grease-packed outer bearing into position.
21   Install the washer and spindle nut. Tighten the nut only slightly (no more than 12 ft-lbs of torque).
22   Spin the hub in a forward direction while tightening the spindle nut to approximately 20 ft-lbs to seat the bearings and remove any grease or burrs which could cause excessive bearing play later.
23   Loosen the spindle nut 1/4-turn, then using your hand (not a wrench of any kind), tighten the nut until it's snug. Install the nut lock and a new cotter pin through the hole in the spindle and the slots in the nut lock. If the nut lock slots don't line up, remove the nut lock and turn it slightly until they do.
24   Bend the ends of the cotter pin until they're flat against the nut. Cut off any extra length which could interfere with the dust cap.
25   Install the dust cap, tapping it into place with a hammer.
26   Place the brake caliper near the rotor and carefully remove the wood spacer. Install the caliper (see Chapter 9).
27   Install the wheel on the hub and tighten the lug nuts.
28   Grasp the top and bottom of the tire and check the bearings in the manner described earlier in this Section.
29   Lower the vehicle.

---

34   Cooling system servicing (draining, flushing and refilling)

Refer to illustrations 34.3 and 34.4

Warning: *Do not allow antifreeze to come in contact with your skin or painted surfaces of the vehicle. Rinse off spills immediately with plenty of water. Antifreeze is highly toxic if ingested. Never leave antifreeze lying around in an open container or in puddles on the floor; children and pets are attracted by it's sweet smell and may drink it. Check with local authorities about disposing of used antifreeze. Many communities have collection centers which will see that antifreeze is disposed of safely.*

1   Periodically, the cooling system should be drained, flushed and refilled to replenish the antifreeze mixture and prevent formation of rust and corrosion, which can impair the performance of the cooling system and cause engine damage. When the cooling system is serviced, all hoses and the radiator cap should be checked and replaced if necessary.
2   Apply the parking brake and block the wheels. If the vehicle has just been driven, wait several hours to allow the engine to cool down before beginning this procedure.
3   Move a large container under the radiator drain to catch the coolant. Attach a 3/8-inch diameter hose to the drain fitting (if possible) to direct the coolant into the container, then open the drain fitting **(see illustration)** (a pair of pliers may be required to turn it).
4   On four-cylinder engines, remove the water box drain/fill plug **(see illustration)**.
5   After coolant stops flowing out of the coolant reservoir, remove the radiator cap, allow the radiator to drain, then, on V6 models, move the container under the engine block drain plugs – there's one on each side of the block. Remove the plugs and allow the coolant in the block to drain.
6   While the coolant is draining, check the condition of the radiator hoses, heater hoses and clamps (refer to Section 9 if necessary).
7   Replace any damaged clamps or hoses.
8   Once the system is completely drained, flush the radiator with fresh water from a garden hose until it runs clear at the drain. The flushing action of the water will remove sediments from the radiator but will not remove rust and scale from the engine and cooling tube surfaces.
9   These deposits can be removed with a chemical cleaner. Follow the procedure outlined in the manufacturer's instructions. If the radiator is severely corroded, damaged or leaking, it should be removed (Chapter 3) and taken to a radiator repair shop.
10   Remove the overflow hose from the coolant reservoir and flush the reservoir with clean water, then reconnect the hose.
11   Close and tighten the radiator drain fitting. Install and tighten the block drain plugs, if equipped.
12   Place the heater temperature control in the maximum heat position.
13   Slowly add new coolant (a 50/50 mixture of water and antifreeze) to the radiator until it's full. On four-cylinder engines, fill the radiator until coolant starts to come out the drain/fill plug opening in the water box (this will bleed the air out of the system), install the plug, then finish the filling procedure. Add coolant to the reservoir up to the lower mark.
14   Leave the radiator cap off and run the engine in a well-ventilated area until the thermostat opens (coolant will begin flowing through the radiator and the upper radiator hose will become hot).
15   Turn the engine off and let it cool. Add more coolant mixture to bring the level back up to the lip on the radiator filler neck.

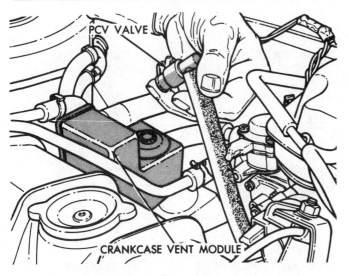

35.1a   On earlier four-cylinder models, the PCV valve is located in the vent module

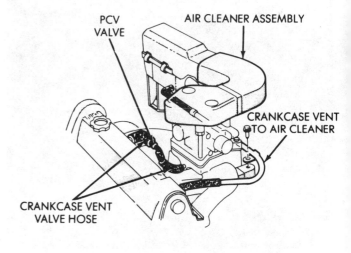

35.1b   On later four-cylinder models, the PCV valve is in the crankcase vent hose

16   Squeeze the upper radiator hose to expel air, then add more coolant mixture if necessary. Replace the radiator cap.
17   Start the engine, allow it to reach normal operating temperature and check for leaks.

35   Positive Crankcase Ventilation (PCV) valve check and replacement

Refer to illustration 35.1a, 35.1b and 35.2
1   The PCV valve is located in the valve cover on V6 and V8 models. On four-cylinder models the PCV valve is located in the crankcase vent module (early models) or the crankcase vent hose between the valve cover and the intake manifold **(see illustrations)**.
2   With the engine idling at normal operating temperature, pull the valve (with hose attached) from the rubber grommet in the cover **(see illustration)**.
3   Place your finger over the valve opening. If there's no vacuum at the valve, check for a plugged hose, manifold port, or the valve itself. Replace any plugged or deteriorated hoses.
4   Turn off the engine and shake the PCV valve, listening for a rattle. If the valve doesn't rattle, replace it with a new one.
5   To replace the valve, pull it from the end of the hose, noting its installed position.
6   When purchasing a replacement PCV valve, make sure it's for your particular vehicle and engine size. Compare the old valve with the new one to make sure they're the same.
7   Push the valve into the end of the hose until it's seated.
8   Inspect the rubber grommet for damage and hardening. Replace it with a new one if necessary.
9   Push the PCV valve and hose securely into position.

36   Evaporative emissions control system check

Refer to illustrations 36.2a and 36.2b
1   The function of the evaporative emissions control system is to draw fuel vapors from the gas tank and fuel system, store them in a charcoal canister and route them to the intake manifold during normal engine operation.

35.2   The PCV valve fits into the valve cover on V6 and V8 models

2   The most common symptom of a fault in the evaporative emissions system is a strong fuel odor in the engine compartment. If a fuel odor is detected, inspect the charcoal canister, located in the engine compartment or under the vehicle **(see illustrations)**. Check the canister and all hoses for damage and deterioration.
3   The evaporative emissions control system is explained in more detail in Chapter 6.

37   Exhaust Gas Recirculation (EGR) system check

Refer to illustration 37.2
Note: *On 1992 and later V6 and V8 engines, the EGR valve is operated electrically and also by vacuum. This check does not pertain to these models. For more information relating to these models, refer to Chapter 6.*

1   The EGR valve is usually located on the intake manifold, adjacent to the carburetor or throttle body. These models are equipped with backpressure type EGR valves which are operated by engine vacuum. Most of the time when a problem develops in the emissions system, it's due to a stuck or corroded EGR valve or a damaged or leaking hose or vacuum diaphragm.
2   Warm the engine up to operating temperature and allow it to idle with the transmission in Neutral. Accelerate the engine abruptly up to about 2000 rpm and look under the valve housing to make sure the movement marker groove in the stem moves **(see illustration)**.

36.2a   On earlier models, the evaporative emissions (charcoal) canister is located under the truck bed

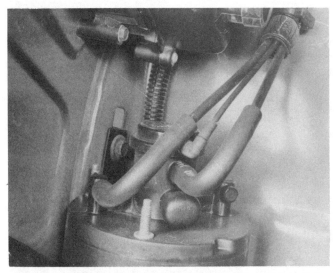

36.2b   On later models the evaporative emissions canister is in the engine compartment

3   If the stem doesn't move, check all the vacuum hose for leaks or damage. If the hoses are not damaged, check the EGR valve operation. Disconnect the vacuum hose, connect a hand vacuum pump and apply 10 in Hg of vacuum. If the valve stem still does not move, the valve itself is faulty and should be replaced.
4   If the valve stem moves, clamp the hose and make sure the valve stays open (diaphragm holds vacuum) 30 seconds or more. If it doesn't, the diaphragm is faulty and the valve should be replaced.
5   Refer to Chapter 6 for more information on the EGR system.

38   Thermostatic air cleaner check (four-cylinder and 1987 through 1991 V6 and V8 models)

Note: *1992 and later V6 and V8 models are not equipped with this system.*
Refer to illustration 38.3
1   These models are equipped with a thermostatically controlled air cleaner which draws air to the carburetor/throttle body from different locations, depending upon engine temperature.
2   This is a visual check. If access is limited, a small mirror may have to be used.
3   Open the hood and locate the damper door inside the air cleaner assembly **(see illustration)**.

4   If there is a flexible air duct attached to the end of the air cleaner, disconnect it at the air cleaner. This will enable you to see the damper inside.
5   The check should be done when the engine is cold. Start the engine and look at the damper, which should move to a closed position. With the damper closed, air cannot enter through the air cleaner opening, but instead enters the air cleaner through a flexible duct attached to a heat stove on the exhaust manifold.
6   As the engine warms up to operating temperature, the damper should open to allow air through the air cleaner opening. Depending on outside temperature, this may take 10 to 15 minutes. To speed up this check you can reconnect the air duct, drive the vehicle, then check to see if the damper is completely open.
7   If the thermo-controlled air cleaner is not operating properly, see Chapter 6 for more information.

39   Crankcase inlet filter – cleaning (1987 through 1991 V6 and V8 models only)

Refer to illustration 39.3
1   Disconnect the hose and pull the crankcase inlet filter out of the valve cover.
2   Wash the inside of the filter with solvent.

37.2   Look under the EGR valve housing (arrow) to make sure the stem moves

38.3   The damper door (arrow) is located in the air cleaner housing (V6 model shown)

39.3   Lubricate the filter by pouring clean engine oil into the large opening until it drains out of the smaller opening (V6 and V8 models only)

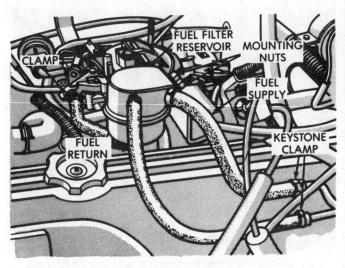

40.1a   Fuel filter/reservoir details (four-cylinder carbureted models)

3   Lubricate the filter by pouring clean engine oil into the large opening and allowing into to drain out through the smaller (inlet) opening **(see illustration)**.
4   Reinstall the filter in the valve cover and connect the hose.

---

40   Fuel filter replacement

Warning: *Gasoline is extremely flammable, so take extra precautions when working on any part of the fuel system. Don't smoke or allow open flames or bare light bulbs in or near the work area, and don't work in a garage where a natural gas-type appliance (such as a water heater or clothes dryer) with a pilot light is present. If you spill fuel on your skin, rinse it off immediately with soap and water. Have a Class B fire extinguisher on hand.*

Carbureted models

Refer to illustrations 40.1a, 40.1b and 40.4

1   On four-cylinder models the fuel filter (which incorporates a reservoir) is located in the fuel line adjacent to the carburetor **(see illustration)**. On V6 models, the fuel filter is mounted below the fuel pump **(see illustration)**.
2   Place rags or newspapers under the filter to absorb any spilled fuel. Use wire cutters to cut the Keystone clamps securing the fuel and vapor return hoses to the filter, then detach the hoses from the filter.
3   On four-cylinder models, remove the two mounting nuts and lift the filter off the bracket.
4   Installation is the reverse of removal. Use new screw-type clamps to replace the Keystone clamps. On V6 models, make sure the vapor return line is routed correctly **(see illustration)**.

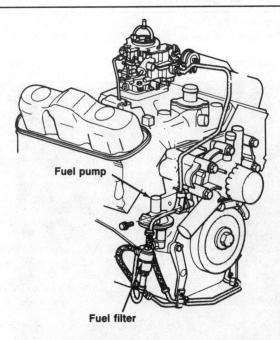

40.1b   Fuel filter installation details (carbureted V6 models)

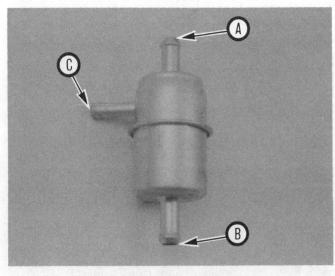

40.4   Carbureted V6 fuel filter details

A   *Outlet to carburetor*   C   *Vapor return line to tank*
B   *Inlet from fuel pump*

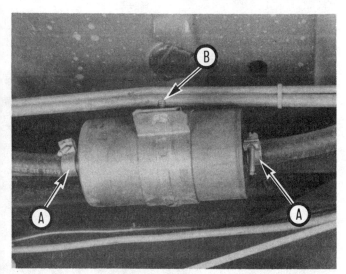

40.7   On fuel-injected models, disconnect the fuel hoses (A), then remove the bracket bolt (B) and lower the filter

Fuel-injected models

Refer to illustration 40.7

5   All models employ an in-line fuel filter. Refer to Chapter 4 and relieve fuel system pressure before proceeding. The filter is located on the left side frame rail, under the bed.

6   With the engine cold, place a container, newspapers or rags under the fuel filter.

7   Use a screwdriver to disconnect the fuel lines and detach the filter from the frame bracket **(see illustration)**.

8   Install the new filter by reversing the removal procedure. Make sure the arrow on the filter points toward the engine, not the fuel tank.

---

41   Exhaust manifold heat control valve – check and servicing (V6 engines through 1991 only)

1   The manifold heat control valve is located on the left exhaust manifold.

Check

2   Allow the engine to warm up to normal operating temperature, then have an assistant accelerate the engine from idle. The valve counterweight should move counterclockwise when the engine accelerates.

3   If it doesn't, deposits have probably built up on the valve shaft which inhibit its movement.

Servicing

Refer to illustration 41.4

4   With the engine cold, spray MOPAR Manifold Heat Control Valve solvent or equivalent to each end of the shaft **(see illustration)**.

5   Allow the solvent to soak in for a few minutes, then work the valve shaft back and forth by hand until it moves freely.

---

42   Carburetor choke check and shaft cleaning

Refer to illustration 42.3, 42.9a and 42.9b

1   The choke operates when the engine is cold, so this check can only be performed before the vehicle has been started for the day.

2   Open the hood and remove the top plate of the air cleaner assembly (Section 27). If any vacuum hoses must be disconnected, make sure you tag the hoses for reinstallation in their original positions. Place the top plate and wing nut aside, out of the way of moving engine components.

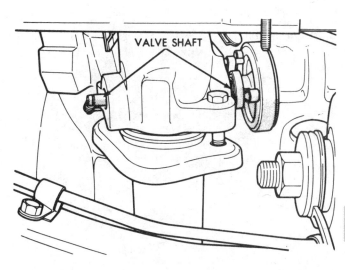

41.4   Spray the solvent at both ends of the valve shaft, let it penetrate, then work the valve back and forth to loosen any deposits which will cause binding

42.3   The choke plate (arrow) is located in the center of the carburetor

3   Look at the center of the air cleaner housing. You will notice a flat plate at the carburetor opening **(see illustration)**.

4   Press the accelerator pedal to the floor. The plate should close completely. Start the engine while you watch the plate at the carburetor. **Warning:** *Do not position your face directly over the carburetor, as the engine could backfire, causing serious burns.* When the engine starts, the choke plate should open slightly.

5   Allow the engine to continue running at an idle speed. As the engine warms up to operating temperature, the plate should slowly open, allowing more air to enter through the top of the carburetor.

6   After a few minutes, the choke plate should be fully open to the vertical position. Lightly tap the accelerator to make sure the fast idle cam disengages.

7   You will notice that the engine speed corresponds with the plate opening. With the plate fully closed, the engine should run at a fast idle speed. As the plate opens and the throttle is moved to disengage the fast idle cam, the engine speed will decrease.

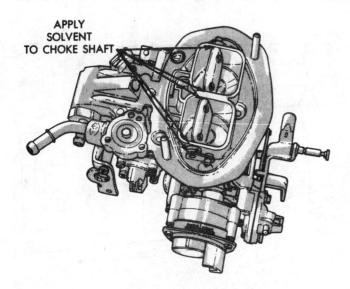

42.9a Apply the solvent to the areas indicated to prevent binding

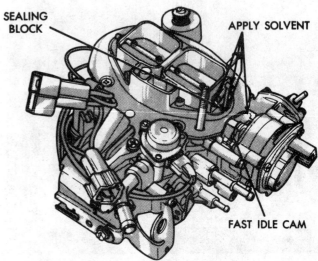

42.9b On four-cylinder engines, apply the solvent to the link between the choke shaft and the thermostat, as well as to the sealing block

8   Refer to Chapter 4 for specific information on adjusting and servicing the choke components.
9   At the specified intervals, or when the choke shaft binds, apply MO-PAR Combustion Chamber Conditioner 4318001 or equivalent to the choke shaft and fast idle cam contact surfaces to remove deposits and ensure free movement **(see illustrations)**.

43 Spark plug replacement

Refer to illustrations 43.2, 43.5a, 43.5b, 43.6 and 43.10

1   Open the hood and label each spark plug wire to ensure proper installation.
2   In most cases, the tools necessary for spark plug replacement include a spark plug socket which fits onto a ratchet (spark plug sockets are padded inside to prevent damage to the porcelain insulators on the new plugs), various extensions and a gap gauge to check and adjust the gaps on the new plugs **(see illustration)**. A special plug wire removal tool is available for separating the wire boots from the spark plugs, but it isn't absolutely necessary. A torque wrench should be used to tighten the new plugs.
3   The best approach when replacing the spark plugs is to purchase the new ones in advance, adjust them to the proper gap and replace them one at a time. When buying the new spark plugs, be sure to obtain the correct plug type for your particular engine. This information can be found on the Emission Control Information label located under the hood and in the factory owner's manual. If differences exist between the plug specified on the emissions label and in the owner's manual, assume that the emissions label is correct.
4   Allow the engine to cool completely before attempting to remove any of the plugs. While you're waiting for the engine to cool, check the new plugs for defects and adjust the gaps.
5   The gap is checked by inserting the proper thickness gauge between the electrodes at the tip of the plug **(see illustration)**. The gap between the electrodes should be the same as the one specified on the Emissions Control Information label. The wire should just slide between the electrodes with a slight amount of drag. If the gap is incorrect, use the adjuster on the gauge body to bend the curved side electrode slightly until the prop-

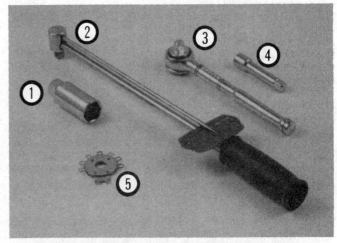

43.2 Tools required for changing spark plugs

1   *Spark plug socket – This will have special padding inside to protect the spark plug's porcelain insulator*
2   *Torque wrench – Although not mandatory, using this tool is the best way to ensure the plugs are tightened properly*
3   *Ratchet – Standard hand tool to fit the spark plug socket*
4   *Extension – Depending on model and accessories, you may need special extensions and universal joints to reach one or more of the plugs*
5   *Spark plug gap gauge – This gauge for checking the gap comes in a variety of styles. Make sure the gap for your engine is included.*

er gap is obtained **(see illustration)**. If the side electrode is not exactly over the center electrode, bend it with the adjuster until it is. Check for cracks in the porcelain insulator (if any are found, the plug should not be used).
6   With the engine cool, remove the spark plug wire from one spark plug. Pull only on the boot at the end of the wire – do not pull on the wire. A plug wire removal tool should be used if available **(see illustration)**.

43.5a   Spark plug manufacturers recommend using a wire-type gauge when checking the gap – if the wire does not slide between the electrodes with a slight drag, adjustment is required

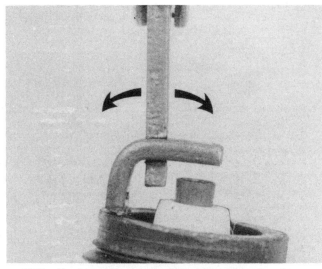

43.5b   To change the gap, bend the side electrode only, as indicated by the arrows, and be very careful not to crack or chip the porcelain insulator surrounding the center electrode

7   If compressed air is available, use it to blow any dirt or foreign material away from the spark plug hole. A common bicycle pump will also work. The idea here is to eliminate the possibility of debris falling into the cylinder as the spark plug is removed.

8   Place the spark plug socket over the plug and remove it from the engine by turning it in a counterclockwise direction.

9   Compare the spark plug to those shown in the color photos on page 1–37 to get an indication of the general running condition of the engine.

10   Thread one of the new plugs into the hole until you can no longer turn it with your fingers, then tighten it with a torque wrench (if available) or the ratchet. It might be a good idea to slip a short length of rubber hose over the end of the plug to use as a tool to thread it into place (see illustration). The hose will grip the plug well enough to turn it, but will start to slip if the plug begins to cross-thread in the hole – this will prevent damaged threads and the accompanying repair costs.

11   Before pushing the spark plug wire onto the end of the plug, inspect it following the procedures outlined in Section 44.

12   Attach the plug wire to the new spark plug, again using a twisting motion on the boot until it's seated on the spark plug.

13   Repeat the procedure for the remaining spark plugs, replacing them one at a time to prevent mixing up the spark plug wires.

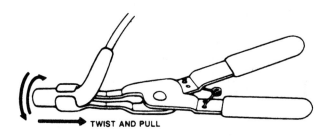

43.6   When removing the spark plug wires, grasp the boot and use a twisting/pulling motion

---

44   Spark plug wire and distributor cap and rotor – check and replacement

---

Refer to illustrations 44.6, 44.10 and 44.13

1   The spark plug wires should be checked at the recommended intervals and whenever new spark plugs are installed in the engine.

2   The wires should be inspected one at a time to prevent mixing up the order, which is essential for proper engine operation. On some models it will be necessary to remove the two screws and detach the distributor splash shield for access.

3   Disconnect the plug wire from one spark plug. To do this, grab the rubber boot, twist slightly and pull the wire free. Do not pull on the wire itself, only on the rubber boot (see illustration 43.6).

4   Check inside the boot for corrosion, which will look like a white crusty powder. Push the wire and boot back onto the end of the spark plug. It should be a tight fit on the plug. If it isn't, remove the wire and use a pair of pliers to carefully crimp the metal connector inside the boot until it fits securely on the end of the spark plug.

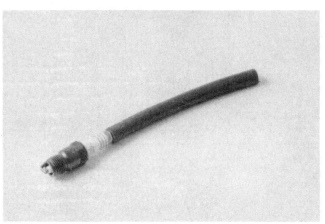

43.10   A length of 3/16-inch ID rubber hose will save time and prevent damaged threads when installing the spark plugs

5   Using a clean rag, wipe the entire length of the wire to remove any built-up dirt and grease. Once the wire is clean, check for holes, burned areas, cracks and other damage. Don't bend the wire excessively or the conductor inside might break.

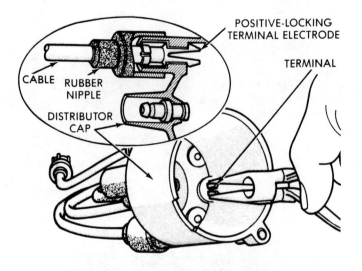

44.6   When replacing the spark plug wires on four-cylinder models, use pliers to compress the terminal tangs

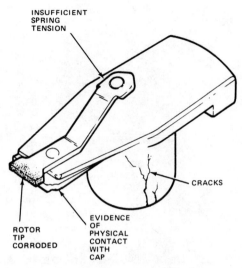

44.10   The ignition rotor should be checked for wear and corrosion as indicated here (if in doubt about its condition, buy a new one)

6   Disconnect the wire from the distributor cap. On four-cylinder engines, you must remove the cap first (see Step 9) so you can compress the terminal tangs from the inside **(see illustration)**. Pull the wire straight out of the cap. Pull only on the rubber boot during removal. Check for corrosion and a tight fit in the same manner as the spark plug end. Reattach the wire to the distributor cap.

7   Check the remaining spark plug wires one at a time, making sure they are securely fastened at the distributor and the spark plug when the check is complete.

8   If new spark plug wires are required, purchase a new set for your specific engine model. Wire sets are available pre-cut, with the rubber boots already installed. Remove and replace the wires one at a time to avoid mix-ups in the firing order. The wire routing is extremely important, so be sure to note exactly how each wire is situated before removing it.

9   Release the distributor cap clips or loosen the screw latches. Pull up on the cap, with the wires attached, to separate it from the distributor, then position it to one side.

10   The rotor is now visible on the end of the distributor shaft. Check it carefully for cracks and carbon tracks. Make sure the center terminal spring tension is adequate and look for corrosion and wear on the rotor tip **(see illustration)**. If in doubt about its condition, replace it with a new one.

11   If replacement is required, detach the rotor from the shaft and install a new one. The rotor is press fit on the shaft and can be pried or pulled off.

12   The rotor is indexed to the shaft so it can only be installed one way. It has an internal key that must line up with a slot in the end of the shaft (or vice versa).

13   Check the distributor cap for carbon tracks, cracks and other damage. Closely examine the terminals on the inside of the cap for excessive corrosion and damage **(see illustration)**. Slight deposits are normal. Again, if in doubt about the condition of the cap, replace it with a new one. Be sure to apply a small dab of silicone dielectric grease to each terminal before installing the cap. Also, make sure the carbon brush (center terminal) is correctly installed in the cap – a wide gap between the brush and rotor will result in rotor burn-through and/or damage to the distributor cap.

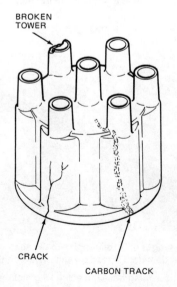

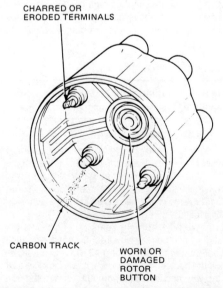

44.13   Shown here are some of the common defects to look for when inspecting the distributor cap (if in doubt about its condition, install a new one)

CARBON DEPOSITS

Symptoms: Dry sooty deposits indicate a rich mixture or weak ignition. Causes misfiring, hard starting and hesitation.

Recommendation: Check for a clogged air cleaner, high float level, sticky choke and worn ignition points. Use a spark plug with a longer core nose for greater anti-fouling protection.

OIL DEPOSITS

Symptoms: Oily coating caused by poor oil control. Oil is leaking past worn valve guides or piston rings into the combustion chamber. Causes hard starting, misfiring and hesition.

Recommendation: Correct the mechanical condition with necessary repairs and install new plugs.

TOO HOT

Symptoms: Blistered, white insulator, eroded electrode and absence of deposits. Results in shortened plug life.

Recommendation: Check for the correct plug heat range, over-advanced ignition timing, lean fuel mixture, intake manifold vacuum leaks and sticking valves. Check the coolant level and make sure the radiator is not clogged.

PREIGNITION

Symptoms: Melted electrodes. Insulators are white, but may be dirty due to misfiring or flying debris in the combustion chamber. Can lead to engine damage.

Recommendation: Check for the correct plug heat range, over-advanced ignition timing, lean fuel mixture, clogged cooling system and lack of lubrication.

HIGH SPEED GLAZING

Symptoms: Insulator has yellowish, glazed appearance. Indicates that combustion chamber temperatures have risen suddenly during hard acceleration. Normal deposits melt to form a conductive coating. Causes misfiring at high speeds.

Recommendation: Install new plugs. Consider using a colder plug if driving habits warrant.

GAP BRIDGING

Symptoms: Combustion deposits lodge between the electrodes. Heavy deposits accumulate and bridge the electrode gap. The plug ceases to fire, resulting in a dead cylinder.

Recommendation: Locate the faulty plug and remove the deposits from between the electrodes.

NORMAL

Symptoms: Brown to grayish-tan color and slight electrode wear. Correct heat range for engine and operating conditions.

Recommendation: When new spark plugs are installed, replace with plugs of the same heat range.

ASH DEPOSITS

Symptoms: Light brown deposits encrusted on the side or center electrodes or both. Derived from oil and/or fuel additives. Excessive amounts may mask the spark, causing misfiring and hesitation during acceleration.

Recommendation: If excessive deposits accumulate over a short time or low mileage, install new valve guide seals to prevent seepage of oil into the combustion chambers. Also try changing gasoline brands.

WORN

Symptoms: Rounded electrodes with a small amount of deposits on the firing end. Normal color. Causes hard starting in damp or cold weather and poor fuel economy.

Recommendation: Replace with new plugs of the same heat range.

DETONATION

Symptoms: Insulators may be cracked or chipped. Improper gap setting techniques can also result in a fractured insulator tip. Can lead to piston damage.

Recommendation: Make sure the fuel anti-knock values meet engine requirements. Use care when setting the gaps on new plugs. Avoid lugging the engine.

SPLASHED DEPOSITS

Symptoms: After long periods of misfiring, deposits can loosen when normal combustion temperature is restored by an overdue tune-up. At high speeds, deposits flake off the piston and are thrown against the hot insulator, causing misfiring.

Recommendation: Replace the plugs with new ones or clean and reinstall the originals.

MECHANICAL DAMAGE

Symptoms: May be caused by a foreign object in the combustion chamber or the piston striking an incorrect reach (too long) plug. Causes a dead cylinder and could result in piston damage.

Recommendation: Remove the foreign object from the engine and/or install the correct reach plug.

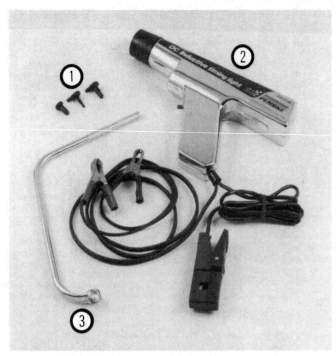

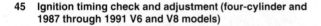

45.2   Tools needed to check and adjust the ignition timing

1   *Vacuum plugs* – *Vacuum hoses will, in most cases, have to be disconnected and plugged. Molded plugs in various shapes and sizes are available for this.*
2   *Inductive pick-up timing light* – *Flashes a bright concentrated beam of light when the number one spark plug fires. Connect the leads according to the instructions supplied with the light.*
3   *Distributor wrench* – *On some models, the hold-down bolt for the distributor is difficult to reach and turn with conventional wrenches or sockets. A special wrench like this must be used.*

14   To replace the cap, simply separate it from the distributor and transfer the spark plug wires, one at a time, to the new cap. Be very careful not to mix up the wires!
15   Reattach the cap to the distributor, then reposition the clips or tighten the screw latches to hold it in place.

---

45   Ignition timing check and adjustment (four-cylinder and 1987 through 1991 V6 and V8 models)

Refer to illustrations 45.2, 45.5a and 45.5b

Note: *On 1992 and later V6 and V8 models, the base ignition timing is NOT adjustable. Do not attempt to adjust ignition timing by rotating the distributor. All ignition timing functions are controlled by the Single Board Engine Controller II (SBEC II) described in Chapter 4.*

1   All vehicles are equipped with an Emissions Control Information label inside the engine compartment. The label contains important ignition timing specifications and the proper timing procedure for your specific vehicle. If the information on the emissions label is different from the information included in this Section, follow the procedure on the label.
2   At the specified intervals, or when the distributor has been removed, the ignition timing must be checked and adjusted if necessary. Tools required for this procedure include an inductive pick-up timing light, a tachometer, a distributor wrench and, in some cases, a means of plugging vacuum hoses **(see illustration)**.
3   Before you check the timing, make sure the idle speed is correct (carbureted models only – Chapter 4) and the engine is at normal operating temperature.

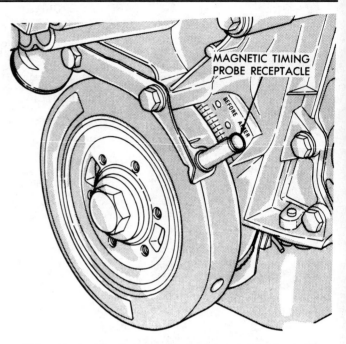

45.5a   The ignition timing marks are located at the front of the engine on V6 models

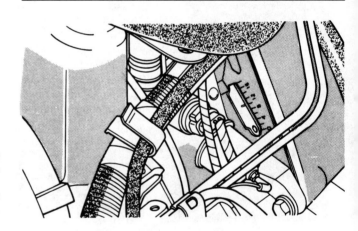

45.5b   On four-cylinder models, the timing marks are located at the rear of the engine on the bellhousing

---

4   With the engine off, connect a timing light in accordance with the manufacturer's instructions. Usually, the light must be connected to the battery and the number one spark plug in some fashion. The number one spark plug wire or terminal should be marked at the distributor; trace it back to the spark plug and attach the timing light lead near the plug. On fuel-injected engines, connect a tachometer to the engine.
5   Locate the numbered timing scale on the front cover of the engine (V6 engines) or the timing window in the transmission bellhousing (four-cylinder engines) **(see illustrations)**.
6   Locate the notched groove across the crankshaft pulley or the flywheel. It may be necessary to have an assistant temporarily turn the ignition on and off in short bursts without starting the engine in order to bring the groove into a position where it can easily be cleaned and marked. **Warning:** *Stay clear of all moving engine components when the engine is turned over in this manner.*
7   Use white soap-stone, chalk or paint to mark the groove in the pulley or flywheel. Also, put a mark on the timing scale corresponding to the num-

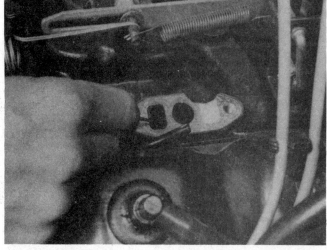

47.2   Disconnect the vacuum hose (A), remove the bolts (B) and lift the EGR valve off the manifold

47.4   Use a thin tool to scrape deposits from the EGR passages

ber of degrees specified on the Emission Control Information label in the engine compartment.

8   On fuel-injected engines, unplug the coolant temperature sensor located in the thermostat housing on four-cylinder engines or just below the housing on V6 engines. The cooling fan light and instrument panel light should come on and stay on and the engine speed should now be as specified on the Emissions Control Information label.

9   On carbureted V6 models, connect a jumper wire between the idle contact button and a good ground. Disconnect the air switching valve at the air pump. Disconnect and plug the vacuum hose at the Spark Control Computer.

10   On 1988 four-cylinder carbureted models, unplug the connector at the carburetor, remove the purple wire from the connector and plug the connector back in. Make sure the wiring for the timing light is clear of all moving engine components, start the engine and increase the engine speed to approximately 1200 rpm and release the throttle. If the engine speed is at or below the speed specified on the emission control information label, proceed to the next Step. If the speed is too high, adjust it (see Chapter 4).

11   Aim the timing light at the marks, again being careful not to come into contact with moving parts. The marks made should appear stationary. If the marks are in alignment, the timing is correct. If the marks are not aligned, turn off the engine.

12   Loosen the hold-down bolt or nut at the base of the distributor. Loosen the bolt/nut only slightly, just enough to turn the distributor (see Chapter 5).

13   Now restart the engine and turn the distributor very slowly until the timing marks are aligned.

14   Shut off the engine and tighten the distributor bolt/nut, being careful not to move the distributor.

15   Start the engine and recheck the timing to make sure the marks are still in alignment.

16   Disconnect the timing light and tachometer and reconnect any components which were disconnected for this procedure.

46   Oxygen sensor replacement

1   The oxygen sensor must be replaced at the specified interval. The sensor is threaded into the exhaust pipe or manifold. It may be necessary on some models to raise the front of the vehicle and support it securely on jackstands for access to the underside of the engine compartment.

2   Disconnect the oxygen sensor wire by unplugging the connector.

3   Unscrew the sensor with a box-end wrench.

4   Use a tap to clean the threads in the exhaust pipe or manifold.

5   If the old sensor is to be reinstalled, apply anti-seize compound to the the threads. New sensors will already have the anti-seize compound on the threads.

6   Install the sensor, tighten it to the torque listed in this Chapter's Specifications and plug in the connector.

47   Exhaust Gas Recirculation (EGR) valve replacement and passage cleaning (V6 engines only through 1991)

Refer to illustrations 47.2 and 47.4

1   The EGR valve must be replaced and the manifold passages cleaned at the specified intervals.

2   Pull off the vacuum hose(s), remove the bolts and lift the EGR valve off **(see illustration)**.

3   Clean the gasket surface of the manifold.

4   Spray carburetor cleaner into the manifold EGR opening and use a screwdriver or narrow scraper tool to clean the deposits from the passages **(see illustration)**.

5   Place the new EGR valve and gasket in position, install the bolts and tighten them to the torque listed in this Chapter's Specifications. Connect the vacuum hose(s).

Contents

Specifications

General

Cylinder numbers (front-to-rear)	1–2–3–4
Firing order	1-3-4-2

Camshaft

Journal diameter
Standard	1.375 to 1.376 in (34.939 to 34.960 mm)
Oversize	1.395 to 1.396 in (35.439 to 35.460 mm)

**ENGINE
FIRING ORDER**

1-3-4-2

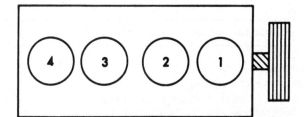

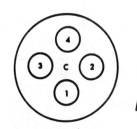

**Cylinder numbering and
distributor terminal locations**

Lobe lift wear limit .... 0.010 in (0.25 mm)
Endplay
    Standard .... 0.005 to 0.013 in (0.13 to 0.33 mm)
    Service limit .... 0.020 in (0.50 mm)
Intermediate shaft journal diameter
    Large journal .... 1.6812 to 1.6822 in (42.670 to 42.695 mm)
    Small journal .... 0.7750 to 0.7760 in (19.670 to 19.695 mm)

Torque specifications

Ft-lbs (unless otherwise indicated)

Cylinder head bolts
    Step 1 45
    Step 2 65
    Step 3 65
    Step 4 .... 1/4 additional turn after reaching torque specified in Step 3
Camshaft sprocket bolt 65
Camshaft bearing cap nuts 14
Crankshaft sprocket bolt 50
Exhaust manifold nuts 17
Flywheel or driveplate-to-crankshaft bolts 55
Front oil seal housing bolts .... 144 in-lbs
Intermediate shaft retainer bolts .... 108 in-lbs
Intermediate shaft sprocket bolt 65
Intake manifold bolt 17
Oil pan bolts
    6 mm .... 144 in-lbs
    8 mm 17
Oil pump cover bolts .... 106 in-lbs
Oil pump mounting bolt 17
Oil pump pickup 21
Rear oil seal housing bolts .... 108 in-lbs
Valve cover bolts .... 78 in-lbs

---

1   General information

This Part of Chapter 2 is devoted to in-vehicle repair procedures for four-cylinder engines. All information concerning engine removal and installation and engine block and cylinder head overhaul can be found in Part C of this Chapter.

Since the repair procedures included in this Part are based on the assumption that the engine is still installed in the vehicle, if they are being used during a complete engine overhaul (with the engine already out of the vehicle and on a stand) many of the steps included here will not apply.

The specifications included in this Part of Chapter 2 apply only to the procedures found here. The specifications necessary for rebuilding the block and cylinder heads are included in Part C.

The four-cylinder engines used in Dodge Dakota trucks through 1988 displace 2.2 liters. 1989 and newer engines displace 2.5 liters. The 2.2L/2.5L engine is an inline four with a belt-driven overhead camshaft. The belt also turns an intermediate shaft, mounted low in the block, which drives the oil pump and distributor.

The 2.2 and 2.5 liter engines used in these models are virtually identical in design except that the 2.5 liter engine features a longer stroke (for increased displacement).

Lubrication is handled by an eccentric rotor-type oil pump mounted in the oil pan and driven by the intermediate shaft.

2   Repair operations possible with the engine in the vehicle

Many major repair operations can be accomplished without removing the engine from the vehicle.

Clean the engine compartment and the exterior of the engine with some type of pressure washer before any work is done. A clean engine will make the job easier and will help keep dirt out of the internal areas of the engine.

Depending on the components involved, it may be a good idea to remove the hood to improve access to the engine as repairs are performed (refer to Chapter 11 if necessary).

If oil or coolant leaks develop, indicating a need for gasket or seal replacement, the repairs can generally be made with the engine in the vehicle. The oil pan gasket, camshaft cover gasket, cylinder head gasket, intake and exhaust manifold gaskets and crankshaft oil seals are accessible with the engine in place.

Exterior engine components, such as the water pump, the starter motor, the alternator, the distributor and the carburetor or fuel injection unit, as well as the intake and exhaust manifolds, can be removed for repair with the engine in place.

Since the cylinder heads can be removed without pulling the engine, valve component servicing can also be accomplished with the engine in the vehicle.

Replacement of, repairs to or inspection of the timing belt and sprockets and the oil pump are all possible with the engine in place.

In extreme cases caused by a lack of necessary equipment, repair or replacement of piston rings, pistons, connecting rods and rod bearings is possible with the engine in the vehicle. However, this practice is not recommended because of the cleaning and preparation work that must be done to the components involved.

3   Valve cover – removal and installation

Removal

Refer to illustrations 3.4 and 3.5

1   Disconnect the negative cable from the battery.
2   Remove the air cleaner assembly (see Chapter 4).
3   Label and disconnect all wiring routed over the camshaft cover.
4   Disconnect the crankcase breather hose (**see illustration**).

3.4 Detach the crankcase breather hose from the valve cover

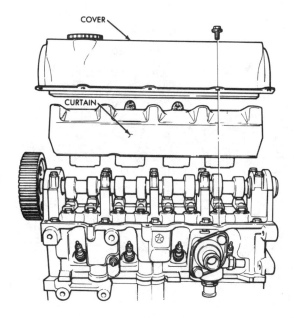

3.5 Valve cover installation details

2A

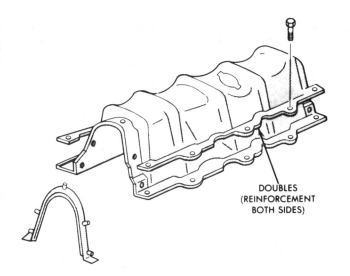

3.10a Valve cover components – exploded view
(1987 models)

3.10b Seat the new end seals in the valve cover by pulling the
tabs through the holes with pliers

5   Remove the valve cover bolts **(see illustration)**.
6   Using a soft face hammer, tap the side of the valve cover to break the gasket seal. Lift the cover from the engine.
7   The curtain (baffle) may be removed, if necessary. Lift it from the distributor side and turn it at an angle to detach it from the cylinder head.

Installation

Refer to illustrations 3.10a, 3.10b and 3.11

8   Thoroughly clean all components, be sure to remove all traces of old gasket material. Use acetone or lacquer thinner to remove any oil film from the sealing surfaces.
9   Reinstall the curtain, if removed.
10   On 1987 models, install a new seal at the front of the valve cover by pulling the tabs through the holes **(see illustrations)**. Apply a bead of RTV sealant to the cover mating surface and install the cover.
11   On 1988 and newer models, install a new gasket onto the valve cover. Hold it in place by pushing the tabs through the slots in the cover **(see illustration)**.

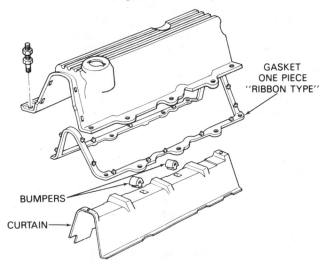

3.11 Valve cover components – exploded view (1988-on)

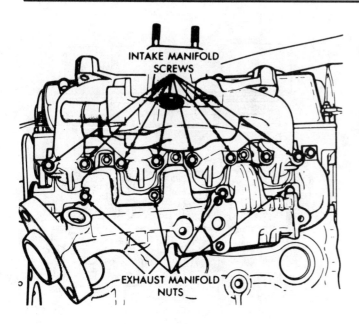

4.10   Intake/exhaust manifold fastener locations

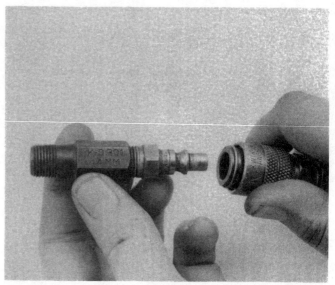

5.4   This is what the air hose adapter that threads into the spark plug hole looks like – they're commonly available from auto parts stores

12 Tighten the cover retaining bolts to the torque listed in this Chapter's Specifications.
13 Install the remaining components in the reverse order of removal.
14 Run the engine and check for oil leaks.

4   Intake and exhaust manifold – removal and installation

Removal

Refer to illustration 4.10
1   On fuel injected models, relieve the fuel pressure (see Chapter 4).
2   Disconnect the negative cable from the battery.
3   Drain the cooling system (see Chapter 1).
4   Remove the air cleaner assembly and the carburetor or throttle body (see Chapter 4).
5   Label and disconnect any remaining electrical wiring, coolant and vacuum hoses and fuel lines from the intake and exhaust manifolds.
6   Disconnect the air injection and EGR tubes and remove the diverter valve and air pump, if equipped (see Chapter 6).
7   Unbolt the power steering pump (if equipped) and set it aside without disconnecting the hoses (see Chapter 10). Unbolt the mounting bracket from the engine block.
8   Set the parking brake and block the rear wheels. Raise the front of the vehicle and support it with jackstands.
9   Working underneath the vehicle, apply penetrating oil to the front exhaust pipe-to-manifold fasteners. Remove the fasteners and separate the pipe from the manifold.
10 Remove the intake and exhaust manifold fasteners **(see illustration)** and lift the manifolds from the vehicle.
11 Thoroughly clean the manifold and cylinder head mating surfaces, removing all traces of old gasket material.
12 Inspect the manifolds and fasteners for cracks and damage. If the gasket was leaking, the mating surfaces may be warped. Have an automotive machine shop resurface the manifold as needed.

Installation

13 Apply a light coat of Mopar sealant 3419115 (or equivalent) to the manifold side of a new gasket and slip it into position over the mounting studs.

14 Install the exhaust manifold and tighten the mounting nuts to the torque listed in this Chapter's Specifications, working from the center out.
15 Install the intake manifold and tighten the mounting screws to the torque listed in this Chapter's Specifications, working from the center out.
16 Reinstall the remaining components in the reverse order of removal.
17 Refill the cooling system, run the engine and check for vacuum, coolant and exhaust leaks.

5   Valve springs, retainers and seals – replacement in the vehicle

Refer to illustrations 5.4, 5.6, 5.15 and 5.18
Note: *Broken valve springs and defective valve stem seals can be replaced without removing the cylinder head. Two special tools and a compressed air source are normally required to perform this operation, so read through this Section carefully and rent or buy the tools before beginning the job. If compressed air is not available, a length of nylon rope can be used to keep the valves from falling into the cylinder during this procedure.*
1   Refer to Section 3 and remove the valve cover from the cylinder head.
2   Remove the spark plug from the cylinder which has the defective component. If all of the valve stem seals are being replaced, all of the spark plugs should be removed.
3   Turn the crankshaft until the piston in the affected cylinder is at top dead center on the compression stroke (refer to Chapter 2, Part C for instructions). If you are replacing all of the valve stem seals, springs or retainers, begin with cylinder number one and work on the valves for one cylinder at a time. Move from cylinder-to-cylinder following the firing order sequence (see the Specifications Section).
4   Thread an adapter into the spark plug hole and connect an air hose from a compressed air source to it **(see illustration)**. Most auto parts stores can supply an air hose adapter. **Note:** *Many cylinder compression gauges utilize a screw-in fitting that may work with your air hose quick-disconnect fitting.*
5   Apply compressed air to the cylinder. The valves should be held in place by the air pressure. If the valve faces or seats are in poor condition, leaks may prevent the air pressure from retaining the valves – refer to the alternative procedure below.
6   Compress the valve spring with a special tool and slip the rocker arm out **(see illustration)**. Store the rocker arms in order to assure installation

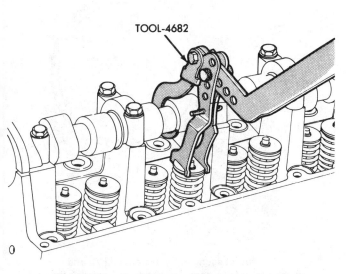

5.6 The same tool can be used to remove the rocker arms and compress the springs for keeper removal

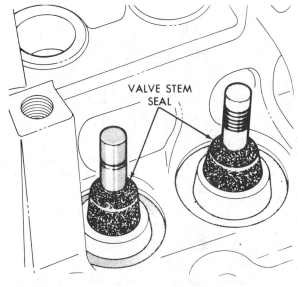

5.15 The valve seals should be seated as shown here

in the same position. If all of the valve stem seals are being replaced, all of the rocker arms should be removed.

7   If you do not have access to compressed air, an alternative method can be used. Position the piston at a point just before TDC on the compression stroke, then feed a long piece of nylon rope through the spark plug hole until it fills the combustion chamber. Be sure to leave the end of the rope hanging out of the engine so it can be removed easily. Use a large breaker bar and socket to rotate the crankshaft in the normal direction of rotation (clockwise) until slight resistance is felt as the piston comes up against the rope in the combustion chamber.

8   Stuff shop rags into the cylinder head holes around the valves to prevent parts and tools from falling into the engine, then use a valve spring compressor to compress the spring assembly. Remove the keepers with a pair of small needle-nose pliers or a magnet.

9   Remove the spring retainer and valve spring assembly. **Note:** *If air pressure fails to hold the valve in the closed position during this operation, the valve face or seat is probably damaged. If so, the cylinder head will have to be removed for additional repair operations.*

10   Wrap a rubber band or tape around the top of the valve stem so the valve will not fall into the combustion chamber, then release the air pressure. **Note:** *If a rope was used instead of air pressure, turn the crankshaft slightly in the direction opposite normal rotation.*

11   Inspect the valve stem for damage. Rotate the valve in the guide and check the end for eccentric movement, which would indicate that the valve is bent.

12   Move the valve up-and-down in the guide and make sure it doesn't bind. If the valve stem binds, either the valve is bent or the guide is damaged. In either case, the head will have to be removed for repair.

13   Inspect the rocker arms for wear and replace as necessary.

14   Reapply air pressure to the cylinder to retain the valve in the closed position, then remove the tape or rubber band from the valve stem. If a rope was used instead of air pressure, rotate the crankshaft in the normal direction of rotation until slight resistance is felt.

15   Lubricate the valve stem with engine oil and install a new oil seal **(see illustration)**.

16   Install the spring assembly in position over the valve.

17   Install the valve spring retainer and compress the valve spring assembly.

18   Position the keepers in the upper groove. Apply a small dab of grease to the inside of each keeper to hold it in place if necessary **(see illustration)**. Remove the pressure from the spring tool and make sure the keepers are seated.

5.18 Keepers don't always stay in place, so apply a small dab of grease to each one as shown here before installation – it'll hold them in place on the valve stem as the spring is released

19   Lubricate the rocker arms with moly-based grease. Compress the valve spring and slip the rocker arm(s) into position.

20   Disconnect the air hose and remove the adapter from the spark plug hole. If a rope was used in place of air pressure, pull it out of the cylinder.

21   Install the spark plugs and connect the wires.

22   Refer to Section 3 and install the valve cover.

23   Start and run the engine, then check for oil leaks and unusual sounds coming from the valve cover area.

---

6   Timing belt and sprockets – removal, inspection and installation

Removal

Refer to illustrations 6.2, 6.3, 6.4, 6.5, 6.6, 6.7

1   Disconnect the cable from the negative battery terminal.

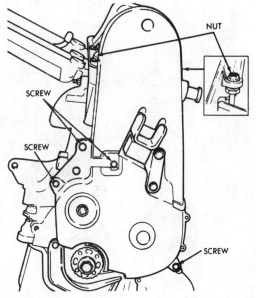

6.2   The timing belt cover is removed in two sections

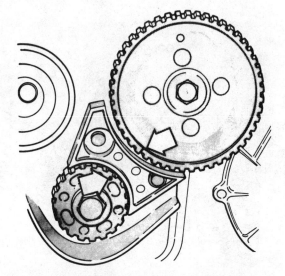

6.3   Correct alignment of the crankshaft and intermediate shaft sprocket marks (arrows) with the number one piston at TDC on the compression stroke

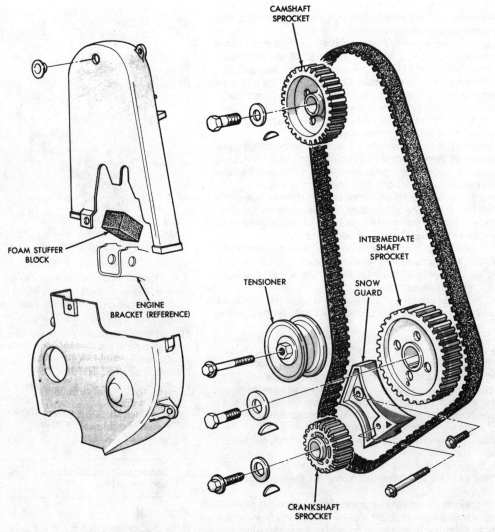

6.4   Timing belt components – exploded view

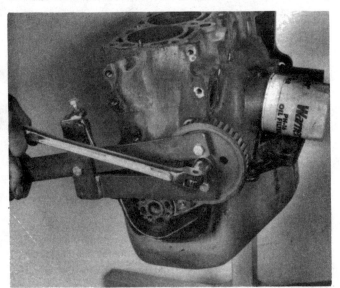

6.5   Hold the intermediate shaft sprocket with a tool to keep it from turning as the bolt is loosened

6.6   A puller must be used to remove the crankshaft sprocket

2   Remove the timing belt cover (see illustration).
3   Locate the number one piston at top dead center on the compression stroke by removing the spark plug, placing your finger over the hole and turning the crankshaft clockwise until pressure is felt. Align the marks on the crankshaft and intermediate shaft sprocket (see illustration) and line up the arrows on the camshaft sprocket with the bearing cap parting line (see illustration 6.16).
4   Use one wrench to hold the tensioner pulley nut (see illustration) while using another wrench or socket to loosen the center bolt, releasing the tension from the timing belt. Remove the belt. Remove the tensioner pulley assembly for inspection.
5   If you intend to remove the intermediate shaft sprocket, remove the sprocket bolt while holding the sprocket with the special tool (no. C-4687) or a homemade substitute (see illustration). Pull the sprocket off the shaft.
6   If you need to remove the crankshaft sprocket, remove the bolt and use a puller to remove the sprocket (see illustration).
7   If the camshaft sprocket needs to be removed, hold the camshaft sprocket as described in Step 5 and remove the bolt (see illustration), then detach the sprocket from the cam.

Inspection

8   Inspect the timing belt for wear, signs of stretching and damaged teeth. Check for signs of contamination by oil, gasoline, coolant and other liquids, which could cause the belt to break down and stretch. **Note:** *Unless the vehicle has very low mileage, it is a good idea to replace the timing belt with a new one any time it is removed.*
9   Inspect the tensioner pulley for damage, distortion and nicked or bent flanges. Turn the pulley and check for bearing play and roughness. Replace the tensioner with a new one if necessary.
10   Inspect the camshaft, crankshaft and intermediate shaft sprockets for wear, damage, cracks, corrosion and rounding of the teeth. Replace them with new ones if necessary as damaged or worn sprockets could cause the belt to slip and alter camshaft timing.
11   Inspect the crankshaft and intermediate shaft seals for signs of oil leakage and replace them with new ones if necessary (Sections 9 and 12).

Installation

Refer to illustrations 6.13, 6.14, 6.16, 6.19, 6.20 and 6.21

12   When installing the timing belt, the keys on all shafts must be at the 12 o'clock position (pointing up).
13   Install the crankshaft and intermediate shaft sprockets (if removed), then turn the shafts until the marks are aligned (see illustration).

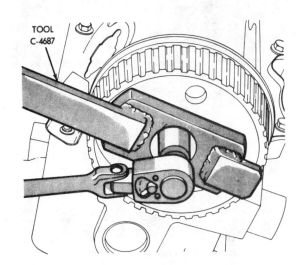

6.7   Removing the camshaft sprocket bolt using a special tool to keep the sprocket from turning

6.13   Use a straightedge to make sure the marks line up with the center of the sprocket bolt holes

6.14   A large screwdriver wedged in the flywheel/driveplate teeth will keep the crankshaft from turning as the sprocket bolt is tightened

6.16   The small hole must be at the top and the arrows on the camshaft sprocket hub must be aligned with the bearing cap parting line when installing the timing belt

6.19   Use a ruler to measure timing belt deflection

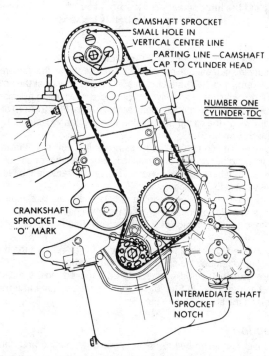

CAMSHAFT SPROCKET
SMALL HOLE IN VERTICAL CENTER LINE
PARTING LINE — CAMSHAFT CAP TO CYLINDER HEAD
NUMBER ONE CYLINDER-TDC
CRANKSHAFT SPROCKET "O" MARK
INTERMEDIATE SHAFT SPROCKET NOTCH

6.20   All of the timing marks must align at once

14   Install the crankshaft sprocket bolt, lock the crankshaft to keep it from rotating and tighten the bolt to the torque listed in this Chapter's Specifications (see illustration).

15   Install the intermediate shaft sprocket and bolt (if removed) and tighten it to the torque listed in this Chapter's Specifications. Double-check to make sure the marks are aligned as shown in illustration 6.13.

16   Install the camshaft sprocket and bolt (if removed). Tighten the bolt to the torque listed in this Chapter's Specifications. The arrows on the sprocket hub must align with the camshaft bearing cap parting line (see illustration).

17   Install the timing belt without turning any of the sprockets.

18   Install the tensioner pulley with the bolt finger tight.

19   With the help of an assistant, apply tension to the timing belt and temporarily tighten the tensioner bolt. Measure the deflection of the belt between the camshaft and tensioner pulley. Adjust the tensioner until belt deflection is approximately 5/16-inch, under moderate pressure (see illustration).

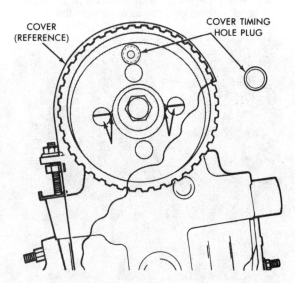

COVER (REFERENCE)
COVER TIMING HOLE PLUG

6.21   To check the cam timing with the cover in place, see if the small hole in the camshaft sprocket is aligned with the hole in the cover

20 Turn the crankshaft two complete revolutions and recheck the timing marks **(see illustration)**. This will align the belt on the pulleys. Recheck the belt deflection and tighten the tensioner pulley.

21 Recheck the camshaft timing with the timing belt cover installed and the number one piston at TDC on the compression stroke. The small hole in the camshaft sprocket must be centered in the timing belt cover hole **(see illustration)**.

7 Camshaft and rocker arms – removal, inspection and installation

Removal

Refer to illustrations 7.1, 7.3, 7.4, 7.6 and 7.8

1 Remove the timing belt cover and timing belt. Unbolt the camshaft sprocket from the camshaft (see Section 6). Keep tension on the timing belt to prevent the sprockets from moving in relation to the belt **(see illustration)**. If the belt slips, the timing procedure MUST be done.

2 Remove the valve cover (see Section 3).

3 Loosen the camshaft bearing caps **(see illustration)**. Work from the ends toward the center, in 1/4-turn increments, until they can be removed by hand.

(ENGINE SUPPORT)

2A

7.1 Hold the timing belt in position on the sprockets by lightly tensioning the camshaft sprocket

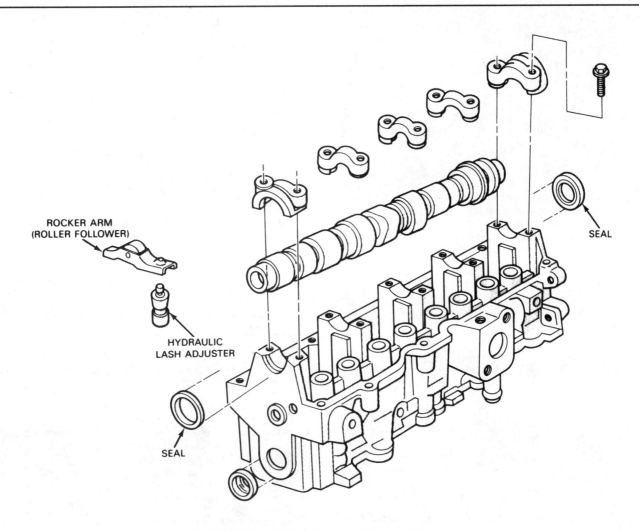

ROCKER ARM (ROLLER FOLLOWER)

HYDRAULIC LASH ADJUSTER

SEAL

SEAL

7.3 Camshaft and related components – exploded view

7.4   Tap the rear of the camshaft lightly with a soft-face hammer to dislodge the bearing caps

7.6   Lift straight up on the camshaft to avoid damage to the thrust bearing surfaces

7.8   Label the rocker arms so they can be reinstalled in their original locations

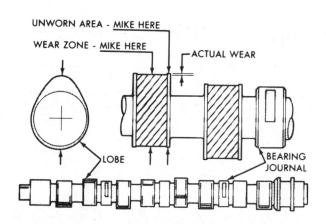

7.10   Four-cylinder engine cam lobe wear can be determined by measuring each lobe at the edge and in the center and subtracting the two measurements

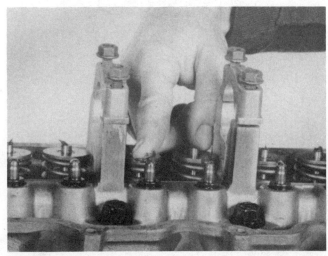

7.14   Apply assembly lubricant to the lash adjusters and the ends of the valve stems

7.15   Seat the rocker arms on the valves and adjusters, then apply assembly lubricant to the cam lobe faces

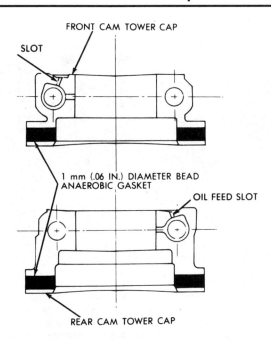

7.16a   Apply anaerobic-type gasket sealant to the dark areas of the front and rear bearing caps (don't get it in the oil passages)

7.16b   Install the camshaft bearing caps in numerical sequence with the arrows pointing toward the timing belt

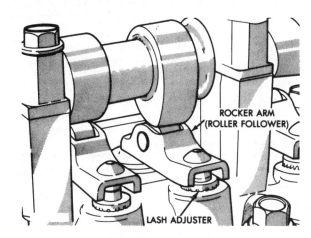

7.17   Be sure the rocker arms and lash adjusters are seated properly

4   Lift off the cam bearing caps. It may be necessary to tap the rear of the camshaft lightly with a soft-faced hammer to loosen them **(see illustration)**.
5   Store the bearing caps in order so they can be reinstalled in their original positions.
6   Remove the camshaft **(see illustration)**. **Caution:** *If the camshaft is cocked as it is removed the thrust bearings could be damaged.*
7   Reinstall the caps finger tight temporarily to protect the studs and bearing surfaces.
8   Remove the rocker arms and lash adjusters **(see illustration)**. Either mark them or place them in a marked container so they may be reinstalled in their original locations.

Inspection

Refer to illustrations 7.10 and 7.14

9   After the camshaft has been removed from the engine, cleaned with solvent and dried, inspect the bearing surfaces for uneven wear, pitting and evidence of seizure.
10   Measure the camshaft lobes and bearing journals with a micrometer to determine if they are excessively worn or out-of-round **(see illustration)**.
11   Check the camshaft lobes and journals for heat discoloration, score marks, chipped areas, pitting and uneven wear. If the lobes and journals are in good condition and if the lobe lift measurements are as listed in this Chapter's Specifications, the camshaft can be reused.
12   Clean the lash adjusters with solvent and dry them thoroughly without mixing them up.
13   On models with roller rocker arms, check the rollers carefully for wear and damage and make sure they turn freely without excessive play.

Installation

Refer to illustrations 7.15, 7.16a, 7.16b, 7.17 and 7.18

14   Lubricate the camshaft lobes, bearing journals, rocker arms and oil seal lips (use new seals) with moly-base grease or engine assembly lube **(see illustration)**. **Note:** *1987 models use a plug instead of a seal at the rear of the camshaft.*
15   Install the lash adjusters and rocker arms **(see illustration)**. Slip new oil seal(s) onto the ends of the camshaft with the lips facing in. Remove the bearing caps and place the camshaft into the cylinder head.

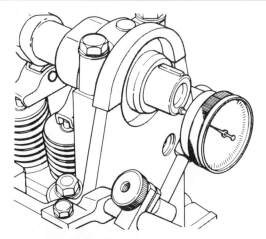

7.18   Move the camshaft back and forth and check the endplay with a dial indicator

16   Apply anaerobic-type sealant to the contact surfaces of the front and rear bearing caps **(see illustration)**. Install the caps in the proper order **(see illustration)** and finger tighten the bolts. Be sure the oil seals are positioned correctly.
17   Working from the center out in a criss-cross pattern, tighten each bolt 1/4-turn at a time until the torque listed in this Chapter's Specifications is reached. Be sure the rocker arms and lash adjusters are properly seated **(see illustration)**.
18   Push the camshaft to the rear and mount a dial indicator **(see illustration)**. Zero the dial indicator and pry the camshaft forward. Compare the reading to the endplay listed in this Chapter's Specifications.

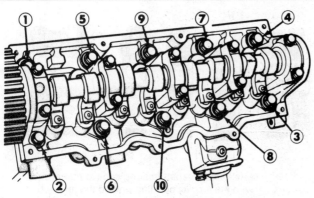

8.9   Cylinder head bolt *loosening* sequence

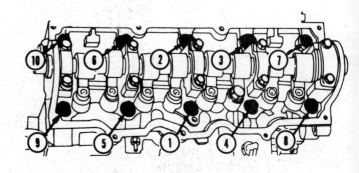

8.13   Cylinder head bolt *tightening* sequence

19   Refer to Section 6 and install the timing belt and sprocket.
20   The remaining installation steps are the reverse of removal.
21   Run the engine and check for oil leaks and proper operation.
Note: *The lash adjusters may take as long as one hour to purge themselves of air and operate quietly.*

---

8   Cylinder head – removal and installation

Caution: *Allow the engine to cool completely before following this procedure*

Removal

Refer to illustration 8.9
1   Position the number one piston at Top Dead Center (see Chapter 2, Part C).
2   Disconnect the negative cable from the battery.
3   Drain the cooling system and remove the spark plugs (see Chapter 1).
4   Remove the intake and exhaust manifolds (see Section 4).
5   Disconnect the dipstick tube from the thermostat housing and turn the bracket away from the stud.
6   Remove the valve cover (see Section 3).
7   Remove the camshaft, rockers and lash adjusters (see Section 7).
8   On air conditioned models, unbolt the compressor and set it aside without disconnecting the refrigerant hoses. Remove the mounting bracket from the engine.
9   Loosen the cylinder head bolts, 1/4-turn at a time, in the sequence shown **(see illustration)** until they can be removed by hand.

9.6   The retainer must be removed to withdraw the intermediate shaft

10   Carefully lift the cylinder head straight up and place the head on wooden blocks to prevent damage to the sealing surfaces. If the head sticks to the engine block, dislodge it by placing a block of wood against the head casting and tapping the wood with a hammer. Cylinder head disassembly and inspection procedure are covered in Chapter 2, Part C. Check the head for warpage, even if you're just replacing the gasket.
Note: *Some engines come from the factory with oversize camshaft bearings and journals. Cylinder heads with oversize bearings may be identified by green painted caps and O/SJ stamped on the end of the head. Oversize camshafts are painted green and stamped O/SJ.*
11   Remove all traces of old gasket material from the block and head. Do not allow anything to fall into the engine. Clean and inspect all threaded fasteners and be sure the threaded holes in the block are clean and dry.

Installation

Refer to illustration 8.13
12   Place a new gasket and the cylinder head in position.
13   The cylinder head bolts should be tightened in four stages following the proper sequence **(see illustration)** to the torque listed in this Chapter's Specifications. If bolt torque is not over 90 lb/ft after the 1/4-additional turn, replace the bolts. **Caution:** *Head bolt diameter is 11mm. 10 mm bolts will thread into the holes but will strip the holes.*
14   Reinstall the camshaft, rockers and timing belt (see Sections 6 and 7).
15   Reinstall the remaining parts in the reverse order of removal.
16   Be sure to refill the cooling system and check all fluid levels. Rotate the crankshaft clockwise slowly by hand through two complete revolutions. Recheck the camshaft timing marks (see Section 6).
17   Run the engine until normal operating temperature is reached. Check for leaks and proper operation. shut off the engine. Remove the valve cover and retorque the cylinder head bolts, unless the gasket manufacturer states otherwise.

---

9   Intermediate shaft and seal – removal, inspection and installation

---

Removal

Refer to illustration 9.6
1   Remove the distributor (see Chapter 5).
2   Remove the oil pump (see Section 11).
3   On carbureted models, remove the fuel pump (see Chapter 4).
4   Remove the timing belt and intermediate shaft sprocket (see Section 6).
5   Inspect the sprocket and belt as described in Section 6.
6   Unbolt and remove the shaft retainer **(see illustration)**.
7   If you need to remove the shaft, remove the radiator (see Chapter 3). Grasp the shaft and carefully withdraw it from the engine.
8   Clean the shaft thoroughly with solvent and inspect the gear, bearing surfaces and lobes for wear and damage.

9.9   With the retainer on a flat surface, carefully tap the new seal into place with a soft-face hammer

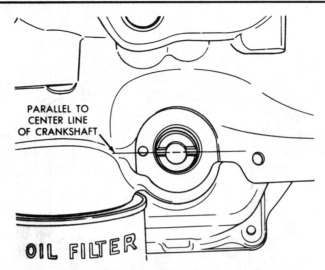

9.10   When viewed through the distributor hole, the oil pump shaft slot must be parallel to the crankshaft centerline

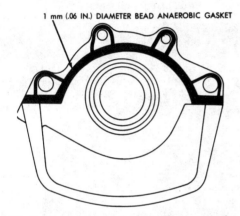

9.11   Apply a 1 mm bead of anaerobic sealant to the retainer as shown here

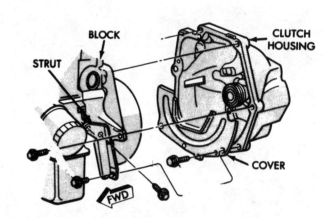

10.5   Remove the strut and cover

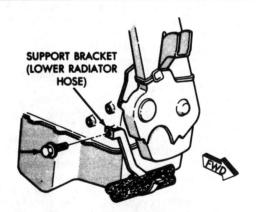

10.6   Unbolt the lower radiator support bracket

Installation

Refer to illustrations 9.9, 9.10 and 9.11

9   Use a punch to drive the old oil seal out of the retainer. Apply a thin coat of RTV sealant to the inner surface of the retainer and tap the new seal into place with a soft-face hammer **(see illustration)**.

10   Lightly lubricate the gear, lobes and bearing surfaces with engine assembly lubricant and carefully insert the shaft into place. After installation, make sure the shaft is securely in place in the oil pump. The oil pump slot must be parallel to the crankshaft centerline and the intermediate shaft keyway must be in the 12 o'clock position **(see illustration)**.

11   Apply a 1 mm wide bead of anaerobic (form-in-place) sealant to the contact surface of the retainer **(see illustration)** and place it in position over the end of the shaft. Install the retaining bolts and tighten them to the torque listed in this Chapter's Specifications.

12   Install the remaining components in the reverse order of removal.

13   Add oil and coolant as needed. Run the engine, set the ignition timing and check for oil leaks.

10   Oil pan – removal and installation

Removal

Refer to illustrations 10.5 and 10.6

1   Disconnect the negative cable from the battery.

2   Detach the hose from the air pump relief valve.

3   Set the parking brake and block the rear wheels. Raise the front of the vehicle and support it securely on jackstands.

4   Drain the engine oil and replace the oil filter (see Chapter 1).

5   Remove the engine block-to-bellhousing strut and the lower inspection cover **(see illustration)**.

6   Detach the lower radiator hose support bracket **(see illustration)**.

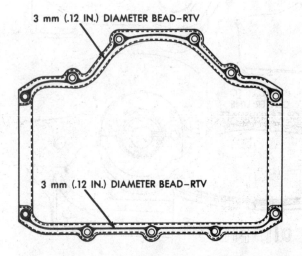

10.16a   Apply a continuous bead of sealant around the oil pan flange, making sure it is applied on the inside of the bolt holes

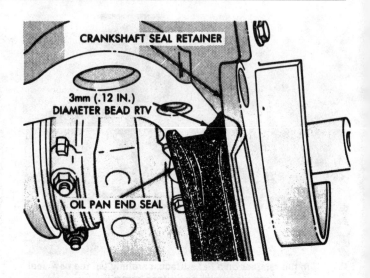

10.16b Apply a bead of RTV sealant completely around the oil pan gasket surface

11.2   Remove the bolt and lower the oil pickup

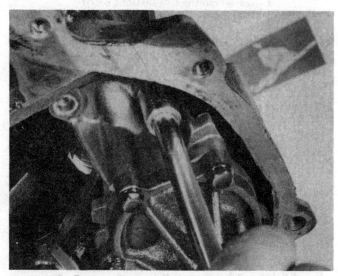

11.3   Remove the mounting bolts from the oil pump

7   Loosen the engine mount through bolts.
8   Loosen the transmission-to-crossmember mounting bracket.
9   Position a jack under the oil pan. Place a block of wood on the jack pad to protect the oil pan.
10   Raise the left side of the engine about two inches. Slip a block of wood into the engine mount to hold the engine up.
11   Lower the jack and move it aside.
12   Remove the bolts securing the oil pan to the engine block.
13   Tap on the pan with a soft-face hammer to break the gasket seal and lower the oil pan from the engine. Don't pry between the pan and the block, as the gasket mating surfaces may be damaged.
14   Using a gasket scraper, scrape off all traces of the old gasket from the engine block and oil pan. Remove the end seals from the oil seal retainers.
15   Clean the oil pan with solvent and dry it thoroughly. Check the gasket sealing surfaces for distortion.

Installation
Refer to illustrations 10.16a and 10.16b

16   Before installing the oil pan, install new end seals in the oil seal retainers. Apply a 3/16-inch bead of RTV sealant completely around the oil pan gasket surface of the engine block, including the end seals (see illustrations).
17   Gently position the oil pan on the engine.

18   Install the bolts and tighten them to the torque listed in this Chapter's Specifications, starting with the bolts closest to the center of the pan and working out in a criss-cross pattern. Do not overtighten them or leakage may occur.
19   Reinstall the remaining components in the reverse order of removal.
20   Add oil, run the engine and check for oil leaks.

11   Oil pump – removal and installation

Removal
Refer to illustrations 11.2 and 11.3

1   Remove the oil pan (see Section 10).
2   Unbolt and remove the oil pickup (see illustration).
3   Unbolt and remove the oil pump (see illustration).

Installation
Refer to illustrations 11.6 and 11.8

4   Unscrew the bolts and remove the cover from the pump. Pack the pump with petroleum jelly to prime it, then install the cover, tightening the bolts to the torque listed in this Chapter's Specifications.
5   Apply sealant (Loctite 515, or equivalent) to the pump body-to-engine block surface.

11.8 Lubricate the new O-ring and install it in the oil pump before attaching the pickup tube

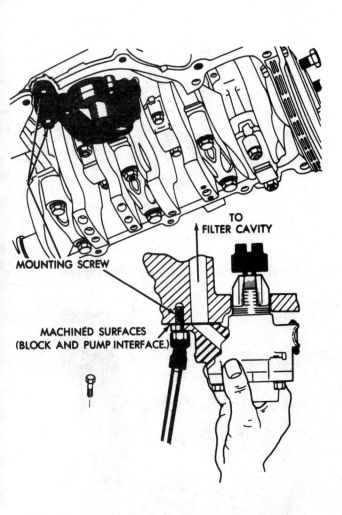

11.6 Be sure the pump is fully seated before installing the bolts

6   Lubricate the driven gear with engine oil. Install the oil pump so the slot in the gear aligns with the drive tang on the distributor **(see illustration)**. If the slot does not align properly, the pump will not seat fully – don't force it! **Note:** *If you can't get the pump slot aligned, turn the engine to Top Dead Center (see Chapter 2C) and remove the distributor (see Chapter 5). Install the oil pump and then install the distributor.*

7   Hold the oil pump against the block and install the mounting bolts. Tighten the bolts to the torque listed in this Chapter's Specifications.

8   Lubricate a new O-ring and install it in the oil pump before attaching the pickup assembly **(see illustration)**.

9   Slip the oil pickup into place and install the mounting bolt. Tighten the bolt to the torque listed in this Chapter's Specifications.

10   Reinstall the remaining parts in the reverse order of removal.

11   Add oil and run the engine. Check for oil pressure and leaks.

12   Front oil seal and housing – removal and installation

Removal

Refer to illustrations 12.1a, 12.1b

1   With the timing belt, crankshaft sprocket, intermediate shaft sprocket and the oil pan removed for access, unbolt and remove the oil seal housing **(see illustrations)**.

2   Use a punch and hammer to drive the old oil seal from the housing.

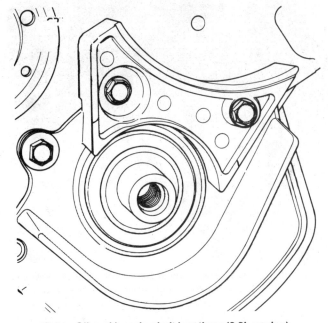

12.1a Oil seal housing bolt locations (2.2L engine)

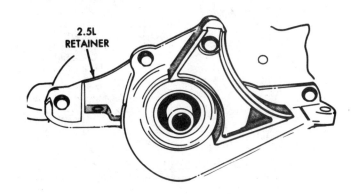

12.1b Oil seal housing bolt locations (2.5L engine)

**12.3   Tap the new front oil seal into place with a
soft-face hammer**

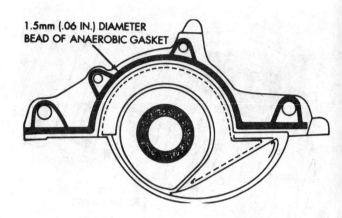

12.4   Apply sealant to the mating surface as shown

**13.3   Pull the rear oil seal housing away from the crankshaft and
detach it from the engine**

**13.6   Tap the new rear oil seal squarely into place with a
soft-face hammer**

Installation

Refer to illustrations 12.3 and 12.4

3   Place the new seal in place and carefully tap it into position with a soft-face hammer **(see illustration)**.

4   Apply a thin coat of anaerobic sealant to the inner surface of the housing **(see illustration)**.

5   Lubricate the inner circumference of the seal with white lithium base grease and apply a 1 mm bead of anaerobic gasket sealant to the engine block mating surfaces of the seal housing. Position the housing on the engine. Install the retaining bolts and tighten them to the torque listed in this Chapter's Specifications.

6   Reinstall the remaining parts in the reverse order of removal.

7   Run the engine and check for oil leaks.

---

13   Rear oil seal and housing – removal and installation

Removal

Refer to illustration 13.3

1   Remove the transmission (see Chapter 7).

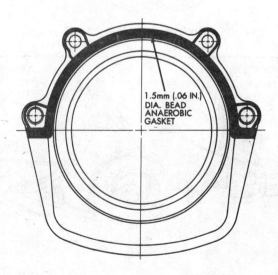

13.8   Apply a bead of anaerobic sealant to the mating surface

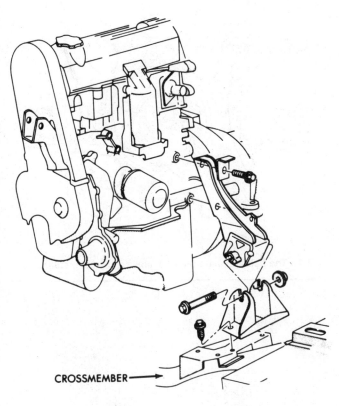

CROSSMEMBER

14.7a Left engine mount – exploded view

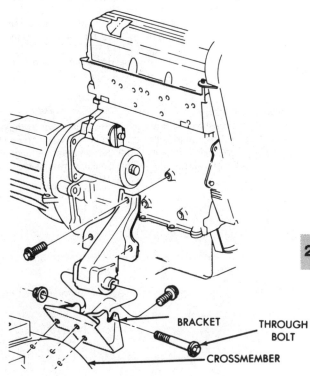

BRACKET THROUGH BOLT

CROSSMEMBER

14.7b Right engine mount – exploded view

2A

2   Remove the flywheel/driveplate (see Section 15).
3   Remove the four bolts and detach the housing and seal from the rear of the engine block **(see illustration)**.
4   Using a hammer and punch, drive the old seal from the housing.
5   Clean the seal surface thoroughly with solvent and inspect it for nicks and other damage.

Installation

Refer to illustrations 13.6 and 13.8

6   Apply a thin coat of RTV sealant to the inner circumference of the housing, lay the new seal in place and tap it squarely into position with a soft-face hammer **(see illustration)**.
7   Lubricate the seal inner surface with white lithium-base grease.
8   Apply a 1.5 mm bead of anaerobic gasket sealant to the engine block mating surfaces of the seal housing **(see illustration)**.
9   Place the assembly in position, install the bolts and tighten them to the torque listed in this Chapter's Specifications.

14   Engine mounts – check and replacement

1   Engine mounts seldom require attention, but broken or deteriorated mounts should be replaced immediately or the added strain placed on the driveline components may cause damage.

Check

2   During the check, the engine must be raised slightly to remove the weight from the mounts.

3   Raise the vehicle and support it securely on jackstands, then position the jack under the engine oil pan. Place a large block of wood between the jack head and the oil pan, then carefully raise the engine just enough to take the weight off the mounts.
4   Check the mounts to see if the rubber is cracked, hardened or separated from the metal plates. Sometimes the rubber will split right down the center. Rubber preservative may be applied to the mounts to slow deterioration.
5   Check for relative movement between the mount plates and the engine or frame (use a large screwdriver or pry bar to attempt to move the mounts). If movement is noted, lower the engine and tighten the mount fasteners.

Replacement

Refer to illustrations 14.7a and 14.7b

6   Disconnect the negative cable from the battery, then raise the vehicle and support it securely on jackstands.
7   Remove the nut and withdraw the through-bolt from the bracket **(see illustrations)**.
8   Raise the engine slightly, then remove the mount-to-engine block bolts and detach the mount.
9   Installation is the reverse of removal. Use thread locking compound on the mount bolts and be sure to tighten them securely.

15   Flywheel/driveplate – removal and installation

Removal

1   Refer to Chapter 7 and remove the transmission. If your vehicle has a manual transmission, the pressure plate and clutch will also have to be removed (see Chapter 8).

2   Jam a large screwdriver in the starter ring gear (on manual transmission models) or through a hole in the driveplate (on automatic transmission models) to keep the crankshaft from turning, then remove the mounting bolts. Since it's fairly heavy, support the flywheel as the last bolt is removed.

3   Pull straight back on the flywheel/driveplate to detach it from the crankshaft.

Installation

Refer to illustration 15.4

4   Installation is the reverse of removal. Be sure to align the holes in the flywheel/driveplate with the offset holes in the crankshaft **(see illustration)**. Use a thread locking compound on the bolt threads and tighten them to the torque listed in this Chapter's Specifications in a criss-cross pattern.

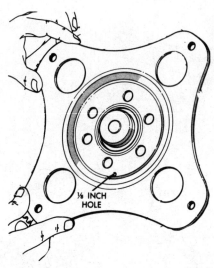

15.4   The bolt holes are offset to ensure correct installation

Chapter 2 Part B   V6 and V8 Engines

Contents

Specifications

General
Cylinder numbers (front-to-rear)
    Left (driver's) side 1-3-5
    Right side 2-4-6
Firing order
    V6 engine 1-6-5-4-3-2
    V8 engine 1-8-4-3-6-5-7-2
Direction distributor rotor rotates .... clockwise

---

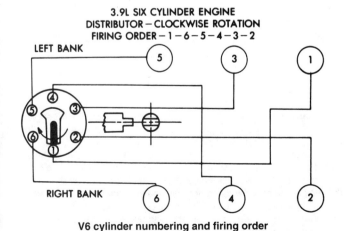

V6 cylinder numbering and firing order

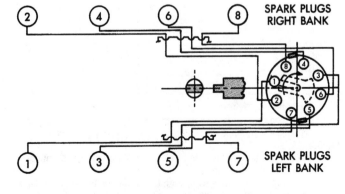

V8 cylinder numbering and firing order

Camshaft (V6 engine)

Bearing journal diameter
No. 1	1.998 to 1.999 in
No. 2	1.967 to 1.968 in
No. 3	1.951 to 1.952 in
No. 4	1.5605 to 1.5615 in

Lobe lift (measured at valve)
Intake	0.373 in
Exhaust	0.400 in

Endplay
Standard	0.002 to 0.010 in
Limit	0.010 in

Camshaft (V8 engine)

Bearing journal diameter
No. 1	2.000 to 2.001 in
No. 2	1.984 to 1.985 in
No. 3	1.969 to 1.970 in
No. 4	1.953 to 1.954 in
No. 5	1.5625 to 1.5635 in

Lobe lift (measured at valve)	not available

End play
Standard	0.002 to 0.010 in
Limit	not available

Torque specifications
Ft-lbs (unless otherwise indicated)

Camshaft sprocket bolt	50
Camshaft thrust plate bolt	210 in-lbs
Cylinder head bolts	
Step one	50
Step two	105
Exhaust manifold	
1987 through 1991	
Bolts	20
Nuts	15
1992 and later (bolts and nuts)	25
Flywheel/driveplate bolt	55
Intake manifold bolts	
1987 through 1991	
Step one	25
Step two	45
1992 and later	
Step one	72 in-lbs
Step two	144 in-lbs
Main bearing cap bolts	85
Oil pan bolts	200 in-lbs
Oil pump mounting bolts	30
Timing cover bolts	35
Rocker arm shaft bolts (1987 through 1991)	200 in-lbs
Rocker arm pedestal bolts (1992 and later)	21
Valve cover	
1987 through 1991	
Nuts	80 in-lbs
Studs	115 in-lbs
1992 and later (bolts)	95 in-lbs
Vibration damper bolt	
1987 through 1991	100
1992 and later	135

1   General information

This part of Chapter 2 is devoted to in-vehicle repair procedures for the 3.9L V6 and 5.2L V8 engines. All information concerning engine removal and installation and engine block and cylinder head overhaul can be found in Part C of this Chapter.

The V6 and V8 engines are from the same engine family and are modular in design. The main difference between the two engines is the addition of two cylinders to enlarge the V6 to a V8. The majority of the photographs and illustrations in this Part of Chapter 2 relate to the V6 engine. Specifications for both engines are almost identical and, where differences occur between the V6 and V8, they are identified.

Since the repair procedures included in this Part are based on the assumption that the engine is still installed in the vehicle, if they are being used during a complete engine overhaul (with the engine already out of the vehicle and on a stand) many of the steps included here will not apply.

The specifications included in this Part of Chapter 2 apply only to the procedures found here. The specifications necessary for rebuilding the block and cylinder heads are included in Part C.

3.4   Remove the PCV valve or breather tube and move the spark plug wires aside

1   *PCV valve*
2   *Spark plug wires*

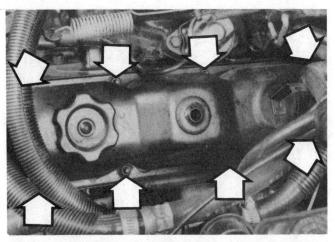

3.5a   Valve cover mounting nuts (arrows) – drivers' side shown

3.5b   Valve cover mounting nuts (arrows) – passengers' side shown

3.6   Move the wires and hoses aside and guide the valve cover out

2   Repair operations possible with the engine in the vehicle

Many major repair operations can be accomplished without removing the engine from the vehicle.

Clean the engine compartment and the exterior of the engine with some type of pressure washer before any work is done. A clean engine will make the job easier and will help keep dirt out of the internal areas of the engine.

Depending on the components involved, it may be a good idea to remove the hood to improve access to the engine as repairs are performed (refer to Chapter 11 if necessary).

If oil or coolant leaks develop, indicating a need for gasket or seal replacement, the repairs can generally be made with the engine in the vehicle. The oil pan gasket, the cylinder head gaskets, intake and exhaust manifold gaskets, timing cover gaskets and the crankshaft oil seals are accessible with the engine in place.

Exterior engine components, such as the water pump, the starter motor, the alternator, the distributor and the carburetor or fuel injection unit, as well as the intake and exhaust manifolds, can be removed for repair with the engine in place.

Since the cylinder heads can be removed without pulling the engine, valve component servicing can also be accomplished with the engine in the vehicle.

Replacement of, repairs to or inspection of the timing chain and sprockets and the oil pump are all possible with the engine in place.

In extreme cases caused by a lack of necessary equipment, repair or replacement of piston rings, pistons, connecting rods and rod bearings is possible with the engine in the vehicle. However, this practice is not recommended because of the cleaning and preparation work that must be done to the components involved.

3   Valve covers – removal and installation

Removal

Refer to illustrations 3.4, 3.5a, 3.5b and 3.6

1   Disconnect the negative cable from the battery.

2   Remove the air cleaner assembly (see Chapter 4).

3   Refer to Chapter 6 and detach any air management components that are in the way, if equipped.

4   Remove the breather tube or PCV valve **(see illustration)**. Label the spark plug wires and position the brackets/wires out of the way.

5   Remove the valve cover mounting nuts/bolts **(see illustrations)**.

6   Remove the valve cover **(see illustration)**. **Note:** *If the cover is stuck to the head, bump the cover with a block of wood and a hammer to release it. If it still will not come loose, try to slip a flexible putty knife between the head and cover to break the seal. Don't pry at the cover-to-head joint, as damage to the sealing surface and cover flange will result and oil leaks will develop.*

2B

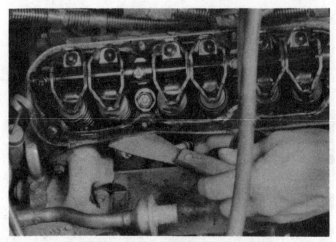

3.7   Remove all traces of old gasket material

4.2   Loosen the bolts (arrows) a little at a time until they're all loose (1987 through 1991 models)

Installation

Refer to illustration 3.7

7   The mating surfaces of each cylinder head and valve cover must be perfectly clean when the covers are installed. Use a gasket scraper to remove all traces of sealant or old gasket **(see illustration)**, then wipe the mating surfaces with a cloth saturated with lacquer thinner or acetone. If there is sealant or oil on the mating surfaces when the cover is installed, oil leaks may develop.

8   Make sure any threaded holes are clean. Run a tap into them to remove corrosion and restore damaged threads.

9   Mate the new gaskets to the covers before the covers are installed. Apply a thin coat of RTV sealant to the cover flange, then position the gasket inside the cover lip and allow the sealant to set up so the gasket adheres to the cover (if the sealant is not allowed to set, the gasket may fall out of the cover as it is installed on the engine).

10   Carefully position the cover on the head and install the nuts/bolts.

11   Tighten the nuts/bolts in three steps to the torque listed in this Chapter's Specifications.

12   The remaining installation steps are the reverse of removal.

13   Start the engine and check carefully for oil leaks as the engine warms up.

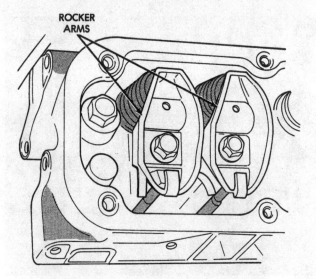

4.3   On 1992 and later models, each individual rocker arm is secured by a bolt and pedestal – store each pedestal together with its rocker arm so they can be reinstalled in exactly the location where they were removed

4   Rocker arms and pushrods – removal, inspection and installation

Removal

Refer to illustrations 4.2, 4.3 and 4.4

1   Refer to Section 3 and detach the valve covers from the cylinder heads.

2   On 1987 through 1991 models, loosen the rocker arm bolts **(see illustration)** a little at a time, working back and forth until they're all loose. Lift off the rocker arm and shaft assembly with the bolts in place and keep the rocker arms in order if they are removed from the shafts (the rocker arms and shafts must be reinstalled in their original positions).

3   On 1992 and later models, beginning at the front of one cylinder head, loosen and remove the rocker arm bolts **(see illustration)**. Store them separately in marked containers to ensure that they will be reinstalled in their original locations. **Note:** *If the pushrods are the only items being removed, loosen each bolt just enough to allow the rocker arm to be rotated to the side so the pushrods can be lifted out.*

4   Remove the pushrods and store them separately to make sure they don't get mixed up during installation **(see illustration)**.

Inspection

5   Check each rocker arm for wear, cracks and other damage, especially where the pushrods and valve stems contact the rocker arm faces.

6   Make sure the hole at the pushrod end of each rocker arm is open.

4.4   Store the pushrods in a box like this to keep them separate

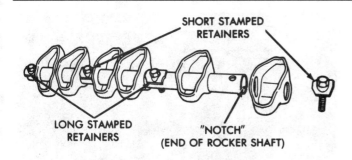

4.9a   Assemble the rocker arms as shown
(1987 through 1991 models)

4.10   Rocker arm identification details (1987 through
1991 models)

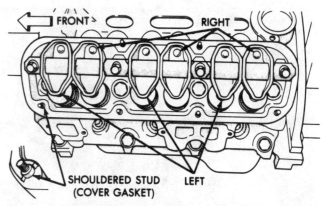

4.9b   Rocker arm location – left bank
(1987 through 1991 models)

4.12   Lubricate the pushrod ends and valve stems with
moly-base grease before installing the rocker arms

14   On 1992 and later models, set the rocker arms in place, then install the pedestals and bolts. Apply moly-base grease to the pedestals to prevent damage to the mating surface before engine oil pressure builds up. Tighten the bolts to the torque listed in this Chapter's Specifications.
15   Refer to Section 3 and install the valve covers. Start the engine, listen for unusual valve train noses and check for oil leaks at the valve cover joints.

7   Check each rocker arm pivot area and shaft for wear, cracks and galling. If the rocker arms or shafts are worn or damaged, replace them with new ones.
8   Inspect the pushrods for cracks and excessive wear at the ends. Roll each pushrod across a piece of plate glass to see if it is bent (if it wobbles, it is bent).

Installation

Refer to illustrations 4.9a, 4.9b, 4.10 and 4.12

9   On 1987 through 1991 models, assemble the rocker arms with the notch on the end of the rocker arm shaft pointing toward the centerline of the engine, and toward the front of the engine on the driver's (left) side or toward the rear on the passenger's (right) side **(see illustrations)**.
10   On engines with exhaust valve rotators, exhaust rockers must have clearance reliefs **(see illustration)**.
11   Lubricate the lower end of each pushrod with clean engine oil or moly-base grease and install them in their original locations. Make sure each pushrod seats completely in the lifter socket.
12   Apply moly-base grease to the ends of the valve stems and the upper ends of the pushrods before positioning the rocker arms over the studs **(see illustration)**.
13   On 1987 through 1991 models, set the rocker arm shaft in place, then tighten the bolts evenly, working back and forth. Apply moly-base grease to the contact surfaces to prevent damage before engine oil pressure builds up. Tighten the bolts to the torque listed in this Chapter's Specifications.

5   Valve springs, retainers and seals – replacement

Refer to illustrations 5.7, 5.15 and 5.17

Note: *Broken valve springs and defective valve stem seals can be replaced without removing the cylinder head. Two special tools and a compressed air source are normally required to perform this operation, so read through this Section carefully and rent or buy the tools before beginning the job. If compressed air isn't available, a length of nylon rope can be used to keep the valves from falling into the cylinder during this procedure.*

1   Remove the valve covers and the spark plugs (see Section 3 and Chapter 1).
2   Turn the crankshaft until the number one piston is at top dead center on the compression stroke (see Chapter 2C).
3   Remove the rocker arm assemblies (see Section 4). If you intend to use a lever-type spring compressor, install a dummy shaft in place of the rocker arm shaft.
4   Thread an adapter (C-3907, or equivalent) into the spark plug hole and connect an air hose from a compressed air source to it. Most auto parts stores can supply the air hose adapter. **Note:** *Many cylinder compression gauges utilize a screw-in fitting that may work with your air hose quick-disconnect fitting.*
5   Apply compressed air to the cylinder. The valves should be held in place by the air pressure. If the valve faces or seats are in poor condition,

5.7   Once the spring is depressed, the keepers can be removed with a small magnet or needle-nose pliers (a magnet is preferred to prevent dropping the keepers)

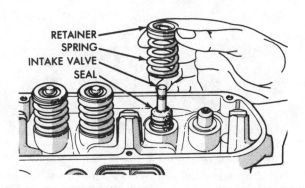

5.17   Install the seal, spring and retainer or rotator

leaks may prevent the air pressure from retaining the valves – valve reconditioning is indicated.

6   If you don't have access to compressed air, an alternative method can be used. Position the piston at a point just before TDC on the compression stroke, then feed a long piece of nylon rope through the spark plug hole until it fills the combustion chamber. Be sure to leave the end of the rope hanging out of the engine so it can be removed easily. Use a large breaker bar and socket to rotate the crankshaft in the normal direction of rotation (clockwise) until slight resistance is felt.

7   Stuff shop rags into the cylinder head holes around the valves to prevent parts and tools from falling into the engine, then use a valve spring compressor to compress the spring. Remove the keepers with small needle-nose pliers or a magnet **(see illustration)**. **Note:** *Several different types of tools are available for compressing the valve springs with the head in place. One type grips the lower spring coils and presses on the retainer as the knob is turned, while the lever-type (C-3906, or equivalent) utilizes the rocker arm dummy shaft for leverage. Both types work very well, although the lever type is usually less expensive.*

8   **Caution:** *Different length springs are used on the intake and exhaust valves – accidentally installing an intake spring on an exhaust valve can cause major engine damage!*

9   Remove the valve spring and retainer (intake valve) or rotator (exhaust valve).

10   Remove the old valve stem seals.

11   Wrap a rubber band or tape around the top of the valve stem so the valve won't fall into the combustion chamber, then release the air pressure. **Note:** *If a rope was used instead of air pressure, turn the crankshaft slightly in the direction opposite normal rotation.*

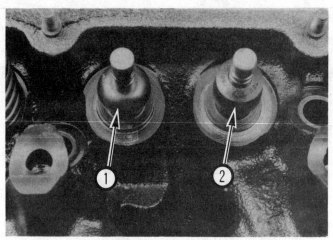

5.15   Be sure to install the seals on the correct bosses

1   Exhaust seal   *2   Intake seal*

12   Inspect the valve stem for damage. Rotate the valve in the guide and check the end for eccentric movement, which would indicate that the valve is bent.

13   Move the valve up-and-down in the guide and make sure it doesn't bind. If the valve stem binds, either the valve is bent or the guide is damaged. In either case, the head will have to be removed for repair.

14   Reapply air pressure to the cylinder to retain the valve in the closed position, then remove the tape or rubber band from the valve stem. If a rope was used instead of air pressure, rotate the crankshaft in the normal direction of rotation until slight resistance is felt.

15   If you're working on an exhaust valve, install the cup shield (seal) on the valve stem and push it down against the valve guide **(see illustration)**.

16   If you're working on an intake valve, push a new valve stem seal down over the valve, using the valve stem as a guide, but don't force the seal against the top of the guide.

17   Install the spring and retainer or rotator in position over the valve **(see illustration)**.

18   Compress the valve spring assembly only enough to install the keepers in the valve stem.

19   Position the keepers in the valve stem groove. Apply a small dab of grease to the inside of each keeper to hold it in place if necessary. Remove the pressure from the spring tool and make sure the keepers are seated.

20   Disconnect the air hose and remove the adapter from the spark plug hole. If a rope was used in place of air pressure, pull it out of the cylinder.

21   Repeat the above procedure on the remaining cylinders, following the firing order sequence (see the Specifications). Bring each piston to top dead center on the compression stroke before applying air pressure or inserting the rope into the cylinder.

22   Reinstall the rocker arm assemblies and the valve covers.

23   Start the engine, then check for oil leaks and unusual sounds coming from the valve cover area.

6   Intake manifold – removal and installation

Removal

Refer to illustrations 6.9a and 6.9b

1   On fuel injected models, relieve fuel pressure (see Chapter 4).

2   Disconnect the negative cable from the battery, then refer to Chapter 1 and drain the cooling system.

3   Remove the air cleaner assembly. If you intend to resurface or replace the manifold, remove the throttle body or carburetor (see Chapter 4).

4   Remove the distributor and alternator (see Chapter 5).

5   On air conditioned models, unbolt the compressor and set it aside without disconnecting the refrigerant hoses (see Chapter 3). Remove the rear compressor bracket from the manifold.

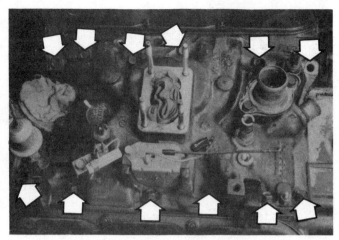

6.9a   Intake manifold bolt locations (typical)

6.9b   Pry up on the corners of the manifold if necessary

2B

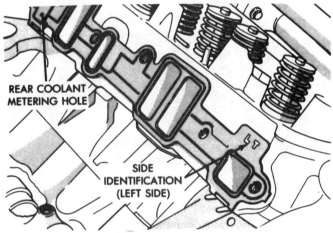

6.13a   The gaskets must be installed on the proper side as marked (1987 through 1991 models)

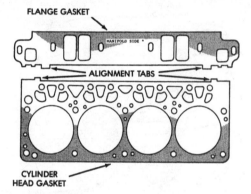

6.13b   The manifold must be installed with the vertical alignment port tab correctly aligned and with the MANIFOLD SIDE mark visible (1992 and later models)

6   Label and then disconnect any fuel lines, wires and vacuum hoses that run from the vehicle to the intake manifold and carburetor or throttle body.

7   Detach the coolant hoses from the intake manifold.

8   Disconnect the accelerator linkage and, if so equipped, the speed control and transmission kickdown cables.

9   Loosen the intake manifold mounting bolts **(see illustration)** in 1/4-turn increments until they can be removed by hand. The manifold will probably be stuck to the cylinder heads and force may be required to break the gasket seal. A pry bar can be positioned to pry up the front of the manifold **(see illustration)**. **Caution:** *Do not pry between the block and manifold or the heads and manifold or damage to the gasket sealing surfaces may result and vacuum leaks could develop.*

Installation

Refer to illustrations 6.13a, 6.13b, 6.14, 6.16a, 6.16b, 6.16c and 6.16d
Note: *The mating surfaces of the cylinder heads, block and manifold must be perfectly clean when the manifold is installed. Gasket removal solvents in aerosol cans are available at most auto parts stores and may be helpful when removing old gasket material that is stuck to the heads and manifold. Be sure to follow the directions printed on the container.*

10   Remove carbon deposits from the exhaust crossover passages. Use a gasket scraper to remove all traces of sealant and old gasket material, then wipe the mating surfaces with a cloth saturated with lacquer thinner or acetone. If there is old sealant or oil on the mating surfaces when the manifold is installed, oil or vacuum leaks may develop. Cover the lifter valley with shop rags to keep debris out of the engine. Use a vacuum cleaner to remove any gasket material that falls into the intake ports in the heads.

11   Use a tap of the correct size to chase the threads in the bolt holes, then use compressed air (if available) to remove the debris from the holes. **Warning:** *Wear safety glasses or a face shield to protect your eyes when using compressed air.*

12   Apply a thin coat of RTV sealant to the cylinder head side of the new intake manifold gaskets.

13   On 1987 through 1991 models, position the side gaskets on the cylinder heads. The gaskets are marked LT for left or RT for right **(see illustration)**. Make sure they are installed on the correct side and all intake port openings, coolant passage holes and bolt holes are aligned correctly. On 1992 and later models, be sure that the vertical port alignment tab is resting on the deck face of the block. Also the horizontal alignment tabs must be in position with the mating cylinder head gasket tabs **(see illustration)**. Also the MANIFOLD SIDE must be visible on the center of each flange.

14   Install the front and rear end seals on the block. Apply a thin, uniform coating of quick dry cement to the intake manifold end seals and the cylinder block contact surfaces. Engage the dowels and the end tangs **(see illustration)**. Refer to the instructions with the gasket set for further information.

15   Carefully set the manifold in place. Do not disturb the gaskets and do not move the manifold fore-and-aft after it contacts the front and rear seals.

16   Install the bolts and hand tighten them. Then tighten the bolts following the tightening sequence **(see illustrations)** to the torque listed in this Chapter's Specifications as Step One.

17   Tighten the bolts following the tightening sequence to the torque listed in this Chapter's Specifications as Step Two.

18   The remaining installation steps are the reverse of removal. Change the engine oil and filter and add coolant. Start the engine and check carefully for oil, vacuum and coolant leaks at the intake manifold joints.

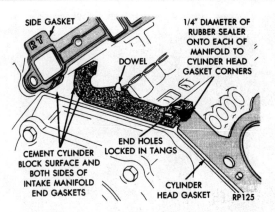

6.14   Fit the end seals over the dowels and engage the end tangs with the holes

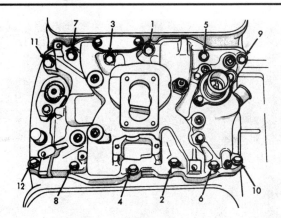

6.16a   Intake manifold bolt tightening sequence (1987 through 1991 models)

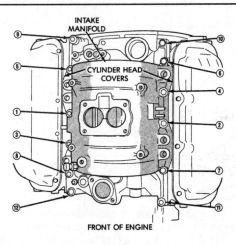

6.16b   Intake manifold bolt tightening sequence (1992 and later V6 engine)

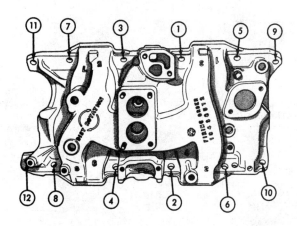

6.16c   Intake manifold bolt tightening sequence (1991 V8 engine)

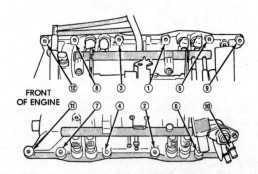

6.16d   Intake manifold bolt tightening sequence (1992 and later V8 engine)

7   Exhaust manifolds – removal and installation

Removal

Warning: *Allow the engine to cool completely before performing this procedure.*

1   Disconnect the negative cable from the battery.

2   Disconnect the spark plug wires and the spark plugs (refer to Chapter 1 if necessary). If there is any danger of mixing the plug wires up, we recommend labeling them with pieces of numbered tape.

7.3   Remove the nuts (arrows) and detach the air pre-heater stove (if equipped)

Right (passenger's) side

Refer to illustrations 7.3 and 7.4

3   Remove the air cleaner assembly and duct for access to the manifold. Detach the air injection hose and then remove the air pre-heater stove, if equipped **(see illustration)**.

4   Unbolt the air injection tube, if equipped **(see illustration)**.

Left (driver's) side

5   If you are removing the left (driver's) side manifold, unplug the electrical connector to the oxygen sensor.

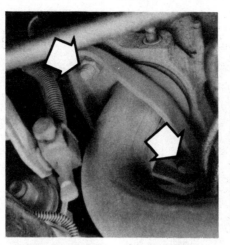

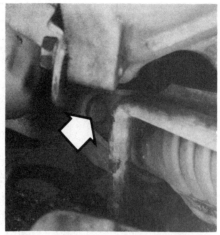

7.4   Unbolt the air injection tube (arrow) (if equipped)

7.7a   Remove the nuts (arrows) from the left (drivers') side exhaust pipe

7.7b   On the right side, one bolt is hidden by the catalytic converter (arrow)

Both sides

Refer to illustrations 7.7a, 7.7b, 7.8a and 7.8b

6   Set the parking brake and block the rear wheels. Raise the front of the vehicle and support it securely on jackstands.

7   Disconnect the exhaust pipe from the manifold outlets **(see illustrations)**. **Note:** *Often a short period of soaking with penetrating oil is necessary to remove frozen exhaust attaching nuts/bolts.*

8   Loosen the outer fasteners first, then the center ones to separate the manifold from the head **(see illustration)**. **Note:** *If the studs come out with the nuts, install new studs. Apply sealant to the coarse thread ends or coolant leaks may develop* **(see illustration)**.

Installation

9   Installation is basically the reverse of the removal procedure. Clean the manifold and head gasket surfaces and check the manifold heat control valve for ease of operation. If the valve is stuck, free it with penetrating oil.

10   Install two bolts and conical washers at the inner ends of the exhaust manifold outboard arms. Install two bolts without washers on the center arm of the manifold. Tighten them to the torque listed in this Chapter's Specifications. Work from the center to the ends and approach the final torque in three steps.

11   Apply anti-seize compound to the exhaust manifold-to-exhaust pipe bolts and tighten them securely.

---

8   Cylinder heads – removal and installation

Removal

Refer to illustrations 8.5, 8.6 and 8.7

1   Refer to Section 3 and remove the valve covers.

2   Refer to Section 6 and remove the intake manifold. Note that the cooling system must be drained (see Chapter 1) to prevent coolant from getting into internal areas of the engine when the manifold and heads are removed.

3   Refer to Section 7 and detach both exhaust manifolds.

4   Refer to Section 4 and remove the rocker arms and pushrods.

5   Using a new head gasket, outline the cylinders and bolt pattern on a piece of cardboard **(see illustration)**. Be sure to indicate the front of the engine for reference. Punch holes at the bolt locations.

6   Loosen the head bolts in 1/4-turn increments until they can be removed by hand. On V6 engines, work from bolt-to-bolt in the sequence shown **(see illustration)**. On V8 engines, reverse the sequence shown in illustration 8.16c. On all engines, store the bolts in the cardboard holder as they are removed. This will ensure that the bolts are reinstalled in their original holes.

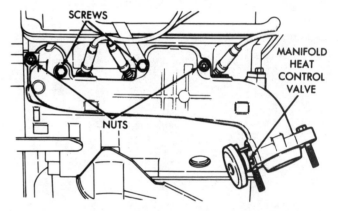

7.8a   Typical V6 engine exhaust manifold fastener locations (left side shown, right side similar) – note that V8 models have two additional fasteners

7.8b   Use sealant on the studs (arrow) where they screw into the heads (if new studs are being installed)

7   Lift the heads off the engine. If resistance is felt, do not pry between the head and block as damage to the mating surfaces will result. To dislodge the head, place a block of wood against the end of it and strike the wood block with a hammer, or lift on a casting protrusion **(see illustration)**. Store the heads on blocks of wood to prevent damage to the gasket sealing surfaces.

8   Cylinder head disassembly and inspection procedures are covered in detail in Chapter 2, Part C.

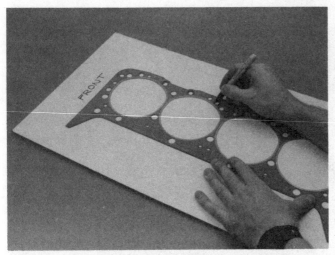

8.5   To avoid mixing up the head bolts, use a new gasket to transfer the bolt hole pattern to a piece of cardboard, then punch holes to accept the bolts (typical gasket shown)

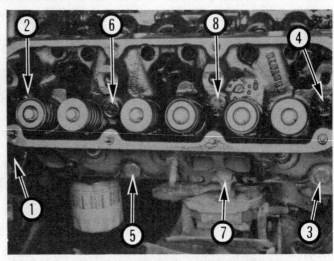

8.6   Cylinder head bolt *loosening* sequence (V6 engine shown, V8 engine similar)

8.7   Pry on a casting protrusion to break the head loose

8.10   Remove all traces of old gasket material (V6 engine shown, V8 engine similar)

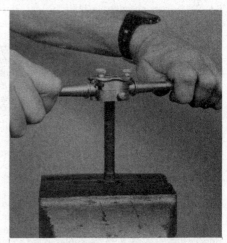

8.12   A die should be used to remove sealant and corrosion from the bolt threads prior to installation

8.13   Install the new gasket over the dowels (arrows) (V6 engine shown, V8 engine similar)

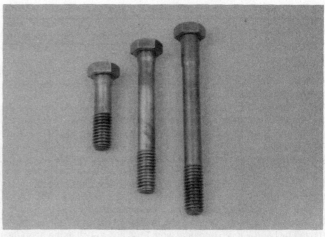

8.16a   The two long bolts go in positions 1 and 3, the middle length bolts go in positions 5 and 7 and the short bolts go in positions 2, 4, 6 and 8 in the tightening sequence (1987–1991 V6 engine)

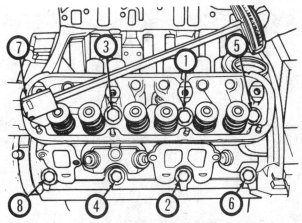

8.16b Cylinder head bolt tightening sequence (V6 engine)

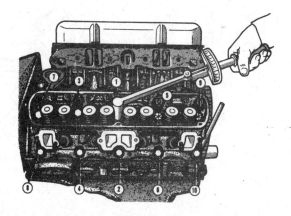

8.16c Cylinder head bolt tightening sequence (V8 models)

9.3 Remove the crankshaft pulley bolts and the vibration damper bolt (viewed from below)

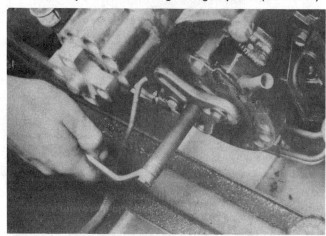

9.6 Use a bolt-type puller to remove the vibration damper

Installation

Refer to illustrations 8.10, 8.12, 8.13, 8.16a, 8.16b and 8.16c

9   The mating surfaces of the cylinder heads and block must be perfectly clean when the heads are installed.

10   Use a gasket scraper to remove all traces of carbon and old gasket material **(see illustration)**, then wipe the mating surfaces with a cloth saturated with lacquer thinner or acetone. If there is oil on the mating surfaces when the heads are installed, the gaskets may not seal correctly and leaks may develop. When working on the block, cover the lifter valley with shop rags to keep debris out of the engine. Use a vacuum cleaner to remove any debris that falls into the cylinders.

11   Check the block and head mating surfaces for nicks, deep scratches and other damage. If damage is slight, it can be removed with emery cloth. If it is excessive, machining may be the only alternative.

12   Use a tap of the correct size to chase the threads in the head bolt holes in the block. Mount each bolt in a vise and run a die down the threads to remove corrosion and restore the threads **(see illustration)**. Dirt, corrosion, sealant and damaged threads will affect torque readings.

13   Position the new gaskets over the dowels in the block **(see illustration)**.

14   Carefully position the heads on the block without disturbing the gaskets.

15   Before installing the head bolts, coat the threads with a nonhardening sealant such as Permatex No. 2.

16   Install the bolts in their original locations and tighten them finger tight. Following the recommended sequence, tighten the bolts in several steps to the torque listed in this Chapter's Specifications **(see illustrations)**.

17   The remaining installation steps are the reverse of removal.

18   Add coolant and change the oil and filter (see Chapter 1). Start the engine, set the ignition timing and check the engine for proper operation and coolant or oil leaks.

---

9   Timing cover, chain and sprockets – removal, inspection and installation

Cover removal

Refer to illustrations 9.3 and 9.6

1   Detach any accessories such as the power steering pump, alternator and air conditioning compressor that block access to the timing chain cover. Leave the hoses/wires connected and tie the units aside. Refer to Chapters 3, 5 and 10 for additional information. Unbolt the accessory brackets from the front of the engine **(see illustration)**.

2   Refer to Chapter 3 and remove the water pump. **Note:** *Some engines have a bolt-on timing tab. Note the location and be sure to reinstall it in the same way.*

3   Remove the bolts **(see illustration)** and separate the crankshaft pulley from the vibration damper.

4   Refer to Chapter 2C and position the number one piston at TDC on the compression stroke. **Caution:** *Once this has been done, do not turn the crankshaft until the timing chain and sprockets have been reinstalled.*

5   Remove the vibration damper bolt **(see illustration 9.3)**. To keep the crankshaft from turning, remove the bellhousing cover and have an assistant jam a large screwdriver against the ring gear teeth.

6   Use a puller (nos. C-3688 and C-3732-A, or equivalent) to detach the vibration damper **(see illustration)**. **Caution**: *Do not use a puller with jaws that grip the outer edge of the damper. The puller must be the type that utilizes bolts to apply force to the damper hub only.*

7   On carbureted engines, remove the fuel pump and cap the lines (see Chapter 4).

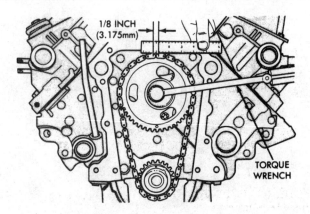

9.10   Position a ruler over the chain to measure slack

9.12a   With the timing marks aligned, remove the camshaft sprocket bolt

1   Timing marks   *2   Camshaft sprocket bolt*

9.12b   Pry the sprocket off the camshaft with a slight rocking motion

8   The front oil pan bolts will have to be removed for the timing cover to be detached. If the pan has been in place for an extended period of time it is likely the pan gasket will break when the cover is removed. In this case the pan should be removed and a new gasket installed.

9   Remove the mounting bolts and separate the timing chain cover from the block. The cover may be stuck; if so, use a putty knife to break the gasket seal. The cover is easily damaged, so do not attempt to pry it off.

Chain inspection
Refer to illustration 9.10

10   Place an accurate ruler over the timing chain **(see illustration)**. Using a torque wrench, apply torque to the camshaft sprocket bolt in a clockwise direction. If the rocker arms and pushrods are in place, use 30 lb/ft, if the rockers and pushrods are removed, use 15 lb/ft. **Note:** *Do not allow the crankshaft to move during this procedure.*

11   Apply an equal amount of torque in the opposite direction and note chain movement. Replace the timing chain and sprockets if the amount of movement exceeds 1/8 inch (3.175 mm).

Chain removal
Refer to illustrations 9.12a, 9.12b

12   Be sure the timing marks are aligned. Hold a pry bar through one of the camshaft sprocket holes to prevent the camshaft from turning. Remove the bolt from the camshaft sprocket **(see illustration)**, then detach the fuel pump eccentric (if equipped), and the camshaft sprocket and chain as an assembly **(see illustration)**.

13   The sprocket on the crankshaft can be removed with a two or three jaw puller, but be careful not to damage the threads in the end of the crankshaft. **Note:** *If the timing chain cover oil seal has been leaking, refer to Section 13 and install a new one.*

Installation
Refer to illustrations 9.17a, 9.17b and 9.17c

14   Use a gasket scraper to remove all traces of old gasket material and sealant from the cover and engine block. Stuff a shop rag into the opening at the front of the oil pan to keep debris out of the engine. Wipe the cover and block sealing surfaces with a cloth saturated with lacquer thinner or acetone.

15   Check the cover flange for distortion, particularly around the bolt holes.

16   If a new crankshaft sprocket is being installed, be sure to align the keyway in the crankshaft sprocket with the Woodruff key in the end of the crankshaft. **Note:** *Timing chains must be replaced as a set with the camshaft and crankshaft gears. Never put a new chain on old gears.* Align the sprocket with the Woodruff key and press the sprocket onto the crankshaft with the vibration damper bolt, a large socket and some washers or tap it gently into place until it is completely seated. **Caution:** *If resistance is encountered, do not hammer the sprocket onto the crankshaft. It may eventually move onto the shaft, but it may be cracked in the process and fail later, causing extensive engine damage.*

17   Loop the new chain over the camshaft sprocket, then turn the sprocket until the timing mark is at the bottom **(see illustration)**. Mesh the chain with the crankshaft sprocket and position the camshaft sprocket on the end of the cam **(see illustration)**. If necessary, turn the camshaft so the key fits into the sprocket keyway with the timing mark in the 6 o'clock position. When the chain is installed, the timing marks MUST align as shown **(see illustration)**. **Note:** *The number one piston must be at TDC on the compression stroke as the chain and sprockets are installed (see Step 4 above).*

18   Apply a thread locking compound to the camshaft sprocket bolt threads, then install the fuel pump eccentric (if equipped) and tighten the bolt to the torque listed in this Chapter's Specifications.

19   Lubricate the chain with clean engine oil.

20   Check for cracks and deformation of the oil pan gasket before installing the timing cover. If the gasket has deteriorated it must be replaced before reinstalling the timing cover.

21   Apply a thin layer of RTV sealant to both sides of the new cover gasket and the corners of the pan and block, then position it on the engine. The dowel pins and sealant will hold it in place.

22   Install the timing chain cover on the block, tightening the bolts finger tight.

23   Tighten the timing chain cover bolts to the torque listed in this Chapter's specifications.

24   Install the oil pan bolts, bringing the oil pan up against the timing chain cover.

25   Lubricate the oil seal contact surface of the vibration damper hub with moly-base grease or clean engine oil, then install the damper on the end of

9.17a   Slip the chain and camshaft sprocket in place over the crankshaft sprocket with the timing mark (arrow) at the bottom

9.17b   The keyway must align with the key (arrows)

9.17c   The timing marks MUST align as shown here

10.3   When checking the camshaft lobe lift, the dial indicator plunger must be positioned directly above and in-line with the pushrod

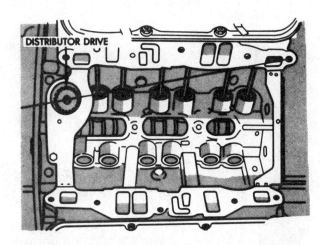

10.9   Pull up on the distributor driveshaft to remove it – upon installation, be sure the slot is aligned as shown

the crankshaft. The keyway in the damper must be aligned with the Woodruff key in the crankshaft nose. If the damper cannot be seated by hand, slip the large washer over the bolt, install the bolt and tighten it to pull the damper into place. Tighten the bolt to the torque listed in this Chapter's Specifications.

26   The remaining installation steps are the reverse of removal.

27   Add coolant and check the oil level. Run the engine and check for oil and coolant leaks.

---

10   Camshaft, bearings and lifters – removal, inspection and installation

Camshaft lobe lift check

Refer to illustration 10.3

1   In order to determine the extent of cam lobe wear, the lobe lift should be checked prior to camshaft removal. Refer to Section 3 and remove the valve covers.

2   Position the number one piston at TDC on the compression stroke (see Chapter 2C).

3   Beginning with the number one cylinder, mount a dial indicator on the engine and position the plunger against the top surface of the first rocker arm. The plunger should be directly above and in line with the pushrod **(see illustration)**.

4   Zero the dial indicator, then very slowly turn the crankshaft in the normal direction of rotation (clockwise) until the indicator needle stops and begins to move in the opposite direction. The point at which it stops indicates maximum cam lobe lift.

5   Record this figure for future reference, then reposition the piston at TDC on the compression stroke.

6   Move the dial indicator to the other number one cylinder rocker arm and repeat the check. Be sure to record the results for each valve.

7   Repeat the check for the remaining valves. Since each piston must be at TDC on the compression stroke for this procedure, work from cylinder-to-cylinder following the firing order sequence.

8   After the check is complete, compare the results to the specifications in this Chapter. If camshaft lobe lift is less than specified, cam lobe wear has occurred and a new camshaft should be installed.

Removal

Refer to illustrations 10.9, 10.11a, 10.11b, 10.12a, 10.12b, 10.13

9   Refer to the appropriate Sections and remove the intake manifold, the rocker arms, pushrods and the timing chain and camshaft sprocket. Once the manifold is out of the way, remove the distributor driveshaft **(see illustration)**. The radiator should be removed as well (see Chapter 3). **Note:** *If the vehicle is equipped with air conditioning it may be necessary to remove the air conditioning condenser to remove the camshaft. If the condenser must be removed the system must first be depressurized by a dealer service department or air conditioning shop. Do not disconnect any air conditioning lines until the system has been properly depressurized.*

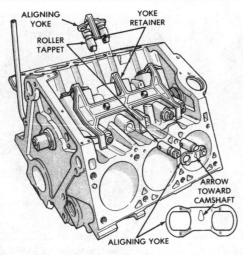

10.11a Unbolt the yoke retainer and pull the lifters out in pairs, then slip off the aligning yoke – be sure to keep the lifters in order

10.11b The lifters in an engine that has accumulated many miles may have to be removed with a special tool (arrow) – store them in an organized manner to make sure they're reinstalled in their original locations

10.12a Remove the camshaft thrust plate and oil tab bolts

1 Oil tab bolt   *2* Thrust plate bolt

10.12b Thread a long bolt into the camshaft sprocket bolt hole to use as a handle

10.13 Carefully guide the camshaft out of the block

10   There are several ways to extract the lifters from the bores. A special tool designed to grip and remove lifters is manufactured by many tool companies and is widely available, but it may not be required in every case. On newer engines without a lot of varnish buildup, the lifters can often be removed with a small magnet or even with your fingers. A machinist's scribe with a bent end can be used to pull the lifters out by positioning the point under the retainer ring inside the top of each lifter. **Caution:** *Do not use pliers to remove the lifters unless you intend to replace them with new ones (along with the camshaft). The pliers will damage the precision machined and hardened lifters, rendering them useless.*

11   Before removing the lifters, arrange to store them in a clearly labelled box to ensure that they are reinstalled in their original locations. **Note:** *On engines equipped with roller lifters, the yoke retainer must be removed before the lifters are withdrawn* **(see illustration)**. Remove the lifters and store them where they will not get dirty **(see illustration)**. Do not attempt to withdraw the camshaft with the lifters in place.

12   Remove the camshaft thrust plate and oil tab **(see illustration)**. Thread a long bolt into the camshaft sprocket bolt hole to use as a handle when removing the camshaft from the block **(see illustration)**.

13   Carefully pull the camshaft out. Support the cam near the block so the lobes do not nick or gouge the bearings as it is withdrawn **(see illustration)**.

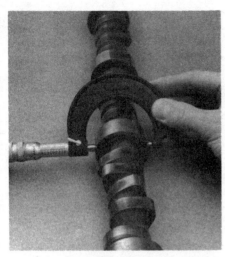

10.15 Check the diameter of each camshaft bearing journal to pinpoint excessive wear and out-of-round conditions

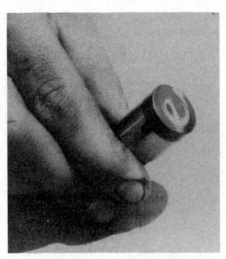

10.18a If the bottom of any lifter is worn concave, scratched or galled, replace the entire set with new lifters

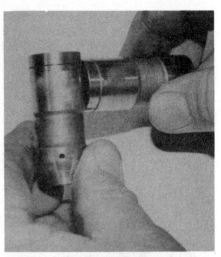

10.18b The foot of each lifter should be slightly convex – the side of another lifter can be used as a straightedge to check it; if it appears flat, it is worn and must not be reused

2B

10.18c If the lifters are pitted or rough, they shouldn't be reused

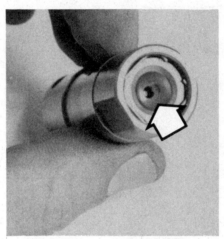

10.18d Check the pushrod seat (arrow) in the top of each lifter for wear

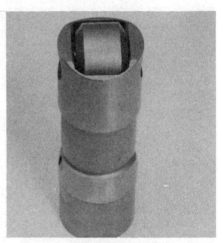

10.20 The roller on roller lifters must turn freely – check for wear and excessive play as well

Inspection

Refer to illustrations 10.15, 10.18a, 10.18b, 10.18c, 10.18d and 10.20

Camshaft and bearings

14 After the camshaft has been removed from the engine, cleaned with solvent and dried, inspect the bearing journals for uneven wear, pitting and evidence of seizure. If the journals are damaged, the bearing inserts in the block are probably damaged as well. Both the camshaft and bearings will have to be replaced. Replacement of the camshaft bearings requires special tools and techniques which place it beyond the scope of the home mechanic. The block will have to be removed from the vehicle and taken to an automotive machine shop for this procedure.

15 Measure the bearing journals with a micrometer to determine if they are excessively worn or out-of-round **(see illustration)**.

16 Check the camshaft lobes for heat discoloration, score marks, chipped areas, pitting and uneven wear. If the lobes are in good condition and if the lobe lift measurements are as specified in this Chapter, the camshaft can be reused.

Conventional lifters

Note: *Some engines are fitted with 0.008 inch oversize lifters at the facto-*

ry. These may be identified by a 3/8 inch diamond shaped stamp on the top pad at the front of the engine and a flat ground on the outside surface of each oversize lifter bore.

17 Clean the lifters with solvent and dry them thoroughly without mixing them up.

18 Check each lifter wall, pushrod seat and foot for scuffing, score marks and uneven wear. Each lifter foot (the surface that rides on the cam lobe) must be slightly convex, although this can be difficult to determine by eye. If the base of the lifter is concave **(see illustrations)**, the lifters and camshaft must be replaced. If the lifter walls are damaged or worn (which is not very likely), inspect the lifter bores in the engine block as well. If the pushrod seats are worn, check the pushrod ends.

19 If new lifters are being installed, a new camshaft must also be installed. If a new camshaft is installed, then use new lifters as well. Never install used lifters unless the original camshaft is used and the lifters can be installed in their original locations.

Roller lifters

20 Check the rollers carefully for wear and damage and make sure they turn freely without excessive play **(see illustration)**. The inspection procedure for conventional lifters also applies to roller lifters.

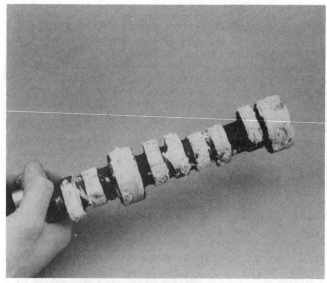

10.22   Be sure to apply moly-base grease or engine assembly lube to the cam lobes and bearing journals before installing the camshaft

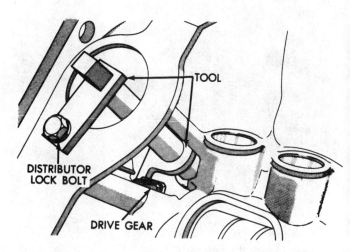

10.23   Camshaft holding tool C-3509 (installed position)

28   Lubricate the lifters with clean engine oil and install them in the block. If the original lifters are being reinstalled, be sure to return them to their original locations. If a new camshaft was installed, be sure to install new lifters as well.
29   The remaining installation steps are the reverse of removal.
30   Change the oil, add Mopar Crankcase Conditioner part no. 3419130, or equivalent, and install a new oil filter (see Chapter 1).
31   Start the engine, check for oil pressure and leaks and set the ignition timing.

11   Oil pan – removal and installation

Refer to illustrations 11.13 and 11.15

Removal
1   Disconnect the negative cable from the battery.
2   Raise the vehicle and support it securely on jackstands.
3   Drain the engine oil and replace the oil filter (see Chapter 1).
4   Detach the exhaust crossover pipe (see Chapter 4).
5   Remove the engine oil dipstick.
6   Remove the lower bellhousing cover and the starter, if necessary for clearance (see Chapter 5).

2WD models only
7   Remove the distributor cap to prevent breakage against the firewall as the engine is lifted.
8   Unbolt the fan shroud and move it back over the fan (see Chapter 3).
9   Using a floor jack under the oil pan, support the engine. Use a block of wood between the jack pad and the oil pan. **Caution:** *On most engines the oil pump pickup is very close to the bottom of the oil pan, and it can be damaged easily if concentrated pressure from a jack is applied to the pan.* Remove the engine mount through bolts.
10   Raise the engine approximately four inches.
11   Temporarily reinstall the engine mount through bolts and lower the engine onto them.

4WD models only
12   Remove the front drive axle (see Chapter 8).

All models
13   Remove the oil pan bolts **(see illustration)** and lower the pan from the vehicle.

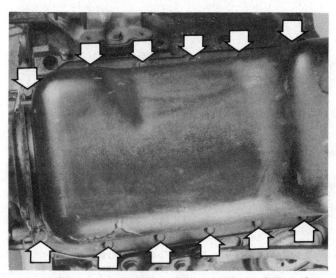

11.13 Remove   the bolts (arrows) around the perimeter of the oil pan (typical)

21   Used roller lifters can be reinstalled with a new camshaft and the original camshaft can be used if new lifters are installed.

Installation
Refer to illustrations 10.22 and 10.23
22   Lubricate the camshaft bearing journals and cam lobes with moly-base grease or engine assembly lube **(see illustration)**.
23   Position a camshaft holding tool (C-3509, or equivalent) through the distributor hole **(see illustration)**. This tool will prevent the camshaft from being pushed in too far and prevents the welch plug in the back of the block from being knocked out. The tool should remain in place until the timing chain has been installed. **Note:** *If the tool is unavailable, work carefully to avoid knocking the plug out.*
24   Slide the camshaft into the engine. Support the cam near the block and be careful not to scrape or nick the bearings.
25   Turn the camshaft until the dowel pin is in the 4 o'clock position.
26   Refer to Section 9 and install the timing chain and sprockets.
27   Mount a dial indicator to the front of the engine and check camshaft endplay. Compare the result to the Specifications in this Chapter and replace the thrust plate if endplay is incorrect.

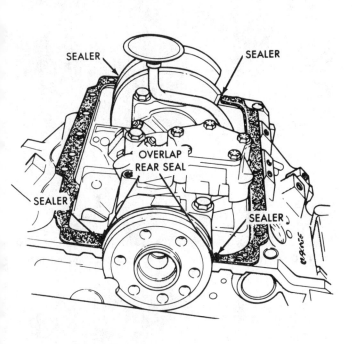

11.15   Add sealer to the four corners as shown

12.2   Remove the bolts (arrows) and lower the oil pump

Installation

14   Wash out the oil pan with solvent. Thoroughly clean the mounting surfaces of the oil pan and engine block of old gasket material and sealer.

15   Place a bead of RTV sealant along the timing cover-to-block parting line and to the oil pan gaskets. Install the gaskets and put additional sealant in the four corners **(see illustration)**.

16   Lift the pan into position, being careful not to disturb the gasket, and install the bolts finger tight.

17   Starting at the ends and alternating from side-to-side towards the center, tighten the bolts to the torque listed in this Chapter's Specifications.

18   The remainder of the installation procedure is the reverse of removal. Add oil, start the engine and check for leaks before placing the vehicle back in service.

12   Oil pump – removal and installation

Refer to illustrations 12.2 and 12.5

Removal

1   Remove the oil pan as described in Section 11.

2   While supporting the oil pump, remove the pump-to-rear main bearing cap bolts **(see illustration)**.

3   Lower the pump from the vehicle and clean the gasket surfaces.

Installation

4   Prime the pump by pouring clean motor oil into the pickup tube.

5   Position the pump on the engine with a new gasket and make sure the hex-shaped driveshaft is aligned with the oil pump **(see illustration)**.

6   Install the mounting bolts and tighten them to the torque listed in this Chapter's Specifications.

12.5   The oil pump driveshaft (arrow) must align with the pump

7   Install the oil pan and add oil.

8   Run the engine and check for oil pressure and leaks.

13   Crankshaft oil seals – replacement

Front seal

Refer to illustrations 13.2 and 13.4

1   Remove the vibration damper as described in Section 9.

2   Carefully pry the seal out of the cover with a seal puller or a large screwdriver **(see illustration)**. Be careful not to distort the cover or scratch the wall of the seal bore.

3   Clean the bore to remove any old seal material and corrosion. Position the new seal in the bore with the spring end of the seal facing IN. A small amount of oil applied to the outer edge of the new seal will make installation easier – don't overdo it!

13.2   Pry the old seal out with a seal puller or screwdriver

13.4   Drive the new seal into place with a socket and hammer

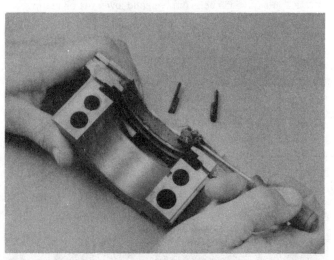

13.8   Lift the old seal section out of the bearing cap with a small screwdriver

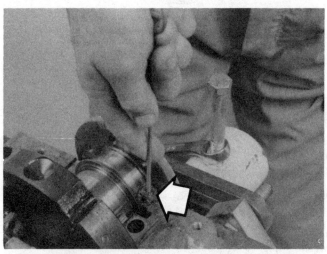

13.9   Screw a removal tool into one end of the old upper seal section and pull it out (engine removed for clarity)

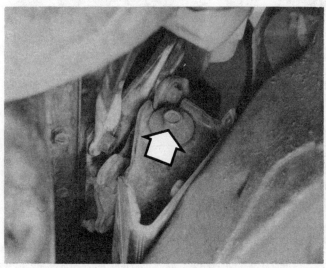

14.7a   The engine mount through bolt (arrow) . . .

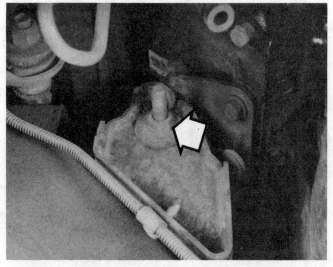

14.7b   . . . is secured by a nut on the other side (arrow)

4   Drive the seal into the bore with a large socket and hammer until it's completely seated **(see illustration)**. Select a socket that's the same outside diameter as the seal.
5   Lubricate the seal lips with engine oil and reinstall the vibration damper.

Rear seal

Refer to illustrations 13.8 and 13.9

6   The rear main seal can be replaced with the engine in the vehicle. Refer to the appropriate Sections and remove the oil pan and oil pump. **Note:** *This procedure is for the factory "rope" type seal. If you install an aftermarket neoprene seal, follow the instructions provided with the seal kit.*
7   Remove the bolts and detach the rear main bearing cap from the engine.
8   The seal section in the bearing cap can be pried out with a screwdriver **(see illustration)**.
9   To remove the upper seal section from the block, screw a seal removal tool (KD-492, or equivalent) into the old seal and pull it out **(see illustration)**. Be very careful not to nick or scratch the crankshaft journal or seal surface as this is done.
10   Inspect the bearing cap and engine block mating surfaces, as well as the cap seal grooves, for nicks, burrs and scratches. Remove any defects with a fine file or deburring tool.
11   Lubricate the seal halves with clean engine oil.
12   Install one seal section in the cap. Roll it into place with a hammer handle. Make sure it is completely seated and then, using a new single edge razor blade, cut the ends flush with the mating surface of the cap.
13   Pull the upper portion of the seal into position with the seal installation tool. Turning the crankshaft may help to draw the seal into place.
14   Carefully trim any excess seal material as described in Step 12.
15   Lubricate the bearing and seal with clean engine oil. Position the bearing cap on the block, install the bolts and tighten them to the torque listed in this Chapter's Specifications.

16   Install the oil pump and oil pan.
17   Add oil, run the engine and check for oil leaks.

14   Engine mounts – check and replacement

Refer to illustrations 14.7a, 14.7b, 14.8, 14.9a and 14.9b

1   Engine mounts seldom require attention, but broken or deteriorated mounts should be replaced immediately or the added strain placed on the driveline components may cause damage.

14.8   On 2WD models, the engine mount bolts to the engine block bracket (arrows) as shown here

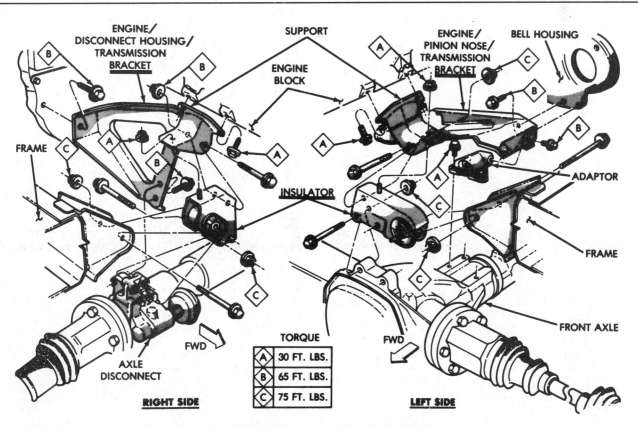

14.9a   4WD engine mount details – exploded view

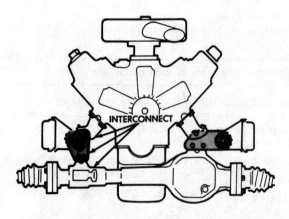

14.9b   On 4WD models, the engine mounts interconnect with the front axle

Check

2   During the check, the engine must be raised slightly to remove the weight from the mounts. Refer to Chapter 1 and remove the distributor cap before raising the engine.

3   Raise the vehicle and support it securely on jackstands, then position the jack under the engine oil pan. Place a large block of wood between the jack head and the oil pan, then carefully raise the engine just enough to take the weight off the mounts.

4   Check the mounts to see if the rubber is cracked, hardened or separated from the metal plates. Sometimes the rubber will split right down the center. Rubber preservative may be applied to the mounts to slow deterioration.

5   Check for relative movement between the mount plates and the engine or frame (use a large screwdriver or pry bar to attempt to move the mounts). If movement is noted, lower the engine and tighten the mount fasteners.

Replacement

6   Disconnect the negative cable from the battery, then raise the vehicle and support it securely on jackstands.

7   Remove the nut and withdraw the mount through bolt from the bracket **(see illustrations)**.

8   Raise the engine slightly, then remove the mount-to-bracket bolts **(see illustration)**.

9   Installation is the reverse of removal **(see illustrations)**. Use thread locking compound on the mount bolts and be sure to tighten them securely.

---

15   Flywheel/driveplate – removal and installation

Refer to Chapter 2, Part A, Section 15 for this procedure, but be sure to use the torque value listed in this Chapter's Specifications.

Chapter 2 Part C
General engine overhaul procedures

Contents

Specifications

Four-cylinder engines

General

Compression pressure	100 psi minimum
Maximum variation between cylinders	25%
Oil pressure	
At idle	4 psi
At 3000 rpm	25 to 80 psi

Engine block

Cylinder bore diameter (nominal)	3.44 in
Taper limit	0.005 in
Out-of-round limit	0.002 in

Pistons and rings

Piston diameter	3.443 to 3.445 in

Piston ring-to-groove clearance
  Standard
    Top ring . . . . 0.0015 to 0.0031 in
    Second ring . . . . 0.0015 to 0.0037 in
    Oil ring . . . . 0.008 in
  Service limit
    Top ring . . . . 0.004 in
    Second ring . . . . 0.004 in
Piston ring end gap
  Top ring
    Standard . . . . 0.010 to 0.020 in
    Service limit . . . . 0.039 in
  Second ring
    Standard . . . . 0.009 to 0.019 in
    Service limit . . . . 0.039 in
  Oil ring
    Standard . . . . 0.015 to 0.055 in
    Service limit . . . . 0.074 in

Crankshaft and flywheel

Main journal
  Diameter . . . . 2.362 to 2.363 in
  Taper limit . . . . 0.0004 in
  Out-of-round limit . . . . 0.0005 in
Main bearing oil clearance
  Standard . . . . 0.0003 to 0.0031 in
  Service limit . . . . 0.004 in
Connecting rod journal diameter . . . . 1.968 to 1.969 in
Connecting rod bearing oil clearance
  Standard . . . . 0.0008 to 0.0034 in
  Service limit . . . . 0.004 in
Connecting rod side clearance . . . . 0.005 to 0.013 in
Crankshaft endplay
  Standard . . . . 0.002 to 0.007 in
  Service limit . . . . 0.014 in

Cylinder head and valve train

Head warpage limit . . . . 0.004 in
Valve margin width (minimum)
  Intake . . . . 1/32 in
  Exhaust . . . . 3/64 in
Valve stem diameter
  Intake . . . . 0.3124 in
  Exhaust . . . . 0.3103 in
Valve stem-to-guide clearance
  Intake . . . . 0.0009 to 0.0026 in
  Exhaust . . . . 0.0030 to 0.0047 in
Valve spring free length . . . . 2.39 in
Valve spring installed height . . . . 1.62 to 1.68 in

Intermediate shaft

Journal diameter
  Large . . . . 1.6812 to 1.6822 in
  Small . . . . 0.775 to 0.776 in
Bearing inside diameter
  Large . . . . 1.6836 to 1.6844 in
  Small . . . . 0.777 to 0.778 in
Oil clearance (maximum) . . . . 0.003 in

Torque specifications   **Ft-lbs** (unless otherwise indicated)

Main bearing cap bolt 30*
Connecting rod bearing cap nut 40*
Crankshaft oil seal housing bolts . . . . 108 in-lbs
*Plus an additional 1/4-turn

V6 and V8 engines

General

Compression pressure . . . . 100 psi minimum
Maximum variation between cylinders 25%
Oil pressure (minimum)
  At idle . . . . 6 psi
  At 3000 rpm . . . . 30 to 80 psi

Engine block

Bore diameter	3.910 to 3.912 in
Taper limit	0.010 in
Out-of-round wear limit	0.005 in

Cylinder heads and valve train

Warpage limit	0.009 in per 12 in
Minimum valve margin	3/64 in
Valve stem-to-valve guide clearance	
Intake valves	0.001 to 0.003 in
Exhaust valves	0.002 to 0.004 in
Valve spring free length	
Intake	2.00 in
Exhaust	1.81 in
Valve spring installed height	
Intake	1-5/8 to 1-11/16 in
Exhaust	1-29/64 to 1-33/64 in

Crankshaft and connecting rods

Main journal diameter	2.4995 to 2.5005 in
Main journal taper limit	0.001 in
Main journal out-of-round limit	0.001 in
Main bearing oil clearance	
1 (standard)	0.0005 to 0.0015 in
1 (limit)	0.0015 in
2, 3 and 4 (standard)	0.0005 to 0.0020 in
2, 3 and 4 (limit)	0.0025 in
Connecting rod journal	
Diameter	2.124 to 2.125 in
Taper limit	0.001 in
Out-of-round limit	0.001 in
Connecting rod bearing oil clearance	
Standard	0.0005 to 0.0022 in
Limit	0.0022 in
Connecting rod endplay	0.006 to 0.014 in
Crankshaft endplay	
Standard	0.002 to 0.007 in
Limit	0.010 in

Pistons and rings

Piston-to-bore clearance (measured at	
top of skirt)	0.0005 to 0.0015 in
Piston ring side clearance	
Compression (both)	0.0015 to 0.0030 in
Oil control	0.002 to 0.005 in
Piston ring end gap	
Compression	0.010 to 0.020 in
Oil control	
Original rings	0.015 to 0.055 in
Service rings	0.010 to 0.062 in

Torque specifications

	Ft-lbs
Connecting rod cap nuts	45
Main bearing cap bolts	85

1 General information

Included in this portion of Chapter 2 are the general overhaul procedures for cylinder heads and internal engine components. The information ranges from advice concerning preparation for an overhaul and the purchase of replacement parts to detailed, step-by-step procedures covering removal and installation of internal engine components and the inspection of parts.

The following Sections have been written based on the assumption that the engine has been removed from the vehicle. For information concerning in-vehicle engine repair, as well as removal and installation of the external components necessary for the overhaul, see Parts A and B of this Chapter and Section 7 of this Part.

The Specifications included here in Part C are only those necessary for the inspection and overhaul procedures which follow. Refer to Parts A and B for additional Specifications.

2 Engine removal – methods and precautions

If you have decided that an engine must be removed for overhaul or major repair work, several preliminary steps should be taken.

Locating a suitable work area is extremely important. A shop is, of course, the most desirable place to work. Adequate work space, along with storage space for the vehicle, will be needed. If a shop or garage is not available, at the very least a flat, level, clean work surface made of concrete or asphalt is required.

3.4a   Remove the oil pressure sending unit (arrow) – on V6 and V8 models it's located adjacent to the distributor

3.4b   Connect a gauge to check the oil pressure

Cleaning the engine compartment and engine before beginning the removal procedure will help keep tools clean and organized.

An engine hoist or A-frame will be needed. Make sure that the equipment is rated in excess of the combined weight of the engine and its accessories. Safety is of primary importance, considering the potential hazards involved in lifting the engine out of the vehicle.

If the engine is being removed by a novice, a helper should be available. Advice and aid from someone more experienced would also be helpful. There are many instances when one person cannot simultaneously perform all of the operations required when lifting the engine out of the vehicle.

Plan the operation ahead of time. Arrange for or obtain all of the tools and equipment you will need prior to beginning the job. Some of the equipment necessary to perform engine removal and installation safely and with relative ease are (in addition to an engine hoist) a heavy duty floor jack, complete sets of wrenches and sockets as described in the front of this manual, wooden blocks and plenty of rags and cleaning solvent for mopping up spilled oil, coolant and gasoline. If the hoist is to be rented, make sure that you arrange for it in advance and perform beforehand all of the operations possible without it. This will save you money and time.

Plan for the vehicle to be out of use for a considerable amount of time. A machine shop will be required to perform some of the work which the do-it-yourselfer cannot accomplish due to a lack of special equipment. These shops often have a busy schedule, so it would be wise to consult them before removing the engine in order to accurately estimate the amount of time required to rebuild or repair components that may need work.

Always use extreme caution when removing and installing the engine. Serious injury can result from careless actions. Plan ahead, take your time and a job of this nature, although major, can be accomplished successfully.

3   Engine overhaul – general information

Refer to illustrations 3.4a, 3.4b and 3.4c

It is not always easy to determine when, or if, an engine should be completely overhauled, as a number of factors must be considered.

High mileage is not necessarily an indication that an overhaul is needed, while low mileage does not preclude the need for an overhaul. Frequency of servicing is probably the most important consideration. An engine that has had regular and frequent oil and filter changes, as well as other required maintenance, will most likely give many thousands of miles of reliable service. Conversely, a neglected engine may require an overhaul very early in its life.

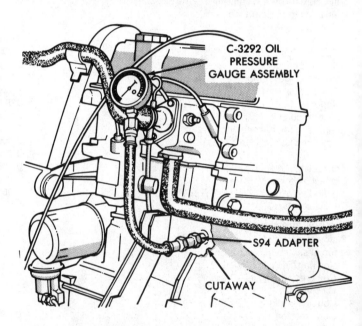

3.4c   On four-cylinder models, the oil pressure port is located on the driver's side near the transmission

Excessive oil consumption is an indication that piston rings and/or valve guides are in need of attention. Make sure that oil leaks are not responsible before deciding that the rings and/or guides are bad. Test the cylinder compression (see Section 5) or have a leakdown test performed by an experienced tune-up mechanic to determine the extent of the work required.

If the engine is making obvious knocking or rumbling noises, the connecting rod and/or main bearings are probably at fault. To accurately test oil pressure, temporarily connect a mechanical oil pressure gauge in place of the oil pressure sending unit **(see illustrations)**. Compare the reading to the pressure listed in this Chapter's Specifications. If the pressure is extremely low, the bearings and/or oil pump are probably worn out.

Loss of power, rough running, excessive valve train noise and high fuel consumption rates may also point to the need for an overhaul, especially if they are all present at the same time. If a complete tune-up does not remedy the situation, major mechanical work is the only solution.

An engine overhaul involves restoring the internal parts to the specifications of a new engine. During an overhaul, the piston rings are replaced and the cylinder walls are reconditioned (rebored and/or honed). If a re-

4.4 Mark the base of the distributor below the number one spark plug terminal (arrows) – V6 shown, V8 and four-cylinder similar

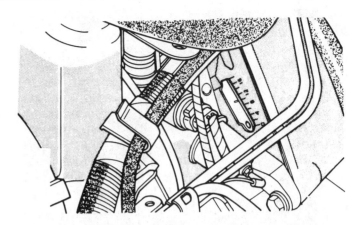

4.6 On four-cylinder engines, the timing indicator is located on the bellhousing – align the mark on the flywheel/driveplate with the "O " mark on the housing

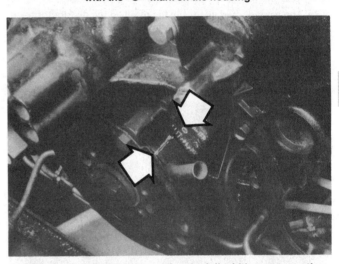

4.6b On V6 and V8 engines, align the full-width groove on the damper with the "O" or "TDC" mark on the timing cover (arrows)

2C

bore is done, new pistons are required. The main bearings, connecting rod bearings and camshaft bearings are generally replaced with new ones and, if necessary, the crankshaft may be reground to restore the journals. Generally, the valves are serviced as well, since they are usually in less-than-perfect condition at this point. While the engine is being overhauled, other components, such as the distributor, starter and alternator, can be rebuilt as well. The end result should be a like new engine that will give many trouble free miles. **Note:** *Critical cooling system components such as the hoses, the drivebelts, the thermostat and the water pump MUST be replaced with new parts when an engine is overhauled. The radiator should be checked carefully to ensure that it isn't clogged or leaking. If in doubt, replace it with a new one. Also, we do not recommend overhauling the oil pump – always install a new one when an engine is rebuilt.*

Before beginning the engine overhaul, read through the entire procedure to familiarize yourself with the scope and requirements of the job. Overhauling an engine is not difficult, but it is time consuming. Plan on the vehicle being tied up for a minimum of two weeks, especially if parts must be taken to an automotive machine shop for repair or reconditioning. Check on availability of parts and make sure that any necessary special tools and equipment are obtained in advance. Most work can be done with typical hand tools, although a number of precision measuring tools are required for inspecting parts to determine if they must be replaced. Often an automotive machine shop will handle the inspection of parts and offer advice concerning reconditioning and replacement. **Note:** *Always wait until the engine has been completely disassembled and all components, especially the engine block, have been inspected before deciding what service and repair operations must be performed by an automotive machine shop.* Since the block's condition will be the major factor to consider when determining whether to overhaul the original engine or buy a rebuilt one, never purchase parts or have machine work done on other components until the block has been thoroughly inspected. As a general rule, time is the primary cost of an overhaul, so it does not pay to install worn or substandard parts.

As a final note, to ensure maximum life and minimum trouble from a rebuilt engine, everything must be assembled with care in a spotlessly clean environment.

---

4 Top Dead Center (TDC) for number one piston – locating

Refer to illustrations 4.4, 4.6a, 4.6b, 4.7a and 4.7b

1   Top Dead Center (TDC) is the highest point in the cylinder that each piston reaches as it travels up-and-down when the crankshaft turns. Each piston reaches TDC on the compression stroke and again on the exhaust stroke, but TDC generally refers to piston position on the compression stroke. The timing marks are referenced to the number one piston at TDC on the compression stroke.

2   Positioning the pistons at TDC is an essential part of many procedures such as camshaft removal, timing belt or chain and sprocket replacement and distributor removal.

3   In order to bring any piston to TDC, the crankshaft must be turned using one of the methods outlined below. When looking at the front of the engine, normal crankshaft rotation is clockwise. **Warning:** *Before beginning this procedure, be sure to place the transmission in Neutral and disable the ignition system by disconnecting the coil wire from the distributor cap and grounding it.*

    a) The preferred method is to turn the crankshaft with a large socket and breaker bar attached to the large bolt that is threaded into the front of the crankshaft.

    b) A remote starter switch, which may save some time, can also be used. Attach the switch leads to the S (switch) and B (battery) terminals on the starter solenoid. Once the piston is close to TDC, use a socket and breaker bar as described in the previous paragraph.

    c) If an assistant is available to turn the ignition switch to the Start position in short bursts, you can get the piston close to TDC without a remote starter switch. Use a socket and breaker bar as described in Paragraph (a) to complete the procedure.

4   Scribe or paint a small mark on the distributor body directly below the number one spark plug wire terminal in the distributor cap **(see illustration)**.

5   Remove the distributor cap as described in Chapter 1.

6   Turn the crankshaft (see Step 3 above) until the line on the flywheel/driveplate (four-cylinder models) or vibration damper (V6 models) is aligned with the zero or "TDC" mark on the timing indicator **(see illustrations)**. On four-cylinder engines, the timing indicator is located at the rear

4.7a The rotor should align with the mark on the distributor base (arrows) below the number one terminal on the cap (1987 through 1991 V6 shown, four-cylinder similar)

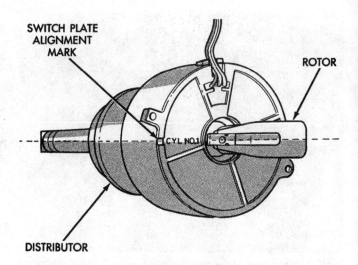

4.7b The rotor should align with the switch plate alignment mark on the switch plate assembly (1992 on V6 and V8 engines)

5.4 A compression gauge with a threaded fitting for the spark plug hole is preferred over the type that requires hand pressure to maintain the seal

of the engine on the driver's side of the bellhousing. On V6 engines, the timing indicator is located below the water pump on the driver's side.

7   The rotor should now be pointing directly at the mark on the distributor base **(see illustrations)**. If it is 180-degrees off, the piston is at TDC on the exhaust stroke.

8   If the rotor is 180-degrees off, turn the crankshaft one complete turn (360-degrees) clockwise. The rotor should now be pointing at the mark. When the rotor is pointing at the number one spark plug wire terminal in the distributor cap (which is indicated by the mark on the distributor body or intake manifold) and the timing marks are aligned, the number one piston is at TDC on the compression stroke.

9   After the number one piston has been positioned at TDC on the compression stroke, TDC for any of the remaining cylinders can be located by turning the crankshaft 180-degrees on four-cylinder engines or 120-degrees on V6's or 90-degrees on V8's and following the firing order (refer to the Specifications in Chapter 2A or 2B).

5   Compression check

Refer to illustration 5.4

1   A compression check will tell you what mechanical condition the upper end (pistons, rings, valves, head gaskets) of your engine is in. Specifically, it can tell you if the compression is down due to leakage caused by worn piston rings, defective valves and seats or a blown head gasket. **Note:** *The engine must be at normal operating temperature for this check and the battery must be fully charged.*

2   Begin by cleaning the area around the spark plugs before you remove them (compressed air works best for this). This will prevent dirt from getting into the cylinders as the compression check is being done. Remove all of the spark plugs from the engine.

3   Block the throttle wide open and disconnect the primary wires from the coil.

4   With the compression gauge in the number one spark plug hole, crank the engine over at least four compression strokes and watch the gauge **(see illustration)**. The compression should build up quickly in a healthy engine. Low compression on the first stroke, followed by gradually increasing pressure on successive strokes, indicates worn piston rings. A low compression reading on the first stroke, which does not build up during successive strokes, indicates leaking valves or a blown head gasket (a cracked head could also be the cause). Record the highest gauge reading obtained.

5   Repeat the procedure for the remaining cylinders and compare the results to the Specifications.

6   Add some engine oil (about three squirts from a plunger-type oil can) to each cylinder, through the spark plug hole, and repeat the test.

7   If the compression increases after the oil is added, the piston rings are definitely worn. If the compression does not increase significantly, the leakage is occurring at the valves or head gasket. Leakage past the valves may be caused by burned valve seats and/or faces or warped, cracked or bent valves.

8   If two adjacent cylinders have equally low compression, there is a strong possibility that the head gasket between them is blown. The appearance of coolant in the combustion chambers or the crankcase would verify this condition.

9   If the compression is unusually high, the combustion chambers are probably coated with carbon deposits. If that is the case, the cylinder heads should be removed and decarbonized.

10   If compression is way down or varies greatly between cylinders, it would be a good idea to have a leak-down test performed by an automotive repair shop. This test will pinpoint exactly where the leakage is occurring and how severe it is.

7.10   Unbolt the compressor and set it aside without disconnecting the hoses, if possible

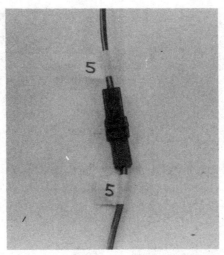

7.13   Label both ends of each wire before unplugging the connector

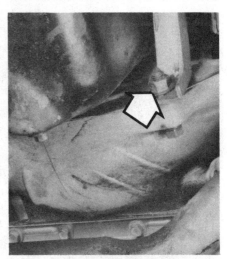

7.21a   Unbolt the engine-to-transmission brace (arrow) and move it aside

6   Engine rebuilding alternatives

The do-it-yourselfer is faced with a number of options when performing an engine overhaul. The decision to replace the engine block, piston/connecting rod assemblies and crankshaft depends on a number of factors, with the number one consideration being the condition of the block. Other considerations are cost, access to machine shop facilities, parts availability, time required to complete the project and the extent of prior mechanical experience on the part of the do-it-yourselfer.

Some of the rebuilding alternatives include:

Individual parts – If the inspection procedures reveal that the engine block and most engine components are in reusable condition, purchasing individual parts may be the most economical alternative. The block, crankshaft and piston/connecting rod assemblies should all be inspected carefully. Even if the block shows little wear, the cylinder bores should be surface honed.

Crankshaft kit – This rebuild package consists of a reground crankshaft and a matched set of pistons and connecting rods. The pistons will already be installed on the connecting rods. Piston rings and the necessary bearings will be included in the kit. These kits are commonly available for standard cylinder bores, as well as for engine blocks which have been bored to a regular oversize.

Short block – A short block consists of an engine block with a crankshaft and piston/connecting rod assemblies already installed. All new bearings are incorporated and all clearances will be correct. The existing cylinder head(s), camshaft, valve train components and external parts can be bolted to the short block with little or no machine shop work necessary.

Long block – A long block consists of a short block plus an oil pump, oil pan, cylinder head(s), valve cover(s), camshaft and valve train components, timing sprockets, belt or chain and timing cover. All components are installed with new bearings, seals and gaskets incorporated throughout. The installation of manifolds and external parts is all that is necessary.

Give careful thought to which alternative is best for you and discuss the situation with local automotive machine shops, auto parts dealers or parts store countermen before ordering or purchasing replacement parts.

7   Engine – removal and installation

Refer to illustrations 7.10, 7.13, 7.21a, 7.21b, 7.23, 7.28a, 7.28b, 7.28c and 7.28d

Warning: Gasoline is extremely flammable, so take extra precautions when disconnecting any part of the fuel system. Don't smoke or allow open flames or bare light bulbs in or near the work area and don't work in a garage where a natural gas appliance (such as a clothes dryer or water heater) is installed. If you spill gasoline on your skin, rinse it off immediately. Have a fire extinguisher rated for gasoline fires handy and know how to use it! Also, the air conditioning system is under high pressure – have a dealer service department or service station discharge the system before disconnecting any of the hoses or fittings.

Note: Read through the following steps carefully and familiarize yourself with the procedure before beginning work.

Removal

1   On air conditioned models, inspect the compressor mounting to determine if the compressor can be unbolted and moved aside without disconnecting the refrigerant lines. If this is not possible, have the system discharged by a dealer or service station (see Warning above).

2   Remove the hood (see Chapter 11).

3   On fuel injected models, relieve fuel pressure (see Chapter 4).

4   Remove the battery (see Chapter 5).

5   Remove the air cleaner assembly (see Chapter 4).

6   Drain the cooling system and remove the drivebelts (see Chapter 1).

7   Remove the radiator, shroud and fan (see Chapter 3).

8   Detach the radiator and heater hoses from the engine.

9   Remove the accelerator cable and kickdown linkage (if used) from the carburetor or throttle body.

10   Remove the air conditioning compressor (if equipped) without disconnecting the lines and set it out of the way **(see illustration)**.

11   Remove the power steering pump (if equipped) without disconnecting the hoses and tie it out of the way (see Chapter 10).

12   Remove the alternator (see Chapter 5).

13   Label and disconnect all wires from the engine **(see illustration)**. Masking tape and/or a touch up paint applicator work well for marking items. Take instant photos or sketch the locations of components and brackets.

14   Disconnect the fuel lines at the engine (see Chapter 4) and plug the lines to prevent fuel loss.

15   Label and remove all vacuum lines from the intake manifold.

16   Raise the vehicle and support it securely on jackstands.

17   Drain the engine oil (see Chapter 1).

18   Disconnect the exhaust pipe(s) from the exhaust manifold(s).

19   Remove the flywheel or torque converter inspection cover.

20   Disconnect the wires from the starter solenoid and remove the starter (see Chapter 5).

21   If equipped with an automatic transmission, remove the torque converter-to-driveplate bolts **(see illustrations)**.

2C

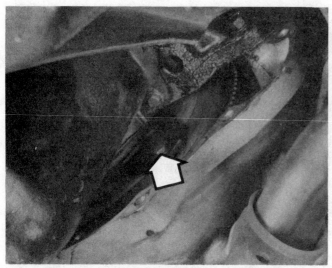

7.21b   Remove the torque converter bolts one at a time, turning the crankshaft to bring them into view

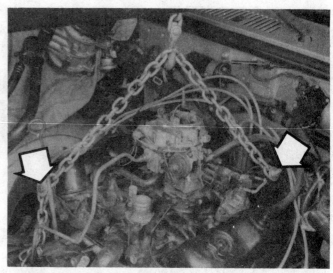

7.23   Attach the chain or hoist cable to the engine lifting brackets (arrows)

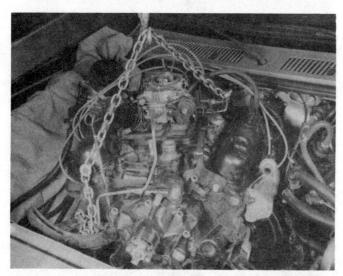

7.28a   Maneuver the engine as it is raised to clear obstructions

7.28b   Watch for interference between the exhaust manifold and firewall-mounted components

22   Support the transmission with a floor jack.
23   Attach an engine hoist to the engine and take the weight off the engine mounts **(see illustration)**.
24   Remove the bellhousing-to-engine bolts.

4WD models only
25   Remove the engine-to-transmission braces and engine mount (insulator) bracket-to-axle bolts (see Chapter 2B).

All models
26   Remove the engine mount through bolts (see Chapter 2A or 2B).
27   Lift the engine slightly and separate the engine from the transmission. Carefully work it forward to separate it from the transmission. If you're working on a vehicle with an automatic transmission, be sure the torque converter stays in the transmission (clamp a pair of locking pliers to the housing to keep the converter from sliding out). If you're working on a vehicle with a manual transmission, the input shaft must be completely disengaged from the clutch.
28   Check to make sure everything is disconnected, then lift the engine out of the vehicle **(see illustrations)**. Warning: *Do not place any part of your body under the engine when it is supported only by a hoist or other lifting device.*

7.28c   Move the engine forward as it is raised

7.28d   Raise the engine until it is completely clear of the vehicle, then move it forward

8.3a   V6 engine – front view (V8 similar)

8.3b   V6 engine – left (drivers' side) view (V8 similar)

8.3c   V6 engine – right (passengers' side) view (V8 similar)

29   Remove the flywheel/driveplate and mount the engine on an engine stand.

Installation

30   Check the engine mounts. If they're worn or damaged, replace them.
31   On manual transmission models, inspect the clutch components (see Chapter 8). On automatic models, inspect the converter seal and bushing.
32   Apply a dab of grease to the pilot bushing on manual transmission models or to the converter seal on automatics.
33   Attach the hoist to the engine and carefully lower the engine into the engine compartment.
34   Carefully guide the engine into place. Follow the procedure outlined in Chapter 7 for transmission attachment. **Caution:** *Do not use the bolts to force the engine and transmission into alignment. It may crack or damage major components.*
35   Align the engine to the engine mounts. Install the through bolts and tighten them securely.
36   Reinstall the remaining components in the reverse order of removal.
37   Add coolant, oil, power steering and transmission fluid as needed (see Chapter 1).
38   Run the engine and check for proper operation and leaks. Shut off the engine and recheck fluid levels.

8   Engine overhaul – disassembly sequence

Refer to illustrations 8.3a, 8.3b, 8.3c and 8.5

1   It is much easier to disassemble and work on the engine if it is mounted on a portable engine stand. These stands can often be rented quite cheaply from an equipment rental yard. Before the engine is mounted on a stand, the flywheel/driveplate should be removed from the engine (refer to Chapter 2A or 2B).
2   If a stand is not available, it is possible to disassemble the engine with it blocked up on a sturdy workbench or on the floor. Be extra careful not to tip or drop the engine when working without a stand.
3   If you are going to obtain a rebuilt engine, all external components **(see illustrations)** must come off first, to be transferred to the replacement engine, just as they will if you are doing a complete engine overhaul yourself. These include:

Alternator and brackets
Emissions control components
Distributor, spark plug wires and spark plugs
Thermostat and housing cover
Water pump

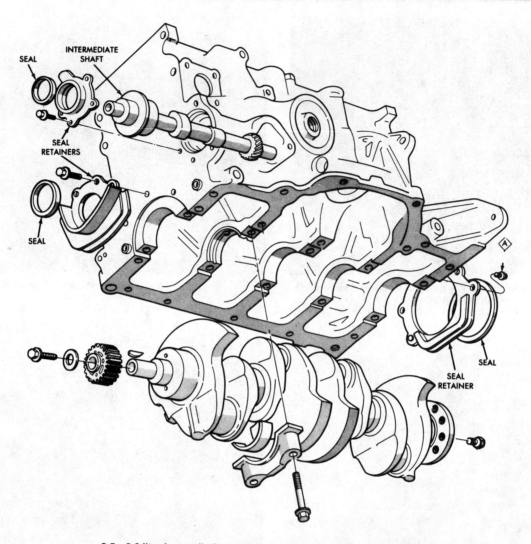

8.5   2.2 liter four-cylinder engine block components – exploded view

Carburetor or EFI components
Intake/exhaust manifolds
Oil filter
Engine mounts
Clutch and flywheel/driveplate

Note: *When removing the external components from the engine, pay close attention to details that may be helpful or important during installation. Note the installed position of gaskets, seals, spacers, pins, washers, bolts and other small items.*

4   If you are obtaining a short block, which consists of the engine block, crankshaft, pistons and connecting rods all assembled, then the cylinder heads, oil pan and oil pump will have to be removed as well. See Engine rebuilding alternatives for additional information regarding the different possibilities to be considered.

5   If you are planning a complete overhaul, the engine must be disassembled and the internal components **(see illustration)** removed in the following order:

Four-cylinder engines

Valve cover
Intake and exhaust manifolds
Timing belt cover
Timing belt
Camshaft and rockers

Cylinder head
Oil pan
Oil pump
Intermediate shaft
Front and rear oil seal housings
Piston/ connecting rod assemblies
Crankshaft and main bearings

V6 and V8 engines

Valve covers
Intake and exhaust manifolds
Rocker arms and pushrods
Valve lifters
Cylinder heads
Oil pan
Timing chain cover
Timing chain and sprockets
Oil pump
Camshaft
Piston/connecting rod assemblies
Crankshaft and main bearings

6   Critical cooling system components such as the hoses, the drivebelts, the thermostat and the water pump MUST be replaced with new parts when an engine is overhauled. Also, we do not recommend overhauling the oil pump – always install a new one when an engine is rebuilt.

9.2   Have several plastic bags ready (one for each valve) before disassembling the head – label each bag and put the entire contents of each valve assembly in one bag as shown

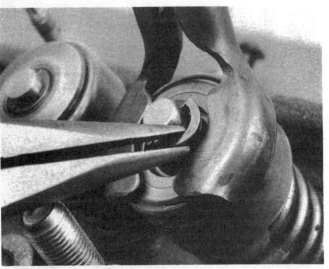

9.3a   Use a valve spring compressor to compress the springs, then remove the keepers from the valve stem with a magnet or small needle-nose pliers

2C

7   Before beginning the disassembly and overhaul procedures, make sure the following items are available:

Common hand tools
Small cardboard boxes or plastic bags for storing parts
Gasket scraper
Ridge reamer
Vibration damper puller (V6 and V8)
Micrometers
Telescoping gauges
Dial indicator set
Valve spring compressor
Cylinder surfacing hone
Piston ring groove cleaning tool
Electric drill motor
Tap and die set
Wire brushes
Oil gallery brushes
Cleaning solvent

9.3b   If you can't pull the valve through the guide, deburr the edge of the stem end and the area around the top of the keeper groove with a file or whetstone

9   Cylinder head – disassembly

Refer to illustrations 9.2, 9.3a and 9.3b
Note: *New and rebuilt cylinder heads are commonly available for most engines at dealerships and auto parts stores. Due to the fact that some specialized tools are necessary for the disassembly and inspection procedures, and replacement parts may not be readily available, it may be more practical and economical for the home mechanic to purchase replacement heads rather than taking the time to disassemble, inspect and recondition the originals.*

1   Cylinder head disassembly involves removal of the intake and exhaust valves and related components. If they are still in place, remove the rocker arms. Label the parts or store them separately so they can be reinstalled in their original locations.
2   Before the valves are removed, arrange to label and store them, along with their related components, so they can be kept separate and reinstalled in the same valve guides they are removed from **(see illustration)**.
3   Compress the springs on the first valve with a spring compressor and remove the keepers **(see illustration)**. Carefully release the valve spring compressor and remove the retainer and (if used) rotators, the shield, the springs and the spring seat or shims (if used). Remove the oil seal(s) from the valve stem and the umbrella-type seal from over the guide boss (if

used), then pull the valve from the head. If the valve binds in the guide (won't pull through), push it back into the head and deburr the area around the keeper groove with a fine file or whetstone **(see illustration)**.
4   Repeat the procedure for the remaining valves. Remember to keep all the parts for each valve together so they can be reinstalled in the same locations.
5   Once the valves and related components have been removed and stored in an organized manner, the head should be thoroughly cleaned and inspected. If a complete engine overhaul is being done, finish the engine disassembly procedures before beginning the cylinder head cleaning and inspection process.

10   Cylinder head – cleaning and inspection

Refer to illustrations 10.12, 10.14, 10.15, 10.16, 10.17, 10.18 and 10.19
1   Thorough cleaning of the cylinder heads and related valve train components, followed by a detailed inspection, will enable you to decide how much valve service work must be done during the engine overhaul.

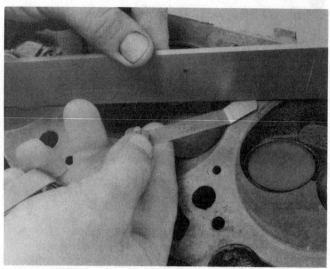

10.12   Check the cylinder head gasket surface for warpage by trying to slip a feeler gauge under the straightedge (see this Chapters' Specifications for the maximum warpage allowed and use a feeler gauge of that thickness)

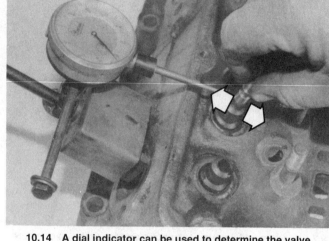

10.14   A dial indicator can be used to determine the valve stem-to-guide clearance – move the valve stem as indicated by the arrows

Cleaning

2   Scrape away all traces of old gasket material and sealing compound from the head gasket, intake manifold and exhaust manifold sealing surfaces. Be very careful not to gouge the cylinder head. Special gasket removal solvents, which soften gaskets and make removal much easier, are available at auto parts stores.

3   Remove any built up scale from the coolant passages.

4   Run a stiff wire brush through the various holes to remove any deposits that may have formed in them.

5   Run an appropriate size tap into each of the threaded holes to remove any corrosion and thread sealant that may be present. If compressed air is available, use it to clear the holes of debris produced by this operation.

6   Check the condition of the spark plug threads.

7   Clean the cylinder head with solvent and dry it thoroughly. Compressed air will speed the drying process and ensure that all holes and recessed areas are clean. **Note:** *Decarbonizing chemicals are available and may prove very useful when cleaning cylinder heads and valve train components. They are very caustic and should be used with caution. Be sure to follow the instructions on the container.*

8   On V6 models, clean the rocker arms, shafts and pushrods with solvent and dry them thoroughly (don't mix them up during the cleaning process). Compressed air will speed the drying process and can be used to clean out the oil passages.

9   Clean all the valve springs, shields, keepers and retainers (or rotators) with solvent and dry them thoroughly. Do the components from one valve at a time to avoid mixing up the parts.

10   Scrape off any heavy deposits that may have formed on the valves, then use a motorized wire brush to remove deposits from the valve heads and stems. Again, make sure the valves do not get mixed up.

Inspection

Cylinder head

11   Inspect the head very carefully for cracks, evidence of coolant leakage and other damage. If cracks are found, a new cylinder head should be obtained.

12   Using a straightedge and feeler gauge, check the head gasket mating surface for warpage **(see illustration)**. If the warpage exceeds the limit specified in this Chapter, it can be resurfaced at an automotive machine shop. **Note:** *On V6 engines, if the heads are resurfaced, the intake manifold flanges will also require machining.*

13   Examine the valve seats in each of the combustion chambers. If they are pitted, cracked or burned, the head will require valve service that is beyond the scope of the home mechanic.

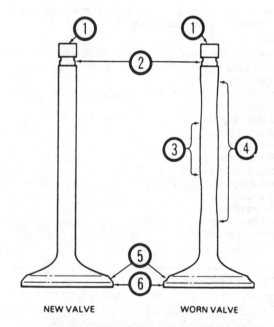

10.15   Check for valve wear at the points shown here

1	Valve tip	4	Stem (most worn area)
2	Keeper groove	5	Valve face
3	Stem (least worn area)	6	Margin

14   Check the valve stem-to-guide clearance by measuring the lateral movement of the valve stem with a dial indicator attached securely to the head **(see illustration)**. The valve must be in the guide and approximately 1/16-inch off the seat. The total valve stem movement indicated by the gauge needle must be divided by two to obtain the actual clearance. After this is done, if there is still some doubt regarding the condition of the valve guides they should be checked by an automotive machine shop (the cost should be minimal).

Valves

15   Carefully inspect each valve face for uneven wear **(see illustration)**, deformation, cracks, pits and burned spots. Check the valve stem for scuffing and galling and the neck for cracks. Rotate the valve and check for

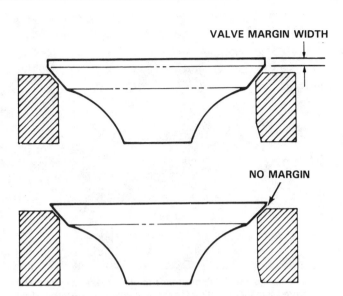

10.16   The margin width on each valve must be as specified
(if no margin exists, the valve cannot be reused)

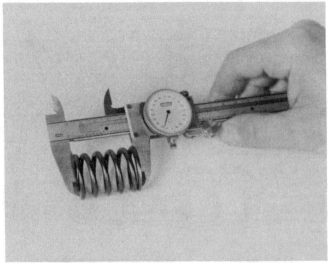

10.17   Measure the free length of each valve spring with a dial
or vernier caliper

any obvious indication that it is bent. Look for pits and excessive wear on the end of the stem. The presence of any of these conditions indicates the need for valve service by an automotive machine shop.

16   Measure the margin width on each valve. Any valve with a margin narrower than 3/64 inch will have to be replaced with a new one (see illustration).

Valve components

17   Check each valve spring for wear (on the ends) and pits. Measure the free length and compare it to the Specifications in this Chapter (see illustration). Any springs that are shorter than specified have sagged and should not be reused. The tension of all springs should be checked with a special fixture before deciding that they are suitable for use in a rebuilt engine (take the springs to an automotive machine shop for this check).

18   Stand each spring on a flat surface and check it for squareness (see illustration). If any of the springs are distorted or sagged, replace all of them with new parts.

19   Check the spring retainers (or rotators) and keepers for obvious wear (see illustration) and cracks. Any questionable parts should be replaced

with new ones, as extensive damage will occur if they fail during engine operation.

Rocker arm components (V6 engines)

20   Check the rocker arm faces (the areas that contact the pushrod ends and valve stems) for pits, wear, galling, score marks and rough spots. Check the rocker arm pivot contact areas and shafts. Look for cracks in each rocker arm.

21   Inspect the pushrod ends for scuffing and excessive wear. Roll each pushrod on a flat surface, such as plate glass, to determine if it is bent.

22   Check the rocker arm bolt holes in the cylinder heads for damaged threads.

23   Any damaged or excessively worn parts must be replaced with new ones.

24   If the inspection process indicates that the valve components are in generally poor condition and worn beyond the limits specified in this Chapter, which is usually the case in an engine that is being overhauled, reassemble the valves in the cylinder head and refer to Section 11 for valve servicing recommendations.

25   If the inspection turns up no excessively worn parts, and if the valve faces and seats are in good condition, the valve train components can be reinstalled in the cylinder head without major servicing. Refer to the appropriate Section for the cylinder head reassembly procedure.

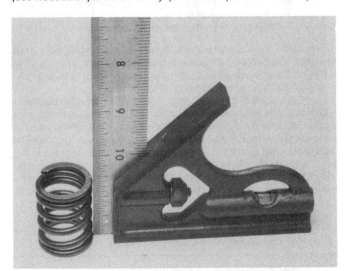

10.18   Check each valve spring for squareness

10.19   The exhaust valve rotators can be checked by turning the
inner and outer sections in opposite directions to feel for
smooth movement and excessive play

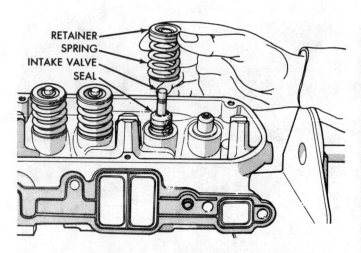

12.5   The intake valves have retainers, the exhaust valves use rotators

12.6   Apply a small dab of grease to each keeper as shown here before installation – it'll hold them in place on the valve stem as the spring is released

11   Valves – servicing

1   Because of the complex nature of the job and the special tools and equipment needed, servicing of the valves, the valve seats and the valve guides, commonly known as a valve job, is best left to a professional.
2   The home mechanic can remove and disassemble the heads, do the initial cleaning and inspection, then reassemble and deliver the heads to a dealer service department or an automotive machine shop for the actual valve servicing.
3   The dealer service department, or automotive machine shop, will remove the valves and springs, recondition or replace the valves and valve seats, recondition the valve guides, check and replace the valve springs, spring retainers or rotators and keepers (as necessary), replace the valve seals with new ones, reassemble the valve components and make sure the installed spring height is correct. The cylinder head gasket surface will also be resurfaced if it is warped.
4   After the valve job has been performed by a professional, the head will be in like new condition. When the head is returned, be sure to clean it again before installation on the engine to remove any metal particles and abrasive grit that may still be present from the valve service or head resurfacing operations. Use compressed air, if available, to blow out all the oil holes and passages.

12   Cylinder head – reassembly

Refer to illustrations 12.5, 12.6 and 12.8
1   Regardless of whether or not the heads were sent to an automotive machine shop for valve servicing, make sure they are clean before beginning reassembly.
2   If the heads were sent out for valve servicing, the valves and related components will already be in place. Begin the reassembly procedure with Step 8.
3   Beginning at one end of the head, lubricate and install the first valve. Apply moly-base grease or clean engine oil to the valve stem.
4   Different types of valve stem oil seals are used on the intake and exhaust. On some applications, an umbrella type seal which extends down over the valve guide boss is used over the valve stem (**see illustration 5.15 in Chapter 2, Part B**).
5   Drop the spring seat or shim(s) over the valve guide and set the valve spring and retainer (or rotator) in place (**see illustrations**).
6   Compress the springs with a valve spring compressor. Make sure the seal is not twisted – it must lie perfectly flat in the groove. Position the keepers in the upper groove, then slowly release the compressor and

12.8   Be sure to check the valve spring installed height (the distance from the top of the seat/shims to the top of the shield or the bottom of the retainer)

make sure the keepers seat properly. Apply a small dab of grease to each keeper to hold it in place if necessary (**see illustration**).
7   Repeat the procedure for the remaining valves. Be sure to return the components to their original locations – do not mix them up!
8   Check the installed valve spring height with a ruler graduated in 1/32-inch increments (**see illustration**) or a dial caliper. If the heads were sent out for service work, the installed height should be correct (but don't automatically assume that it is). The measurement is taken from the top of each spring seat or shim(s) to the bottom of the retainer/rotator. If the height is greater than listed in this Chapter's specifications, shims can be added under the springs to correct it. **Caution:** *Do not, under any circumstances, shim the springs to the point where the installed height is less than specified.*

13   Piston/connecting rod assembly – removal

Refer to illustrations 13.1, 13.3, 13.4 and 13.5
Note: *Prior to removing the piston/connecting rod assemblies, remove the cylinder head(s), the oil pan and the oil pump by referring to the appropriate Sections in Chapter 2, Part A or Part B.*

13.1   A ridge reamer is required to remove the ridge from the top of each cylinder – do this before removing the pistons!

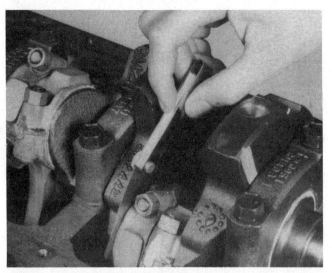

13.3   Check the connecting rod side clearance with a feeler gauge as shown

1   Completely remove the ridge at the top of each cylinder with a ridge reaming tool **(see illustration)**. Follow the manufacturer's instructions provided with the tool. Failure to remove the ridge before attempting to remove the piston/connecting rod assemblies will result in piston breakage.

2   After the cylinder ridges have been removed, turn the engine upside-down so the crankshaft is facing up.

3   Before the connecting rods are removed, check the endplay (side clearance) with feeler gauges. Slide them between the first connecting rod and the crankshaft throw until the play is removed **(see illustration)**. The endplay is equal to the thickness of the feeler gauge(s). If the endplay exceeds the service limit listed in this Chapter's specifications, new connecting rods will be required. If new rods (or a new crankshaft) are installed, the endplay may fall under the specified minimum. If it does, the rods will have to be machined to restore it – consult an automotive machine shop for advice if necessary. Repeat the procedure for the remaining connecting rods.

4   Check the connecting rods and caps for identification marks **(see illustration)**. If they are not plainly marked, use a small center punch to make the appropriate number of indentations on each rod and cap.

5   Loosen each of the connecting rod cap nuts 1/2-turn at a time until they can be removed by hand. Remove the number one connecting rod

cap and bearing insert. Do not drop the bearing insert out of the cap. Slip a short length of plastic or rubber hose over each connecting rod cap bolt to protect the crankshaft journal and cylinder wall when the piston is removed **(see illustration)**. Push the connecting rod/piston assembly out through the top of the engine. Use a wooden hammer handle to push on the upper bearing insert in the connecting rod. If resistance is felt, double-check to make sure that all of the ridge was removed from the cylinder.

6   Repeat the procedure for the remaining cylinders. After removal, reassemble the connecting rod caps and bearing inserts in their respective connecting rods and install the cap nuts finger tight. Leaving the old bearing inserts in place until reassembly will help prevent the connecting rod bearing surfaces from being accidentally nicked or gouged.

14   Crankshaft – removal

Refer to illustrations 14.2, 14.3, 14.4a, 14.4b and 14.4c
Note: *The crankshaft can be removed only after the engine has been removed from the vehicle. It is assumed that the flywheel or driveplate, vibration damper or crankshaft pulley, timing belt or chain, oil pan, oil pump and piston/connecting rod assemblies have already been removed.*

13.4   The connecting rods and caps should be marked to indicate which cylinders they're installed in – if they aren't, mark them with a center punch to avoid confusion during reassembly

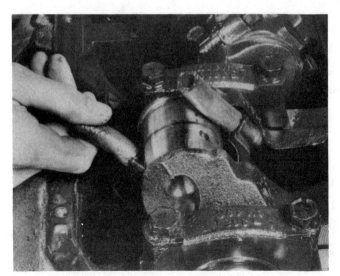

13.5   To prevent damage to the crankshaft journals and cylinder walls, slip sections of hose over the rod bolts before removing the pistons

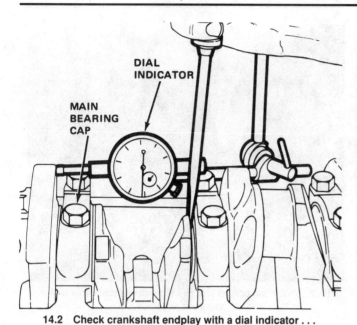

14.2   Check crankshaft endplay with a dial indicator . . .

14.3   . . . or slip feeler gauges between the crankshaft and main bearing thrust surfaces – the endplay is equal to the feeler gauge thickness

1   Before the crankshaft is removed, check the endplay. Mount a dial indicator with the stem in line with the crankshaft and touching one of the crank throws.

2   Push the crankshaft all the way to the rear and zero the dial indicator. Next, pry the crankshaft to the front as far as possible and check the reading on the dial indicator (see illustration). The distance that it moves is the endplay. If it is greater than the maximum listed in this Chapter's Specifications, check the crankshaft thrust surfaces for wear. If no wear is evident, new main bearings should correct the endplay.

3   If a dial indicator is not available, feeler gauges can be used. Gently pry or push the crankshaft all the way to the front of the engine. Slip feeler gauges between the crankshaft and the front face of the thrust main bearing to determine the clearance (see illustration).

4   Check the main bearing caps to see if they are marked to indicate their locations. They should be numbered consecutively from the front of the engine to the rear (see illustration). If they aren't, mark them with number stamping dies or a center punch (see illustration). Main bearing caps generally have a cast-in arrow (see illustration), which points to the front of the engine. Loosen each of the main bearing cap bolts 1/4-turn at a time

each, until they can be removed by hand.

5   Gently tap the caps with a soft-face hammer, then separate them from the engine block. If necessary, use the bolts as levers to remove the caps. Try not to drop the bearing inserts if they come out with the caps.

6   Carefully lift the crankshaft out of the engine. It is a good idea to have an assistant available, since the crankshaft is quite heavy. With the bearing inserts in place in the engine block and main bearing caps, return the caps to their respective locations on the engine block and tighten the bolts finger tight.

15   Engine block – cleaning

Refer to illustrations 15.1, 15.8 and 15.10

Note: The core plugs (also known as freeze or soft plugs) may be difficult or impossible to retrieve if they're driven into the block coolant passages.

1   Remove the core plugs from the engine block. To do this, drill a small hole in the center of each one and pull them out with an auto body type dent puller (see illustration).

14.4a   V6 and V8 engines use the same caps – this cap is number two on a V6 engine

14.4b   Use a center punch or number stamping dies to mark the main bearing caps to ensure installation in their original locations on the block (make the punch marks near one of the bolt heads)

14.4c The arrow on the main bearing cap indicates the front of the engine

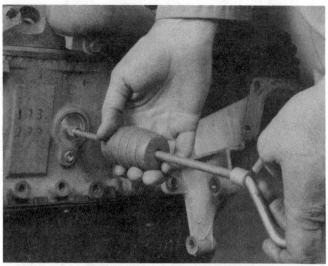

15.1 Remove the core plugs with a puller – if they're driven into the block, they may be impossible to retrieve

2 Using a gasket scraper, remove all traces of gasket material from the engine block. Be very careful not to nick or gouge the gasket sealing surfaces.

3 Remove the main bearing caps and separate the bearing inserts from the caps and the engine block. Tag the bearings, indicating which cylinder they were removed from and whether they were in the cap or the block, then set them aside.

4 Using a 1/4-inch drive breaker bar or ratchet, remove all of the threaded oil gallery plugs from the rear of the block. Discard the plugs and use new ones when the engine is reassembled.

5 If the engine is extremely dirty it should be taken to an automotive machine shop to be steam cleaned or hot tanked.

6 After the block is returned, clean all oil holes and oil galleries one more time. Brushes specifically designed for this purpose are available at most auto parts stores. Flush the passages with warm water until the water runs clear, dry the block thoroughly and wipe all machined surfaces with a light, rust preventive oil. If you have access to compressed air, use it to speed the drying process and to blow out all the oil holes and galleries.

7 If the block is not extremely dirty or sludged up, you can do an adequate cleaning job with warm soapy water and a stiff brush. Take plenty of time and do a thorough job. Regardless of the cleaning method used, be sure to clean all oil holes and galleries very thoroughly, dry the block completely and coat all machined surfaces with light oil.

8 The threaded holes in the block must be clean to ensure accurate torque readings during reassembly. Run the proper size tap into each of the holes to remove any rust, corrosion, thread sealant or sludge and to restore any damaged threads (see illustration). If possible, use compressed air to clear the holes of debris produced by this operation. Now is a good time to clean the threads on the head bolts and the main bearing cap bolts as well.

9 Reinstall the main bearing caps and tighten the bolts finger tight.

10 After coating the sealing surfaces of the new core plugs with RTV sealant, install them in the engine block. Make sure they are driven in straight and seated properly or leakage could result. Special tools are available for this purpose, but equally good results can be obtained using a large socket, with an outside diameter that will just slip into the plug, and a hammer (see illustration).

11 Apply non-hardening sealant (such as Permatex Number 2 or Teflon tape) to the new oil gallery plugs and thread them into the holes at the rear of the block. Make sure they are tightened securely.

12 If the engine is not going to be reassembled right away, cover it with a large plastic trash bag to keep it clean.

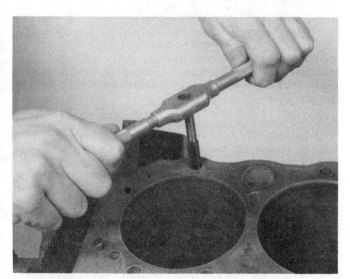

15.8 Clean and restore all threaded holes in the block – especially the main bearing cap and head bolt holes – with a tap (be sure to remove debris from the holes when you're done)

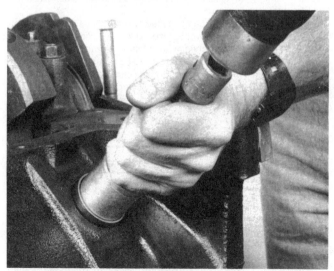

15.10 A large socket on an extension can be used to drive the new core plugs into the bores

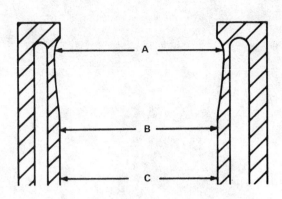

16.4a   Measure the diameter of each cylinder just under the wear ridge (A), at the center (B) and at the bottom (C)

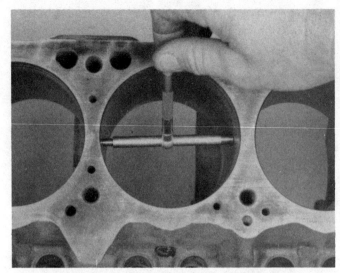

16.4b   The ability to "feel" when the telescoping gauge is at the correct point will be developed over time, so work slowly and repeat the check until you're satisfied the bore measurement is accurate

16   Engine block – inspection

Refer to illustrations 16.4a, 16.4b and 16.4c

1   Before the block is inspected, it should be cleaned as described in Section 15. Double-check to make sure that the ridge at the top of each cylinder has been completely removed.

2   Visually check the block for cracks, rust and corrosion. Look for stripped threads in the threaded holes. It is also a good idea to have the block checked for hidden cracks by an automotive machine shop that has the special equipment to do this type of work. If defects are found, have the block repaired, if possible, or replaced.

3   Check the cylinder bores for scuffing and scoring.

4   Measure the diameter of each cylinder at the top (just under the ridge area), center and bottom of the cylinder bore, parallel to the crankshaft axis **(see illustrations)**. **Note:** *These measurements should not be made with the bare block mounted on an engine stand – the cylinders may be distorted and the measurements may be inaccurate.*

5   Next, measure each cylinder's diameter at the same three locations across the crankshaft axis. Compare the results to the Specifications in this Chapter.

6   If the cylinder walls are badly scuffed or scored, or if they are out-of-round or tapered beyond the limits given in the Specifications, have the engine block rebored and honed at an automotive machine shop. If a rebore is done, oversize pistons and rings will be required.

7   If the cylinders are in reasonably good condition and not worn to the outside of the limits, and if the piston-to-cylinder clearances can be maintained properly, then they do not have to be rebored. Honing is all that is necessary (see Section 17).

17   Cylinder honing

Refer to illustrations 17.3a and 17.3b

1   Prior to engine reassembly, the cylinder bores must be honed so the new piston rings will seat correctly and provide the best possible combustion chamber seal. **Note:** *If you do not have the tools or do not want to tackle the honing operation, most automotive machine shops will do it for a reasonable fee.*

2   Before honing the cylinders, install the main bearing caps and tighten the bolts to the specified torque.

3   Two types of cylinder hones are commonly available – the flex hone or "bottle brush" type and the more traditional surfacing hone with spring-

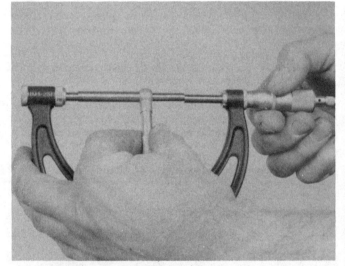

16.4c   The gauge is then measured with a micrometer to determine bore size

loaded stones. Both will do the job, but for the less experienced mechanic the "bottle brush" hone will probably be easier to use. You will also need plenty of light oil or honing oil, some rags and an electric drill motor. Proceed as follows:

  a) Mount the hone in the drill motor, compress the stones and slip it into the first cylinder **(see illustration)**.

  b) Lubricate the cylinder with plenty of oil, turn on the drill and move the hone up-and-down in the cylinder at a pace which will produce a fine crosshatch pattern on the cylinder walls. Ideally, the crosshatch lines should intersect at approximately a 60-degree angle **(see illustration)**. Be sure to use plenty of lubricant and do not take off any more material than is absolutely necessary to produce the desired finish. **Note:** *Piston ring manufacturers may specify a smaller crosshatch angle than the traditional 60-degrees – read and follow any instructions printed on the piston ring packages.*

  c) Do not withdraw the hone from the cylinder while it is running. Instead, shut off the drill and continue moving the hone up-and-down in the cylinder until it comes to a complete stop, then compress the stones and withdraw the hone. If you are using a "bottle brush" type hone, stop the drill motor, then turn the chuck in the normal direction of rotation while withdrawing the hone from the cylinder.

17.3a   If this is the first time you've ever honed cylinders, you'll get better results with a "bottle brush" hone than you will with a traditional spring-loaded hone

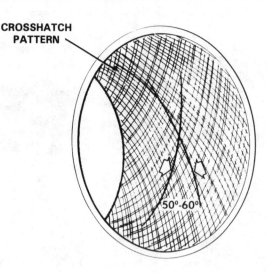

17.3b   The cylinder hone should leave a smooth, crosshatch pattern with the lines intersecting at approximately a 60-degree angle

2C

d)   Wipe the oil out of the cylinder and repeat the procedure for the remaining cylinders.

4   After the honing job is complete, chamfer the top edges of the cylinder bores with a small file so the rings will not catch when the pistons are installed. Be very careful not to nick the cylinder walls with the end of the file.

5   The entire engine block must be washed again very thoroughly with warm, soapy water to remove all traces of the abrasive grit produced during the honing operation. **Note:** *The bores can be considered clean when a white cloth – dampened with clean engine oil – used to wipe down the bores does not pick up any more honing residue, which will show up as gray areas on the cloth. Be sure to run a brush through all oil holes and galleries and flush them with running water.*

6   After rinsing, dry the block and apply a coat of light rust preventive oil to all machined surfaces. Wrap the block in a plastic trash bag to keep it clean and set it aside until reassembly.

---

18   Piston/connecting rod assembly – inspection

Refer to illustrations 18.4a, 18.4b, 18.10, 18.11a, 18.11b and 18.11c

1   Before the inspection process can be carried out, the piston/connect-

ing rod assemblies must be cleaned and the original piston rings removed from the pistons. **Note:** *Always use new piston rings when the engine is reassembled.*

2   Using a piston ring installation tool, carefully remove the rings from the pistons. Be careful not to nick or gouge the pistons in the process.

3   Scrape all traces of carbon from the top (known as the crown) of the piston. A hand-held wire brush or a piece of fine emery cloth can be used once the majority of the deposits have been scraped away. Do not, under any circumstances, use a wire brush mounted in a drill motor to remove deposits from the pistons. The piston material is soft and will be eroded away by the wire brush.

4   Use a piston ring groove cleaning tool to remove carbon deposits from the ring grooves **(see illustration)**. If a tool is not available, a piece broken off the old ring will do the job **(see illustration)**. Be very careful to remove only the carbon deposits – don't remove any metal and do not nick or scratch the sides of the ring grooves.

5   Once the deposits have been removed, clean the piston/rod assemblies with solvent and dry them with compressed air (if available). Make sure that the oil return holes in the back sides of the ring grooves are clear.

6   If the pistons are not damaged or worn excessively, and if the engine block is not rebored, new pistons will not be necessary. Normal piston

18.4a   The piston ring grooves can be cleaned with a special tool, as shown here . . .

18.4b   . . . or a piece of broken piston ring

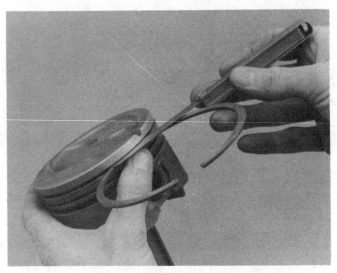

18.10   Check the ring side clearance with a feeler gauge at several points around the groove

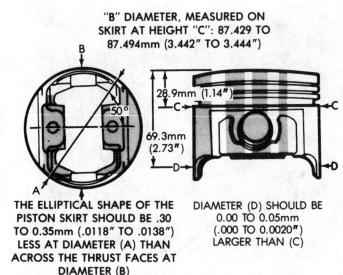

"B" DIAMETER, MEASURED ON SKIRT AT HEIGHT "C": 87.429 TO 87.494mm (3.442" TO 3.444")

28.9mm (1.14")

69.3mm (2.73")

50°

THE ELLIPTICAL SHAPE OF THE PISTON SKIRT SHOULD BE .30 TO 0.35mm (.0118" TO .0138") LESS AT DIAMETER (A) THAN ACROSS THE THRUST FACES AT DIAMETER (B)

DIAMETER (D) SHOULD BE 0.00 TO 0.05mm (.000 TO 0.0020") LARGER THAN (C)

18.11a   On 2.2 liter engines, measurements should be taken at C and D, perpendicular to the piston pin

wear appears as even vertical wear on the piston thrust surfaces and slight looseness of the top ring in its groove. New piston rings, on the other hand, should always be used when an engine is rebuilt.

7   Carefully inspect each piston for cracks around the skirt, at the pin bosses and at the ring lands.

8   Look for scoring and scuffing on the thrust faces of the skirt, holes in the piston crown and burned areas at the edge of the crown. If the skirt is scored or scuffed, the engine may have been suffering from overheating and/or abnormal combustion, which caused excessively high operating temperatures. The cooling and lubrication systems should be checked thoroughly. A hole in the piston crown is an indication that abnormal combustion (preignition) was occurring. Burned areas at the edge of the piston crown are usually evidence of spark knock (detonation). If any of the above problems exist, the causes must be corrected or the damage will occur again.

9   Corrosion of the piston, in the form of small pits, indicates that coolant is leaking into the combustion chamber and/or the crankcase. Again, the cause must be corrected or the problem may persist in the rebuilt engine.

10   Measure the piston ring side clearance by laying a new piston ring in each ring groove and slipping a feeler gauge in beside it **(see illustration)**. Check the clearance at three or four locations around each groove. Be sure to use the correct ring for each groove; they are different. If the side clearance is greater than listed in this Chapter's specifications, new pistons will have to be used.

11   Check the piston-to-bore clearance by measuring the bore (see Section 16) and the piston diameter. Make sure that the pistons and bores are correctly matched. Four-cylinder engines have two different piston measurement points, depending on the engine **(see illustrations)**. On V6 and V8 engines, measure the piston across the skirt, at a 90-degree angle to and in line with the piston pin **(see illustration)**. Subtract the piston diameter from the bore diameter to obtain the clearance. If it is greater than spe-

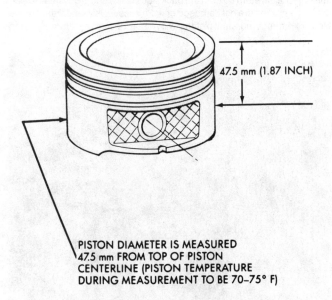

47.5 mm (1.87 INCH)

PISTON DIAMETER IS MEASURED 47.5 mm FROM TOP OF PISTON CENTERLINE (PISTON TEMPERATURE DURING MEASUREMENT TO BE 70–75° F)

18.11b   On 2.5 liter engines, the piston is measured 1.87 inch (47.5 mm) below the crown, perpendicular to the piston pin

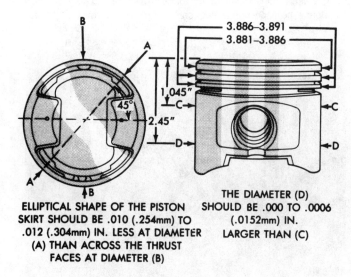

3.886–3.891
3.881–3.886

1.045"
2.45"
45°

ELLIPTICAL SHAPE OF THE PISTON SKIRT SHOULD BE .010 (.254mm) TO .012 (.304mm) IN. LESS AT DIAMETER (A) THAN ACROSS THE THRUST FACES AT DIAMETER (B)

THE DIAMETER (D) SHOULD BE .000 TO .0006 (.0152mm) IN. LARGER THAN (C)

18.11c   Measure the V6 and V8 pistons as shown

19.1 Clean the crankshaft oil passages with a wire or stiff plastic bristle brush and flush them out with solvent

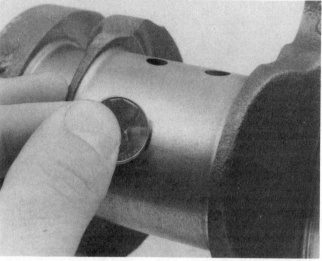

19.3 Rubbing a penny lengthwise on each journal will give you a quick idea of its condition – if copper rubs off the penny and adheres to the crankshaft, the journals should be reground

cified, the block will have to be rebored and new pistons and rings installed.

12 Check the piston-to-rod clearance by twisting the piston and rod in opposite directions. Any noticeable play indicates that there is excessive wear, which must be corrected. The piston/connecting rod assemblies should be taken to an automotive machine shop to have the pistons and rods rebored and new pins installed.

13 If the pistons must be removed from the connecting rods for any reason, they should be taken to an automotive machine shop. While they are there have the connecting rods checked for bend and twist, since automotive machine shops have special equipment for this purpose. **Note:** *Unless new pistons and/or connecting rods must be installed, do not disassemble the pistons and connecting rods.*

14 Check the connecting rods for cracks and other damage. Temporarily remove the rod caps, lift out the old bearing inserts, wipe the rod and cap bearing surfaces clean and inspect them for nicks, gouges and scratches. After checking the rods, replace the old bearings, slip the caps into place and tighten the nuts finger tight.

2C

19   Crankshaft – inspection

Refer to illustrations 19.1, 19.3, 19.4, 19.5, 19.6a, 19.6b and 19.6c

1   Clean the crankshaft with solvent and dry it with compressed air (if available). Be sure to clean the oil holes with a stiff brush **(see illustration)** and flush them with solvent. **Warning:** *Wear eye protection when using compressed air.*

2   Check the main and connecting rod bearing journals for uneven wear, scoring, pits and cracks. Check the rest of the crankshaft for cracks and other damage.

3   Rub a penny across each journal several times **(see illustration)**. If a journal picks up copper from the penny, it's too rough and must be reground.

4   Remove all burrs from the crankshaft oil holes with a stone, file or scraper **(see illustration)**.

5   Check the rest of the crankshaft for cracks and other damage **(see illustration)**. It should be magnafluxed to reveal hidden cracks – an automotive machine shop will handle the procedure.

19.4 Chamfer the oil holes to remove sharp edges that might gouge or scratch the new bearings

19.5 If the seal lips have worn grooves in the crankshaft journals, or if the seal journals are nicked or scratched, the new seal will leak

19.6a   Measure the diameter of each crankshaft journal at several points to detect taper and out-of-round conditions

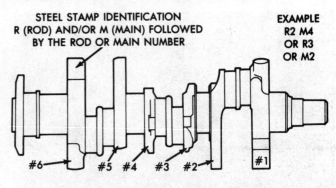

19.6b   V6 engine crankshafts may have a letter/number stamped into the counterweight of the number six journal – this marking will reveal the location (journal number) of undersize rod (R) or main (M) journal bearing(s)

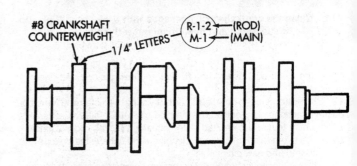

19.6c   The V8 engine crankshaft may have a letter/number stamped into the counterweight of the number eight journal – this marking will reveal the location (journal number) of the undersize rod (R) or (M) main journal bearing(s)

6   Using a micrometer, measure the diameter of the main and connecting rod journals and compare the results to this Chapter's Specifications **(see illustration)**. By measuring the diameter at a number of points around each journal's circumference, you will be able to determine whether or not the journal is out-of-round. Take the measurement at each end of the journal, near the crank throws, to determine if the journal is tapered. **Note:** *Some V6 crankshafts may have one or more journal bearings that are undersize. In this case, there will be a letter and number stamped near the notch of the number six counterweight* **(see illustration)**.

7   If the crankshaft journals are damaged, tapered, out-of-round or worn beyond the limits given in the Specifications, have the crankshaft reground by an automotive machine shop. Be sure to use the correct size bearing inserts if the crankshaft is reconditioned.

8   Refer to Section 20 and examine the main and rod bearing inserts.

20   Main and connecting rod bearings – inspection

Refer to illustration 20.1

1   Even though the main and connecting rod bearings should be replaced with new ones during the engine overhaul, the old bearings should be retained for close examination, as they may reveal valuable information about the condition of the engine **(see illustration)**.

2   Bearing failure occurs because of lack of lubrication, the presence of dirt or other foreign particles, overloading the engine and corrosion. Regardless of the cause of bearing failure, it must be corrected before the engine is reassembled to prevent it from happening again.

3   When examining the bearings, remove them from the engine block, the main bearing caps, the connecting rods and the rod caps and lay them out on a clean surface in the same general position as their location in the engine. This will enable you to match any bearing problems with the corresponding crankshaft journal.

4   Dirt and other foreign particles get into the engine in a variety of ways. If may be left in the engine during assembly, or it may pass through filters or the PCV system. It may get into the oil, and from there into the bearings. Metal chips from machining operations and normal engine wear are often present. Abrasives are sometimes left in engine components after reconditioning, especially when parts are not thoroughly cleaned using the proper cleaning methods. Whatever the source, these foreign objects often end up embedded in the soft bearing material and are easily recognized. Large particles will not embed in the bearing and will score or gouge the bearing and journal. The best prevention for this cause of bearing failure is to clean all parts thoroughly and keep everything spotlessly clean during engine assembly. Frequent and regular engine oil and filter changes are also recommended.

5   Lack of lubrication (or lubrication breakdown) has a number of interrelated causes. Excessive heat (which thins the oil), overloading (which

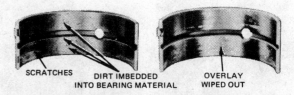

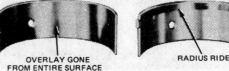

20.1   Typical bearing failures

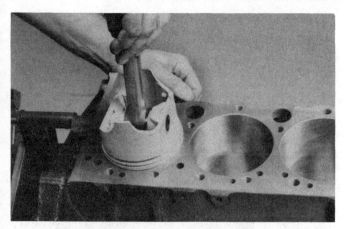

22.3   When checking piston ring end gap, the ring must be square in the cylinder bore – this is done by pushing it down with the top of a piston

22.4   Once the ring is at the lower limit of travel and square in the cylinder, measure the end gap with a feeler gauge

squeezes the oil from the bearing face) and oil leakage or throw off (from excessive bearing clearances, worn oil pump or high engine speeds) all contribute to lubrication breakdown. Blocked oil passages, which usually are the result of misaligned oil holes in a bearing shell, will also oil starve a bearing and destroy it. When lack of lubrication is the cause of bearing failure, the bearing material is wiped or extruded from the steel backing of the bearing. Temperatures may increase to the point where the steel backing turns blue from overheating.

6   Driving habits can have a definite effect on bearing life. Full throttle, low speed operation in too high a gear (lugging the engine) puts very high loads on bearings, which tends to squeeze out the oil film. These loads cause the bearings to flex, which produces fine cracks in the bearing face (fatigue failure). Eventually the bearing material will loosen in pieces and tear away from the steel backing. Short trip driving leads to corrosion of bearings because insufficient engine heat is produced to drive off the condensed water and corrosive gases. These products collect in the engine oil, forming acid and sludge. As the oil is carried to the engine bearings, the acid attacks and corrodes the bearing material.

7   Incorrect bearing installation during engine assembly will lead to bearing failure as well. Tight fitting bearings leave insufficient bearing oil clearance and will result in oil starvation. Dirt or foreign particles trapped behind a bearing insert result in high spots on the bearing which lead to failure.

21   Engine overhaul – reassembly sequence

1   Before beginning engine reassembly, make sure you have all the necessary new parts, gaskets and seals as well as the following items on hand:

Common hand tools
1/2-inch drive torque wrench
Piston ring installation tool
Piston ring compressor
Short lengths of rubber or plastic hose to fit over connecting rod bolts
Plastigage
Feeler gauges
A fine-tooth file
New engine oil
Engine assembly lube or moly-base grease
RTV-type gasket sealant
Anaerobic-type gasket sealant
Thread locking compound

2   In order to save time and avoid problems, engine reassembly must be done in the following general order:

Four-cylinder engines
Crankshaft and main bearings
Piston/ connecting rod assemblies
Front and rear oil seal housings
Intermediate shaft
Oil pump
Oil pan
Cylinder head
Camshaft and rockers
Timing belt
Timing belt cover
Intake and exhaust manifolds
Valve cover

V6 and V8 engines
New camshaft bearings (must be done by an automotive
    machine shop)
Crankshaft and main bearings
Piston rings
Piston/connecting rod assemblies
Camshaft
Oil pump
Timing chain and sprockets
Timing chain cover
Oil pan
Cylinder heads
Valve lifters
Rocker arms and pushrods
Intake and exhaust manifolds
Valve covers
Flywheel/driveplate

22   Piston rings – installation

Refer to illustrations 22.3, 22.4, 22.5, 22.9a, 22.9b and 22.12

1   Before installing the new piston rings, the ring end gaps must be checked. It is assumed that the piston ring side clearance has been checked and verified correct (see Section 18).

2   Lay out the piston/connecting rod assemblies and the new ring sets so the ring sets will be matched with the same piston and cylinder during the end gap measurement and engine assembly.

3   Insert the top (number one) ring into the first cylinder and square it up with the cylinder walls by pushing it in with the top of the piston **(see illustration)**. The ring should be near the bottom of the cylinder, at the lower limit of ring travel.

4   To measure the end gap, slip feeler gauges between the ends of the ring until a gauge equal to the gap width is found **(see illustration)**. The feeler gauge should slide between the ring ends with a slight amount of drag. Compare the measurement to that listed in this Chapter's Specifications. If the gap is larger or smaller than specified, double-check to make sure that you have the correct rings before proceeding.

2C

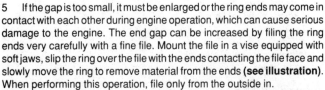

22.5   If the end gap is too small, clamp a file in a vise and file the ring ends (from the outside in only) to enlarge the gap slightly

22.9a   Install the three-piece oil control ring first, one part at a time beginning with the spacer/expander . . .

5   If the gap is too small, it must be enlarged or the ring ends may come in contact with each other during engine operation, which can cause serious damage to the engine. The end gap can be increased by filing the ring ends very carefully with a fine file. Mount the file in a vise equipped with soft jaws, slip the ring over the file with the ends contacting the file face and slowly move the ring to remove material from the ends **(see illustration)**. When performing this operation, file only from the outside in.
6   Excess end gap is not critical unless it is greater than 0.040-inch. Again, double-check to make sure you have the correct rings for your engine.
7   Repeat the procedure for each ring that will be installed in the first cylinder and for each ring in the remaining cylinders. Remember to keep rings, pistons and cylinders matched up.
8   Once the ring end gaps have been checked/corrected, the rings can be installed on the pistons.
9   The oil control ring (lowest one on the piston) is installed first. It is composed of three separate components. Slip the spacer/expander into the groove **(see illustration)**. If an anti-rotation tang is used, make sure it is inserted into the drilled hole in the ring groove. Install the lower side rail. Do not use a piston ring installation tool on the oil ring side rails, as they may

be damaged. Instead, place one end of the side rail into the groove between the spacer/expander and the ring land, hold it firmly in place and slide a finger around the piston while pushing the rail into the groove **(see illustration)**. Next, install the upper side rail in the same manner.
10   After the three oil ring components have been installed, check to make sure that both the upper and lower side rails can be turned smoothly in the ring groove.
11   The number two (middle) ring is installed next. It is stamped with a mark which must face up, toward the top of the piston. **Note:** *Always follow the instructions printed on the ring package or box – different manufacturers may require different approaches.* Do not mix up the top and middle rings, as they have different cross sections.
12   Use a piston ring installation tool and make sure that the identification mark is facing the top of the piston, then slip the ring into the middle groove on the piston **(see illustration)**. Do not expand the ring any more than is necessary to slide it over the piston.
13   Install the number one (top) ring in the same manner. Make sure the mark is facing up. Be careful not to confuse the number one and number two rings.
14   Repeat the procedure for the remaining pistons and rings.

22.9b   . . . followed by the side rails – DO NOT USE a piston ring installation tool to install the oil ring side rails

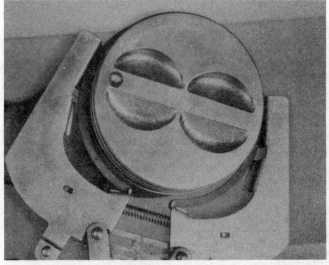

22.12   Install the compression rings with a ring expander – the mark (arrow) must face up

23.10   Lay the Plastigage strips (arrow) on the main bearing journals, parallel to the crankshaft centerline

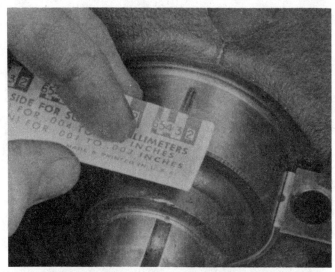

23.14   Compare the width of the crushed Plastigage to the scale on the envelope to determine the main bearing oil clearance (always take the measurement at the widest point of the Plastigage); be sure to use the correct scale – standard and metric ones are included

2C

23   Crankshaft – installation and main bearing oil clearance check

Refer to illustrations 23.10 and 23.14

1   Crankshaft installation is the first step in engine reassembly. It is assumed at this point that the engine block and crankshaft have been cleaned, inspected and repaired or reconditioned.

2   Position the engine with the bottom facing up.

3   Remove the main bearing cap bolts and lift out the caps. Lay them out in the proper order to ensure that they are installed correctly.

4   If they are still in place, remove the old bearing inserts from the block and the main bearing caps. Wipe the main bearing surfaces of the block and caps with a clean, lint free cloth. They must be kept spotlessly clean.

Main bearing oil clearance check

Note: *Don't touch the faces of the new bearings with your fingers. Oil and acids from your skin can etch the bearings.*

5   Clean the back sides of the new main bearing inserts and lay one bearing half in each main bearing saddle in the block. Lay the other bearing half from each bearing set in the corresponding main bearing cap. Make sure the tab on the bearing insert fits into the recess in the block or cap. Also, the oil holes in the block must line up with the oil holes in the bearing insert. Do not hammer the bearing into place and do not nick or gouge the bearing faces. No lubrication should be used at this time.

6   The flanged thrust bearing must be installed in the third cap and saddle on four-cylinder engines and in the second cap and saddle on V6 engines.

7   Clean the faces of the bearings in the block and the crankshaft main bearing journals with a clean, lint free cloth. Check or clean the oil holes in the crankshaft, as any dirt here can go only one way – straight through the new bearings.

8   Once you are certain that the crankshaft is clean, carefully lay it in position (an assistant would be very helpful here) in the main bearings.

9   Before the crankshaft can be permanently installed, the main bearing oil clearance must be checked.

10   Trim several pieces of the appropriate size of Plastigage (they must be slightly shorter than the width of the main bearings) and place one piece on each crankshaft main bearing journal, parallel with the journal axis **(see illustration)**.

11   Clean the faces of the bearings in the caps and install the caps in their respective positions (do not mix them up) with the arrows pointing toward the front of the engine. Do not disturb the Plastigage.

12   Starting with the center main and working out toward the ends, tighten the main bearing cap bolts, in three steps, to the torque listed in this Chapter's specifications. Do not rotate the crankshaft at any time during this operation.

13   Remove the bolts and carefully lift off the main bearing caps. Keep them in order. Do not disturb the Plastigage or rotate the crankshaft. If any of the main bearing caps are difficult to remove, tap them gently from side-to-side with a soft-face hammer to loosen them.

14   Compare the width of the crushed Plastigage on each journal to the scale printed on the Plastigage container to obtain the main bearing oil clearance **(see illustration)**. Check the Specifications in this Chapter to make sure it is correct.

15   If the clearance is not as specified, the bearing inserts may be the wrong size (which means different ones will be required). Before deciding that different inserts are needed, make sure that no dirt or oil was between the bearing inserts and the caps or block when the clearance was measured. If the Plastigage was wider at one end than the other, the journal may be tapered (refer to Section 19).

16   Carefully scrape all traces of the Plastigage material off the main bearing journals and/or the bearing faces. Do not nick or scratch the bearing faces – use your fingernail or a credit card.

Final crankshaft installation

17   Carefully lift the crankshaft out of the engine. Clean the bearing faces in the block, then apply a thin, uniform layer of clean moly-base grease or engine assembly lube to each of the bearing surfaces. Be sure to coat the thrust faces as well as the journal face of the rear bearing.

18   If you're working on a V6 engine, install the rear main oil seal halves into the engine block and rear main bearing cap (refer to Chapter 2, Part B, for main seal installation details).

19   Make sure the crankshaft journals are clean, then lay the crankshaft back in place in the block. Clean the faces of the bearings in the caps, then apply lubricant to them. Install the caps in their respective positions with the arrows pointing toward the front of the engine. Install the bolts.

20   Tighten all *except* the thrust bearing cap bolts (third on four-cylinder and second on V6 models) to the torque listed in this Chapter's Specifications. Work from the center out and approach the final torque in three steps. Tighten the thrust cap bolts to 10-to-12 ft-lbs. Tap the ends of the crankshaft forward and backward with a lead or brass hammer to line up the main bearing and crankshaft thrust surfaces. Retighten all main bearing cap bolts to the specified torque, starting with the center main and working out toward the ends.

24.3   Make sure the bearing tang fits securely into the notch in the rod cap

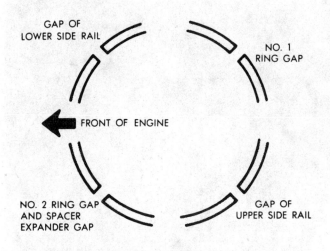

24.5   Position the ring end gaps as shown here before installing the pistons in the block

21   On manual transmission equipped models, install a new pilot bushing in the end of the crankshaft (see Chapter 8).

22   Rotate the crankshaft a number of times by hand to check for any obvious binding.

23   Check the crankshaft endplay with a feeler gauge or a dial indicator as described in Section 14. The endplay should be correct if the crankshaft thrust faces are not worn or damaged and new bearings have been installed.

24   If you're working on a four-cylinder engine, install the crankshaft rear oil seal and housing (refer to Chapter 2, Part A, for main seal installation details).

---

24   Piston/connecting rod assembly – installation and rod bearing oil clearance check

---

Refer to illustrations 24.3, 24.5, 24.8a, 24.8b, 24.9, 24.11 and 24.13

1   Before installing the piston/connecting rod assemblies the cylinder walls must be perfectly clean, the top edge of each cylinder must be chamfered, and the crankshaft must be in place.

2   Remove the connecting rod cap from the end of the number one connecting rod. Remove the old bearing inserts and wipe the bearing surfaces

of the connecting rod and cap with a clean, lint free cloth. They must be kept spotlessly clean.

Connecting rod bearing oil clearance check

Note: *Don't touch the faces of the new bearing inserts with your fingers. Oil and acids from your skin can etch the bearings.*

3   Clean the back side of the new upper bearing half, then lay it in place in the connecting rod. Make sure the tang on the bearing fits into the notch in the rod cap **(see illustration)**. Do not hammer the bearing insert into place and be very careful not to nick or gouge the bearing face. Do not lubricate the bearing at this time.

4   Clean the backside of the other bearing insert and install it in the rod cap. Again, make sure the tab on the bearing fits into the recess in the cap, and do not apply any lubricant. It is critically important that the mating surfaces of the bearing and connecting rod are perfectly clean and oil free when they are assembled.

5   Space the piston ring gaps around the piston **(see illustration)**, then slip a section of plastic or rubber hose over each connecting rod cap bolt.

6   Lubricate the piston and rings with clean engine oil and attach a piston ring compressor to the piston. Leave the skirt protruding about 1/4-inch to guide the piston into the cylinder. The rings must be compressed until they are flush with the piston.

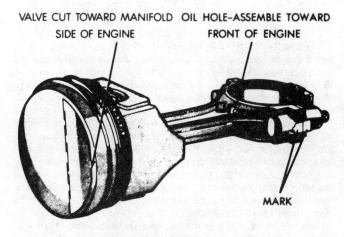

24.8a   On four-cylinder engines, the valve cut goes toward the manifold side of the engine

24.8b   The pistons are numbered (arrow) to their corresponding cylinders

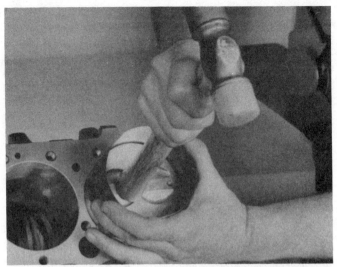

24.9   Drive the piston gently into the cylinder bore with the end of a wooden or plastic hammer handle

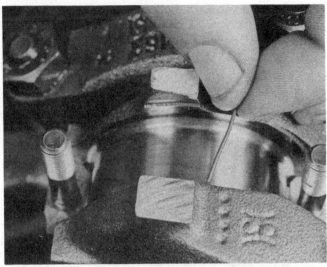

24.11   Lay the Plastigage strips on each rod bearing journal, parallel to the crankshaft centerline

2C

7   Rotate the crankshaft until the number one connecting rod journal is at BDC (bottom dead center) and apply a coat of engine oil to the cylinder walls.

8   On four-cylinder engines, the valve cut **(see illustration)** must be installed on the manifold side of the engine. On V6 and V8 engines, align the notch on top of the piston to face the front of the engine. The pistons are numbered to indicate which cylinder they must be installed into **(see illustration)**. Gently insert the piston/connecting rod assembly into the number one cylinder bore and rest the bottom edge of the ring compressor on the engine block. Tap the top edge of the ring compressor to make sure it is contacting the block around its entire circumference.

9   Carefully tap on the top of the piston with the end of a wooden hammer handle while guiding the end of the connecting rod into place on the crankshaft journal **(see illustration)**. The piston rings may try to pop out of the ring compressor just before entering the cylinder bore, so keep some downward pressure on the ring compressor. Work slowly, and if any resistance is felt as the piston enters the cylinder, stop immediately. Find out what is hanging up and fix it before proceeding. Do not, for any reason, force the piston into the cylinder, as you will break a ring and/or the piston.

10   Once the piston/connecting rod assembly is installed, the connecting rod bearing oil clearance must be checked before the rod cap is permanently bolted in place.

11   Cut a piece of the appropriate size Plastigage slightly shorter than the width of the connecting rod bearing and lay it in place on the number one connecting rod journal, parallel with the crankshaft centerline **(see illustration)**.

12   Clean the connecting rod cap bearing face, remove the protective hoses from the connecting rod bolts and install the rod cap. Make sure the mating mark on the cap is on the same side as the mark on the connecting rod. Install the nuts and tighten them to the torque listed in this Chapter's specifications, working up to it in three steps. **Note:** *Use a thin-wall socket to avoid erroneous torque readings that can result if the socket becomes wedged between the rod cap and nut. Do not rotate the crankshaft at any time during this operation.*

13   Remove the rod cap, being very careful not to disturb the Plastigage. Compare the width of the crushed Plastigage to the scale printed on the Plastigage container to obtain the oil clearance **(see illustration)**. Compare it to the Specifications in this Chapter to make sure the clearance is correct. If the clearance is not as specified, the bearing inserts may be the wrong size (which means different ones will be required). Before deciding that different inserts are needed, make sure that no dirt or oil was between the bearing inserts and the connecting rod or cap when the clearance was measured. Also, recheck the journal diameter. If the Plastigage was wider at one end than the other, the journal may be tapered (refer to Section 19).

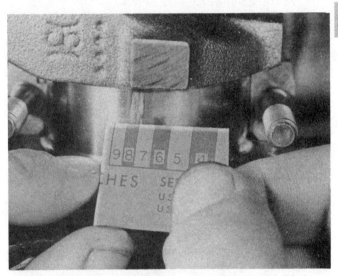

24.13   Measure the width of the crushed Plastigage with the scale on the envelope to determine the rod bearing oil clearance (be sure to use the correct scale – standard and metric ones are included)

Final connecting rod installation

14   Carefully scrape all traces of the Plastigage material off the rod journal and/or bearing face. Be very careful not to scratch the bearing – use your fingernail or a credit card. Make sure the bearing faces are perfectly clean, then apply a uniform layer of clean moly-base grease or engine assembly lube to both of them. You will have to push the piston into the cylinder to expose the face of the bearing insert in the connecting rod – be sure to slip the protective hoses over the rod bolts first.

15   Slide the connecting rod back into place on the journal, remove the protective hoses from the rod cap bolts, install the rod cap and tighten the nuts to the torque listed in this Chapter's specifications. Again, work up to the torque in three steps.

16   Repeat the entire procedure for the remaining piston/connecting rod assemblies. Keep the backsides of the bearing inserts and the inside of the connecting rod and cap perfectly clean when assembling them. Make sure you have the correct piston for the cylinder. On four-cylinder engines, align the valve cuts toward the manifold side. On V6 and V8 engines, ensure that the notch on the piston faces to the timing chain end of the engine

when the piston is installed. Remember, use plenty of oil to lubricate the piston before installing the ring compressor. Also, when installing the rod caps for the final time, be sure to lubricate the bearing faces adequately.

17   After all the piston/connecting rod assemblies have been properly installed, rotate the crankshaft a number of times by hand to check for any obvious binding.

18   As a final step, the connecting rod endplay must be checked. Refer to Section 13 for this procedure. Compare the measured endplay to the Specifications in this Chapter to make sure it is correct. If it was correct before disassembly and the original crankshaft and rods were reinstalled, it should still be right. If new rods or a new crankshaft were installed, the endplay may be too small. If so, the rods will have to be removed and taken to an automotive machine shop for resizing.

---

25   Initial start-up and break-in after overhaul

---

1   Once the engine has been installed in the vehicle, double-check the engine oil and coolant levels. Add one pint of Chrysler Crankcase Conditioner (part no. 4318002) or equivalent.

Four-cylinder engines

2   With the spark plugs out of the engine and the ignition disabled by disconnecting the primary wires to the coil, crank the engine until oil pressure registers on the gauge.

3   Install the spark plugs, hook up the plug wires and reconnect the wires to the coil.

All engines

4   Start the engine. It may take a few moments for the gasoline to reach the carburetor or fuel injection unit, but the engine should start without a great deal of effort.

5   After the engine starts, it should be allowed to warm up to normal operating temperature. While the engine is warming up, make a thorough check for oil and coolant leaks.

6   Shut the engine off and recheck the engine oil and coolant levels.

7   Drive the vehicle to an area with minimum traffic, accelerate at full throttle from 30 to 50 mph, then allow the vehicle to slow to 30 mph with the throttle closed. Repeat the procedure 10 or 12 times. This will load the piston rings and cause them to seat properly against the cylinder walls. Check again for oil and coolant leaks.

8   Drive the vehicle gently for the first 500 miles (no sustained high speeds) and keep a constant check on the oil level. It is not unusual for an engine to use oil during the break-in period.

9   At approximately 500 to 600 miles, change the oil and filter.

10   For the next few hundred miles, drive the vehicle normally. Do not pamper it or abuse it.

11   After 2000 miles, change the oil and filter again and consider the engine fully broken in.

Chapter 3   Cooling, heating and air conditioning systems

Contents

Specifications

General

Coolant capacity .... See Chapter 1
Drivebelt tension .... See Chapter 1
Radiator pressure cap rating .... 14 to 15 psi
Thermostat opening temperature .... 195-degrees F

Torque specifications   **Ft-lbs** (unless otherwise indicated)

V6 and V8 fan-to-water pump hub bolts
  With fan clutch (A/C) 20
  With solid hub (non-A/C) 17
Thermostat cover bolts 17
Water pump attaching bolts
  Four-cylinder engine
    Upper bolts 21
    Lower bolts 40
    Water pump housing-to-cover bolts .... 105 in-lbs
  V6 and V8 engine (all) 30

1   General information

The cooling system consists of a radiator, a thermostat and a crankshaft pulley-driven water pump.

On V6 models, the radiator cooling fan is mounted on the front of the water pump and incorporates a fluid drive fan clutch, saving horsepower and reducing noise. A fan shroud is mounted on the rear of the radiator. Four cylinder models are equipped with electrically powered fans mounted to the radiator.

The system is pressurized by a spring-loaded radiator cap, which increases the boiling point of the coolant. If the coolant temperature goes above this increased boiling point, the extra pressure in the system forces the radiator cap valve off its seat and exposes the overflow pipe. The overflow pipe leads to a coolant recovery system. This consists of a plastic reservoir into which the coolant that normally escapes due to expansion is retained. When the engine cools, the excess coolant is drawn back into the radiator, maintaining the system at full capacity. This is a continuous

3.2a   Disconnect the upper radiator hose and, on four-cylinder models, unclip the fan shroud

1 Hose	2 Fan shroud clip

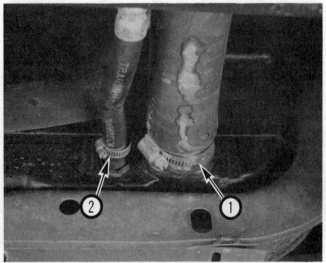

3.2b   Detach the lower radiator hose and cooler line, if equipped (viewed from below)

1 Lower radiator hose	2 Cooler line

process and provided the level in the reservoir is correctly maintained, it is not necessary to add coolant to the radiator.

Coolant in the right side of the radiator circulates up the lower radiator hose to the water pump, where it is forced through the water passages in the cylinder block. The coolant then travels up into the cylinder head, circulates around the combustion chambers and valve seats, travels out of the cylinder head past the open thermostat into the upper radiator hose and back into the radiator.

When the engine is cold, the thermostat restricts the circulation of coolant to the engine. When the minimum operating temperature is reached, the thermostat begins to open, allowing coolant to return to the radiator.

Automatic transmission-equipped models have a cooler element incorporated into the radiator to cool the transmission fluid.

The heating system works by directing air through the heater core mounted in the dash and then to the interior of the vehicle by a system of ducts. Temperature is controlled by mixing heated air with fresh air, using a system of flapper doors in the ducts, and a heater motor.

Air conditioning is an optional accessory, consisting of an evaporator core located under the dash, a condenser in front of the radiator, a receiver-drier in the engine compartment and a belt-driven compressor mounted at the front of the engine.

2   Antifreeze – general information

Warning: *Do not allow antifreeze to come in contact with your skin or painted surfaces of the vehicle. Rinse off spills immediately with plenty of water. Antifreeze is highly toxic if ingested. Never leave antifreeze lying around in an open container or in puddles on the floor; children and pets are attracted by it's sweet smell and may drink it. Check with local authorities about disposing of used antifreeze. Many communities have collection centers which will see that antifreeze is disposed of safely.*

The cooling system should be filled with a water/ethylene glycol based antifreeze solution which will prevent freezing down to at least -20-degrees F (even lower in cold climates). It also provides protection against corrosion and increases the coolant boiling point.

The cooling system should be drained, flushed and refilled at least every other year (see Chapter 1). The use of antifreeze solutions for periods of longer than two years is likely to cause damage and encourage the formation of rust and scale in the system.

Before adding antifreeze to the system, check all hose connections. Antifreeze can leak through very minute openings.

The exact mixture of antifreeze to water which you should use depends on the relative weather conditions. The mixture should contain at least 50-percent antifreeze, but should never contain more than 70-percent antifreeze.

3   Radiator – removal and installation

Refer to illustrations 3.2a, 3.2b, 3.5 and 3.6
Warning: *The engine must be completely cool when this procedure is performed.*

Removal

1   Disconnect the negative cable at the battery.
2   Drain the cooling system as described in Chapter 1, then disconnect the overflow, heater and upper and lower radiator hoses from the radiator **(see illustrations)**.
3   If equipped with an automatic transmission or engine oil cooler, remove the cooler lines from the radiator – be careful not to damage the lines or fittings. Plug the ends of the disconnected lines to prevent leakage and stop dirt from entering the system. Have a drip pan ready to catch any spills.
4   On four-cylinder models, remove the engine cooling fan (see Section 5).
5   On V6 and V8 models, unbolt the fan shroud **(see illustration)** and slip it back over the fan.

3.5 Remove the fan shroud bolts (arrow) from both sides of the radiator

3.6 Remove the radiator mounting bolts (arrow) from both sides of the radiator

6   Remove the radiator mounting bolts **(see illustration)** and lift the radiator from the engine compartment. Take care not to contact the fan blades.
7   Prior to installation of the radiator, replace any damaged hose clamps and radiator hoses.

Installation
8   Radiator installation is the reverse of removal. When installing the radiator, make sure it seats properly in the lower saddles and that the rubber mounts are intact.
9   After installation, fill the system with the proper mixture of antifreeze, and also check the automatic transmission fluid level, where applicable.

---

4   Thermostat – check and replacement

Refer to illustrations 4.7, 4.8, 4.9, 4.10, 4.11a and 4.11b

Warning: *The engine must be completely cool when this procedure is performed.*

Note: *Don't drive the vehicle without a thermostat! The computer may stay in open loop and emissions and fuel economy will suffer.*

Check
1   Before condemning the thermostat, check the coolant level, drivebelt tension, drivebelt tension and temperature gauge (or light) operation.
2   If the engine takes a long time to warm up, the thermostat is probably stuck open. Replace the thermostat.
3   If the engine runs hot, check the temperature of the upper radiator hose. If the hose isn't hot, the thermostat is probably stuck shut. Replace the thermostat.
4   If the upper radiator hose is hot, it means the coolant is circulating and the thermostat is open. Refer to the Troubleshooting section for the cause of overheating.
5   If an engine has been overheated, you may find damage such as leaking head gaskets, scuffed pistons and warped or cracked cylinder heads.

Replacement
6   Drain coolant (about 3 quarts) from the radiator, until the coolant level is below the thermostat housing (See Chapter 1).
7   Disconnect the upper radiator hose from the thermostat cover, which is located on the driver's side of the engine on four-cylinder engines **(see illustration)** or at the forward end of the intake manifold on V6 models. **Note:** *It may be necessary to remove the air cleaner assembly on V6 models for access.*
8   Remove the bolts **(see illustration)** and lift the cover off. It may be necessary to tap the cover with a soft-face hammer to break the gasket seal.

3

4.7 On four-cylinder engines, the thermostat is mounted in a housing on the driver's side (arrow)

4.8 Remove the bolts (arrows) and lift the cover off (V6 shown, V8 and four cylinder similar)

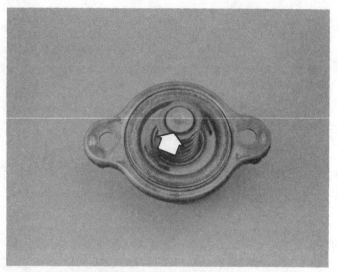

4.9   The thermostat is marked with it's opening temperature (arrow) – the spring side goes into the engine

4.10   Remove all traces of old gasket material, but avoid gouging the soft aluminum

9   Note how it's installed, then remove the thermostat **(see illustration)**. Be sure to use a replacement thermostat with the correct opening temperature (see this Chapter's Specifications).

10   Use a scraper or putty knife to remove all traces of old gasket material and sealant from the mating surfaces **(see illustration)**. Make sure no gasket material falls into the coolant passages; it is a good idea to stuff a rag in the passage. Wipe the mating surfaces with a rag saturated with lacquer thinner or acetone.

11   On four-cylinder engines, dip the replacement gasket in water before installation. On V6 models, apply a thin layer of RTV sealant to the gasket mating surfaces of the housing and cover, then install the new thermostat and gasket **(see illustrations)**. Make sure the correct end faces out – the spring is directed toward the engine.

12   Position a new gasket on the engine side and make sure the gasket holes line up with the bolt holes in the housing.

13   Carefully position the cover and install the bolts. Tighten them to the torque listed in this Chapter's Specifications – do not overtighten them or the cover may be distorted.

14   Reattach the radiator hose to the cover and tighten the clamp – now may be a good time to check and replace the hoses and clamps (see Chapter 1).

15   Refer to Chapter 1 and refill the system, then run the engine and check carefully for leaks. **Note:** *On four-cylinder models air must be bled from the cooling system (see Chapter 1).*

5   Cooling fan and fan clutch – removal and installation

Warning: *The cooling fan should be replaced if the blades become damaged or bent.*

Four-cylinder engines

Refer to illustration 5.5

1   Disconnect the negative cable from the battery.
2   Label and disconnect the fan wiring at the motor.

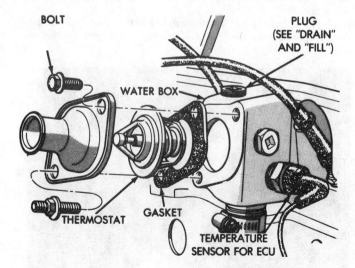

4.11a   Four-cylinder thermostat components – exploded view

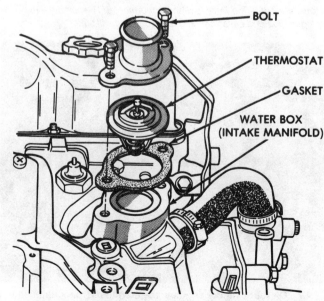

4.11b   V6 and V8 thermostat components – exploded view

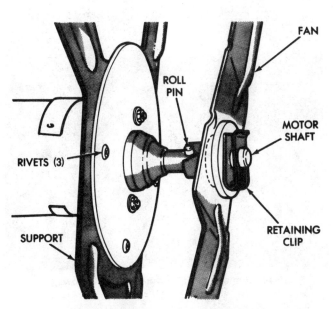

5.5   Remove the clip from the motor shaft

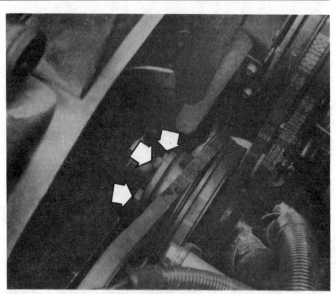

5.9   Loosen the water pump pulley bolts (arrows) – lower bolt obscured

3   If necessary for clearance, drain about two quarts of coolant (see Chapter 1) and detach the upper hose from the radiator.

4   Remove the clips **(see illustration 3.2a)** and lift the fan assembly from the engine compartment.

5   Remove the clip from the motor shaft **(see illustration)** and slip the fan blade off the shaft.

6   Installation is the reverse of removal.

V6 and V8 engines

Refer to illustrations 5.9, 5.13a, 5.13b and 5.14

7   Air conditioned models have a viscous drive fan clutch, while non-air conditioned models use a solid spacer between the fan and water pump pulley. On air conditioned models, the viscous drive fan clutch is disengaged when the engine is cold, or at high engine speeds. Symptoms of failure of the fan clutch are continuous noisy operation, looseness leading to vibration and evidence of silicone fluid leaks.

8   Disconnect the negative cable from the battery.

9   Loosen the water pump pulley bolts **(see illustration)**. **Note:** *On non-air conditioned models, the bolts go through the fan and spacer.*

10   Remove the drivebelts from the water pump pulley (see Chapter 1).

11   Drain about two quarts of coolant (see Chapter 1) and detach the upper hose from the radiator.

12   Unbolt the fan assembly and detach it from the water pump.

13   Remove the fan shroud bolts and lift the fan and shroud from the vehicle **(see illustrations)**.

3

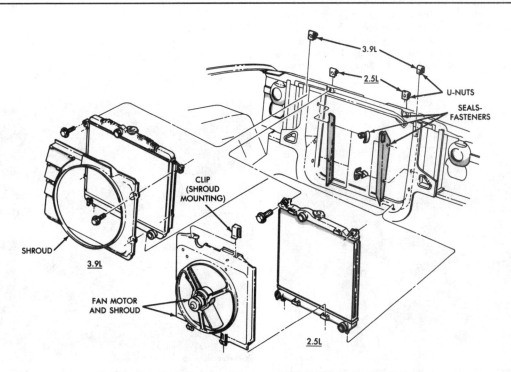

5.13a   Fan shroud and radiator mounting details – exploded view

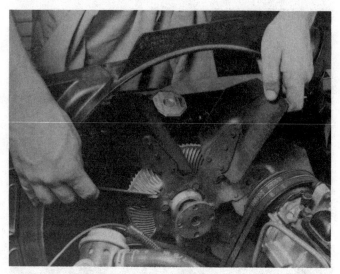

5.13b   Lift the fan and shroud as an assembly

5.14   Remove the fan mounting bolts (arrows)

14   The fan clutch (if equipped) can be unbolted from the fan blade assembly for replacement **(see illustration)**.
15   Installation is the reverse of removal.

---

6   Water pump – check

Refer to illustrations 6.3 and 6.5

1   Water pump failure can cause overheating and serious damage to the engine. There are three ways to check the operation of the water pump while it is installed on the engine. If any one of the three following quick checks indicates water pump problems, it should be replaced immediately.
2   Start the engine and warm it up to normal operating temperature. Squeeze the upper radiator hose. If the water pump is working properly, you should feel a pressure surge as the hose is released.
3   A seal protects the water pump impeller shaft bearing from contamination by engine coolant. If this seal fails, a weep hole in the water pump snout will leak coolant **(see illustration)** (an inspection mirror can be used to look at the underside of the pump if the hole isn't on top). If the weep hole is leaking, shaft bearing failure will follow. Replace the water pump immediately.

4   Besides contamination by coolant after a seal failure, the water pump impeller shaft bearing can also be prematurely worn out by an improperly tensioned drivebelt. When the bearing wears out, it emits a high pitched squealing sound. If such a noise is coming from the water pump during engine operation, the shaft bearing has failed – replace the water pump immediately. **Note:** *Do not confuse belt noise with bearing noise.*
5   To identify excessive bearing wear before the bearing actually fails, grasp the water pump pulley and try to force it up-and-down or from side-to-side **(see illustration)**. If the pulley can be moved either horizontally or vertically, the bearing is nearing the end of its service life. Replace the water pump.

---

7   Water pump – removal and installation

Refer to illustrations 7.5, 7.6, 7.7a, 7.7b, 7.7c and 7.8

Removal

1   Disconnect the negative cable at the battery.
2   Drain the coolant (see Chapter 1).
3   Loosen the water pump pulley bolts (on four-cylinder) or fan mounting bolts (on V6 and V8) and then remove the drivebelts (see Chapter 1).

6.3   Check the weep hole (arrow) for leakage (pump removed for clarity)

6.5   Check the pump for loose or rough bearings

7.5   On V6 and V8 models, detach the heater, bypass and lower radiator hoses (arrows)

7.6   On this V6 model, all the water pump bolts (arrows) secure mounting brackets

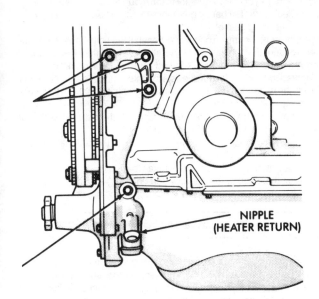

7.7a   Remove the housing-to-block bolts (arrows)

NIPPLE
(HEATER RETURN)

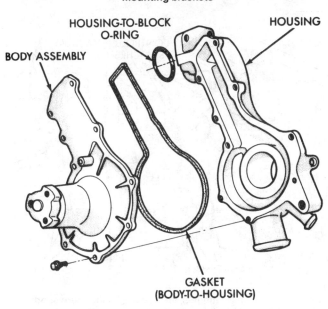

HOUSING-TO-BLOCK
O-RING

BODY ASSEMBLY

HOUSING

GASKET
(BODY-TO-HOUSING)

7.7b   Four-cylinder water pump components – exploded view

3

4   Remove the fan and shroud assembly (see Section 5) and water pump pulley.

5   Detach the coolant hoses from the water pump **(see illustration)**.

6   On some models the compressor, alternator, power steering and air pump brackets may attach to the water pump **(see illustration)**. Where necessary, loosen or remove the components so that the brackets can be moved aside and the water pump bolts removed. **Note:** *Do not disconnect the power steering or compressor hoses; unbolt the units and tie them aside.* On four-cylinder models with air conditioning, remove the solid mount accessory bracket (see Section 13).

7   On four-cylinder models, unbolt the water pump housing from the block. Remove the water pump mounting bolts and detach it. It may be necessary to tap the pump with a soft-face hammer to break the gasket seal **(see illustrations)**.

Installation

8   Clean the sealing surfaces on both the water pump and housing **(see illustration)**. Wipe the mating surfaces with a rag saturated with lacquer thinner or acetone.

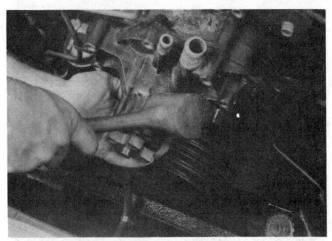

7.7c   Strike the water pump with a soft-face hammer to break the gasket seal

7.8   Remove all traces of old gasket material – use care to avoid gouging the soft aluminum

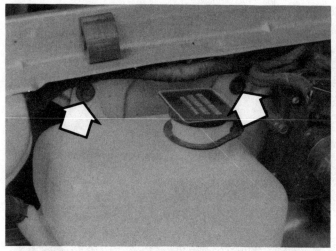

8.2   The coolant reservoir is secured to the inner fender by two bolts (arrows)

9   Apply a thin layer of RTV sealant to the mounting surfaces. On for-cylinder engines, install the housing-to-block O-ring. Then install a new water pump-to-housing gasket.

10   Place the water pump in position and install the bolts finger tight. Use caution to ensure that the gaskets do not slip out of position. Remember to replace any mounting brackets secured by the water pump mounting bolts. Tighten the bolts to the torque listed in this Chapter's specifications.

11   Install the water pump pulley and fan assembly and tighten the pulley bolts by hand.

12   Install the coolant hoses and hose clamps. Tighten the hose clamps securely.

13   Install the drivebelts (see Chapter 1) and tighten the fan/pulley mounting bolts securely.

14   Add coolant to the specified level (see Chapter 1).

15   Connect the cable to the negative terminal of the battery.

16   Start the engine and check the water pump and hoses for leaks.

---

8   Coolant reservoir – removal and installation

Refer to illustration 8.2

1   Remove the coolant overflow hose from the reservoir.

2   Remove the bolts and detach the reservoir **(see illustration)**. Note: *Some later model reservoirs slip into the mounting bracket without bolts.*

3   Prior to installation make sure the reservoir is clean and free of debris which could be drawn into the radiator (wash it with soap and water if necessary).

4   Installation is the reverse of removal.

---

9   Coolant temperature sending unit – check and replacement

Refer to illustrations 9.1a and 9.1b
Warning: *Wait until the engine is completely cool before beginning this procedure.*

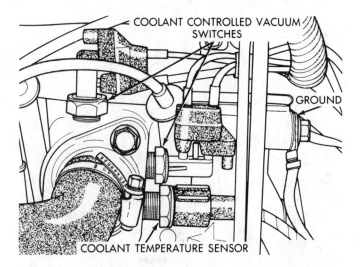

9.1a   On four-cylinder models, the coolant temperature sending unit is located adjacent to the thermostat housing

Check

1   The coolant temperature indicator system is composed of a light or temperature gauge mounted in the instrument panel and a coolant temperature sending unit mounted on the engine **(see illustrations)**. Some vehicles have more than one sending unit, but only one is used for the indicator system. **Warning:** *If the vehicle is equipped with an electric cooling fan, stay clear of the fan blades. The fan can come on at any time.*

2   If an overheating indication occurs, check the coolant level in the system and then make sure the wiring between the light or gauge and the sending unit is secure and all fuses are intact.

3   When the ignition switch is turned on and the starter motor is turning, the indicator light (if equipped) should be on (overheated engine indication).

9.1b   On V6 and V8 models, the coolant temperature sending unit (arrow) is located near the front of the intake manifold

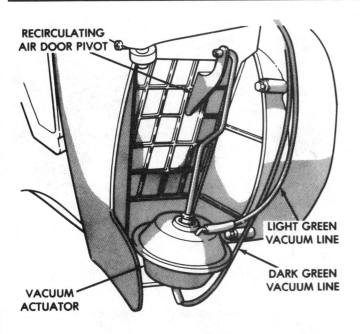

10.4   Disconnect the vacuum hoses from the recirculating air door vacuum actuator

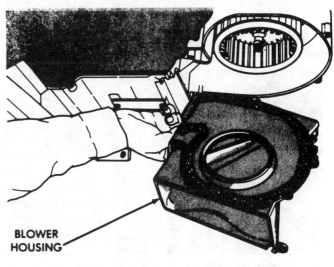

10.7   Remove the screws and detach the blower housing

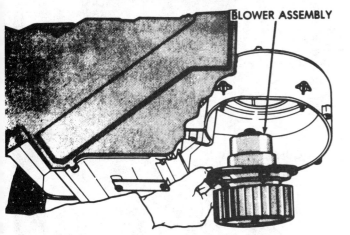

10.8   Remove the blower assembly

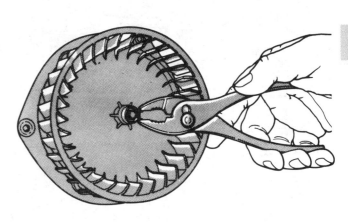

10.9   Squeeze the clip with a pair of pliers, then slip the fan off the shaft

3

4   If the light is not on, the bulb may be burned out, the ignition switch may be faulty or the circuit may be open. Test the circuit by grounding the wire to the sending unit while the ignition is on (engine not running for safety). If the gauge deflects full scale or the light comes on, replace the sending unit.

5   As soon as the engine starts, the light should go out and remain out unless the engine overheats. Failure of the light to go out may be due to a grounded wire between the light and the sending unit, a defective sending unit or a faulty ignition switch. Check the coolant to make sure it's the proper type. Plain water may have too low a boiling point to activate the sending unit.

Replacement

6   If the sending unit must be replaced, simply unscrew it from the engine and install the replacement. Use sealant on the threads. Make sure the engine is cool before removing the defective sending unit. There will be some coolant loss as the unit is removed, so be prepared to catch it. Check the coolant level after the replacement has been installed.

10   Heater and air conditioner blower motor – removal and installation

Refer to illustrations 10.4, 10.7, 10.8 and 10.9

1   Disconnect the negative cable at the battery.
2   Drain the cooling system (see Chapter 1).
3   Remove the lower instrument panel.
4   On air conditioned models, disconnect the two vacuum lines from the recirculating air door actuator (see illustration).
5   Disconnect the blower motor wiring.
6   Remove the two screws that secure the unit cover to the top of the bower housing.
7   Remove the five screws from the perimeter of the blower housing and detach the blower housing (see illustration).
8   Remove the three blower-to-housing screws and lower the blower from the housing (see illustration).
9   To remove the fan from the blower, squeeze the spring clip together (see illustration) and slip the fan off the shaft.
10   Installation is the reverse of removal.

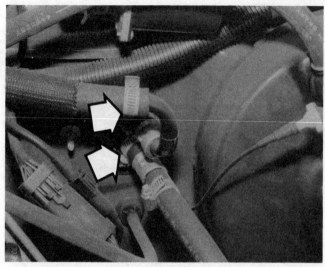

11.4 Disconnect the heater hoses (arrows) where they attach to the heater core at the firewall

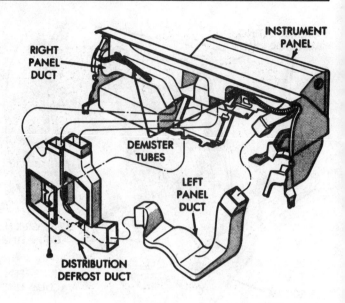

11.6 Remove the center air distribution duct

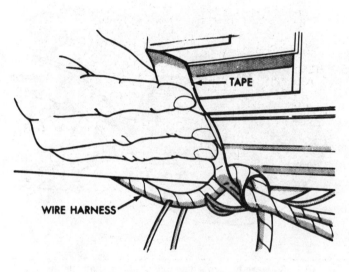

11.7 Tape the wires out of the way

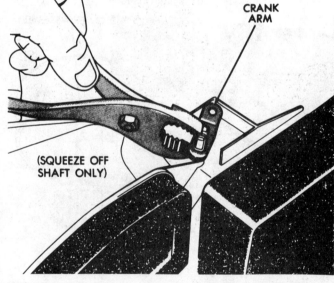

11.11 Use a pair of pliers to remove the clip and crank arm from the shaft of the blend air door

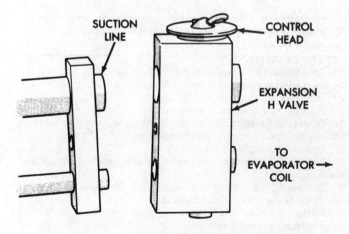

11.12 On air conditioned models, disconnect the expansion valve

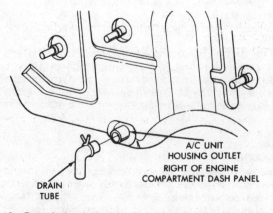

11.13 Detach the drain tube from the evaporator housing

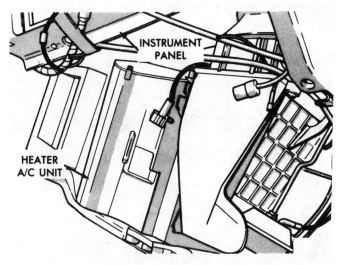

11.16a   Lower the unit from the dash

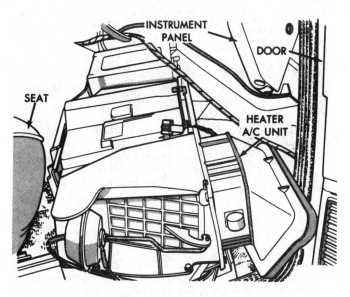

11.16b   Turn the heater unit and lift it out

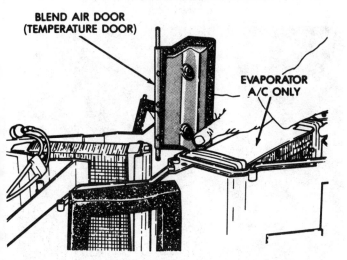

11.17   Remove one 1/4-20 nut from the pivot shaft of the blend air door

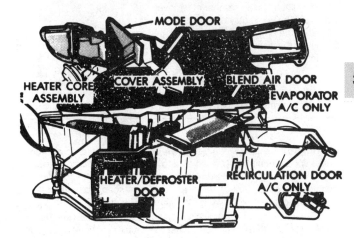

11.19   Remove the cover assembly

11   Heater core – replacement

Refer to illustrations 11.4, 11.6, 11.7, 11.11, 11.12, 11.13, 11.16a, 11.16b, 11.17, 11.19 and 11.20

Warning: *The air conditioning system is under high pressure. DO NOT disconnect any refrigerant fittings until after the system has been discharged by a dealer service department or service station.*

1   On air conditioned models, have the system discharged (see the Warning above).
2   Disconnect the negative cable from the battery.
3   Drain the cooling system (see Chapter 1).
4   Disconnect the heater hoses at the heater core inlet and outlet **(see illustration)** and plug the open fittings.
5   Remove the lower instrument panel.
6   Remove the center (defrost) air distribution duct **(see illustration)**.
7   Label and disconnect the wiring harness. Tape the wires out of the way **(see illustration)**. Remove the terminal insulator retainer from the heater housing support brace.
8   Detach the antenna cable from the retaining clip on the right end of the heater housing.

9   Remove the defroster hoses from the tee fitting at the top of the heater unit.
10   Disconnect the heater control (see Section 16) and the vacuum feed line from the check valve. Label and disconnect any remaining vacuum hoses.
11   Detach the self-adjusting clip and crank from the shaft of the blend air door **(see illustration)**.
12   On air conditioned models, disconnect the refrigerant lines and remove the expansion valve **(see illustration)**. Cap the open fittings to keep dirt and moisture out.
13   On air conditioned models, detach the evaporator housing drain tube **(see illustration)**.
14   Remove the four heater housing mounting nuts from the firewall.
15   Unbolt the support brace and move it aside.
16   Move the heater housing to the rear until the studs clear the holes, then turn the unit so the studs point down. Lift the unit from the vehicle **(see illustrations)**.
17   Remove one 1/4-20 nut from the pivot shaft of the blend air door **(see illustration)**.
18   Label and then disconnect the vacuum lines from the defrost and panel mode vacuum actuators and position them aside.
19   Remove the screws from the heater housing cover and lift the cover off **(see illustration)**.

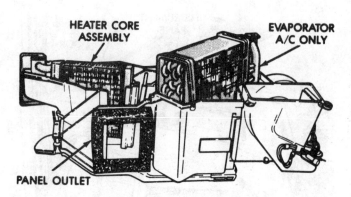

11.20 Remove the heater core mounting screw and lift the core out

20 Remove the mounting screw from the heater core retaining bracket and lift the core from the housing **(see illustration)**.
21 Installation is the reverse of removal.
22 Refill the cooling system (see Chapter 1).
23 Start the engine and check for proper operation.
24 Have the air conditioning system (if equipped) evacuated, recharged and leak tested.

12 Air conditioning system – check and maintenance

Refer to illustrations 12.6 and 12.8
Warning: *The air conditioning system is pressurized at the factory and requires special equipment for service and repair. The system should be discharged by your dealer servicing department or an automotive air conditioning shop. Do not, under any circumstances, disconnect the air conditioning hoses while the system is under pressure.*

1 The following maintenance steps should be performed on a regular basis to ensure that the air conditioner continues to operate at peak efficiency.
  a) Check the tension of the drivebelt and adjust if necessary (see Chapter 1).
  b) Check the condition of the hoses. Look for cracks, hardening and deterioration. **Warning:** *Do not replace air conditioning hoses until the system has been discharged by a dealer or air conditioning shop.*
  c) Check the fins of the condenser for leaves, bugs and other foreign material. A soft brush and compressed air can be used to remove them.
  d) Check the wire harness for correct routing, broken wires, damaged insulation, etc. Make sure the harness connections are clean and tight.
  e) Maintain the correct refrigerant charge.
2 The system should be run for about 10 minutes at least once a month. This is particularly important during the winter months because long-term non-use can cause hardening of the internal seals.
3 Because of the complexity of the air conditioning system and the special equipment required to effectively work on it, accurate troubleshooting of the system should be left to a professional technician. One probable cause for poor cooling that can be determined by the home mechanic is low refrigerant charge. Should the system lose its cooling ability, the following procedure will help you pinpoint the cause.

Check

4 Warm the engine up to normal operating temperature.
5 Place the air conditioning temperature selector at the coldest setting and put the blower at the highest setting. Open the doors (to make sure the

12.6 The sight glass (arrow) is located on the top of the receiver-drier

12.8 Connect the charging kit to the low side fitting on the compressor (marked "S" for suction)

air conditioning system doesn't cycle off as soon as it cools the passenger compartment).
6 With the compressor engaged – the clutch will make an audible click and the center of the clutch will rotate – inspect the sight glass **(see illustration)**. If the refrigerant looks foamy, it's low. Charge the system as described later in this Section. If the refrigerant appears clear, the system is properly charged.

Adding refrigerant

Note: *Due to recent environmental legislation, 14-ounce refrigerant cans may not be available in your area. If this is the case, take the vehicle to a dealer service department or automotive air conditioning shop to have refrigerant added.*

7 Buy an automotive charging kit at an auto parts store. A charging kit includes a 14-ounce can of refrigerant, a tap valve and a short section of hose that can be attached between the tap valve and the system low side service valve. Because one can of refrigerant may not be sufficient to bring the system charge up to the proper level, it's a good idea to buy a few additional cans. Make sure the first can contains red refrigerant dye. If the system is leaking, the red dye will leak out with the refrigerant and help you pinpoint the location of the leak. **Warning:** *Never add more than three cans of refrigerant to the system.*
8 Connect the charging kit by following the manufacturer's instructions **(see illustration)**. **Warning:** *DO NOT hook the charging kit hose to the system high pressure side! Always wear eye protection!*

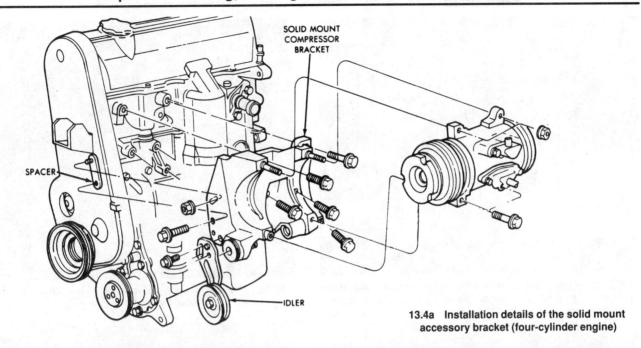

SOLID MOUNT
COMPRESSOR
BRACKET

SPACER

IDLER

13.4a Installation details of the solid mount
accessory bracket (four-cylinder engine)

13.4b Compressor mounting bolt locations
(arrows) – four-cylinder engine

13.4c Remove the brace bolt (arrow) – V6 shown (V8 similar)

13.4d Remove the mounting bolts/nuts on the passenger's side
(arrows) – V6 shown (V8 similar)

13.4e Remove the mounting bolts/nuts on the driver's
side – V6 shown (V8 similar)

3

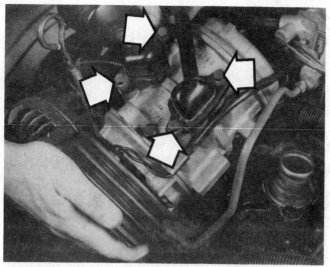

13.4f The compressor on V6 and V8 engines must be tilted down in front and pushed back to clear the rear bracket – if you intend to disconnect the refrigerant hoses, remove the bolts (arrows)

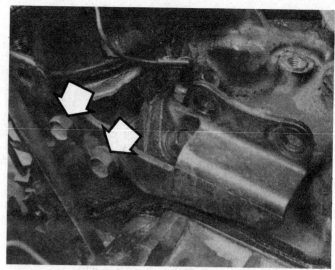

13.4g The rear mounting bracket on V6 and V8 engines is secured by two bolts (arrows)

9　Warm up the engine and turn on the air conditioner. Keep the charging kit hose away from the fan and other moving parts.

10　Place a thermometer in the dashboard vent nearest the evaporator and add refrigerant until the indicated temperature is around 40 to 45-degrees F.

13　Air conditioning compressor – removal and installation

Refer to illustrations 13.4a through 13.4g

Warning: *Have the air conditioning system discharged by a dealer service department or an air conditioning shop before disconnecting refrigerant hoses.*

Removal

1　Disconnect the negative cable at the battery.

2　Disconnect the electrical wiring from the air conditioning compressor

and remove the line fitting bolts from the top of the compressor.

3　Remove the drivebelts (refer to Chapter 1).

4　Remove the compressor-to-bracket bolts and nuts and lift the compressor from the engine compartment **(see illustrations)**.

Installation

5　Place the compressor in position on the bracket and install the nuts and bolts finger tight. Once all the compressor mounting nuts and bolts are installed, tighten them securely.

6　Install the drivebelt (see Chapter 1).

7　Connect the electrical connector to the compressor. Install the line fitting bolt to the compressor, using new O-rings lubricated with clean refrigeration oil, and tighten it securely.

8　Connect the cable to the negative terminal of the battery.

9　Take the vehicle to a dealer service department or an air conditioning shop and have the system evacuated and recharged. **Note:** *If the compressor is replaced, add 7.25 oz of refrigerant oil to it.*

14.4 Remove the vertical support brace bolts (arrow)

14.5 Unbolt the refrigerant line fitting (arrow)

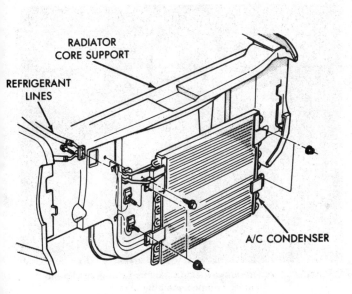

14.6   Condenser mounting details

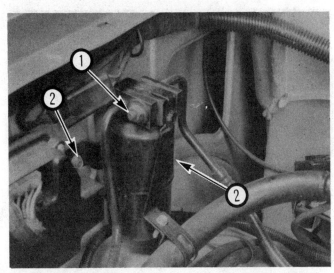

15.2   Remove the through-bolt and mounting bolts – one mounting bolt is located on the far side of the receiver-drier

1   *Through-bolt*   2   *Mounting bolts*

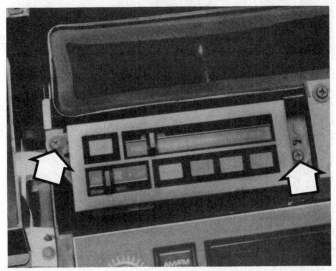

16.3   Remove the screws securing the control assembly to the dash (arrows)

---

14   Air conditioning condenser – removal and installation

Refer to illustrations 14.4, 14.5 and 14.6
Warning: *Have the air conditioning system discharged by a dealer service department or an air conditioning shop before beginning this procedure.*

1   Disconnect the negative cable at the battery.
2   Remove the radiator (see Section 3).
3   Remove the grille assembly (see Chapter 11).
4   Remove the vertical support brace **(see illustration)**.
5   Disconnect the refrigerant line fittings **(see illustration)** and cap the open fittings.
6   Remove the condenser mounting bolts/nuts **(see illustration)**.
7   Lift the condenser from the vehicle.
8   Installation is the reverse of removal. Be sure to use new O-rings on the refrigerant line fittings (lubricate the O-rings with clean refrigerant oil).

9   Have the system evacuated, recharged and leak tested by the shop that discharged it. If a new condenser is installed, add 1 oz of refrigerant oil.

---

15   Air conditioning receiver-drier – removal and installation

Refer to illustration 15.2
Warning: *Have the air conditioning system discharged by a dealer service department or an air conditioning shop before beginning this procedure.*

Removal
1   Disconnect the negative cable at the battery.
2   Remove the through-bolt and disconnect the refrigerant inlet and outlet lines **(see illustration)**. Cap or plug the open lines immediately.
3   Remove the mounting bolts and detach the receiver-drier assembly.

Installation
4   If you are replacing the receiver-drier, add one ounce of fresh refrigerant oil to the new unit.
5   Place the new receiver-drier into position, install the mounting bolts and tighten them securely.
6   Install the inlet and outlet lines, using clean refrigerant oil on the new O-rings. Tighten the through-bolt securely.
7   Connect the cable to the negative terminal of the battery.
8   Have the system evacuated, recharged and leak tested by a dealer service department or an air conditioning shop.

---

16   Air conditioner and heater control assembly – removal and installation

Refer to illustrations 16.3, 16.5, 16.6a, 16.6b and 16.7
1   Disconnect the negative cable from the battery.
2   Remove the steering column cover and detach the instrument panel bezel (see Chapter 11).
3   Remove the two mounting screws from the air conditioning/heater control assembly **(see illustration)**.
4   Pull the control out from the dash enough to detach the cables and hoses and wiring.

16.5 Working from below the control, unclip the electrical connector (arrow) and disconnect it

16.6a Push in on the locking tab (arrow) and unclip the cable assembly

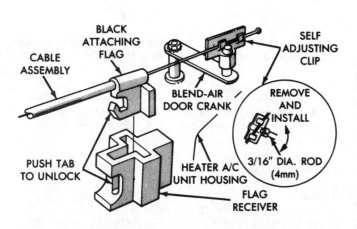

16.6b Use a 3/16-inch diameter rod (a drill bit will work) to remove or install the self adjusting clip

16.7 Disconnect the color-coded vacuum hoses

5   Detach the electrical connector by bending back the locking tab **(see illustration)**.
6   Release the locking tab on the temperature control cable with a 3/16-inch diameter rod **(see illustrations)**.

7   Disconnect the vacuum hoses from the control assembly **(see illustration)**.
8   To install the control, reverse the removal procedure.

Chapter 4   Fuel and exhaust systems

Contents

Specifications

Carburetor adjustments

Accelerator pump stroke (distance between top of pump lever to top of bowl vent cover surface) – 3.9L (Holley 6280) ..	1/8 to 9/64 in
Choke unloader (gap between choke plate and air horn)	
3.9L (Holley 6280)	
Holley No. R-40218A	1/4 in
All others	11/32 in
Choke vacuum kick	
2.2L (Holley 6520)	5/64 in
3.9L (Holley 6280)	
Auto. Trans	9/64 in
Manual Trans	5/32 in
Fast idle speed	refer to the Vehicle Emissions Control Information (VECI) label
Fast idle cam (gap between choke plate and air horn) – 3.9L (Holley 6520)	1/16 in

Idle speed	refer to the Vehicle Emissions Control Information (VECI) label
Float drop – 2.2L (Holley 6520)	1-7/8 in
Float level	
2.2L (Holley 6520)	1/2 in
3.9L (Holley 6280)	9/32 in

Fuel Pressure

Carbureted	
2.2L	4-1/2 to 6 psi
3.9L	4 to 7-1/4 psi
Fuel injection	
TBI	14.5 psi
MPI	
At idle with vacuum hose connected to the pressure regulator ..	31 psi
At idle with vacuum hose disconnected from the pressure regulator	39 psi

Torque specifications   **Ft–lbs** (unless otherwise indicated)

Fuel fitting on TBI unit	15
Pressure regulator retaining screws (TBI)	40 in–lbs
Throttle body mounting bolts	
TBI system	
Four–cylinder engine	175 in–lbs
V6 and V8 engines	168 in–lbs
MPI system	200 in–lbs

1   General information

These models may be equipped with either a carburetor or an Electronic Fuel Injection (EFI) system. Two types of EFI systems are used: a Muti-Port Injection (MPI) system and a Throttle Body Injection (TBI) system. The fuel system consists of a rear mounted fuel tank, a mechanical (mounted on the engine – carbureted models) or electric (located in the fuel tank – EFI models) fuel pump which supplies fuel to the carburetor or fuel injection system, and associated hoses, lines and filters. The exhaust system is made up of pipes, heat shields, a muffler and catalytic converter(s). The use of the catalytic converter(s) requires that only unleaded fuel be used in the vehicle.

2   Fuel pressure relief procedure (fuel-injection models)

Refer to illustrations 2.4, 2.7a and 2.7b
Warning: *Gasoline is extremely flammable, so take extra precautions when you work on any part of the fuel system. Don't smoke or allow open flames or bare light bulbs near the work area, and don't work in a garage where a natural gas-type appliance (such as a water heater or clothes dryer) with a pilot light is present. If you spill any fuel on your skin, rinse it off immediately with soap and water. When you perform any kind of work on the fuel system, wear safety glasses and have a Class B type fire extinguisher on hand.*
1   The fuel system on fuel injected models is pressurized, even when the engine is off. Consequently, any time the fuel system is worked on (such as when the fuel filter is replaced) the system must be depressurized to avoid the dangerous release of fuel when a component is disconnected.

Thottle body injection

2   Loosen the fuel tank cap to release any pressure in the tank.
3   Unplug the electrical connector from the fuel injector.
4   Ground the injector terminal No. 1 and connect a jumper wire between terminal No. 2 and battery voltage **(see illustration)**. Be very careful not to create a direct short by touching the jumper wires together. **Caution:** *Do not ground the injector terminal for more than five seconds. To avoid damage to the fuel injector, it is recommended that the pressure*

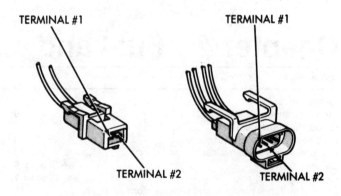

2.4   To relieve the fuel pressure, ground the injector terminal #1 and apply battery voltage to terminal #2 (be careful not to cause a direct short or energize the injector for more than five seconds)

be bled in several spurts of one or two seconds to make sure the injector is not damaged. The fuel pressure can be heard escaping into the throttle body or combustion chamber; when the sound is no longer heard, the system is depressurized.

Multi-point injection

5   Loosen the fuel tank cap to release any pressure in the fuel tank.
6   Detach the cable from the negative terminal of the battery.
7   Remove the protective cap from the pressure test port **(see illustrations)**.
8   Disconnect the gauge, in the special fuel pressure gauge tool set (Chrysler tool number 5069, or equivalent), from the fuel hose in the tool set. Place the gauge end of the hose into an approved gasoline container.
9   Wrap a shop towel around the test port fitting.
10   To release the pressure, screw the other end of the hose onto the fuel pressure port and drain the fuel into the container. Be careful not to let the fuel spray into the engine compartment.
11   Unscrew the hose from the fitting and reinstall the protective cap.

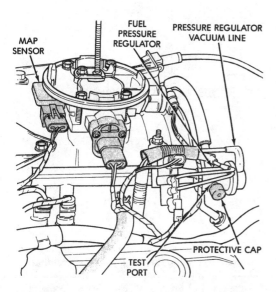

2.7a Remove the protective cap from the pressure test port (V6 engine)

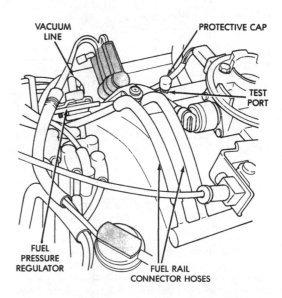

2.7b Test port location on V8 engines

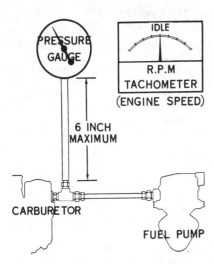

3.1 When checking the fuel pressure, attach the T-fitting as close to the carburetor as possible and use a six-inch maximum length hose

3   Fuel pump – testing

Warning: *Gasoline is extremely flammable, so take extra precautions when you work on any part of the fuel system. Don't smoke or allow open flames or bare light bulbs near the work area, and don't work in a garage where a natural gas-type appliance (such as a water heater or clothes dryer) with a pilot light is present. If you spill any fuel on your skin, rinse it off immediately with soap and water. When you perform any kind of work on the fuel system, wear safety glasses and have a Class B type fire extinguisher on hand.*

2.2L carbureted engine

Refer to illustration 3.1

1   Disconnect the fuel line from the carburetor and install a T-fitting. Connect a fuel pressure gauge to the T-fitting with a section of fuel hose that is no longer than six inches **(see illustration)**.

2   Disconnect the gauge from the end of the fuel hose and direct the end of the hose into a metal container. Operate the starter until fuel spurts out of the hose, to bleed the hose (this eliminates any air in the hose, which could affect the pressure reading). Reattach the gauge to the fuel hose.
3   Start the engine and allow it to idle. The pressure on the gauge should be as listed in this Chapter's Specifications, remain constant and return to zero slowly when the engine is shut off.
4   An instant pressure drop indicates a faulty outlet valve and the fuel pump must be replaced.
5   If the pressure is too high, check the air vent to see if it is plugged before replacing the pump.
6   If the pressure is too low, be sure the fuel inlet line is not plugged before replacing the pump.

Fuel-injected engines

Preliminary inspection
7   If the fuel system fails to deliver the proper amount of fuel, or any fuel at all, to the fuel-injection system, inspect it as follows.
8   Always make sure there's fuel in the tank.
9   With the engine running, check for leaks at the threaded fittings at both ends of the fuel lines. Tighten any loose connections. Inspect all hoses for flat spots and kinks which would restrict the flow of fuel.
10   Be sure the fuel pump operates when the engine is cranked over. This can be determined by removing the fuel filler cap and listening for the characteristic whirring noise of the pump, as an assistant turns the ignition key to the Start position. If it doesn't make any noise, the electrical circuitry to the pump, or the pump itself, is bad. **Note:** *The auto shutdown relay must receive a tachometer signal from the distributor in order to for the fuel pump power circuit to be energized.*

Pressure check
11   Relieve the fuel system pressure (see Section 2).
12   On TBI models, disconnect the fuel feed hose at the inlet fitting and attach a fuel pressure gauge using a T-fitting.
13   On multi–port injection (MPI) models, disconnect the vacuum supply line from the fuel pressure regulator. **Note:** *This vacuum line must be disconnected to obtain an accurate fuel pressure reading.*
14   On MPI models, remove the protective cap from the test port, then connect the fuel pressure test gauge (Chrysler tool 5069, or equivalent) to the test port **(see illustration 2.7a or 2.7b)**.
15   Crank the engine (if it won't start) or start the engine. if the pressure is within the range listed in this Chapter's Specifications, no further testing is necessary. If the pressure is higher than specified, check for a restricted fuel return line. If the line is okay, replace the fuel pressure regulator.

4

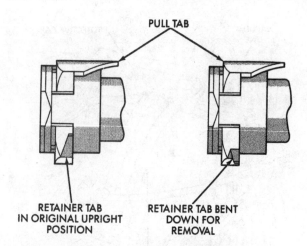

4.11a Bend the retaining tab down with your fingers

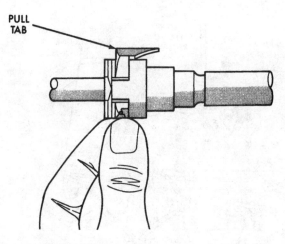

4.11b Push up on the bottom side of the pull tab, then release the retainer legs by pulling them away from each other

16   If the pressure was less than specified, pinch the hose between the gauge and the TBI unit or fuel rail (while cranking or running the engine). If the pressure increases, replace the fuel pressure regulator. If there isn't any pressure, check for a plugged fuel filter, plugged fuel pump inlet filter or restricted fuel line. If the filters and lines are not obstructed, replace the fuel pump.

---

4   Fuel lines and fittings – repair and replacement

Warning: *Gasoline is extremely flammable, so take extra precautions when you work on any part of the fuel system. Don't smoke or allow open flames or bare light bulbs near the work area, and don't work in a garage where a natural gas-type appliance (such as a water heater or clothes dryer) with a pilot light is present. If you spill any fuel on your skin, rinse it off immediately with soap and water. When you perform any kind of work on the fuel system, wear safety glasses and have a Class B type fire extinguisher on hand.*

Inspection

1   Once in a while, you will have to raise the vehicle to service or replace some component (an exhaust pipe hanger, for example). Whenever you work under the vehicle, always inspect the fuel lines and fittings for possible damage or deterioration.
2   Check all hoses and pipes for cracks, kinks, deformation or obstructions.
3   Make sure all hose and pipe clips attach their associated hoses or pipes securely to the underside of the vehicle.
4   Verify all hose clamps attaching rubber hoses to metal fuel lines or pipes are snug enough to assure a tight fit between the hoses and pipes.

Replacement (1987 through 1991)

5   If you must replace any damaged sections, use original equipment replacement hoses or pipes constructed from exactly the same material as the section you are replacing. Do not install substitutes constructed from inferior or inappropriate material, as this could result in a fuel leak or a fire.
6   Always, before detaching or disassembling any part of the fuel line system, note the routing of all hoses and pipes and the orientation of all clamps and clips to assure that replacement sections are installed in exactly the same manner.
7   Before detaching any part of the fuel system, be sure to relieve the fuel tank pressure by removing the fuel filler cap. On fuel injected vehicles, also relieve the fuel system pressure (see Section 2).
8   Whenever fittings that are sealed by copper washers are removed, be sure to replace the washers with new ones. Also, use new hose clamps after loosening or removing them.
9   While you're under the vehicle, it's a good idea to check the following related components:

a) Check the condition of the fuel filter – make sure that it's not clogged or damaged (see Chapter 1).
b) Inspect the evaporative emission control system. Verify that all hoses are attached and in good condition (see Chapter 6).

Replacement (1992 and later)

Refer to illustrations 4.11a and 4.11b
Warning: *The fuel pressure must be relieved before any lines can be disconnected (see Section 2).*
10   Quick–disconnect–type fittings are used at various locations in the fuel system. These fittings must be disconnected correctly; otherwise they will be damaged. **Caution:** *If the retainer tab or removable pull tab is not bent down correctly prior to disconnecting the fitting, the connector could be damaged and must be replaced.*
11   Bend the retainer tab down **(see illustration)**. While pushing up on the bottom side of the pull tab, release the retainer legs by pulling them away from each other **(see illustration)**.
12   Raise the pull tab until the hooks on the retainer legs clear the stop on the fuel line nipple.
13   Grasp the connector and pull it straight off the fuel line. Some adhesion between the seals in the connector and the fuel line will occur over a period of time. Twist the fitting on the fuel line, then push and pull the fitting until it moves freely.
14   Inspect the connector body and retainer for damage. Inspect the inside of the fitting to ensure that it's free of dirt and/or obstructions. Replace as necessary.
15   Before reinstalling the fuel line into the connector, wipe the fuel line end with a clean cloth, then apply clean engine oil to the outer surface of the fuel line.
16   To reinstall the fuel line into the connector, align them and push the fuel line into place until it stops. Push the retainer down until it locks in place. Pull on the connector to ensure that it's completely engaged.
17   After reassembly, run the engine and check for fuel leaks.

---

5   Fuel tank – removal and installation

Refer to illustrations 5.6a, 5.6b, 5.6c, 5.6d and 5.9
Warning: *Gasoline is extremely flammable, so take extra precautions when you work on any part of the fuel system. Don't smoke or allow open flames or bare light bulbs near the work area, and don't work in a garage where a natural gas-type appliance (such as a water heater or clothes dryer) with a pilot light is present. If you spill any fuel on your skin, rinse it off immediately with soap and water. When you perform any kind of work on the fuel system, wear safety glasses and have a Class B type fire extinguisher on hand.*
Note: *The following procedure is much easier to perform if the fuel tank is empty. Some tanks have a drain plug for this purpose. If the tank does not*

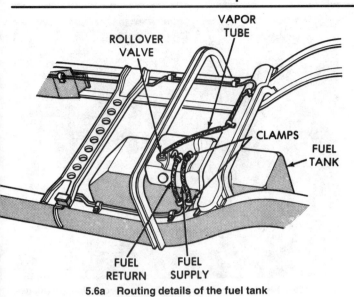

5.6a   Routing details of the fuel tank lines (2.2L engine)

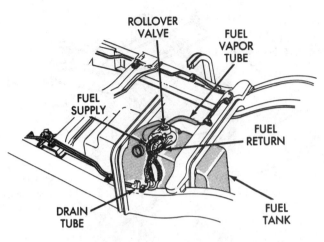

5.6b   Routing details of the fuel tank lines (2.5L, 3.9L and 5.2L engines)

have a drain plug, drain the fuel into an approved fuel container using a commercially available siphoning kit (NEVER start a siphoning action by mouth) or wait until the fuel tank is nearly empty, if possible.

1   Remove the fuel tank filler cap to relieve fuel tank pressure.
2   If the vehicle is fuel-injected, relieve the fuel system pressure (see Section 2).
3   Detach the cable from the negative terminal of the battery.
4   If the tank still has fuel in it, you can drain it at the fuel feed line after raising the vehicle. If the tank has a drain plug, remove it and allow the fuel to collect in an approved gasoline container.
5   Raise the vehicle and place it securely on jackstands.
6   Disconnect the fuel lines, the vapor return line and the fuel filler tube **(see illustrations). Note:** *The fuel feed and return lines and the vapor return line are three different diameters, so reattachment is simplified. If you have any doubts, however, clearly label the three lines and the fittings. Be sure to plug the hoses to prevent leakage and contamination of the fuel system.*
7   If there is still fuel in the tank, siphon it out from the fuel feed port. Remember – NEVER start the siphoning action by mouth! Use a siphoning kit, which can be purchased at most auto parts stores.

8   Support the fuel tank with a floor jack. Position a piece of wood between the jack head and the fuel tank to protect the tank.
9   Disconnect both fuel tank retaining straps and pivot them down until they are hanging out of the way **(see illustration)**.
10   Lower the tank enough to disconnect the electrical wires and ground strap from the fuel pump/fuel gauge sending unit, if you have not already done so.
11   Remove the tank from the vehicle.
12   Installation is the reverse of removal.

6   Fuel tank cleaning and repair – general information

1   All repairs to the fuel tank or filler neck should be carried out by a professional who has experience in this critical and potentially dangerous work. Even after cleaning and flushing of the fuel system, explosive fumes can remain and ignite during repair of the tank.
2   If the fuel tank is removed from the vehicle, it should not be placed in an area where sparks or open flames could ignite the fumes coming out of the tank. Be especially careful inside garages where a natural gas-type appliance is located, because the pilot light could cause an explosion.

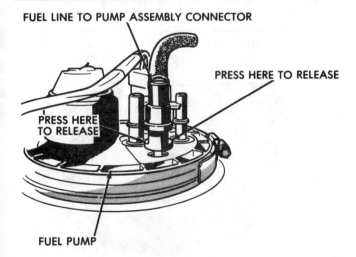

5.6c   The bottom of the hose connector for the fuel feed line must be squeezed to release it from the pump (EFI engines)

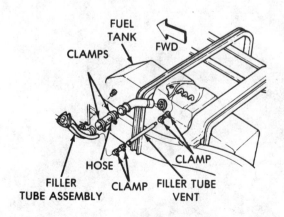

5.6d   Details of the fuel filler tube (midframe-mounted 15 and 22 gallon fuel tanks)

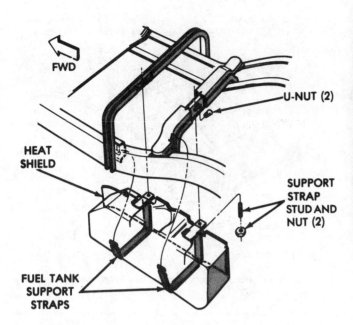

5.9   To remove the fuel tank, support the tank and remove the support strap nuts, then carefully lower the straps, then the tank

---

7   Fuel pump – removal and installation

Warning: *Gasoline is extremely flammable, so take extra precautions when you work on any part of the fuel system. Don't smoke or allow open flames or bare light bulbs near the work area, and don't work in a garage where a natural gas-type appliance (such as a water heater or clothes dryer) with a pilot light is present. If you spill any fuel on your skin, rinse it off immediately with soap and water. When you perform any kind of work on the fuel system, wear safety glasses and have a Class B type fire extinguisher on hand.*

Mechanical fuel pump (carbureted models)
Refer to illustrations 7.3 and 7.4

1   On 3.9L engines, the fuel pump is bolted to the right front of the engine block. On 2.2L engines, the fuel pump is mounted on the left front of the engine.

7.4   A ratchet, socket and proper length extension makes removing the fuel pump easier

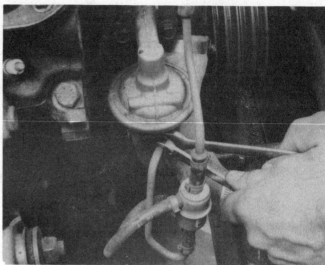

7.3   When breaking the lines loose for the mechanical pump, use a flare-nut wrench and a backup wrench

2   On all models, place rags under the fuel pump to catch any gasoline which is spilled during removal.
3   Carefully unscrew the fuel line fittings and detach the lines from the pump. A flare-nut wrench along with a backup wrench should be used to prevent damage to the line fittings **(see illustration)**.
4   Unbolt and remove the fuel pump **(see illustration)**.
5   Before installation, coat both sides of the gasket surface with RTV sealant, position the gasket and fuel pump against the block and install the bolts, tightening them securely.
6   Attach the lines to the pump and tighten the fittings securely (use a flare-nut wrench, if one is available, to prevent damage to the fittings).
7   Run the engine and check for leaks.

Electric fuel pump (models with throttle body injection)
Refer to illustrations 7.9 and 7.12

8   Remove fuel tank from the vehicle (see Section 5).
9   Push down on the fuel pump (it's under slight spring tension), then loosen the retaining clamp which secures the fuel pump to the fuel tank **(see illustration)**.
10   Carefully lift the unit from the tank.
11   Wipe the sealing area of tank clean and place a new O-ring seal in position on the fuel pump assembly.

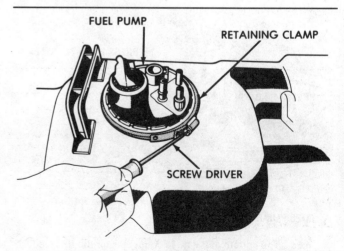

7.9   To remove the fuel pump from the fuel tank, you must remove the retaining clamp

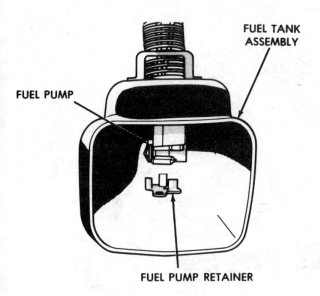

7.12   When installing the fuel pump, be sure to align it with the retainer at the bottom of the tank

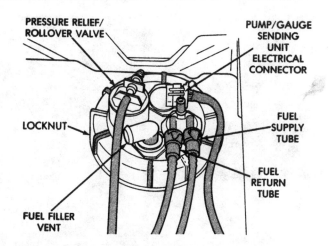

7.17   Unscrew the large locknut securing the fuel pump assembly to the fuel tank

12   Align the fuel pump with the retainer on the bottom of the tank and push the pump into the retainer **(see illustration)**.
13   Install and tighten the holding clamp.
14   The remainder of installation is the reverse of removal.
15   Be sure to check for any fuel leaks and repair if necessary.

Electric fuel pump (models with multi–port injection)

Refer to illustration 7.17
Caution: *Whenever the fuel pump unit is serviced, the lock nut and gasket must be replaced.*

16   Remove the fuel tank from the vehicle (see Section 5).
17   Unscrew the large locknut securing the fuel pump assembly to the fuel tank **(see illustration)**. If the locknut cannot be loosened by hand, use a brass punch (not steel!) and hammer and carefully tap on one of the raised ridges to break it loose.
18   Carefully lift the unit from the tank and discard the gasket.
19   Wipe the sealing area of the tank clean and place a new gasket in position on the fuel pump assembly.
20   Install the fuel pump unit into the fuel tank and install the new locknut. Tighten the locknut securely.
21   The remainder of the installation is the reverse of removal.
22   Be sure to check for fuel leaks and repair if necessary.

8   Carburetor – diagnosis and overhaul

Warning: *Gasoline is extremely flammable, so take extra precautions when you work on any part of the fuel system. Don't smoke or allow open flames or bare light bulbs near the work area, and don't work in a garage where a natural gas-type appliance (such as a water heater or clothes dryer) with a pilot light is present. If you spill any fuel on your skin, rinse it off immediately with soap and water. When you perform any kind of work on the fuel system, wear safety glasses and have a Class B type fire extinguisher on hand.*

Diagnosis

1   A thorough road test and check of carburetor adjustments should be done before any major carburetor service work. Specifications for some adjustments are listed on the Vehicle Emissions Control Information (VECI) label found in the engine compartment.

2   Carburetor problems usually show up as flooding, hard starting, stalling, severe backfiring and poor acceleration. A carburetor that's leaking fuel and/or covered with wet looking deposits definitely needs attention.
3   Some performance complaints directed at the carburetor are actually a result of loose, out-of-adjustment or malfunctioning engine or electrical components. Others develop when vacuum hoses leak, are disconnected or are incorrectly routed. The proper approach to analyzing carburetor problems should include the following items:

  a)   Inspect all vacuum hoses and actuators for leaks and correct installation (see Chapters 1 and 6).
  b)   Tighten the intake manifold and carburetor mounting nuts/bolts evenly and securely.
  c)   Perform a cylinder compression test (see Chapter 2).
  d)   Clean or replace the spark plugs as necessary (see Chapter 1).
  e)   Check the spark plug wires (see Chapter 1).
  f)   Inspect the ignition primary wires.
  g)   Check the ignition timing (follow the instructions printed on the Emissions Control Information label).
  h)   Check the fuel pump pressure/volume (see Section 2).
  i)   Check the heat control valve in the air cleaner for proper operation (see Chapter 1).
  j)   Check/replace the air filter element (see Chapter 1).
  k)   Check the PCV system (see Chapter 6).
  l)   Check/replace the fuel filter (see Chapter 1). Also, the strainer in the tank could be restricted.
  m)   Check for a plugged exhaust system.
  n)   Check EGR valve operation (see Chapter 6).
  o)   Check the choke – it should be completely open at normal engine operating temperature (see Chapter 1).
  p)   Check for fuel leaks and kinked or dented fuel lines (see Chapters 1 and 4)
  q)   Check accelerator pump operation with the engine off (remove the air cleaner cover and operate the throttle as you look into the carburetor throat – you should see a stream of gasoline enter the carburetor).
  r)   Check for incorrect fuel or bad gasoline.
  s)   Check the valve clearances (if applicable) and camshaft lobe lift (see Chapters 1 and 2)
  t)   Have a dealer service department or repair shop check the electronic engine and carburetor controls.

4   Diagnosing carburetor problems may require that the engine be started and run with the air cleaner off. While running the engine without the air cleaner, backfires are possible. This situation is likely to occur if the carburetor is malfunctioning, but just the removal of the air cleaner can lean the fuel/air mixture enough to produce an engine backfire. **Warning:** *Do not position any part of your body, especially your face, directly over the carburetor during inspection and servicing procedures. Wear eye protection!*

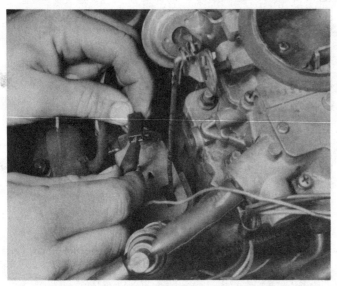

9.1   Apply 12-volts to the choke heater connector. The choke should open in about five minutes (2.2L carbureted)

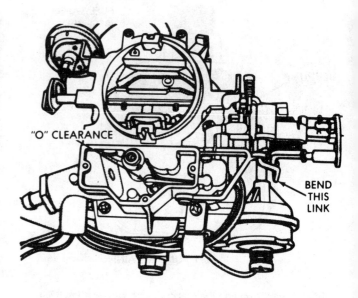

10.3   Adjust the accelerator pump stroke by bending the linkage (3.9L models)

Overhaul

5   Once it's determined that the carburetor needs an overhaul, several options are available. If you're going to attempt to overhaul the carburetor yourself, first obtain a good quality carburetor rebuild kit (which will include all necessary gaskets, internal parts, instructions and a parts list). You'll also need some special solvent and a means of blowing out the internal passages of the carburetor with air.

6   An alternative is to obtain a new or rebuilt carburetor. They are readily available from dealers and auto parts stores. Make absolutely sure the exchange carburetor is identical to the original. A tag is usually attached to the top of the carburetor or a number is stamped on the float bowl. It will help determine the exact type of carburetor you have. When obtaining a rebuilt carburetor or a rebuild kit, make sure the kit or carburetor matches your application exactly. Seemingly insignificant differences can make a large difference in engine performance.

7   If you choose to overhaul your own carburetor, allow enough time to disassemble it carefully, soak the necessary parts in the cleaning solvent (usually for at least one-half day or according to the instructions listed on the carburetor cleaner) and reassemble it, which will usually take much longer than disassembly. When disassembling the carburetor, match each part with the illustration in the carburetor kit and lay the parts out in order on a clean work surface. Overhauls by inexperienced mechanics can result in an engine which runs poorly or not at all. To avoid this, use care and patience when disassembling the carburetor so you can reassemble it correctly.

8   Because carburetor designs are constantly modified by the manufacturer in order to meet increasingly more stringent emissions regulations, it isn't feasible to include a step-by-step overhaul of each type. You'll receive a detailed, well illustrated set of instructions with the carburetor overhaul kit.

9   Automatic choke – testing

Refer to illustration 9.1

Caution: *If there is any loss of electrical current to the choke heater, operation of any type, including idling, should be avoided. Loss of power to the choke will cause the choke to remain fully on (closed) during engine operation. A very rich air-to-fuel mixture will be created and result in abnormally high exhaust system temperatures, which may cause damage to the catalytic converter or other underbody parts of the vehicle.*

1   Using a jumper wire, apply 12-volts to the electrical connector at the choke heater. Be sure it opens completely in about five minutes or replacement is necessary **(see illustration)**.

2   If the choke heater tests okay but the choke valve does not open, check for voltage to the choke heater when oil pressure is above four psi.

3   If no voltage is present in Step 2, repair the open in the power circuit to the choke heater.

10   Carburetor adjustments

Accelerator pump stroke (3.9L models)

Refer to illustration 10.3

1   Remove the cover plate and the gasket for the bowl vent.

2   With the pump links and levers installed, back out the idle speed screw to close the throttle plate.

3   By bending the pump linkage, set the distance from the top of the pump lever to the top of bowl vent cover to the value listed in this Chapter's Specifications **(see illustration)**. There should be no clearance between the end of the pump lever and the pump plunger. **Note:** *Be sure wide open throttle can be obtained without binding.*

4   Install the gasket and the bowl vent cover plate.

5   Reset the idle speed.

Air conditioning idle speed (2.2L models)

Refer to illustration 10.8

Note: *Air conditioned vehicles are equipped with a solenoid kicker. It is not possible to set the air conditioning idle speed, but the kicker operation should be checked.*

6   Run engine until normal operating temperature is reached.

7   Turn on the air conditioning and set the temperature control lever to the coldest position.

8   As the air conditioning compressor clutch cycles off and on, the kicker plunger should move in and out **(see illustration)**. If the plunger moves in and out as the compressor cycles, go to step 11. If the plunger does not operate properly go to the next step.

9   Remove the air cleaner.

10   Check the kicker vacuum hoses for leaks and check the operation of the vacuum solenoid. If no problems are found, turn off the engine and replace the kicker. Repeat Steps 6 through 8.

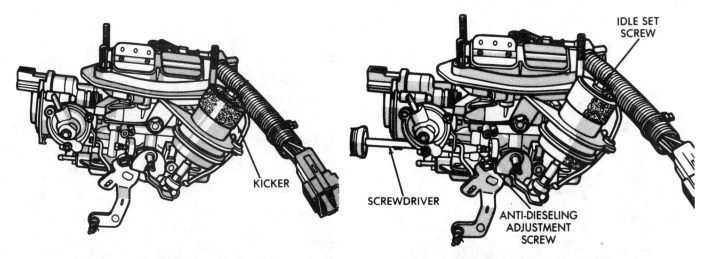

10.8   The kicker plunger should extend and raise the idle when the air conditioning compressor cycles on (2.2L models)

10.17   With the throttle kicker solenoid deactivated, adjust the anti-dieseling stop screw so the engine idle is 700 RPM (2.2L models)

11   Turn off the air conditioning.
12   Turn off the engine and install the air cleaner if removed.

Anti-dieseling adjustment (2.2L models)

Refer to illustration 10.17

13   Check ignition timing and adjust it if necessary (see Chapter 1).
14   With the engine fully warmed up, place the transaxle in neutral and set the parking brake.
15   Be sure the headlights and accessories are off.
16   Remove the red wire from the six-way electrical connector on the carburetor side of the connector.
17   Adjust the anti-dieseling stop screw so the engine speed is at 700 rpm **(see illustration)**.
18   Reconnect the red wire at the connector.

Choke unloader adjustment (3.9L models)

Refer to illustration 10.21

19   With the engine off, hold the throttle valve in the wide open position.
20   Using light pressure on the choke shaft lever, move the choke valve toward the closed position.

21   Using the specified thickness gauge (or drill bit), measure the clearance between the center of the choke valve and the air horn **(see illustration)**.
22   Adjust the clearance by bending the tang on the accelerator pump lever.

Choke vacuum kick adjustment

2.2L models

Refer to illustration 10.27

23   Open the throttle, close the choke and close the throttle to catch the fast idle system in a closed choke condition.
24   Disconnect vacuum hose from choke diaphragm.
25   Using a vacuum pump, apply fifteen or more inches to the choke diaphragm.
26   Use just enough force to position the choke valve at it's smallest opening possible without distorting the linkage.
27   Measure the choke opening by inserting a drill bit or gauge in the center of the area between top of the choke valve and air horn wall **(see illustration)**. For the drill or the gauge size to be used, see the Specifications at the beginning of this Chapter.

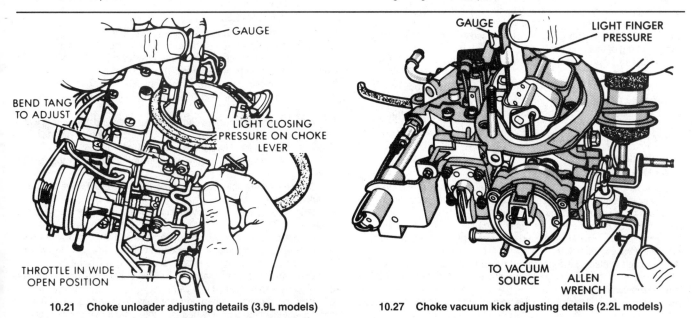

10.21   Choke unloader adjusting details (3.9L models)

10.27   Choke vacuum kick adjusting details (2.2L models)

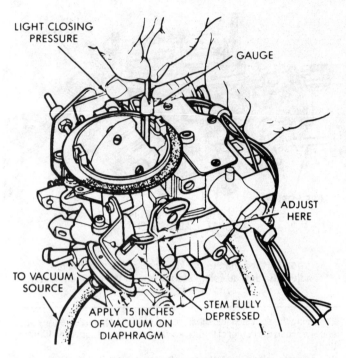

10.34   Choke vacuum kick adjusting details (3.9L models)

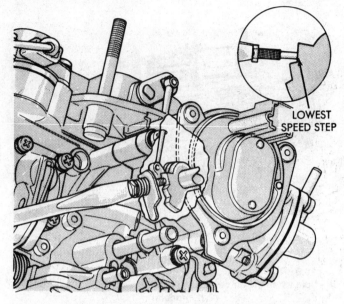

10.50   Adjust fast idle on the lowest step of the fast idle cam (2.2L models)

28   Adjust the choke opening by rotating the Allen head screw located in the center of the diaphragm housing.
29   Replace the vacuum hose on the choke diaphragm.

3.9L models

Refer to illustration 10.34

30   Open the throttle, close the choke and close the throttle to trap the fast idle cam at the closed choke position.
31   Disconnect the choke diaphragm vacuum hose from the carburetor.
32   Using a vacuum pump, apply fifteen or more inches of vacuum to the choke diaphragm.
33   Apply just enough closing force on the choke shaft lever to completely compress the spring in the diaphragm stem. **Note:** *The stem of the diaphragm extends to a stop as the spring compresses.*
34   Measure the choke opening by inserting a drill bit or gauge in the center of the area between top of the choke valve and air horn wall **(see illustration)**. For the drill or the gauge size to be used, see the Specifications at the beginning of this Chapter.
35   Adjust the clearance by bending the U-bend in the diaphragm linkage open or closed.
36   Check for free movement between the open and closed positions. Adjust any interference or misalignment.
37   Reconnect the vacuum hose on the proper carburetor fitting.

Fast idle speed adjustment

2.2L models

Refer to illustration 10.50

38   Check the ignition timing and adjust if necessary (see Section 1).
39   Set the parking brake and place the transmission in neutral.
40   Turn off the lights and the accessories.
41   Connect a tachometer to the ignition coil.
42   Start the engine and warm it up to normal operating temperature.
43   Allow the engine to idle.
44   Unplug the electrical connector at the radiator fan.
45   Using a jumper wire, apply battery voltage to the fan connector (so the fan will run continuously).
46   Remove the PCV valve from the engine and allow the valve to suck air.

47   Disconnect the electrical connector from the kicker vacuum control solenoid.
48   Disconnect the vacuum hoses from the Coolant Vacuum Switch Cold Closed (CVSCC) valve and plug both hoses.
49   Place the fast idle speed screw on the lowest step of the fast idle cam.
50   With the choke fully open, adjust the fast idle speed screw to the correct RPM by turning the fast idle speed screw **(see illustration)**. Return the engine speed to idle.
51   Reposition the adjusting screw on the lowest step of the fast idle cam and verify the fast idle speed. Readjust if necessary.
52   Return the engine to idle, remove the jumper wire and reconnect the radiator fan connector.
53   Reconnect the PCV valve, the kicker vacuum control solenoid harness and the CVSCC hoses.

3.9L models

Refer to illustration 10.56

54   Check the ignition timing and adjust if necessary.
55   To gain access to the fast idle cam, remove the air cleaner assembly.
56   Place the fast idle speed adjusting screw on the second highest step on the fast idle cam **(see illustration)**.
57   Use light closing pressure on the choke lever.
58   Measure the clearance between center of choke plate and air horn wall.
59   Adjust the clearance between the choke plate and the air horn wall to the gap listed in this Chapter's Specifications, by opening or closing the U-bend in the fast idle linkage **(see illustration 10.56).**
60   Using a jumper wire, ground the carburetor switch on the vacuum kicker.
61   Disconnect and plug the vacuum hoses at the EGR valve and the air switching valve.
62   Disconnect and plug the 3/16-inch diameter canister purge control hose.
63   Remove the PCV valve from the engine and allow it to suck air.
64   Connect a tachometer to the ignition coil.
65   Start and run the engine to normal operating temperature.
66   Open the throttle and place the fast idle adjusting screw on the second highest step of the fast idle cam.
67   With the choke fully open, turn the fast idle adjusting screw until the correct fast idle speed is obtained (see this Chapter's Specifications).

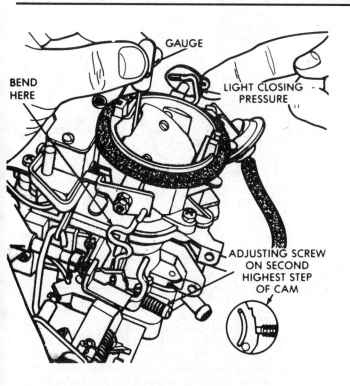

10.56   Fast idle cam adjusting details (3.9L models)

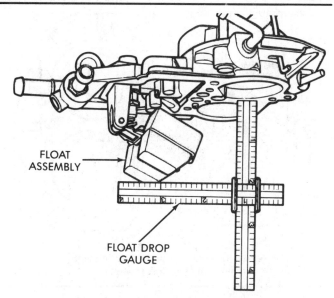

10.76   Check the float drop with the gasket removed
(2.2L models)

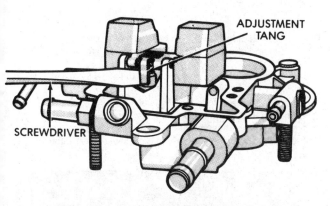

10.77   Use a screwdriver to adjust the float drop
(2.2L models)

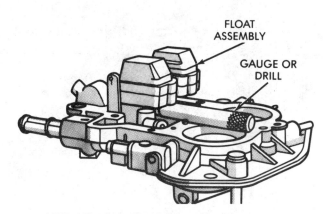

10.78   Check the float level setting as shown
(2.2L models)

76   With the gasket removed, measure from the mating surface of the top of the carburetor to the lowest part of the float **(see illustration)**.
77   Using a small screwdriver, bend the limiting tang and adjust the float drop to the correct level **(see illustration)**.

Float level adjustment

2.2L models

Refer to illustrations 10.78 and 10.79

78   With the top of the carburetor removed and held upside down, insert a 1/2-inch thick gauge between the air horn and float **(see illustration)**.
79   Using a small screwdriver, bend the adjustment tang for the float setting to obtain the proper level **(see illustration)**.

3.9L models

Refer to illustration 10.82

80   Turn the main body upside down (be careful not to lose the pump intake check ball if the venturi cluster has been removed) so the weight of the floats is forcing the needle against it's seat.
81   Hold your finger against the hinge pin retainer to fully seat it in the float pin cradle.
82   Using a ruler, check the float setting from the mating surface of the fuel bowl to the toe of each float **(see illustration)**.
83   If adjustment is necessary, bend the float tang.
84   To equalize float positions, bend either float arm.

68   To verify the fast idle speed is correct, return the engine to idle, then reposition the adjusting screw on the second highest step of the fast idle cam. Readjust the fast idle speed if necessary.
69   Return the engine to idle and turn the engine off. **Note:** *Idle speeds with the engine in normal operating condition (everything connected) may vary from the set speeds. Don't attempt to readjust the idle speed.*
70   Unplug and reconnect the vacuum hoses to the EGR valve, canister and air switching valve.
71   Reinstall the air cleaner assembly.
72   Remove the jumper wire from the vacuum kicker.
73   Disconnect the tachometer.
74   Reinstall the PCV valve.

Float drop adjustment (2.2L models)

Refer to illustrations 10.76 and 10.77

75   With the top of the carburetor removed, hold the top of the carburetor so the float will hang free.

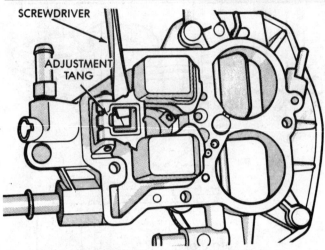

10.79   Adjust the float level setting by bending the adjustment tang (2.2L models)

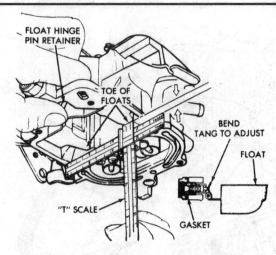

10.82   Float level adjustment details (3.9L models)

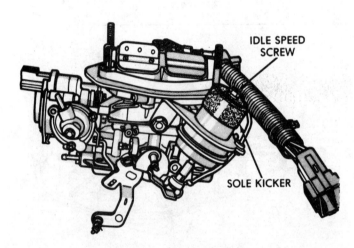

10.93   To raise the idle speed, adjust the screw on the solenoid kicker (2.2L models)

Idle speed adjustment

2.2L models
Refer to illustration 10.93

85   Before checking or adjusting the idle speed, be sure the ignition timing is set to specifications (see Chapter 1).
86   Set the parking brake and place the transmission in neutral.
87   Turn the lights and the accessories off.
88   Connect a tachometer to the ignition coil.
89   Start the engine and warm the engine up to normal operating temperature.
90   Unplug the electrical connector from the radiator fan and use a jumper wire to apply battery voltage to the fan connector (so the fan will run continuously).
91   Remove the PCV valve from the crankcase vent and allow the valve to suck air.
92   Disconnect the wiring from the kicker vacuum control solenoid located on the firewall above the right inner fender.
93   If idle speed is not to specifications (refer to the VECI label under the hood), turn the idle speed screw on top of the solenoid kicker to obtain the

correct idle speed **(see illustration)**.
94   Reconnect the PCV valve and the solenoid wiring.
95   Rev the engine to 2500 rpm for 15 seconds.
96   Remove the jumper wire and reconnect the connector for the radiator fan. **Note:** *The idle speed may change a little when everything is reconnected. This is normal and the engine speed should not be readjusted.*

3.9L models
Refer to illustration 10.104

97   Before checking or adjusting the idle speed, check the ignition timing and adjust it if necessary (see Chapter 1).
98   Using a jumper wire, ground the carburetor switch on the vacuum kicker.
99   Disconnect and plug the vacuum hose at the air switching valve.
100 Disconnect and plug the 3/16-inch diameter canister purge hose at the solenoid.
101 Remove the PCV valve from the engine and allow the valve to suck air.
102 Connect a tachometer to the ignition coil.
103 Start and run the engine to operating temperature.
104 With the engine speed stabilized, turn the idle speed screw to obtain the idle speed listed on the engine compartment sticker **(see illustration)**.

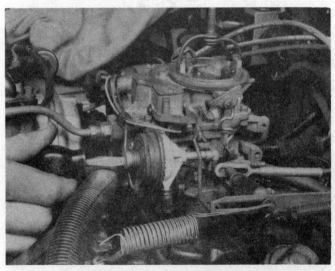

10.104   Be sure the engine speed is stabilized before adjusting the idle speed (3.9L models)

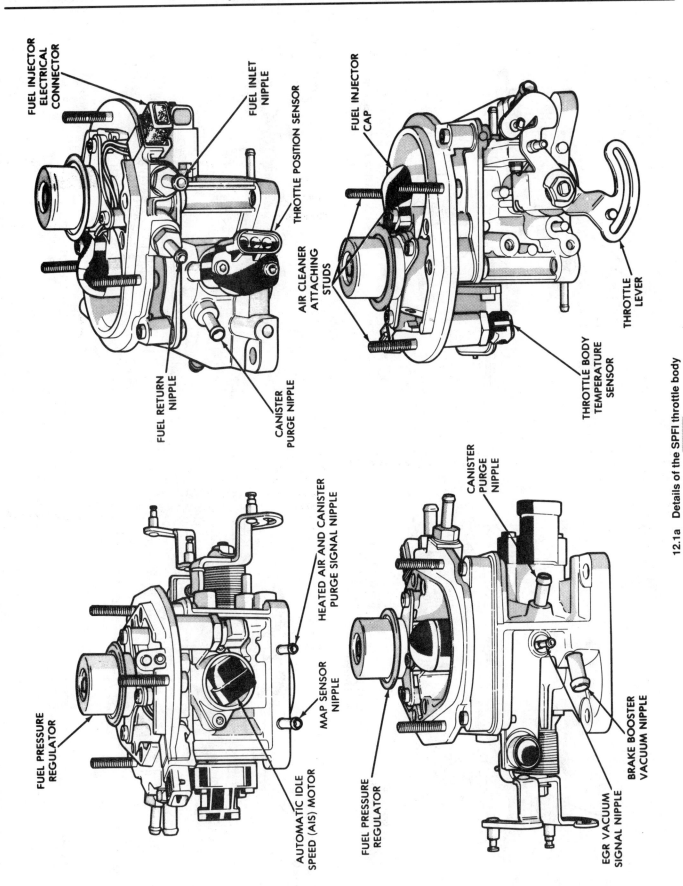

FUEL INJECTOR ELECTRICAL CONNECTOR

FUEL INLET NIPPLE

THROTTLE POSITION SENSOR

AIR CLEANER ATTACHING STUDS

FUEL RETURN NIPPLE

CANISTER PURGE NIPPLE

FUEL INJECTOR CAP

THROTTLE LEVER

THROTTLE BODY TEMPERATURE SENSOR

FUEL PRESSURE REGULATOR

HEATED AIR AND CANISTER PURGE SIGNAL NIPPLE

MAP SENSOR NIPPLE

AUTOMATIC IDLE SPEED (AIS) MOTOR

CANISTER PURGE NIPPLE

FUEL PRESSURE REGULATOR

EGR VACUUM SIGNAL NIPPLE

BRAKE BOOSTER VACUUM NIPPLE

12.1a   Details of the SPFI throttle body

4

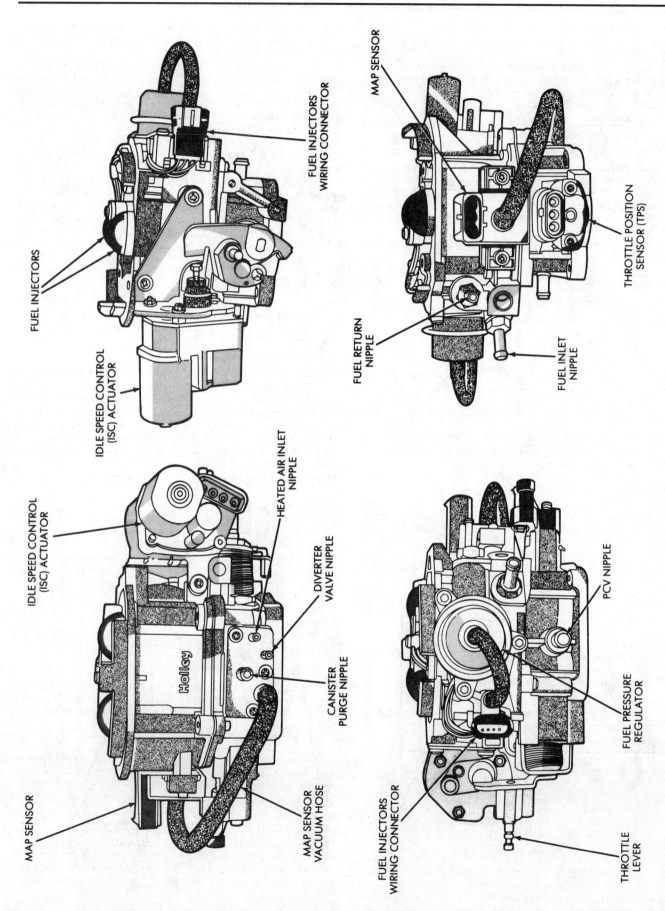

FUEL INJECTORS WIRING CONNECTOR

FUEL INJECTORS

IDLE SPEED CONTROL (ISC) ACTUATOR

MAP SENSOR

THROTTLE POSITION SENSOR (TPS)

FUEL RETURN NIPPLE

FUEL INLET NIPPLE

IDLE SPEED CONTROL (ISC) ACTUATOR

HEATED AIR INLET NIPPLE

DIVERTER VALVE NIPPLE

CANISTER PURGE NIPPLE

MAP SENSOR

MAP SENSOR VACUUM HOSE

PCV NIPPLE

FUEL PRESSURE REGULATOR

FUEL INJECTORS WIRING CONNECTOR

THROTTLE LEVER

12.1b   Details of the DPFI throttle body

105 Turn off the engine.

106 Unplug and reconnect the vacuum hoses at the canister, and the air switching valve.

107 Reinstall the PCV valve and remove the tachometer. **Note:** *The idle speed may change a little when everything is reconnected. This is normal and the engine speed should not be readjusted.*

11 Carburetor – removal and installation

Warning: *Gasoline is extremely flammable, so take extra precautions when you work on any part of the fuel system. Don't smoke or allow open flames or bare light bulbs near the work area, and don't work in a garage where a natural gas-type appliance (such as a water heater or clothes dryer) with a pilot light is present. If you spill any fuel on your skin, rinse it off immediately with soap and water. When you perform any kind of work on the fuel system, wear safety glasses and have a Class B type fire extinguisher on hand.*

Removal

1   Remove the fuel filler cap to relieve fuel tank pressure.

2   Remove the air cleaner from the carburetor. Be sure to label all vacuum hoses attached to the air cleaner housing.

3   Disconnect the throttle cable from the throttle lever (see Section 15).

4   If the vehicle is equipped with an automatic transmission, disconnect the kickdown cable from the throttle lever.

5   Clearly label all vacuum hoses and fittings, then disconnect the hoses.

6   Disconnect the fuel line from the carburetor.

7   Label the wires and terminals, then unplug all the electrical connectors.

8   Remove the mounting fasteners and detach the carburetor from the intake manifold. Remove the carburetor mounting gasket. Stuff a shop rag into the intake manifold openings.

Installation

9   Use a gasket scraper to remove all traces of gasket material and sealant from the intake manifold (and the carburetor, if it's being reinstalled), then remove the shop rag from the manifold openings. Clean the mating surfaces with lacquer thinner or acetone.

10   Place a new gasket on the intake manifold.

11   Position the carburetor on the gasket and install the mounting fasteners.

12   To prevent carburetor distortion or damage, tighten the fasteners to the torque listed in this Chapter's Specifications in a criss-cross pattern, 1/4-turn at a time.

13   The remaining installation steps are the reverse of removal.

14   Check and, if necessary, adjust the idle speed.

15   If the vehicle is equipped with an automatic transmission, refer to Chapter 7B for the kickdown cable adjustment procedure.

16   Start the engine and check carefully for fuel leaks.

12 Throttle Body Fuel Injection (TBI) system – general information

Refer to illustrations 12.1a and 12.1b

Two types of Throttle Body fuel Injection (TBI) systems are used on these models: Single Point Fuel Injection (SPFI) and Dual Point Fuel Injection (DPFI) **(see illustrations)**. The SPFI system is used on all 2.5L four–cylinder engines and the DPFI system is used on 3.9L V6 engines through 1991 and on the 1991 5.2L V8 engine.

Both types are similar in operation and are controlled by a computer called a Single Module Engine Controller (SMEC) or Single Board Engine Controller (SBEC) in combination with a variety of sensors and switches. On both systems the conventional carburetor is replaced by a throttle body which is capable of very precise fuel metering for every driving condition. The fuel is mixed with air and sprayed into the intake manifold, which directs it to the intake ports and cylinders.

The EFI system consists of a throttle body mounted on the intake manifold which houses the fuel injector(s), fuel pressure regulator and Throttle Position Sensor (TPS). On Single Point Fuel Injection an Automatic Idle Speed (AIS) motor and throttle body temperature sensor are used. On Dual Point Fuel Injection an Idle Speed Control (ISC) actuator is used.

Due to the complexity of the EFI system, the home mechanic can do very little in the way of diagnosis because of the special techniques and equipment required. However, checking of the EFI system components and electrical and vacuum connections to make sure they are secure and not obviously damaged is one thing the home mechanic can do which can often detect a potential or current problem. Since the SMEC and SBEC are completely dependent on the information provided by the many sensors and vacuum connections, a simple visual check and tightening of loose connections can save diagnostic time and possibly an unnecessary trip to the dealer service department.

Damaged or faulty TBI components can be replaced using the procedures in the following Sections. Further information on the TBI system can be found in Chapters 5 and 6.

13 Throttle Body Injection (TBI) unit – removal and installation

Refer to illustrations 13.7a and 13.7b

Warning: *Gasoline is extremely flammable, so take extra precautions when you work on any part of the fuel system. Don't smoke or allow open flames or bare light bulbs near the work area, and don't work in a garage where a natural gas-type appliance (such as a water heater or clothes dryer) with a pilot light is present. If you spill any fuel on your skin, rinse it off immediately with soap and water. When you perform any kind of work on the fuel system, wear safety glasses and have a Class B type fire extinguisher on hand.*

Note: *This procedure applies to SPFI and DPFI models.*

Removal

1   Remove the air cleaner.

2   Relieve the fuel system pressure (see Section 2).

3   Disconnect the negative cable from the battery.

4   Disconnect the vacuum hoses and wire harness connectors from the throttle body. Label them to ensure reinstallation in the same locations.

5   Remove the throttle return spring, cable and bracket, and, if equipped, the speed control cable and transmission kickdown linkage.

6   Disconnect the fuel supply and return hoses. Position rags under the fittings to catch any fuel spillage.

7   Remove the throttle body mounting bolts and lift the throttle body assembly off the intake manifold **(see illustrations)**.

Installation

8   Installation is the reverse of the removal procedure. Be sure to use a new gasket between the throttle body and intake manifold. Tighten the mounting bolts, in a criss-cross pattern, to the torque listed in this Chapter's Specifications.

14 Throttle Body Injection (TBI) unit – component replacement

Warning: *Gasoline is extremely flammable, so take extra precautions when you work on any part of the fuel system. Don't smoke or allow open flames or bare light bulbs near the work area, and don't work in a garage where a natural gas-type appliance (such as a water heater or clothes dryer) with a pilot light is present. If you spill any fuel on your skin, rinse it off immediately with soap and water. When you perform any kind of work on the fuel system, wear safety glasses and have a Class B type fire extinguisher on hand.*

Note: *These procedures apply to DPFI and SPFI models.*

4

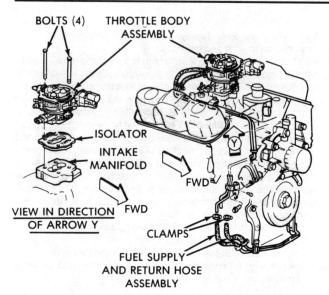

13.7a   Mounting details of the Dual Point Fuel Injection (DPFI) throttle body unit

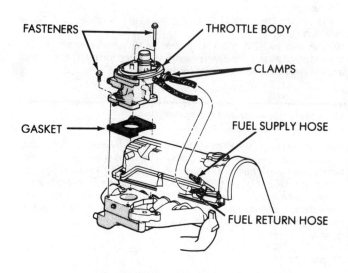

13.7b   Mounting details of the Single Point Fuel Injection (SPFI) throttle body unit

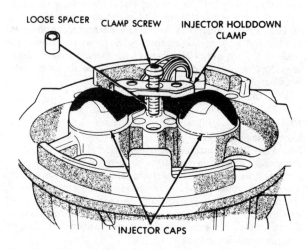

14.4   Note the spacer under the fuel injector hold-down clamp

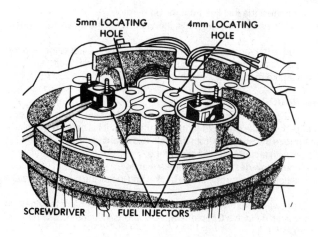

14.6   Use a small screwdriver to pry the fuel injectors out of the throttle body

Fuel injector(s)

Refer to illustrations 14.4, 14.6, 14.7 and 14.8

1   Remove the air cleaner.
2   Relieve the fuel system pressure.
3   Disconnect the negative cable from the battery.
4   Remove the Torx screw holding the injector hold-down clamp. Be careful not to lose the spacer under the clamp **(see illustration)**.
5   Using a small screwdriver, lift the top off the injector(s).
6   Using a small screwdriver placed in the hole in front of the electrical connector, gently pry the fuel injector(s) from the throttle body **(see illustration)**.
7   Make sure the lower O-ring came out of the throttle body with the injector(s) **(see illustration)**.
8   To reinstall an injector, align the injector cap with the locating notch on the injector **(see illustration)**.
9   Press the injector into the cap until the upper O-ring flange is flush with the lower surface of the cap.

10   Lightly lubricate the upper and lower O-rings with petroleum jelly.
11   Insert the injector and cap into the throttle body and align the cap locating pin with the locating hole in the casting. Note that on DPFI models the left and right injectors have different size locating pins and matching locating holes and will not interchange.
12   Press firmly on the injector caps until the injectors are flush with the casting surface.
13   While aligning the holes in the clamp with the pins on the caps, place the injector hold-down clamp and spacer on the rear of the caps.
14   Since squeezing the O-rings may cause the caps to lift, press firmly on both caps with one hand while installing the clamp screw.
15   The remainder of installation is the reverse of the removal procedure.

Fuel pressure regulator

Refer to illustrations 14.21a and 14.21b

16   Remove the air cleaner assembly.
17   Release the fuel system pressure.

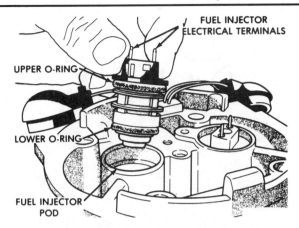

14.7   Make sure the lower O-ring comes out of the throttle body with the injector

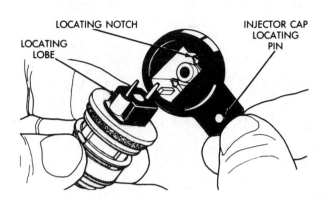

14.8   Align the injector cap with the locating notch on the injector

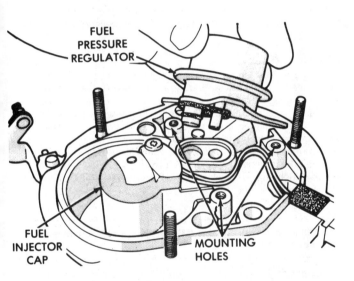

14.21a   Remove the retaining screws and the fuel pressure regulator (SPFI)

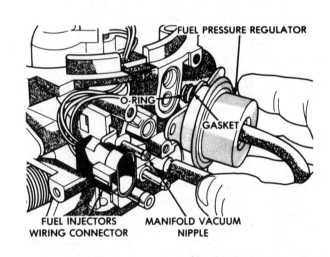

14.21b   Details of the fuel pressure regulator (DPFI)

18   Disconnect the negative cable at the battery.
19   Remove the screws mounting the pressure regulator to the throttle body.
20   Wrap a cloth around the fuel inlet chamber to catch any residual fuel, which is under pressure.
21   Withdraw the pressure regulator from the throttle body **(see illustrations)**.
22   Carefully remove the O-ring from the pressure regulator, followed by the gasket.
23   Place a new gasket in position on the pressure regulator and carefully install a new O-ring.
24   Place the pressure regulator in position on the throttle body, press it into position and install the retaining screws.
25   Tighten the screws securely.
26   Connect the negative battery cable.
27   Install the air cleaner assembly.
28   Start the engine and check for fuel leaks.

Idle Speed Control (ISC) motor or actuator

29   For information on the ISC motor or actuator, see Chapter 6.

Throttle body temperature sensor (SPFI only)

30   For information on the throttle body temperature sensor, see Chapter 6.

Throttle Position Sensor (TPS)

31   For information on the TPS see Chapter 6.

15   Multi–Port fuel Injection (MPI) system – general information

The Multi–Port Fuel Injection (MPI) system is used on 1992 and later 3.9L V6 and 5.2L V8 engines.

This system is controlled by a dual microprocessor digital computer called the Single Board Engine Controller II (SBEC II) that works in conjunction with a variety of sensors and switches. The SBEC II regulates ignition timing, air–fuel ratio, emission control devices, charging system, speed control, air conditioning compressor clutch engagement and engine idle speed.

The MPI system consists of a throttle body mounted on the intake manifold, six or eight individual fuel injectors attached to the fuel rail assembly on the intake manifold, a fuel pressure regulator, a crankshaft position sensor, an engine coolant temperature sensor, an idle air control (IAC)

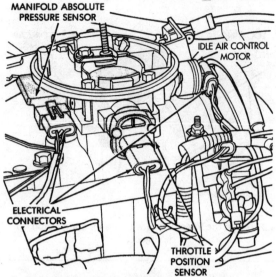

16.4 Locations of the wire harness connectors on the throttle body – the Idle Air Control (IAC) motor can be easily removed after disconnecting its electrical connector and removing the two TORX screws that secure it to the throttle body assembly

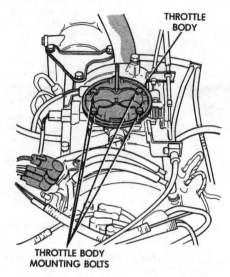

16.7 Remove the throttle body mounting bolts

motor, a manifold absolute pressure (MAP) sensor, an oxygen sensor, a powertrain control module and the vehicle speed sensor.

Due to the complexity of the MPI system, the home mechanic can do very little in a the way of diagnosis because of the special techniques and equipment required. However, checking of the electrical and vacuum connections to make sure they are secure and not obviously damaged is one thing the home mechanic can do which can often detect a potential or current problem. Since the MPI system is completely dependent on the information provided by the many sensors and vacuum connections, a simple visual check and tightening of loose connections can save diagnostic time and possibly an unnecessary trip to the dealer service department.

Damaged or faulty MPI components can be replaced using the procedures in the following Sections. Further information on the MPI system can be found in Chapters 5 and 6.

16   Multi–Point fuel Injection (MPI) throttle body – removal and installation

Refer to illustrations 16.4 and 16.7

Warning: *Gasoline is extremely flammable, so extra precautions must be taken when working on any part of the fuel system. DO NOT smoke or allow open flames or bare light bulbs near the work area. Also, don't work in a garage where a natural gas–type appliances (such as a water heater or clothes dryer) with a pilot light is present. If you spill any fuel on your skin, rinse it off immediately with soap and water. When you perform any kind of work on the fuel system, wear safety glasses and have a Class B fire extinguisher on hand.*

Removal

1   Remove the air filter.
2   Relieve the fuel system pressure (see Section 2).
3   Disconnect the negative cable from the battery.
4   Disconnect the vacuum hoses and wire harness connectors from the throttle body **(see illustration)**. Label them to ensure reinstallation in the same location.
5   Disconnect the throttle cable and, if equipped, the speed control cable and transmission kickdown linkage (see Section 18).
6   Disconnect the fuel supply and return hoses. Position rags under the fittings to catch any fuel spillage.
7   Remove the throttle body mounting bolts and lift the throttle body off the intake manifold **(see illustration)**.

8   Cover the openings in the intake manifold to prevent the entry of foreign matter.

Installation

9   Using a scraper, remove all traces of old gasket material from the mating surfaces of the intake manifold and throttle body. Be very careful not to scratch or gouge the delicate aluminum surfaces. Gasket removal solvents are available at auto parts stores and may prove helpful. Make sure the surfaces are perfectly clean and not oily. Remove any oily residue with a rag soaked in lacquer thinner or acetone.
10   The remainder of installation is the reverse of the removal procedure. Be sure to install a new gasket between the throttle body and the intake manifold. Tighten the mounting bolts to the torque listed in this Chapter's Specifications.

17   Multi–Point fuel Injection (MPI) system – component replacement

Warning: *Gasoline is extremely flammable, so extra precautions must be taken when working on any part of the fuel system. DO NOT smoke or allow open flames or bare light bulbs near the work area. Also, don't work in a garage where a natural gas–type appliances (such as a water heater or clothes dryer) with a pilot light is present. If you spill any fuel on your skin, rinse it off immediately with soap and water. When you perform any kind of work on the fuel system, wear safety glasses and have a Class B fire extinguisher on hand.*

Note: *For information on the information sensors used with this system, see Chapter 6.*

Fuel rail and fuel injector assembly

Refer to illustrations 17.6, 17.11 and 17.14

1   Remove the air filter.
2   Relieve the fuel system pressure (see Section 2).
3   Disconnect the negative cable from the battery.
4   Remove the throttle body from the intake manifold (see Section 16).
5   If equipped, remove the air conditioning bracket from the intake manifold. Move the compressor and bracket out of the way without disconnecting the refrigerant lines. **Warning:** *Never disconnect any refrigerant lines until the system has been depressurized by a dealer service department or automotive air conditioning shop.*
6   Carefully lift the retaining clip (a pointed tool will probably be necessary) and disconnect the wire harness connectors from each individual injector **(see illustration)**. The connectors are identified for injector position identification.
7   Disconnect the vacuum line from the fuel pressure regulator.

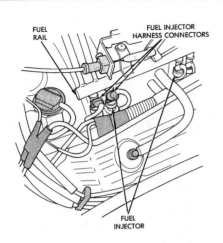

17.6 Disconnect the wire harness connectors from
each individual injector

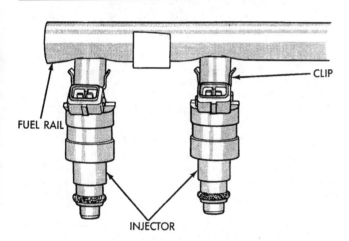

17.14 Remove the clip and carefully pull the fuel
injector from the fuel rail

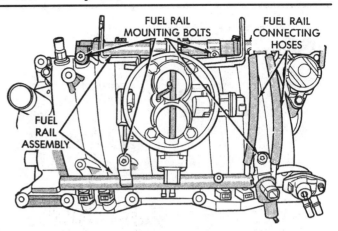

17.11 Remove the remaining fuel rail mounting bolts

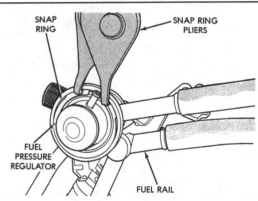

17.26 On V6 engines, remove the snap ring securing
the pressure regulator to the fuel rail

8   On V6 models only, disconnect the wire connector from the air temperature sensor. Do not remove the sensor.

9   Remove the EVAP canister purge solenoid/bracket assembly from the intake manifold. There is one nut on V6 engines or one bolt on V8 engines.

10   Disconnect the two fuel lines at the rear of the fuel rails. Refer to Section 4 regarding quick–disconnect fittings.

11   Remove the remaining fuel rail mounting bolts **(see illustration)**.

12   Gently rock and pull the LEFT fuel rail until the fuel injectors just start to clear the intake manifold. Gently rock and pull the RIGHT fuel rail until the fuel injectors just start to clear the intake manifold. Repeat this step until all fuel injectors are clear of their receptacles in the intake manifold.

13   Pull the fuel rail assembly straight up and remove it from the engine. Make sure the O–ring is still installed on each fuel injector. If any O–ring(s) are missing, check and remove them from the receptacles in the intake manifold. **Note:** *Don't drop the O–rings into the intake manifold.*

14   To remove any individual fuel injector(s) from the fuel rail, remove the clip and carefully pull the fuel injector(s) from the fuel rail **(see illustration)**.

15   Inspect each injector O–ring for signs of deterioration. Replace as required. **Note:** *We recommend replacing the O–rings whenever the injectors are removed, since an O–ring that does not seal will cause a vacuum or fuel leak.*

16   Lubricate all fuel injector O–rings with light grade engine oil. **Note:** *Do not use silicone grease as it will clog the injectors.*

17   If removed, install the fuel injector(s) into the fuel rail and install the

clip. Make sure the fuel injector is seated properly and the clip is holding securely.

18   Correctly position the fuel rail assembly over the engine and guide each fuel injector into its receptacle in the intake manifold. **Note:** *Be careful not to tear the injector O–rings during installation.*

19   Push the RIGHT fuel rail down until each fuel injector's shoulder has bottomed out in the intake manifold. Push the LEFT fuel rail down until each fuel injector's shoulder has bottomed out in the intake manifold.

20   Gently rock the fuel rail to make sure all fuel injectors are properly seated. Install the mounting bolts and tighten them securely.

21   The remainder of the installation procedure is the reverse of removal. Make sure all wire connectors are tight and that all vacuum lines are installed completely onto their respective fittings. Tighten the throttle body mounting bolts to the torque listed in this Chapter's Specifications. Start the engine and check for fuel leaks.

Fuel pressure regulator

Refer to illustration 17.26

22   Remove the air filter.

23   Relieve the fuel system pressure (see Section 2).

24   Disconnect the negative cable from the battery.

25   Disconnect the vacuum line from the pressure regulator.

26   On V6 engines, remove the snap ring from the pressure regulator, then remove the pressure regulator from the fuel rail **(see illustration)**.

27   On V8 engines, remove the mounting bolt and remove the pressure regulator from the fuel rail.

28   Install a new O–ring to the pressure regulator.

29   On V6 engines, mount the pressure regulator onto the fuel rail with the vacuum fitting pointing straight up. Install the snap ring and make sure it is properly seated.

30   The remainder of the installation procedure is the reverse of removal. Start the engine and check for fuel leaks.

4

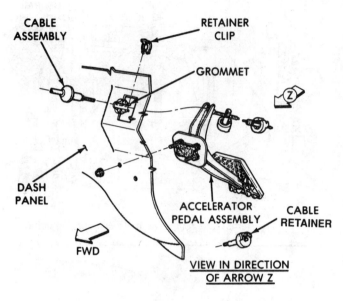

18.1　Interior mounting details of the throttle cable

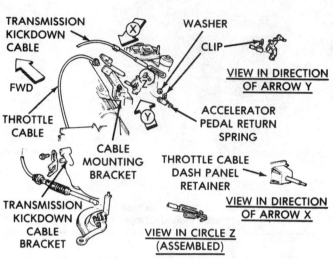

18.4a　Throttle cable-to-engine attaching details
(2.2L models)

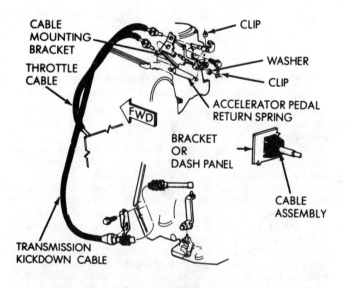

18.4b　Throttle cable-to-engine attaching details
(2.5L models)

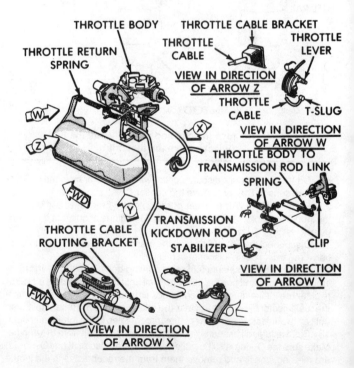

18.4c　Throttle cable-to-engine attaching details (3.9L SPFI
shown, carbureted models similar)

18　Throttle cable – removal and installation

Refer to illustrations 18.1, 18.4a, 18.4b, 18.4c and 18.4d

1　From inside the vehicle, remove the clip retaining the cable housing to the firewall. Remove the cable retainer at the pedal **(see illustration)**.
2　Remove the cable from the pedal arm.
3　From the engine compartment, pull the cable housing out of the firewall grommet.
4　Disconnect the cable from the throttle lever **(see illustration)**.
5　Use pliers to compress the tabs on the cable retainer at the cable mounting bracket. Push the retainer through the bracket.
6　Remove the cable.
7　Installation is the reverse of removal.

19　Exhaust system – servicing and general information

Refer to illustration 19.1

Warning: *Inspection and repair of exhaust system components should be done only after enough time has elapsed after driving the vehicle to allow* *the system components to cool completely. Also, when working under the vehicle, make sure it is securely supported on jackstands.*

1   The exhaust system consists of the exhaust manifold(s), the catalytic converter(s), the muffler, the tailpipe and all connecting pipes, brackets, hangers and clamps **(see illustration)**. The exhaust system is attached to the body with mounting brackets and rubber hangers. If any of the parts are improperly installed, excessive noise and vibration will be transmitted to the body.

2   Conduct regular inspections of the exhaust system to keep it safe and quiet. Look for any damaged or bent parts, open seams, holes, loose connections, excessive corrosion or other defects which could allow exhaust fumes to enter the vehicle. Deteriorated exhaust system components should not be repaired; they should be replaced with new parts.

3   If the exhaust system components are extremely corroded or rusted together, welding equipment will probably be required to remove them. The convenient way to accomplish this is to have a muffler repair shop remove the corroded sections with a cutting torch. If, however, you want to save money by doing it yourself (and you don't have a welding outfit with a

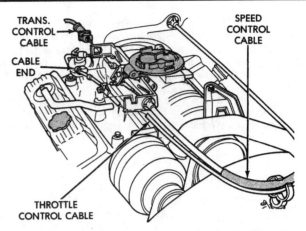

18.4d   Throttle cable-to-engine attaching details (V6 and V8 models with MPI – 1992 and later)

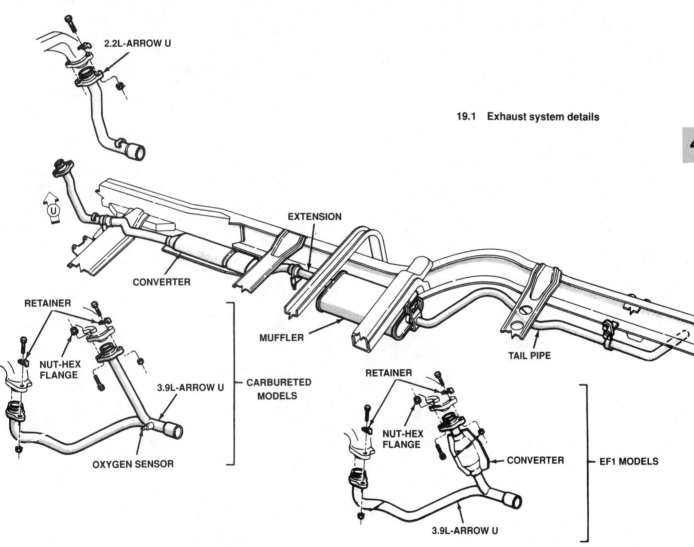

19.1   Exhaust system details

4

cutting torch), simply cut off the old components with a hacksaw. If you have compressed air, special pneumatic cutting chisels can also be used. If you do decide to tackle the job at home, be sure to wear safety goggles to protect your eyes from metal chips and work gloves to protect your hands.

4   Here are some simple guidelines to follow when repairing the exhaust system:

a) Work from the back to the front when removing exhaust system components.

b) Apply penetrating oil to the exhaust system component fasteners to make them easier to remove.

c) Use new gaskets, hangers and clamps when installing exhaust system components.

d) Apply anti-seize compound to the threads of all exhaust system fasteners during reassembly.

e) Be sure to allow sufficient clearance between newly installed parts and all points on the underbody to avoid overheating the floor pan and possibly damaging the interior carpet and insulation. Pay particularly close attention to the catalytic converter and heat shield.

Chapter 5   Engine electrical systems

Contents

Specifications

Ignition coil resistance

Primary	
1987 through 1990	1.34 to 1.55 ohms
1991 and later	0.95 to 1.20 ohms
Secondary	
Prestolite coil	9,400 to 11,700 ohms
Essex coil	9,000 to 12,200 ohms
Diamond coil	
1987 through 1990	15,000 to 19,000 ohms
1991	15,000 to 19,000 ohms
1992 on	11,300 to 15,300 ohms
Toyodenso coil (1992 and later)	11,300 to 13,300 ohms

1   General information and precautions

The engine electrical systems include all ignition, charging and starting components. Because of their engine-related functions, these components are discussed separately from chassis electrical devices such as the lights, the instruments, etc. (which are included in Chapter 12).

Always observe the following precautions when working on the electrical systems:

a) Be extremely careful when servicing engine electrical components. They are easily damaged if checked, connected or handled improperly.

b) The alternator is driven by an engine drivebelt which could cause serious injury if your hands, hair or clothes become entangled in it with the engine running.

c) Both the alternator and the starter are connected directly to the battery and could arc or even cause a fire if mishandled, overloaded or shorted out.

d) Never leave the ignition switch on for long periods of time with the engine off.

e) Don't disconnect the battery cables while the engine is running.

f) Maintain correct polarity when connecting a battery cable from another source, such as a vehicle, during jump starting.

g) Always disconnect the negative cable first and hook it up last or the battery may be shorted by the tool being used to loosen the cable clamps.

It's also a good idea to review the safety-related information regarding the engine electrical systems located in the Safety First section near the front of this manual before beginning any operation included in this Chapter.

2   Battery – removal and installation

Warning: *Hydrogen gas is produced by the battery, so keep open flames, bare light bulbs and lighted tobacco away from it at all times. Always wear eye protection when working around a battery. Rinse off spilled electrolyte immediately with large amounts of water.*

1   Disconnect both cables from the battery terminals. **Caution:** *Always disconnect the negative cable first and hook it up last or the battery may be shorted by the tool being used to loosen the cable clamps.*

2   Remove the battery hold-down clamp.

3   Lift out the battery. Use the proper lifting technique – the battery is heavy.

4   While the battery is out, inspect the battery carrier (tray) for corrosion (see Chapter 1).

5   If you are replacing the battery, make sure that you get an identical battery, with the same dimensions, amperage rating, "cold cranking" rating, etc.

6   Installation is the reverse of removal.

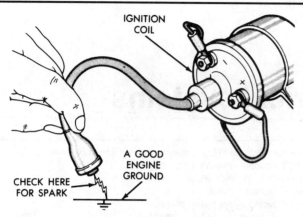

6.1   The spark at the coil wire must be bright blue and well defined

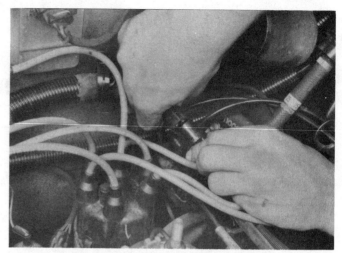

7.1   When disconnecting the primary connector at the distributor, don't pull on the wires

On vehicles equipped with carbureted engines, the ignition system consists of a switch, the ignition coil, the distributor, the spark plugs and wires, and a Spark Control Computer (SCC). The spark timing is constantly adjusted by the computer and distributor in response to input from the various sensors located on the engine.

On fuel–injected models, the ignition system works in conjunction with the fuel injection computer. The ignition system interacts with the Single Module Engine Controller (SMEC) on the TBI fuel injection system or with the Single Board Engine Controller II (SBEC II) on the MPI fuel injection system. These computer-controlled systems provide the proper fuel flow and ignition timing for all driving conditions.

3   Battery – emergency jump starting

Refer to the Booster battery (jump) starting procedure at the front of this manual.

4   Battery cables – check and replacement

1   Periodically inspect the entire length of each battery cable for damage, cracked or burned insulation and corrosion. Poor battery cable connections can cause starting problems and decreased engine performance.
2   Check the cable-to-terminal connections at the ends of the cables for cracks, loose wire strands and corrosion. The presence of white, fluffy deposits under the insulation at the cable terminal connection is a sign that the cable is corroded and should be replaced. Check the terminals for distortion, missing mounting bolts and corrosion.
3   When removing the cables, always disconnect the negative cable first and hook it up last or the battery may be shorted by the tool used to loosen the cable clamps. Even if only the positive cable is being replaced, be sure to disconnect the negative cable from the battery first (see Chapter 1 for further information regarding battery cable removal).
4   Disconnect the old cables from the battery, then trace each of them to their opposite ends and detach them from the starter solenoid and ground. Note the routing of each cable to insure correct installation.
5   If you are replacing either or both of the old cables, take them with you when buying new cables. It is vitally important that you replace the cables with identical parts. Cables have characteristics that make them easy to identify: positive cables are usually red, larger in cross-section and have a larger diameter battery post clamp; ground cables are usually black, smaller in cross-section and have a slightly smaller diameter clamp for the negative post.
6   Clean the threads of the solenoid or ground connection with a wire brush to remove rust and corrosion. Apply a light coat of battery terminal corrosion inhibitor, or petroleum jelly, to the threads to prevent future corrosion.
7   Attach the cable to the solenoid or ground connection and tighten the mounting nut/bolt securely.
8   Before connecting a new cable to the battery, make sure that it reaches the battery post without having to be stretched.
9   Connect the positive cable first, followed by the negative cable.

5   Ignition system – general information

The ignition system is designed to ignite the fuel/air charge entering each cylinder at just the right moment. It does this by producing a high voltage electrical spark between the electrodes of each spark plug.

6   Ignition system – check

Refer to illustration 6.1
1   Remove the high voltage coil wire from the distributor cap and, using an insulated tool, hold the end about 1/4-inch from a good engine ground. Operate the starter and look for a series of bright blue sparks at the coil wire **(see illustration)**.
2   If sparks occur, and they are bright blue and well defined, continue to operate the starter while slowly moving the coil wire away from the ground. As this is done, look for arcing and sparking at the coil tower. If it occurs, replace the coil with a new one. If arcing does not occur at the coil tower, the ignition system is producing the necessary high secondary voltage. However, make sure the voltage is getting to the spark plugs by checking the rotor, distributor cap, spark plug wires and spark plugs as described in Chapter 1. If the results are positive but the engine still won't start, the ignition system is not at fault.
3   If no sparks occurred from the coil wire, or if they were weak or intermittent, the problem could be an open in the coil wire (see Chapter 1), the coil (see Section 10), the Hall Effect pick-up (see Section 7), any of the related electrical circuits, or the SCC or SMEC.

7   Hall Effect pick-up (TBI models) or Signal Generator switch plate (MPI models) – check and replacement

Note: *There is no check procedure for MPI-equipped models.*

Check (TBI models only)
Refer to illustrations 7.1, 7.2 and 7.7
1   Disconnect the primary electrical connector from the distributor **(see illustration)**.
2   Jump cavity number 2 to cavity number 3 of the connector **(see illustration)**.
3   Turn the ignition switch to the On position.

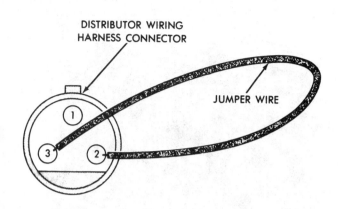

7.2   The jumper wire must be connected between cavities No. 2 and 3 in the distributor wiring harness connector

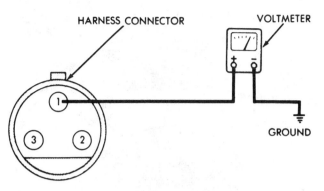

7.7   Checking for voltage between the distributor connector cavity No. 1 and ground

7.11   Lift the Hall Effect pick-up assembly off the distributor shaft (four-cylinder models)

4   While holding the coil wire 1/4-inch from a good ground **(see illustration 6.1)**, make and break the connection at cavity two or cavity three several times.

5   If spark is not present at the coil wire in Step 4, the circuit connected to cavity number two and/or number three is open, or the coil is bad (see Section 10).

6   If spark is present at the coil wire in Step 4, go to the next Step.

7   Measure voltage at cavity number 1 of the distributor connector – it should be within one volt of battery voltage **(see illustration)**.

8   If battery voltage is within specification, replace the Hall Effect pick-up. If battery voltage is not present, repair open in the circuit connected to cavity number one.

Replacement

Four-cylinder models
Refer to illustration 7.11

9   Disconnect the negative cable at the battery.

10   Remove the distributor splash shield and cap (see Chapter 1).

11   Lift the rotor off the shaft, followed by the pick-up assembly **(see illustration)**.

12   To install the pick-up assembly, place it carefully into position, making sure the wiring grommet is seated in its locating hole. Install the rotor.

13   Install the distributor cap and splash shield and connect the negative battery cable.

V6 and V8 models equipped with TBI (1991 and earlier)
Refer to illustration 7.15

14   Disconnect the negative cable at the battery.

15   Remove the distributor cap and rotor (see Chapter 1). Unscrew the two Hall Effect pick-up screws (located on opposite sides of each other on

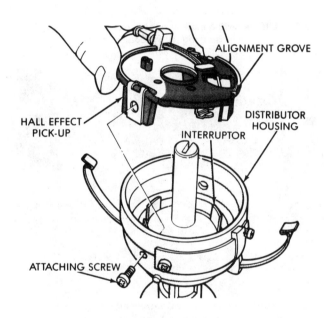

7.15   To remove the Hall Effect pick-up, remove the two attaching screws

the distributor housing) **(see illustration)**. Be careful not to drop them.

16   Carefully lift the Hall Effect pick-up assembly from the distributor housing.

17   Installation is the reverse of removal.

V6 and V8 models
Refer to illustration 7.21

18   Disconnect the negative cable from the battery.

19   Remove the distributor cap and rotor (see Chapter 1).

20   Disconnect the switch plate electrical connector from the engine wire harness.

21   Lift the switch plate assembly from the distributor housing **(see illustration)**.

22   Installation is the reverse of removal.

---

8   **Electronic control unit – removal and installation**

Spark Control Computer (SCC) – carbureted models
Refer to illustration 8.2

1   Disconnect the negative battery cable.

5

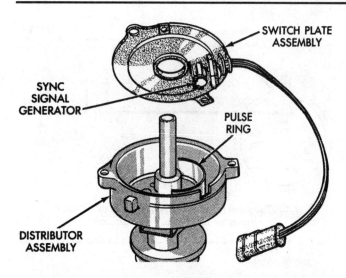

7.21   Lift the switch plate assembly out of the distributor housing (MPI models)

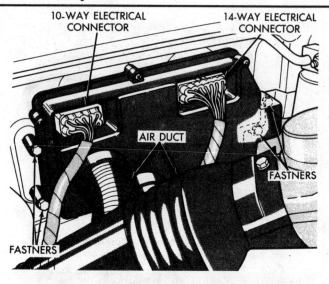

8.2   To remove the Spark Control Computer (SCC), disconnect the wiring and hoses and remove the fasteners

8.9   The Single Module Engine Controller (SMEC) is mounted on the right fender. Two mounting bolt locations are shown (arrows)

9.3   Mark the position of the distributor body in relation to the engine

2   Disconnect the vacuum hose from the transducer in the SCC and unplug the electrical connectors **(see illustration)**. Disengage the assembly from the outside air duct.

3   Remove the mounting fasteners and detach the SCC assembly from the vehicle.

4   To install the computer, place it in position, engage it with the air duct and install the screws mounting it to the fender. Connect the vacuum hose.

Note: *Do not remove the grease from the connectors or cavities. There should be at least a 1/8-inch thick film of grease in the cavities to prevent the intrusion of moisture. If there is not, apply multi-purpose grease to the cavities.*

5   Plug in the electrical connectors.

6   Reconnect the battery.

Single Module Engine Controller (SMEC) or single Board Engine Controller (SBEC) – fuel injected models

Refer to illustration 8.9

7   Disconnect the negative battery cable.

8   Detach the air cleaner duct from the SMEC/SBEC (if equipped).

9   Remove the mounting screws **(see illustration)**.

10   Unscrew the bolt securing the large electrical connector and unplug the connector from the SMEC/SBEC (if equipped).

11   Remove the SMEC/SBEC (if equipped).

12   Installation is the reverse of removal.

---

9   Distributor – removal and installation

Refer to illustrations 9.3, 9.4 and 9.14

Removal

1   On models equipped with TBI fuel injection, unplug the primary electrical connector from the distributor. On models equipped with MPI fuel injection, disconnect the switch plate wire connector from the engine harness **(see illustration 7.21)**.

2   Look for a raised "1" on the distributor cap. This marks the location for the number one cylinder spark plug wire terminal. If the cap doesn't have a mark for the number one terminal, locate the number one spark plug and trace the wire back to the terminal on the cap.

3   Mark the relationship of the distributor base to the engine block to ensure the distributor is installed correctly **(see illustration)**. Remove the distributor cap (see Chapter 1) and turn the engine over until the rotor is pointing toward the number one spark plug terminal (see locating TDC procedure in Chapter 2).

9.4   Make a mark on the distributor housing to show where the rotor is pointing

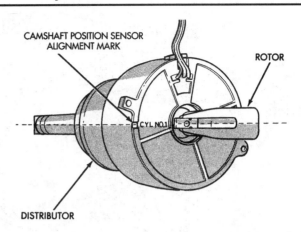

9.14   Slowly rotate the distributor until the rotor is aligned with the "CYL. NO. 1" alignment mark on the switch plate

4   Make a mark on the edge of the distributor base directly below the rotor tip and in line with it **(see illustration)**.
5   Remove the distributor hold-down bolt and clamp, then pull the distributor straight up to remove it. **Caution:** *DO NOT turn the crankshaft while the distributor is out of the engine or the alignment marks will be useless.*

Installation

Note: *If the crankshaft has been turned while the distributor is out, the number one piston must be repositioned at TDC. This can be done by feeling for compression pressure at the number one plug hole as the crankshaft is turned. Once compression is felt, align the crankshaft timing mark with the zero on the engine timing scale.*

6   Insert the distributor into the engine in exactly the same relationship to the block that it was in when removed.
7   To mesh the helical gears on the camshaft and distributor, you may have to turn the rotor slightly. Recheck the alignment marks between the distributor base and the block to verify the distributor is in the same position it was before removal. Also check the rotor to see if it's aligned with the mark you made on the edge of the distributor base.
8   On models with TBI fuel injection, place the hold–down clamp in position and loosely install the bolt. On models with MPI fuel injection, tighten the bolt at this time, providing correct alignment was achieved in Step 7. If correct alignment cannot be achieved or if the engine was rotated any amount with the distributor removed, proceed to Step 14.
9   Install the distributor cap.
10   On TBI systems, plug in the primary electrical connector. On MPI systems, connect the switch plate wire connector.
11   Reattach the spark plug wires to the plugs (if removed).
12   Connect the cable to the negative terminal of the battery.
13   On TBI models, check the ignition timing (refer to Chapter 1) and tighten the distributor hold-down bolt securely.
14   On MPI models, if the engine was rotated with the distributor removed, perform the following:
   a)   Rotate the crankshaft until the number one piston is at top dead center (TDC) on the compression stroke. The mark on the damper should be aligned with the 0 degree (TDC) mark on the timing chain case.
   b)   Install the distributor rotor onto the distributor shaft. Rotate the rotor approximately to the "CYL NO. 1" alignment mark on the switch plate **(see illustration)**.
   c)   Install the distributor into the engine (to its original position). Engage the distributor shaft with the slot in the oil pump drive gear.
   d)   Install the distributor hold–down clamp and bolt. Do not tighten it at this time.
   e)   Slowly rotate the distributor until the rotor is aligned with the "CYL. NO. 1" alignment mark on the switch plate.
   f)   Tighten the hold-down clamp bolt securely.
   g)   Install the distributor cap.

10   Ignition coil – check, removal and installation

Check

1   Mark the wires and terminals with pieces of numbered tape, then remove the primary wires and the high-tension lead from the coil.
2   Clean the outer case and check it for cracks and other damage.
3   Clean the coil primary terminals and check the coil tower terminal for corrosion. Clean it with a wire brush if any corrosion is found.
4   Check the coil primary resistance by attaching the leads of an ohmmeter to the positive and negative terminals. Compare the measured resistance to the value listed in this Chapter's Specifications.
5   Check the coil secondary resistance by hooking one of the ohmmeter leads to one of the primary terminals and the other ohmmeter lead to the large center terminal. Compare the measured resistance to the value listed in this Chapter's Specifications.
6   If the measured resistances are not as specified, the coil is defective and should be replaced with a new one.
7   It is essential for proper operation of the ignition system that all coil terminals and wires be kept clean and dry.

Removal and installation

8   To remove the coil, loosen the screw on the mounting clamp and slide the coil out of clamp.
9   Installation is the reverse of removal.

11   Starting system – general information and precautions

The sole function of the starting system is to turn over the engine quickly enough to allow it to start.
The starting system consists of the battery, the starter motor, the starter relay, the starter solenoid and the wires connecting them. The solenoid is mounted directly on the starter motor or is a separate component located in the engine compartment.
The solenoid/starter motor assembly is installed on the lower part of the engine, next to the transmission bellhousing.
When the ignition key is turned to the Start position, the starter solenoid is actuated through the starter relay and control circuit. The starter solenoid then connects the battery to the starter. The battery supplies the electrical energy to the starter motor, which does the actual work of cranking the engine.
The starter motor on a vehicle equipped with a manual transmission can only be operated when the clutch pedal is depressed; the starter on a vehicle equipped with an automatic transmission can only be operated when the transmission selector lever is in Park or Neutral.

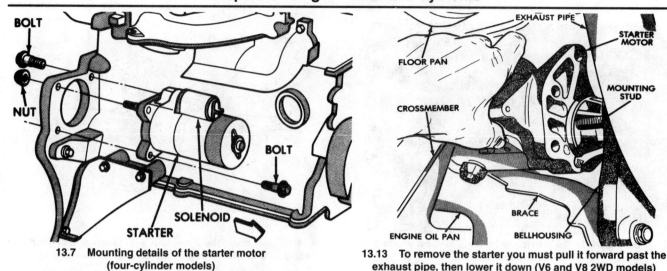

13.7   Mounting details of the starter motor (four-cylinder models)

13.13   To remove the starter you must pull it forward past the exhaust pipe, then lower it down (V6 and V8 2WD models)

Always observe the following precautions when working on the starting system:

a) Excessive cranking of the starter motor can overheat it and cause serious damage. Never operate the starter motor for more than 15 seconds at a time without pausing to allow it to cool for at least two minutes.

b) The starter is connected directly to the battery and could arc or cause a fire if mishandled, overloaded or shorted out.

c) Always detach the cable from the negative terminal of the battery before working on the starting system.

---

12   Starter motor – testing in vehicle

Note: *Before diagnosing starter problems, make sure the battery is fully charged.*

1   If the starter motor does not turn at all when the ignition switch is operated, make sure the shift lever is in Neutral or Park.

2   Make sure that the battery is charged and that all cables, both at the battery and starter solenoid terminals, are clean and secure.

3   If the starter motor spins but the engine is not cranking, the overrunning clutch in the starter motor is slipping and the starter motor must be replaced.

4   If, when the switch is actuated, the starter motor does not operate at all but the solenoid clicks, then the problem lies with either the battery, the starter relay, the main solenoid contacts or the starter motor itself, or the engine is seized.

5   If the solenoid plunger cannot be heard when the switch is actuated, the battery is bad, the fusible link is burned (the circuit is open) or the solenoid itself is defective.

6   To check the solenoid, connect a jumper lead between the battery (positive terminal) and the ignition switch terminal (the small terminal) on the solenoid. If the starter motor now operates, the solenoid is OK and the problem is in the ignition switch, neutral start switch or in the wiring.

7   If the starter motor still does not operate, remove the starter/solenoid unit for disassembly, testing and repair.

8   If the starter motor cranks the engine at an abnormally slow speed, first make sure that the battery is charged and that all terminal connections are tight. If the engine is partially seized, or has the wrong viscosity oil in it, it will crank slowly.

9   Run the engine until normal operating temperature is reached, then disconnect the coil wire from the distributor cap and ground it on the engine.

10   Connect a voltmeter positive lead to the battery positive post and then connect the negative lead to the negative post.

11   Crank the engine and take the voltmeter readings as soon as a steady figure is indicated. Do not allow the starter motor to turn for more than 15 seconds at a time. A reading of nine volts or more, with the starter motor turning at normal cranking speed, is normal. If the reading is nine volts or

more but the cranking speed is slow, the motor is faulty. If the reading is less than nine volts and the cranking speed is slow, the solenoid contacts are probably burned, the starter motor is bad, the battery is discharged or there is a bad connection.

---

13   Starter motor – removal and installation

Four-cylinder models

Refer to illustration 13.7

1   Disconnect the cable from the negative terminal of the battery.

2   Remove the clamp mounting the heat shield (if equipped).

3   Remove the heat shield (if equipped).

4   Loosen the air pump tube at the exhaust manifold and swivel the tube bracket away from the starter (if equipped).

5   Detach the battery cable from the starter.

6   Disconnect the solenoid wire from the solenoid.

7   Remove the nut and bolts attaching the starter to the bellhousing **(see illustration)**.

8   Remove the starter assembly.

9   Installation is the reverse of removal.

V6 and V8 2WD models

Refer to illustration 13.13

10   Disconnect the cable from the negative terminal of the battery.

11   Disconnect the wiring from the starter.

12   Remove the mounting nut and bolt for the starter.

13   Move the starter forward and lower it past the exhaust pipe **(see illustration)**.

14   Installation is the reverse of removal.

V6 and V8 4WD models

Refer to illustration 13.18

15   Disconnect the cable from the negative terminal of the battery.

16   Disconnect the steering shaft coupling from the steering gear and position the shaft out of the way (see Chapter 10).

17   Remove the mounting fasteners for the starter.

18   Move the starter forward and lift it up and out **(see illustration)**.

19   Installation is the reverse of removal.

---

14   Starter solenoid – removal and installation

Four-cylinder models (Bosch)

Refer to illustrations 14.1 and 14.4

1   Remove the starter from the vehicle (see Section 13), then remove the field terminal nut **(see illustration)**.

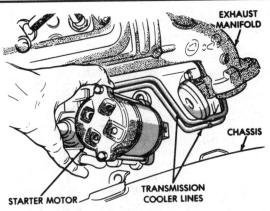

13.18   To remove the starter you must pull it forward and lift it up and out (V6 4WD models)

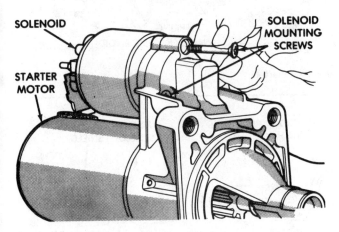

14.4   Remove the solenoid mounting screws (Bosch)

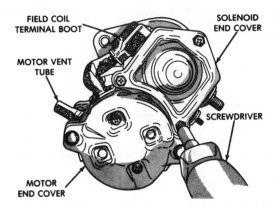

14.10   Remove the screws retaining the solenoid end cover (Nippondenso)

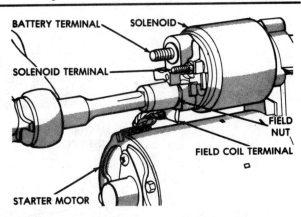

14.1   Remove the field terminal nut (Bosch)

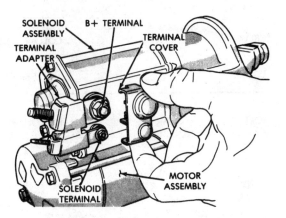

14.8   Remove the terminal cover to expose the terminals (Nippondenso)

5

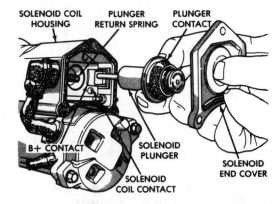

14.11   Remove the solenoid plunger and check for damage

2   Remove the field terminal.
3   Remove the field washer.
4   Remove the three solenoid mounting screws (**see illustration**).
5   Work the solenoid off the shift fork and remove the solenoid.
6   Installation is the reverse of removal.

V6 and V8 models
1987 only (1.8 h.p. reduction gear starter)

7   Refer to Section 14 for the solenoid removal and installation procedure.

1988 and later (Nippondenso reduction gear starter)

Refer to illustrations 14.8, 14.10 and 14.11

8   Remove the starter from the vehicle (see Section 13), then remove the terminal cover (**see illustration**).
9   Remove the nuts mounting the terminal adapter, then remove the adapter.
10   Remove the screws retaining the end cover and separate the end cover from the solenoid housing (**see illustration**).
11   Pull the solenoid plunger from the solenoid housing and inspect the contact and sliding surfaces for damage and excessive wear (**see illustration**).
12   Installation is the reverse of removal.

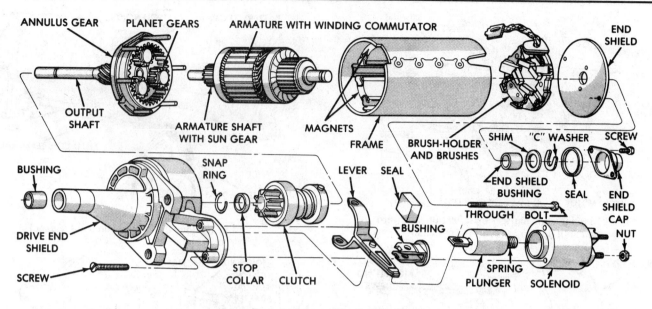

15.1a   Exploded view of the Bosch starter

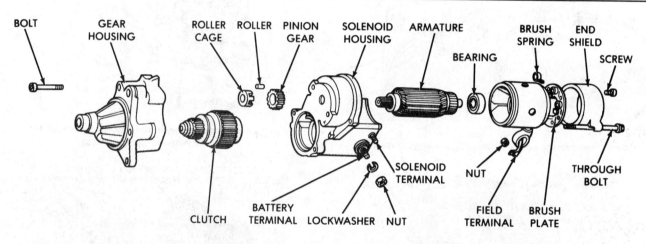

15.1b   Exploded view of the Nippondenso starter

15   Starter motor brushes – replacement

All four-cylinder and 1988 and later V6 and V8 models (Bosch and Nippondenso)

Refer to illustrations 15.1a and 15.1b

1   With the starter removed from the vehicle (see Section 13), remove the through bolts at the end of the starter **(see illustration)**.

2   Remove the end shield from the starter.

3   Remove the brush holder screws and lift the assembly from the starter.

4   On four-cylinder models, remove the brush holder and replace it as an assembly if the brushes are worn. On V6 and V8 models, unsolder the brush leads and solder the new brush leads into place.

5   To install the brush holder assembly, insert the brushes into their receptacles and hold them there, lower the holder assembly down over the commutator and install the screws. Install the end shield.

1987 V6 models (1.8 h.p. reduction gear starter)

Refer to illustrations 15.6, 15.9 and 15.23

6   With the starter removed from the vehicle, remove the through bolts and separate the end head from the field frame assembly **(see illustration)**.

7   Carefully pull the armature out of the gear housing and field frame assembly.

8   Pull the field frame assembly away from the gear housing just far enough to expose the terminal screw.

9   Remove the brush terminal screw **(see illustration)**.

10   Remove the field frame assembly.

11   Remove the mounting nuts from the solenoid and brush holder assembly and separate the assembly from the gear housing.

12   Remove the nut and washers from the solenoid terminal.

13   Unwind the solenoid wire from the starter brush terminal.

14   Separate the solenoid and solenoid wire from the brush plate.

15   The brushes can now be removed from the brush holders and new ones installed.

16   Check the condition of the contacts in the brush holder plate. If they are badly burned, replace the plate and brushes as an assembly.

17   Use a new gasket when attaching the brush holder plate to the solenoid. If a new gasket is not available, apply a thin bead of RTV-type sealant to the outside edge of the gasket.

18   Insert the solenoid wire through the hole in the brush holder.

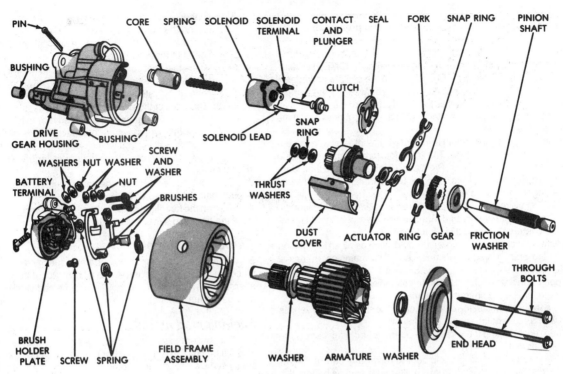

15.6   Exploded view of the 1.8 h.p. reduction gear starter (1987 V6 models)

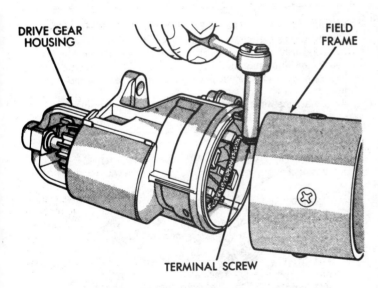

15.9   Removing the brush terminal screw from the
starter motor field frame assembly (1987 V6 models)

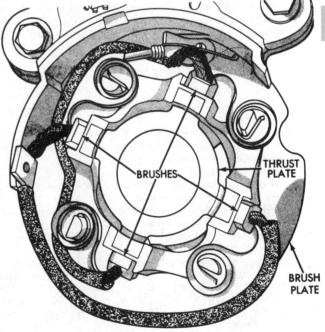

15.23   Correct positioning of the starter brushes
(1987 V6 models)

19   Install the brush holder plate mounting bolts and attach the plate to the solenoid.
20   Install the nut and washers on the solenoid terminal.
21   Wind the solenoid wire tightly around the brush terminal and solder it in place with a high-temperature resin core solder and resin flux.
22   Carefully install the solenoid and brush plate assembly in the gear housing and install the bolts.
23   Position the brushes against the thrust plate (see illustration).
24   Install the brush terminal screw.

25   Carefully install the field frame assembly and armature. Rotate the armature shaft slightly to engage it with the reduction gear.
26   Install the thrust washer on the armature shaft.
27   Install the end head and through bolts. Tighten the through bolts securely.

16   Charging system – general information and precautions

The charging system includes the alternator with either an external voltage regulator or the Single Module Engine Controller (SMEC) regulating the charging system output. Also included in the system is a charge indicator, the battery, a fusible link and the wiring between all the components. The charging system supplies electrical power for the ignition system, the lights, the radio, etc. The alternator is driven by a drivebelt at the front of the engine.

The fusible link is a short length of insulated wire integral with the engine compartment wiring harness. The link is four wire gauges smaller in diameter than the circuit it protects. Production fusible links and their identification flags are identified by the flag color. See Chapter 12 for additional information regarding fusible links.

The charging system doesn't ordinarily require periodic maintenance. However, the drivebelt, battery and wires and connections should be inspected at the intervals outlined in Chapter 1.

The dashboard charge warning light should come on when the ignition key is turned to Start, then go off immediately. If it remains on, there is a malfunction in the charging system (see Section 17). Some vehicles are also equipped with a voltmeter. If the voltmeter indicates abnormally high or low voltage, check the charging system

Be very careful when making electrical circuit connections to a vehicle equipped with an alternator and note the following:

a) When reconnecting the wires to the alternator from the battery, be sure to note the polarity.

b) Before using arc welding equipment to repair any part of the vehicle, disconnect the wires from the alternator and the battery terminals.

c) Never start the engine with a battery charger connected.

d) Always disconnect both battery leads before using a battery charger.

e) The alternator is turned by an engine drivebelt which could cause serious injury if your hands, hair or clothes become entangled in it with the engine running.

f) Because the alternator is connected directly to the battery, it could arc or cause a fire if overloaded or shorted out.

g) Wrap a plastic bag over the alternator and secure it with rubber bands before steam cleaning the engine.

17   Charging system – check

1   If a malfunction occurs in the charging circuit, don't automatically assume that the alternator is causing the problem.

First check the following items:

a) Check the drivebelt tension and condition (see Chapter 1). Replace it if it's worn or deteriorated.

b) Make sure the alternator mounting and adjustment bolts are tight.

c) Inspect the alternator wiring harness and the electrical connectors at the alternator and voltage regulator (if equipped). They must be in good condition and tight.

d) Check the fusible link (if equipped) located between the starter solenoid and the alternator. If it's burned, determine the cause, repair the circuit and replace the link (the vehicle won't start and/or the accessories won't work if the fusible link blows). Sometimes a fusible link may look good, but still be bad. If in doubt, remove it and check for continuity.

e) Start the engine and check the alternator for abnormal noises (a shrieking or squealing sound indicates a bad bearing).

f) Check the specific gravity of the battery electrolyte. If it's low, charge the battery (doesn't apply to maintenance free batteries).

g) Make sure the battery is fully charged (one bad cell in a battery can cause overcharging by the alternator).

h) Disconnect the battery cables (negative first, then positive). Inspect the battery posts and the cable clamps for corrosion. Clean them thoroughly if necessary (see Chapter 1). Reconnect the cable to the positive terminal.

i) With the key off, connect a test light between the negative battery post and the disconnected negative cable clamp.

1) If the test light does not come on, reattach the clamp and proceed to the next Step.

2) If the test light comes on, there is a short (drain) in the electrical system of the vehicle. The short must be repaired before the charging system can be checked.

3) Disconnect the alternator wiring harness.

(a) If the light goes out, the alternator is bad.

(b) If the light stays on, pull each fuse until the light goes out (this will tell you which component is shorted).

2   Using a voltmeter, check the battery voltage with the engine off. If should be approximately 12-volts.

3   Start the engine and check the battery voltage again. It should now be approximately 14-to-15 volts.

4   Turn on the headlights. The voltage should drop, and then come back up, if the charging system is working properly.

Carbureted models

5   If the voltage reading is more than the specified charging voltage, replace the voltage regulator (refer to Section 20). If the voltage is less, the alternator diode(s), stator or rectifier may be bad or the voltage regulator may be malfunctioning.

Fuel-injected models

6   This system is very complex and includes the use of the SMEC or SBEC II for voltage regulation. For further checking, take the vehicle to a dealer service department or other repair shop capable of doing electrical troubleshooting and repairs.

18   Alternator – removal and installation

Refer to illustrations 18.2a, 18.2b, 18.2c and 18.4

1   Detach the cable from the negative terminal of the battery.

2   Loosen the alternator adjustment and pivot bolts and detach the drivebelt **(see illustrations)**.

3   Remove the adjustment and pivot bolts and separate the alternator from the engine.

4   Detach the wires from the alternator **(see illustration)**.

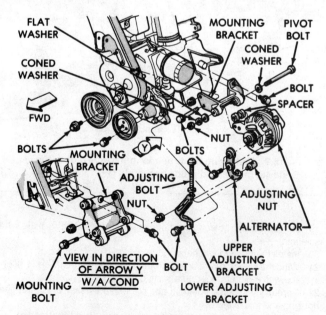

18.2a   Alternator mounting details (four-cylinder models)

18.2b   Loosen the adjustment bolt ...

18.2c   ... and the pivot bolt (V6 model shown)

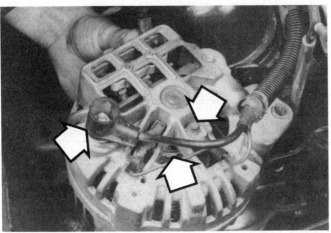
18.4   Disconnect the wires from the back of the alternator

19.2   On Bosch alternators, remove the screws evenly so the holder won't be damaged

5   If you are replacing the alternator, take the old alternator with you when purchasing a replacement unit. Make sure the new/rebuilt unit is identical to the old alternator. Look at the terminals – they should be the same in number, size and location as the terminals on the old alternator. Finally, look at the identification markings – they will be stamped in the housing or printed on a tag or plaque affixed to the housing. Make sure these numbers are the same on both alternators.

6   Many new/rebuilt alternators do not have a pulley installed, so you may have to switch the pulley from the old unit to the new/rebuilt one. When buying an alternator, find out the shop's policy regarding pulleys – some shops will perform this service free of charge.

7   Installation is the reverse of removal.

8   After the alternator is installed, adjust the drivebelt tension (see Chapter 1).

9   Check the charging voltage to verify proper operation of the alternator (see Section 17).

19   Alternator brushes – replacement

Bosch (1988 and 1989)

Refer to illustrations 19.2, 19.3, 19.5 and 19.6

1   Remove the alternator from the vehicle (if necessary).

2   Remove the brush holder mounting screws a little at a time to prevent distortion of the holder (see illustration).

3   Rotate the brush holder and separate it from the rear of the alternator (see illustration).

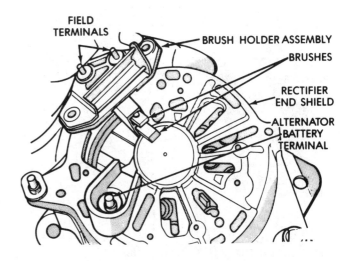
19.3   Rotate the brush holder out of the alternator housing (Bosch)

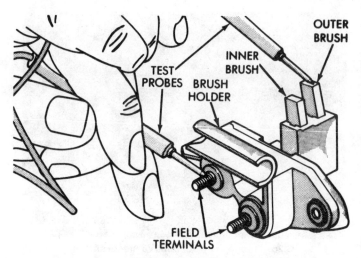

19.5   Be sure continuity exists between each brush and the appropriate field terminal before installing the brush holder assembly (Bosch)

19.6   Push the brush holder into place making sure the brushes (which are spring loaded) seat securely (Bosch)

19.9a   The mounting screw locations for the alternator field brushes (Chrysler 78 amp alternator)

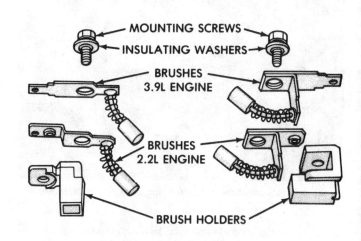

19.9b   Details of the Chrysler 78 amp alternator brushes

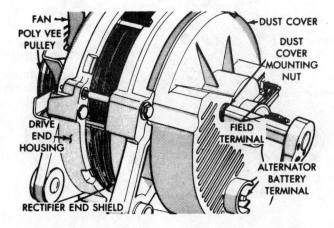

19.12   Remove the nut and detach the dust cover

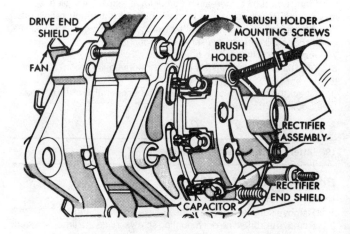

19.13a   Remove the brush holder mounting screws

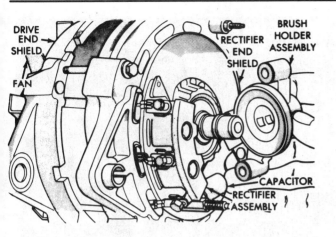

19.13b   Detach the brush holder to service the brushes

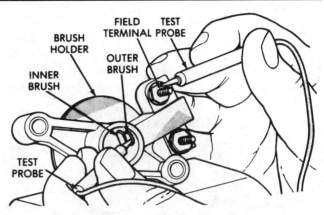

19.14   Using an ohmmeter, check for continuity between the brushes and the appropriate field terminals before installing the brush holder assembly

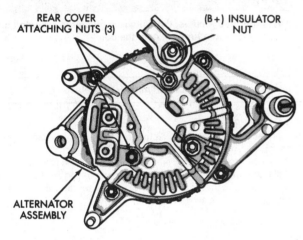

19.17   Remove the B+ insulator (Nippondenso)

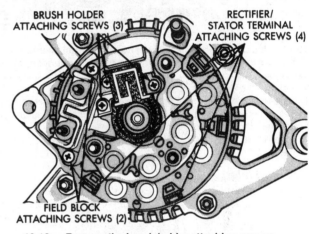

19.19a   Remove the brush holder attaching screws (Nippondenso)

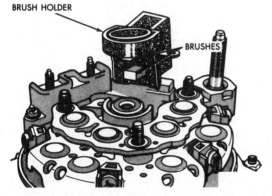

19.19b   Lift the brush holder from the alternator (Nippondenso)

4   If the brushes are worn badly, or if they do not move smoothly in the brush holder, replace the brush holder assembly with a new one.

5   Before installing the brush holder assembly, check for continuity between each brush and the appropriate field terminal **(see illustration)**.

6   Insert the holder into position, making sure the brushes seat correctly **(see illustration)**

7   Hold the brush holder securely in place and install the screws. Tighten them evenly, a little at a time, so the holder is not distorted. Once the screws are snug, tighten them securely.

8   Connect the negative battery cable.

Chrysler
78 amp model (1987)
Refer to illustrations 19.9a and 19.9b

9   With the alternator removed, remove the brush screws and insulating washers, then lift the brush and holder assemblies from the alternator **(see illustrations)**.

10   Installation is the reverse of removal.

11   Be sure the brushes are not grounded.

All others (1987 through 1989)
Refer to illustrations 19.12, 19.13a, 19.13b and 19.14

12   With the alternator removed from the vehicle, remove the nut retaining the dust cover. Remove the dust cover **(see illustration)**.

13   Remove the brush holder mounting screws and separate the brush holder from the end shield **(see illustrations)**.

14   Before installing the new brush holder assembly, check for continuity between each brush and the appropriate field terminal **(see illustration)**.

15   Installation is the reverse of removal.

16   Be careful when slipping the brushes over the slip rings and do not overtighten the brush holder mounting screws.

Nippondenso (1988 and 1989)
Refer to illustrations 19.17, 19.19a, 19.19b and 19.21

17   With the alternator removed from the vehicle, remove the B+ insulator nut and insulator **(see illustration)**.

18   Remove rear cover attaching nuts and remove the rear cover.

19   Remove the brush holder attaching screws and lift the brush holder from the alternator **(see illustrations)**.

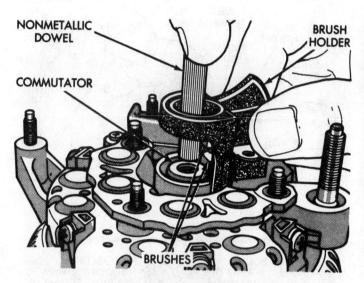

19.21   Using a non-metallic dowel, push the brushes into their holders and guide the assembly into place (Nippondenso)

20   Reverse the removal procedure to install the brushes.

21   When installing the brush holder, use a non-metallic dowel to hold the brushes in the holder, then slide the assembly over the commutator slip rings and screw it into place **(see illustration)**.

22   When installing the B+ insulator, align the guide boss with the hole in the rear cover.

1990 and later

The manufacturer does not recommend servicing alternators on 1990 and later models. If faulty in any way, replace the alternator as a unit.

20.1   On carbureted models, the voltage regulator is mounted on the firewall, near the coil

20   Voltage regulator (carbureted models) – replacement

Refer to illustration 20.1

1   Disconnect the electrical connector from the voltage regulator **(see illustration)**.

2   Remove the mounting screws and regulator from the firewall.

3   Installation is the reverse of removal. Before mounting the regulator to the firewall, make sure the regulator and the firewall are clean (bare metal) so a good ground will be achieved.

Chapter 6   Emissions control systems

Contents

6

---

1   General information

Refer to illustration 1.6a and 1.6b

1   To prevent pollution of the atmosphere from incompletely burned and evaporating gases, and to maintain good driveability and fuel economy, a number of emission control systems are incorporated. They include the:

Electronic Engine Control system
Exhaust Gas Recirculation (EGR) system
Air Injector Reactor (AIR) system
Fuel evaporative emission control (EVAP) system
Positive Crankcase Ventilation (PCV) system
Heated air Inlet system
Catalytic converter

All of these systems are linked, directly or indirectly, to the emission control system.
2   The Sections in this Chapter include general descriptions, checking procedures within the scope of the home mechanic and component replacement procedures (when possible).

3   Before assuming that an emissions control system is malfunctioning, check the fuel and ignition systems carefully. The diagnosis of some emission control devices requires specialized tools, equipment and training. If checking and servicing become too difficult or if a procedure is beyond your ability, consult a dealer service department. Remember, the most frequent cause of emissions problems is simply a loose or broken vacuum hose or wire, so always check the hose and wiring connections first.
4   This doesn't mean, however, that emission control systems are particularly difficult to maintain and repair. You can quickly and easily perform many checks and do most of the regular maintenance at home with common tune-up and hand tools. **Note:** *Because of a Federally mandated extended warranty (five years or 50,000 miles at the time this manual was written) which covers the emission control system components, check with your dealer about warranty coverage before working on any emissions-related systems. Once the warranty has expired, you may wish to perform some of the component checks and/or replacement procedures in this Chapter to save money.*
5   Pay close attention to any special precautions outlined in this Chapter. It should be noted that the illustrations of the various systems may not exactly match the system installed on your vehicle because of changes made by the manufacturer during production or from year-to-year.

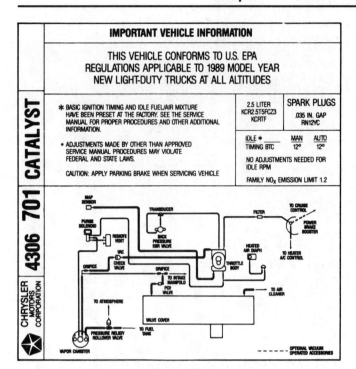

1.6a   A typical Emissions Adjustment and Routing (EAR) information label

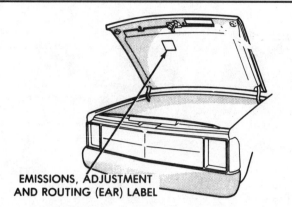

EMISSIONS, ADJUSTMENT AND ROUTING (EAR) LABEL

1.6b   The EAR label is attached to the inside of the hood

6   An Emissions Adjustment and Routing (EAR) information label is located in the engine compartment **(see illustrations)**. This label contains important emissions specifications and adjustment information, as well as a vacuum hose schematic with emissions components identified. When servicing the engine or emissions systems, the EAR label in your particular vehicle should always be checked for up-to-date information.

2   Check Engine light (fault codes) and electronic control system components

Check Engine light (Fuel-injected models only)

1   The Check Engine light, located at the lower left corner of the instrument cluster, comes on each time the ignition key is turned to the On posi-

tion. It should stay on for three seconds. This lets you know the Check Engine light is functioning properly.
2   If the SMEC receives an incorrect signal or no signal from certain sensors or emission related systems, the Check Engine light will illuminate and the SMEC will revert to a "limp in" mode, allowing the vehicle to be driven in for servicing. If the Check Engine light comes on while the vehicle is being driven, service the vehicle as soon as possible. On fuel-injected models, the first step in servicing should be checking to see what fault code(s) are stored. These codes can be very helpful in diagnosing the problem(s).

Obtaining fault codes (Fuel-injected models only)

3   The "Check Engine" light flashes any stored fault code(s) after the ignition switch is cycled twice from On to Off, then to On within five seconds.
4   The codes are two-digit numbers. The start of test (88) code (eight flashes, a pause and eight more flashes) is flashed first. After this code, any stored fault codes will be flashed in order. After the last code is flashed, the end of code output (55) code (five flashes, a pause and five more flashes) is flashed.
5   Refer to the accompanying fault code chart to determine the problem(s) indicated by the code(s). Most of the fault codes identify a problem in a particular circuit or component. Check the vacuum hoses, wires and connections in the circuit identified. Make sure all vacuum hoses are routed properly (refer to the EAR label attached to the inside of the hood). Keep in mind that replacing the component identified may not solve the problem in all cases. If you're not sure what's causing the problem in the circuit, take the vehicle to a dealer service department for further diagnosis. Remember that electrical parts usually cannot be returned, and many of the sensors and actuators used on these vehicles are quite expensive.

Note: *These codes apply only to fuel-injected models. Codes cannot be retrieved from carbureted models.*

Fault code	Circuit or component affected
88 (8 flashes, pause, 8 flashes)	Start of test
11 (3.9L and 5.2L models) (1 flash, pause, 1 flash)	No distributor input signal
11 (3.9L models) (1 flash, pause, 1 flash)	No distributor input signal
12 (1 flash, pause, 2 flashes)	Memory standby power lost
13* (1 flash, pause, 3 flashes)	MAP sensor vacuum circuit
14* (1 flash, pause, 4 flashes)	MAP sensor electrical circuit

Fault code	Circuit or component affected
15** (1 flash, pause, 5 flashes)	Vehicle speed/distance sensor circuit
16* (1 flash, pause, 6 flashes)	Loss of battery voltage
17 (1 flash, pause, 7 flashes)	Engine running too cold
21** (2 flashes, pause, 1 flash)	Oxygen sensor circuit
22* (2 flashes, pause, 2 flashes)	Coolant temperature sensor circuit
23 (2 flashes, pause, 3 flashes)	Throttle body temperature sensor circuit (2.5L and 3.9L models) Charge air temperature sensor circuit (5.2L models)
24* (2 flashes, pause, 4 flashes)	Throttle position sensor circuit
25** (2 flashes, pause, 5 flashes)	Idle Speed Control (ISC) motor driver circuit
26* (2.5L models) (2 flashes, pause, 6 flashes)	Peak injector current has not been reached
26 (3.9L models) (2 flashes, pause, 6 flashes)	Injector circuit(s) have high resistance
27* (2.5L models) (2 flashes, pause, 7 flashes)	Fuel injector control circuit
27 (3.9L and 5.2L models) (2 flashes, pause, 7 flashes)	Injector output circuit not responding
31** (3 flashes, pause, 1 flash)	Canister purge solenoid circuit
32** (3 flashes, pause, 2 flashes)	EGR system
33 (3 flashes, pause, 3 flashes)	A/C clutch cutout relay circuit
34 (3 flashes, pause, 4 flashes)	Speed control vacuum or vent control solenoid circuit(s)
35 (3 flashes, pause, 5 flashes)	Idle switch circuit
36* (3 flashes, pause, 6 flashes)	*Air switching solenoid circuit
37 (3 flashes, pause, 7 flashes)	Part throttle unlock solenoid driver circuit (Automatic transmission only)
41 (4 flashes, pause, 1 flash)	Charging system excess or lack of field current
42 (4 flashes, pause, 2 flashes)	Automatic shutdown relay driver circuit
43 (4 flashes, pause, 3 flashes)	Ignition coil control circuit
44 (4 flashes, pause, 4 flashes)	Loss of FJ2 to logic board

6

Fault code	Circuit or component affected
46* (4 flashes, pause, 6 flashes)	Battery voltage too high
47 (4 flashes, pause, 7 flashes)	Battery voltage too low
51* (5 flashes, pause, 1 flash)	Oxygen sensor stuck at lean position
52* (5 flashes, pause, 2 flashes)	Oxygen sensor stuck at rich position
53 (5 flashes, pause, 3 flashes)	Module internal problem
55 (5 flashes, pause, 5 flashes)	End of code output
62 (6 flashes, pause, 2 flashes)	Emissions reminder light mileage is not being updated
63 (6 flashes, pause, 3 flashes)	EEPROM write denied

* Activates Check Engine light

** Activates Check Engine light (California models only)

Electronic control system components

Note: *The following information is for some of the components used in the engine's electronic control system. The other Sections in this Chapter have checking and component replacement information for other emissions control system components.*

Automatic Idle Speed Motor (AIS) (all four-cylinder and 1992 and later V6 and V8 engines)

General description

6   The AIS motor is an output device controlled by the SMEC or SBEC II. It controls the idle rpm according to engine load.

Replacement

Refer to illustrations 2.9 and 2.13

7   Disconnect the negative cable at the battery.
8   Remove the air cleaner assembly.

9   Unplug the connector on the AIS motor **(see the accompanying illustration or illustration 16.4 in Chapter 4).**
10   On 2.5L engines, remove the throttle body temperature sensor.
11   Remove the two Torx retaining screws.
12   Withdraw the AIS motor from the throttle body, making sure that the O-ring does not fall into the throttle body opening.
13   On 2.5L engines, prior to installation, make sure the pintle is in the retracted position. If the retracted pintle measurement is more than one inch (25 mm) **(see illustration)**, the AIS motor must be taken to a dealer service department or properly equipped shop to be retracted.
14   Install a new O-ring and insert the AIS motor into the housing, making sure the O-ring is not dislodged.
15   Install the two retaining screws and tighten them securely.
16   Plug the four-way connector into the AIS motor.
17   On 2.5L engines, install the throttle body temperature sensor.
18   Install the air cleaner assembly and connect the negative battery cable.

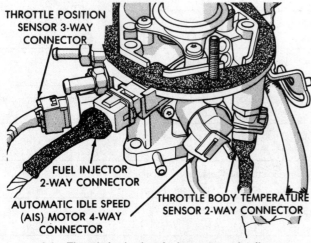

2.9   Throttle body electrical connector details (2.5L engine models)

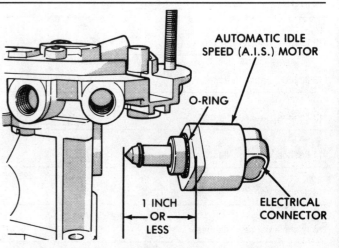

2.13   Be sure the AIS pintle extends one inch or less (2.5L engine)

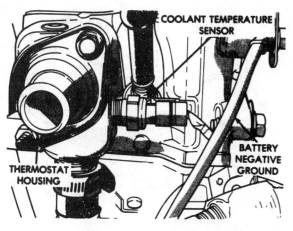

2.19a   The location of the coolant temperature sensor (four-cylinder engines)

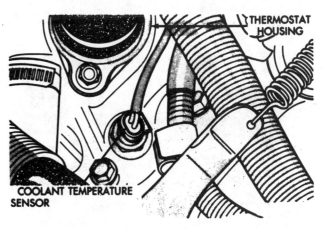

2.19b   The location of the coolant temperature sensor (V6 and V8 engine)

Coolant temperature sensor

Refer to illustrations 2.19a and 2.19b

General description

19   Located on or near the thermostat housing (see illustrations), this temperature sensitive variable resistor inputs the coolant temperature to the SCC, SMEC or SBEC II.

Replacement

20   Disconnect the electrical connector.
21   Unscrew the sensor from the engine.
22   Wrap the threads of the sensor with Teflon tape.
23   Install the sensor and tighten it securely.

Emissions maintenance (MAINT REQD) reminder light

24   This light illuminates to remind the driver that it is time to have the emissions control devices checked for proper operation.
25   To turn off the light on 1987 and 1988 models, insert a small screwdriver into the hole in the module (located on the back of the instrument cluster, on a bracket below the headlight switch) and depress the reset switch.

Note: *A special DRB-II scan tool is required to reset the MAINT REQD light on 1989 and later models. Take the vehicle to a dealer service department that has the correct tool.*

Idle speed control actuator (fuel-injected V6 and V8 engines through 1991)

Refer to illustrations 2.29 and 2.38

General description

26   The idle speed control actuator is an output device controlled by the SMEC. It controls idle rpm according to engine load.

Replacement

27   Remove the air cleaner.
28   Disconnect the negative cable from the battery.
29   Disconnect the electrical connector from the actuator (see illustration).
30   Remove the three nuts and detach the actuator from the bracket.
31   Install the new actuator in the bracket with the three nuts and washers.
32   Attach the electrical connector.
33   Connect the negative battery cable.
34   Start the engine and allow it to run for two minutes.
35   Shut off the engine and allow 60 seconds for the actuator to fully engage.
36   Disconnect the electrical connector from the actuator.
37   Disconnect the electrical connector from the coolant temperature sensor.
38   Hook up a tachometer, start the engine and adjust the adjustment screw on the actuator until the rpm is between 2500 and 2600 (see illustration).

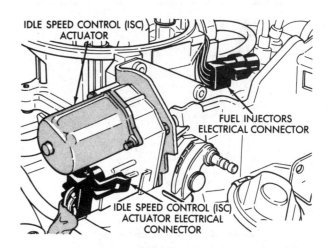

2.29   Lightly pry on the retaining clip and remove the ISC actuator electrical connector

6

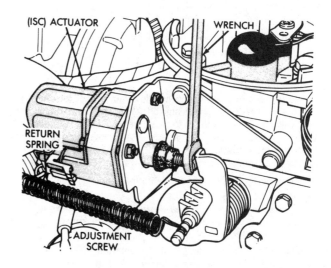

2.38   Turn the adjustment screw until the specified rpm is obtained

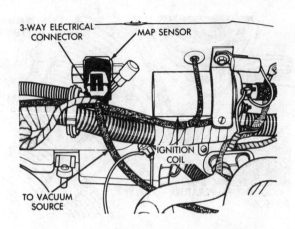

2.40a   Manifold Absolute Pressure (MAP) sensor mounting details (all four-cylinder and 1988 V6 engines)

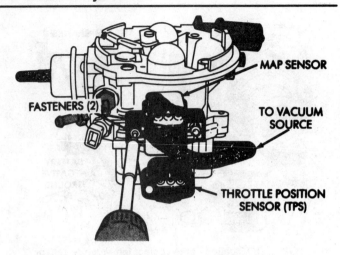

2.40b   Manifold Absolute Pressure (MAP) sensor mounting details (1989 through 1991 V6 and V8 engines)

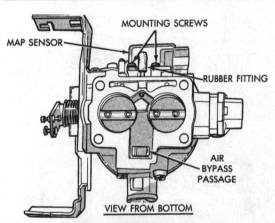

2.45   Remove the MAP sensor mounting screws and, while removing the MAP sensor, disconnect the L–shaped vacuum fitting from the throttle body

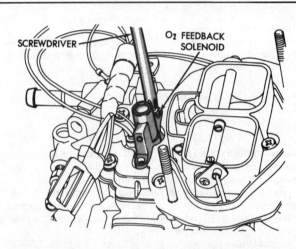

2.48   Remove the screws retaining the oxygen feedback solenoid

39   Shut off the engine, remove the tachometer and reconnect the actuator and coolant temperature sensor.

Manifold Absolute Pressure (MAP) sensor (fuel-injected models)
Refer to illustrations 2,40a, 2.40b and 2.45

General description
40   This sensor provides an intake manifold vacuum signal to the SMEC or SBEC II. The MAP sensor is located on the engine compartment side of the firewall **(see illustration)** on four-cylinder and 1988 V6 engines. On 1989 through 1991 V6 and V8 engines the MAP sensor is mounted on the throttle body **(see illustration)**. On 1992 and later V6 and V8 models it is also located on the throttle body **(see illustration 16.4 in Chapter 4)**.

Replacement (four-cylinder and 1989 through 1991 V6 and V8 engines)
41   Remove the vacuum hose and electrical connector from the sensor.
42   Push down on the mounting clip and remove the sensor.
43   Installation is the reverse of the removal procedure.

Replacement (1992 and later V6 and V8 engines)
44   Remove the throttle body (see Chapter 4).
45   Remove the MAP sensor mounting screws. While removing the MAP sensor, slide the vacuum rubber L-shaped fitting from the throttle body **(see illustration)**.

46   Installation is the reverse of the removal procedure.

Oxygen feedback solenoid (carbureted models)
Refer to illustrations 2.48, 2.49 and 2.51

General description
47   This output device is controlled by the Spark Control Computer (SCC). It is located in the carburetor and is controlled in response to the oxygen sensor input.

Replacement
48   Remove the two screws retaining the feedback solenoid **(see illustration)**.
49   Disconnect the electrical connector and lift the solenoid from the carburetor **(see illustration)**.
50   Position a new solenoid gasket on the carburetor.
51   Install a new O-ring on the solenoid **(see illustration)**.
52   Apply a thin film of grease to the O-ring and install the solenoid assembly into the carburetor.
53   Install and tighten the retaining screws securely.

Oxygen sensor

General description
54   By measuring the exhaust content, this input device reports to the computer how rich or lean the engine is running. This sensor is located in the exhaust manifold.

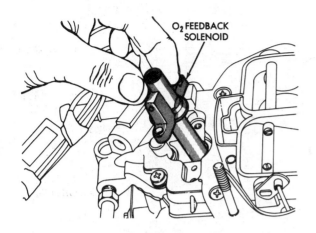

2.49 Pull up on the solenoid and remove it from the carburetor

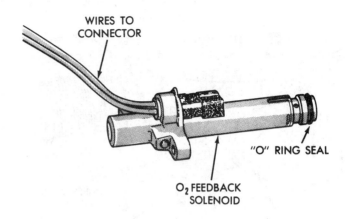

2.51 Before installing the solenoid, replace the O-ring and lubricate it with a thin film of grease

55 Unlike other inputs it is not a variable resistor; it actually produces up to one volt of electricity (at full rich condition). **Caution:** *Never use a voltmeter without a 10 mega-ohm impedance to check the output of the oxygen sensor.*
56 The oxygen sensor must be replaced at the specified interval (see Chapter 1). The sensor is threaded into the exhaust manifold. On some models it may be necessary to raise the front of the vehicle and support it securely on jackstands to gain access from the underside of the engine compartment.

Replacement
Refer to illustration 2.57

57 Disconnect the oxygen sensor wire by unplugging the connector **(see illustration)**.
58 With the engine warmed up, use a wrench to unscrew the sensor.
59 Use a tap to clean the threads in the exhaust manifold.
60 New sensors should already have anti-seize compound on their threads, so you shouldn't need to apply any.
61 Install and tighten the sensor.
62 Plug in the connector.

Single Module Engine Controller (SMEC) (TBI fuel injection) or Single Board Engine Controller II (SBEC II) (MPI fuel injection)

63 This is the computer for fuel-injected engines. It makes calculations based on inputs from the various sensors and in turn sends out signals to control the various output controlled devices. See Chapter 5 for more information on this component.

Spark Control Computer (SCC)

64 This is the computer for carbureted engines. It makes calculations based on inputs from the various sensors and in turn sends out signals to control the various output controlled devices. See Chapter 5 for more information on this component.

Throttle body temperature sensor (fuel-injected four-cylinder models)
Refer to illustration 2.70

General description
65 This is a temperature sensitive variable resistor acting as an input for the SMEC. It is mounted on the throttle body and reports the throttle body temperature.

Replacement
66 Disconnect the negative cable at the battery.
67 Remove the air cleaner assembly.
68 Disconnect the throttle cable from the throttle body, remove the two cable bracket screws and lay the bracket aside.
69 Unplug the electrical connector by pulling down on it.

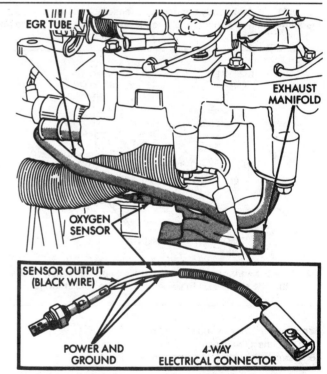

2.57 It's sometimes easier to remove the oxygen sensor with the engine warmed up – be careful not to burn yourself on the hot exhaust manifold! (2.2L and 2.5L oxygen sensor shown; others are similar)

70 Remove the sensor by unscrewing it **(see illustration)**.
71 Apply a thin coat of heat transfer compound to the tip of the new sensor.
72 Screw the new sensor into the throttle body and tighten it securely.
73 Plug in the electrical connector.
74 Connect the throttle cable and bracket.
75 Install the air cleaner and connect the negative battery cable.

Throttle Position Sensor (TPS) (fuel-injected models)
Refer to illustrations 2.81 and 2.91

General description
76 The throttle position sensor is a variable resistor acting as an input for the SMEC. It is located on the throttle shaft and reports the throttle position.

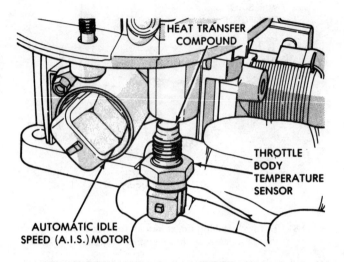

2.70   Throttle body temperature sensor location – when installing the new sensor, apply heat transfer compound to the tip

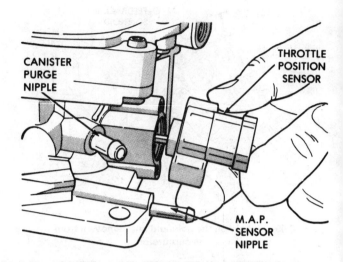

2.81   Remove the mounting screws and pull off the throttle position sensor (TPS) (V6 and V8 engines through 1991)

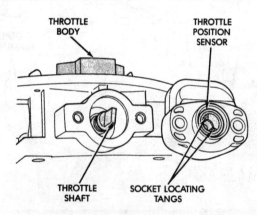

2.91   If the sensor won't rotate, remove and reinstall it so the throttle shaft is on the other side of the socket tangs

Replacement (four-cylinder models)
77 Disconnect the negative cable at the battery.
78 Remove the air cleaner assembly.

79 Unplug the electrical connector at the TPS.
80 Remove the two TPS-to-throttle body screws.
81 Pull the TPS off the throttle shaft (see illustration).
82 Remove the O-ring.
83 Install the TPS with a new O-ring on the throttle body and install the screws. Tighten the screws securely.
84 Plug in the electrical connector at the TPS.
85 Install the air cleaner assembly.
86 Connect the negative battery cable.

Replacement (V6 and V8 engines)
87 Remove the air cleaner assembly.
88 Disconnect the negative cable from the battery.
89 Disconnect the electrical connector from the throttle position sensor.
90 On V6 and V8 engines through 1991, remove the two screws and lift the throttle position sensor off the throttle shaft (see illustration 2.81). On 1992 and later V6 and V8 engines, remove the two screws and remove the throttle position sensor from the throttle shaft.
91 Installation is the reverse of the removal procedure. On 1992 and later V6 and V8 engines, install the throttle position sensor onto the throttle

shaft so that it can be rotated a few degrees in either direction. If the sensor won't rotate, remove the sensor and reinstall it so the throttle shaft is on the other side of the socket tangs (see illustration), then tighten the screws securely.

Crankshaft Position Sensor (CPS) (1992 and later V6 and V8 engines)
Refer to illustrations 2.93 and 2.97

General description
92 The crankshaft position sensor is located at the rear of the engine next to the flywheel. It measures flywheel or flexplate rotations and sends signals to the SBEC II. The output from the CPS and distributor sync signal is used to differentiate between spark or fuel injection events.

Replacement
93 Remove the spark plug wire loom and spark plug wires from the right valve cover mounting stud (see illustration). Position the spark plug cables on top of the valve cover.
94 Disconnect the two hoses from the EGR valve. Mark the hoses to ensure proper reinstallation.
95 Disconnect the wire connector and hoses from the EGR transducer. Mark the hoses to ensure proper reinstallation.
96 Remove the mounting bolts and the EGR valve and gasket.
97 Disconnect the electrical wire from the engine oil pressure sending unit. Use special tool (C-4597) and remove the oil pressure sending unit from the engine (see illustration).
98 Loosen the EGR tube mounting nuts on the intake manifold. Remove the mounting bolts at the exhaust manifold and remove the EGR tube, discarding the gasket at the exhaust manifold end.
99 Disconnect the electrical wire from the crankshaft position sensor (see illustration 2.93).
100 Remove the sensor mounting bolts and remove the sensor.
101 Installation is the reverse of the removal procedure. Apply thread sealant to the oil pressure sending unit prior to installation. Don't let any of the sealant into the sending unit opening. Install new gaskets where applicable.

Vehicle Speed Sensor (1992 and later V6 and V8 engines)

General description
102 The sensor input is used to determine vehicle speed and distance traveled.

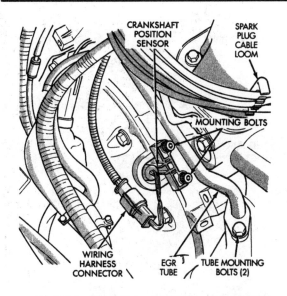

2.93 Crankshaft position sensor and related components (1992 and later V6 and V8 engines)

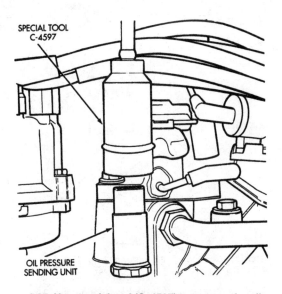

2.97 Use special tool (C–4597) to remove the oil pressure sending unit from the engine

Replacement

103 Raise the vehicle and support is securely on jackstands.
104 Disconnect the wire connector from the sensor and unscrew the speedometer cable.
105 Remove the speed sensor mounting bolts and remove the sensor from the transmission extension housing or transfer case.
106 Installation is the reverse of the removal procedure.

3   Heated air inlet system

General description

Refer to illustration 3.1

Note: *The heated air inlet system is used on all 2.5L engines and on V6 engines through 1991.*

1   This system is designed to improve driveability, reduce emissions and prevent icing in cold weather by directing hot air from around the exhaust manifold to the air cleaner intake **(see illustration)**.
2   The intake air system is made up of two circuits. When the outside air temperature is cold and the engine is cold the intake air flows through the heated air duct, up through the air cleaner and into the carburetor or throttle body.
3   When the air temperature is warm or hot, air enters the air cleaner through the fresh air duct.

4   A valve in the air cleaner assembly is controlled by a vacuum diaphragm which is actuated by a bi-metal temperature sensor. The sensor reacts to both intake manifold vacuum and the air temperature inside the air cleaner itself.
5   When the air temperature inside the air horn is cold, the air bleed valve in the sensor remains closed and intake manifold vacuum opens the air control valve to direct heated air to the intake.
6   When the air temperature inside the air cleaner is hot, the sensor air bleed valve opens the air control valve, allowing outside air directly into the carburetor. At temperatures between the two extremes, the sensor provides a blend of outside and heated air to the intake.

Checking

Refer to illustrations 3.8a, 3.8b, 3.8c, 3.11, 3.14a, 3.14b, and 3.15

7   Refer to Chapter 1 for the general checking procedure. If the system is not operating properly, check the individual components as follows.
8   Check all vacuum hoses for cracks, kinks, proper routing and broken sections. Make sure the shrouds and ducts are in good condition as well **(see illustrations)**.

6

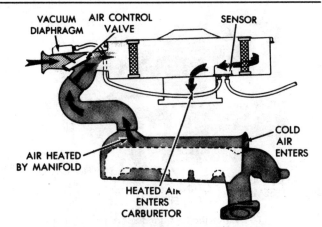

3.1   A typical heated air inlet system

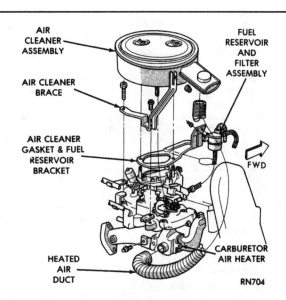

3.8a   Heated air inlet system details (2.2L)

RN704

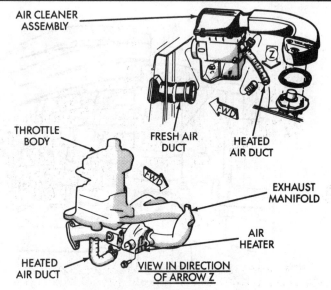

3.8b   Heated air inlet system details (2.5L)

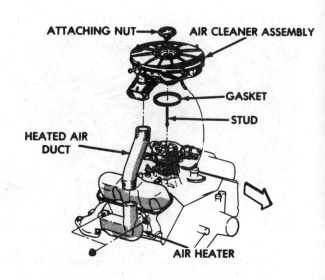

3.8c   Heated air inlet system details (3.9L through 1991)

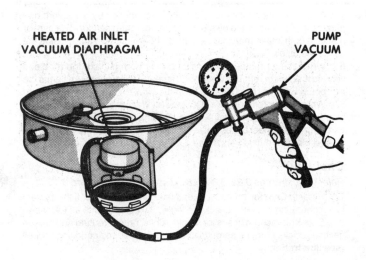

3.11   The door should open when vacuum is applied to the diaphragm (3.9L shown, others similar)

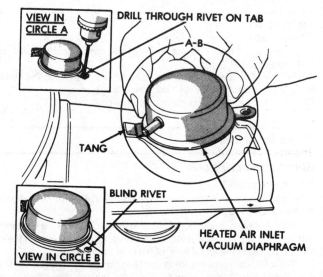

3.14a   To remove the vacuum diaphragm drill out the blind rivet (2.2L and 1987 through 1991 3.9L)

9   Remove the air cleaner assembly from the engine and allow it to cool to 110-degrees F (44-degrees C). Apply 20-inches of vacuum to the sensor with a hand vacuum pump.

10   The door should be in the up (heat on) position with the vacuum applied. If it is not, check the vacuum diaphragm.

11   To check the diaphragm, slowly apply vacuum with the hand pump while watching the door **(see illustration)**.

12   The door should not begin to open at less than two inches and should be fully open at four inches or less. With 25-inches applied, the diaphragm should not bleed down more than ten inches in five minutes.

13   Replace the sensor and/or vacuum diaphragm with new units if they fail any of the tests. Test the new unit(s) as described before reinstalling the air cleaner assembly.

Component replacement
Vacuum diaphragm
Refer to illustrations 3.14a, 3.14b and 3.15

14   With the air cleaner removed, disconnect the vacuum hose and drill out the blind rivet **(see illustrations)**.

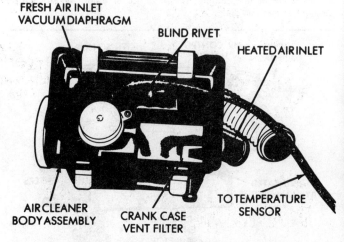

3.14b   To remove the vacuum diaphragm, drill out the blind rivet (2.5L)

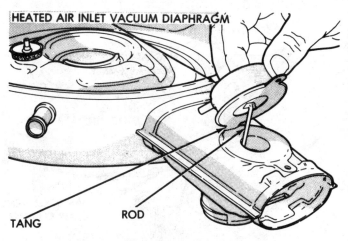

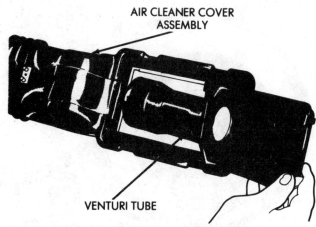

3.15   Pull the diaphragm away from the air cleaner assembly and disconnect the rod (3.9L is shown, others are similar)

3.19   To remove the temperature sensor, you must slide the venturi tube away from the air cleaner assembly (2.5L models)

15   Lift up on the diaphragm, disconnect the rod and disengage the tang from the air cleaner housing **(see illustration)**.
16   Check the control door for free travel by raising it to the full up position and allowing it to fall closed. If it does not close easily, free it up. Check the hinge pin for free movement also, using compressed air or spray cleaner to remove any foreign matter.
17   To install the diaphragm, insert the rod end into the control door and position the diaphragm tang in the slot, turning the diaphragm clockwise until it engages. Rivet the tab in place.
18   Connect the vacuum hose.

Temperature sensor
Refer to illustrations 3.19, 3.20, 3.22a, 3.22b and 3.25

2.5L models
19   With the air cleaner housing removed, remove the venturi tube **(see illustration)**.
20   Remove the retaining clip, the sensor and the gasket **(see illustration)**.
21   Installation is the reverse of removal.

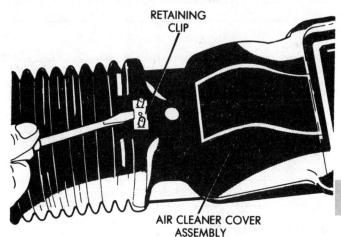

3.20   Use a screwdriver to pop up the clip retaining the temperature sensor

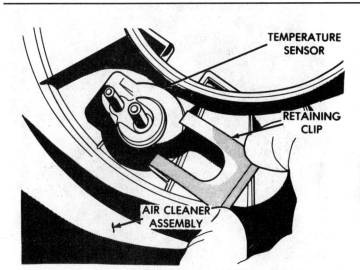

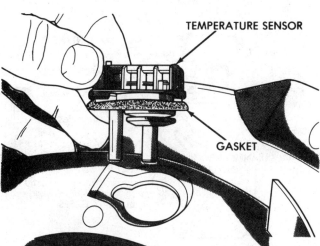

3.22a   Slide the retaining clip away from the heated air temperature sensor (2.2L and 1987 through 1991 3.9L) and . . .

3.22b   . . . detach the sensor from the housing – be sure to install a new gasket if it's damaged

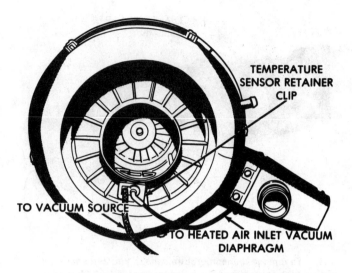

3.25   Vacuum hose routing for the heated air inlet system (2.2L and 1987 through 1991 3.9L)

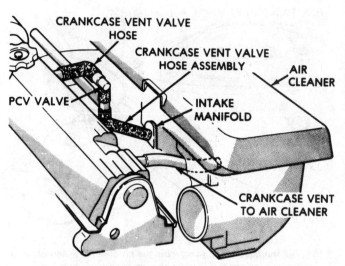

4.2a   A typical Positive Crankcase Ventilation (PCV) system (2.5L four-cylinder)

All others

22   Remove the air cleaner assembly. Disconnect the vacuum hoses and use a screwdriver to pry the retaining clip off **(see illustration)**. Detach the sensor from the housing **(see illustration)**.

23   To install the sensor, place the gasket on it and insert it into the housing.

24   Hold the sensor in place so that the gasket is compressed to form a good seal and install the new retaining clip.

25   Connect the vacuum hoses **(see illustration)**.

4   Positive Crankcase Ventilation (PCV) system

General description

Refer to illustrations 4.2a, 4.2b and 4.3

1   This system is designed to reduce hydrocarbon emissions (HC) by routing blow-by gases (fuel/air mixture that escapes from the combustion chamber past the piston rings into the crankcase) from the crankcase to the intake manifold and combustion chambers, where they are burned during engine operation.

2   The system is very simple and consists of rubber hoses and a small, replaceable metering valve (PCV valve) **(see illustrations)**.

Checking and component replacement

3   With the engine running at idle, pull the PCV valve out of the engine or crankcase vent valve hose and place your finger over the valve inlet **(see illustration)**. A strong vacuum will be felt and a hissing noise will be heard if the valve is operating properly. Replace the valve with a new one if it is not functioning as described. Do not attempt to clean the old valve.

4   To replace the PCV valve, simply pull it from the hose or vent module and install a new one.

5   Inspect the hose prior to installation to ensure that it isn't plugged or damaged. Compare the new valve with the old one to make sure they are the same. Chapter 1 contains additional PCV valve information.

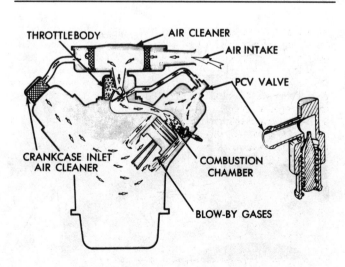

4.2b   A typical Positive Crankcase Ventilation (PCV) system (V6 and V8)

4.3   With the engine running, be sure you can feel vacuum at the PCV valve

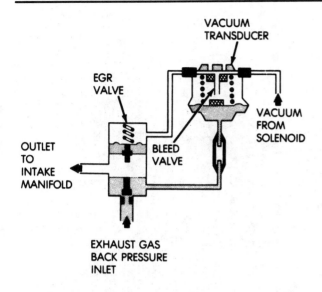

5.3 Backpressure type EGR system schematic (fuel-injected models)

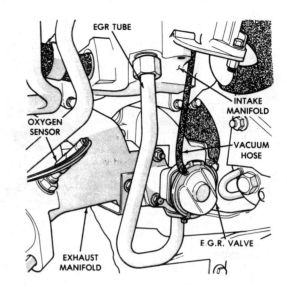

5.6 Inspect all EGR hoses and connections for leaks (2.2L)

5   Exhaust Gas Recirculation (EGR) system

General description

Refer to illustration 5.3

1   This system recirculates a portion of the exhaust gases into the intake manifold or carburetor in order to reduce the combustion temperatures and decrease the amount of nitrogen oxide (NOx) produced. The main component in the system is the EGR valve.

Carbureted models

2   The EGR valve operates in conjunction with the Coolant Vacuum Switch Cold Closed (CVSCC) valve. The CVSCC and the EGR valves remain shut at low engine temperatures. When the engine is operating at normal temperatures, the CVSCC valve opens, allowing vacuum to be applied to the EGR valve so exhaust gas can recirculate.

Fuel-injected models

3   The EGR valve is a backpressure type. The amount of exhaust gas admitted is regulated by engine vacuum and the backpressure transducer. The transducer uses exhaust system backpressure to control the EGR valve vacuum, bleeding the vacuum off to the atmosphere whenever the backpressure at the valve itself drops below the calibrated level **(see illustration)**.

4   In accordance with engine temperature and driving conditions, the EGR valve and transducer are controlled by the EGR solenoid (which is operated by the SMEC) which controls the vacuum flow to the EGR valve.

5   Symptoms of problems associated with the EGR system are rough idling or stalling, rough engine performance during light throttle application and stalling during deceleration.

Checking

Refer to illustrations 5.6, 5.12, 5.16, 5.18a and 5.18b

Carbureted models

6   Check all hoses for cracks, kinks, broken sections and proper connection **(see illustration)**. Inspect all system connections for damage, cracks and leaks.

7   To check the EGR system operation, bring the engine up to operating temperature and, with the transmission in Neutral (parking brake set and tires blocked to prevent movement), allow it to idle for 70 seconds. Open the throttle abruptly so the engine speed is between 2000 and 3000 rpm and then allow it to close. The EGR valve stem should move if the control system is working properly. The test should be repeated several times. Movement of the stem indicates the control system is functioning correctly.

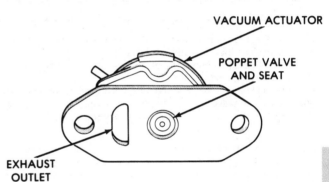

5.12 If the EGR valve is suspected of leaking exhaust into the intake at idle (and causing a rough idle), it should be removed and inspected for deposits between the poppet and seat

8   If the EGR valve stem does not move, check all of the hose connections to make sure they are not leaking or clogged. Disconnect the vacuum hose and apply ten inches of vacuum with a hand pump. If the stem still does not move, replace the EGR valve with a new one. If the valve does open, measure the valve travel to make sure it is approximately 1/8-inch. Also, the engine should run roughly when the valve is open. If it doesn't, the passages are probably clogged (see Step 11)

9   Apply vacuum with the pump and then clamp the hose shut. The valve should stay open for 30 seconds or longer. If it does not, the diaphragm is leaking and the valve should be replaced with a new one.

10   Using a 3/16-inch diameter hose, bypass the Coolant Vacuum Switch Cold Closed (CVSCC) valve located in the thermostat housing. If the EGR valve did not operate under the conditions described in Step 7, but does operate properly with the CVSCC bypassed, the CVSCC is defective and should be replaced.

11   If the EGR valve does not operate with the CVSCC bypassed, the carburetor must be removed to check and clean the slotted port in the throttle bore and the vacuum passages and orifices in the throttle body. Use solvent to remove deposits and check for flow with light air pressure.

12   If the engine idles roughly and it is suspected the EGR valve is not closing, remove the EGR valve and inspect the poppet and seat area for deposits **(see illustration)**.

6

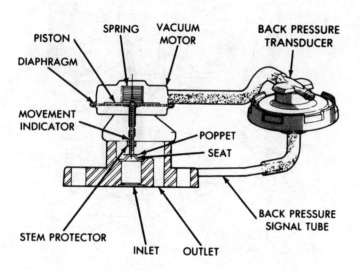

5.16   To test the EGR valve assembly on fuel-injected models, disconnect the vacuum inlet line to the transducer (shown disconnected in this illustration) and apply vacuum (see text)

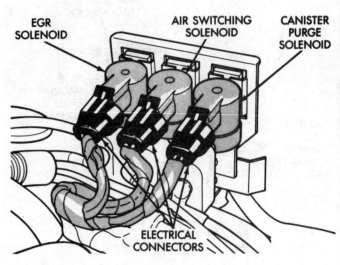

5.18a   EGR solenoid location (3.9L and 5.2L through 1991)

13   If the deposits are more than a thin film of carbon, the valve should be cleaned. To clean the valve, apply solvent and allow it to penetrate and soften the deposits, making sure that none gets on the valve diaphragm, as it could be damaged.

14   Use a vacuum pump to hold the valve open and carefully scrape the deposits from the seat and poppet area with a tool. Inspect the poppet and stem for wear and replace the valve with a new one if wear is found.

Fuel-injected models

15   To check the EGR valve operation, bring the engine up to operating temperature with the transmission in Neutral (tires blocked and parking brake set to prevent movement).

16   Disconnect the vacuum inlet hose from the transducer and connect a vacuum pump **(see illustration)**. Start the engine, raise the engine speed to approximately 2000 rpm, hold it there and apply ten inches of vacuum with the pump. The EGR valve stem should move and stay open for at least 30 seconds if the control system is working properly.

17   Measure the valve travel to make sure it's approximately 1/8-inch. If the stem moves but will not stay open, the EGR valve/backpressure transducer assembly is faulty and must be replaced with a new one.

18   If the EGR valve stem does not move except when vacuum from the pump is applied, check the EGR solenoid for proper operation **(see illustrations)**. If the solenoid is allowing vacuum to the EGR transducer, remove the throttle body (see Chapter 4) and clean the EGR ports in the throttle bore and body with solvent.

19   If the engine exhibits rough idle, dies when returned to idle or the idle is both rough and slow, the EGR valve may be leaking in the closed position. Inspect the EGR tube for leaks at the connection to the manifold. Loosen the tube connection and then tighten it securely. Remove the EGR valve and transducer assembly and inspect the poppet to make sure it is seated. If it is not, replace the EGR valve transducer assembly with a new one; do not attempt to clean the EGR valve.

Component replacement

Coolant Vacuum Switch Cold Closed (CVSCC) valve

Refer to illustration 5.20

20   Remove the vacuum hoses and unscrew the valve from the thermostat housing **(see illustration)**.

21   Installation is the reverse of removal.

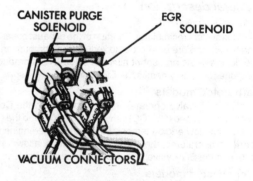

5.18b   EGR solenoid location (2.5L)

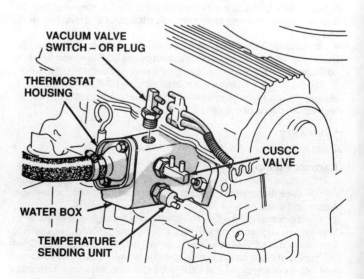

5.20   CVSCC valve location (2.2L shown, 2.5L similar)

5.25   EGR valve location details (3.9L carbureted model shown)

EGR valve
Refer to illustrations 5.25, 5.29a and 5.29b

2.2L carbureted models
22   Unscrew the fitting attaching the EGR valve tube to the intake manifold **(see illustration 5.6)**. Remove the two nuts retaining the valve and remove the assembly.
23   Check the tube for signs of leaking or cracks.
24   Installation is the reverse of removal.

3.9L carbureted models
25   Disconnect the hose to the valve **(see illustration)**.
26   Remove the two nuts retaining the valve and remove the valve.
27   Check the passages in the intake manifold for deposits and clean them with solvent, if necessary.
28   Installation is the reverse of removal.

Fuel-injected models
29   Disconnect the hose to the valve **(see illustrations)**.
30   Remove the two bolts retaining the valve and remove the valve.
31   On four-cylinder models, check the tube for cracks and damage. On V6 models, check the passages in the intake manifold for deposits and clean them with solvent, if necessary.
32   Installation is the reverse of removal.

EGR solenoid (fuel-injected models through 1991)
33   Label and disconnect the vacuum hoses and electrical connectors from the solenoid pack **(see illustrations 5.18a and 5.18b)**.

5.29b   EGR valve location (typical V6 and V8 fuel-injected models)

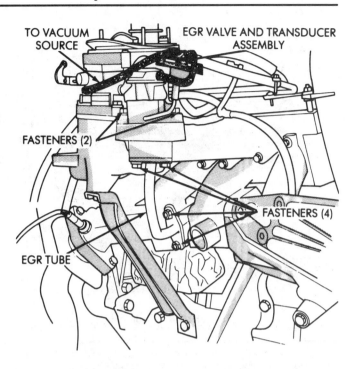

5.29a   EGR valve installation details (2.5L)

34   Remove the mounting fastener(s) and remove the pack.
35   Depress the tab on top of the EGR solenoid and slide it down and out of the bracket.
36   Installation is the reverse of removal.

6   Fuel evaporative emissions control system

General description
Refer to illustrations 6.2a, 6.2b, 6.5a, 6.5b, 6.5c and 6.8
1   This system is designed to trap and store fuel that evaporates from the fuel system that would normally enter the atmosphere in the form of hydrocarbon (HC) emissions.
2   The system consists of a charcoal-filled vapor canister, a damping canister (3.9L carbureted models) **(see illustrations)**, an external bowl

6.2a   The vapor canister is located in the right front corner of the engine compartment (all except 1987 models)

6

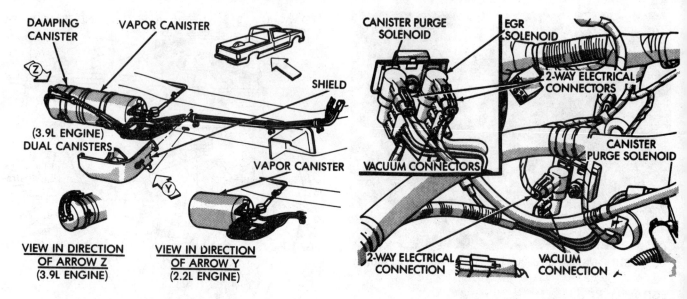

6.2b   1987 vapor canister mounting details

6.5a   Canister purge solenoid details (2.5L)

vent valve and thermal bowl vent valve (2.2L models), a purge solenoid, a combination rollover/separator valve (fuel-injected models) or a rollover valve and Vacuum Controlled Orificed Tank Vapor Valve (VCOTVV) (carbureted models), and connecting lines and hoses (see the EAR label attached to the inside of the hood).

3   When the engine is off and pressure begins to build up in the fuel tank (caused by fuel expansion), the charcoal in the canister absorbs the fuel vapor. When the engine is started (cold), the charcoal continues to absorb and store fuel vapor. As the engine warms up, the stored fuel vapors are routed to the intake manifold or air cleaner and combustion chambers where they are burned during normal vehicle operation.

4   On 3.9L carbureted engines, a damping canister is used in conjunction with the vapor canister. It is connected to the purge line in series with the primary canister and the intake manifold port. Sudden releases of rich vapors pass through the damping canister and are momentarily held before being drawn into the intake manifold.

5   The canister is purged using engine vacuum via the purge solenoid **(see illustrations)** which is controlled by the Single Module Engine Controller (SMEC) on EFI models, or the Spark Control Computer (SCC) on

carbureted engines.

6   On all engines, before the SCC or SMEC will energize the purge control solenoid for canister purging, the following conditions must be met:
  a) The coolant temperature must be above 90-degrees F.
  b) The engine must have been running for approximately 1.5 minutes.
  c) The vehicle speed must be above 5 mph (15 mph on 1989 and later models).
  d) The engine speed must be above 800 rpm (1200 rpm on 1989 and later models).
  e) The engine vacuum must be below 30 inches.
  f) The carburetor or throttle body switch must be open.

7   Carbureted engines are also equipped with an external bowl vent valve which is controlled by air pump operation, and a thermal bowl vent valve (located in the bowl vent line to the canister) which is controlled by engine temperature to aid in cold starting.

8   All models are equipped with a relief valve, mounted in the fuel tank filler cap, which is calibrated to open when the fuel tank vacuum or pressure reaches a certain level **(see illustration)**. This vents the fuel tank and relieves extreme tank vacuum or pressure.

6.5b   The canister purge solenoid on 1991 and earlier V6 and V8 models (arrow)

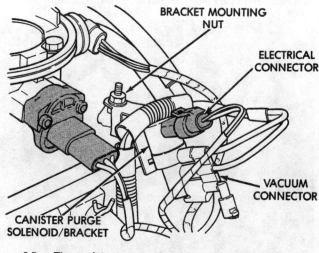

6.5c   The canister purge solenoid on 1992 and later V6 and V8 models

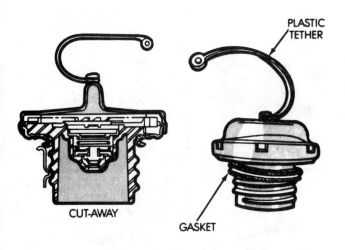

6.8 The fuel tank cap is equipped with a relief valve to equalize the tank pressure

7 Air injection reactor system

Note: *The air injection system is not used on 1992 and later models.*

General description

Refer to illustrations 7.1a, 7.1b, 7.4a, 7.4b, 7.5a, 7.5b and 7.7

1   The air injection reactor system is employed to reduce carbon monoxide and hydrocarbon emissions. The system consists of a belt-driven air pump, an air switching/relief valve, an air switching solenoid (3.9L and 5.2L fuel-injected models), a diverter valve, a check valve, injection tubes and connecting hoses **(see illustrations)**.

2   The air system continues combustion of unburned gases after they leave the combustion chamber by injecting fresh air into the hot exhaust stream. At this point, the fresh air mixes with hot exhaust gases to promote further burning of hydrocarbons and carbon monoxide. During some modes of operation, such as high engine speeds, the switch/relief valve dumps the air into the atmosphere to prevent overheating of the exhaust system.

Check valve

3   This is a one-way valve (reed valve) that lets air enter the exhaust gas stream, but doesn't let the exhaust enter the air injection stream.

Diverter valve

4   This is a vacuum sensitive valve, which dumps air into the atmosphere upon sudden deceleration to prevent backfiring **(see illustrations)**.

Switch/relief valve

5   The switch portion of the switch/relief valve, directs air injection flow to either the exhaust manifold (via the diverter valve when the engine is cold) or to the catalytic converter, depending on engine temperature or, on 3.9L fuel-injected engines, open loop idle condition **(see illustrations)**.

6   On all models, the relief portion of the switch/relief valve diverts excessive pump output at higher engine speeds to the atmosphere.

Switching solenoid

7   When the engine is cold, vehicle speed is less than four miles per hour or the throttle switch is closed, the switching solenoid **(see illustration)** is de-energized to allow air injection to the exhaust manifolds via the switch/relief valve.

Checking

Refer to illustration 7.22

Air pump

8   Check and adjust the drivebelt tension (refer to Chapter 1).

9   Disconnect the air supply hose or switching relief valve at the pump outlet port.

10   The pump is operating satisfactorily if air flow is felt at the pump outlet with the engine running at idle, increasing as the engine speed is increased.

6

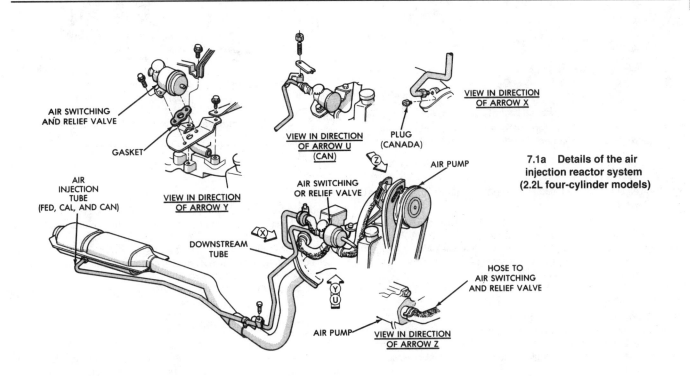

7.1a   Details of the air injection reactor system (2.2L four-cylinder models)

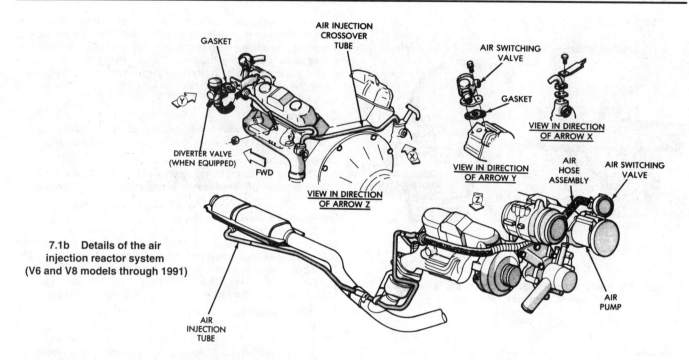

7.1b   Details of the air
injection reactor system
(V6 and V8 models through 1991)

7.4a   The diverter valve (arrow) vents pump pressure to the
atmosphere on deceleration (V6 shown, others similar)

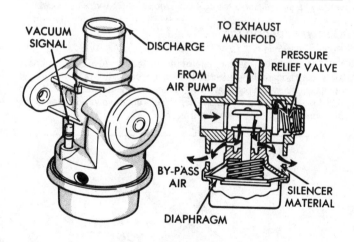

7.4b   A cutaway view of the diverter valve

11   If the air pump does not successfully pass the above tests, replace it with a new or rebuilt unit.

Diverter valve and relief portion of the switch/relief valve

12   Failure of the relief portion of the switch/relief valve or diverter valve will cause excessive noise and air pump output at the valve.
13   There should be little or no air escaping from the silencer on the switch/relief valve while the engine is running.
14   If the system does not pass these tests, the diverter valve or switch/relief valve is malfunctioning.

Switch portion of the switch/relief valve

15   If air injection flow is being directed to both the upstream and downstream inlets simultaneously, the switch/relief valve is malfunctioning.
16   There should be no air escaping from the switch/relief valve silencer at idle speed.
17   If these tests indicate a faulty switch/relief, valve the unit should be

replaced.

Check valve

18   The check valve, located on the injection tube assembly, can be tested by removing the air hose from the valve inlet tube.
19   Start the engine and check for exhaust gas escaping from the valve inlet tube. **Caution:** *Do not put any part of your body near the inlet tube – the hot exhaust gasses can burn you.*
20   If there is exhaust escaping, the check valve is faulty and should be replaced.

Component replacement

Check valve and air control valve

21   These valves may be replaced by disconnecting the hoses leading to them (be sure to label the hoses as they are disconnected to facilitate reconnection), replacing the faulty valve with a new one and reconnecting

7.5a   Location of the switch/relief valve (arrow)

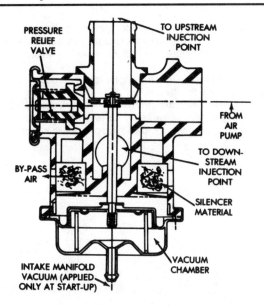

7.5b   A cutaway view of the switch/relief valve

the hoses to the proper ports. Be sure to use new gaskets and remove all traces of the old gasket, where applicable. Make sure that the hoses are in good condition. If not, replace them with new ones.

Air pump

22   Loosen the appropriate engine drivebelt(s) (refer to Chapter 1), then remove the faulty pump from the mounting bracket **(see illustration)**, labeling all wires and hoses as they are removed to facilitate installation of the new unit.

23   After the new pump is installed, adjust the drivebelt(s) to the specified tension (refer to Chapter 1).

Air switching solenoid

24   Disconnect the vacuum and the electrical connections.

25   Slide the solenoid out of the bracket

26   Installation is the reverse of removal

---

8   Catalytic converter

Note: *Because of a Federally-mandated extended warranty (five years or 50,000 miles at the time this manual was written) which covers emissions-related components such as the catalytic converter, check with a dealer service department before replacing the converter at your own expense.*

General description

1   The catalytic converter is an emission control device added to the exhaust system to reduce pollutants from the exhaust gas stream. There are two types of converters. The conventional oxidation catalyst reduces the levels of hydrocarbon (HC) and carbon monoxide (CO). The three-way catalyst lowers the levels of nitrogen oxides (NOx) as well as hydrocarbons (HC) and carbon monoxide (CO).

Checking

2   The test equipment for a catalytic converter is expensive and highly sophisticated. If you suspect that the converter on your vehicle is malfunctioning, take it to a dealer or authorized emissions inspection facility for diagnosis and repair.

3   Whenever the vehicle is raised for servicing of underbody components, check the converter for leaks, corrosion, dents and other damage. Check the welds/flange bolts that attach the front and rear ends of the converter to the exhaust system. If damage is discovered, the converter should be replaced.

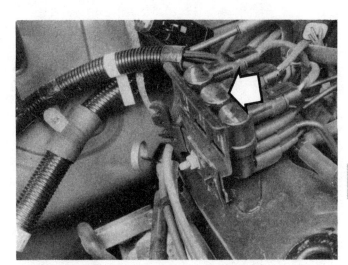

7.7   The switching solenoid (arrow) controls the vacuum to the switch/relief valve

7.22   The air pump on V6 models is secured by a through-bolt on the right side (arrow) and another on the left side that's not visible in this photo

6

4   Although catalytic converters don't break too often, they do become plugged. The easiest way to check for a restricted converter is to use a vacuum gauge to diagnose the effect of a blocked exhaust on intake vacuum.

   a) Open the throttle until the engine speed is about 2000 RPM.
   b) Release the throttle quickly.
   c) If there is no restriction, the gauge will quickly drop to not more than 2 in Hg or more above its normal reading.
   d) If the gauge does not show 5 in Hg or more above its normal read-ing, or seems to momentarily hover around its highest reading for a moment before it returns, the exhaust system, or the converter, is plugged (or an exhaust pipe is bent or dented, or the core inside the muffler has shifted).

Component replacement

5   Refer to the exhaust system removal and installation section in Chapter 4.

Chapter 7 Part A   Manual transmission

Contents

Specifications

General

Transmission lubricant type .... See Chapter 1

Torque specifications   **Ft-lbs**

Access cover bolt 21
Input shaft bearing bolt 21
Shift lever 30
Shift assembly-to-extension housing bolts 40
Extension housing-to-case bolts 40
Transmission-to-clutch housing bolts 50
Drain and fill plugs 30

1   General information

Vehicles covered by this manual are equipped with a five-speed manual or a three or four-speed automatic transmission. Information on the manual transmission is included in this Part of Chapter 7. Information on the automatic transmission can be found in Part B of this Chapter. Information on the transfer case used on 4WD models is in Part C.

The manual transmission used on these models is a 5-speed unit with the 5th gear being an overdrive.

Depending on the expense involved in having a transmission overhauled, it may be a better idea to consider replacing it with either a used or rebuilt one. Your local dealer or transmission shop should be able to supply information concerning cost, availability and exchange policy. Regardless of how you decide to remedy a transmission problem, you can still save a lot of money by removing and installing the unit yourself.

2   Shift lever – removal and installation

Refer to illustrations 2.1, 2.4a, 2.4b and 2.5

1987 through 1991 models

Removal
1   Unscrew the shift lever and remove it, along with the boot **(see illustration)**.
2   Use a screwdriver to carefully pry the insert out for access to the bezel screws. Remove the screws and lift the bezel off.
3   Remove the bolts and detach the bezel support and lower boot.
4   Remove the bolts and use a screwdriver to pry the shifter assembly free, then lift the assembly off the case **(see illustrations)**.

Installation
5   Apply a 1/4-inch wide bead of RTV sealant around the contact surface of the shifter housing, lower it into place and install the bolts **(see illustration)**. Tighten the bolts to the torque listed in this Chapter's Specifications.
6   The remainder of installation is the reverse of removal.

1992 and later models

On these models, the gearshift lever is removed during transmission removal. It cannot be removed without partially removing the transmission from the frame.

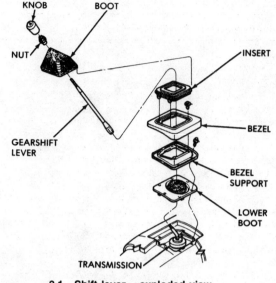

2.1   Shift lever – exploded view
(1987 through 1991 models)

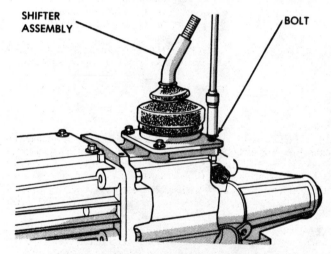

2.4a   Remove the shifter housing bolts
(1987 through 1991 models)

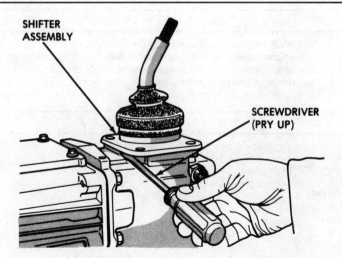

2.4b   Pry the shifter housing from the transmission
with a screwdriver (1987 through 1991 models)

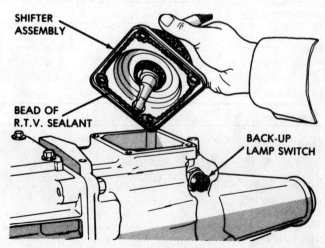

2.5   Apply a bead of RTV sealant to the shifter housing
surfaces prior to installation (1987 through 1991 models)

3   Transmission – removal and installation

Removal

Refer to illustration 3.14

1   Disconnect the negative cable from the battery.
2   Working inside the vehicle, shift the transmission into neutral. On 1987 through 1991 models, unscrew the shift lever and remove the boot (see Section 2).
3   Raise the vehicle and support it securely on jackstands.
4   On 1992 and later models, mark the location of the engine timing sensor. Remove the mounting bolts and remove the sensor.
5   Remove the skid plate, if equipped.
6   On 1992 and later models, disconnect the vehicle speed sensor and speedometer cable (see Chapter 6). On all other models, disconnect the speedometer cable and wire harness connectors from the transmission.
7   On 2WD models, remove the driveshaft (see Chapter 8). Use a plastic bag to cover the end of the transmission to prevent fluid loss and contamination.
8   On 4WD models, remove the transfer case (see Chapter 7 Part C).
9   Remove the exhaust system components as necessary for clearance (see Chapter 4).
10   Support the engine. This can be done from above with an engine hoist, or by placing a jack (with a block of wood as an insulator) under the engine oil pan. The engine should remain supported at all times while the transmission is out of the vehicle.
11   Support the transmission with a jack – preferably a special jack made for this purpose. Safety chains will help steady the transmission on the jack.
12   Remove the rear transmission support-to-crossmember nuts and bolts.
13   Remove the nuts from the crossmember bolts. Raise the transmission slightly and remove the crossmember.
14   On 1992 and later models, lower the transmission approximately 3 inches. Reach up around the transmission case and unseat the shift lever dust boot from the shift tower. Move the boot up to gain access to the shift lever retainer. Press the shift lever retainer down with your fingers then turn it clockwise to release it **(see illustration)**. Lift the lever and retainer up and out of the shift tower. Leave the shift lever and boot in place in the floorpan.
15   On some 4WD models, it may be necessary to remove the front axle struts (see Chapter 10) and the oil filter to gain sufficient clearance for transmission removal. Remove these components only if necessary.
16   Remove the bolts securing the transmission to the clutch housing.
17   Make a final check that all wires and hoses have been disconnected from the transmission and then move the transmission and jack toward the rear of the vehicle until the transmission input shaft is clear of the clutch housing. Keep the transmission level as this is done.
18   Once the input shaft is clear, lower the transmission and remove it from under the vehicle. **Caution:** *Do not depress the clutch pedal while the transmission is out of the vehicle.*
19   The clutch components can be inspected by removing the clutch housing from the engine (see Chapter 8). In most cases, new clutch components should be routinely installed if the transmission is removed.

Installation

20   Insert a small amount of multi-purpose grease into the pilot bushing in the crankshaft and lubricate the inner surface of the bushing. Make sure no grease gets on the input shaft, clutch disc splines or the release lever.
21   If removed, install the clutch components (see Chapter 8).
22   If removed, attach the clutch housing to the engine and tighten the bolts to the specified torque (see Chapter 8).
23   With the transmission secured to the jack as on removal, raise the transmission into position behind the clutch housing and then carefully slide it forward, engaging the input shaft with the clutch plate hub. Do not use excessive force to install the transmission – if the input shaft does not slide into place, readjust the angle of the transmission so it is level and/or turn the input shaft so the splines engage properly with the clutch.

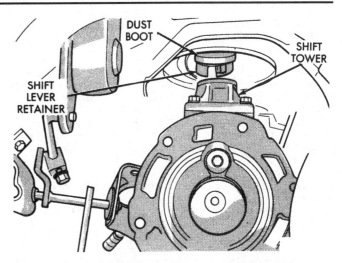

3.14 Shift lever retainer location (1992 and later models)

24   Install the transmission-to-clutch housing bolts. Tighten the bolts to the torque listed in this Chapter's Specifications.
25   On 1992 and later models, reach up and around the transmission and insert the shift lever into the shift tower. Press the lever retainer down and turn it clockwise to lock it in place. Pull the lever dust boot down onto the shift tower.
26   Install the crossmember and transmission support. Tighten all nuts and bolts securely.
27   Remove the jacks supporting the transmission and the engine.
28   Install the various items removed previously, referring to Chapter 8 for the installation of the driveshaft and Chapter 4 for information regarding the exhaust system components.
29   Make a final check that all wires, hoses and the speedometer cable have been connected and that the transmission has been filled with lubricant to the proper level (see Chapter 1). Lower the vehicle.
30   On 1987 through 1991 models, working inside the vehicle, install the shift lever (see Section 2).
31   Connect the negative battery cable. Road test the vehicle for proper operation and check for leakage.

4   Transmission overhaul – general information

Overhauling a manual transmission is a difficult job for the do-it-yourselfer. It involves the disassembly and reassembly of many small parts. Numerous clearances must be precisely measured and, if necessary, changed with select fit spacers and snap-rings. As a result, if transmission problems arise, it can be removed and installed by a competent do-it-yourselfer, but overhaul should be left to a transmission repair shop. Rebuilt transmissions may be available – check with your dealer parts department and auto parts stores. At any rate, the time and money involved in an overhaul is almost sure to exceed the cost of a rebuilt unit.

Nevertheless, it's not impossible for an inexperienced mechanic to rebuild a transmission if the special tools are available and the job is done in a deliberate step-by-step manner so nothing is overlooked.

The tools necessary for an overhaul include internal and external snap-ring pliers, a bearing puller, a slide hammer, a set of pin punches, a dial indicator and possibly a hydraulic press. In addition, a large, sturdy workbench and a vise or transmission stand will be required.

During disassembly of the transmission, make careful notes of how each piece comes off, where it fits in relation to other pieces and what holds it in place.

Before taking the transmission apart for repair, it will help if you have some idea what area of the transmission is malfunctioning. Certain problems can be closely tied to specific areas in the transmission, which can make component examination and replacement easier. Refer to the Troubleshooting section at the front of this manual for information regarding possible sources of trouble.

Chapter 7 Part B Automatic transmission

Contents

Specifications

Torque specifications

Ft-lb (unless otherwise indicated)

Kickdown band
    Adjusting screw . . . . 72 in-lbs
    Adjusting screw locknut 30
Reverse band
    Adjusting screw . . . . 72 in-lbs
    Adjusting screw locknut 25
Neutral start/backup light switch 25
Transmission fluid pan bolts . . . . See Chapter 1
Transmission-to-engine bolts 30
Torque converter-to-driveplate bolts 22

7B

1 General information

All vehicles covered in this manual come equipped with either a 5-speed manual transmission or an automatic transmission. All information on the automatic transmission is included in this Part of Chapter 7. Information on the manual transmission can be found in Part A of this Chapter. You'll also find certain procedures common to both automatic and manual transmissions - such as oil seal replacement – here in Part B. Information on the transfer case used on 4WD models is in Part C.

Automatic transmission models are equipped with either a three-speed (A-998) or four-speed (A-500, 42RH or 46RH, all of which are basically the A-998 with overdrive). All transmissions are equipped with a lock-up torque converter that engages in high gear. The lock-up torque converter provides a direct connection between the engine and the drive wheels for improved efficiency and economy.

Due to the complexity of the automatic transmissions covered in this manual and the need for specialized equipment to perform most service operations, this Chapter contains only general diagnosis, routine maintenance, adjustment and removal and installation procedures.

If the transmission requires major repair work, it should be left to a dealer service department or an automotive or transmission repair shop. You can, however, remove and install the transmission yourself and save the expense, even if the repair work is done by a transmission shop.

2 Diagnosis – general

Note: *Automatic transmission malfunctions may be caused by five general conditions: poor engine performance, improper adjustments, hydraulic malfunctions, mechanical malfunctions or malfunctions in the computer or its signal network. Diagnosis of these problems should always begin with a check of the easily repaired items: fluid level and condition (see Chapter 1), shift linkage adjustment and throttle rod linkage adjustment. Next, perform a road test to determine if the problem has been corrected or if more diagnosis is necessary. If the problem persists after the preliminary tests and corrections are completed, additional diagnosis should be done by a dealer service department or transmission repair shop. Refer to the Troubleshooting Section at the front of this manual for information on symptoms of transmission problems.*

Preliminary checks

1   Drive the vehicle to warm the transmission to normal operating temperature.
2   Check the fluid level as described in Chapter 1:
    a) If the fluid level is unusually low, add enough fluid to bring the level within the designated area of the dipstick, then check for external leaks (see below).

b) If the fluid level is abnormally high, drain off the excess, then check the drained fluid for contamination by coolant. The presence of engine coolant in the automatic transmission fluid indicates that a failure has occurred in the internal radiator walls that separate the coolant from the transmission fluid (see Chapter 3).

c) If the fluid is foaming, drain it and refill the transmission, then check for coolant in the fluid or a high fluid level.

3   Check the engine idle speed. **Note:** *If the engine is malfunctioning, do not proceed with the preliminary checks until it has been repaired and runs normally.*

4   Check the throttle rod for freedom of movement. Adjust it if necessary (see Section 5). **Note:** *The throttle rod may function properly when the engine is shut off and cold, but it may malfunction once the engine is hot. Check it cold and at normal engine operating temperature.*

5   Inspect the shift control linkage (see Section 4). Make sure it's properly adjusted and that the linkage operates smoothly.

Fluid leak diagnosis

6   Most fluid leaks are easy to locate visually. Repair usually consists of replacing a seal or gasket. If a leak is difficult to find, the following procedure may help.

7   Identify the fluid. Make sure it's transmission fluid and not engine oil or brake fluid (automatic transmission fluid is a deep red color).

8   Try to pinpoint the source of the leak. Drive the vehicle several miles, then park it over a large sheet of cardboard. After a minute or two, you should be able to locate the leak by determining the source of the fluid dripping onto the cardboard.

9   Make a careful visual inspection of the suspected component and the area immediately around it. Pay particular attention to gasket mating surfaces. A mirror is often helpful for finding leaks in areas that are hard to see.

10   If the leak still cannot be found, clean the suspected area thoroughly with a degreaser or solvent, then dry it.

11   Drive the vehicle for several miles at normal operating temperature and varying speeds. After driving the vehicle, visually inspect the suspected component again.

12   Once the leak has been located, the cause must be determined before it can be properly repaired. If a gasket is replaced but the sealing flange is bent, the new gasket will not stop the leak. The bent flange must be straightened.

13   Before attempting to repair a leak, check to make sure that the following conditions are corrected or they may cause another leak. **Note:** *Some of the following conditions cannot be fixed without highly specialized tools and expertise. Such problems must be referred to a transmission repair shop or a dealer service department.*

Gasket leaks

14   Check the pan periodically. Make sure the bolts are tight, no bolts are missing, the gasket is in good condition and the pan is flat (dents in the pan may indicate damage to the valve body inside).

15   If the pan gasket is leaking, the fluid level or the fluid pressure may be too high, the vent may be plugged, the pan bolts may be too tight, the pan sealing flange may be warped, the sealing surface of the transmission housing may be damaged, the gasket may be damaged or the transmission casting may be cracked or porous. If sealant instead of gasket material has been used to form a seal between the pan and the transmission housing, it may be the wrong sealant.

Seal leaks

16   If a transmission seal is leaking, the fluid level or pressure may be too high, the vent may be plugged, the seal bore may be damaged, the seal itself may be damaged or improperly installed, the surface of the shaft protruding through the seal may be damaged or a loose bearing may be causing excessive shaft movement.

17   Make sure the dipstick tube seal is in good condition and the tube is properly seated. Periodically check the area around the speedometer gear or sensor for leakage. If transmission fluid is evident, check the O-ring for damage.

Case leaks

18   If the case itself appears to be leaking, the casting is porous and will have to be repaired or replaced.

19   Make sure the oil cooler hose fittings are tight and in good condition.

Fluid comes out vent pipe or fill tube

20   If this condition occurs, the transmission is overfilled, there is coolant in the fluid, the case is porous, the dipstick is incorrect, the vent is plugged or the drain-back holes are plugged.

---

3   Oil seal replacement

Refer to illustrations 3.4, 3.6, 3.9, 3.10, 3.12a, 3.12b and 3.13

1   Oil leaks frequently occur due to wear of the extension housing oil seal, and/or the speedometer drive gear oil seal and O-ring. Replacement of these seals is relatively easy, since the repairs can usually be performed without removing the transmission from the vehicle.

Extension housing oil seal

2   The extension housing oil seal is located at the extreme rear of the transmission, where the driveshaft is attached. If leakage at the seal is suspected, raise the vehicle and support it securely on jackstands. If the seal is leaking, transmission lubricant will be built up on the front of the driveshaft and may be dripping from the rear of the transmission.

3   Refer to Chapter 8 and remove the driveshaft.

3.4   **Use a hammer and chisel to dislodge the oil seal**

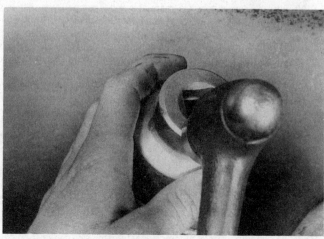

3.6   **A large socket can be used to drive the new seal evenly into the bore**

4   Using a chisel, screwdriver or prybar, carefully pry the oil seal out of the rear of the transmission **(see illustration)**. Do not damage the splines on the transmission output shaft.

5   If the oil seal and bushing cannot be removed with a chisel, screwdriver or pry bar, a special oil seal removal tool (available at auto parts stores) will be required.

6   Using a large section of pipe or a very large deep socket as a drift, install the new oil seal **(see illustration)**. Drive it into the bore squarely and make sure it's completely seated.

7   Lubricate the splines of the transmission output shaft and the outside of the driveshaft sleeve yoke with lightweight grease, then install the driveshaft. Be careful not to damage the lip of the new seal.

Speedometer or speed sensor driven gear seal

8   The speedometer cable and driven gear housing is located on the side of the extension housing. Look for transmission oil around the cable housing to determine if the seal and O-ring are leaking.

9   On vehicles equipped with a speed sensor, disconnect the electrical connector from the sensor. On all models, disconnect the speedometer cable **(see illustration)**.

10 Remove the retainer clip with a small screwdriver and, using a hook, remove the seal **(see illustration)**.

11 Using a small socket as a drift, install the new seal.

12 Mark the relationship of the driven gear housing to the transmission, then remove the bolt and detach the driven gear housing **(see illustrations)**.

13 Install a new O-ring in the driven gear housing and reinstall the driven gear housing and cable assembly on the extension housing **(see illustration)**.

3.12a   Remove the bolt . . .

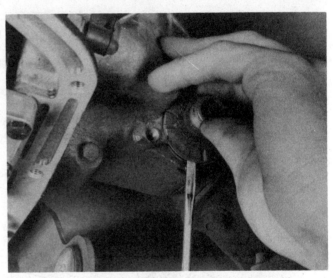

3.12b   . . . and pry the driven gear housing out with a screwdriver

7B

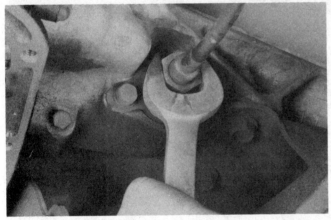

3.9   Unscrew the speedometer cable collar with a wrench

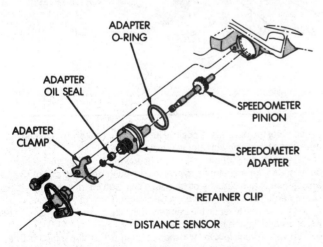

3.10   Details of the speedometer cable driven gear, O-ring and oil seal

ADAPTER O-RING

ADAPTER OIL SEAL

ADAPTER CLAMP

SPEEDOMETER PINION

SPEEDOMETER ADAPTER

RETAINER CLIP

DISTANCE SENSOR

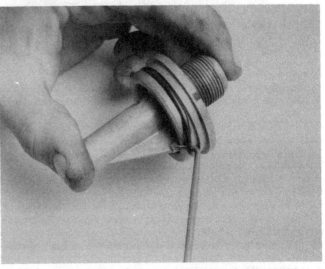

3.13   Use a hooked tool to remove the driven gear O-ring

4   Shift linkage – check and adjustment

Refer to illustration 4.3

1   Check the operation of the shift linkage, making sure the lever is within the stops and the engine starts only in the Park or Neutral.

2   Raise the front of the vehicle and support it securely on jackstands. In the passenger compartment, place the shift lever in Park.

3   In the engine compartment, loosen the adjustment swivel lockscrew **(see illustration)**. If the swivel block binds at all on the shift rod, clean off any corrosion, dirt or grease with solvent and a wire brush before proceeding.

4   Under the vehicle, move the shift lever on the transmission all the way to the rear (Park) position by hand.

5   Hold pressure on the transmission shift lever and tighten the lockscrew securely.

6   Lower the vehicle and check the shift linkage operation, again making sure the engine starts only in Park or Neutral.

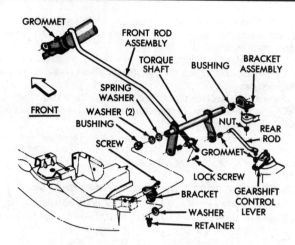

4.3   Shift linkage details (typical)

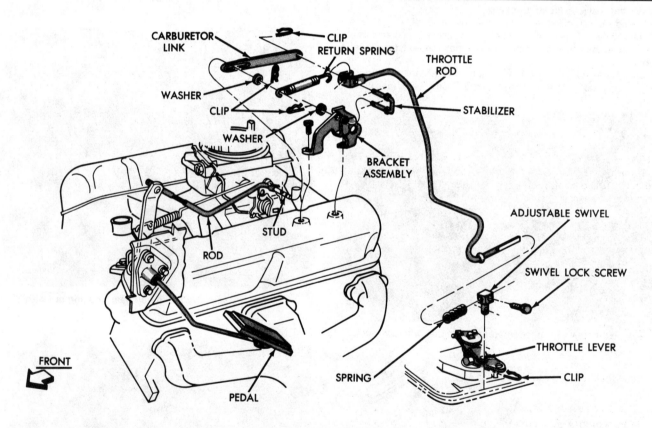

5.4   Throttle rod details (typical)

5   Throttle rod adjustment

Refer to illustration 5.4

1   The throttle rod controls a valve in the transmission which governs shift quality and speed. If shifting is harsh or erratic, the throttle rod should be adjusted.

2   The adjustment must be made with the engine at normal operating temperature. On 1990 models, the Idle Speed Control (ISC) actuator must be retracted. With the engine off, unplug the ISC connector. Connect jumper wires to the battery terminals, then connect the negative jumper to

the actuator top pin and the positive jumper to the second pin, for no more than 5 seconds. The actuator is now retracted.

3   Raise the front of the vehicle and support it securely on jackstands.

4   Loosen the adjustment swivel lockscrew **(see illustration)**. Before adjustment, make sure the block doesn't bind on the rod. If it does, clean the rod and block with solvent and a wire brush.

5   Hold the shift lever on the transmission fully forward (against it's internal stop) and tighten the lockscrew securely.

6   Lower the vehicle. On 1990 models, plug in the ISC connector. Check the adjustment by moving the throttle rod rearward, then slowly releasing it. If properly adjusted, the throttle rod will return completely when released. If it doesn't, repeat the adjustment procedure.

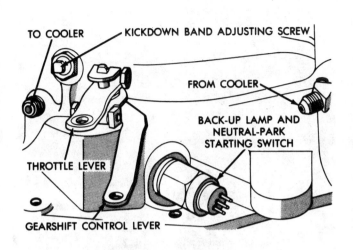

6.2   Location of the kickdown band adjusting screw

6.7   Loosen the Low-Reverse band locknut (arrow)

6   Band adjustment

Refer to illustrations 6.2 and 6.7

1   The transmission bands should be adjusted at the specified interval when the transmission fluid and filter are replaced (see Chapter 1).

Kickdown band

2   The kickdown band adjusting screw is located on the left side of the transmission **(see illustration)**.
3   Raise the front of the vehicle and support it securely on jackstands.
4   Loosen the adjusting screw locknut approximately five turns. Make sure the adjusting screw turns freely, with no binding; lubricate it with penetrating oil if necessary.
5   Tighten the adjusting screw to the torque specified at the beginning of this Chapter, then back it off exactly two and one-half turns. Hold the adjusting screw so it can't turn and tighten the locknut to the torque specified at the beginning of this Chapter.

Low-Reverse (rear) band

6   To gain access to the Low-Reverse band, the fluid pan must be removed (see Chapter 1).
7   Loosen the adjusting screw locknut and back it off four turns **(see illustration)**. Make sure the screw turns freely in the lever.
8   Tighten the adjusting screw to the torque listed in this Chapter's Specifications, then back it off exactly four turns. Hold the screw from turning, then tighten the locknut securely.
9   Install the transmission fluid pan (Chapter 1).

7   Neutral start/backup light switch – check and replacement

Refer to illustration 7.3

1   The Neutral start/backup switch is threaded into the lower left front edge of the transmission case. The Neutral start and backup light switch functions are combined into one unit, with the center terminal of the switch grounding the starter solenoid circuit when the transmission is in Park or Neutral, allowing the engine to start. The outer terminals make up the backup light switch circuit.

Check

2   Prior to checking the switch, make sure the shift linkage is properly adjusted (see Section 4).
3   Unplug the connector and use an ohmmeter to check for continuity between the center terminal and the transmission case **(see illustration)**. Continuity should exist only when the transmission is in Park or Neutral.

7.3   Unplug the electrical connector from the switch for access to the terminals (arrow)

7B

4   Check for continuity between the two outer terminals. There should be continuity only when the transmission is in Neutral. There should be no continuity between either of the outer terminals and the transmission case.

Replacement

5   Place a container under the transmission to catch the fluid which will be released, then use a box-end wrench to remove the switch.
6   Move the shift lever from Park to Neutral while checking to see that the switch operating fingers are centered in the opening. If they aren't, there is an internal problem with transmission.
7   Install the new switch, tighten it to the torque listed in this Chapter's Specifications, then repeat the checks before plugging in the connector.

8   Transmission mount – check and replacement

Refer to illustration 8.2

Check

1   Raise the vehicle and support it securely on jackstands. Insert a large screwdriver or prybar into the space between the transmission extension housing and the crossmember and try to pry the transmission up slightly.

2   The transmission should not move away from the mount much at all **(see illustration)**.

Replacement

3   To replace the mount, remove the bolts attaching the mount to the crossmember and the bolts attaching the mount to the transmission.
4   Raise the transmission slightly with a jack and remove the insulator, noting which holes are used in the crossmember for proper alignment during installation.
5   Installation is the reverse of the removal procedure. Be sure to tighten the nuts/bolts securely.

---

9   Automatic transmission – removal and installation

Removal

1   Disconnect the negative cable from the battery.
2   Raise the vehicle and support it securely on jackstands.
3   On 4WD models, remove the transfer case (see Chapter 7, Part C).
4   Drain the transmission fluid (see Chapter 1), then reinstall the pan.
5   Remove the torque converter cover.
6   If so equipped, remove the engine-to-transmission struts.
7   Mark the relationship of the torque converter and driveplate with white paint so they can be installed in the same position.
8   Remove the torque converter-to-driveplate bolts. Turn the crankshaft for access to each bolt. Turn the crankshaft in a clockwise direction only (as viewed from the front).
9   Remove the starter motor (see Chapter 5).
10   Remove the driveshaft (see Chapter 8).
11   Disconnect the speedometer cable.
12   Detach the wire harness connectors from the transmission.
13   Remove any exhaust components which will interfere with transmission removal (see Chapter 4).
14   Disconnect the throttle rod.
15   Disconnect the shift linkage.
16   Support the engine with a jack. Use a block of wood under the oil pan to spread the load.
17   Support the transmission with a jack – preferably a jack made for this purpose. Safety chains will help steady the transmission on the jack.
18   Remove the rear mount-to-crossmember bolts and the crossmember-to-frame bolts.
19   Remove the engine rear support-to-transmission extension housing bolts.
20   Raise the transmission enough to allow removal of the crossmember.
21   Remove the bolts securing the transmission to the engine.
22   Lower the transmission slightly and disconnect and plug the transmission fluid cooler lines.
23   Remove the transmission dipstick tube.
24   Move the transmission to the rear to disengage it from the engine block dowel pins and make sure the torque converter is detached from the driveplate. Secure the torque converter to the transmission so it won't fall out during removal.

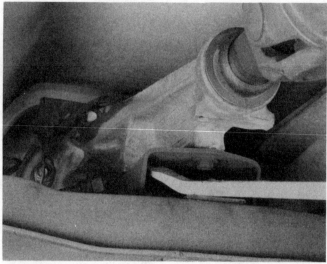

8.2   Pry up on the transmission – there should be very little movement

Installation

25   Prior to installation, make sure the torque converter hub is securely engaged in the pump.
26   With the transmission secured to the jack, raise it into position. Be sure to keep it level so the torque converter does not slide forward. Connect the transmission fluid cooler lines.
27   Turn the torque converter to line up the studs with the holes in the driveplate. The white paint mark on the torque converter and the stud made in Step 5 must line up.
28   Move the transmission forward carefully until the dowel pins and the torque converter are engaged.
29   Install the transmission housing-to-engine bolts. Tighten them securely.
30   Install the torque converter-to-driveplate bolts. Tighten the nuts to the specified torque.
31   Install the transmission mount crossmember and through-bolts. Tighten the bolts and nuts securely.
32   Remove the jacks supporting the transmission and the engine.
33   Install the dipstick tube and engine-to-transmission bolts.
34   Install the starter motor (see Chapter 5).
35   Connect the shift and throttle rod linkage.
36   Plug in the transmission wire harness connectors.
37   Install the torque converter cover.
38   Install the driveshaft.
39   Connect the speedometer cable.
40   Adjust the shift linkage.
41   Install any exhaust system components that were removed or disconnected.
42   Lower the vehicle.
43   Fill the transmission with the specified fluid (see Chapter 1), run the engine and check for fluid leaks.

Chapter 7 Part C Transfer case

Contents

Specifications

General
Transfer case lubricant type .... See Chapter 1

Torque specifications   **Ft-lbs** (unless otherwise indicated)
Adapter-to-transfer case
   Nut 26
   Bolt 24
Driveshaft yoke nut 110
Shift linkage clamp bolt .... 94 in-lbs
Transfer case-to-transmission bolts 26
Drain and fill plugs 35

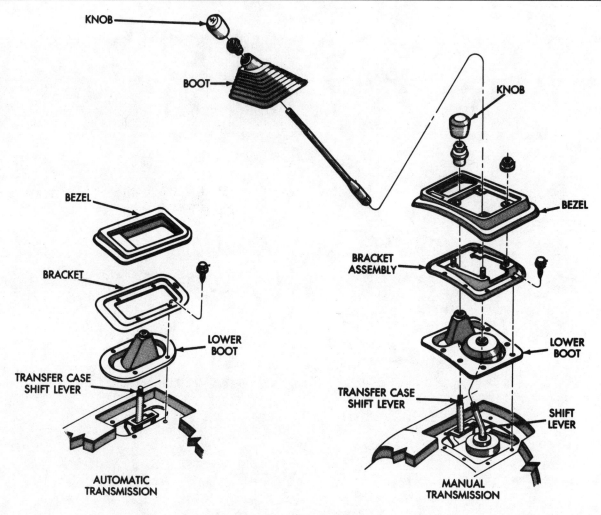

2.3   Transfer case shift boot details

1   General information

Four-wheel drive (4WD) models are equipped with a transfer case mounted on the rear of the transmission. Power is transmitted from the engine, through the transmission and the transfer case to the front and rear axles by driveshafts. 1987 models use a New Process model 207 transfer case. 1988 and later models are equipped with a New Process model 231 unit.

2   Shift linkage – check and adjustment

Refer to illustrations 2.3 and 2.5

1   Raise the vehicle and support it securely on jackstands.
2   Place the shift lever in the 4H position.
3   Remove the screws which attach the shift boot to the floor, then slide the boot up for access **(see illustrations)**.
4   Place a 1/8-in spacer (a 1/8-in drill bit will suffice) between the console shift lever and the forward edge of the shift gate. Secure the lever and spacer in position.
5   Loosen the clamp bolt for the shift rod so the rod will slide easily in the link **(see illustration)**.
6   Shift the transfer case into the 4H position.
7   Position the shift rod so it fits freely in the transfer case shift lever, then tighten the clamp bolt securely.
8   Remove the spacer, install the shift boot and lower the vehicle.

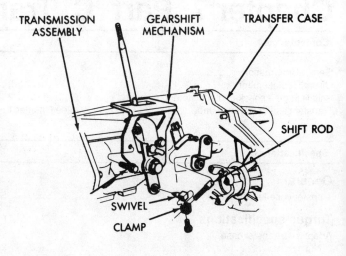

2.5   Transfer case shift mechanism details

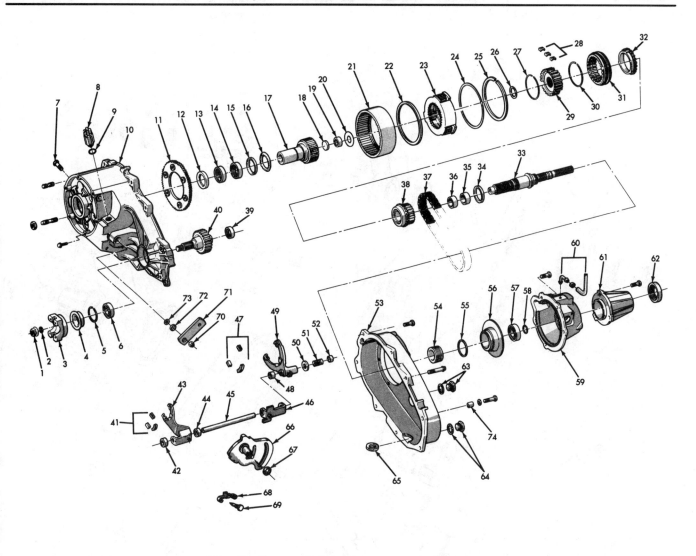

5.4a New Process 207 transfer case – exploded view

1	Front yoke nut	26	Snap-ring	50	Mode fork cup
2	Front yoke seal	27	Synchronizer front spring	51	Mode fork spring
3	Front yoke	28	Synchronizer struts	52	Mode fork rear bushing
4	Front output shaft seal	29	Synchronizer hub	53	Rear case
5	Bearing snap-ring	30	Synchronizer rear spring	54	Oil pump
6	Front output shaft bearing	31	Synchronizer sleeve	55	Pump housing seal
7	Case plug	32	Synchronizer stop-ring	56	Oil pump housing
8	Vacuum switch	33	Mainshaft	57	Mainshaft rear bearing
9	Gasket	34	Thrust washer	58	Rear bearing snap-ring
10	Front case	35	Drive sprocket rear bearing	59	Rear retainer
11	Low range lock plate	36	Drive sprocket front bearing	60	Vent assembly
12	Input gear seal	37	Drive chain	61	Extension housing
13	Input gear front bearing	38	Drive sprocket	62	Extension housing seal
14	Input gear rear bearing	39	Front output shaft rear bearing	63	Fill plug
15	Thrust bearing washer	40	Front output shaft	64	Drain plug
16	Input gear thrust bearing	41	Range fork pads	65	Magnet
17	Input gear	42	Range fork front bushing	66	Shift sector
18	Input gear cup plug	43	Range fork	67	Shift sector spacer
19	Mainshaft pilot bearing	44	Range fork rear bushing	68	Sector detent spring
20	Planetary thrust washer	45	Shift rail	69	Detent spring bolt
21	Annuls gear	46	Shift rail bracket	70	Range lever nut
22	Front thrust ring	47	Mode fork pads	71	Range lever
23	Planetary gear	48	Mode fork front bushing	72	O-ring retainer
24	Rear thrust ring	49	Mode fork	73	O-ring
25	Planetary retaining ring			74	Dowel

7C

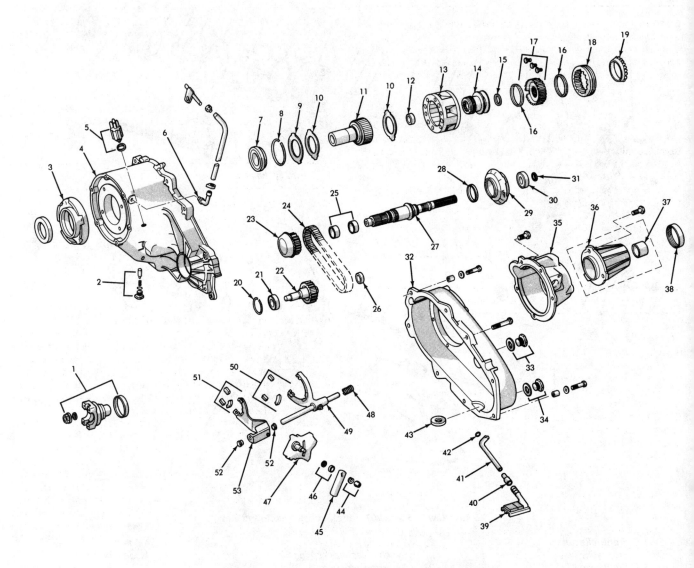

5.4b   New Process 241 and 231 transfer case – exploded view

1	Front yoke nut, seal washer, yoke and oil seal
2	Shift detent plug, spring and pin
3	Front retainer and seal
4	Front case
5	Vacuum switch and seal
6	Vent assembly
7	Input gear bearing and snap-ring
8	Low range gear snap-ring
9	Input gear retainer
10	Low range gear thrust washers
11	Input gear
12	Input gear pilot bearing
13	Low range gear
14	Range fork shift hub
15	Synchronizer hub snap-ring
16	Synchronizer hub springs
17	Synchronizer hub and inserts
18	Synchronizer sleeve
19	Synchronizer stop-ring
20	Snap-ring
21	Output shaft front bearing
22	Output shaft (front)
23	Drive sprocket
24	Drive chain
25	Drive sprocket bearings
26	Output shaft rear bearing
27	Mainshaft
28	Oil seal
29	Oil pump assembly
30	Rear bearing
31	Snap-ring
32	Rear case
33	Fill plug and gasket
34	Drain plug and gasket
35	Rear retainer
36	Extension housing
37	Bushing
38	Oil seal
39	Oil pickup screen
40	Tube connector
41	Oil pickup tube
42	Pickup tube O-ring
43	Magnet
44	Range lever nut and washer
45	Range lever
46	O-ring and seal
47	Sector
48	Mode spring
49	Mode fork
50	Mode fork inserts
51	Range fork inserts
52	Range fork bushings
53	Range fork

3 Oil seal replacement

Note: *This procedure applies to both the front output shaft or rear extension housing oil seals.*

1 Oil leaks frequently occur due to wear of the output oil seals and or/the speedometer drive gear seal and O-ring. Replacement of these seals is relatively easy, since the repairs can be performed without removing the transfer case from the vehicle. Refer to Chapter 7, Part B for the speedometer drive gear oil seal replacement procedure.
2 Raise the vehicle and place it securely on jackstands.
3 Remove the driveshaft (front or rear, as applicable) (see Chapter 8).
4 Remove the nut and the driveshaft yoke (if equipped) **(see illustrations 6.4a and 6.4b)**. A puller tool may be required to draw the yoke off.
5 Pry out the seal with a screwdriver. Take care not to damage the seal bore.
6 Lubricate the new seal lips with automatic transmission fluid or petroleum jelly.
7 Drive the seal into place with a large socket. The O.D. of the socket should be slightly smaller than the O.D. of the seal.
8 The remainder of installation is the reverse of removal. Be sure to tighten the yoke nut to the torque listed in this Chapter's Specifications.

4 Transfer case – removal and installation

Removal

1 Disconnect the negative cable from the battery.
2 Raise the vehicle and support it securely on jackstands.
3 Remove the skid plate (if equipped).
4 Drain the transfer case lubricant (see Chapter 1).
5 Remove the front and rear driveshafts (see Chapter 8).
6 On vehicles equipped with a speed sensor, disconnect the electrical connector from the sensor. Disconnect the speedometer cable and vacuum connectors from the transfer case.
7 Disconnect the shift linkage.
8 Remove the exhaust system, if necessary, for clearance (see Chapter 4).
9 Support the transmission with a jack or jackstand. The transmission should remain supported at all times while the transfer case is out of the vehicle.
10 Support the transfer case with a jack – preferably a special jack made for this purpose. Safety chains will help steady the transfer case on the jack.

11 Remove the rear crossmember.
12 Remove the nuts securing the transmission to the transfer case.
13 Make a final check that all wires and hoses have been disconnected from the transfer case, then move the transfer case and jack toward the rear of the vehicle until the transfer case is clear of the transmission. Keep the transfer case level as this is done. Once the input shaft is clear, lower the transfer case and remove it from under the vehicle.

Installation

14 Prior to installation, clean the gasket surfaces of the transfer case and transmission adapter housing. Apply RTV sealant to both sides of a new gasket and place it position on the transmission. Installation is the reverse of removal. Be sure to tighten the transfer case-to-transmission nuts.

5 Transfer case overhaul – general information

Refer to illustrations 5.4a and 5.4b

Overhauling a transfer case is a difficult job for the do-it-yourselfer. It involves the disassembly and reassembly of many small parts. Numerous clearances must be precisely measured and, if necessary, changed with select fit spacers and snap-rings. As a result, if transfer case problems arise, it can be removed and installed by a competent do-it-yourselfer, but overhaul should be left to a transfer case repair shop. Rebuilt transfer cases may be available – check with your dealer parts department and auto parts stores. At any rate, the time and money involved in an overhaul is almost sure to exceed the cost of a rebuilt unit.

Nevertheless, it's not impossible for an inexperienced mechanic to rebuild a transfer case if the special tools are available and the job is done in a deliberate step-by-step manner so nothing is overlooked.

The tools necessary for an overhaul include internal and external snap-ring pliers, a bearing puller, a slide hammer, a set of pin punches, a dial indicator and possibly a hydraulic press. In addition, a large, sturdy workbench and a vise or transmission stand will be required.

During disassembly of the transfer case, make careful notes of how each piece comes off, where it fits in relation to other pieces and what holds it in place. Exploded views are included to show where the parts go – but actually noting how they are installed when you remove the parts will make it much easier to get transfer case back together **(see illustration)**.

Before taking the transfer case apart for repair, it will help if you have some idea what area of the transfer case is malfunctioning. Certain problems can be closely tied to specific areas in the transfer case, which can make component examination and replacement easier. Refer to the Troubleshooting section at the front of this manual for information regarding possible sources of trouble.

7C

Chapter 8 Clutch and driveline

Contents

Specifications

General

Clutch hydraulic fluid type	See Chapter 1
Clutch disc lining thickness	1/16 in (above rivet)

Torque specifications

Ft-lbs (unless otherwise indicated)

Clutch

Pressure plate-to-flywheel bolts	21
Release fork pivot stud	16
Bellhousing-to-engine bolts	50
Release cylinder mounting bolts	16

Driveshaft

U-joint strap bolts	14
Center support bearing bolts	50

Rear axle

Pinion shaft lock bolt	96 in-lbs

Front differential (4WD models)

Driveaxle-to-differential shaft bolts	65
Differential cover bolts	35
Driveaxle hub nut	190
Driveaxle flange bolts/nuts	75
Pinion shaft lock bolt	96 in-lbs
Right differential shaft retainer screws	17
Shift motor cover bolts	120 in-lbs

8

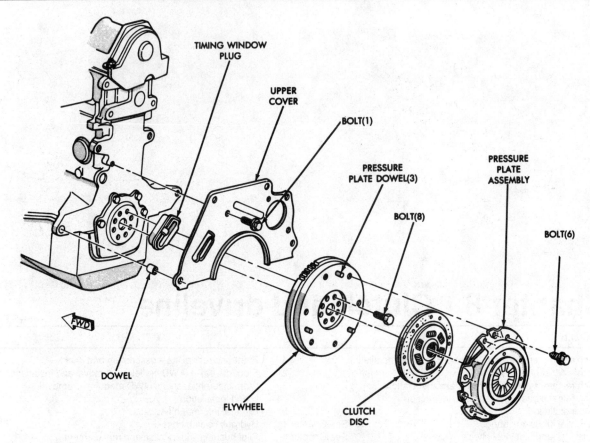

2.1   Exploded view of the clutch components

1   General information

The information in this Chapter deals with the components from the rear of the engine to the rear wheels, except for the transmission, which is dealt with in the previous Chapter. For the purposes of this Chapter, these components are grouped into three categories: clutch, driveshaft and axles. Separate Sections within this Chapter offer general descriptions and checking procedures for components in each of the three groups.

Since nearly all the procedures covered in this Chapter involve working under the vehicle, make sure it's securely supported on sturdy jackstands or on a hoist where the vehicle can be easily raised and lowered.

2   Clutch – description and check

Refer to illustration 2.1

1   All vehicles with a manual transmission use a single dry plate, diaphragm spring type clutch **(see illustration)**. The clutch disc has a splined hub which allows it to slide along the splines of the transmission input shaft. The clutch and pressure plate are held in contact by spring pressure exerted by the diaphragm in the pressure plate.

2   The clutch release system is operated by hydraulic pressure. The hydraulic release system consists of the clutch pedal, a master cylinder and fluid reservoir, the hydraulic line, a release (or slave) cylinder which actuates the clutch release lever and the clutch release (or throwout) bearing.

3   When pressure is applied to the clutch pedal to release the clutch, hydraulic pressure is exerted against the outer end of the clutch release lever. As the lever pivots the shaft fingers push against the release bearing. The bearing pushes against the fingers of the diaphragm spring of the pressure plate assembly, which in turn releases the clutch plate.

4   Terminology can be a problem when discussing the clutch components because common names are in some cases different from those used by the manufacturer. For example, the driven plate is also called the clutch plate or disc, the clutch release bearing is sometimes called a throwout bearing, the release cylinder is sometimes called the operating or slave cylinder.

5   Other than to replace components with obvious damage, some preliminary checks should be performed to diagnose clutch problems.

a) The first check should be of the fluid level in the clutch master cylinder. If the fluid level is excessively low, add fluid as necessary and inspect the hydraulic system for leaks (fluid level will actually rise as the clutch wears).

b) To check "clutch spin down time," run the engine at normal idle speed with the transmission in Neutral (clutch pedal up – engaged). Disengage the clutch (pedal down), wait several seconds and shift the transmission into Reverse. No grinding noise should be heard. A grinding noise would most likely indicate a problem in the pressure plate or the clutch disc.

c) To check for complete clutch release, run the engine (with the parking brake applied to prevent movement) and hold the clutch pedal approximately 1/2-inch from the floor. Shift the transmission between First gear and Reverse several times. If the shift is hard or the transmission grinds, component failure is indicated. Check the release cylinder pushrod travel. With the clutch pedal depressed completely, the release cylinder pushrod should extend substantially. If it doesn't, check the fluid level in the clutch master cylinder (see Chapter 1).

d) Visually inspect the pivot bushing at the top of the clutch pedal to make sure there is no binding or excessive play.

e) Crawl under the vehicle and make sure the clutch release lever is solidly mounted on the ball stud.

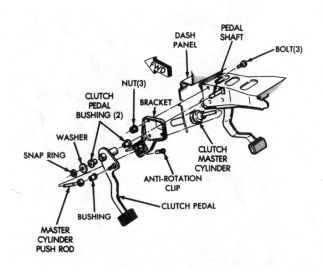

3.2 The anti-rotation clip must be removed before clutch master cylinder can be removed.

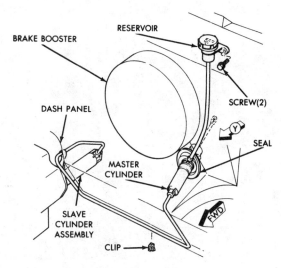

3.7. Mounting details of the clutch master cylinder and fluid reservoir

3 Clutch release system – removal and installation

Refer to illustrations 3.2, 3.7 and 3.11

Note: *The clutch release system is serviced as a complete unit and has been bled of air at the factory, as individual components or rebuild kits are not available separately. There are no provisions for adjustment of clutch pedal height or freeplay.*

Removal

1   Disconnect the negative cable from the battery.

Master cylinder

2   Carefully remove the anti-rotation clip from the clutch master cylinder mounting bracket **(see illustration)**.
3   Remove the retaining ring, wave washer and flat washer that attaches the clutch master cylinder pushrod to the clutch pedal.
4   Slide the clutch master cylinder pushrod off the clutch pedal pin.
5   Inspect the condition of the bushing on the clutch pedal pin and replace it if it's worn or damaged.
6   To avoid spillage during removal, verify that the cap on the clutch master cylinder reservoir is tight.
7   Remove the screws attaching the clutch fluid reservoir to the engine firewall **(see illustration)**.
8   Pull the clutch master cylinder rubber seal from the firewall.
9   Rotate the clutch master cylinder 45-degrees counterclockwise to unlock it and remove the cylinder. Using a piece of wire, secure the cylinder and reservoir to a nearby component while the release cylinder is removed.

Release cylinder

10   Raise the vehicle and support it securely on jackstands.
11   Remove the two release cylinder mounting nuts **(see illustration)**.
12   Remove the release cylinder.
13   If the entire system is being removed or replaced, carefully lift the system from the engine compartment.

Installation

14   Installation is the reverse of removal. If the fluid level is extremely low, fill the clutch master cylinder reservoir with the fluid recommended in the Chapter 1 Specifications Section. Don't add too much, though, because the fluid level actually rises as the clutch components wear.

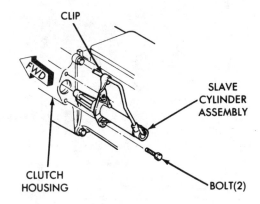

3.11   Mounting details of the clutch release cylinder

4 Clutch components – removal, inspection and installation

Warning: *Dust produced by clutch wear and deposited on clutch components may contain asbestos, which is hazardous to your health. DO NOT blow it out with compressed air and DO NOT inhale it. DO NOT use gasoline or petroleum-based solvents to remove the dust. Brake system cleaner should be used to flush the dust into a drain pan.*

After the clutch components are wiped clean with a rag, dispose of the contaminated rags and cleaner in a covered, marked container.

Removal

Refer to illustration 4.7

1   Access to the clutch components is normally accomplished by removing the transmission, leaving the engine in the vehicle. If, of course, the engine is being removed for major overhaul, then check the clutch for wear and replace worn components as necessary. However, the relatively low cost of the clutch components compared to the time and trouble spent gaining access to them warrants their replacement anytime the engine or transmission is removed, unless they are new or in near perfect condition. The following procedures are based on the assumption the engine will stay in place.

2   Referring to Chapter 7 Part A, remove the transmission from the vehicle. Support the engine while the transmission is out. Preferably, an engine hoist should be used to support it from above. However, if a jack is

8

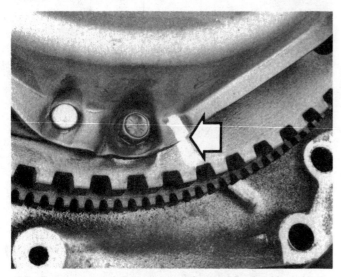

4.7   Be sure to mark the pressure plate and flywheel in order to insure proper alignment during installation (this won't be necessary if a new pressure plate is to be installed)

4.10   Check the flywheel for cracks, hot spots and other obvious defects (slight imperfections can be removed by a machine shop)

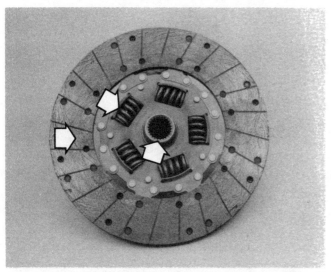

4.12   The clutch plate lining, springs and splines (arrows) should be checked for wear

used underneath the engine, make sure a piece of wood is positioned between the jack and oil pan to spread the load. **Caution:** *The pickup for the oil pump is very close to the bottom of the oil pan. If the pan is bent or distorted in any way, engine oil starvation could occur.*

3   Unbolt the release (slave) cylinder and position it out of the way (see Section 3).

4   Remove the bellhousing-to-engine bolts and then detach the housing. It may have to be gently pried off the alignment dowels with a screwdriver or pry bar.

5   The clutch fork and release bearing can remain attached to the housing for the time being.

6   To support the clutch disc during removal, install a clutch alignment tool through the clutch disc hub.

7   Carefully inspect the flywheel and pressure plate for indexing marks. The marks are usually an X, an O or a white letter. If they cannot be found, scribe marks yourself so the pressure plate and the flywheel will be in the same alignment during installation **(see illustration)**.

8   Turning each bolt only 1/4-turn at a time, loosen the pressure plate-to-flywheel bolts. Work in a criss-cross pattern until all spring pressure is relieved. Then hold the pressure plate securely and completely remove the bolts, followed by the pressure plate and clutch disc.

Inspection

Refer to illustrations 4.10, 4.12 and 4.14

9   Ordinarily, when a problem occurs in the clutch, it can be attributed to wear of the clutch driven plate assembly (clutch disc). However, all components should be inspected at this time.

10   Inspect the flywheel for cracks, heat checking, grooves and other obvious defects **(see illustration)**. If the imperfections are slight, a machine shop can machine the surface flat and smooth, which is highly recommended regardless of the surface appearance. Refer to Chapter 2 for the flywheel removal and installation procedure.

11   Inspect the pilot bushing (see Section 6).

12   Inspect the lining on the clutch disc. There should be at least 1/16-inch of lining above the rivet heads. Check for loose rivets, distortion, cracks, broken springs and other obvious damage **(see illustration)**. As mentioned above, ordinarily the clutch disc is routinely replaced, so if in doubt about the condition, replace it with a new one.

13   The release bearing should also be replaced along with the clutch disc (see Section 5).

14   Check the machined surfaces and the diaphragm spring fingers of the pressure plate **(see illustration)**. If the surface is grooved or otherwise damaged, replace the pressure plate. Also check for obvious damage, distortion, cracking, etc. Light glazing can be removed with medium grit emery cloth. If a new pressure plate is required, new and factory-rebuilt units are available.

Installation

Refer to illustration 4.16

15   Before installation, clean the flywheel and pressure plate machined surfaces with lacquer thinner or acetone. It's important that no oil or grease is on these surfaces or the lining of the clutch disc. Handle the parts only with clean hands.

16   Position the clutch disc and pressure plate against the flywheel with the clutch held in place with an alignment tool **(see illustration)**. Make sure it's installed properly (most replacement clutch plates will be marked "flywheel side" or something similar – if not marked, install the clutch disc with the damper springs toward the transmission).

17   Tighten the pressure plate-to-flywheel bolts only finger tight, working around the pressure plate.

18   Center the clutch disc by ensuring the alignment tool extends through the splined hub and into the pilot bushing in the crankshaft. Wiggle the tool up, down or side-to-side as needed to bottom the tool in the pilot bushing. Tighten the pressure plate-to-flywheel bolts a little at a time, working in a criss-cross pattern to prevent distorting the cover. After all of the bolts are

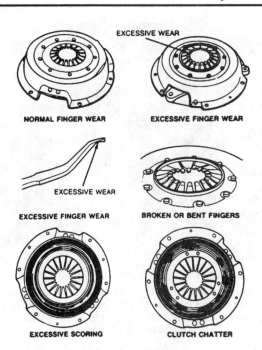

4.14   Replace the pressure plate if excessive wear or damage is noted

4.16   Center the clutch disc using a clutch alignment tool

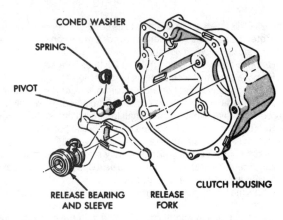

5.4   To remove the release bearing, pop the release fork off the pivot stud and remove the release bearing and sleeve from the fork.

snug, tighten them to the torque listed in this Chapter's Specifications. Remove the alignment tool.

19   Using high-temperature grease, lubricate the inner groove of the release bearing (see Section 5). Also place grease on the release lever contact areas and the transmission input shaft bearing retainer.

20   Install the clutch release bearing as described in Section 5.

21   Install the bellhousing and tighten the bolts to the torque listed in this Chapter's Specifications.

22   Install the transmission, release cylinder and all components removed previously. Tighten all fasteners to the proper torque specifications.

---

5   Clutch release bearing – removal, inspection and installation

Refer to illustration 5.4

Warning: *Dust produced by clutch wear and deposited on clutch components may contain asbestos, which is hazardous to your health. DO NOT blow it out with compressed air and DO NOT inhale it. DO NOT use gasoline or petroleum-based solvents to remove the dust. Brake system cleaner should be used to flush the dust into a drain pan. After the clutch components are wiped clean with a rag, dispose of the contaminated rags and cleaner in a covered, marked container.*

Removal

1   Disconnect the negative cable from the battery.

2   Remove the transmission (see Chapter 7 Part A).

3   Remove the bellhousing from the engine.

4   Remove the clutch release fork from the pivot stud, then remove the bearing and sleeve from the fork **(see illustration)**.

Inspection

5   Hold the center of the bearing and rotate the outer portion while applying pressure. If the bearing doesn't turn smoothly or if it's noisy, remove it from the sleeve and replace it with a new one. Wipe the bearing with a clean rag and inspect it for damage, wear and cracks. Don't immerse the bearing in solvent – it's sealed for life and to do so would ruin it. Also check the release fork for cracks and other damage.

Installation

6   Lightly lubricate the clutch fork crown and spring retention crown where they contact the bearing sleeve with high-temperature grease. Fill the inner groove of the bearing with the same grease.

7   Attach the release bearing sleeve to the clutch fork.

8   Lubricate the fork ball socket with high-temperature grease and push the fork onto the pivot stud until it's firmly seated.

9   Apply a light coat of high-temperature grease to the face of the release bearing, where it contacts the pressure plate diaphragm fingers.

10   Install the bellhousing and tighten the bolts to the torque listed in this Chapter's Specifications.

11   Prior to installing the transmission, apply a light coat of grease to the transmission front bearing retainer.

12   The remainder of installation is the reverse of the removal procedure.

---

6   Pilot bushing – inspection and replacement

Refer to illustrations 6.8 and 6.9

1   The clutch pilot bushing is an oil-impregnated type bushing which is pressed into the rear of the crankshaft. It is greased at the factory and does not require additional lubrication. Its primary purpose is to support the front of the transmission input shaft. The pilot bushing should be inspected whenever the clutch components are removed from the engine. Due to its

8

6.8   Fill the cavity behind the pilot bushing with grease . . .

6.9   . . . then force the bushing out hydraulically with a steel rod slightly smaller than the bore in the bushing – when the hammer strikes the rod, the grease will transmit force to the backside of the bushing and push it out

inaccessibility, if you are in doubt as to its condition, replace it with a new one. **Note:** *If the engine has been removed from the vehicle, disregard the following steps which do not apply.*

2   Remove the transmission (refer to Chapter 7 Part A).

3   Remove the clutch components (see Section 4).

4   Inspect for any excessive wear, scoring, lack of grease, dryness or obvious damage. If any of these conditions are noted, the bushing should be replaced. A flashlight will be helpful to direct light into the recess.

5   Removal can be accomplished with a special puller and slide hammer, but an alternative method also works very well.

6   Find a solid steel bar which is slightly smaller in diameter than the bushing. Alternatives to a solid bar would be a wood dowel or a socket with a bolt fixed in place to make it solid.

7   Check the bar for fit – it should just slip into the bushing with very little clearance.

8   Pack the bushing and the area behind it (in the crankshaft recess) with heavy grease. Pack it tightly to eliminate as much air as possible **(see illustration)**.

9   Insert the bar into the bushing bore and strike the bar sharply with a hammer which will force the grease to the back side of the bushing and push it out **(see illustration)**. Remove the bushing and clean all grease from the crankshaft recess.

10   To install the new bushing, lightly lubricate the outside surface with lithium-based grease, then drive it into the recess with a soft-face hammer. Most new bushings come already lubricated, but if it is dry, apply a thin coat of high-temperature grease to it.

11   Install the clutch components, transmission and all other components removed previously, tightening all fasteners properly.

---

7   Driveshaft(s) and universal joints – general information

Refer to illustration 7.1a and 7.1b

1   A driveshaft is a tube, or a pair of tubes, that transmits power between the transmission (or transfer case on 4WD models) and the differential **(see illustrations)**. Universal joints are located at either end of the driveshaft and in the center on two-piece driveshafts.

2   Driveshafts on 2WD models employ a splined yoke at the front, which slips into the extension housing of the transmission. This arrangement allows the driveshaft to slide back-and-forth within the transmission during vehicle operation. An oil seal prevents leakage of fluid at this point and keeps dirt from entering the transmission. If leakage is evident at the front of the driveshaft, replace the oil seal (see Chapter 7, Part B).

3   If two-piece driveshafts are used, a slip joint is usually employed at the front of the rear driveshaft section.

4   Center bearings support the driveline when two-piece driveshafts are used. The center bearing is a ball-type bearing mounted in a rubber cushion attached to a frame crossmember. The bearing is pre-lubricated and sealed at the factory.

5   On 4WD models, driveshafts have either a splined yoke or companion flange at the transfer case.

6   On all models, the driveshaft assembly requires very little service. The universal joints are lubricated for life and must be replaced if problems develop. The driveshaft must be removed from the vehicle for this procedure.

7   Since the driveshaft is a balanced unit, it's important that no undercoating, mud, etc. be allowed to stay on it. When the vehicle is raised for service it's a good idea to clean the driveshaft and inspect it for any obvious damage. Also, make sure the small weights used to originally balance the driveshaft are in place and securely attached. Whenever the driveshaft is removed it must be reinstalled in the same relative position to preserve the balance.

8   Problems with the driveshaft are usually indicated by a noise or vibration while driving the vehicle. A road test should verify if the problem is the driveshaft or another vehicle component. Refer to the Troubleshooting section at the front of this manual. If you suspect trouble, inspect the driveline (see the next Section).

---

8   Driveline inspection

1   Raise the rear of the vehicle and support it securely on jackstands. Block the front wheels to keep the vehicle from rolling off the stands.

2   Crawl under the vehicle and visually inspect the driveshaft. Look for any dents or cracks in the tubing. If any are found, the driveshaft must be replaced.

3   Check for oil leakage at the front and rear of the driveshaft. Leakage where the driveshaft enters the transmission or transfer case indicates a defective transmission/transfer case seal (see Chapter 7). Leakage where the driveshaft enters the differential indicates a defective pinion seal (see Section 16).

4   While under the vehicle, have an assistant rotate a rear wheel so the driveshaft will rotate. As it does, make sure the universal joints are operating properly without binding, noise or looseness. Listen for any noise from the center bearing (if equipped), indicating it's worn or damaged. Also check the rubber portion of the center bearing for cracking or separation, which will necessitate replacement.

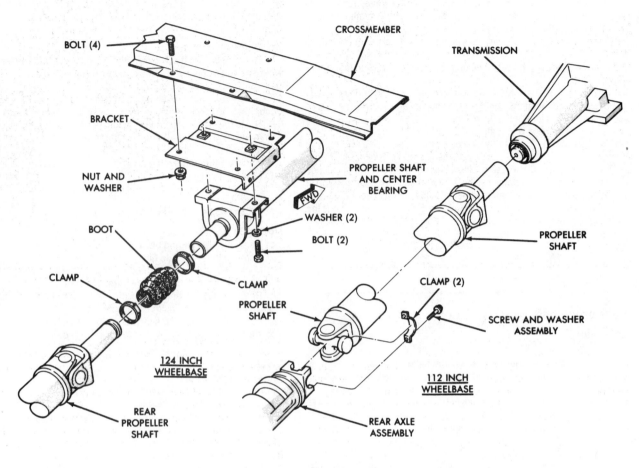

BOLT (4)

CROSSMEMBER

TRANSMISSION

BRACKET

NUT AND WASHER

PROPELLER SHAFT AND CENTER BEARING

FWD

WASHER (2)

BOOT

BOLT (2)

CLAMP

CLAMP

PROPELLER SHAFT

PROPELLER SHAFT

CLAMP (2)

SCREW AND WASHER ASSEMBLY

124 INCH WHEELBASE

112 INCH WHEELBASE

REAR PROPELLER SHAFT

REAR AXLE ASSEMBLY

7.1a   Details of the driveshafts on 2WD models

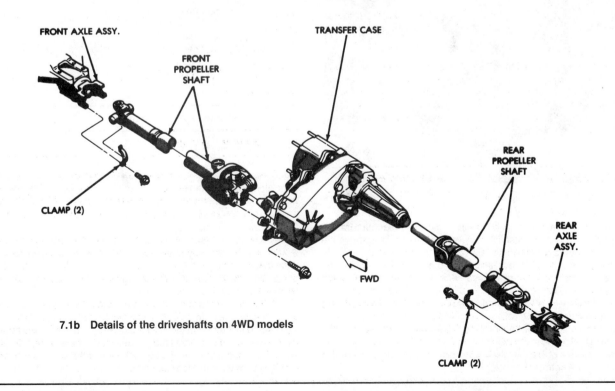

FRONT AXLE ASSY.

FRONT PROPELLER SHAFT

TRANSFER CASE

REAR PROPELLER SHAFT

CLAMP (2)

FWD

REAR AXLE ASSY.

CLAMP (2)

7.1b   Details of the driveshafts on 4WD models

8

5   The universal joint can also be checked with the driveshaft motion-
less, by gripping your hands on either side of the joint and attempting to
twist the joint. Any movement at all in the joint is a sign of considerable
wear. Lifting up on the shaft will also indicate movement in the universal
joints.
6   Finally, check the driveshaft mounting bolts at the ends to make sure
they're tight.
7   On 4WD models, the above driveshaft checks should be repeated on
all driveshafts. In addition, check for grease leakage around the sleeve
yoke, indicating failure of the yoke seal.
8   Check for leakage where the driveshafts connect to the transfer case
and front differential. Leakage indicates worn oil seals.
9   At the same time, check for looseness in the joints of the front driveaxles. Also check for grease or oil leakage from around the driveaxles
by inspecting the rubber boots and both ends of each axle. Oil leakage at
the differential junction indicates a defective side oil seal. Grease leakage
at the wheel side indicates a defective front hub seal, while leakage at the
boots means a damaged rubber boot. For servicing of these components,
see the appropriate Sections.

---

9   Driveshaft(s) – removal and installation

Rear driveshaft

Removal

Refer to illustration 9.3
1   Disconnect the negative cable from the battery.
2   Raise the vehicle and support it securely on jackstands. Place the
transmission in Neutral with the parking brake off.
3   Make reference marks on the driveshaft and the pinion flange in line
with each other **(see illustration)**. This is to make sure the driveshaft is
reinstalled in the same position to preserve the balance.

9.3   Mark the relationship of the driveshaft to the pinion flange

4   Remove the rear universal joint bolts and clamps **(see illustration
7.1a or 7.1b)**. Turn the driveshaft (or wheels) as necessary to bring the
bolts into the most accessible position.
5   If the vehicle is a 4WD model and has a companion flange where the
driveshaft connects to the transfer case, remove the four bolts, nuts and
washers from the flange.
6   On vehicles with a two-piece driveshaft, unbolt the center support
bearing **(see illustration 7.1a)**.
7   On all models, tape the bearing caps to the spider to prevent the caps
from coming off during removal.
8   Lower the rear of the driveshaft. Slide the front of the driveshaft out of
the transmission or transfer case.

9   Wrap a plastic bag over the transmission or transfer case housing and
hold it in place with a rubber band. This will prevent loss of fluid and protect
against contamination while the driveshaft is out.

Installation

10   Remove the plastic bag from the transmission or transfer case and
wipe the area clean. Inspect the oil seal carefully. Procedures for replacement of this seal can be found in Chapter 7.
11   Slide the front of the driveshaft into the transmission or transfer case
or connect the companion flange, installing the fasteners finger-tight.
12   Raise the rear of the driveshaft into position, checking to be sure the
marks are in alignment. If not, turn the rear wheels to match the pinion
flange and the driveshaft.
13   Remove the tape securing the bearing caps and install the clamps
and bolts. Tighten all bolts to the torque listed in this Chapter's Specifications. Lower the vehicle and connect the negative battery cable.

Front driveshaft (4WD models)

Removal

14   Raise the vehicle and place it securely on jackstands.
15   Remove the skid plate (if equipped).
16   Mark the relationship of the driveshaft to the front differential flange
and the transfer case flange **(see illustration 9.3)**.
17   Remove the bolts and clamps **(see illustration 7.1b)** from the differential flange and the transfer case flange.
18   Push the rear half of the driveshaft forward far enough to separate it
from the transfer case flange, then lower it and separate it at the differential
flange.

Installation

19   Attach the front end of the driveshaft to the front differential flange and
install the clamps and bolts finger-tight.
20   Extend or compress the driveshaft as necessary, attach the rear end
to the transfer case flange, install the clamps and bolts and tighten all bolts
to the torque listed in this Chapter's Specifications.
21   Install the skid plate (if equipped).
22   Lower the vehicle and connect the negative battery cable.

---

10   Driveshaft center support bearing – removal and installation

1   Remove the rear driveshaft (see Section 9).
2   Loosen the boot clamps and slide the boot and clamps to the rear of
the driveshaft **(see illustration 9.1a)**.
3   Separate the two sections of the driveshaft, then slide the collar and
bearing off the front section.
4   Installation is the reverse of removal.

---

11   Universal joints – replacement

*Refer to illustrations 11.2, 11.3, 11.5a, 11.5b, 11.7a, 11.7b, 11.9a and
11.9b*
Note: *A press or large vise will be required for this procedure. It may be a
good idea to take the driveshaft to a repair or machine shop where the universal joints can be replaced for you, normally at a reasonable charge.*
1   Remove the driveshaft as outlined in Section 9.
2   On joints retained by an outer snap-ring, use a small pair of pliers to
remove the snap-rings from the spider **(see illustration)**.
3   On joints retained by inner snap-rings, use a screwdriver and hammer
to tap the snap-rings off **(see illustration)**.
4   Supporting the driveshaft, place it in position on either an arbor press
or on a workbench equipped with a vise.
5   Place a piece of pipe or a large socket with the same inside diameter
over one of the bearing caps. Position a socket which is of slightly smaller
diameter than the cap on the opposite bearing cap **(see illustration)** and
use the vise or press to force the cap out (inside the pipe or large socket),
stopping just before it comes completely out of the yoke. Use the vise or
large pliers to work the cap the rest of the way out **(see illustration)**.

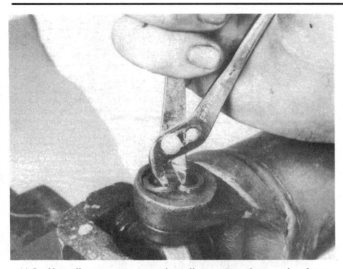

11.2   Use pliers to remove or install an external snap-ring from the U-joint

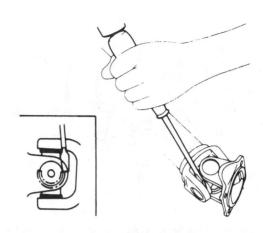

11.3   Remove inner snap-rings from the U-joint by tapping them off with a screwdriver and hammer

11.5a   Removing the bearing caps from the yoke with sockets and a large vise

11.5b   Pliers can be used to grip the cup to detach it from the yoke after it has been pushed out

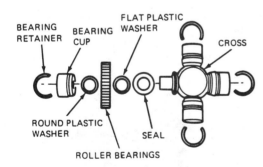

11.7a   The U-joint repair kit will contain all necessary new parts and, in some cases, complete instructions – follow them carefully!

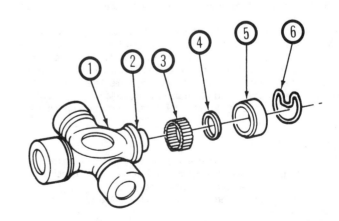

11.7b   Repair kit components for the outer snap-ring type joint

1	Trunnion (cross)	4	Washer
2	Seal	5	Cup
3	Needle rollers	6	Snap-ring

6   Transfer the sockets to the other side and press the opposite bearing cap out in the same manner.

7   Pack the new universal joint bearings with chassis grease. Position the spider in the yoke and partially install one bearing cap in the yoke (**see illustrations**). If the replacement spider is equipped with a grease fitting, be sure it's offset in the proper direction (toward the driveshaft).

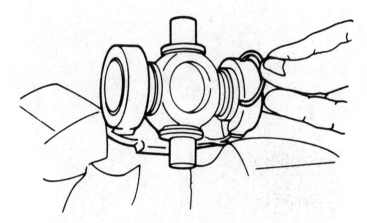

11.9a   Press the bearing cap into place and install the snap-ring in the groove

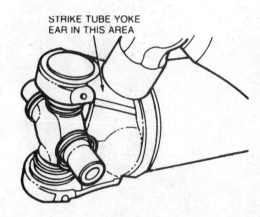

STRIKE TUBE YOKE EAR IN THIS AREA

11.9b   Strike the yoke with a hammer to reposition the retainer groove (this will also relieve stress in the joint caused by pressing the bearing caps in)

8   Start the spider into the bearing cap and then partially install the other cap. Align the spider and press the bearing caps into position, being careful not to damage the dust seals.
9   Install the snap-rings. If difficulty is encountered in seating the snap-rings, strike the driveshaft yoke sharply with a hammer. This will spring the yoke ears slightly and allow the snap-rings to seat in the groove **(see illustrations)**.
10   Install the grease fitting (if equipped) and fill the joint with grease. Be careful not to overfill the joint, as this could blow out the grease seals.
11   Install the driveshaft (see Section 9).

12   Front and rear axles – description and check

Description

1   The rear axle assembly is a hypoid, semi-floating type (the centerline of the pinion gear is below the centerline of the ring gear). The differential carrier is a casting with a pressed steel cover and the axle tubes are made of steel, pressed and welded into the carrier.
2   An optional locking rear axle is also available. This differential allows for normal operation until one wheel loses traction. The unit utilizes multi-disc clutch packs and a speed sensitive engagement mechanism which locks both axleshafts together, applying equal rotational power to both wheels.
3   On 4WD models, a fully independent front axle assembly is used. This consists of a differential and a pair of driveaxles. Each driveaxle has an inner and outer Constant Velocity (CV) joint. Because the differential – like the transfer case – is offset to the left, the distance between the differential and the right front wheel is greater than the distance from the differential to the left wheel. In order to use two equal-length driveaxles, an extension axleshaft is employed on the right side to make up the difference.

Check

4   On all models, many times a problem is suspected in an axle area when, in fact, it lies elsewhere. For this reason, a thorough check should be performed before assuming an axle problem.
5   The following noises are those commonly associated with axle diagnosis procedures:
  a) Road noise is often mistaken for mechanical faults. Driving the vehicle on different surfaces will show whether the road surface is the cause of the noise. Road noise will remain the same if the vehicle is under power or coasting.
  b) Tire noise is sometimes mistaken for mechanical problems. Tires which are worn or low on pressure are particularly susceptible to

emitting vibrations and noises. Tire noise will remain about the same during varying driving situations, where axle noise will change during coasting, acceleration, etc.
  c) Engine and transmission noise can be deceiving because it will travel along the driveline. To isolate engine and transmission noises, make a note of the engine speed at which the noise is most pronounced. Stop the vehicle and place the transmission in Neutral and run the engine to the same speed. If the noise is the same, the axle is not at fault.
6   Overhaul and general repair of the front or rear axle differential is beyond the scope of the many special tools and critical measurements required. Thus, the procedures listed here will involve axleshaft removal and installation, axleshaft oil seal replacement, axleshaft bearing replacement and removal of the entire unit for repair or replacement.

13   Rear axleshaft – removal and installation

Refer to illustrations 13.3 and 13.4
1   Raise the rear of the vehicle, support it securely and remove the wheel and brake drum (refer to Chapter 9).
2   Remove the cover from the differential carrier and allow the oil to drain into a container.
3   Remove the lock bolt from the differential pinion shaft. Remove the pinion shaft **(see illustration)**.

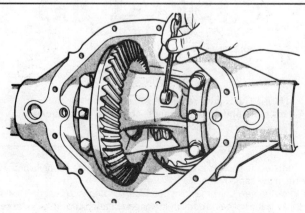

13.3   Removing the pinion shaft lock bolt

13.4 With an assistant pressing the axleshaft into the differential, the C-lock can be pulled out of the groove in the end of the axleshaft

14.2 The end of the axleshaft can be used to pry the old seal out of the axle housing

4 Push the outer (flanged) end of the axleshaft in and remove the C-lock from the inner end of the shaft **(see illustration)**.

5 Withdraw the axleshaft, taking care not to damage the oil seal in the end of the axle housing as the splined end of the axleshaft passes through it.

6 Installation is the reverse of removal. Tighten the lock bolt to the torque listed in the Chapter 1 Specifications.

7 Always use a new cover gasket and tighten the cover bolts to the torque listed in the Chapter 1 Specifications.

8 Refill the axle with the correct quantity and grade of lubricant (see Chapter 1).

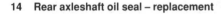

14 Rear axleshaft oil seal – replacement

Refer to illustrations 14.2 and 14.3

1 Remove the axleshaft (see Section 13).

2 Pry the oil seal out of the end of the axle housing with a large screw-driver or the inner end of the axleshaft **(see illustration)**.

3 Apply high-temperature grease to the oil seal recess and tap the new seal evenly into place with a hammer and seal installation tool **(see illustration)**, large socket or piece of pipe so the lips are facing in and the metal face is visible from the end of the axle housing. When correctly installed, the face of the oil seal should be flush with the end of the axle housing.

15 Rear axle bearing – replacement

Refer to illustrations 15.3 and 15.4

1 Remove the axleshaft (see Section 13) and the oil seal (see Section 14).

2 A bearing puller which grips the bearing from behind will be required for this job.

3 Attach a slide hammer to the puller and extract the bearing from the axle housing **(see illustration)**.

8

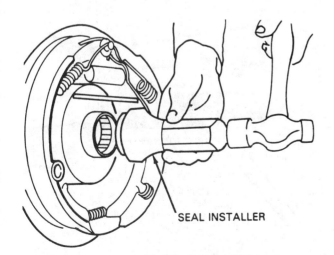

SEAL INSTALLER

14.3 Use a seal installer tool, large socket or piece of pipe to tap the seal evenly into place

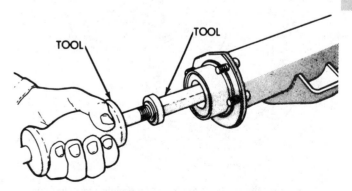

TOOL   TOOL

15.3 Use a slide hammer to remove the axleshaft bearing

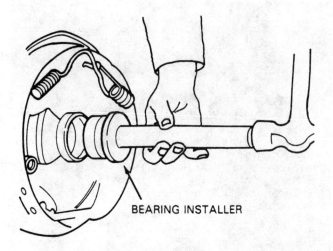

15.4 Use a special bearing installer tool, large socket or piece of pipe to tap the bearing evenly into the axle housing

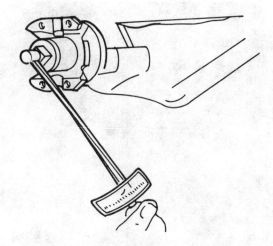

16.4 Use an in-lbs torque wrench to check the torque necessary to move the pinion shaft

4   Clean out the bearing recess and drive in the new bearing with a bearing installer or a piece of pipe positioned against the outer bearing race **(see illustration)**. Make sure the bearing is tapped in to the full depth of the recess and the numbers on the bearing are visible from the outer end of the axle housing.

5   Install a new oil seal (see Section 14), then install the axleshaft.

16 Pinion oil seal – replacement

Refer to illustrations 16.4, 16.5, 16.7 and 16.11

1   Raise the front (for front differential) or rear (for rear differential) of the vehicle and support it securely on jackstands. Block the opposite set of wheels to keep the vehicle from rolling off the stands.

2   Disconnect the driveshaft and fasten it out of the way.

3   On the front differential of 4WD models, be sure that the transfer case is in 2WD.

4   On all models, use an inch-pound torque wrench to check the torque required to rotate the pinion. Record it for use later **(see illustration)**.

5   Scribe or punch alignment marks on the pinion shaft, nut and flange **(see illustration)**.

6   Count the number of threads visible between the end of the nut and the end of the pinion shaft and record it for use later.

7   A special tool (C-3717 for 7-1/4 inch axles or C-4040 for 8-1/4 inch axles or an equivalent tool) can be used to keep the companion flange from moving while the self-locking pinion nut is loosened **(see illustration)**. If the special tool isn't available, try using a large pair of pliers.

8   Remove the pinion nut.

9   Withdraw the companion flange. It may be necessary to use a two or three-jaw puller engaged behind the flange to draw it out. Do Not attempt to pry behind the flange or hammer on the end of the pinion shaft.

10 Pry out the old seal and discard it.

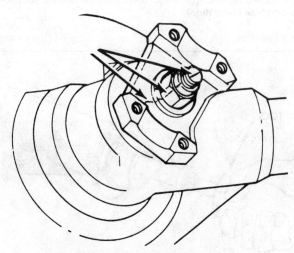

16.5 Mark the relative positions of the pinion, nut and flange (arrows) before removing the nut

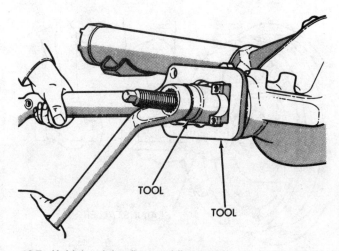

16.7 Hold the pinion flange while removing the lock nut

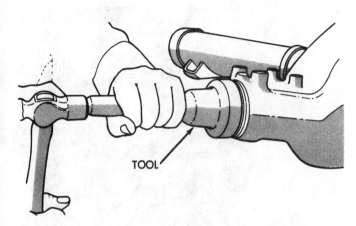

16.11   Use the proper size driver to install the pinion seal

11   Lubricate the lips of the new seal with high-temperature grease and tap it evenly into position with a seal installation tool or a large socket. Make sure it enters the housing squarely and is tapped in to its full depth **(see illustration)**.
12   Align the mating marks made before disassembly and install the companion flange. If necessary, tighten the pinion nut to draw the flange into place. Do not try to hammer the flange into position.
13   Apply non-hardening sealant to the ends of the splines visible in the center of the flange so oil will be sealed in.
14   Install the washer (if equipped) and pinion nut. Tighten the nut carefully until the original number of threads are exposed.
15   Measure the torque required to rotate the pinion and tighten the nut in small increments until it matches the figure recorded in Step 4. In order to compensate for the drag of the new oil seal, the nut should be tightened more until the rotational torque of the pinion exceeds earlier recording by 10 in-lbs. with a torque reading of at least 210 ft-lbs. on the nut.
16   Connect the driveshaft and lower the vehicle.

17   Rear axle assembly – removal and installation

Removal

1   Loosen the rear wheel lug nuts, raise the rear of the vehicle and support it securely on jackstands. Block the front wheels to keep the vehicle from rolling off the stands. Remove the rear wheels.
2   Position a jack under the rear axle differential case.
3   Disconnect the driveshaft from the rear axle companion flange. Fasten the driveshaft out of the way with a piece of wire from the underbody.
4   Disconnect the shock absorbers at the lower mounts, then compress them to get them out of the way.
5   If equipped, disconnect the vent hose from the fitting on the axle housing and fasten it out of the way.
6   Disconnect the brake hose from the junction block on the axle housing, then plug the hose to prevent fluid leakage.
7   Remove the brake drums.
8   Disconnect the parking brake cables from the actuating levers and the backing plate (see Chapter 9).
9   Disconnect the spring U-bolts. Remove the spacers and clamp plates.
10   Disconnect any wiring interfering with removal.
11   Lower the jack under the differential, then remove the rear axle assembly from under the vehicle.

Installation

12   Installation is the reverse of removal. Lower the vehicle weight onto the wheels before tightening the U-bolt nuts completely.
13   Bleed the brakes (see Chapter 9).

18   Front driveaxle (4WD models) – removal and installation

Refer to illustration 18.1

Removal

1   Remove the hub cotter pin, nut lock and spring washer on the side the axle is being removed from **(see illustration)**.

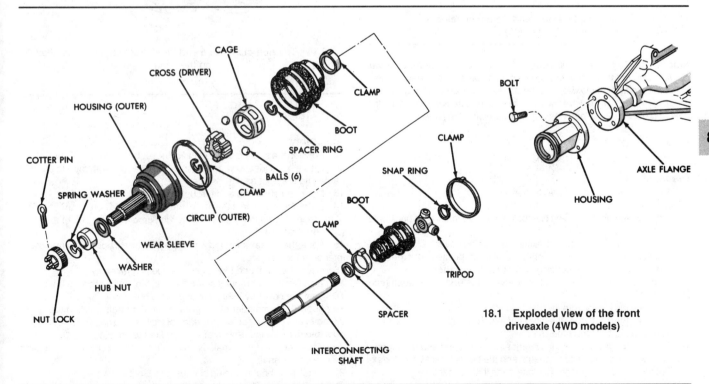

18.1   Exploded view of the front driveaxle (4WD models)

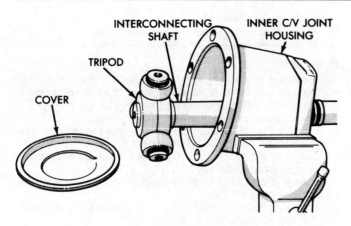

19.5   Use a soft-faced hammer to tap on the axle and knock off the inner CV joint housing cover

19.6   The tripod is held on the shaft with a snap-ring

2   Loosen the hub nut 1/4-turn, then raise the vehicle and support it securely on jackstands.
3   Remove the skid plate.
4   Remove the hub nut and washer.
5   Remove the driveaxle flange bolts. Separate the driveaxle from the differential flange.
6   Using a plastic or rubber mallet, tap the end of the driveaxle out of the hub. If it's stuck, it can be pressed out with a two-jaw puller. Carefully guide the driveaxle out from under the vehicle.

Installation

7   Installation is the reverse of removal. Be sure to tighten the hub nut and the flange bolts to the torque listed in this Chapter's Specifications.

---

19   Driveaxle boot replacement and Constant Velocity (CV) joint overhaul (4WD models)

Note: *If the CV joints exhibit wear, indicating the need for an overhaul (usually due to torn boots), explore all options before beginning the job. Complete rebuilt driveaxles may be available on an exchange basis, which eliminates a lot of time and work. Whatever is decided, check on the cost and availability of parts before disassembling the joints.*

Inner CV joint

Refer to illustrations 19.5, 19.6 and 19.14

Disassembly

1   Remove the driveaxle (see Section 18).
2   Mount the inner CV joint in a bench vise.
3   Remove the boot retaining clamps and pull the inner boot back onto the shaft.
4   Place the shaft and tripod against the housing cover.
5   Using a soft-faced hammer, lightly tap on the opposite end of the shaft to loosen and remove the housing cover **(see illustration)**.
6   Remove the snap-ring from the groove at the end of the shaft **(see illustration)**.
7   Remove the tripod from the shaft.
8   Remove the shaft from the inner CV joint housing.
9   Remove the boot from the shaft.
10   Remove the grease from the interior of the housing and the tripod.
11   Check the the tripod components and the bearing raceways for excessive wear and/or damage. Replace parts if necessary.

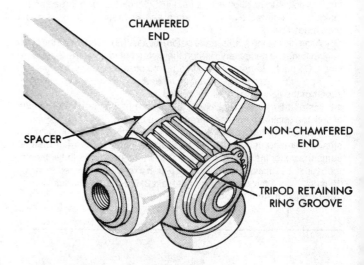

19.14   The non-chamfered end must face out when installed on the shaft

Assembly

12   Position the small-diameter end of the rubber boot over the end of the shaft. It's a good idea to wrap the splines of the axle with tape to prevent damaging the boot as it is installed.
13   Insert the shaft into and through the inner CV joint housing.
14   Install the tripod onto the end of the shaft with the non-chamfered end of the tripod facing the snap-ring retaining groove at the end of the shaft **(see illustration)**.
15   Apply the grease included with the replacement boot to the tripod and interior of the housing.
16   Insert the shaft and tripod into the housing raceway.
17   With the tripod properly seated, install the cover over the housing.
18   Seat the cover by lightly tapping it into position.
19   Apply the remainder of the grease into the boot. Position the large-diameter end of the boot over the edge of the housing and seat the lip of the boot into the locating groove at the edge of the housing.
20   Insert the lip of the small-diameter end of the boot into the locating groove on the shaft.
21   Install new boot retaining clamps (see Step 46).

19.24a   The outer joint housing can be dislodged from the shaft circlip with a soft-faced hammer . . .

19.24b   . . . and removed by hand

Outer CV joint

Refer to illustrations 19.24a, 19.24b, 19.30, 19.31, 19.33, 19.34, 19.37, 19.41, 19.43 and 19.45

Disassembly

22   Mount the axleshaft in a vise with wood blocks to protect it, remove the boot clamps and push the boot back.
23   Wipe the grease from the joint.
24   While supporting the CV joint, use a soft-faced hammer to rap on the housing outer edge to dislodge it from the internal circlip installed on the shaft **(see illustrations)**.
25   Unless the shaft is damaged and replacement is necessary, do not remove the spacer ring from the shaft.
26   Slide the boot off the driveaxle. If the CV joint was operating properly and the grease does not appear to be contaminated, just replace the boot. Bypass the following disassembly procedure. If the CV joint was noisy,

proceed with the disassembly procedure to determine if it should be replaced with a new one.
27   Remove the circlip from the driveaxle groove and discard it (the rebuild kit will include a new circlip).
28   Clean the axle spline area and inspect for wear, damage, corrosion and broken splines.
29   Clean the outer CV joint bearing assembly with a clean cloth to remove excess grease.
30   Mark the relative position of the bearing cage, cross and housing **(see illustration)**.
31   With the housing shaft securely mounted in the wood blocks in the vise, push down one side of the cage and remove the ball bearing from the opposite side **(see illustration)**.
32   Repeat this procedure in a criss-cross pattern until all of the balls are removed. If the joint is tight, tap on the cross (not the cage) with a hammer and brass drift.

19.30   Mark the bearing cage, cross and housing relationship after removing the grease

19.31   With the cage and cross tilted, the balls can be removed one at a time

8

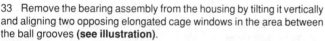

19.33   Align one of the elongated windows in the cage with one of the lands on the housing (outer race), then rock the cage and inner race out of the housing

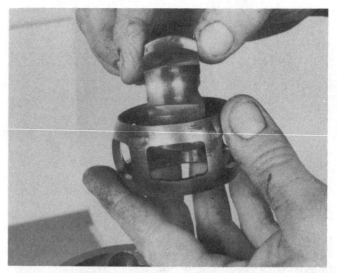

19.34   Tilt the inner race 90-degrees, align the race lands with the windows in the cage, then separate the two components

33   Remove the bearing assembly from the housing by tilting it vertically and aligning two opposing elongated cage windows in the area between the ball grooves **(see illustration)**.

34   Turn the cross 90-degrees to the cage and align one of the spherical lands with an elongated cage window. Raise the land into the window and swivel the cross out of the cage **(see illustration)**.

35   Clean all of the parts with solvent and dry them with compressed air (if available).

36   Inspect the housing, splines, balls and races for damage, corrosion, wear and cracks. Check the bearing cross for wear and scoring in the races. If any of the components are not serviceable, the entire CV joint assembly must be replaced with a new one.

37   Check the outer housing wear sleeve for damage and distortion. If it is damaged or worn, pry the sleeve from the housing **(see illustration)** and replace it with a new one. A special tool is made for this purpose, but a large section of pipe will work if care is exercised (do not nick or gouge the seal mating surface).

Assembly

38   Apply a thin coat of oil to all CV joint components before beginning reassembly.

39   Align the marks and install the cross in the cage so one of the cross lands fits into the elongated window **(see illustration 19.34)**.

40   Rotate the cross into position in the cage and install the assembly in the CV joint housing, again using the elongated window for clearance **(see illustration 19.33)**.

41   Rotate the cage into position in the housing. Be sure the large cross counterbore faces out **(see illustration)**. The marks made during disassembly should face out and be aligned.

42   Pack the lubricant from the kit into the ball races and grooves.

43   Install the balls into the elongated holes, one at a time, until they are all in position. Fill the joint with grease through the splined hole, then insert a wooden dowel into the splined hole to force the grease into the joint **(see illustration)**.

44   Place the driveaxle in the vise and slide the boot over it (wrap the shaft splines with tape to prevent damaging the boot). Install a new circlip in the axle groove, taking care not to twist it.

19.37   The wear sleeve can be pried off the housing with a large screwdriver if replacement is necessary

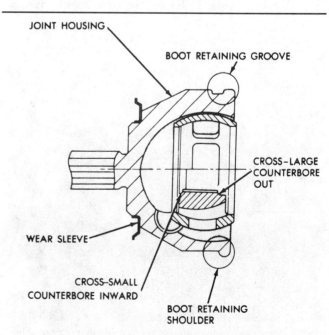

19.41   Make sure the large cross counterbore faces OUT when the CV joint is reassembled

19.43   Apply grease through the splined hole, then insert a wooden dowel into the hole and push down – the dowel will force the grease into the joint

19.45   Strike the end of the housing shaft with a soft-faced hammer to engage it with the shaft circlip

45   Place the CV joint housing in position on the axle, align the splines and rap it sharply with a soft-face hammer **(see illustration)**. Make sure it is seated on the circlip by attempting to pull it from the shaft.

Boot clamp installation

Refer to illustrations 19.46, 19.47, 19.49, 19.50, 19.52a, 19.52b, 19.53, 19.54a, 19.54b and 19.54c

Metal ladder-type clamps (for the small end of the boot)

46   Make sure the boot is properly located on the shaft, then locate the metal clamp tangs in the slots, making the clamp as tight as possible by hand **(see illustration)**.

47   Squeeze the clamp bridge with tool number C-4124 or equivalent clamp crimping tool to complete the tightening procedure **(see illustration)**. Do not cut through the clamp bridge or damage the rubber boot.

Strap and buckle clamp (large diameter of the boot)

48   Locate the large end of the boot over the shoulder or in the groove in the housing (make sure the boot is not twisted).

49   Wrap the clamping strap around the boot twice, plus 2-1/2 inches, and cut it off **(see illustration)**.

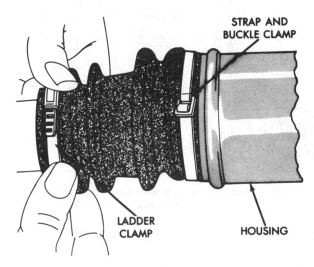

19.46   Tighten the clamp by hand ...

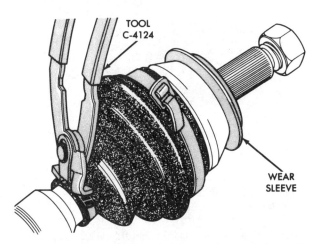

19.47   ... then crimp it with a pair of clamp-crimping pliers

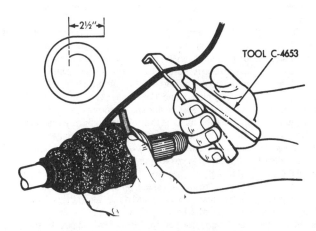

19.49   Wrap the clamp around the boot twice, leaving 2-1/2 inches of extra material, then cut it off

8

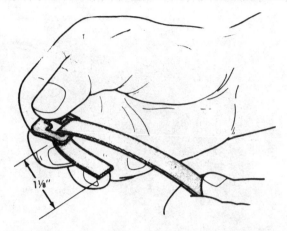

19.50   Pass the strap through the buckle and fold it back about 1-1/8 inch on the inside of the buckle

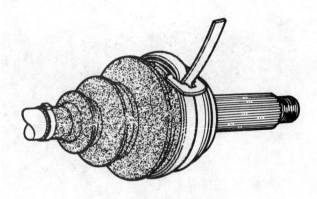

19.52a   After installing it on the boot, bend the strap back so it doesn't unwind

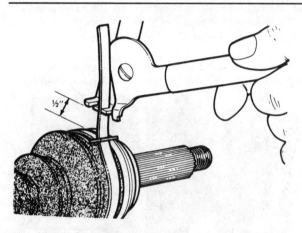

19.52b   Attach the special tool about 1/2-inch from the buckle . . .

19.53   . . . then push the tool forward and up and engage the hook in the buckle eye

50   Pass the end of the strap through the buckle opening and fold it back about 1-1/8 inch on the inside of the buckle **(see illustration)**.

51   Position the clamping strap around the boot, on the clamping surface, with the eye of the buckle toward you. Wrap the strap around the boot once and pass it through the buckle, then wrap it around a second time and pass it through the buckle again.

52   Fold the strap back slightly to prevent it from unwinding itself **(see illustration)**, then open the special tool (C-4653) and place the strap in the narrow slot, about 1/2-inch from the buckle **(see illustration)**.

53   Hold the strap with one hand and push the tool forward and up slightly, then fit the tool hook into the buckle eye **(see illustration)**.

54   Tighten the strap by closing the tool handles **(see illustration)**, then rotate the tool down slowly while releasing the pressure on the handles **(see illustration)**. Allow the handles to open progressively, then open the tool all the way and slide it sideways off the strap. **Caution:** *Never fold the strap back or rotate the tool down while squeezing the handles together (if this is done, the strap will be broken)* **(see illustration)**.

55   If the strap is not tight enough, repeat the procedure. Always engage the tool about 1/2-inch from the buckle. Make sure the strap moves smoothly as tightening force is applied and do not allow the buckle to fold over as the strap passes through it.

56   When the strap is tight, cut it off 1/8-inch above the buckle and fold it back neatly. It must not overlap the edge of the buckle.

57   Repeat the procedure for the remaining boot clamp.

58   Install the driveaxle (see Section 18).

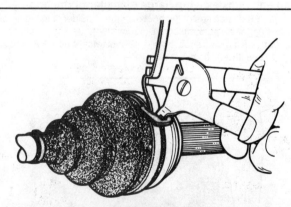

19.54a   Close the tool handles slowly to tighten the clamp strap . . .

20   Front differential shafts (4WD models) – removal and installation

1   Loosen the wheel lug nuts, raise the front of the vehicle and support it securely on jackstands. Remove the front wheels.

2   Reference mark and disconnect the driveaxle(s) from the axleshaft flanges at the differential.

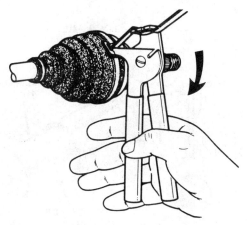

19.54b . . . then rotate the tool down while releasing the pressure on the handles (allow the handles to open)

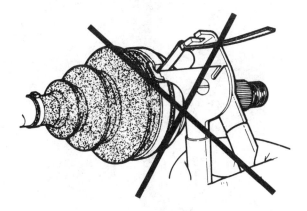

19.54c DO NOT rotate the tool down while applying pressure to the handles

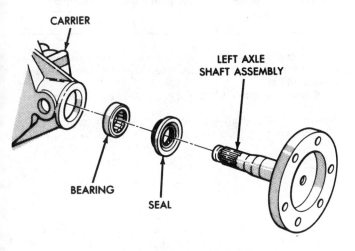

20.7 Be careful not to damage the bearing when removing the left front axle

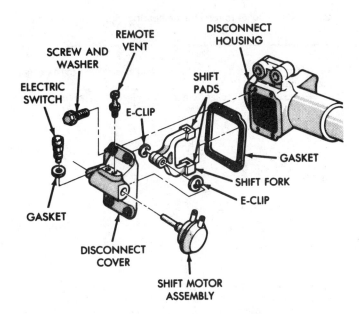

20.8 Exploded view of the shift motor and housing

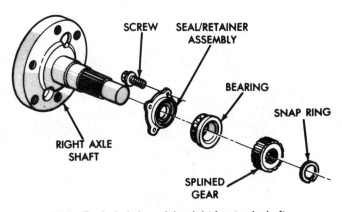

20.9 Exploded view of the right front axleshaft

3   Remove the differential housing cover bolts, drain the lubricant and remove the cover.

4   Rotate the differential case so the pinion shaft lock bolt is accessible **(see illustration 13.3)**.

5   Remove the lock bolt and pinion shaft.

Left axle

6   Force the left axleshaft toward the center of the vehicle and remove the C-clip retainer from the recessed groove at the axleshaft end **(see illustration 13.4)**.

7   Using care to prevent damage to the axleshaft bearing, remove the left axleshaft from the differential housing **(see illustration)**.

Right axle

8   Remove the four bolts retaining the shift motor cover and remove the complete shifting assembly from the intermediate axle housing **(see illustration)**.

9   Working through the holes in the axle flange, remove the seal and bearing retainer bolts **(see illustration)**.

10   Remove the outer axleshaft from the differential housing and tube.

11   Remove the snap-ring and the splined gear from the outer axleshaft.

8

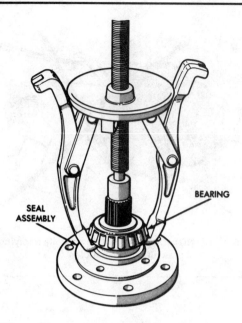

20.12　Use a puller to remove the bearing (right front axleshaft)

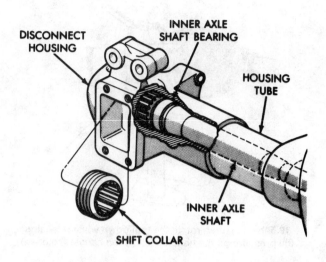

20.13　Remove the shift collar from the disconnect housing

12　Using a puller, remove the bearing and the seal from the outer shaft **(see illustration)**.

13　Remove the shift collar from the disconnect housing **(see illustration)**.

14　Force the inner axleshaft toward the center of the vehicle and remove the axleshaft C-clip retainer from the recessed groove in the shaft **(see illustration 13.4)**.

15　To retain the differential spider gears, install the pinion shaft and the lock bolt.

16　Remove the inner axleshaft from the differential housing and tube.

17　Installation is the reverse of removal.

Chapter 9   Brakes

Contents

Specifications

9

Disc brakes

Brake pad minimum thickness	See Chapter 1
Disc lateral runout limit	0.004 in
Disc minimum thickness	Cast into disc

Drum brakes

Minimum brake lining thickness	See Chapter 1
Maximum drum diameter	Cast into drum

Torque specifications

Ft-lbs (unless otherwise indicated)

Caliper guide pin (mounting) bolts	18 to 26
Caliper adapter-to-steering knuckle bolts	95 to 125
Inlet fitting-to-caliper bolt	30 to 40
Master cylinder mounting nuts	230 to 250 in-lbs
Brake booster mounting nuts	200 to 250 in-lbs

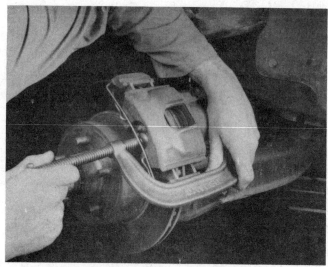

2.3 Using a large C-clamp, push the piston back into the caliper bore – note that one end of the clamp is positioned against the flat end of the piston housing and the screw is pushing against the outer pad

2.4 On 2WD models, remove the hold-down spring by depressing the ends and pulling the spring out

1   General information

General

All models covered by this manual are equipped with hydraulically-operated, four wheel brake systems. All front brakes are discs, all rear brakes are drums.

All brakes are self-adjusting. The front disc brakes automatically compensate for pad wear, while the rear drum brakes incorporate an adjustment mechanism which is activated as the brakes are applied.

The hydraulic system has separate circuits for the front and rear brakes. If one circuit fails, the other circuit will remain functional and a warning indicator will light up on the dashboard when a substantial amount of brake fluid is lost, showing that a failure has occurred.

Master cylinder

The master cylinder is located under the hood on the driver's side, and can be identified by the large fluid reservoir on top. The master cylinder has separate primary and secondary piston assemblies for the front and rear circuits.

Power brake booster

The power brake booster uses engine manifold vacuum to provide assistance to the brakes. It is mounted on the firewall in the engine compartment, directly behind the master cylinder.

Rear Wheel Anti-Lock (RWAL) brake system

A rear wheel anti-lock brake system is used on these vehicles to improve directional stability and control during hard braking.

Parking brake

The parking brake mechanically operates the rear brakes only. The parking brake cables pull on a lever attached to the brake shoe assembly, causing the shoes to expand against the drum.

Precautions

There are some general precautions and warnings related to the brake system:

a) Use only brake fluid conforming to DOT 3 specifications.
b) The brake pads and linings may contain asbestos fibers which are hazardous to your health if inhaled. Whenever you work on brake system components, clean all parts with brake system cleaner or denatured alcohol. Do not allow the fine dust to become airborne.

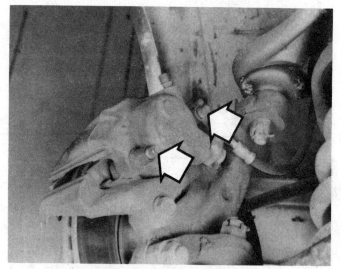

2.5   Remove the caliper pins (arrows)

c) Safety should be paramount whenever any servicing of the brake components is performed. Do not use parts or fasteners which are not in perfect condition, and be sure all clearances and torque specifications are adhered to. If you are at all unsure about a certain procedure, seek professional advice. Upon completion of any brake system work, test the brakes carefully in a controlled area before driving the vehicle in traffic.

If a problem is suspected in the brake system, don't drive the vehicle until it's fixed.

2   Disc brake pads – replacement

Refer to illustrations 2.3, 2.4, 2.5, 2.6, 2.7a, 2.7b and 2.7c
Warning: *Disc brake pads must be replaced on both front wheels at the same time – never replace the pads on only one wheel. Also, the dust created by the brake system may contain asbestos, which is harmful to your health. Never blow it out with compressed air and don't inhale any of it. An approved filtering mask should be worn when working on the brakes. Do not, under any circumstances, use petroleum-based solvents to clean brake parts. Use brake cleaner or denatured alcohol only!*

2.6   Lift the caliper straight up off the brake disc . . .

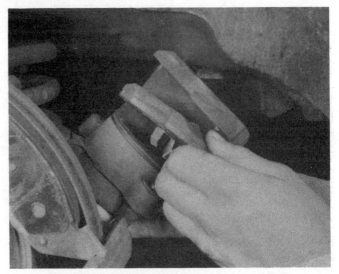

2.7a   Unclip the inner pad from the caliper piston

2.7b   Remove the outer pad from the caliper adapter

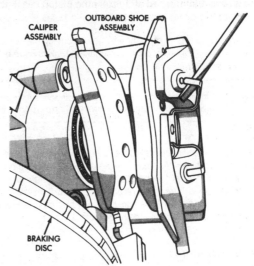

2.7c   On 4WD models, pry the hold-down spring away from the caliper to detach the outer pad

Note: *When servicing the disc brakes, use only high-quality, nationally-recognized, name-brand parts.*

1   Loosen the front wheel lug nuts, raise the front of the vehicle and support it securely on jackstands. Apply the parking brake. Remove the front wheels.

2   Remove about two-thirds of the fluid from the master cylinder reservoir and discard it.

3   Work on one brake assembly at a time. Push the piston back into the bore to provide room for the new brake pads. A C-clamp can be used to accomplish this **(see illustration)**.

4   Remove the C-clamp and, on 2WD models, remove the hold-down spring **(see illustration)**.

5   Remove the two caliper pins (mounting bolts) enough to detach the caliper **(see illustration)**. **Note:** *Don't remove the pins completely unless the sleeves or bushings are to be replaced.*

6   Lift the caliper off the disc **(see illustration)**.

7   Pull the inner pad out of the caliper, then, on 2WD models, remove the outer pad from the caliper adapter **(see illustrations)**. On 4WD models, remove the outer pad from the caliper by prying the hold-down spring away from the caliper **(see illustration)**. Fasten the caliper out of the way with a piece of wire to prevent damage to the brake hose.

8   Inspect the caliper for brake fluid leaks and ruptures of the piston boot. Overhaul or replace the caliper as necessary.

9   Clean the caliper and mounting bolts and check them for corrosion and damage. Replace the bolts with new ones if they're significantly corroded or damaged. Inspect the brake disc carefully as outlined in Section 4. If machining is necessary, follow the information in that Section to remove the disc.

10   If the caliper pin bushings appear worn, replace them as described in Section 3.

11   Remove the protective paper from the noise suppression gasket on the new brake pads (if equipped). Position the inner pad with the clip in the caliper.

12   On 2WD models, position the outer pad in the caliper adapter so the ears on the pad engage the cutouts in the caliper. On 4WD models, attach the outer pad to the caliper, making sure the ends of the hold-down spring engage with the dimples on the caliper frame.

13   Hold the caliper in position over the disc, push the pins through the bushings and thread them into the bracket. Tighten them to the torque listed in this Chapter's Specifications. On 2WD models, install the hold-down spring.

14   Install the brake pads on the opposite wheel, then install the wheels and lower the vehicle. Add brake fluid to the reservoir until it's full (see Chapter 1).

15   Pump the brakes several times to seat the pads against the disc, then check the fluid level again.

9

3.4　With a block of wood placed between the piston and caliper frame, use compressed air to ease the piston out of the bore

16　Check the operation of the brakes before driving the vehicle in traffic. Try to avoid heavy brake applications until the brakes have been applied lightly several times to seat the pads.

3　Disc brake caliper – removal, overhaul and installation

Refer to illustrations 3.4, 3.5a, 3.5b, 3.6, 3.10, 3.11a, 3.11b and 3.12

Note: *If an overhaul is indicated (usually because of fluid leaks, a stuck piston or broken bleeder screw) explore all options before beginning this procedure. New and factory rebuilt calipers are available on an exchange basis, which makes this job quite easy. If you decide to rebuild the calipers, make sure rebuild kits are available before proceeding. Always rebuild or replace the calipers in pairs – never rebuild just one of them.*

Removal

1　Loosen the front wheel lug nuts, raise the vehicle and support it se-curely on jackstands. Remove the front wheels.

2　Remove the brake hose-to-caliper union bolt and detach the hose from the caliper. (If the caliper is only being removed for access to other components, don't disconnect the hose.) Discard the two copper sealing washers on each side of the fitting and use new ones during installation. Wrap a plastic bag around the end of the hose to prevent fluid loss and contamination.

3　Remove the caliper following the first few steps of Section 2 (it's part of the brake pad replacement procedure), then clean it with brake system cleaner. DO NOT use kerosene, gasoline or petroleum-based solvents.

Overhaul

4　Place several shop towels or a block of wood in the center of the caliper to act as a cushion, then use compressed air, directed into the fluid inlet, to remove the piston **(see illustration)**. Use only enough air pressure to ease the piston out of the bore. If the piston is blown out, even with the cushion in place, it may be damaged. **Warning:** *Never place your fingers in front of the piston in an attempt to catch or protect it when applying compressed air, as serious injury could occur.*

5　Pry the dust boot from the caliper bore **(see illustrations)**.

6　Using a wood or plastic tool, remove the piston seal from the groove in the caliper bore **(see illustration)**. Metal tools may cause bore damage.

7　Remove the bleeder screw, then remove and discard the caliper pin bushings and sleeves.

8　Clean the remaining parts with brake system cleaner or clean brake fluid, then blow them dry with compressed air.

9　Inspect the surfaces of the piston for nicks and burrs and loss of plating. If surface defects are present, the caliper must be replaced. Check the caliper bore in a similar way. Light polishing with crocus cloth is permissible to remove slight corrosion and stains. Discard the caliper pins if they're severely corroded or damaged.

10　Lubricate the new piston seal with clean brake fluid and position the seal in the cylinder groove using your fingers only **(see illustration)**.

11　Install the new dust boot in the groove in the end of the piston **(see illustration)**. Dip the piston in clean brake fluid and insert it squarely into the cylinder. Depress the piston to the bottom of the cylinder bore **(see illustration)**.

12　Seat the boot in the caliper counterbore using a boot installation tool or a blunt punch **(see illustration)**.

13　Install the new mounting pin bushings and sleeves.

14　Install the bleeder screw.

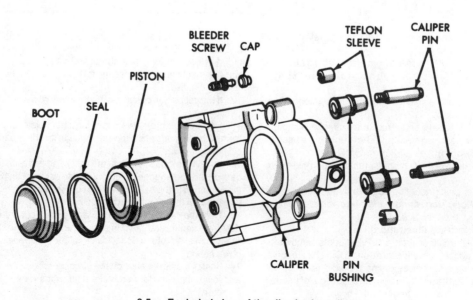

3.5a　Exploded view of the disc brake caliper

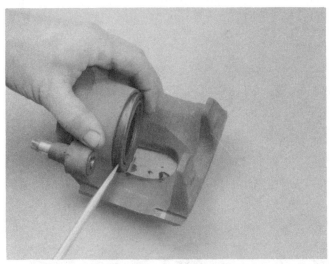

3.5b   Carefully pry the dust boot out of the caliper

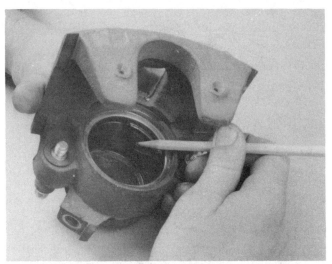

3.6   The piston seal should be removed with a plastic or wooden tool to avoid damage to the bore and seal groove (a pencil will do the job)

3.10   Position the new seal in the cylinder groove – make sure it isn't twisted

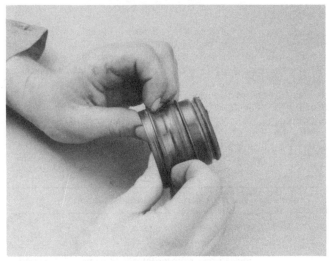

3.11a   Slip the boot over the piston

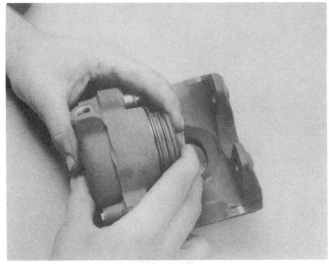

3.11b   Push the piston straight into the cylinder – make sure it doesn't become cocked in the bore

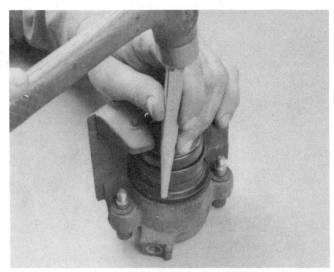

3.12   If you don't have a boot installation tool, gently seat the boot with a drift punch

9

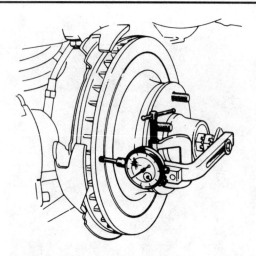

4.3   Use a dial indicator to check disc runout – if the reading exceeds the specified runout limit, the disc will have to be machined or replaced

4.4a   On some models, the minimum thickness is cast into the inside of the disc – on others, it's located on the outside of the disc

Installation

15   Clean the sliding surfaces of the caliper and the caliper adapter.

16   Install the caliper and brake pads as described in Section 2.

17   Using new sealing washers, connect the brake hose to the inlet fitting. Tighten the inlet fitting bolt to the torque listed in this Chapter's Specifications.

18   Bleed the brakes as outlines in Section 10.

19   Install the wheels and lug nuts. Lower the vehicle and tighten the lug nuts to the torque listed in the Chapter 1 Specifications.

20   After the job has been completed, firmly depress the brake pedal a few times to bring the pads into contact with the disc.

21   Check the operation of the brakes before driving the vehicle in traffic.

4   Brake disc – inspection, removal and installation

Refer to illustrations 4.3, 4.4a, 4.4b, 4.5a and 4.5b

Inspection

1   Loosen the wheel lug nuts, raise the front of the vehicle and support it securely on jackstands. Apply the parking brake. Remove the front wheels.

4.4b   Use a micrometer to measure the thickness of the disc at several points

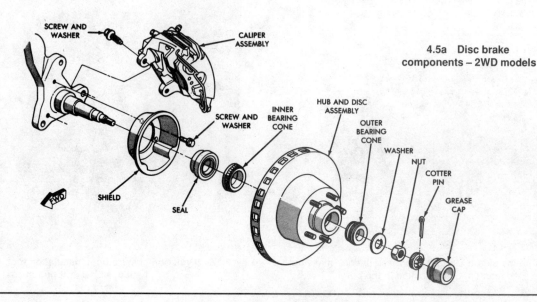

4.5a   Disc brake components – 2WD models

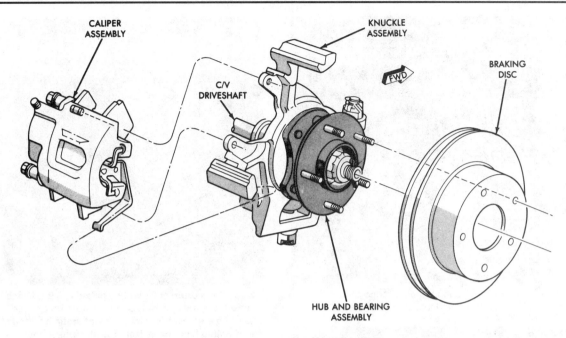

4.5b   Disc brake components – 4WD models

2   Remove the brake caliper as described in Section 2. Visually inspect the disc surface for score marks and other damage. Light scratches and shallow grooves are normal after use and won't affect brake operation. Deep grooves – over 0.015-inch (0.38 mm) deep – require disc removal and refinishing by an automotive machine shop. Be sure to check both sides of the disc.

3   To check disc runout, place a dial indicator at a point about 1/2-inch from the outer edge of the disc **(see illustration)**. On 4WD models, install two lug nuts, with the flat sides facing in, and tighten them securely to hold the disc in place. Set the indicator to zero and turn the disc. The indicator reading should not exceed the runout limit listed in this Chapter's Specifications. If it does, the disc should be refinished by an automotive machine shop. **Note:** *Professionals recommend resurfacing the brake discs regardless of the dial indicator reading (to produce a smooth, flat surface that will eliminate brake pedal pulsations and other undesirable symptoms related to questionable discs). At the very least, if you elect not to have the discs resurfaced, deglaze them with sandpaper or emery cloth.*

4   The disc must not be machined to a thickness less than the specified minimum thickness. The minimum (or discard) thickness is cast into the disc **(see illustration)**. The disc thickness can be checked with a micrometer **(see illustration)**.

Removal and installation

5   On 2WD models, the disc is an integral part of the front hub **(see illustration)**. Hub removal and installation is done as part of the front wheel bearing maintenance procedure (see Chapter 1). On 4WD models, the disc can be pulled off the hub after the wheel and caliper have been removed **(see illustration)**.

---

5   Drum brake shoes – replacement

Refer to illustrations 5.4a through 5.4r and 5.5
Warning: *Drum brake shoes must be replaced on both wheels at the same time – never replace the shoes on only one wheel. Also, the dust created by the brake system may contain asbestos, which is harmful to your health. Never blow it out with compressed air and don't inhale any of it. An approved filtering mask should be worn when working on the brakes. Do not, under any circumstances, use petroleum-based solvents to clean brake parts. Use brake cleaner only!*

Caution: *Whenever the brake shoes are replaced, the retractor and hold-down springs should also be replaced. Due to the continuous heating/ cooling cycle that the springs are subjected to, they lose their tension over a period of time and may allow the shoes to drag on the drum and wear at a much faster rate than normal. When replacing the rear brake shoes, use only high quality, nationally recognized brand-name parts.*

1   Loosen the wheel lug nuts, raise the rear of the vehicle and support it securely on jackstands. Block the front wheels to keep the vehicle from rolling.

2   Release the parking brake.

3   Remove the wheel. **Note:** *All four rear brake shoes must be replaced at the same time, but to avoid mixing up parts, work on only one brake assembly at a time.*

4   Follow the accompanying illustrations **(5.4a through 5.4r)** for the inspection and replacement of the brake shoes. Be sure to stay in order and read the caption under each illustration.

5.4a   If the brake drum cannot be easily pulled off, apply some penetrating oil at the hub-to-drum joint and allow it to soak in, lightly tap the drum to break it loose . . .

9

5.4b   . . . then carefully tap around the outer edge of the drum to drive it off the studs – don't use excessive force!

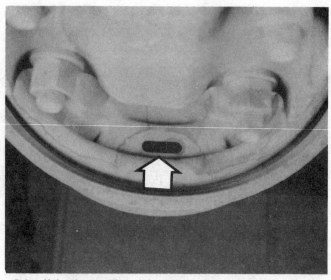

5.4c   If the drum still can't be pulled off, the shoes have worn into the drum and will have to be retracted – this is done by inserting a screwdriver into the slot in the backing plate to hold the adjusting lever away from the star wheel, then turning the star wheel with another screwdriver

5.4d   Before beginning work, wash away all traces of dust with brake system cleaner – DO NOT use compressed air

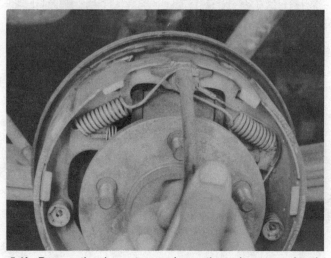

5.4f   Remove the shoe return springs – the spring removal tool shown here can be purchased at most auto parts stores and greatly simplifies this step

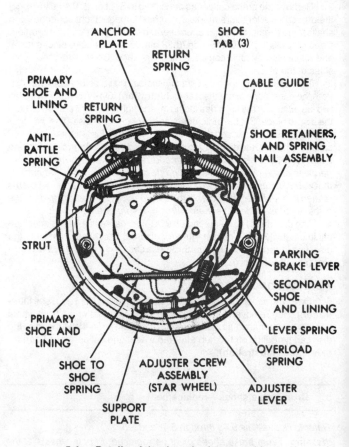

5.4e   Details of the drum brake assembly (left side shown)

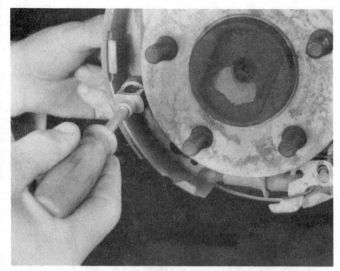

5.4g   Remove the hold-down springs

5.4h   Remove the adjuster cable

5.4i   Remove the cable guide and spring

5.4j   Separate the shoes at the top, lift them away from the backing plate, then detach the parking brake lever from the secondary shoe – the shoes, adjuster and spring can now be separated

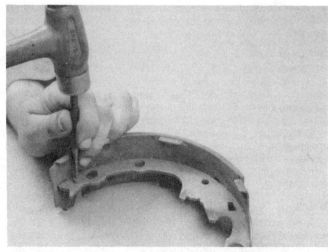

5.4k   Install a new adjuster lever pin to the new shoe

5.4l   Apply high temperature grease to the areas on the backing plate that support the shoes (don't use too much grease or get it on the shoes or drum)

9

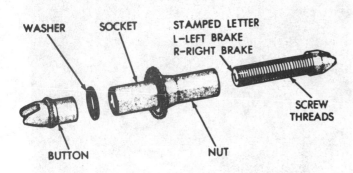

5.4m   Clean the adjuster screw, then lubricate the threads and the sliding surface of the button with high temperature grease

WASHER   SOCKET   STAMPED LETTER
L—LEFT BRAKE
R—RIGHT BRAKE

SCREW
THREADS

BUTTON   NUT

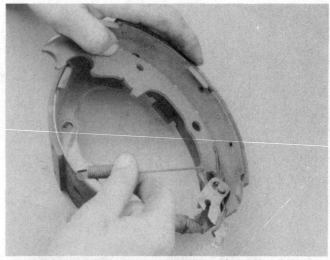

5.4n   Install the shoe-to-shoe spring and adjuster assembly

5.4o   Raise the shoe assembly up to the backing plate and connect the tang on the parking brake lever with its slot in the secondary shoe

5.4p   Fit the shoes over the axle flange, then install the hold-down pins, springs and retainers – make sure the shoes engage with the wheel cylinder pistons (or, on some models, the wheel cylinder pushrods)

5   Before reinstalling the drum it should be checked for cracks, score marks, deep scratches and hard spots, which will appear as small discolored areas. If the hard spots cannot be removed with fine emery cloth or if any of the other conditions listed above exist, the drum must be taken to an automotive machine shop to have it turned. **Note:** *Professionals recommend resurfacing the drums whenever a brake job is done. Resurfacing will eliminate the possibility of out-of-round drums.* If the drums are worn so much that they can't be resurfaced without exceeding the maximum allowable diameter (stamped into the drum) **(see illustration)**, then new ones will be required. At the very least, if you elect not to have the drums resurfaced, remove the glazing from the surface with emery cloth or sandpaper using a swirling motion.

6   Install the brake drum on the axle flange.

7   Mount the wheel, install the lug nuts, then lower the vehicle.

8   Make a number of forward and reverse stops to adjust the brakes until satisfactory pedal action is obtained.

9   Check brake operation before driving the vehicle in traffic.

---

6   Wheel cylinder – removal, overhaul and installation

Refer to illustrations 6.2 and 6.6

Note: *If an overhaul is indicated (usually because of fluid leakage or sticky operation) explore all options before beginning the job. New wheel cylin-* ders are available, which makes this job quite easy. If you decide to rebuild the wheel cylinder, make sure a rebuild kit is available before proceeding. Never overhaul only one wheel cylinder. Always rebuild both of them at the same time.

Removal

1   Refer to Section 5 and remove the brake shoes.

2   Unscrew the brake line fitting from the rear of the wheel cylinder **(see illustration)**. If available, use a flare-nut wrench to avoid rounding off the corners on the fitting. Don't pull the metal line out of the the wheel cylinder – it could bend, making installation difficult.

3   Remove the two bolts securing the wheel cylinder to the brake backing plate.

4   Remove the wheel cylinder.

5   Plug the end of the brake line to prevent the loss of brake fluid and the entry of dirt.

Overhaul

6   To disassemble the wheel cylinder, first remove the rubber boot from each end of the cylinder and push out the two pistons, cups (seals) and spring expander **(see illustration)**. Discard the rubber parts and use new ones from the rebuild kit when reassembling the wheel cylinder.

7   Inspect the pistons for scoring and scuff marks. If present, the pistons should be replaced with new ones.

5.4q   Install the parking brake strut and anti-rattle spring

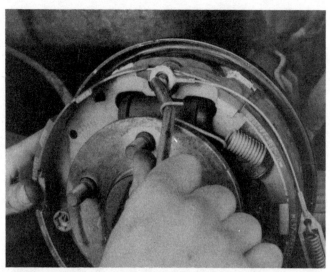

5.4r   Install the return springs, route the adjuster cable around the cable guide and hook it to the adjuster lever – the brake drum can now be installed

5.5   The maximum allowable inside diameter is cast into the outer edge of the drum

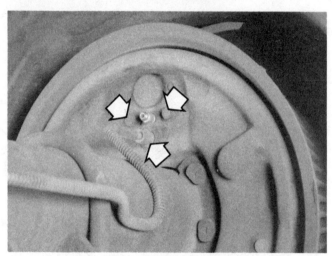

6.2   Disconnect the brake line fitting, then remove the mounting bolts (arrows)

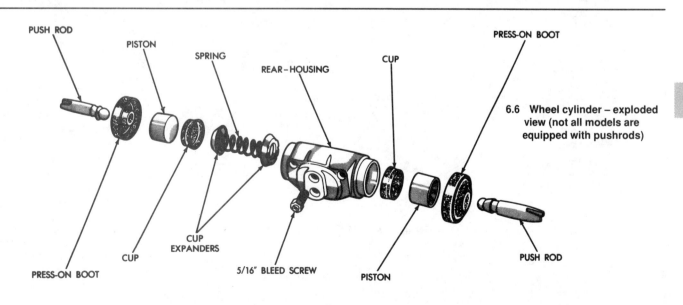

6.6   Wheel cylinder – exploded view (not all models are equipped with pushrods)

9

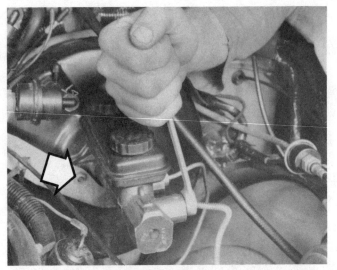

7.2   Use a flare-nut wrench, if available, to loosen and tighten the brake line fittings – the right mounting nut is shown by the arrow – the left mounting nut is obscured

8   Examine the inside of the cylinder bore for score marks and corrosion. If these conditions exist, the cylinder can be honed slightly to restore it, but replacement is recommended.

9   If the cylinder is in good condition, clean it with brake system cleaner or denatured alcohol. **Warning:** *DO NOT, under any circumstances, use gasoline or petroleum-based solvents to clean brake parts!*

10   Remove the bleeder screw and make sure the hole is clean.

11   Lubricate the cylinder bore with clean brake fluid, then insert one of the new rubber cups into the bore. Make sure the lip on the rubber cup faces in.

12   Place the expander spring in the opposite end of the bore and push it in until it contacts the rear of the rubber cup.

13   Install the remaining cup in the cylinder bore.

14   Attach the rubber boots to the pistons, then install the pistons and boots.

15   The wheel cylinder is now ready for installation.

Installation

16   Installation is the reverse of removal. Attach the brake line to the wheel cylinder before installing the mounting bolts and tighten the line fitting after the wheel cylinder mountings bolts have been tightened. If available, use a flare-nut wrench to tighten the line fitting.

17   Bleed the brakes (see Section 10). Don't drive the vehicle in traffic until the operation of the brakes has been thoroughly tested.

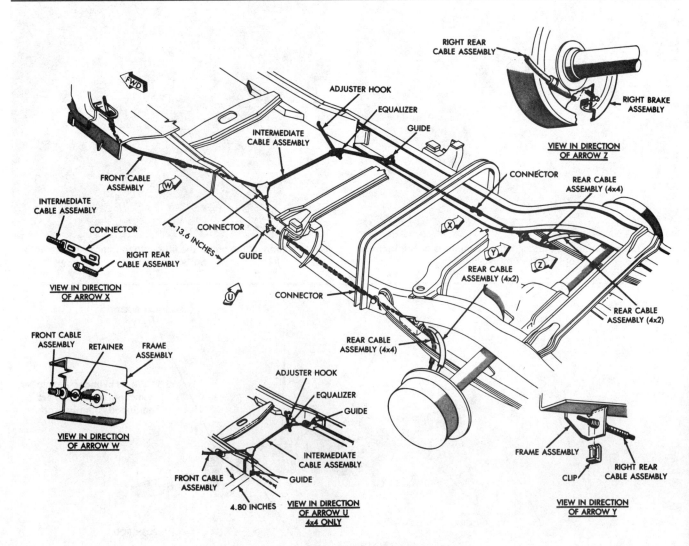

8.2   Routing details of the parking brake cables

8.4 To detach a cable from a connector (arrow), push the cable toward the center opening and pull it out

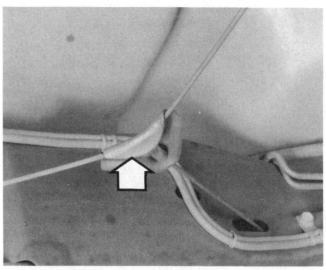

8.5 To remove the intermediate cable, loosen the adjuster nut and pull the cable out of the connector (arrow)

7 Master cylinder – removal and installation

Refer to illustration 7.2

Removal

1   Place rags under the brake line fittings and prepare caps or plastic bags to cover the ends of the lines once they're disconnected. **Caution:** Brake fluid will damage paint. Cover all painted surfaces and avoid spilling fluid during this procedure.

2   Loosen the tube nuts at the ends of the brake lines where they enter the master cylinder. To prevent rounding off the flats on these nuts, a flare-nut wrench, which wraps around the nut, should be used (**see illustration**).

3   Pull the brake lines away from the master cylinder slightly and plug the ends to prevent contamination.

4   Remove the two master cylinder mounting nuts and unbolt the bracket. Move the bracket aside slightly, taking care not to kink the hydraulic lines. Remove the master cylinder from the vehicle.

5   Remove the reservoir caps, then discard any fluid remaining in the reservoir.

Installation

6   Whenever the master cylinder is removed, the entire hydraulic system must be bled. The time required to bleed the system can be reduced if the master cylinder is filled with fluid and bench bled (refer to Steps 7 through 9) before the master cylinder is installed on the vehicle.

7   Fill the reservoirs with brake fluid. The master cylinder should be held in a vise so the brake fluid won't spill during the bench bleeding procedure.

8   Hold your fingers tightly over the holes where the brake lines normally connect to the master cylinder to prevent air from being drawn back into the master cylinder.

9   Stroke the piston several times to ensure all air has been expelled. A large Phillips screwdriver can be used to push on the piston assembly. Wait several seconds each time for brake fluid to be drawn from the reservoir into the piston bore, then depress the piston again, removing your finger as brake fluid is expelled. Be sure to put your fingers back over the holes each time before releasing the piston. When the bleeding procedure is complete, temporarily install plugs in the holes.

10   Carefully install the master cylinder by reversing the removal steps.

11   Bleed the brake system as described in Section 10.

8 Parking brake cables – replacement

Refer to illustrations 8.2, 8.4, 8.5, 8.6a and 8.6b

1   Release the parking brake.

2   Loosen the adjuster nut on the adjuster hook and disconnect the cable from the equalizer (**see illustration**).

3   To remove the front cable, slip the ball at the end of the cable out of the clevis on the parking brake pedal.

4   Slip the front cable out of the connector located below the driver's side of the cab (**see illustration**) and remove the cable from the vehicle.

5   To remove the intermediate cables, loosen the adjuster nut and detach the cable at the connectors (**see illustration**).

6   To remove the rear cable, remove the rear brake shoes as described in Section 5. Disengage the rear cable from the parking brake lever. Compress the tangs of the cable retainer and withdraw the cable assembly from the brake backing plate (**see illustration**). Remove the retaining clip (**see illustration**) and lift the cable from the vehicle.

8.6a   Pinch the retainer tangs together with needle-nose pliers, then push the cable through the backing plate

9

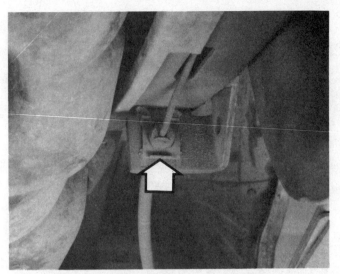

8.6b   Remove the rear cable retaining clip (arrow)

7   Installation is the reverse of removal. Adjust the parking brake as described in Section 9.

9   Parking brake – adjustment

Refer to illustration 9.3

1   The parking brake is pedal operated and is normally self-adjusting through the automatic adjusters in the rear brake drums. However, supplementary adjustment may be needed in the event of cable stretch, wear in the linkage or after installation of new components.
2   Raise the rear of the vehicle until the wheels are clear of the ground, support it securely on jackstands and block the front wheels. Release the parking brake pedal by pulling on the release lever.
3   The adjuster is located on the inside of the frame under catalytic converter. Hold the cable from turning with locking pliers, then loosen the locknut and tighten the adjuster nut **(see illustration)** until a slight drag is felt when the rear wheels are turned. **Note:** *If the threads appear rusty, apply penetrating oil before attempting adjustment.*
4   Loosen the parking brake adjustment until there's no longer any drag when the rear wheels are turned, then loosen the cable adjusting nut two turns.
5   Tighten the locknut, then apply and release the parking brake several times. Confirm that the brake does not drag.
6   Lower the vehicle to the ground.

10   Brake system bleeding

Refer to illustration 10.8
Warning: *Wear eye protection when bleeding the brake system. If the fluid comes in contact with your eyes, immediately rinse them with water and seek medical attention.*
Note: *Bleeding the brake system is necessary to remove any air that's trapped in the system when it's opened during removal and installation of a hose, line, caliper, wheel cylinder or master cylinder.*

1   It will probably be necessary to bleed the system at all four brakes if air has entered the system due to low fluid level, or if the brake lines have been disconnected at the master cylinder.
2   If a brake line was disconnected only at a wheel, then only that caliper or wheel cylinder must be bled.
3   If a brake line is disconnected at a fitting located between the master cylinder and any of the brakes, that part of the system served by the disconnected line must be bled.

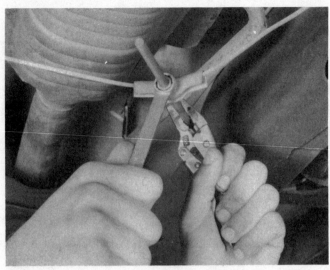

9.3   Hold the cable with locking pliers and turn the adjuster nut with a wrench

4   Remove any residual vacuum from the brake power booster (if equipped) by applying the brake several times with the engine off.
5   Remove the master cylinder reservoir cover and fill the reservoir with brake fluid. Reinstall the cover. **Note:** *Check the fluid level often during the bleeding operation and add fluid as necessary to prevent the fluid level from falling low enough to allow air bubbles into the master cylinder.*
6   Have an assistant on hand, as well as a supply of new brake fluid, an empty clear plastic container, a length of 3/16-inch plastic, rubber or vinyl tubing to fit over the bleeder valve and a wrench to open and close the bleeder valve.
7   Beginning at the right rear wheel, loosen the bleeder screw slightly, then tighten it to a point where it's snug but can still be loosened quickly and easily.
8   Place one end of the tubing over the bleeder screw fitting and submerge the other end in brake fluid in the container **(see illustration)**.

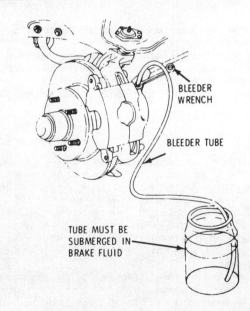

BLEEDER WRENCH

BLEEDER TUBE

TUBE MUST BE SUBMERGED IN BRAKE FLUID

10.8   When bleeding the brakes, a clear piece of tubing is attached to the bleeder screw fitting and submerged in brake fluid – the air bubbles can easily be seen in the tube and container (when no more bubbles appear, the air has been purged from the caliper or wheel cylinder)

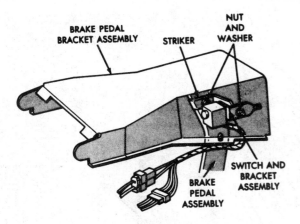

11.3   The brake light switch is mounted above the brake pedal

11   Brake light switch – replacement and adjustment

Refer to illustration 11.3

Replacement

1   Disconnect the negative cable from the battery.
2   The brake light switch is located at the top of the brake pedal.
3   To remove the switch, unplug the electrical connector and unbolt the switch and bracket assembly **(see illustration)**.
4   Installation is the reverse of removal. Reconnect the electrical connector and have an assistant check the brake lights.

Adjustment

5   Push the switch towards the front of the vehicle as far as possible, moving the brake pedal forward slightly.
6   Slowly pull the brake pedal back all the way, causing the switch to ratchet into the correct position.

9   Have the assistant pump the brakes a few times to get pressure in the system, then hold the pedal firmly depressed.
10   While the pedal is held depressed, open the bleeder screw just enough to allow a flow of fluid to leave the valve. Watch for air bubbles to exit the submerged end of the tube. When the fluid flow slows after a couple of seconds, tighten the screw and have your assistant release the pedal.
11   Repeat Steps 9 and 10 until no more air is seen leaving the tube, then tighten the bleeder screw and proceed to the left rear wheel, the right front wheel and the left front wheel, in that order, and perform the same procedure. Be sure to check the fluid in the master cylinder reservoir frequently.
12   Never use old brake fluid. It contains moisture which will deteriorate the brake system components.
13   Refill the master cylinder with fluid at the end of the operation.
14   Check the operation of the brakes. The pedal should feel solid when depressed, with no sponginess. If necessary, repeat the entire process. Bleed the height sensing proportioning valve or anti-lock hydraulic valve, if equipped. **Warning:** *Do not operate the vehicle if you are in doubt about the effectiveness of the brake system.*

12   Brake hoses and lines – check and replacement

Refer to illustration 12.4

1   About every six months, with the vehicle raised and placed securely on jackstands, the flexible hoses which connect the steel brake lines with the front and rear brake assemblies should be inspected for cracks, chafing of the outer cover, leaks, blisters and other damage. These are important and vulnerable parts of the brake system and inspection should be complete. A light and mirror will be needed for a thorough check. If a hose exhibits any of the above defects, replace it with a new one.

Flexible hose replacement

2   Clean all dirt away from the ends of the hose.
3   Disconnect the brake line from the hose fitting using a back-up wrench on the fitting. Be careful not to bend the frame bracket or line. If necessary, soak the connections with penetrating oil.
4   Remove the U-clip (lock) from the female fitting at the bracket **(see illustration)** and remove the hose from the bracket.

9

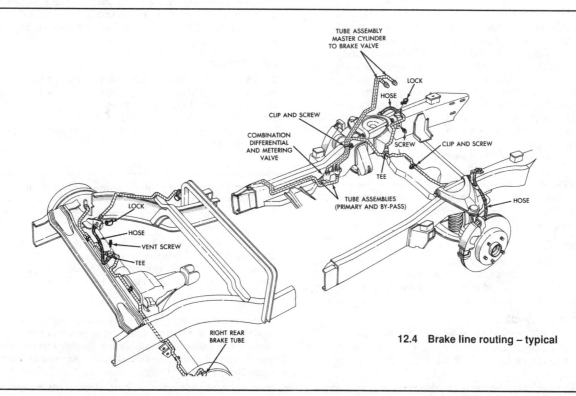

12.4   Brake line routing – typical

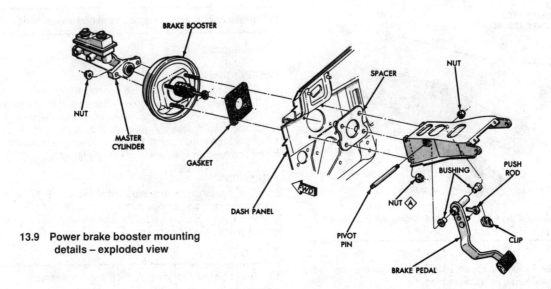

13.9   Power brake booster mounting
details – exploded view

5   Disconnect the hose from the caliper, discarding the copper washers on either side of the fitting.
6   Using new copper washers, attach the new brake hose to the caliper.
7   Pass the female fitting through the frame or frame bracket. With the least amount of twist in the hose, install the fitting in this position. **Note:** *The weight of the vehicle must be on the suspension, so the vehicle should not be raised while positioning the hose.*
8   Install the U-clip (lock) in the female fitting at the frame bracket.
9   Attach the brake line to the hose fitting using a back-up wrench on the fitting.
10   Carefully check to make sure the suspension or steering components don't make contact with the hose. Have an assistant push on the vehicle and also turn the steering wheel lock-to-lock during inspection.
11   Bleed the brake system as described in Section 10.

Metal brake lines

12   When replacing brake lines, be sure to use the correct parts. Don't use copper tubing for any brake system components. Purchase steel brake lines from a dealer parts department or auto parts store.
13   Prefabricated brake line, with the tube ends already flared and fittings installed, is available at auto parts stores and dealer parts departments. These lines are also sometimes bent to the proper shapes.
14   When installing the new line make sure it's well supported in the brackets and has plenty of clearance between moving or hot components.
15   After installation, check the master cylinder fluid level and add fluid as necessary. Bleed the brake system as outlined in Section 10 and test the brakes carefully before placing the vehicle into normal operation.

13   Power brake booster – check, removal and installation

Refer to illustration 13.9

Operating check

1   Depress the brake pedal several times with the engine off and make sure that there is no change in the pedal reserve distance.
2   Depress the pedal and start the engine. If the pedal goes down slightly, operation is normal.

Air tightness check

3   Start the engine and turn it off after one or two minutes.
Depress the brake pedal several times slowly. If the pedal goes down farther the first time but gradually rises after the second or third depression, the booster is air tight.

4   Depress the brake pedal while the engine is running, then stop the engine with the pedal depressed. If there is no change in the pedal reserve travel after holding the pedal for 30 seconds, the booster is air tight.

Removal

5   The power brake booster unit requires no special maintenance apart from periodic inspection of the vacuum hose and the case.
6   Disassembly of the power unit requires special tools and is not ordinarily performed by the home mechanic. If a problem develops, it's recommended that a new or factory rebuilt unit be installed.
7   Remove the master cylinder (refer to Section 7).
8   Disconnect the vacuum hose where it attaches to the power brake booster.
9   Working under the dash, disconnect the power brake pushrod from the top of the brake pedal by prying the clip off **(see illustration)**.
10   Remove the nuts attaching the booster to the firewall.
11   Carefully lift the booster unit away from the firewall and out of the engine compartment.

Installation

12   To install the booster, place it into position and tighten the retaining nuts to the torque listed in this Chapter's Specifications. Connect the brake pedal. **Warning:** *Use a new clip.*
13   Install the master cylinder and vacuum hose.
14   Carefully test the operation of the brakes before placing the vehicle in normal operation.

14   Hydraulic system control valve – check, resetting and replacement

Refer to illustration 14.1

1   All models have a brake warning switch to warn if one side of the hydraulic system fails, and a hold-off (metering) valve to limit the front brake pressure until the rear brake shoes have overcome the return springs and contacted the drums **(see illustration)**.

Check

2   The brake warning light normally comes on during the engine start sequence, then goes off again when the engine starts. It can be checked functionally by opening one bleeder screw slightly while an assistant presses down on the brake pedal. The light should come on with the ignition switch On.

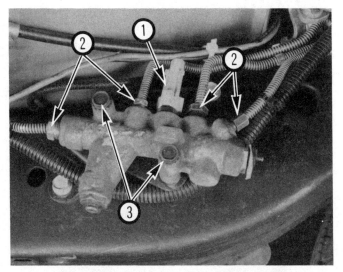

14.1 Hydraulic system control valve assembly

1	Brake warning light connector	2	Brake line unions
		3	Mounting bolts

Resetting

3   If the light for the brake warning system comes on, a leak or problem has occurred in the system and must be corrected. Once the leak or problem has been repaired or if the hydraulic system has been opened up for brake cylinder overhaul or a similar repair, the pressure differential valve must be centered. Once the valve is centered, the brake light on the dash will go out.

4   To center the valve, first fill the master cylinder reservoir and make sure the hydraulic system has been bled.

5   Turn the ignition switch to On or Accessory. Slowly press the brake pedal down and the piston will center itself, causing the light to go out.

6   Check the brake pedal for firmness and proper operation.

Replacement

7   If a pressure differential valve is defective or if it is leaking, it must be replaced. It is a non-serviceable unit and no repair operations are possible by the home mechanic.

8   Disconnect the brake warning light connector from the warning light switch.

9   Disconnect the brake line unions from the valve assembly. Plug the ends of the lines to prevent loss of brake fluid and the entry of dirt.

10   Remove the bolts and nuts securing the valve assembly to the chassis.

11   Remove the valve assembly and bracket.

12   Installation is the reverse of removal.

13   Bleed the system after the replacement valve has been installed.

14   Center the valve as described in Steps 3 through 6 above.

---

15   Height sensing proportioning valve – general information

Refer to illustration 15.1

Note: *Models equipped with anti-lock brakes do not have height sensing proportioning valves.*

The height sensing proportioning valve **(see illustration)** regulates hydraulic pressure to the rear brakes in accordance with the amount of weight present in the rear of the truck. When the truck is unloaded, pressure to the rear brakes will be decreased to prevent brake lockup.

When the vehicle is loaded, the valve senses the lower ride height and allows more hydraulic pressure to the rear brakes.

Due to the special tools, equipment and skills required to diagnose and service the height sensing proportioning valve, we do not recommend that the home mechanic attempt repairs. If service becomes necessary, take the vehicle to a dealer service department or other qualified repair shop.

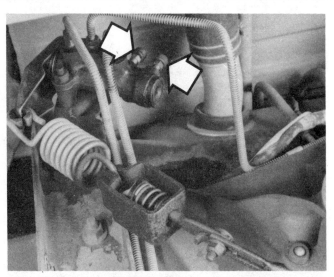

15.1   The height sensing proportioning valve is located adjacent to the rear spring on the driver's side – note the location of the brake bleeders (arrows)

Warning: *Suspension modifications that alter the ride height or spring rate will reduce the effectiveness of the valve. This could lead to inadequate braking characteristics, possibly resulting in an accident.*

---

16   Rear Wheel Anti-lock (RWAL) brake system – general information

Refer to illustrations 16.2, 16.3 and 16.5

1   The Rear Wheel Anti-lock (RWAL) brake system was introduced on the 1990 models. It is designed to maintain vehicle maneuverability, directional stability and optimum deceleration under severe braking conditions on most road surfaces. RWAL does so by monitoring the rotational speed of the rear wheels and controlling the brake line pressure to the rear wheels while braking. This prevents the rear wheels from locking up prematurely during hard braking.

Components

Hydraulic valve

2   The hydraulic valve, which consists of a dump valve and an isolation valve, is located above the rear axle **(see illustration)**. The valve operates by changing the rear brake fluid pressure in response to signals from the control module.

16.2   The hydraulic valve (arrow) is located inside the frame rail on the driver's side, above the rear axle

9

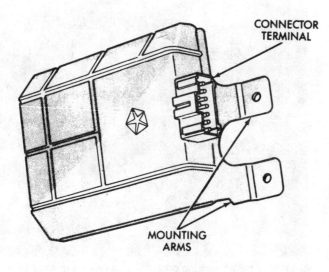

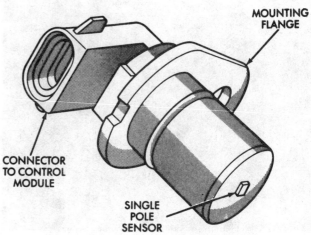

16.3   RWAL electronic control module

16.5   RWAL speed sensor

Control module
3   The RWAL electronic control module **(see illustration)** is mounted under the dash on the passenger's side. The function of the control module is to accept and process information received from the speed sensor and signal the hydraulic valve to control the hydraulic line pressure, avoiding wheel lock-up. The control module also constantly monitors the system, even under normal driving conditions, to find faults within the system.
4   If a problem develops within the system, the ANTILOCK warning light will glow on the dashboard. A diagnostic code will also be stored, which, when retrieved by a service technician, will indicate the problem area or component.

Speed sensor
5   A speed sensor **(see illustration)** is located at the top of the rear differential. The speed sensor sends a signal to the control module indicating rear wheel rotational speed and rate of deceleration.

Diagnosis and repair
6   If the ANTILOCK warning light on the dashboard comes on and stays on, make sure the parking brake is not applied and there's no problem with the standard brake hydraulic system. If neither of these is the cause, the RWAL system is probably malfunctioning. Although a special electronic tester is necessary to properly diagnose the system, the home mechanic can perform a few preliminary checks before taking the vehicle to a dealer service department which is equipped with this tester.
   a) Make sure the brakes, calipers and wheel cylinders are in good condition.
   b) Check the electrical connectors at the control module assembly.
   c) Check the fuses.
   d) Follow the wiring harness to the speed sensor and valve and make sure all connections are secure and the wiring isn't damaged.
If the above preliminary checks don't rectify the problem, the vehicle should be diagnosed by a dealer service department.

---

17   Four–wheel Anti–lock Brake System (ABS) – general information

---

Refer to illustrations 17.2a, 17.2b and 17.5
1   A four–wheel Anti–lock Brake System (ABS) was introduced as an option starting in 1993. It is designed to maintain vehicle maneuverability, directional stability and maximum deceleration under severe braking conditions on most road conditions. Unlike the RWAL system that monitors

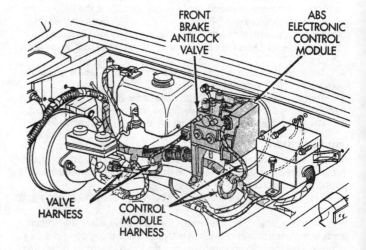

17.2a   Location of the front anti-lock valve assembly, related components and the ECM unit

only the rear two wheels, the four wheel ABS system monitors the rotational speed of all four wheels and controls the brake line pressure to all four wheels while braking. This system prevents all four wheels from locking up prematurely during hard braking.

Components

Anti-lock valves
2   In this system there is a separate anti–lock valve assembly for the front two wheels and one for the rear two wheels. Both valve assemblies are located under the hood with the front valve assembly mounted on the left front inner fender apron **(see illustration)** and the rear valve assembly mounted next to the master cylinder **(see illustration)**. The two valve assemblies are tied together by a brake line from the master cylinder combination valve. Both valve assemblies operate in the same exact manner even though they operate different sets of wheels. These valve assemblies operate by changing the brake fluid pressure in response to signals from the electronic control module.

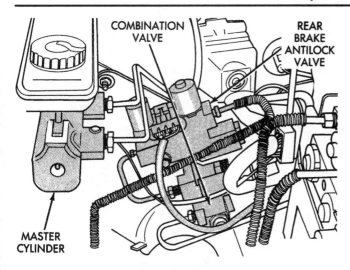

17.2b Location of the rear anti-lock valve assembly and related components

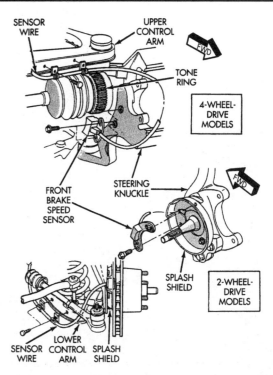

17.5 Locations of the front speed sensors for both 2WD and 4WD models

Electronic control module (ECM)
3   The ECM is mounted under the hood next to the front valve assembly **(see illustration 17.2a)**. The function of the ECM is to accept and process information received from the three speed sensors and signal the hydraulic valves to control hydraulic line pressure, avoiding wheel lock-up. The ECM also constantly monitors the system, even under normal driving conditions, to find faults within the system.
4   If a problem develops within the system, the ANTILOCK warning light will glow on the dashboard. A diagnostic code will also be stored, which, when retrieved by a service technician, will indicate the problem area or components.

Speed sensors
5   The front wheel speed sensors are located on the front spindle on 2WD models or at the outer end of the front drive axles on 4WD models **(see illustration)**. The single rear wheel sensor is mounted at the top of the rear differential. The speed sensors send signals to the ECM indicating the rotational speed and rate of deceleration of all four wheels.

Diagnosis and repair
6   If the ANITLOCK warning light on the dashboard comes on and stays on, make sure the parking brake is not applied and there's no problem with the standard brake hydraulic system. If neither of these is the case, the

ABS system is probably malfunctioning. Although a special electronic tester is necessary to properly diagnose the system, the home mechanic can perform a few preliminary checks before taking the vehicle to a dealer service department which is equipped with the tester.
  a) Make sure the brakes, calipers and wheel cylinders are in good condition.
  b) Check the electrical connectors at the ECM assembly.
  c) Check the fuses.
  d) Follow the wiring harness to all three wheel sensors, to the valve assemblies and to the ECM. Make sure all connections are secure and the wiring isn't damaged.
If the above preliminary checks don't rectify the problem, the vehicle should be diagnosed by a dealer service department.

9

Chapter 10
Suspension and steering systems

Contents

Specifications

Torque specifications

Ft-lbs

Front suspension and steering
Steering wheel nut 45

2WD models
Upper control arm
    Pivot bolt 155
    Balljoint-to-steering knuckle nut 135
    Balljoint-to-upper control arm 125
Lower control arm
    Pivot bolts
        Front 130
        Rear 80
    Balljoint-to-steering knuckle nut 135
Tie-rod stud nut 40
Tie-rod jam nut 55
Steering gear-to-frame bolts 150

4WD models
Upper control arm-to-frame bolts 155
Lower control arm pivot bolts
    Front 130
    Rear 80

10

Balljoint-to-knuckle nut (upper and lower)   80
Hub and bearing-to-steering knuckle bolts   110
Idler arm-to-center link nut   38
Idler arm-to-frame bolts   65
Tie-rod end-to-steering knuckle nut   38
Tie-rod end-to-center link nut   38
Pitman arm-to-center link nut   38
Pitman arm-to-steering gear nut   185
Steering gear-to-frame bolts   100

Rear suspension
Leaf spring-to-front bracket bolt   81
Leaf spring shackle bolt/nut   65
Leaf spring u-bolt nuts
   2WD   65
   4WD   110

---

1   General information

Refer to illustrations 1.1, 1.2 and 1.4

    The steering linkage **(see illustration)** on 4WD models consists of a Pitman (steering gear) arm, idler arm, center link, two adjustable tie-rods and a steering damper (not on all models). When the steering wheel is turned, the gear rotates the Pitman arm which forces the center link to one side. The tie-rods, which are connected to the center link by ball studs, transfer steering force to the wheels. The tie-rods are adjustable and are used for toe-in adjustments. The center link is supported by the Pitman arm and idler arm. The idler arm pivots on a support attached to the frame rail. The steering damper is attached to the frame and center link.

    2WD models use rack and pinion steering connected directly to the tie-rods **(see illustration)**.

    The front suspension is fully independent. Each wheel is connected to the frame by a steering knuckle, upper and lower balljoints and upper and lower control arms. Coil springs and shock absorbers are used on 2WD models; 4WD models use shocks and torsion bars. The coil springs are mounted between the spring pockets on the frame and the lower control arms. The shocks are attached to the lower control arms by bolts and nuts; the upper end of each shock is attached to a bracket on the frame.

    The rear suspension **(see illustration)** consists of a pair of multi-leaf springs and two shock absorbers. The rear axle assembly is attached to

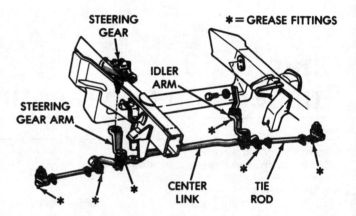

1.1   4WD steering linkage

the leaf springs by U-bolts. The front ends of the springs are attached to the frame at the front hangers, through rubber bushings. The rear ends of the springs are attached to the frame by shackles which allow the springs to alter their length when the vehicle is in operation.

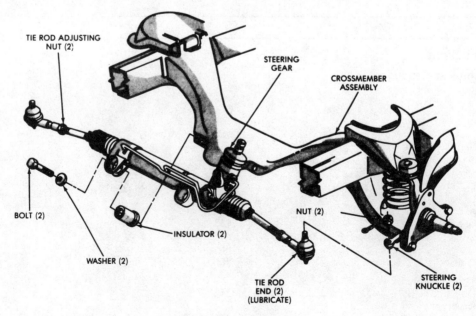

1.2   2WD steering linkage

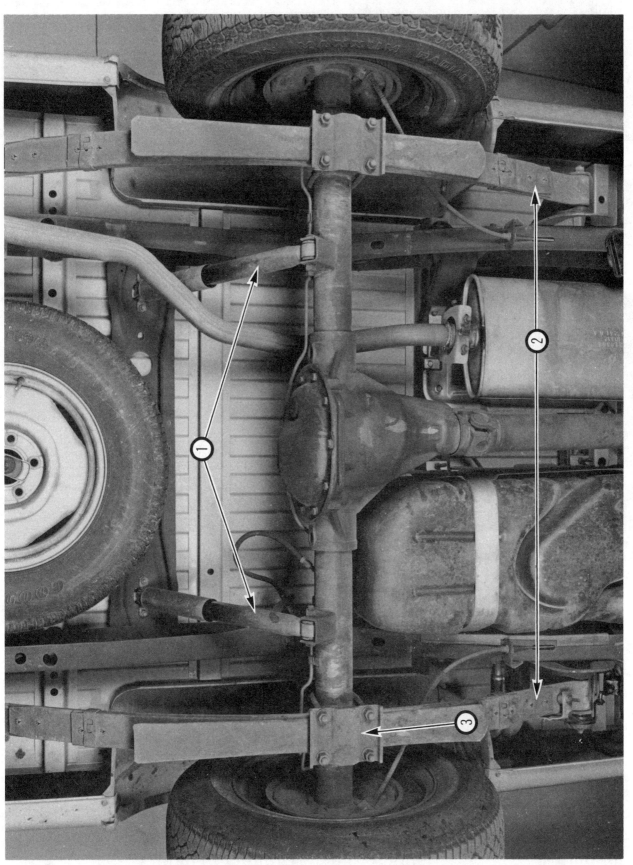

1.4   Rear suspension components

1   Shock absorbers   2   Leaf springs   3   U-bolt anchor plates

10

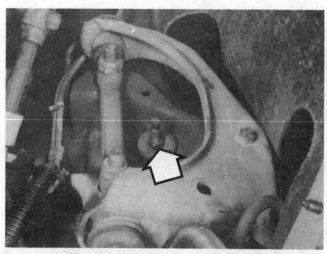

2.1   Remove the shock absorber upper nut (arrow) – 2WD shown, 4WD similar

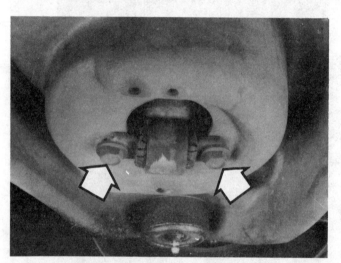

2.4a   Remove the shock absorber lower bolts (arrows)

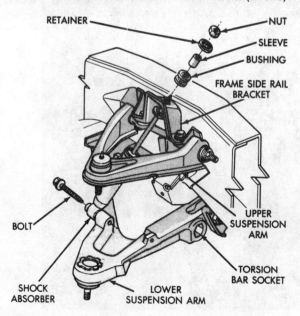

2.4b   4WD shock absorber details – exploded view

Frequently, when working on the suspension or steering system components, you may come across fasteners which seem impossible to loosen. These fasteners on the underside of the vehicle are continually subjected to water, road grime, mud, etc., and can become rusted or "frozen," making them extremely difficult to remove. In order to unscrew these stubborn fasteners without damaging them (or other components), be sure to use lots of penetrating oil and allow it to soak in for a while. Using a wire brush to clean exposed threads will also ease removal of the nut or bolt and prevent damage to the threads. Sometimes a sharp blow with a hammer and punch is effective in breaking the bond between a nut and bolt threads, but care must be taken to prevent the punch from slipping off the fastener and ruining the threads. Heating the stuck fastener and surrounding area with a torch sometimes helps too, but isn't recommended because of the obvious dangers associated with fire. Long breaker bars and extension, or "cheater," pipes will increase leverage, but never use an extension pipe on a ratchet – the ratcheting mechanism could be damaged. Sometimes, turning the nut or bolt in the tightening (clockwise) direction first will help to break it loose. Fasteners that require drastic measures to unscrew should always be replaced with new ones.

Since most of the procedures that are dealt with in this Chapter involve jacking up the vehicle and working underneath it, a good pair of jackstands will be needed. A hydraulic floor jack is the preferred type of jack to lift the vehicle, and it can also be used to support certain components during various operations. **Warning:** *Never, under any circumstances, rely on a jack to support the vehicle while working on it. Also, whenever any of the suspension or steering fasteners are loosened or removed they must be inspected and, if necessary, replaced with new ones of the same part number or of original equipment quality and design. Torque specifications must be followed for proper reassembly and component retention. Never attempt to heat or straighten any suspension or steering component. Instead, replace bent or damaged parts with new ones.*

2   Shock absorber (front) – removal and installation

Refer to illustrations 2.1, 2.4a and 2.4b

1   Using a backup wrench on the stem, remove the upper mounting nut **(see illustration)**.
2   Remove the retainer and grommet.
3   Raise the vehicle and place it securely on jackstands.
4   Working underneath the vehicle, remove the bolt(s) which attach the lower end of the shock absorber to the lower control arm **(see illustrations)** and pull the shock out from below.
5   Remove the lower grommet and retainer from the stem.
6   Fully extend the shock absorber prior to installation. The remaining installation steps are the reverse of removal. Be sure to tighten the upper mounting nut and the lower mounting bolts securely.

3   Stabilizer bar – removal and installation

Refer to illustrations 3.2 and 3.3

1   Raise the vehicle and place it securely on jackstands.
2   On 2WD models, remove the nuts from the link bolts and remove the link bolts **(see illustration)**.
3   On 4WD models, unbolt the retainers from the lower control arms **(see illustration)**.
4   Unscrew the bracket bolts from the frame and remove the stabilizer bar.
5   Remove the rubber bushings.
6   Inspect all parts for wear and damage.
7   Installation is the reverse of removal. Be sure to tighten all fasteners securely.

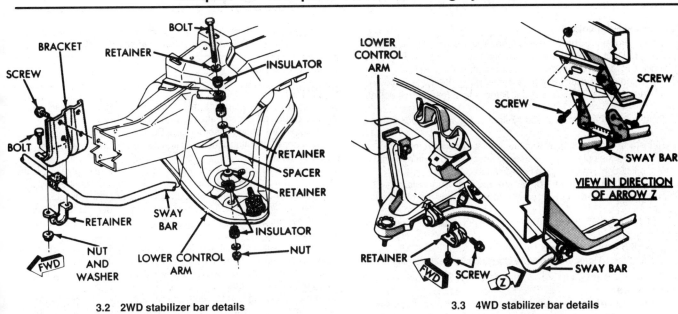

3.2 2WD stabilizer bar details

3.3 4WD stabilizer bar details

---

4   Balljoints – check and replacement

Check

Upper balljoint

1   Loosen the wheel lug nuts, raise the front of the vehicle and support it securely on jackstands. Remove the wheel.

2   Place a floor jack under the lower control arm and raise it slightly. Using a large screwdriver or pry bar, pry up on the upper control arm and watch for movement at the balljoint. Any movement indicates a worn balljoint. Now grasp the steering knuckle and attempt to move the top of it in-and-out – if any play is felt, the balljoint will have to be replaced.

Lower balljoint

3   Place a floor jack under the lower control arm.

4   Grasp the wheel and tire and attempt to move the bottom of it in-and-out – if any play is felt, the balljoint will have to be replaced.

Replacement

Refer to illustrations 4.9 and 4.12

5   Loosen the wheel lug nuts, raise the front of the vehicle and support it securely on jackstands. Remove the wheel.

2WD models

Upper balljoint

6   Remove the brake caliper and tie it out of the way (see Chapter 9).

7   Remove the cotter pin from the upper balljoint and back off the nut several turns.

8   Place a jack or jackstand under the outer end of the lower control arm. **Warning:** *The jack or jackstand must remain under the control arm during removal and installation of the balljoint to hold the spring and control arm in position.*

9   Separate the balljoint from the steering knuckle using tool No. C-3564-A (or equivalent) or a balljoint separator to press the balljoint out of the steering knuckle **(see illustration). Note:** *The use of a "picklefork" type balljoint separator may tear the balljoint boot.*

10   Unscrew the upper balljoint from the control arm using tool No. C-3561, or equivalent. Remove the balljoint and clean the control arm.

Lower balljoint

11   Remove the lower control arm (see Section 8).

12   Using tool No. C-4212 or equivalent, press out the old balljoint **(see illustration).** If this tool isn't available, take the control arm to a dealer device department or other repair shop to have the old balljoint pressed out and the new one installed.

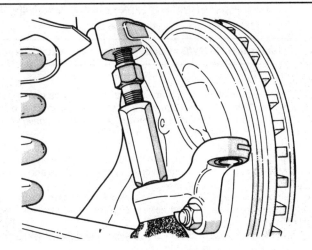

4.9   Install the tool and turn the threaded part until it presses against the upper stud, then strike the knuckle with a hammer

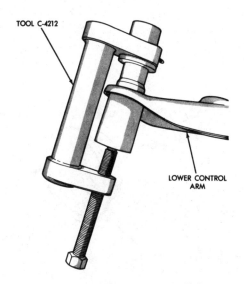

4.12   Removing the lower balljoint

10

Upper or lower balljoint

13   Inspect the tapered holes in the steering knuckle, removing any accumulated dirt. If out-of-roundness, deformation or other damage is noted, the knuckle must be replaced with a new one (see Section 5).
14   Install the new balljoint using the same tool you used to remove it. Tighten the upper balljoint to the torque listed in this Chapter's Specifications.
15   Install a new balljoint boot and retainer using a large socket and a hammer.
16   Reinstall the remaining parts in the reverse order of removal.
17   Reconnect the balljoint to the steering knuckle and tighten the nut to the torque listed in this Chapter's Specifications.
18   If the cotter pin does not line up with the opening in the castellated nut, tighten (never loosen) the nut just enough to allow installation of the cotter pin.
19   Install the grease fittings and lubricate the new balljoints (see Chapter 1).
20   Install the wheels and lower the vehicle.
21   The front end alignment should be checked by a dealer or alignment shop.

4WD models

22   The procedure for replacing the balljoints on a 4WD model is similar to that described above for the lower balljoints on 2WD models. In addition to the above listed steps, remove the driveaxle for access (see Chapter 8).

---

5   Steering knuckle (2WD models) – removal and installation

Refer to illustration 5.5

1   Raise the front of the vehicle and support it securely on jackstands.
2   Support the lower control arm with a jack so the coil spring is compressed to its normal ride height. **Warning:** *The jack must remain in this position throughout the entire procedure.*
3   Remove the wheel.
4   Remove the brake caliper (see Chapter 9) and the brake disc/hub assembly (see Chapter 1, Front wheel bearing check, repack and adjustment).
5   Remove the disc splash shield, if equipped **(see illustration)**.
6   Disconnect the tie-rod end from the steering knuckle (see Section 15).
7   Disconnect the balljoints from the steering knuckle (see Section 4).
8   Remove the steering knuckle.
9   Installation is the reverse of removal. Adjust the front wheel bearings (see Chapter 1) and have the front wheel alignment checked by a dealer service department or alignment shop.

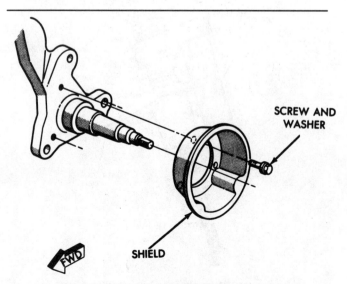

5.5   Unbolt the splash shield from the steering knuckle

6   Coil spring (2WD models) – removal and installation

Refer to illustration 6.5

Removal

1   Loosen the wheel lug nuts, raise the vehicle and support it securely on jackstands placed underneath the frame rails.
2   Remove the shock absorber (see Section 2).
3   Disconnect the stabilizer bar (if equipped) from the lower control arm (see Section 3).
4   Position a spring compressor (tool no. DD-1278, or equivalent) in the spring. **Warning:** *Failure to use this tool could result in severe injury.*
5   Place a floor jack under the lower control arm. Raise the jack slightly to relieve spring pressure from the control arm pivot bolts **(see illustration)**. If they are difficult to remove, tap them out with a hammer and a long, narrow punch.
6   Slowly lower the jack and until the coil spring can be removed. Do not apply downward pressure on the control arm, as it may damage the balljoint. If the upper isolator is not on the top of the spring, reach up into the spring pocket and retrieve it.
7   If the coil spring is to be replaced with a new one, loosen the tool to extend the coil spring fully, then install the tool to the new spring. Tighten the tool to compress the spring sufficiently for installation.

Installation

8   Tape the isolator on top of the coil spring.
9   Install the top of the spring into the spring pocket, and the bottom in the lower control arm.

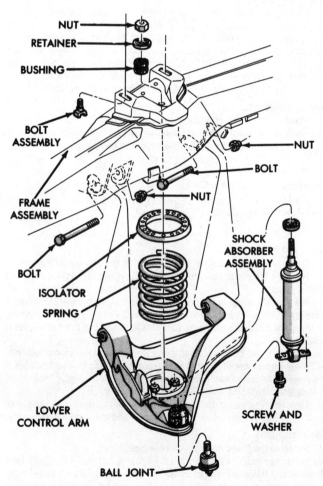

6.5   Coil spring and related parts – exploded view

10 Raise the lower control arm with the jack until the bolt holes are aligned, then install the pivot bolts. The bolts must be inserted from the front. Install the nuts, but don't tighten them completely at this time. Remove the spring compressor tool.

11 Install the shock absorber.

12 Connect the stabilizer bar (if equipped) to the lower control arm.

13 Install the wheel and lug nuts. Lower the vehicle and tighten the lug nuts to the torque specified in Chapter 1.

14 Reach under the vehicle and tighten the pivot bolt nuts to the torque listed in this Chapter's Specifications.

7   Upper control arm – removal and installation

2WD models

Refer to illustration 7.4

Removal

1 Loosen the wheel lug nuts, raise the front of the vehicle and support it securely on jackstands. Remove the wheel.

2 Position a floor jack, with a wood block on the jack head (to act as a cushion), under the lower control arm in the area between the spring seat and the balljoint. Raise the jack slightly to take the spring pressure off the upper control arm. **Warning:** *The jack must remain in this position throughout the entire procedure.*

3 Disconnect the upper balljoint from the steering knuckle (see Section 4). Using a piece of wire or rope, tie the top of the steering knuckle to the coil spring so it doesn't fall and stretch the brake hose.

4 Make matchmarks at the adjustment bolts to facilitate reassembly. Remove the upper control arm bolts and nuts **(see illustration)** and remove the control arm.

5 Inspect the control arm bushings for wear. Replace them if necessary. A hydraulic press may be required to remove and install the bushings, in which case you may have to take them to a dealer service department or other repair shop to have this done.

Installation

6 Position the arm in the frame brackets and install the bolts and nuts.

7 Line up the previously applied matchmarks. Tighten the mounting bolts and nuts to the torque listed in this Chapter's Specifications.

8 Attach the balljoint to the steering knuckle (see Section 4). Tighten the balljoint nut to the torque listed in this Chapter's Specifications.

9 Install the wheel and lug nuts, then lower the vehicle. Tighten the lug nuts to the torque listed in the Chapter 1 Specifications.

10 Have the front end alignment checked and, if necessary, adjusted.

4WD models

Refer to illustration 7.18

Removal

11 Remove the cotter pin, nut lock and spring washer, then loosen the axle hub nut.

12 Loosen the wheel lug nuts, raise the front of the vehicle and support it securely on jackstands. Remove the wheel.

13 Remove the driveaxle (see Chapter 8).

14 Unload the torsion bar (see Section 11). Position a floor jack, with a wood block on the jack head (to act as a cushion), under the lower control arm in the area between the spring seat and the balljoint. Raise the jack slightly to take the spring pressure off the upper control arm. **Warning:** *The jack must remain in this position throughout the entire procedure.*

15 Remove the shock absorber lower mounting bolt.

16 Unbolt the brake hose bracket from the upper control arm.

17 Disconnect the upper balljoint from the steering knuckle (see Section 4).

18 Remove the upper control arm bolts **(see illustration)** and remove the control arm.

19 Inspect the control arm bushings for wear. Replace them if necessary. A hydraulic press may be required to remove and install the bushings, in which case you may have to take them to a dealer service department or other repair shop to have this done.

Installation

20 Position the arm in the frame brackets and install the bolts.

21 Tighten the mounting bolts to the torque listed in this Chapter's Specifications.

22 Attach the balljoint to the steering knuckle (see Section 4).

23 Reinstall the axle and shock absorber.

24 Adjust the torsion bar (see Section 11).

25 Install the wheel and lug nuts, then lower the vehicle. Tighten the lug nuts to the torque listed in the Chapter 1 Specifications.

26 Have the front end alignment checked and, if necessary, adjusted.

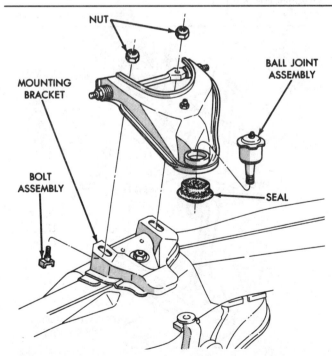

7.4   Mounting details of the upper control arm – 2WD models

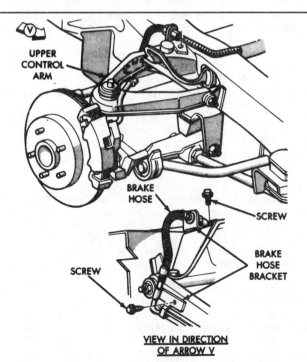

7.18   Mounting details of the upper control arm – 4WD models

10

8   Lower control arm – removal and installation

2WD models

Removal

1   Loosen the wheel lug nuts, raise the vehicle and support it securely on jackstands. Remove the wheel.
2   Remove the coil spring (see Section 6).
3   Disconnect the lower balljoint from the steering knuckle **(see illustration 4.9)** and remove it from the vehicle.

Installation

4   Installation is the reverse of removal. Make sure the pivot bolts are installed from the front **(see illustration 6.5)**, and don't tighten them until the vehicle is at normal ride height. Tighten all nuts to the torque listed in this Chapter's Specifications, and if a new balljoint has been installed, lubricate it on completion.

4WD models

Refer to illustration 8.17

Removal

5   Loosen the wheel lug nuts, raise the vehicle and support it securely on jackstands. Remove the wheel.
6   Remove the front splash shield (if equipped) for access to the front end components.
7   Disconnect the stabilizer bar from the lower control arm (see Section 3).
8   Remove the shock absorber (see Section 2).
9   Disconnect the inner tie-rod end from the center link (see Section 15).
10   Remove the driveaxle (see Chapter 8).
11   Follow the torsion bar back to the crossmember. Measure the distance between the crossmember and the end of the torsion bar anchor and record this measurement for reference when reassembling.
12   Loosen the torsion bar adjusting bolt as much as possible, without removing the bolt completely. This will reduce the tension on the bar.
13   Support the lower control arm with a floor jack. The jack head should be positioned as near to the balljoint as possible, and still allow access to the balljoint stud nut.
14   Disconnect the steering knuckle from the lower balljoint (see Section 4). Lift the knuckle and hub assembly up, then place a block of wood between the upper control arm and the frame to support the assembly out of the way.
15   SLOWLY lower the jack until the pressure from the torsion bar is completely released.
16   Slide the torsion bar forward, out of the anchor arm.
17   Remove the lower control arm pivot bolts and nuts **(see illustration)**. Remove the lower control arm and torsion bar as a unit.
18   Mark the front of the torsion bar with a piece of tape to insure correct installation, then separate the bar from the arm.
19   Check the bushings for damage or wear. If necessary, take the control arm to a dealer service department or other repair shop to have the bushings replaced for you.

Installation

20   Insert the torsion bar into its hole in the lower control arm. Raise the arm and bar up into position, inserting the rear end of the bar into the anchor. Position the lower control arm in the frame brackets, inserting the front portion first.
21   Install the control arm pivot bolts. They must be inserted as shown in illustration 8.17. Install the nuts, but don't tighten them completely at this time.
22   Slide the torsion bar back into the adjusting arm.
23   Carefully raise the lower control arm with the floor jack until the balljoint stud can be inserted into the hole in the steering knuckle. Install the balljoint stud nut, tighten it to the torque listed in this Chapter's Specifications, then install a new cotter pin.
24   Tighten the torsion bar adjusting nut until the distance between the crossmember and the end of the anchor is the same as it was before removal.

25   Install the driveaxle.
26   Connect the inner tie-rod to the center link.
27   Install the shock absorber.
28   Connect the stabilizer bar to the lower control arm.
29   Install the wheel and lug nuts. Lower the vehicle and tighten the lug nuts to the torque listed in the Chapter 1 Specifications.
30   Tighten the lower control arm pivot bolts to the torque listed in this Chapter's Specifications.
31   Install the splash shield, if equipped.
32   Measure the vehicle's ride height on each side, from equal points on the frame to the ground. If the side that has been worked on is higher or lower than the other side, adjust the torsion bars as described in Section 11.

9   Steering knuckle (4WD models) – removal and installation

Removal

1   Remove the hub cover and loosen the driveaxle/hub nut about a quarter of a turn.
2   Loosen the wheel lug nuts, raise the front of the vehicle and support it securely on jackstands. Remove the wheel.
3   Disconnect the tie-rod end from the steering knuckle (see Section 15).
4   Unbolt the brake caliper and hang it out of the way with a piece of wire (see Chapter 9). Remove the brake disc.
5   Remove the driveaxle/hub nut.
6   Support the lower control arm with a floor jack and detach the steering knuckle from the lower balljoint (see Section 4). **Warning:** *The jack must remain in this position throughout the entire procedure.*
7   Support the steering knuckle and separate it from the upper balljoint (see Section 4).
8   Using a puller if necessary, push the driveaxle out of the hub while withdrawing the steering knuckle and hub assembly.
9   Refer to Section 10 for the hub and bearing replacement procedure, if necessary.
10   Inspect the seal on the rear side of the knuckle. If it is damaged or shows signs of deterioration, pry it out with a large screwdriver or pry bar. Install a new seal by driving it in with a socket that has an outside diameter slightly smaller than the seal.

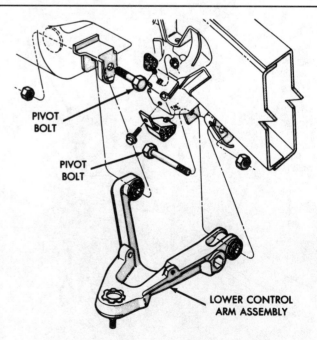

8.17   Details of the lower control arm – 4WD models

Installation

11   Installation is the reverse of the removal procedure. Be sure to lubricate the driveaxle splines with multi-purpose grease, and tighten all of the fasteners to the torque listed in this Chapter's Specifications.

---

10   Front hub and wheel bearing assembly (4WD models) – replacement

Refer to illustration 10.5

Note: *The hub and bearing assembly is a sealed unit and is not serviceable. If found defective, it must be replaced.*

1   Remove the hub cover and loosen the driveaxle/hub nut about a quarter of a turn.
2   Loosen the wheel lug nuts, raise the vehicle and support it securely on jackstands. Remove the wheel.
3   Unbolt the brake caliper and hang it out of the way with a piece of wire (see Chapter 9). Remove the brake disc.
4   Remove the driveaxle/hub nut.
5   Remove the hub assembly-to-steering knuckle bolts **(see illustration)**. Tap the hub assembly from side-to-side to break it loose from the steering knuckle. Using a puller, pull the hub assembly off the end of the driveaxle. Wrap the end of the driveaxle with a rag to prevent damaging it.
6   Installation is the reverse of the removal procedure. Be sure to lubricate the driveaxle splines with multi-purpose grease, and tighten all of the fasteners to the torque listed in this Chapter's Specifications.

---

11   Torsion bar (4WD models) – removal and installation

Refer to illustrations 11.3 and 11.10

Caution: *Do not interchange torsion bars from one side to the other. The bars are marked either "L" or "R" on the ends to indicate the side they must be used on.*

Removal

1   Remove the upper control arm rebound bumper.
2   Raise the front of the vehicle and support it securely on jackstands positioned under the frame.

3   Release tension on the torsion bar by turning the adjusting bolt counterclockwise **(see illustration)**.
4   Remove the adjusting bolt, torsion bar and anchor.
5   Clean and inspect the parts and torsion bar pocket. Replace components as necessary.

Installation

6   Installation is the reverse of removal. After installation, the vehicle ride height must be set.
7   Check and adjust tire pressure (see Chapter 1).
8   Place the vehicle on level, solid pavement. It must be unloaded with a full tank of fuel.
9   Jounce the front bumper up and down several times at least four inches to settle the suspension.
10   Measure the difference between the height of the lower control arm inner pivot and the outer end of the arm **(see illustration)**. This difference should be 1-1/4 inch.
11   Make adjustments by turning the adjusting bolt. After each adjustment, jounce the front bumper again. The final adjustment must be in the up direction. **Note:** *Measure both sides even if only one side was replaced.*
12   Front vehicle height should not vary more than 1/4 inch from the specification and should be within 1/4 inch side to side.

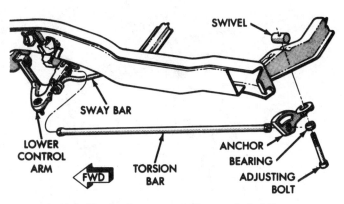

11.3   Torsion bar components – exploded view

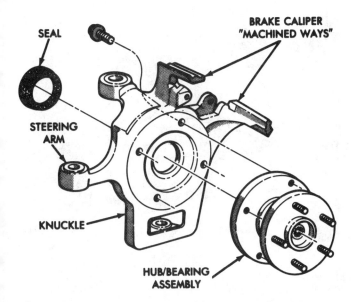

10.5   Hub and bearing installation details (4WD models)

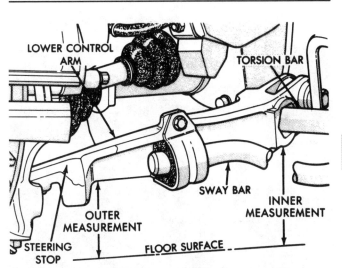

11.10   Measure the height at these points and subtract the outer measurement from the inner measurement

10

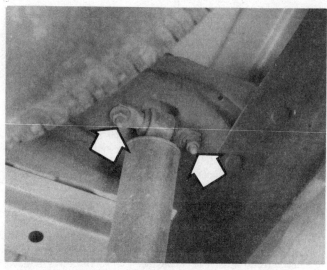

12.2   Remove the upper mounting nuts (arrows)

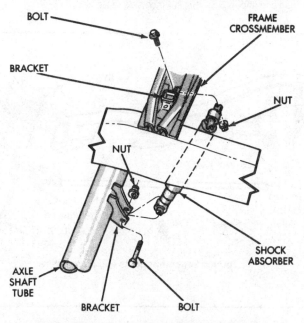

12.3   Rear shock absorber mounting details

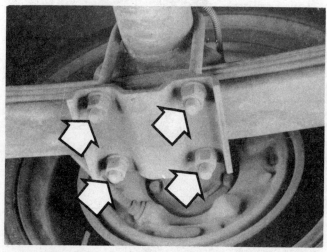

13.2   Remove the nuts and washers (arrows) from the U-bolts

12   Shock absorber (rear) – removal and installation

Refer to illustrations 12.2 and 12.3

1   Raise the rear of the vehicle and place it securely on jackstands.
2   Remove the shock absorber upper mounting nuts and bolts from the frame crossmember **(see illustration)**.
3   Remove the lower mounting nut, washer and bolt from the axle bracket **(see illustration)**.
4   Remove the shock absorber.
5   Installation is the reverse of removal. Make sure you install the nuts and bolts facing in the proper direction.

13   Leaf spring/shackle – removal and installation

Refer to illustrations 13.2, 13.3a, 13.3b, 13.4 and 13.5
Note: *Change one spring at a time, using the other spring to hold the rear axle in position.*

1   Raise the rear of the vehicle and place the frame securely on jackstands. Support the axle with a floor jack and raise it slightly to relieve the tension on the leaf springs.
2   Remove the nuts and washers from the U-bolts **(see illustration)**. Remove the U-bolts.
3   Remove the spring bracket or seat and parking brake cable guide, as applicable **(see illustrations)**.
4   Remove the shackle-to-spring nut and the shackle-to-rear bracket nut **(see illustration)**.
5   Support the front end of the spring. Remove the spring-to-front bracket nut, washers and bolt **(see illustration)** and lower the front of the spring.
6   Support the rear end of the spring and remove the shackle bolts. Remove the spring assembly from the vehicle.
7   Installation is the reverse of removal. Tighten the U-bolt nuts in a diagonal sequence. Tighten all the fasteners to the torque listed in this Chapter's Specifications.

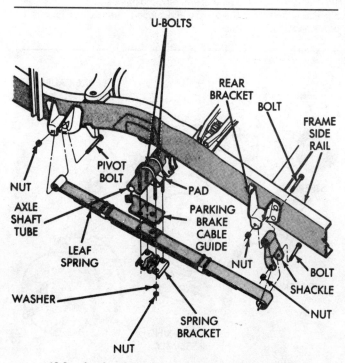

13.3a   Leaf spring mounting details – 2WD models

14   Steering wheel – removal and installation

Refer to illustrations 14.2, 14.3 and 14.4

1   Disconnect the cable from the negative terminal of the battery.

2   Remove the horn pad from the steering wheel by removing the screws from the back side **(see illustration)**. Lift the pad off and disconnect the horn switch wires.

3   Remove the steering wheel retaining nut and mark the position of the steering wheel to the shaft, if marks don't already exist or don't line up **(see illustration)**.

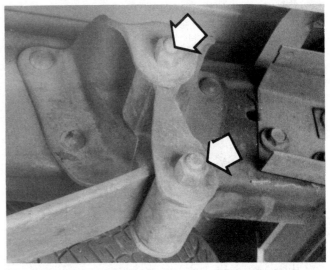

13.4   Remove the shackle-to-spring nuts and the shackle-to-rear bracket nut (arrows)

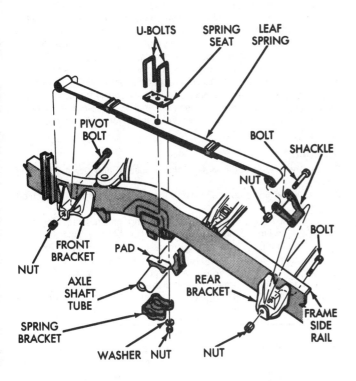

13.3b   Leaf spring mounting details – 4WD models

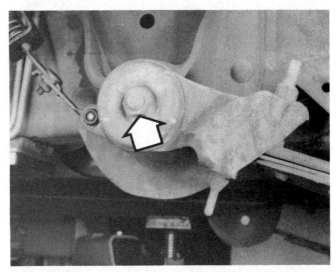

13.5   Remove the spring-to-front bracket nut (arrow)

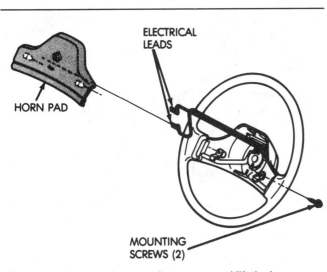

14.2   Remove the mounting screws and lift the horn pad off the wheel

14.3   Mark the position of the wheel relative to the shaft (arrows)

10

14.4   Remove the steering wheel with a bolt-type puller

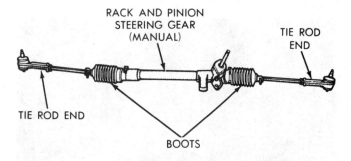

15.1a   Manual steering gear – 2WD models

4   Use a puller to detach the steering wheel from the shaft **(see illustration)**. Don't hammer on the shaft to dislodge the wheel.
5   To install the wheel, align the mark on the steering wheel hub with the mark on the shaft and slide the wheel onto the shaft. Install the nut and tighten it to the torque listed in this Chapter's Specifications.
6   Connect the horn wire and install the horn pad.
7   Connect the cable to the negative terminal of the battery.

15   Steering linkage – inspection, removal and installation

Refer to illustrations 15.1a, 15.1b and 15.6
1   The steering linkage connects the steering gear to the front wheels and keeps the wheels in proper relation to each other. On 2WD models, the steering rack connects directly to the steering knuckles through the tie-rods **(see illustration)**. On 4WD models, the linkage **(see illustration)** consists of the Pitman (or steering gear) arm, the idler arm, the center link, two adjustable tie-rods and, on some models, a steering damper. The Pitman arm, which is fastened to the steering gear shaft, moves the center link back-and-forth. The center link is supported on the other end by a frame-mounted idler arm. The back-and-forth motion of the center link is transmitted to the steering knuckles through a pair of tie-rod assemblies. Each tie-rod is made up of an inner and outer tie-rod end, a threaded adjuster tube and two clamps.

Inspection
2   Set the wheels in the straight ahead position and lock the steering wheel.
3   Raise one side of the vehicle until the tire is approximately 1-inch off the ground.
4   Grasp the front and rear of the tire and using light pressure, wiggle the wheel back-and-forth. There should be no noticeable play. If the play in the steering system is noticeable, inspect each steering linkage pivot point and ballstud for looseness and replace parts if necessary.
5   Raise the front of the vehicle and support it on jackstands. Push up, then pull down on the center link end of the idler arm, exerting a force of approximately 25 pounds each way. If there is any looseness, replace the idler arm.

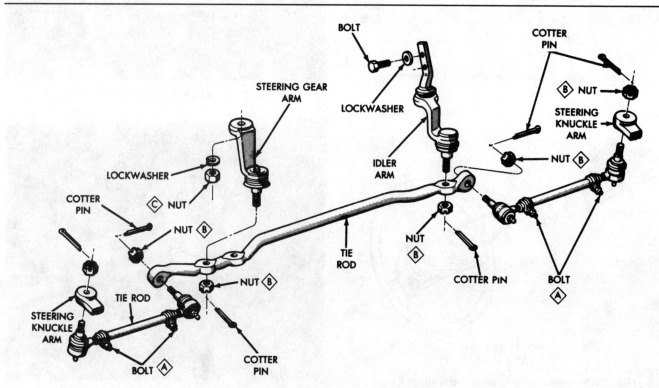

15.1b   4WD steering linkage – exploded view

6   Check for torn rubber boots **(see illustration)**, frozen joints and bent or damaged linkage components.

Removal and installation

All models

Tie-rod

Refer to illustrations 15.8, 15.9, 15.10a, 15.10b, 15.12 and 15.13

7   Loosen the wheel lug nuts, raise the vehicle and support it securely on jackstands. Apply the parking brake. Remove the wheel.

8   Remove the cotter pin and loosen, but do not remove, the castellated nut from the ballstud **(see illustration)**.

9   Using a two-jaw puller, separate the tie-rod end from the steering knuckle **(see illustration)**. Remove the castellated nut and pull the tie-rod end from the knuckle.

10   On 4WD models, if a tie-rod end must be replaced, measure the distance from the end of the adjuster tube to the center of the ballstud and record it **(see illustration)**. Loosen the adjuster tube clamp and unscrew the tie-rod end. On 2WD models, loosen the jam nut **(see illustration)** and count the number of turns required to unscrew the tie-rod end.

11   On 4WD models, remove the nut securing the inner tie-rod end to the center link. Separate the inner tie-rod end from the center link in the same manner as in Step 9.

15.6   Inspect the rubber boots (arrow) for cracks and tears

15.8   Loosen the castellated nut

15.9   Break the tie-rod end loose from the steering knuckle with a two-jaw puller

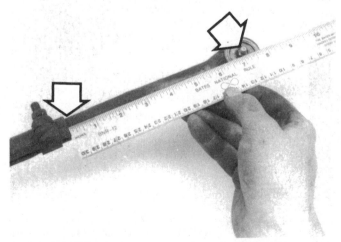

15.10a   Measure the distance from the end of the adjuster tube to the center of the ballstud and record the measurement before loosening the adjuster tube clamp and unscrewing the tie-rod end

15.10b   On 2WD models, loosen the jam nut (arrow) before unscrewing the tie-rod end

10

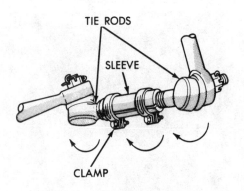

15.12   Make sure the tie-rod can pivot back and forth freely – otherwise, it may bind

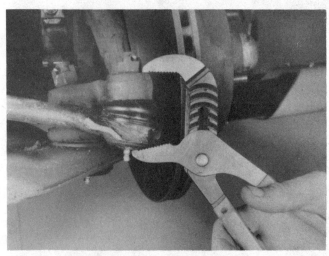

15.13   Press the tie-rod end into the steering knuckle if the ballstud spins when the nut is tightened

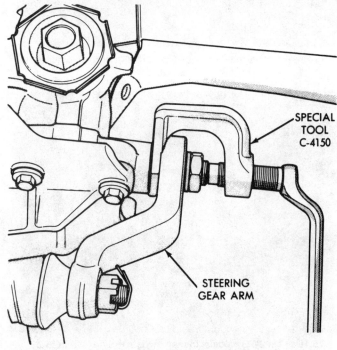

15.33   A puller will be needed to remove the Pitman (steering gear) arm

12   Lubricate the threaded portion of the tie-rod with chassis grease. On 4WD models, screw the new tie-rod end into the adjuster sleeve and adjust the distance from the tube to the ballstud to the previously measured dimension. The number of threads showing on the inner and outer tie-rod ends should be equal within three threads. Don't tighten the clamp nut yet **(see illustration)**.

13   To install the tie-rod, connect the outer tie-rod end to the steering knuckle and install the castellated nut. Tighten the nut to the torque listed in this Chapter's Specifications and install a new cotter pin. If the ballstud spins when attempting to tighten the nut, force it into the tapered hole with a large pair of pliers **(see illustration)**. If necessary, tighten the nut slightly to align a slot in the nut with the cotter pin hole in the ballstud. Install the cotter pin.

14   On 4WD models, insert the inner tie-rod end ballstud into the center link until it's seated. Install the nut and tighten it to the torque listed in this Chapter's Specifications.

15   Tighten the clamp nuts. The center of the bolt should be nearly horizontal and the adjuster tube slot must not line up with the gap in the clamps.

16   Install the wheel and lug nuts, lower the vehicle and tighten the lug nuts to the torque listed in the Chapter 1 Specifications. Drive the vehicle to an alignment shop to have the front end alignment checked and, if necessary, adjusted.

4WD models

Idler arm

17   Raise the vehicle and support it securely on jackstands. Apply the parking brake.

18   Loosen but do not remove the idler arm-to-center link nut.

19   Separate the idler arm from the center link with a two jaw puller **(see illustration 15.9)**. Remove the nut.

20   Remove the idler arm-to-frame bolts **(see illustration 15.1b)**.

21   To install the idler arm, position it on the frame and install the bolts, tightening them to the torque listed in this Chapter's Specifications.

22   Insert the idler arm ballstud into the center link and install the nut. Tighten the nut to the torque listed in this Chapter's Specifications. If the ballstud spins when attempting to tighten the nut, force it into the tapered hole with a large pair of pliers **(see illustration 15.13)**.

Center link

23   Raise the vehicle and support it securely on jackstands. Apply the parking brake.

24   Separate the two inner tie-rod ends from the center link.

25   Separate the center link from the Pitman arm.

26   Separate the center link from the idler arm.

27   Installation is the reverse of the removal procedure. If the ballstuds spin when attempting to tighten the nuts, force them into the tapered holes with a large pair of pliers **(see illustration 15.13)**. Be sure to tighten all of the nuts to the torque listed in this Chapter's Specifications.

Pitman (steering gear) arm

Refer to illustration 15.33

28   Raise the vehicle and place it securely on jackstands.

29   Remove the center link nut from the Pitman arm ballstud. Discard the nut – don't reuse it.

30   Using a puller, separate the center link from the Pitman arm ballstud.

31   Mark the Pitman arm and the steering gear shaft to ensure proper alignment at reassembly time.

32   Remove the Pitman arm nut and washer.

33   Remove the Pitman arm with a Pitman arm puller or a two-jaw puller **(see illustration)**.

34   Inspect the ballstud threads for damage. Inspect the ballstud seals for excessive wear. Clean the threads of the ballstud.

35   Installation is the reverse of removal. Make sure the marks you made on the Pitman arm and Pitman shaft are aligned. **Note:** *If a clamp type Pitman arm is used, spread the arm just enough, with a wedge, to slip the arm onto the Pitman shaft. Don't spread the arm more than necessary to slip it over the shaft with hand pressure. Do not hammer the arm onto the shaft or you may damage the steering gear.*

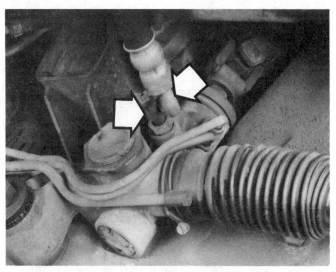

16.2   Disconnect the hose fittings (arrows)

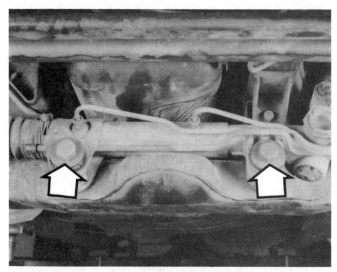

16.5   Remove the steering gear mounting bolts (arrows)

16   Steering gear – removal and installation

2WD models

Refer to illustrations 16.2 and 16.5

Removal
1   Raise the front of the vehicle and support it securely on jackstands. Apply the parking brake.
2   If the vehicle has power steering, place a drain pan under the steering gear. Disconnect the hose fittings **(see illustration)** and cap the ends to prevent excessive fluid loss and contamination.
3   Detach the tie-rod ends from the steering knuckles (see Section 15).
4   Mark the relationship of the steering shaft lower joint to the steering gear input shaft. Unbolt the steering shaft-to-steering gear coupling. Some models use a roll pin instead of a bolt – in this case, drive the roll pin out with a hammer and punch.
5   Remove the steering gear mounting bolts **(see illustration)** and lower the steering gear from the vehicle.

Installation
6   Installation is the reverse of removal. Tighten the bolts to the torque listed in this Chapter's Specifications and use a new roll pin in the steering shaft. On power steering equipped models, be sure to add fluid and bleed the system (see Section 18).

4WD models
Removal
7   Raise the front of the vehicle and support it securely on jackstands. Apply the parking brake.
8   If the vehicle has power steering, place a drain pan under the steering gear. Disconnect the hose fittings and cap the ends to prevent excessive fluid loss and contamination.
9   Mark the relationship of the steering shaft lower joint to the steering gear input shaft. Remove the shaft-to-steering box roll pin with a punch and hammer.
10   Mark the relationship of the Pitman arm to the shaft so it can be installed in the same position. Remove the Pitman arm nut and washer (see Section 15).
11   Remove the Pitman arm from the shaft with a two-jaw puller.
12   Support the steering gear and remove the mounting bolts. Lower the unit, separate the steering shaft from the steering gear input shaft and remove the steering gear from the vehicle.

Installation
13   Raise the steering gear into position and connect the steering shaft, aligning the marks.

14   Install the mounting bolts and washers and tighten them to the torque listed in this Chapter's Specifications.
15   Slide the Pitman arm onto the shaft. Make sure the marks are aligned. Install the washer and nut and tighten the nut to the torque listed in this Chapter's Specifications.
16   Install a new steering shaft pin.
17   Connect the power steering hose fittings to the steering gear and fill the power steering pump reservoir with the recommended fluid (see Chapter 1).
18   Lower the vehicle and bleed the steering system (see Section 18).

17   Power steering pump – removal and installation

Refer to illustrations 17.3, 17.6 and 17.9

Removal
1   Disconnect the cable from the negative terminal of the battery.
2   Remove the power steering drivebelt (see Chapter 1).
3   Detach the cover from the rear of the pump **(see illustration)**.
4   Position a drain pan under the power steering pump. Disconnect the pressure and return hoses from the backside of the pump. Plug the hoses to prevent contaminants from entering.

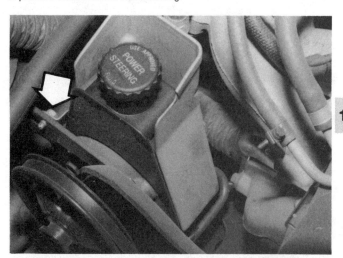

17.3   Remove the cover bolts (arrow) and detach the cover

10

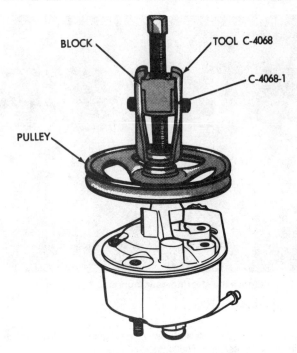

17.6   Remove the pulley with a special tool

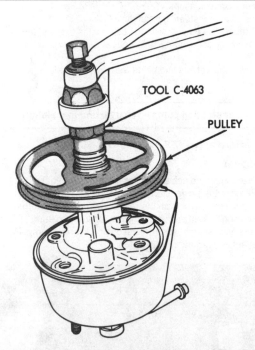

17.9   Use a pulley installation tool – do not hammer the pulley onto the shaft

5   Remove the pump mounting fasteners and lift the pump from the vehicle, taking care not to spill fluid on the painted surfaces.
6   Using a special pulley removal tool (C-4068 or equivalent), remove the pulley from the pump **(see illustration)**.

Installation

7   Position the pump in the mounting bracket and install the bolts/nuts. Tighten the fasteners securely.
8   Connect the hoses to the pump. Tighten the fittings securely and reinstall the cover.

9   Press the pulley onto the shaft using a special pulley installer tool (C-4063, or equivalent) **(see illustration)**. An alternative tool can be fabricated from a long bolt, nut, washer and a socket of the same diameter as the pulley hub. Push the pulley onto the shaft until the front of the hub is flush with the shaft, but no further.
10   Install the drivebelt.
11   Fill the power steering reservoir with the recommended fluid (see Chapter 1) and bleed the system following the procedure described in the next Section.

18   Power steering system – bleeding

1   Following any operation in which the power steering fluid lines have been disconnected, the power steering system must be bled to remove all air and obtain proper steering performance.
2   With the front wheels in the straight ahead position, check the power steering fluid level and, if low, add fluid until it reaches the Cold mark on the dipstick.
3   Start the engine and allow it to run at fast idle. Recheck the fluid level and add more if necessary to reach the Cold mark on the dipstick.
4   Bleed the system by turning the wheels from side-to-side, without hitting the stops. This will work the air out of the system. Keep the reservoir full of fluid as this is done.
5   When the air is worked out of the system, return the wheels to the straight ahead position and leave the vehicle running for several more minutes before shutting it off.
6   Road test the vehicle to be sure the steering system is functioning normally and noise free.
7   Recheck the fluid level to be sure it is up to the Hot mark on the dipstick while the engine is at normal operating temperature. Add fluid if necessary (see Chapter 1).

19   Wheels and tires – general information

Refer to illustration 19.1

All vehicles covered by this manual are equipped with metric-sized radial tires **(see illustration)**. Use of other size or type of tires may affect the ride and handling of the vehicle. Don't mix different types of tires, such as radials and bias belted, on the same vehicle as handling may be seriously affected. It's recommended that tires be replaced in pairs on the same axle, but if only one tire is being replaced, be sure it's the same size, structure and tread design as the other.
   Because tire pressure has a substantial effect on handling and wear, the pressure on all tires should be checked at least once a month or before any extended trips (see Chapter 1).
   Wheels must be replaced if they are bent, dented, leak air, have elongated bolt holes, are heavily rusted, out of vertical symmetry or if the lug nuts won't stay tight. Wheel repairs that use welding or peening are not recommended.
   Tire and wheel balance is important to the overall handling, braking and performance of the vehicle. Unbalanced wheels can adversely affect handling and ride characteristics as well as tire life. Whenever a tire is installed on a wheel, the tire and wheel should be balanced by a shop with the proper equipment.

20   Front end alignment – general information

Refer to illustration 20.1

A front end alignment refers to the adjustments made to the front wheels so they are in proper angular relationship to the suspension and the ground. Front wheels that are out of proper alignment not only affect steering control, but also increase tire wear **(see illustration)**.
   Getting the proper front wheel alignment is a very exacting process, one in which complicated and expensive machines are necessary to perform the job properly. Because of this, you should have a technician with

METRIC TIRE SIZES

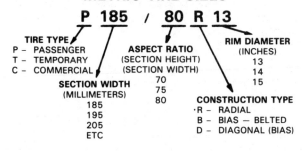

P 185 / 80 R 13

TIRE TYPE
P – PASSENGER
T – TEMPORARY
C – COMMERCIAL

SECTION WIDTH
(MILLIMETERS)
185
195
205
ETC

ASPECT RATIO
(SECTION HEIGHT)
(SECTION WIDTH)
70
75
80

CONSTRUCTION TYPE
·R – RADIAL
B – BIAS — BELTED
D – DIAGONAL (BIAS)

RIM DIAMETER
(INCHES)
13
14
15

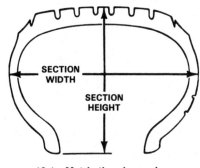

SECTION WIDTH

SECTION HEIGHT

19.1   Metric tire size code

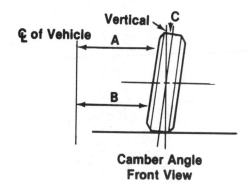

ℂ of Vehicle   Vertical   C
A
B

Camber Angle
Front View

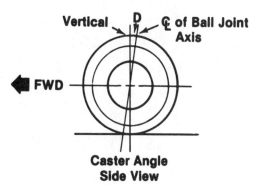

Vertical   D   ℂ of Ball Joint Axis

FWD

Caster Angle
Side View

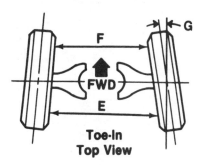

F   G
FWD
E

Toe-In
Top View

20.1   Front end alignment details

A minus B = C (degrees camber)
D = caster (measured in degrees)
E minus F = toe-in (measured in inches)
G = toe-in (expressed in degrees)

the proper equipment perform these tasks. We will, however, use this space to give you a basic idea of what is involved with front end alignment so you can better understand the process and deal intelligently with the shop that does the work.

Toe-in is the turning in of the front wheels. The purpose of a toe specification is to ensure parallel rolling of the front wheels. In a vehicle with zero toe-in, the distance between the front edges of the wheels will be the same as the distance between the rear edges of the wheels. The actual amount of toe-in is normally only a fraction of an inch. Toe-in adjustment is controlled by the tie-rod end position on the tie-rod. Incorrect toe-in will cause the tires to wear improperly by making them scrub against the road surface.

Camber is the tilting of the front wheels from the vertical when viewed from the front of the vehicle. When the wheels tilt out at the top, the camber is said to be positive (+). When the wheels tilt in at the top the camber is negative (-). The amount of tilt is measured in degrees from the vertical and this measurement is called the camber angle. This angle affects the amount of tire tread which contacts the road and compensates for changes in the suspension geometry when the vehicle is cornering or travelling over an undulating surface.

Caster is the tilting of the top of the front steering axis from the vertical. A tilt toward the rear is positive caster and a tilt toward the front is negative caster.

10

Chapter 11 Body

Contents

1 General information

The vehicles covered by this manual have a separate frame and body.

Certain components are particularly vulnerable to accident damage and can be unbolted and repaired or replaced. Among these parts are the body moldings, bumpers, the hood and tailgate and all glass.

Only general body maintenance practices and body panel repair procedures within the scope of the do-it-yourselfer are included in this Chapter.

2 Body – maintenance

1   The condition of your vehicle's body is very important, because the resale value depends a great deal on it. It's much more difficult to repair a neglected or damaged body than it is to repair mechanical components. The hidden areas of the body, such as the wheel wells, the frame and the engine compartment, are equally important, although they don't require as frequent attention as the rest of the body.

2   Once a year, or every 12,000 miles, it's a good idea to have the underside of the body steam cleaned. All traces of dirt and oil will be removed and the area can then be inspected carefully for rust, damaged brake lines, frayed electrical wires, damaged cables and other problems. The

front suspension components should be greased after completion of this job.

3   At the same time, clean the engine and the engine compartment with a steam cleaner or water soluble degreaser.

4   The wheel wells should be given close attention, since undercoating can peel away and stones and dirt thrown up by the tires can cause the paint to chip and flake, allowing rust to set in. If rust is found, clean down to the bare metal and apply an anti-rust paint.

5   The body should be washed about once a week. Wet the vehicle thoroughly to soften the dirt, then wash it down with a soft sponge and plenty of clean soapy water. If the surplus dirt is not washed off very carefully, it can wear down the paint.

6   Spots of tar or asphalt thrown up from the road should be removed with a cloth soaked in solvent.

7   Once every six months, wax the body and chrome trim. If a chrome cleaner is used to remove rust from any of the vehicle's plated parts, remember that the cleaner also removes part of the chrome, so use it sparingly.

3 Vinyl trim – maintenance

Don't clean vinyl trim with detergents, caustic soap or petroleum-based cleaners. Plain soap and water works just fine, with a soft brush to clean dirt that may be ingrained. Wash the vinyl as frequently as the rest

11

of the vehicle.

After cleaning, application of a high quality rubber and vinyl protectant will help prevent oxidation and cracks. The protectant can also be applied to weatherstripping, vacuum lines and rubber hoses, which often fail as a result of chemical degradation, and to the tires.

4   Upholstery and carpets – maintenance

1   Every three months remove the carpets or mats and clean the interior of the vehicle (more frequently if necessary). Vacuum the upholstery and carpets to remove loose dirt and dust.
2   Leather upholstery requires special care. Stains should be removed with warm water and a very mild soap solution. Use a clean, damp cloth to remove the soap, then wipe again with a dry cloth. Never use alcohol, gasoline, nail polish remover or thinner to clean leather upholstery.
3   After cleaning, regularly treat leather upholstery with a leather wax. Never use car wax on leather upholstery.
4   In areas where the interior of the vehicle is subject to bright sunlight, cover leather seats with a sheet if the vehicle is to be left out for any length of time.

5   Body repair – minor damage

See color photo sequence

Repair of minor scratches

1   If the scratch is superficial and does not penetrate to the metal of the body, repair is very simple. Lightly rub the scratched area with a fine rubbing compound to remove loose paint and built up wax. Rinse the area with clean water.
2   Apply touch-up paint to the scratch, using a small brush. Continue to apply thin layers of paint until the surface of the paint in the scratch is level with the surrounding paint. Allow the new paint at least two weeks to harden, then blend it into the surrounding paint by rubbing with a very fine rubbing compound. Finally, apply a coat of wax to the scratch area.
3   If the scratch has penetrated the paint and exposed the metal of the body, causing the metal to rust, a different repair technique is required. Remove all loose rust from the bottom of the scratch with a pocket knife, then apply rust inhibiting paint to prevent the formation of rust in the future. Using a rubber or nylon applicator, coat the scratched area with glaze-type filler. If required, the filler can be mixed with thinner to provide a very thin paste, which is ideal for filling narrow scratches. Before the glaze filler in the scratch hardens, wrap a piece of smooth cotton cloth around the tip of a finger. Dip the cloth in thinner and then quickly wipe it along the surface of the scratch. This will ensure that the surface of the filler is slightly hollow. The scratch can now be painted over as described earlier in this section.

Repair of dents

4   When repairing dents, the first job is to pull the dent out until the affected area is as close as possible to its original shape. There is no point in trying to restore the original shape completely as the metal in the damaged area will have stretched on impact and cannot be restored to its original contours. It is better to bring the level of the dent up to a point which is about 1/8-inch below the level of the surrounding metal. In cases where the dent is very shallow, it is not worth trying to pull it out at all.
5   If the back side of the dent is accessible, it can be hammered out gently from behind using a soft-face hammer. While doing this, hold a block of wood firmly against the opposite side of the metal to absorb the hammer blows and prevent the metal from being stretched.
6   If the dent is in a section of the body which has double layers, or some other factor makes it inaccessible from behind, a different technique is required. Drill several small holes through the metal inside the damaged area, particularly in the deeper sections. Screw long, self tapping screws into the holes just enough for them to get a good grip in the metal. Now the dent can be pulled out by pulling on the protruding heads of the screws with locking pliers.

7   The next stage of repair is the removal of paint from the damaged area and from an inch or so of the surrounding metal. This is easily done with a wire brush or sanding disk in a drill motor, although it can be done just as effectively by hand with sandpaper. To complete the preparation for filling, score the surface of the bare metal with a screwdriver or the tang of a file or drill small holes in the affected area. This will provide a good grip for the filler material. To complete the repair, see the Section on filling and painting.

Repair of rust holes or gashes

8   Remove all paint from the affected area and from an inch or so of the surrounding metal using a sanding disk or wire brush mounted in a drill motor. If these are not available, a few sheets of sandpaper will do the job just as effectively.
9   With the paint removed, you will be able to determine the severity of the corrosion and decide whether to replace the whole panel, if possible, or repair the affected area. New body panels are not as expensive as most people think and it is often quicker to install a new panel than to repair large areas of rust.
10   Remove all trim pieces from the affected area except those which will act as a guide to the original shape of the damaged body, such as headlight shells, etc. Using metal snips or a hacksaw blade, remove all loose metal and any other metal that is badly affected by rust. Hammer the edges of the hole inward to create a slight depression for the filler material.
11   Wire brush the affected area to remove the powdery rust from the surface of the metal. If the back of the rusted area is accessible, treat it with rust inhibiting paint.
12   Before filling is done, block the hole in some way. This can be done with sheet metal riveted or screwed into place, or by stuffing the hole with wire mesh.
13   Once the hole is blocked off, the affected area can be filled and painted. See the following subsection on filling and painting.

Filling and painting

14   Many types of body fillers are available, but generally speaking, body repair kits which contain filler paste and a tube of resin hardener are best for this type of repair work. A wide, flexible plastic or nylon applicator will be necessary for imparting a smooth and contoured finish to the surface of the filler material. Mix up a small amount of filler on a clean piece of wood or cardboard (use the hardener sparingly). Follow the manufacturer's instructions on the package, otherwise the filler will set incorrectly.
15   Using the applicator, apply the filler paste to the prepared area. Draw the applicator across the surface of the filler to achieve the desired contour and to level the filler surface. As soon as a contour that approximates the original one is achieved, stop working the paste. If you continue, the paste will begin to stick to the applicator. Continue to add thin layers of paste at 20-minute intervals until the level of the filler is just above the surrounding metal.
16   Once the filler has hardened, the excess can be removed with a body file. From then on, progressively finer grades of sandpaper should be used, starting with a 180-grit paper and finishing with 600-grit wet-or-dry paper. Always wrap the sandpaper around a flat rubber or wooden block, otherwise the surface of the filler will not be completely flat. During the sanding of the filler surface, the wet-or-dry paper should be periodically rinsed in water. This will ensure that a very smooth finish is produced in the final stage.
17   At this point, the repair area should be surrounded by a ring of bare metal, which in turn should be encircled by the finely feathered edge of good paint. Rinse the repair area with clean water until all of the dust produced by the sanding operation is gone.
18   Spray the entire area with a light coat of primer. This will reveal any imperfections in the surface of the filler. Repair the imperfections with fresh filler paste or glaze filler and once more smooth the surface with sandpaper. Repeat this spray-and-repair procedure until you are satisfied that the surface of the filler and the feathered edge of the paint are perfect. Rinse the area with clean water and allow it to dry completely.
19   The repair area is now ready for painting. Spray painting must be carried out in a warm, dry, windless and dust free atmosphere. These conditions can be created if you have access to a large indoor work area, but if you are forced to work in the open, you will have to pick the day very care-

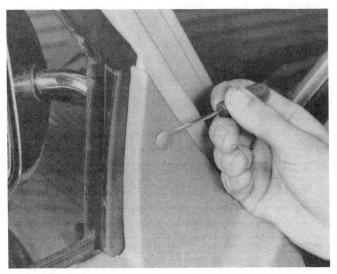

9.2a Use a small screwdriver to remove the covers . . .

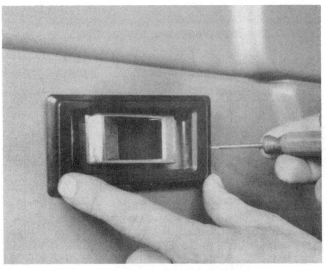

9.2b . . . or bezels covering the retaining screws

fully. If you are working indoors, dousing the floor in the work area with water will help settle the dust which would otherwise be in the air. If the repair area is confined to one body panel, mask off the surrounding panels. This will help minimize the effects of a slight mismatch in paint color. Trim pieces such as chrome strips, door handles, etc., will also need to be masked off or removed. Use masking tape and several thicknesses of newspaper for the masking operations.

20   Before spraying, shake the paint can thoroughly, then spray a test area until the spray painting technique is mastered. Cover the repair area with a thick coat of primer. The thickness should be built up using several thin layers of primer rather than one thick one. Using 600-grit wet-or-dry sandpaper, rub down the surface of the primer until it is very smooth. While doing this, the work area should be thoroughly rinsed with water and the wet-or-dry sandpaper periodically rinsed as well. Allow the primer to dry before spraying additional coats.

21   Spray on the top coat, again building up the thickness by using several thin layers of paint. Begin spraying in the center of the repair area and then, using a circular motion, work out until the whole repair area and about two inches of the surrounding original paint is covered. Remove all masking material 10 to 15 minutes after spraying on the final coat of paint. Allow the new paint at least two weeks to harden, then use a very fine rubbing compound to blend the edges of the new paint into the existing paint. Finally, apply a coat of wax.

6   Body repair – major damage

1   Major damage must be repaired by an auto body shop specifically equipped to perform frame repairs. These shops have the specialized equipment required to do the job properly.

2   If the damage is extensive, the body and frame must be checked for proper alignment or the vehicle's handling characteristics may be adversely affected and other components may wear at an accelerated rate.

3   Due to the fact that all of the major body components (hood, fenders, etc.) are separate and replaceable units, any seriously damaged components should be replaced rather than repaired. Sometimes the components can be found in a wrecking yard that specializes in used vehicle components, often at considerable savings over the cost of new parts.

7   Hinges and locks – maintenance

Once every 3000 miles, or every three months, the hinges and latch assemblies on the doors, hood and trunk should be given a few drops of light oil or lock lubricant. The door latch strikers should also be lubricated

9.3 Use an Allen wrench to remove the window crank

with a thin coat of grease to reduce wear and ensure free movement. Lubricate the door locks with spray-on graphite lubricant.

8   Windshield and fixed glass – replacement

Replacement of the windshield and fixed glass requires the use of special fast-setting adhesive/caulk materials and some specialized tools and techniques. These operations should be left to a dealer service department or a shop specializing in glass work.

9   Door trim panel – removal and installation

Refer to illustrations 9.2a, 9.2b, 9.3 and 9.4

Removal

1   Disconnect the negative cable from the battery.

2   Remove all door trim panel retaining screws and door pull/armrest assemblies **(see illustrations)**.

3   On models equipped with manual window regulators, remove the window crank **(see illustration)**. On power regulator models, pry out the control switch assembly and unplug it.

These photos illustrate a method of repairing simple dents. They are intended to supplement *Body repair - minor damage* in this Chapter and should not be used as the sole instructions for body repair on these vehicles.

1   If you can't access the backside of the body panel to hammer out the dent, pull it out with a slide-hammer-type dent puller. In the deepest portion of the dent or along the crease line, drill or punch hole(s) at least one inch apart . . .

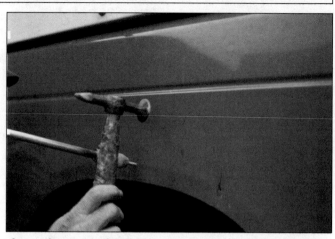

2   . . . then screw the slide-hammer into the hole and operate it. Tap with a hammer near the edge of the dent to help 'pop' the metal back to its original shape. When you're finished, the dent area should be close to its original contour and about 1/8-inch below the surface of the surrounding metal

3   Using coarse-grit sandpaper, remove the paint down to the bare metal. Hand sanding works fine, but the disc sander shown here makes the job faster. Use finer (about 320-grit) sandpaper to feather-edge the paint at least one inch around the dent area

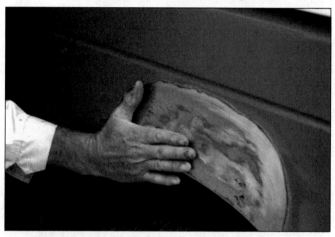

4   When the paint is removed, touch will probably be more helpful than sight for telling if the metal is straight. Hammer down the high spots or raise the low spots as necessary. Clean the repair area with wax/silicone remover

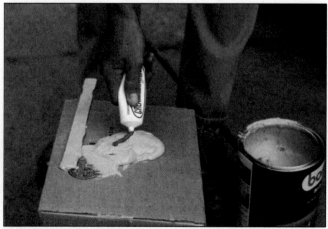

5   Following label instructions, mix up a batch of plastic filler and hardener. The ratio of filler to hardener is critical, and, if you mix it incorrectly, it will either not cure properly or cure too quickly (you won't have time to file and sand it into shape)

6   Working quickly so the filler doesn't harden, use a plastic applicator to press the body filler firmly into the metal, assuring it bonds completely. Work the filler until it matches the original contour and is slightly above the surrounding metal

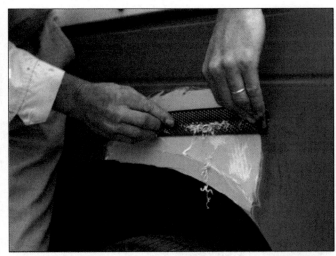

7 Let the filler harden until you can just dent it with your fingernail. Use a body file or Surform tool (shown here) to rough-shape the filler

8 Use coarse-grit sandpaper and a sanding board or block to work the filler down until it's smooth and even. Work down to finer grits of sandpaper - always using a board or block - ending up with 360 or 400 grit

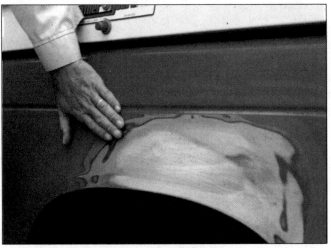

9 You shouldn't be able to feel any ridge at the transition from the filler to the bare metal or from the bare metal to the old paint. As soon as the repair is flat and uniform, remove the dust and mask off the adjacent panels or trim pieces

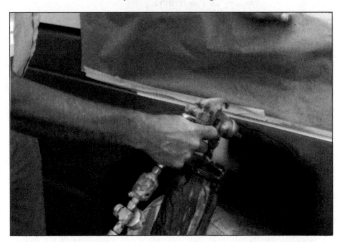

10 Apply several layers of primer to the area. Don't spray the primer on too heavy, so it sags or runs, and make sure each coat is dry before you spray on the next one. A professional-type spray gun is being used here, but aerosol spray primer is available inexpensively from auto parts stores

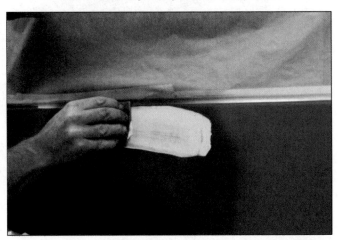

11 The primer will help reveal imperfections or scratches. Fill these with glazing compound. Follow the label instructions and sand it with 360 or 400-grit sandpaper until it's smooth. Repeat the glazing, sanding and respraying until the primer reveals a perfectly smooth surface

12 Finish sand the primer with very fine sandpaper (400 or 600-grit) to remove the primer overspray. Clean the area with water and allow it to dry. Use a tack rag to remove any dust, then apply the finish coat. Don't attempt to rub out or wax the repair area until the paint has dried completely (at least two weeks)

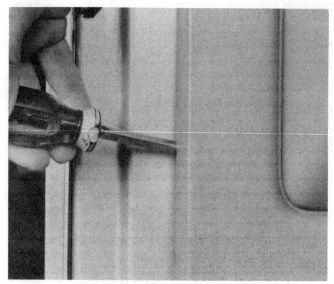

9.4   Pry carefully, working around the panel to disengage the retainers

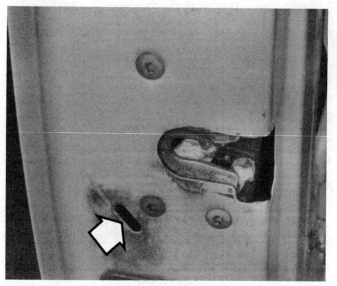

11.4   Insert a screwdriver through the access hole (arrow) to adjust the linkage

4   Insert a putty knife or flat screwdriver between the trim panel and the door and disengage the retainers **(see illustration)**. Work around the outer edge until the panel is free.

5   Once all of the clips are disengaged, detach the trim panel, unplug any wire harness connectors and remove the trim panel from the vehicle.

6   For access to the inner door, carefully peel back the plastic watershield.

Installation

7   Prior to installation of the door panel, be sure to reinstall any clips in the panel which may have come out during the removal procedure and remain in the door itself.

8   Plug in the electrical connectors and place the panel in position on the door. Press the door panel into place until the clips are seated and install the armrest/door pulls. Install the manual regulator window crank or power window switch assembly.

---

10   Door window glass – removal and installation

1   Remove the door trim panel (see Section 9).
2   Lower the window glass.
3   Remove the door belt moulding screws.
4   Detach the glass sliders from the rear glass guide using special tool C-4867 (available from Miller Tool Co.). Use of any other tool will damage the rear glass channel run.
5   Rotate the glass on the regulator roller, then slide it to the rear and up at a 45-degree angle to remove it.
6   If new glass is to be installed, drill out the rivets and detach the lift channel. Transfer the channel to the new glass and secure it with rivets or bolts.
7   Installation is the reverse of removal.

---

11   Door latch, lock cylinder and outside handle – removal and installation

Refer to illustration 11.4

1   Raise the glass fully and remove the door trim panel.

Latch

2   Disconnect the operating links from the latch.
3   Remove the retaining screws and lift the latch out of the door through the opening.

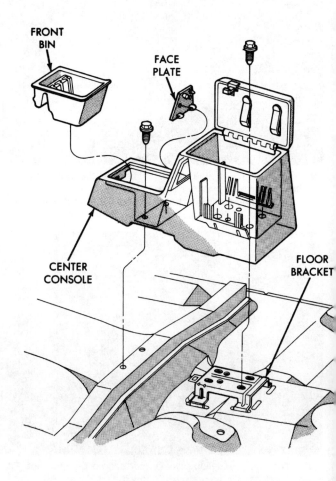

12.2   Center console details

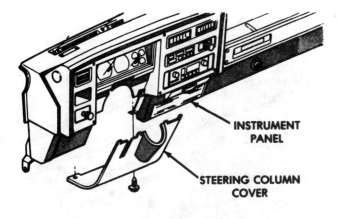

13.1 Remove the screws and lower the steering column cover

4   Installation is the reverse of removal. After installation, loosen the linkage adjusting screw by inserting a screwdriver into the access hole in the end of the door **(see illustration)**. Push up on the latch lever through the access hole to remove all slack from the linkage, then tighten the screw while holding the latch lever in position.

Lock cylinder

5   Disconnect the operating link at the lock cylinder. Use a screwdriver to push the retaining clip off, then withdraw the lock cylinder from the door.
6   Installation is the reverse of removal.

Outside handle

7   Disconnect the operating links from the outside handle.
8   Remove the screws and lift the handle from the door.
9   Installation is the reverse of removal.

12   Center console – removal and installation

Refer to illustration 12.2
1   Open the top of the console for access.
2   Remove the two bolts, detach the console, then lift it out **(see illustration)**.
3   Installation is the reverse of removal.

13   Steering column cover – removal and installation

Refer to illustration 13.1
1   Remove the screws at the base, then rotate the steering column cover out and lower it from the instrument panel **(see illustration)**.
2   Installation is the reverse of removal.

14   Cup holder – removal and installation

Refer to illustrations 14.1 and 14.2
1   Use a #15 Torx head tool to remove the screws and detach the cup holder and bezel assembly from the instrument panel **(see illustration)**.
2   If it is necessary to remove the cup holder from the bezel, pull the holder out to the stop position, the pry the stop up so it can slide under the shelf, allowing the holder to be withdrawn **(see illustration)**.
3   Installation is the reverse of removal.

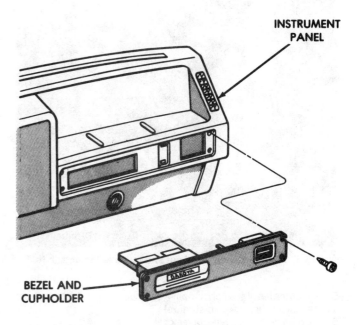

14.1 Remove the Torx head screws and detach the cup holder and bezel assembly

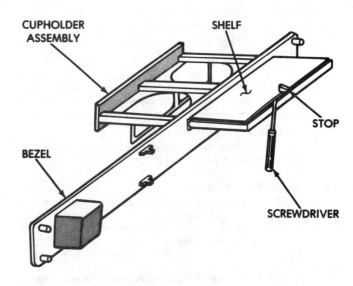

14.2 Pull the cup holder out to the stop, then pry the stop up with a screwdriver so the holder can be removed

15   Instrument cluster bezel – removal and installation

Refer to illustration 15.5
1   Disconnect the negative battery cable.
2   Remove the steering column (see Section 13).
3   Using a #15 Torx head tool, remove the two screws at the bottom edge of the bezel on either side of the steering column, then remove the eight screws along the top of the bezel.
4   On automatic transmission models, shift column shift lever into Low.

11

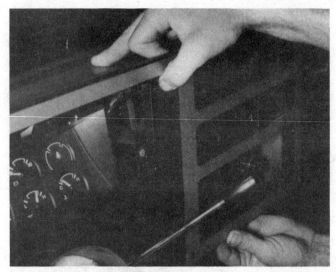

15.5   Pull the cluster bezel out and to the left to detach it

5   Grasp the bezel securely and pull it out and to the left to detach it from the instrument panel **(see illustration)**.
6   Installation is the reverse of removal.

16   Cowl grille – removal and installation

Refer to illustration 16.2
1   Remove the windshield wiper arms and raise the hood.
2   Remove the screws, detach the rear of the grille from the windshield weatherstripping and lift the grille from the vehicle **(see illustration)**.
3   Installation is the reverse of removal.

17   Hood – removal, installation and adjustment

Refer to illustrations 17.2, 17.10 and 17.11
Note: *The hood is heavy and somewhat awkward to remove and install – at least two people should perform this procedure.*

Removal and installation
1   Use blankets or pads to cover the cowl area of the body and the fenders. This will protect the body and paint as the hood is lifted off.
2   Scribe or draw alignment marks around the bolt heads to insure proper alignment during installation **(see illustration)**.
3   Disconnect any cables or wire harnesses which will interfere with removal.
4   Have an assistant support the weight of the hood. Remove the hinge-to-hood bolts.
5   Lift off the hood.
6   Installation is the reverse of removal.

Adjustment
7   Fore-and-aft and side-to-side adjustment of the hood is done by moving the hood in relation to the hinge plate after loosening the bolts or nuts.
8   Scribe a line around the entire hinge plate so you can judge the amount of movement **(see illustration 17.2)**.
9   Loosen the bolts or nuts and move the hood into correct alignment. Move it only a little at a time. Tighten the hinge bolts or nuts and carefully lower the hood to check the alignment.
10   If necessary after installation, the entire hood latch assembly can be adjusted up-and-down as well as from side-to-side on the radiator support so the hood closes securely and is flush with the fenders. To do this, scribe

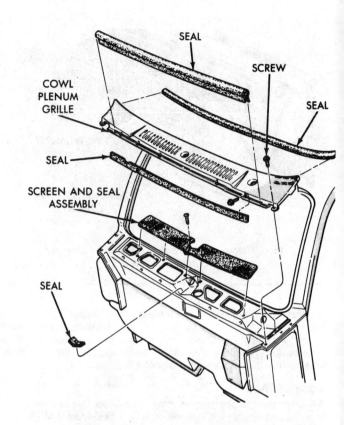

16.2   Cowl grille details

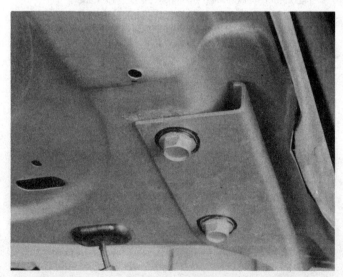

17.2   Scribe or mark around the mounting bolts on the hinge – mark around the entire hinge plate before removing the hood

a line around the hood latch and striker mounting bolts to provide a reference point. Then loosen the bolts and reposition the latch assembly and striker assemblies as necessary. Following adjustment, retighten the mounting bolts **(see illustration)**.
11   Finally, adjust the hood bumpers on the radiator support so the hood, when closed, is flush with the fenders **(see illustration)**.
12   The hood latch assembly, as well as the hinges, should be periodically lubricated with white lithium-base grease to prevent sticking and wear.

17.10   To adjust the hood in relation to the fenders, loosen the hood latch bolts and move the latch as necessary

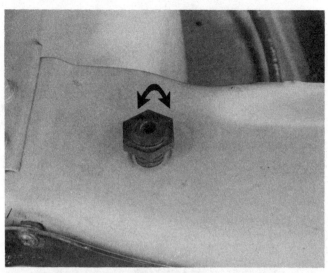

17.11   The hood bumpers can be screwed in or out to adjust the front edge of the hood in relation to the fenders

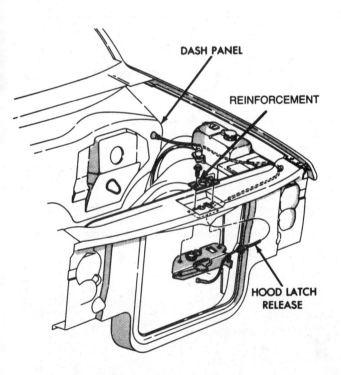

DASH PANEL

REINFORCEMENT

HOOD LATCH RELEASE

18.2   Hood release cable installation details

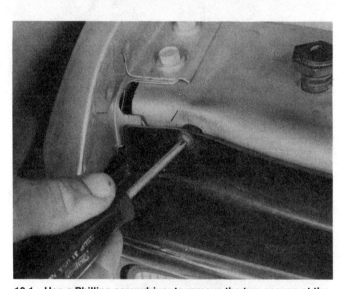

19.1   Use a Phillips screwdriver to remove the two screws at the top of each headlight bezel

5   Connect string or thin wire to the cable in the engine compartment and have an assistant pull the cable assembly through the firewall into the passenger compartment.

6   Connect the string or wire to the new cable assembly and pull it through the firewall into the engine compartment.

7   Place the release handle in position the instrument panel and install the screws. Install the firewall grommet and secure the cable to the clip in the engine compartment.

8   Connect the cable and install the hood latch.

9   Test the hood latch operation, adjusting the latch position as necessary.

10   Install the radiator grille.

---

18   Hood release cable – replacement

Refer to illustration 18.2

1   Open the hood and remove the radiator grille (see Section 19).

2   Remove the bolts, detach the hood latch assembly from the radiator support, then disconnect the cable from the latch **(see illustration)**.

3   In the engine compartment, detach the cable assembly from the clip and remove the grommet from the firewall.

4   In the passenger compartment, remove the screws and detach the release handle from the instrument panel.

---

19   Radiator grille – removal and installation

Refer to illustrations 19.1 and 19.3

1   Remove the headlight bezel screws **(see illustration)**.

2   Detach the bezels and disconnect the bulbs.

11

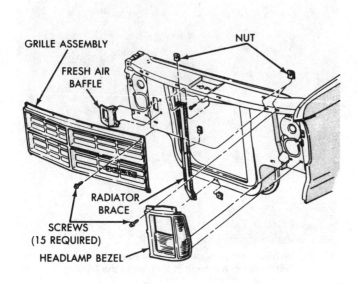

19.3   Radiator grille details

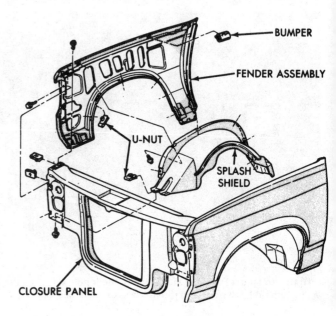

20.3   Front fender installation details

3   Remove the screws and detach the radiator grille **(see illustration)**.
4   Installation is the reverse of removal.

20   Front fender – removal and installation

Refer to illustrations 20.3
1   Raise the vehicle, support it securely on jackstands and remove the front wheel.
2   Disconnect the antenna and all light bulb wiring harness connectors and other components that would interfere with fender removal.
3   Remove the fender mounting bolts **(see illustration)**.
4   Detach the fender. It is a good idea to have an assistant support the fender while it's being moved away from the vehicle to prevent damage to

the surrounding body panels.
5   Installation is the reverse of removal. Tighten all nuts, bolts and screws securely.

21   Bumpers – removal and installation

Refer to illustrations 21.3a and 21.3b
1   Disconnect any wiring or other components that would interfere with bumper removal.
2   Support the bumper with a jack or jackstand. Alternatively, have an assistant support the bumper as the bolts are removed.
3   Remove the retaining bolts and detach the bumper **(see illustrations)**.

21.3a   Front bumper mounting bolts (arrows)

21.3b   Rear bumper bolt locations (arrows)

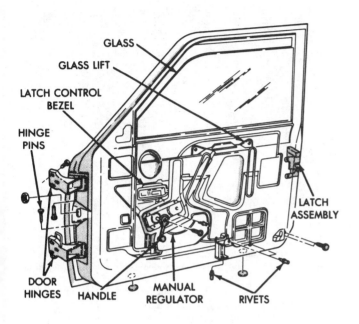

22.4   Door installation details

GLASS

GLASS LIFT

LATCH CONTROL
BEZEL

HINGE
PINS

LATCH
ASSEMBLY

DOOR
HINGES   HANDLE   MANUAL
REGULATOR   RIVETS

4   Installation is the reverse of removal. Tighten the retaining bolts securely.
5   Install the bumper cover and any other components that were removed.

22   Door – removal, installation and adjustment

Refer to illustration 22.4

Removal and installation

1   Remove the door trim panel. Disconnect any wire harness connectors and push them through the door opening so they won't interfere with door removal.
2   Place a jack or jackstand under the door or have an assistant on hand to support it when the hinge bolts are removed. **Note:** *If a jack or jackstand is used, place a rag between it and the door to protect the door's painted surfaces.*
3   Scribe around the door hinges.
4   Remove the hinge-to-door bolts or drive out the pins and carefully lift off the door **(see illustration)**.
5   Installation is the reverse of removal.

Adjustment

6   Following installation of the door, check the alignment and adjust it if necessary as follows:
  a) Up-and-down and forward-and-backward adjustments are made by loosening the hinge-to-body bolts and moving the door as necessary.
  b) The door lock striker can also be adjusted both up-and-down and sideways to provide positive engagement with the lock mechanism. This is done by loosening the mounting bolts and moving the striker as necessary.

23   Tailgate – removal and installation

Refer to illustrations 23.2 and 23.3

1   Open the tailgate.
2   Detach the cables from the pins on the body by positioning the large ends of eyelet openings over the heads of the pins **(see illustration)**.
3   With the cables disconnected, lower the tailgate until the slot in the right side will slide off the hinge pin **(see illustration)**.
4   Slide the left side of the tailgate out of the hinge and remove the tailgate from the vehicle.
5   Installation is the reverse of removal.

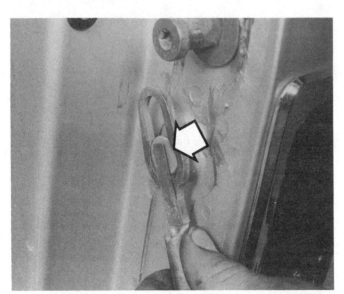

23.2   Slide the widest opening of the eyelet over the head of the pin and lift it off

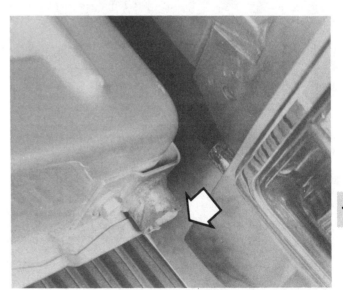

23.3   Lower the tailgate until the slot lines up, then detach the right side from the hinge pin by pulling down and back

11

24.2   Slide the ends of the clips over, then lift the link straight up to disconnect it from the handle mechanism

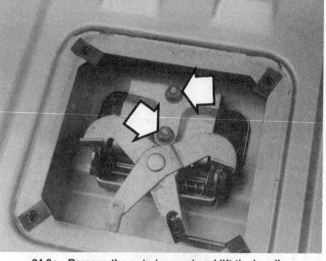

24.3a   Remove the nuts (arrows) and lift the handle mechanism off

---

24   Tailgate latch and linkage – removal and installation

Refer to illustrations 24.2, 24.3a, 24.3b and 24.4

1   Open the tailgate and remove the cover for access to the linkage.

2   Detach the linkage from the handle mechanism **(see illustration)**.
3   Remove the nuts and remove the mechanism and handle **(see illustrations)**.
4   Remove the bolts and withdraw the latch and linkage assemblies from the ends of the tailgate **(see illustration)**.
5   Installation is the reverse of removal.

24.3b   With the mechanism removed, the handle assembly can be easily detached from the tailgate

24.4   Remove the bolts (arrows) and withdraw the latch assembly from the tailgate

Chapter 12   Chassis electrical system

Contents

1   General information

The electrical system is a 12-volt, negative ground type. Power for the lights and all electrical accessories is supplied by a lead/acid-type battery which is charged by the alternator.

This Chapter covers repair and service procedures for the various electrical components not associated with the engine. Information on the battery, alternator, distributor and starter motor can be found in Chapter 5.

It should be noted that when portions of the electrical system are serviced, the negative battery cable should be disconnected from the battery to prevent electrical shorts and/or fires.

2   Electrical troubleshooting – general information

A typical electrical circuit consists of an electrical component, any switches, relays, motors, fuses, fusible links or circuit breakers related to that component and the wiring and connectors that link the component to both the battery and the chassis. To help you pinpoint an electrical circuit problem, wiring diagrams are included at the end of this book.

Before tackling any troublesome electrical circuit, first study the appropriate wiring diagrams to get a complete understanding of what makes up that individual circuit. Trouble spots, for instance, can often be narrowed down by noting if other components related to the circuit are operating properly. If several components or circuits fail at one time, chances are the

12

problem is in a fuse or ground connection, because several circuits are often routed through the same fuse and ground connections.

Electrical problems usually stem from simple causes, such as loose or corroded connections, a blown fuse, a melted fusible link or a bad relay. Visually inspect the condition of all fuses, wires and connections in a problem circuit before troubleshooting it.

If testing instruments are going to be utilized, use the diagrams to plan ahead of time where you will make the necessary connections in order to accurately pinpoint the trouble spot.

The basic tools needed for electrical troubleshooting include a circuit tester or voltmeter (a 12-volt bulb with a set of test leads can also be used), a continuity tester, which includes a bulb, battery and set of test leads, and a jumper wire, preferably with a circuit breaker incorporated, which can be used to bypass electrical components. Before attempting to locate a problem with test instruments, use the wiring diagram(s) to decide where to make the connections.

Voltage checks

Voltage checks should be performed if a circuit is not functioning properly. Connect one lead of a circuit tester to either the negative battery terminal or a known good ground. Connect the other lead to a connector in the circuit being tested, preferably nearest to the battery or fuse. If the bulb of the tester lights, voltage is present, which means that the part of the circuit between the connector and the battery is problem free. Continue checking the rest of the circuit in the same fashion. When you reach a point at which no voltage is present, the problem lies between that point and the last test point with voltage. Most of the time the problem can be traced to a loose connection. **Note:** *Keep in mind that some circuits receive voltage only when the ignition key is in the Accessory or Run position.*

Finding a short

One method of finding shorts in a circuit is to remove the fuse and connect a test light or voltmeter in its place to the fuse terminals. There should be no voltage present in the circuit. Move the wiring harness from side-to-side while watching the test light. If the bulb goes on, there is a short to ground somewhere in that area, probably where the insulation has rubbed through. The same test can be performed on each component in the circuit, even a switch.

Ground check

Perform a ground test to check whether a component is properly grounded. Disconnect the battery and connect one lead of a self-powered test light, known as a continuity tester, to a known good ground. Connect the other lead to the wire or ground connection being tested. If the bulb goes on, the ground is good. If the bulb does not go on, the ground is not good.

Continuity check

A continuity check is done to determine if there are any breaks in a circuit – if it is passing electricity properly. With the circuit off (no power in the circuit), a self-powered continuity tester can be used to check the circuit. Connect the test leads to both ends of the circuit (or to the "power" end and a good ground), and if the test light comes on the circuit is passing current properly. If the light doesn't come on, there is a break somewhere in the circuit. The same procedure can be used to test a switch, by connecting the continuity tester to the switch terminals. With the switch turned On, the test light should come on.

Finding an open circuit

When diagnosing for possible open circuits, it is often difficult to locate them by sight because oxidation or terminal misalignment are hidden by the connectors. Merely wiggling a connector on a sensor or in the wiring harness may correct the open circuit condition. Remember this when an open circuit is indicated when troubleshooting a circuit. Intermittent problems may also be caused by oxidized or loose connections.

Electrical troubleshooting is simple if you keep in mind that all electrical circuits are basically electricity running from the battery, through the wires, switches, relays, fuses and fusible links to each electrical component (light bulb, motor, etc.) and to ground, from which it is passed back to the battery.

Any electrical problem is an interruption in the flow of electricity to and from the battery.

---

3   Fuses – general information

Refer to illustrations 3.1 and 3.3

The electrical circuits of the vehicle are protected by a combination of fuses, circuit breakers and fusible links. The fuse block is located under the instrument panel on the left side of the dashboard **(see illustration)**.

Each of the fuses is designed to protect a specific circuit, and the various circuits are identified on the fuse panel itself.

Miniaturized fuses are employed in the fuse block. These compact fuses, with blade terminal design, allow fingertip removal and replacement. If an electrical component fails, always check the fuse first. A blown fuse is easily identified through the clear plastic body. Visually inspect the element for evidence of damage **(see illustration)**. If the fuse looks good, but you still suspect it's faulty, perform a continuity check at the blade terminal tips exposed in the fuse body.

Be sure to replace blown fuses with the correct type. Fuses of different ratings are physically interchangeable, but only fuses of the proper rating should be used. Replacing a fuse with one of a higher or lower value than specified is not recommended. Each electrical circuit needs a specific amount of protection. The amperage value of each fuse is molded into the fuse body.

If the replacement fuse immediately fails, don't replace it again until the cause of the problem is isolated and corrected. In most cases, the cause will be a short circuit in the wiring caused by a broken or deteriorated wire.

3.1   The fuse block is located under the left side of the instrument panel, next to the parking brake release handle

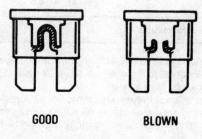

GOOD   BLOWN

3.3   The fuses on these models can be checked visually to determine if they're blown

FUSIBLE LINK CHART

Wire Gauge	Color Code	Color
12 Ga.	BK	Black
14 Ga.	RD	Red
16 Ga.	DB	Dark Blue
18 Ga.	GY	Gray
20 Ga.	OR	Orange
30 Ga.	LG	Light Green

4.2 Always replace a burned out fusible link with one of the same color code from your dealer

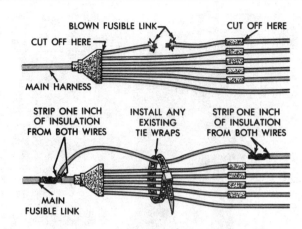

4.3 Fusible link repair details

---

4 Fusible links – general information

Refer to illustrations 4.2 and 4.3

Some circuits are protected by fusible links. The links are used in circuits which are not ordinarily fused, such as the ignition circuit.

Although the fusible links appear to be a heavier gauge than the wire they are protecting, the appearance is due to the thick insulation. All fusible links are several wire gauges smaller than the wire they are designed to protect. The fusible links are color coded and a link should always be replaced with one of the same color obtained from a dealer **(see illustration)**.

Fusible links cannot be repaired, but a new link of the same size wire can be put in its place. The procedure is as follows:

a) Disconnect the negative cable from the battery.
b) Disconnect the fusible link from the wiring harness.
c) Cut the damaged fusible link out of the wiring just behind the connector.
d) Strip the insulation back approximately 1-inch **(see illustration)**.
e) Position the connector on the new fusible link and twist or crimp it into place.
f) Use rosin core solder at each end of the new link to obtain a good solder joint.
g) Use plenty of electrical tape around the soldered joint. No wires should be exposed.
h) Connect the battery ground cable. Test the circuit for proper operation.

5 Circuit breakers – general information

Circuit breakers protect components such as power windows, power door locks and headlights. Some circuit breakers are located in the fuse box.

On some models the circuit breaker resets itself automatically, so an electrical overload in a circuit breaker protected system will cause the circuit to fail momentarily, then come back on. If the circuit does not come back on, check it immediately. Once the condition is corrected, the circuit breaker will resume its normal function.

6 Relays – general information

Several electrical accessories in the vehicle use relays to transmit the electrical signal to the component. If the relay is defective, that component will not operate properly.

The various relays are grouped together in several locations.

If a faulty relay is suspected, it can be removed and tested by a dealer

service department or a repair shop. Defective relays must be replaced as a unit.

---

7 Turn signal and hazard flashers – check and replacement

Refer to illustration 7.1

Turn signal flasher

1 The turn signal flasher, a small canister-shaped unit located in the fuse block **(see illustration)**, flashes the turn signals.

2 When the flasher unit is functioning properly, an audible click can be heard during its operation. If the turn signals fail on one side or the other and the flasher unit does not make its characteristic clicking sound, a faulty turn signal bulb is indicated.

3 If both turn signals fail to blink, the problem may be due to a blown fuse, a faulty flasher unit, a broken switch or a loose or open connection. If a quick check of the fuse box indicates that the turn signal fuse has blown, check the wiring for a short before installing a new fuse.

4 To replace the flasher, simply pull it out of the fuse block or wiring harness.

5 Make sure that the replacement unit is identical to the original. Compare the old one to the new one before installing it.

6 Installation is the reverse of removal.

Hazard flasher

7 The hazard flasher, a small canister-shaped unit located in the fuse block **(see illustration 7.1),** flashes all four turn signals simultaneously when activated.

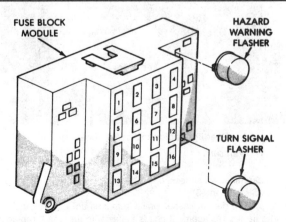

7.1 The turn signal and hazard flashers are located in the fuse block

8.2   A Torx head tool may be necessary for removing the headlight bezel screws

8.3   Remove only the retainer screws (arrows) – do not disturb the headlight aim adjusting screws unless you're adjusting the headlights

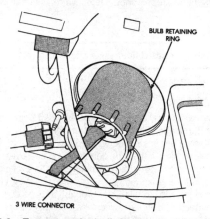

8.8   To remove the bulb from an aerodynamic headlight, disconnect the electrical connector and rotate the retaining ring counterclockwise

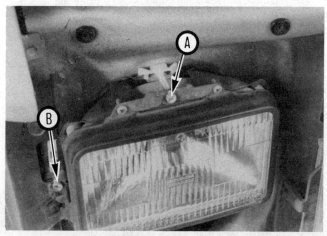

9.1   Headlight adjusting screw locations

A   Vertical   B   Horizontal

8   The hazard flasher is checked in a fashion similar to the turn signal flasher (see Steps 2 and 3).
9   To replace the hazard flasher, pull it from the back of fuse block.
10   Make sure the replacement unit is identical to the one it replaces. Compare the old one to the new one before installing it.
11   Installation is the reverse of removal.

8   Headlights – removal and installation

Sealed-beam type

Refer to illustrations 8.2 and 8.3
1   Disconnect the negative cable from the battery.
2   Remove the retaining screws and detach the headlight bezel **(see illustration)**.
3   Remove the retainer screws, taking care not to disturb the adjusting screws **(see illustration)**.
4   Remove the retainer and pull the headlight out enough to allow the connector to be unplugged.
5   Remove the headlight.
6   To install the headlight, plug the connector in, place the headlight in position and install the retainer and screws. Tighten the screws securely.
7   Place the bezel in position and install the retaining screws.

Bulb-type (aerodynamic)

Refer to illustration 8.8
Caution: *Halogen gas-filled bulbs are under pressure and may shatter if the surface is scratched or the bulb is dropped. Wear eye protection and handle the bulbs carefully, grasping only the base whenever possible. Do not touch the surface of the bulb with your fingers because the oil from your skin could cause the bulb to overheat and fail prematurely. If you do touch the bulb, clean it with rubbing alcohol.*
8   Disconnect the 3-wire electrical connector in the engine compartment, behind the headlight **(see illustration)**.
9   Rotate the bulb retaining ring counterclockwise. Remove the ring and bulb assembly. Installation is the reverse of removal.

9   Headlights – adjustment

Refer to illustration 9.1
Note: *The headlights must be aimed correctly. If adjusted incorrectly they could blind the driver of an oncoming vehicle and cause a serious accident or seriously reduce your ability to see the road. The headlights should be checked for proper aim every 12 months and any time a new headlight is installed or front end body work is performed. It should be emphasized that the following procedure is only an interim step which will provide temporary adjustment until the headlights can be adjusted by a properly equipped shop.*
1   Headlights have two spring loaded adjusting screws, one on the top controlling up-and-down movement and one on the side controlling left-and-right movement **(see illustration)**.

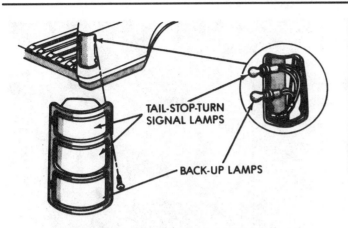

10.1   The rear tail lights are accessible after removing the lens; push the bulbs in and turn counterclockwise to remove them

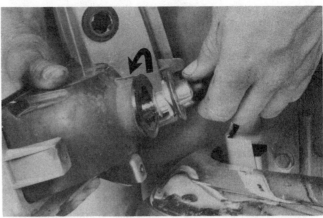

10.3a   Turn the parking light bulb holder to align the tabs, then withdraw it from the bezel housing

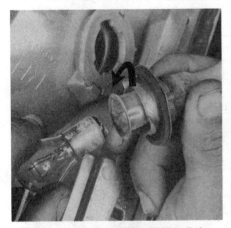

10.3b   Push the parking light bulb in and turn it counterclockwise to remove it

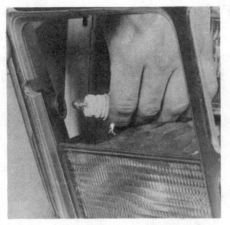

10.3c   Remove the side marker housing from the bezel . . .

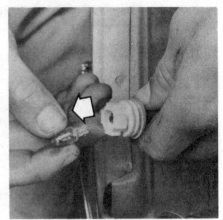

10.3d   . . . then pull the bulb straight out to remove it

2   There are several methods of adjusting the headlights. The simplest method requires a blank wall 25 feet in front of the vehicle and a level floor.

3   Position masking tape vertically on the wall in reference to the vehicle centerline and the centerlines of both headlights.

4   Position a horizontal tape line in reference to the centerline of all the headlights. **Note:** *It may be easier to position the tape on the wall with the vehicle parked only a few inches away.*

5   Adjustment should be made with the vehicle sitting level, the gas tank half-full and no unusually heavy load in the vehicle.

6   Starting with the low beam adjustment, position the high intensity zone so it is two inches below the horizontal line and two inches to the right of the headlight vertical line. Adjustment is made by turning the top adjusting screw clockwise to raise the beam and counterclockwise to lower the beam. The adjusting screw on the side should be used in the same manner to move the beam left or right.

7   With the high beams on, the high intensity zone should be vertically centered with the exact center just below the horizontal line. **Note:** *It may not be possible to position the headlight aim exactly for both high and low beams. If a compromise must be made, keep in mind that the low beams are the most used and have the greatest effect on driver safety.*

8   Have the headlights adjusted by a dealer service department or service station at the earliest opportunity.

---

10   Bulb replacement

Refer to illustrations 10.1, 10.3a, 10.3b, 10.3c, 10.3d and 10.4

1   The lenses of many lights are held in place by screws, which makes it a simple procedure to gain access to the bulbs **(see illustration).**

2   On some lights the lenses are held in place by clips. The lenses can be removed either by unsnapping them or by using a small screwdriver to pry them off.

3   Several types of bulbs are used. Some are removed by pushing in and turning them counterclockwise **(see illustration)**. Others can simply be unclipped from the terminals or pulled straight out of the socket **(see illustrations)**.

4   To gain access to the instrument panel lights, the instrument cluster will have to be removed first **(see illustration)**.

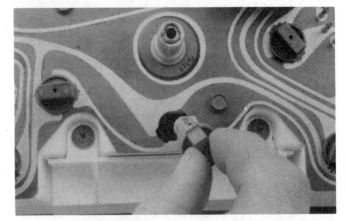

10.4   After removing the instrument cluster, turn the bulb holders counterclockwise, lift them out and pull out the bulbs

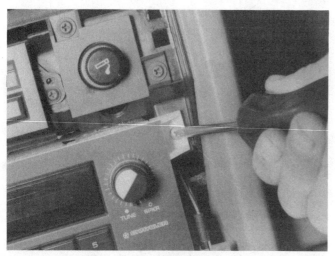

11.3   Use a Phillips head screwdriver to remove the two radio retaining screws

11.4a   Pull the radio out, support it and . . .

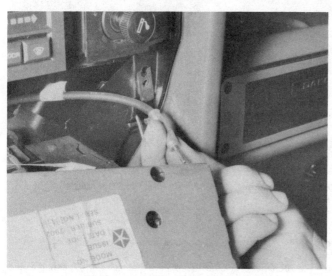

11.4b   . . . unplug the connectors

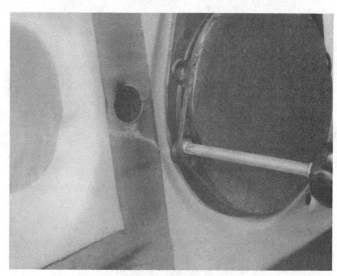

11.7a   Remove the screws . . .

11   Radio and speakers – removal and installation

Radio

Refer to illustrations 11.3, 11.4a and 11.4b

1   Disconnect the negative cable at the battery.
2   Remove the steering column cover and instrument cluster bezel (see Chapter 11).
3   Remove the retaining screws (see illustration).
4   Slide the radio out and support it, disconnect the ground cable, antenna and electrical connectors, then remove the assembly from the instrument panel (see illustrations).
5   Installation is the reverse of removal.

Speakers

Refer to illustrations 11.7a and 11.7b

6   Remove the door trim panel (see Chapter 11).
7   Remove the retaining screws, detach the speaker and pull it out for access to the electrical connector (see illustration). Unplug the connector and remove the speaker (see illustration).
8   Installation is the reverse of removal.

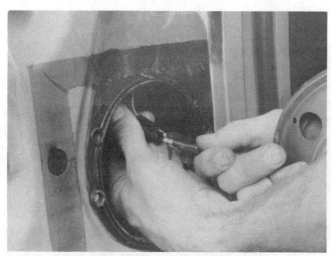

11.7b   . . . then pull the speaker out and support it so you can use both hands to unplug the connector

12.2   Unscrew the antenna mast with a small wrench

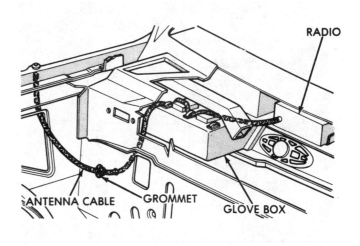

12.6   Antenna cable routing details

12.8a   Unscrew the cap nut with needle-nose pliers – use care so
the pliers don't slip and scratch the fender

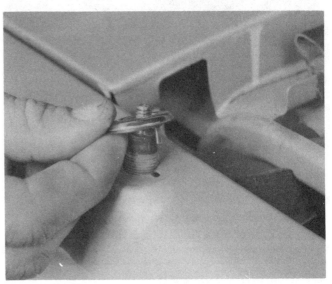

12.8b   Lift the adapter off the fender

12   Antenna – removal and installation

Antenna mast

Refer to illustration 12.2

1   The antenna mast can be unscrewed and replaced with a new one in the event it is damaged, following the procedure below. Follow the procedure beginning with Step 4 to replace the antenna and cable as an assembly.
2   Use a small wrench to unscrew the mast **(see illustration)**
3   Install the new antenna mast finger tight and tighten it securely with the wrench.

Antenna and cable

Refer to illustrations 12.6, 12.8a and 12.8b

4   Disconnect the negative cable at the battery.
5   Remove the glove box, reach around behind the radio and unplug the antenna lead.
6   Working through the glove box opening, detach the antenna cable

from the clips and push the grommet through firewall. Connect a long piece or string or thin wire to the antenna cable **(see illustration)**.
7   Remove the antenna mast (see Steps 1 and 2).
8   Remove the antenna cap nut, using needle-nose pliers, then lift off the adapter **(see illustrations)**. Be very careful – the pliers could slip and scratch the fender. It's a good idea to surround the base of the antenna with rags to prevent against scratching.
9   Install the antenna mast temporarily and push the antenna down far enough so that you can grasp the cable end through the fender opening in the engine compartment.
10   Remove the antenna mast, then pull the cable through the firewall and into the engine compartment.
11   Push the new cable end up through the fender, then install the adapter, cap nut and antenna mast.
12   Connect the string or wire to the radio end of the new cable and pull it through into the passenger compartment.
13   Connect the cable to the radio, secure it with the clips, then push the grommet into place in the firewall.
14   Install the glove box and connect the battery negative cable.

12

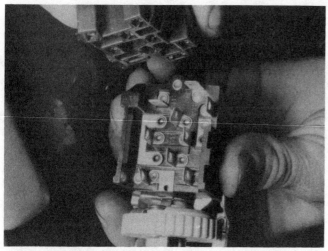

13.3   Unplug the electrical connector from the switch

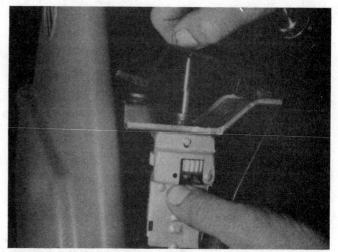

13.5   Hold the release button down and pull the knob shaft out of the switch

13.6   Unscrew the spanner nut with needle-nose pliers

13   Headlight switch – replacement

Refer to illustrations 13.3, 13.5 and 13.6

1   Disconnect the negative cable at the battery.
2   Remove the steering column cover and instrument cluster bezel (see Chapter 11).
3   Remove the switch screws, pull the switch and bracket assembly out, then unplug the electrical connector **(see illustration)**.
4   If there is tinnerman nut retaining the bracket to the switch, remove it.
5   Press the release button on the bottom of the switch and withdraw the switch knob shaft **(see illustration)**.
6   Use needle-nose pliers to remove the spanner nut and separate the switch from the bracket **(see illustration)**.
7   Place the new switch on the bracket and secure it with the spanner nut. Insert the switch knob shaft into the switch. The remainder of installation is the reverse of removal.

14   Headlight dimmer switch – check and replacement (1987 through 1990 models)

Note: *For 1991 and later models, refer to Section 17.*
Refer to illustrations 14.2, 14.3 and 14.6

Check

1   Remove the steering column cover (see Chapter 11).

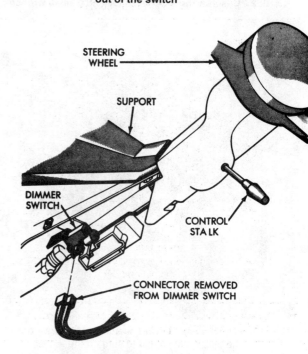

14.2   Unplug the dimmer switch connector (1987 through 1990 models)

2   Unplug the electrical connector from the switch **(see illustration)**.
3   Use an ohmmeter to check the continuity between the switch terminals. There should be continuity between the B and H terminals with the switch in the high beam position and the B and L terminals in the low beam position **(see illustration)**. If there isn't, replace the switch.

Replacement

4   Remove the two bolts and lower the switch from the steering column.
5   Place the new switch in position and install the mounting bolts finger tight.
6   Insert an adjustment pin fabricated from a piece of wire. Push the switch to the rear to take up the slack in the actuator control rod, then tighten the bolts securely **(see illustration)**.
7   Remove the pin, plug in the connector and install the steering column cover.

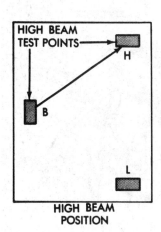 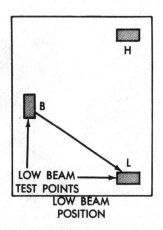

14.3   Dimmer switch continuity check points (1987 through 1990 models)

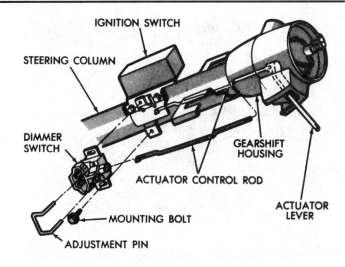

14.6   Dimmer switch adjustment details (1987 through 1990 models)

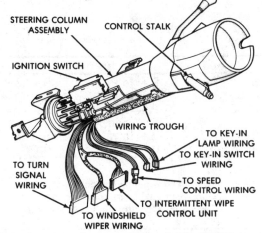

15.4   Steering column connector details (1987 through 1990 models)

SWITCH CONTINUITY CHART			
Turn Signal Switch			
Switch Position:	Left	Neutral	Right
Continuity Between:	7 and 4	10 and 9	7 and 5
Continuity Between:	7 and 8	10 and 8	7 and 9
Continuity Between:	10 and 9	—	10 and 8
Hazard Warning Switch			
Switch Position:	Off	On	
Continuity Between:	10 and 9	6 and 4	
Continuity Between:	10 and 8	6 and 5	
Continuity Between:	—	6 and 8	
Continuity Between:	—	6 and 9	

15.5   Turn signal and hazard switch continuity check details (1987 through 1990 models)

15   Turn signal/hazard switch – check and replacement (1987 through 1990 models)

Note: *For 1991 and later models, refer to Section 17.*

Refer to illustration 15.4, 15.5, 15.8, 15.11 and 15.13

1   The turn signal switch is located at the top end of the steering column and is operated by the multi-function control stalk. The hazard warning switch is mounted under the turn signal switch, next to the ignition key light.

Check

2   Disconnect the negative cable from the battery.
3   Remove the steering column lower cover (see Chapter 11).
4   Unplug the turn signal switch electrical connector **(see illustration)**.
5   Use an ohmmeter or self-powered test light to check for continuity between the indicated switch connector terminals **(see illustration)**.
6   Replace the turn signal or hazard switch if the continuity is not as specified.

Replacement

7   Disconnect the negative battery cable, then remove the steering wheel (see Chapter 10).

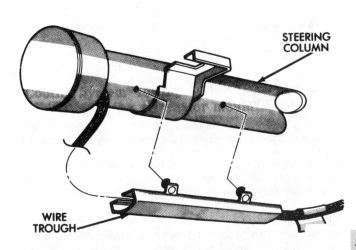

15.8   The wiring harness trough is held in place by clips (1987 through 1990 models)

8   Detach the wiring harness trough from the steering column **(see illustration)**.
9   Unplug the electrical connector **(see illustration 15.4)**.

12

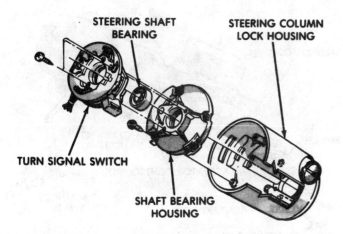

15.11   Turn signal switch mounting details (standard steering column) (1987 through 1990 models)

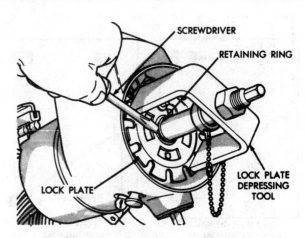

15.13   The retaining ring can be removed with a screwdriver after depressing the lock plate (tilt steering column) (1987 through 1990 models)

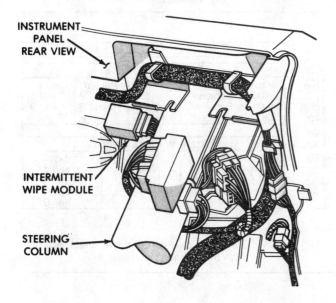

16.1   The intermittent wiper module is located under the instrument panel (1987 through 1990 models)

Off	Low	High
B + to P$_1$	B + to P$_1$	B + to P$_1$
L to P$_2$	B + to L	B + to H
H—Open	P$_2$—Open	P$_2$—Open
	H—Open	L—Open
B + to W	B + to W	B + to W
(In Wash)	(In Wash)	(In Wash)

16.5a   Two-speed wiper switch continuity check chart – continuity should be as specified in the three switch positions (1987 through 1990 models)

16   Unscrew the hazard switch knob.
17   Remove the screws, lift the switches out and guide the wiring harness out of the steering column opening.
18   Installation is the reverse of removal, noting the following: Place the turn signal switch in position in the right turn position, install the screws, then pull the link into position and install the wiper/washer pivot screw. Be sure to install a new lock plate retaining ring.

Standard steering column

10   Remove the wiper/washer switch pivot screw, leaving the control stalk in place.
11   Remove the three screws and detach the turn signal switch **(see illustration)**. Carefully pull the wiring harness out through the top of the steering column.
12   Installation is the reverse of removal, remembering to lubricate the steering shaft contact surfaces with multi-purpose grease and to make sure the dimmer switch rod is located securely in the pocket of the control stalk.

Tilt steering column

13   Depress the lock plate using the factory recommended tool (C-4156), then use a small screwdriver to pry out the retaining ring **(see illustration)**. If the recommended tool is not available, you might be able to depress the lock plate by hand far enough so you can get at the retaining ring.
14   Remove the lock plate, cancelling cam and upper bearing spring.
15   Place the turn signal switch in the right turn position, remove the screw and detach the link between the turn signal switch and the wiper/washer switch pivot.

16   Wiper/washer switch – check and replacement (1987 through 1990 models)

Note: *For 1991 and later models, refer to Section 17.*
Refer to illustration 16.1, 16.5a, 16.5b, 16.11, 16.12, 16.13, 16.22 and 16.24

1   These models are equipped with a a multi-function lever located on the left side of the steering column which controls the wiper/washer, turn signal and dimmer switches. The wipers are two-speed with an optional intermittent feature, operated by a module located under the instrument panel to the right of the steering column **(see illustration)**.

Check

2   Disconnect the negative cable from the battery.
3   Remove the steering column lower cover (see Chapter 11).
4   Unplug the electrical connector **(see illustration 15.4).**
5   Use an ohmmeter or self-powered test light to check for continuity between the switch terminals at the electrical connector **(see illustrations)**.
6   Replace the wiper\washer switch if the continuity is not as specified.

SWITCH POSITION	CONTINUITY BETWEEN
OFF	L and P_2
DELAY	P_1 and I_1 R and I_1* I_2 and G
LOW	P_1 and L
HIGH	P_1 and H

* Resistance at maximum delay position should be between 270,000 ohms and 330,000 ohms.
* Resistance at minimum delay position should be zero with ohmmeter set on the high ohm scale.

16.5b   Intermittent wiper switch continuity check chart – continuity should be as specified in each switch position (1987 through 1990 models)

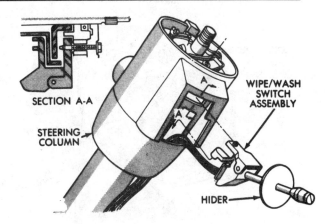

16.11   Wiper/washer switch removal details (1987 through 1990 models)

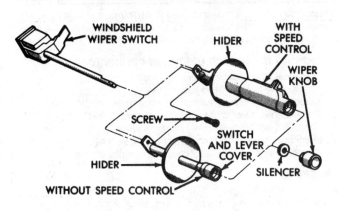

16.12   Wiper/washer stalk details (1987 through 1990 models)

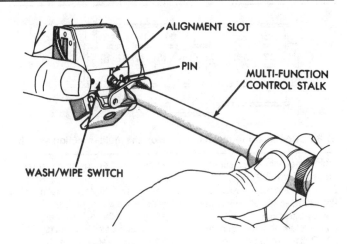

16.13   Line up the pin with the alignment slot and withdraw the multi-function control stalk (1987 through 1990 models)

Replacement

7   Perform the procedures in Steps 2 and 3, then remove the steering wheel (see Chapter 10).
8   Detach the wiring harness trough from the steering column (see illustration 15.8).
9   Unplug the electrical connector (see illustration 15.4).

Standard steering column

10   Remove the lock housing cover screws and pull the cover off.
11   Pull the switch hider out for access (see illustration).
12   Remove the two screws and detach the switch from the stalk, then remove the wiper knob from the end of the stalk (see illustration).
13   Rotate the control stalk fully clockwise, align the slot and pin, then pull the stalk out (see illustration).
14   Installation is the reverse of removal.

Tilt steering column

15   Compress the lock plate and remove the retaining ring (see Step 13 in Section 15).
16   Remove the lock plate, cancelling cam and upper bearing spring.
17   Remove the multi-function stalk retaining screw.
18   Remove the hazard flasher knob by pushing it in and unscrewing it.
19   Unplug the wiper/washer switch electrical connector (see illustration 15.4) and remove the turn signal switch (see Section 15).
20   Remove the ignition key lamp.
21   Remove the lock cylinder (see Section 21).
22   Bend the end of a straightened paper clip into a hook, insert it into the loop of the key buzzer switch wedge spring, then lift the switch out (see illustration).

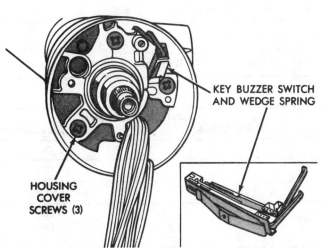

16.22   Hook a piece of wire (a straightened paper clip works well) under the wedge spring and remove the key buzzer switch – the housing cover is retained by three screws (1987 through 1990 models)

12

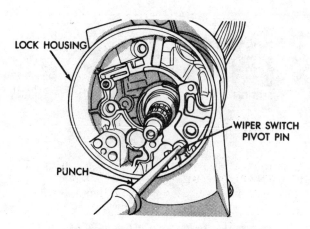

16.24   Use a thin punch or screwdriver to press the pivot pin out (1987 through 1990 models)

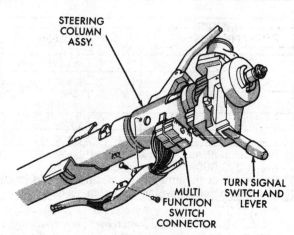

17.6   Unscrew the mounting screw and disconnect the electrical connector from the switch

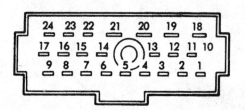

17.8a   Connector terminal numbers on the multi–function switch

23   Remove the three screws and lift off the column housing cover (**see illustration 16.22**).
24   Press the wiper switch pivot pin out with a punch (**see illustration**).
25   Remove the wiper/washer switch (**see illustration 16.11**).
26   Use tape to secure the dimmer switch rod, pull the switch hider up the control stalk, then remove the two screws (**see illustration 16.12**).
27   Pull the knob off the end of the multi-function stalk, turn the stalk fully clockwise, align the pin with the slot and pull the stalk straight out (**see illustration 16.13**).
28   Installation is the reverse of removal.

17   Multi-Function steering column switch – check and replacement (1991 and later models)

Refer to illustrations 17.6, 17.8a, 17.8b, 17.9 and 17.10
1   These models are equipped with a multi-function switch located on the left side of the steering column. The switch controls the following func-

tions: turn signals, hazard warning, headlight dimmer and windshield wiper/washer. If any of the functions of the switch become faulty, the entire switch assembly must be replaced.

Accessing the switch electrical connector

2   Disconnect the negative cable from the battery.
3   Remove the tilt lever (if so equipped).
4   Remove the steering column lower cover (see Chapter 11).
5   Remove the screws and the upper and lower column shrouds.
6   Unscrew the mounting screw (the screw will stay with the connector) and disconnect the electrical connector from the switch (**see illustration**).
7   Reverse this procedure after checking or replacing the switch.

Checking

Note: *Before performing any of the checks below, disconnect the electrical connector from the switch by following Steps 2 through 7 above.*

Turn signal and hazard warning functions
8   Use an ohmmeter or self-powered test light to check for continuity between the turn signal and/or hazard warning switch terminals at the electrical connector (**see illustrations**).

Headlight dimmer function
9   Use an ohmmeter or self-powered test light to check for continuity between the dimmer switch terminals at the electrical connector (**see the accompanying illustration and illustration 17.8a**).

Windshield wiper, intermittent wiper control and windshield washer functions
10   Use an ohmmeter or self-powered test light to check for continuity between the indicated terminals of the switch's electrical connector (**see the accompanying illustration and illustration 17.8a**).

SWITCH POSITIONS		
TURN SIGNAL	**HAZARD WARNING**	**CONTINUITY BETWEEN**
NEUTRAL	OFF	12 AND 14 AND 15
LEFT	OFF	15 AND 16 AND 17
LEFT	OFF	12 AND 14
LEFT	OFF	22 AND 23 WITH OPTIONAL CORNER LAMPS
RIGHT	OFF	11 AND 12 AND 17
RIGHT	OFF	14 AND 15
RIGHT	OFF	23 AND 24 WITH OPTIONAL CORNER LAMPS
NEUTRAL	ON	11 AND 12 AND 13 AND 15 AND 16

17.8b   Turn signal and/or hazard warning switch continuity chart – continuity should be as specified at the three switch positions

SWITCH POSITION	CONTINUITY BETWEEN
LOW BEAM	18 AND 19
HIGH BEAM	19 AND 20
OPTICAL HORN	20 AND 21

17.9 Headlight dimmer switch continuity chart – continuity should be as specified at the three switch positions

SWITCH POSITION	CONTINUITY BETWEEN
OFF	PIN 6 AND PIN 7
DELAY	PIN 8 AND PIN 9
	PIN 2 AND PIN 4
	PIN 1 AND PIN 2
	PIN 1 AND PIN 4
LOW	PIN 4 AND PIN 6
HIGH	PIN 4 AND PIN 5
WASH	PIN 3 AND PIN 4

*RESISTANCE AT MAXIMUM DELAY POSITION SHOULD BE BETWEEN 270,000 OHMS AND 330,000 OHMS.
*RESISTANCE AT MINIMUM DELAY POSITION SHOULD BE ZERO WITH OHMMETER SET ON HIGH OHM SCALE.

17.10 Windshield wiper/washer continuity chart – continuity should be as specified at the five switch positions

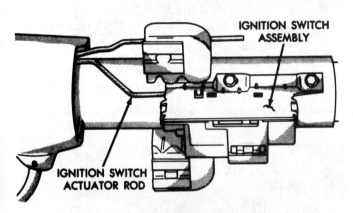

18.1 The ignition switch is located on the right side of the steering column (1987 through 1990 models)

Switch replacement

11 Disconnect the negative cable from the battery.

12 Remove the tilt lever (if so equipped).

13 Remove the steering column lower cover (see Chapter 11).

14 Remove the screws and the upper and lower column shrouds.

15 Loosen, but do not remove, the steering column upper bracket nuts.

16 Move the upper fixed column cover to gain access to the rear of the multi–function switch.

17 Remove the multi–function switch tamper–proof screws with Snap–on TTXR20B2 or an equivalent tool.

18 Gently pull the switch away from the steering column.

19 Unscrew the mounting screw (the screw will stay with the connector) and disconnect the electrical connector from the switch **(see illustration 17.6)**

18 Ignition switch – check and replacement

1987 through 1990 models

Refer to illustrations 18.1 and 18.3

1   The ignition switch is located on the steering column and is actuated by a rod attached to the key lock cylinder **(see illustration)**.

Check

2   Remove the switch (see Steps 5 through 8).

3   Use an ohmmeter or self-powered timing light and the accompanying diagram to check for continuity between the switch terminals.

4   If the switch does not have correct continuity, replace it.

Replacement

5   Disconnect the negative cable from the battery.

6   Insert the key into the lock cylinder and turn it to the Acc position.

7   Remove the steering column cover (see Chapter 11).

8   Unplug the electrical connector, remove the bolts, then detach the switch from the actuator rod and lower it from the steering column.

9   Installation is the reverse of removal. As the switch is engaged to the actuator rod, push up on the switch to remove any slack from the rod before fully tightening the bolts.

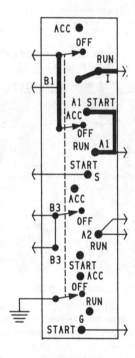

18.3 A schematic diagram of the ignition switch (1987 through 1990 models)

1991 and later models

10 The ignition switch is located on the right side of the steering column.

Check

Refer to illustration 18.12

11 Remove the ignition switch (see Steps 14 through 20).

12 Use an ohmmeter or self-powered test light and the accompanying diagram to check for continuity between the switch terminals **(see illustration)**.

13 If the switch does not have the correct continuity, replace it.

Replacement

Refer to illustration 18.18

14 Disconnect the negative cable from the battery.

15 Remove the tilt lever (if so equipped).

16 Remove the steering column lower cover (see Chapter 11).

17 Remove the screws and the upper and lower column shrouds.

18 Remove the ignition switch mounting screws **(see illustration)**.

19 Gently pull the switch assembly away from the steering column.

12

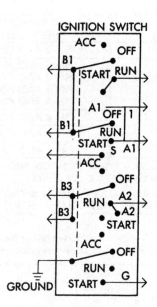

18.12 A schematic diagram of the ignition switch (1991 and later models)

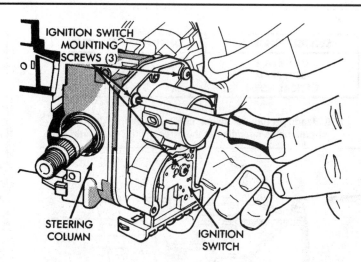

18.18 Remove the ignition switch mounting screws (1991 and later models)

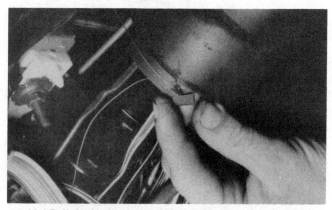

19.4 Pull the U-shaped clip off and disconnect the shift indicator cable

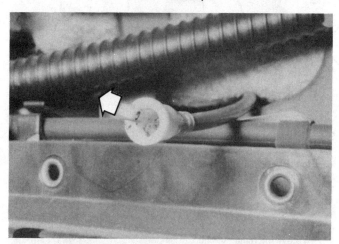

19.5 Pull the clip out to detach the speedometer cable

20   Release the two connector locks on the seven-way electrical connector and disconnect the connector from the switch assembly. Remove the switch.
21   Installation is the reverse of removal.

19   Instrument cluster – removal and installation

Refer to illustrations 19.4 and 19.5
1   Disconnect the negative cable from the battery.
2   Remove the steering column cover (see Chapter 11).
3   Remove the instrument cluster bezel (see Chapter 11).
4   On automatic transmission models, place the shift lever in Drive, remove the U-shaped clip and disconnect the indicator cable **(see illustration)**.
5   Remove the screws and pull the cluster out far enough for access to the electrical and speedometer connectors. On some models it may be necessary to disconnect the speedometer cable at the transmission or cruise control adapter to provide sufficient slack so the cluster can be pulled out (see Section 19). Unplug the connectors, detach the speedometer cable and remove the cluster **(see illustration)**.
6   Installation is the reverse of removal. On automatic transmission models, pull the indicator cable down to position the indicator in Neutral or Reverse, then let the cable snap back to 1. Repeat the procedure, pull the

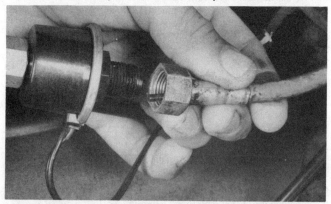

20.2 Unscrew the collar and pull the speedometer cable out of the cruise control adapter (shown) or transmission housing

cable up far enough to connect the end to the slot (don't go past Reverse), then install the clip. Move the shift lever to Park to self adjust the indicator.

20   Speedometer cable – removal and installation

Refer to illustrations 20.2 and 20.3
1   Disconnect the negative cable from the battery.
2   Disconnect the speedometer cable from the transmission or cruise control adapter **(see illustration)**.

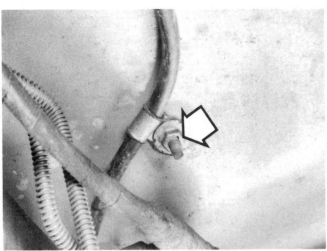

20.3   Remove the nut (arrow) to detach the speedometer cable routing clip

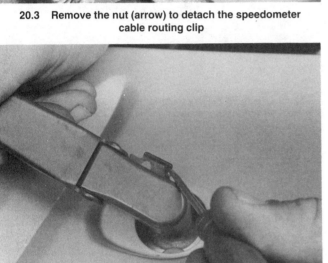

21.9   Pry the release lever out with a screwdriver and lift the wiper arm off

3   Detach the cable from the routing clips in the engine compartment and pull the cable up to provide enough slack to allow disconnection from the speedometer **(see illustration)**.
4   Remove the instrument cluster screws, pull the cluster out and disconnect the speedometer cable from the back of the cluster **(see illustration 18.5)**.
5   Remove the cable from the vehicle.
6   Prior to installation, lubricate the speedometer end of the cable with spray-on speedometer cable lubricant (available at auto parts stores).
7   Installation is the reverse of removal.

21   Windshield wiper motor – check and replacement

Refer to illustrations 21.8 and 21.9

Check

1   If the wiper motor does not run at all, first check the fuse block for a blown fuse (see Section 3).
2   Check the wiper switch (see Section 16).
3   Turn the ignition switch and wiper switch on.
4   Connect a jumper wire between the wiper motor and ground, then retest. If the motor works now, repair the ground connection.
5   If the wipers still don't work, turn on the wipers and check for voltage at the motor connector. If there's voltage, remove the motor and check it off

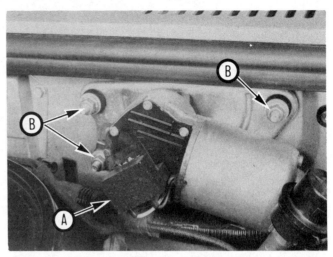

21.8   Unplug the connector (A) and remove the three nuts (B)

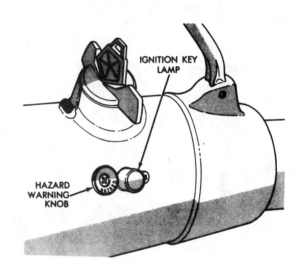

22.3   Ignition key lamp details (1987 through 1990 models)

the vehicle with fused jumper wires from the battery. If the motor now works, check for binding linkage. If the motor still doesn't work, replace it.
6   If there's no voltage at the motor, the problem is in the switch or wiring.
7   Disconnect the negative cable from the battery.
8   Unplug the wiper motor electrical connector and remove the mounting nuts **(see illustration)**.

Replacement

9   Remove the wiper arms **(see illustration)**.
10   Remove cowl grille (see Chapter 11).
11   Hold the motor drive crank with a wrench, remove the crank nut and detach the crank, then lift the motor out.
12   Installation is the reverse of removal.

22   Ignition lock cylinder – removal and installation

1987 through 1990 models
Refer to illustrations 22.3 and 22.5
1   Disconnect the negative cable from the battery.
2   Remove the turn signal/hazard warning switches (see Section 15).
3   Remove the ignition key lamp assembly **(see illustration)**.
4   Place the lock cylinder in the Lock position.

12

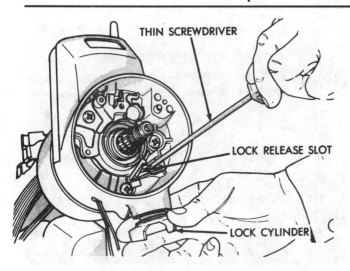

22.5   Insert a thin screwdriver into the lock release slot and press the spring latch while pulling the lock cylinder out (1987 through 1990 models)

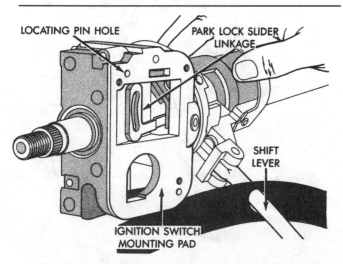

22.16a   Move the column shift lever to the PARK position and make sure the park-lock dowel pin on the ignition switch assembly is engaged with the column park-lock slider linkage

5   Insert a thin screwdriver or punch into the lock release slot located next to the switch mounting screw boss, press down on the spring latch and withdraw the cylinder from the steering column **(see illustration)**.
6   Insert the new lock cylinder (without the key) into position until it contacts the ignition switch actuating rod. Move the rod up and down to remove any slack and align the components. Insert the key and push the lock cylinder in. The lock cylinder will snap into place automatically when the components align themselves, locking it in the housing.
7   The remainder of installation is the reverse of removal.

1991 and later models

Removal
Refer to illustration 22.10
8   Remove the ignition switch (see Section 18).
9   Place the lock cylinder in the LOCK position.
10   Use a small screwdriver to depress the key cylinder retaining pin until it is flush with the key cylinder surface **(see illustration)**.
11   Rotate the key to the OFF position. The key cylinder should now be released and stick about 1/8 inch away from the halo light ring.
12   Rotate the key counterclockwise to the LOCK position and remove the key from the lock cylinder.
13   Remove the lock cylinder.

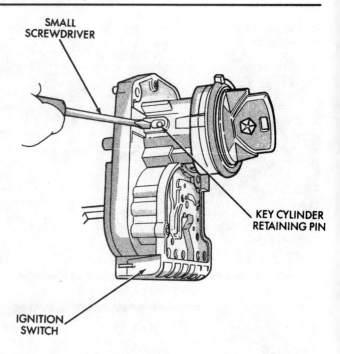

22.10   Depress the key cylinder retaining pin with a small screwdriver until it is flush with the key cylinder surface

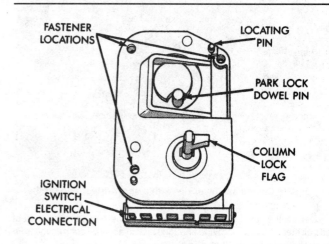

22.16b   Make sure the ignition switch is in the LOCK position – the flag must be parallel with the ignition switch terminals

Installation
Refer to illustrations 22.16a and 22.16b
14   Attach the electrical connector to the ignition switch. Make sure the connector's locking tabs are fully seated in the wire connector.
15   Attach the ignition switch to the steering column (see Section 18).
16   Move the column shift lever to the PARK position. The park–lock dowel pin on the ignition switch assembly must engage with the column park-lock slider linkage **(see illustration)**. Verify that the ignition switch is in the LOCK position. The flag must be parallel with the ignition switch terminals **(see illustration)**.
17   Position the park–lock link and slider to mid–travel. Position the ignition switch against the lock housing face. Be sure the pin is inserted into the park–lock link contour slot and tighten the mounting screws securely.
18   Install the upper and lower column shrouds.
19   Install the steering column lower cover (see Chapter 11).
20   Install the tilt lever (if so equipped).
21   Place the lock cylinder in the LOCK position and gently insert the key cylinder into the lock assembly until it bottoms out.

22   Insert the key and gently push the key cylinder inward toward the ignition switch and rotate the key clockwise to the end of its travel.
23   Turn the key to all of its positions and check for normal operation.
22.10 Depress the key cylinder retaining pin with a small screwdriver until it is flush with the key cylinder surface

23   Power door lock system – description and check

The power door lock system operates the door lock actuators mounted in each door. The system consists of the switches, actuators and associated wiring. Since special tools and techniques are required to diagnose the system, it should be left to a dealer service department or a repair shop. However, it is possible for the home mechanic to make simple checks of the wiring connections and actuators for minor faults which can be easily repaired. These include:
   a) Check the system fuse and/or circuit breaker.
   b) Check the switch wires for damage and loose connections. Check the switches for continuity.
   c) Remove the door panel(s) and check the actuator wiring connections to see if they're loose or damaged. Inspect the actuator rods (if equipped) to make sure they aren't bent or damaged. Inspect the actuator wiring for damaged or loose connections. The actuator can be checked by applying battery power momentarily. A discernible click indicates that the solenoid is operating properly.

24   Power window system – description and check

The power window system operates the electric motors mounted in the doors which lower and raise the windows. The system consists of the control switches, the motors (regulators), glass mechanisms and associated wiring.
   Because of the complexity of the power window system and the special tools and techniques required for diagnosis, repair should be left to a dealer service department or a repair shop. However, it is possible for the home mechanic to make simple checks of the wiring connections and motors for minor faults which can be easily repaired. These include:
   a) Inspect the power window actuating switches for broken wires and loose connections.
   b) Check the power window fuse/and or circuit breaker.
   c) Remove the door panel(s) and check the power window motor wires to see if they're loose or damaged. Inspect the glass mechanisms for damage which could cause binding.

25   Cruise control system – description and check

The cruise control system maintains vehicle speed with a vacuum actuated servo motor located in the engine compartment, which is connected to the throttle linkage by a cable. The system consists of the servo motor, clutch switch, brake switch, control switches, a relay and associated vacuum hoses.
   Because of the complexity of the cruise control system and the special tools and techniques required for diagnosis, repair should be left to a dealer service department or a repair shop. However, it is possible for the home mechanic to make simple checks of the wiring and vacuum connections for minor faults which can be easily repaired. These include:

   a) Inspect the cruise control actuating switches for broken wires and loose connections.
   b) Check the cruise control fuse.
   c) The cruise control system is operated by vacuum so it's critical that all vacuum switches, hoses and connections are secure. Check the hoses in the engine compartment for tight connections, cracks and obvious vacuum leaks.

26   Wiring diagrams – general information

Refer to illustration 26.4
   Since it isn't possible to include all wiring diagrams for every year covered by this manual, the following diagrams are those that are typical and most commonly needed.
   Prior to troubleshooting any circuits, check the fuse and circuit breakers (if equipped) to make sure they're in good condition. Make sure the battery is properly charged and check the cable connections (see Chapter 1).
   When checking a circuit, make sure that all connectors are clean, with no broken or loose terminals. When unplugging a connector, do not pull on the wires. Pull only on the connector housings themselves.
   Refer to the accompanying chart for the wire color codes applicable to your vehicle.

WIRE COLOR CODE CHART					
COLOR CODE	COLOR	STANDARD TRACER COLOR	COLOR CODE	COLOR	STANDARD TRACER CODE
BK	BLACK	WT	PK	PINK	BK OR WH
BR	BROWN	WT	RD	RED	WT
DB	DARK BLUE	WT	TN	TAN	WT
DG	DARK GREEN	WT	VT	VIOLET	WT
GY	GRAY	BK	WT	WHITE	BK
LB	LIGHT BLUE	BK	YL	YELLOW	BK
LG	LIGHT GREEN	BK	*	WITH TRACER	
OR	ORANGE	BK			

26.4   Wiring diagram color codes

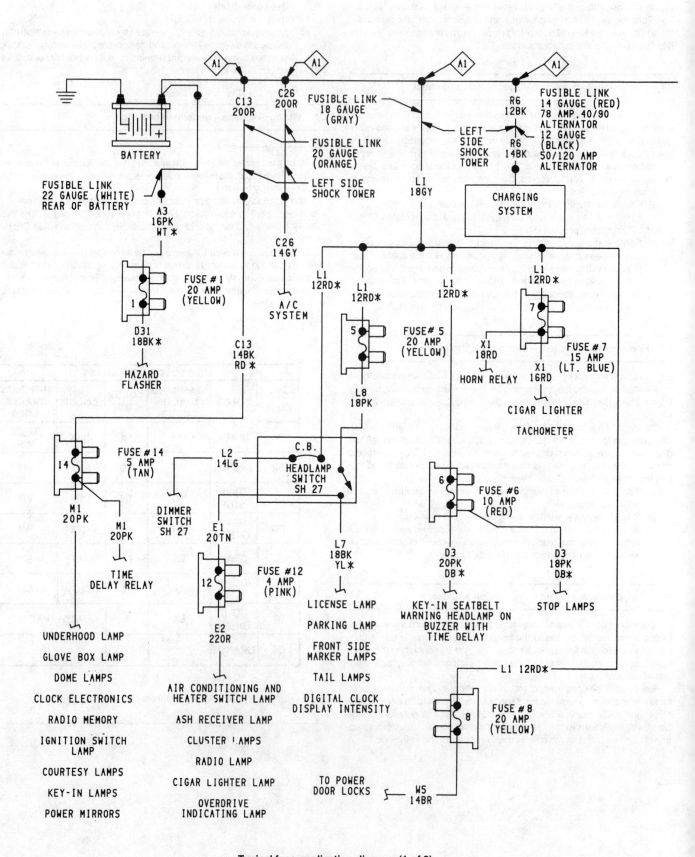

Typical fuse application diagram (1 of 2)

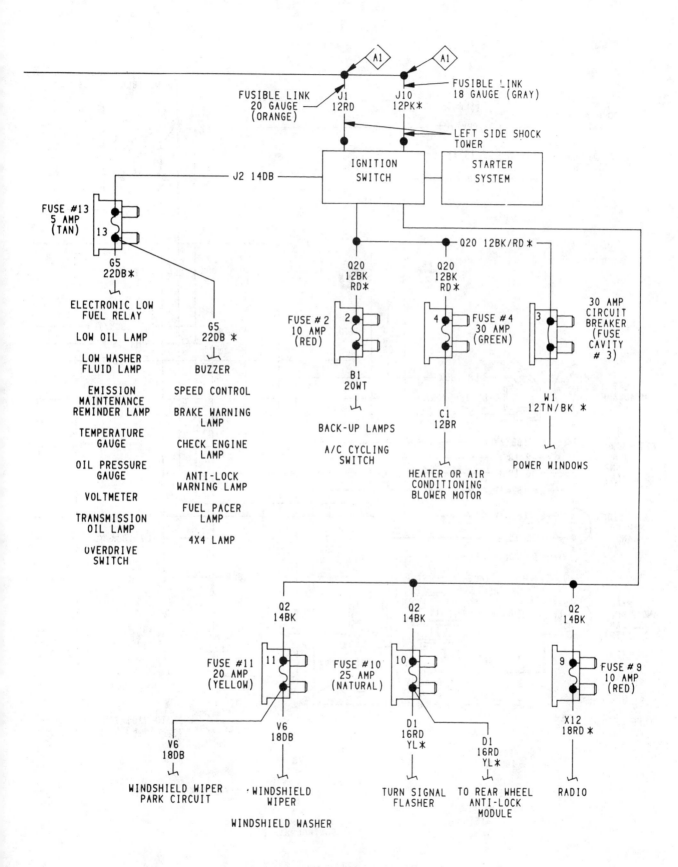

Typical fuse application diagram (2 of 2)

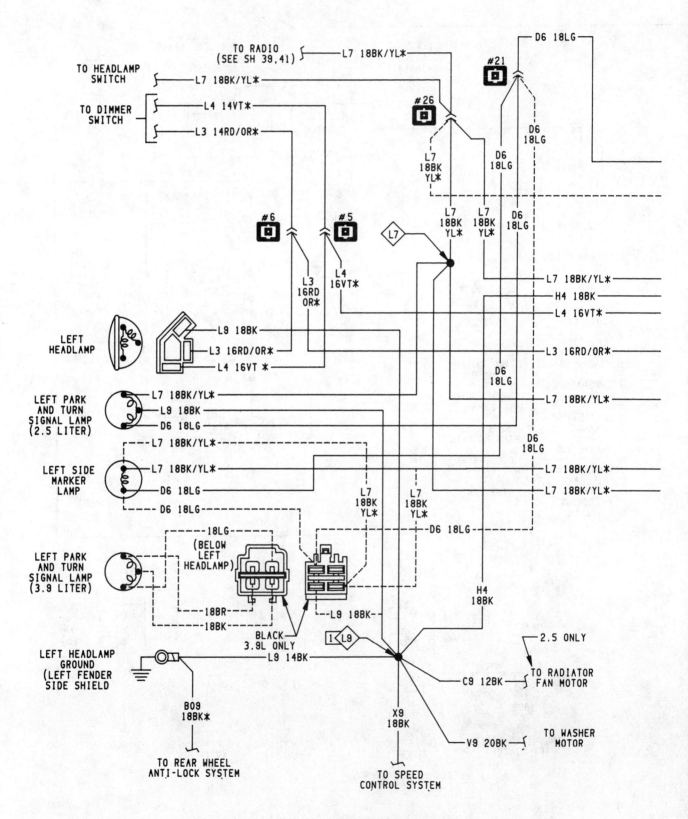

Typical front end lighting wiring diagram (1 of 2)

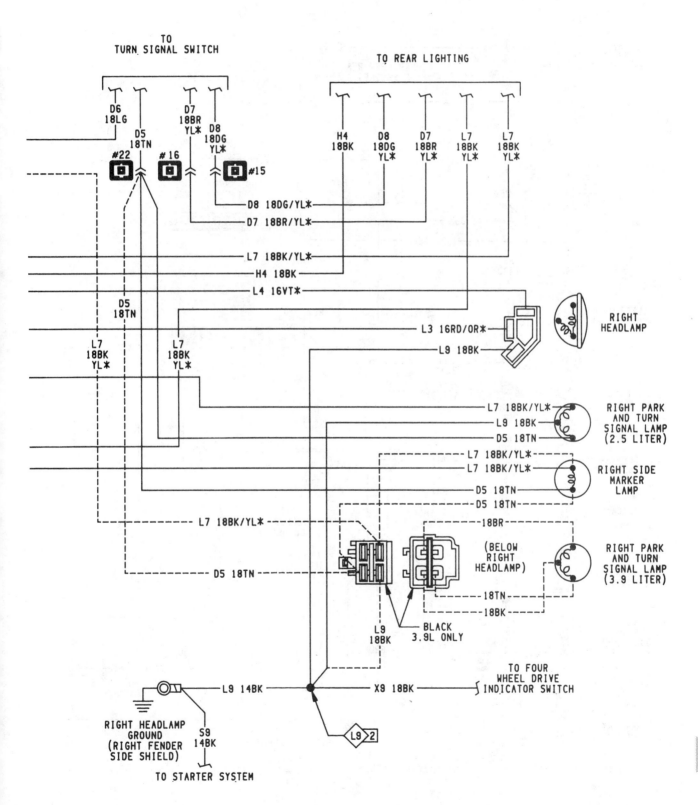

Typical front end lighting wiring diagram (2 of 2)

12

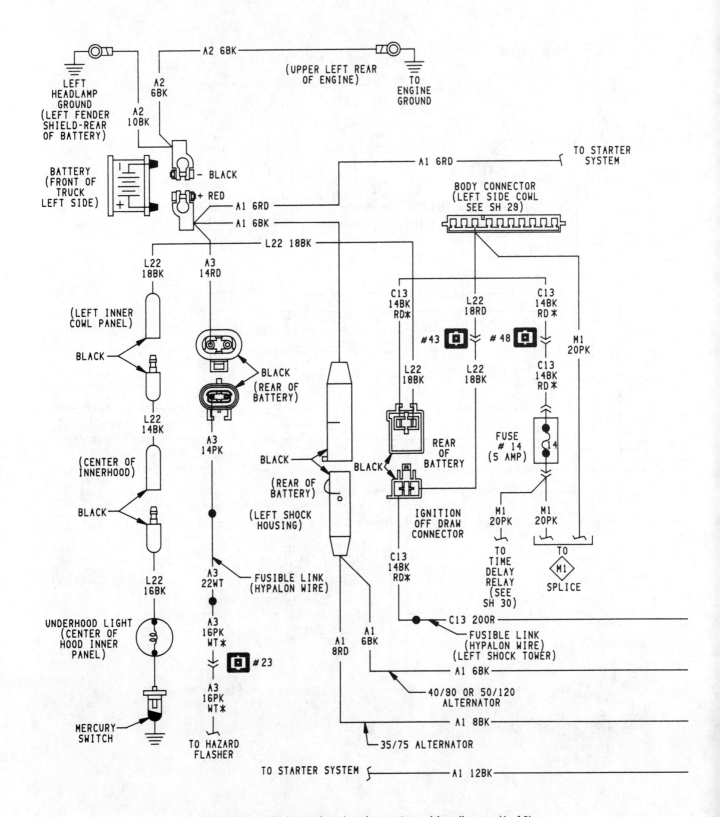

Typical four-cylinder engine charging system wiring diagram (1 of 2)

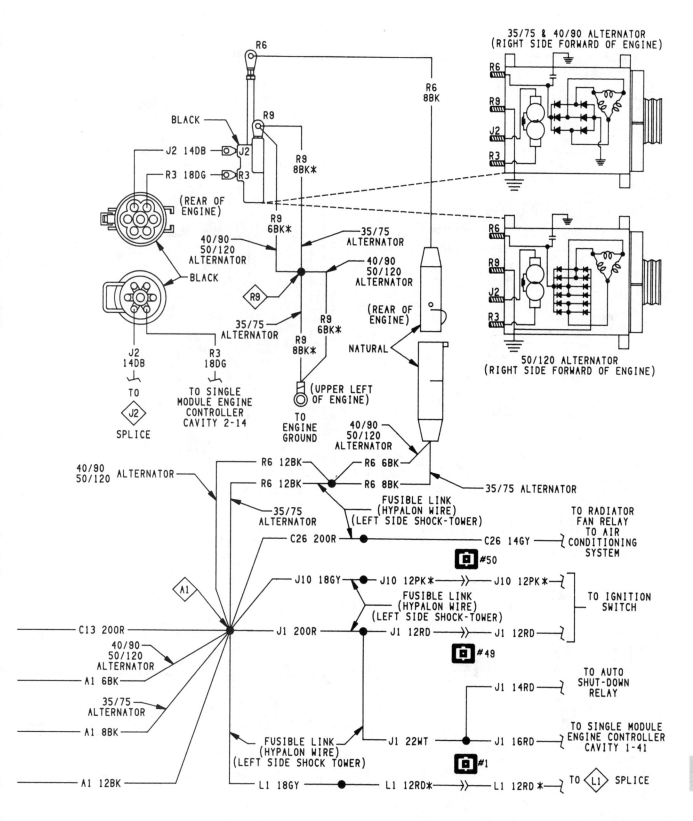

Typical four-cylinder engine charging system wiring diagram (2 of 2)

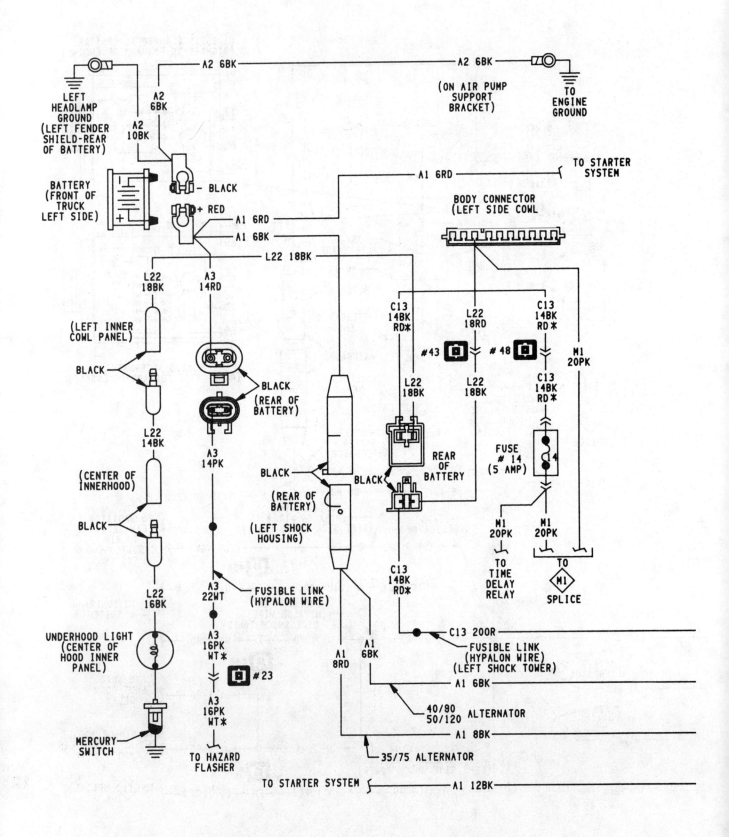

Typical V6 engine charging system wiring diagram (1 of 2)

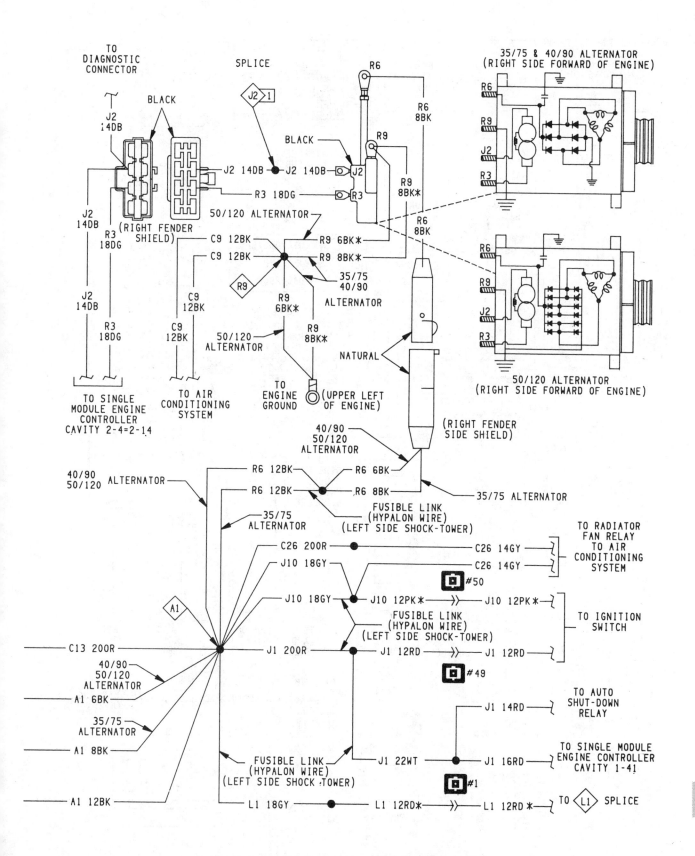

Typical V6 engine charging system wiring diagram (2 of 2)

12

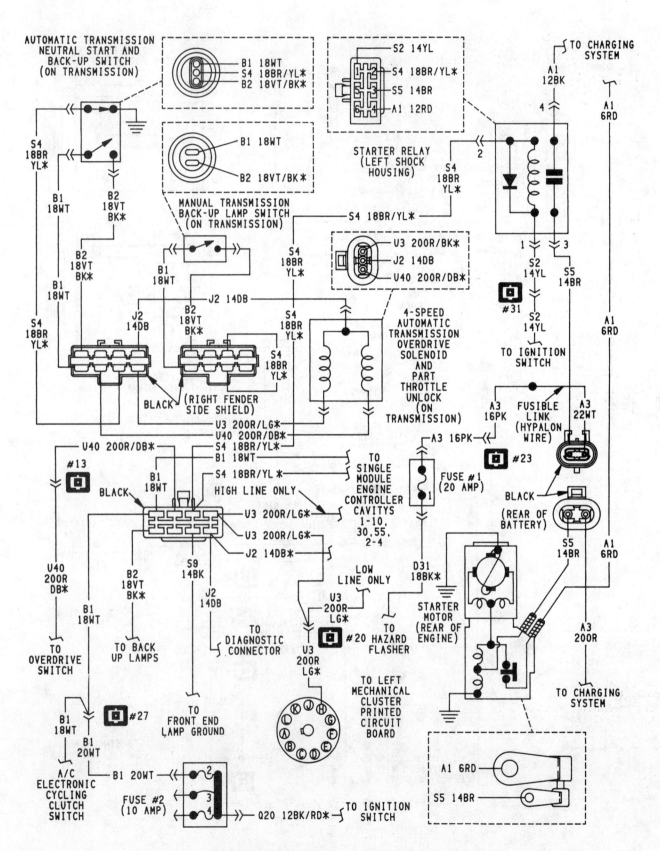

Typical four-cylinder engine starting system wiring diagram

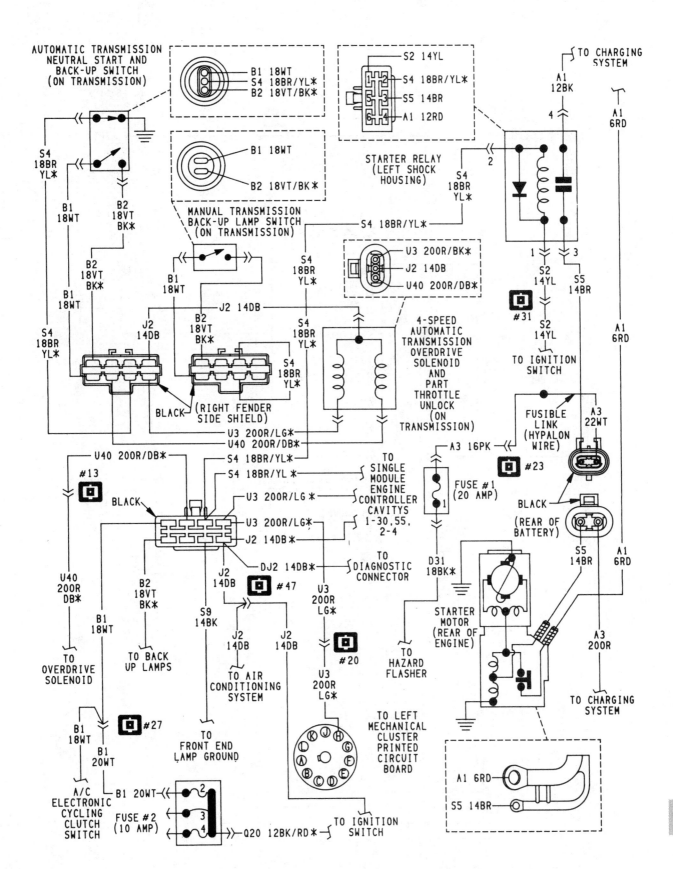

Typical V6 engine starting system wiring diagram

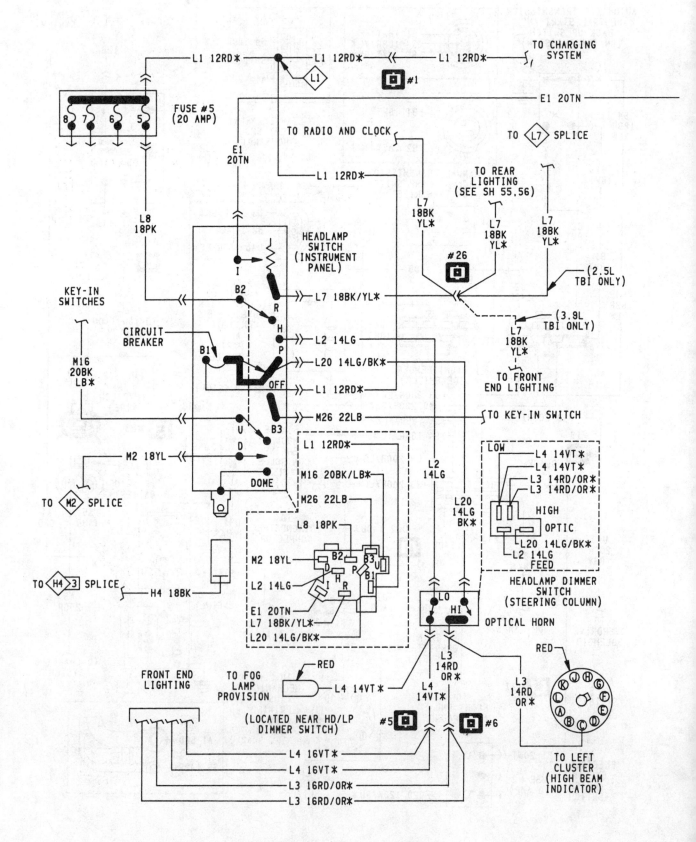

Typical headlight switch wiring diagram

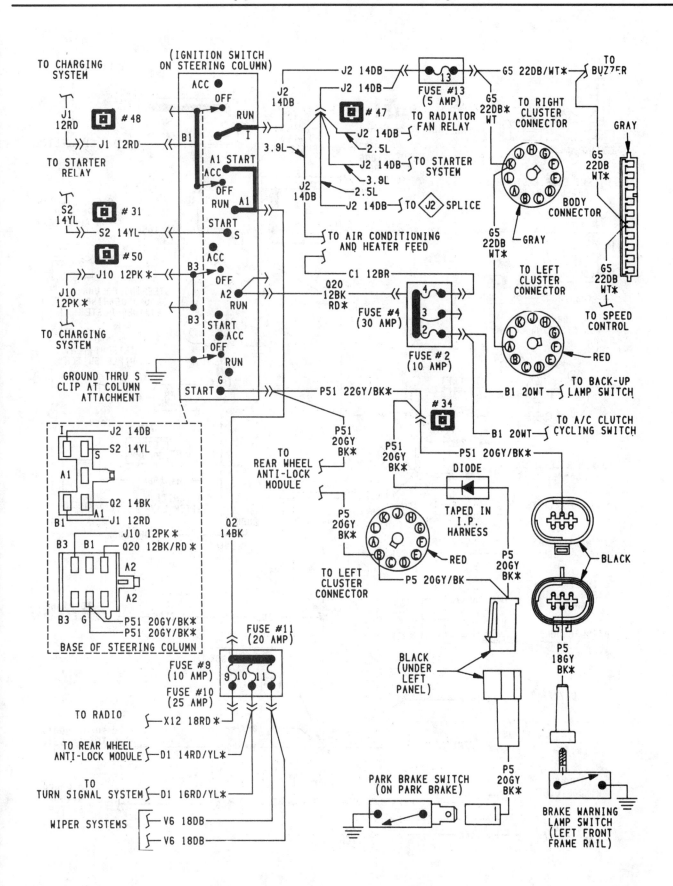

Typical ignition switch wiring diagram

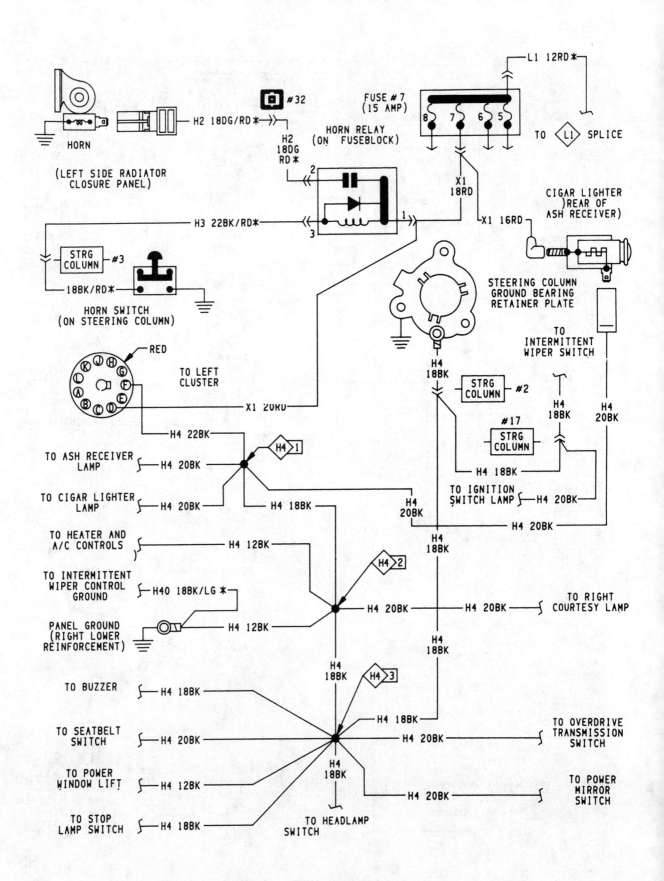

Typical horn system wiring diagram

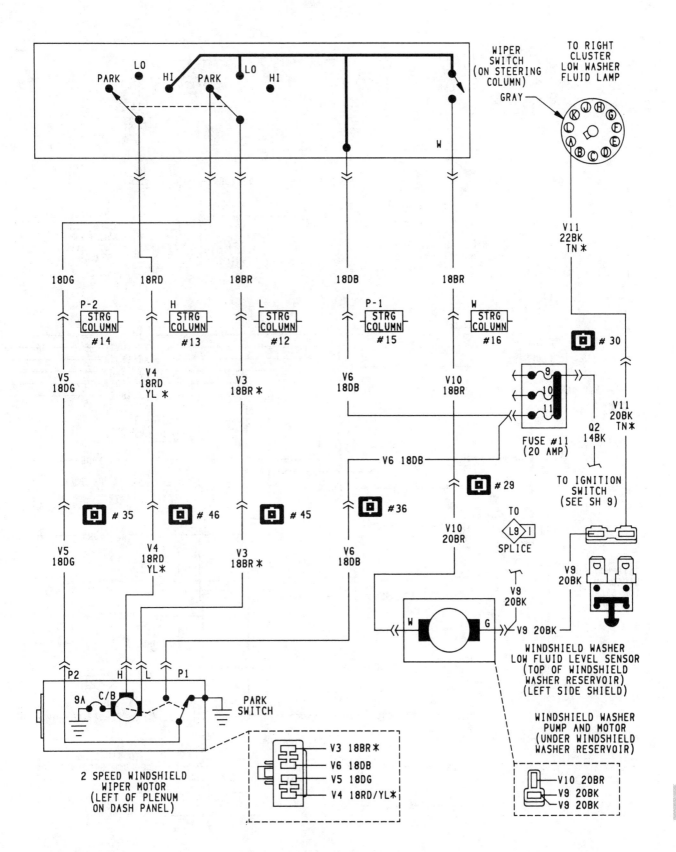

Typical two-speed windshield wiper wiring diagram

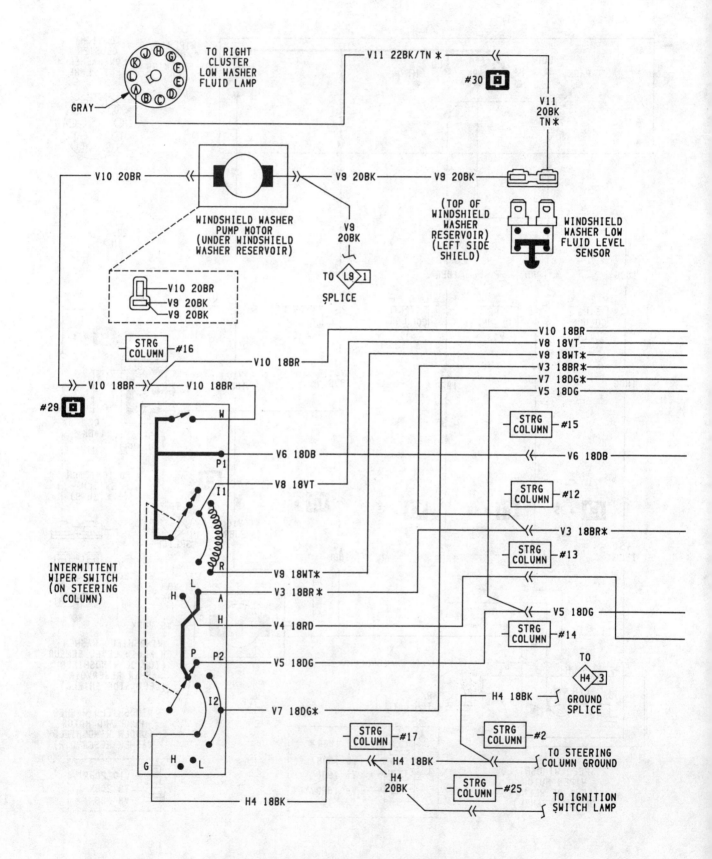

Typical intermittent windshield wiper wiring diagram (1 of 2)

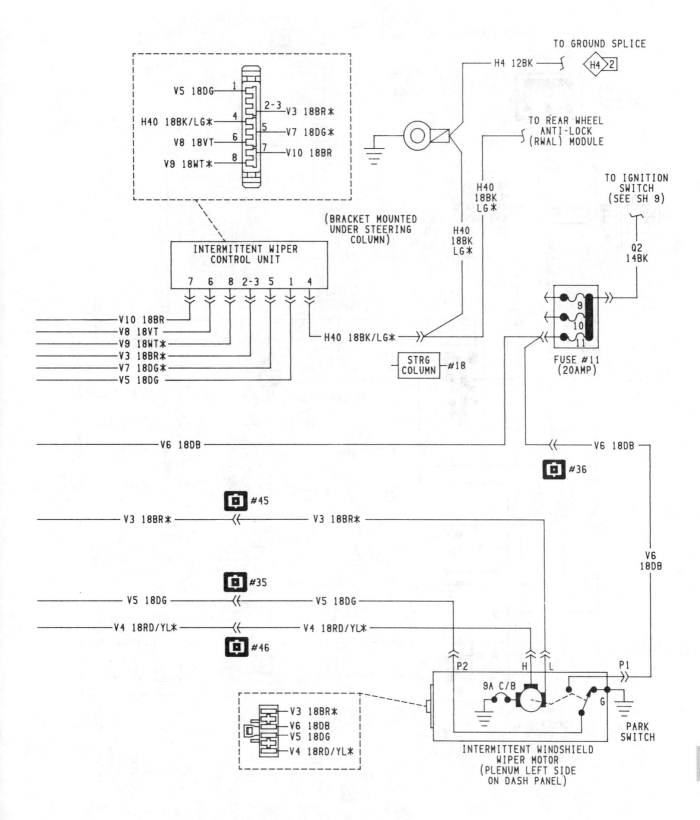

Typical intermittent windshield wiper wiring diagram (2 of 2)

12

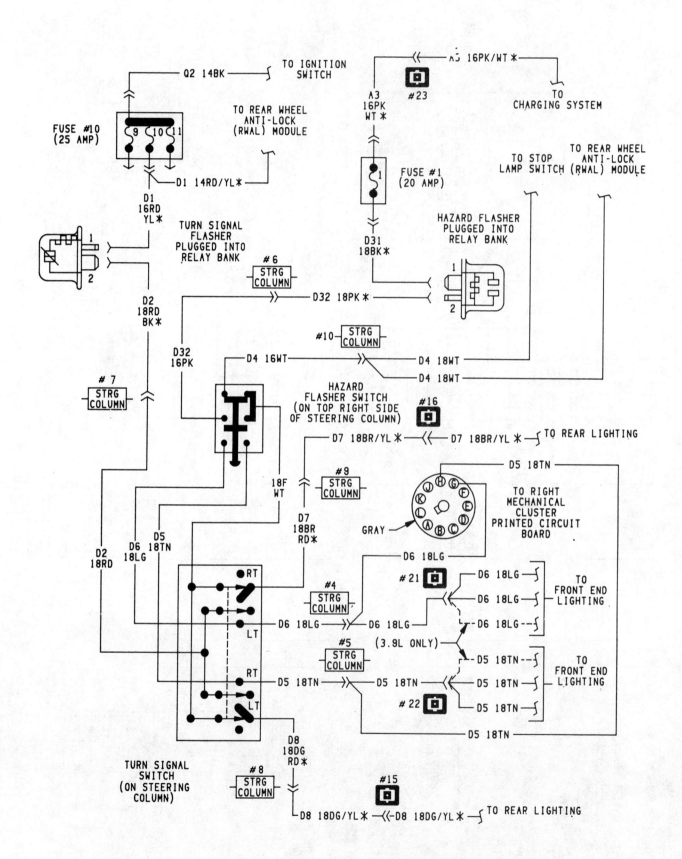

Typical stop/turn and hazard flasher system wiring diagram

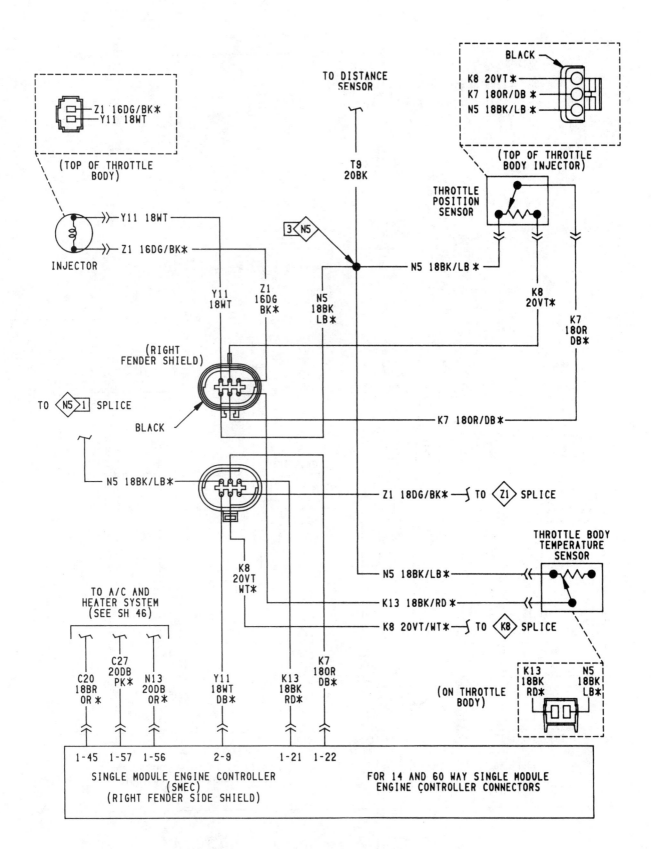

Typical four-cylinder engine fuel injection wiring diagram (1 of 5)

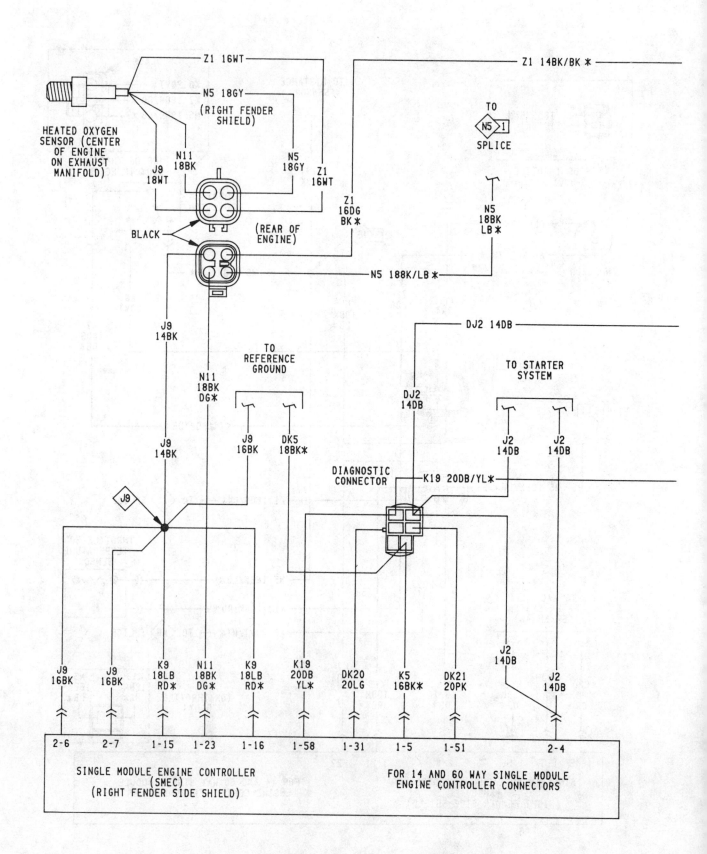

Typical four-cylinder engine fuel injection wiring diagram (2 of 5)

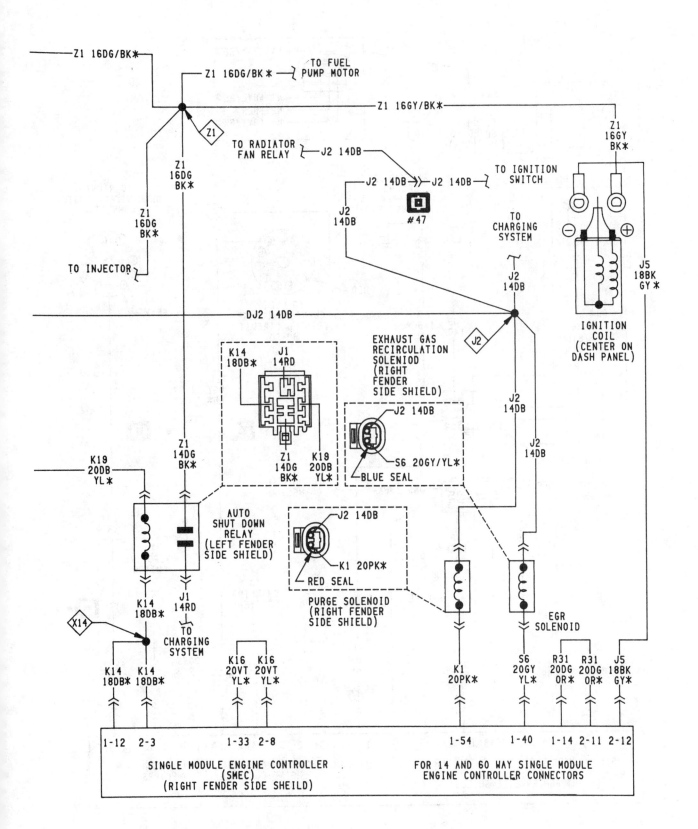

Typical four-cylinder engine fuel injection wiring diagram (3 of 5)

12

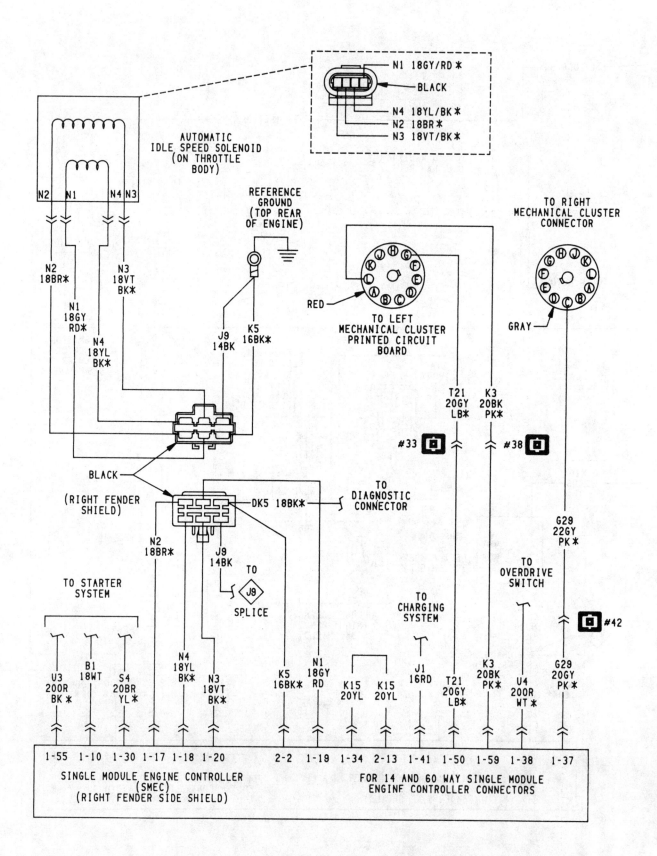

Typical four-cylinder engine fuel injection wiring diagram (4 of 5)

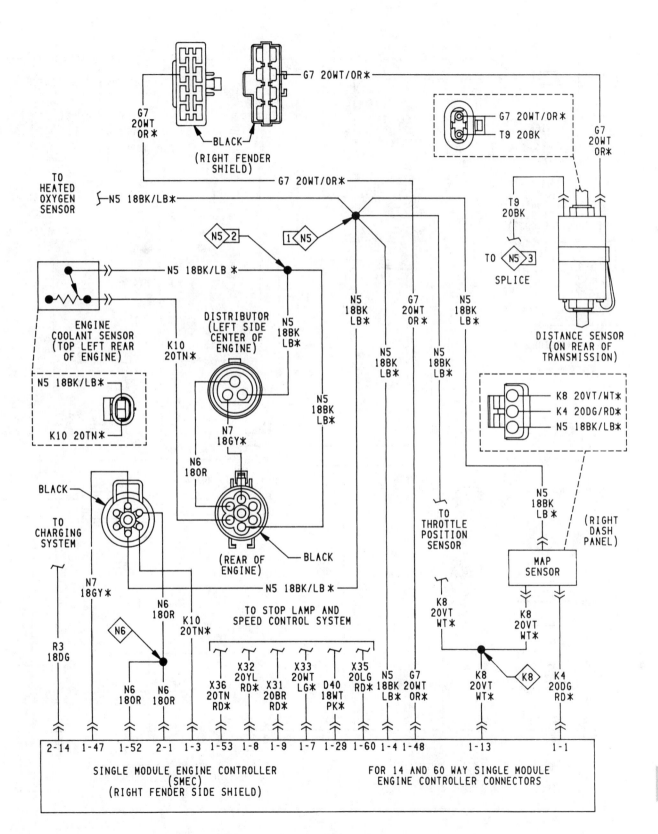

Typical four-cylinder engine fuel injection wiring diagram (5 of 5)

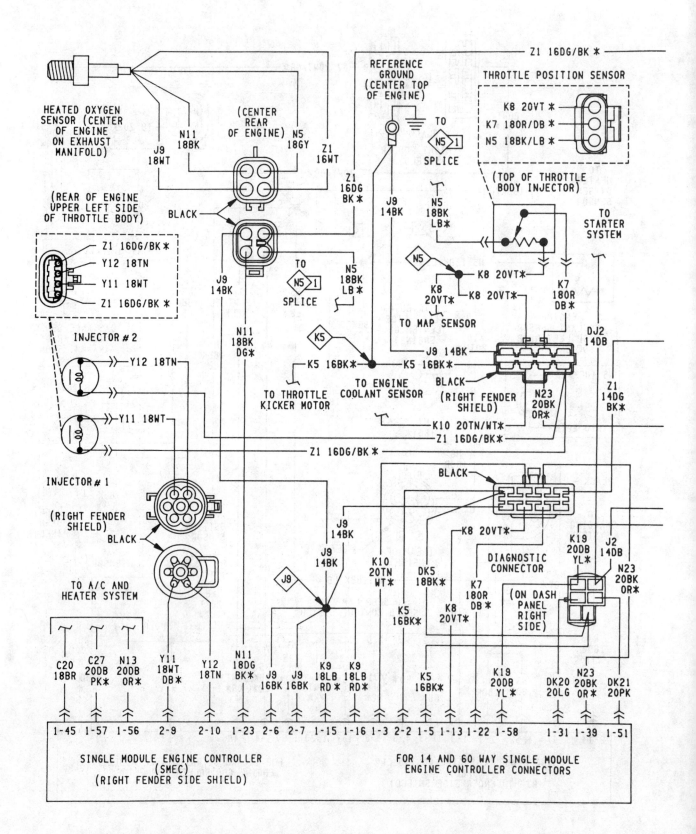

Typical V6 and V8 engine fuel injection wiring diagram – models with Throttle Body Injection (TBI) – (1 of 4)

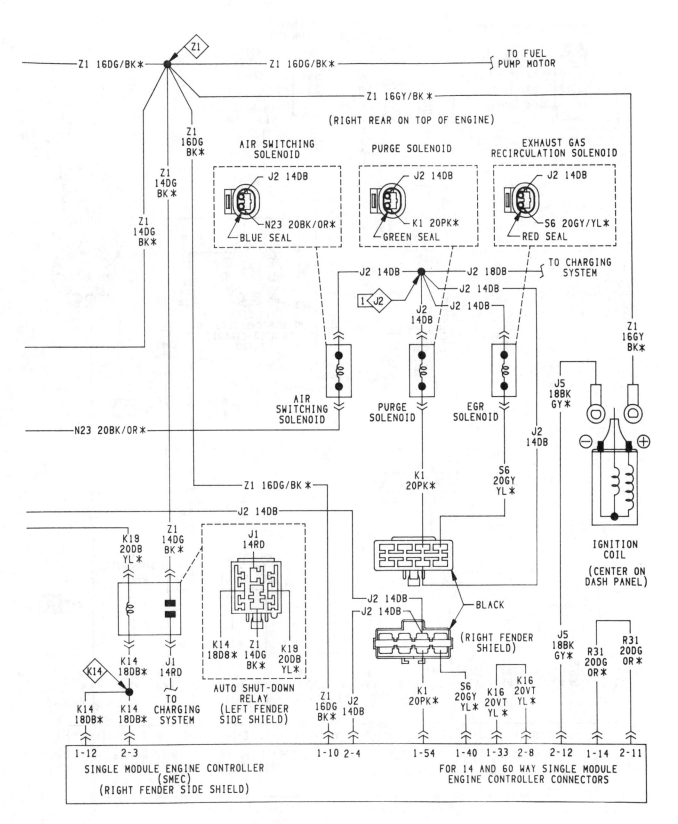

Typical V6 and V8 engine fuel injection wiring diagram – models with Throttle Body Injection (TBI) – (2 of 4)

12

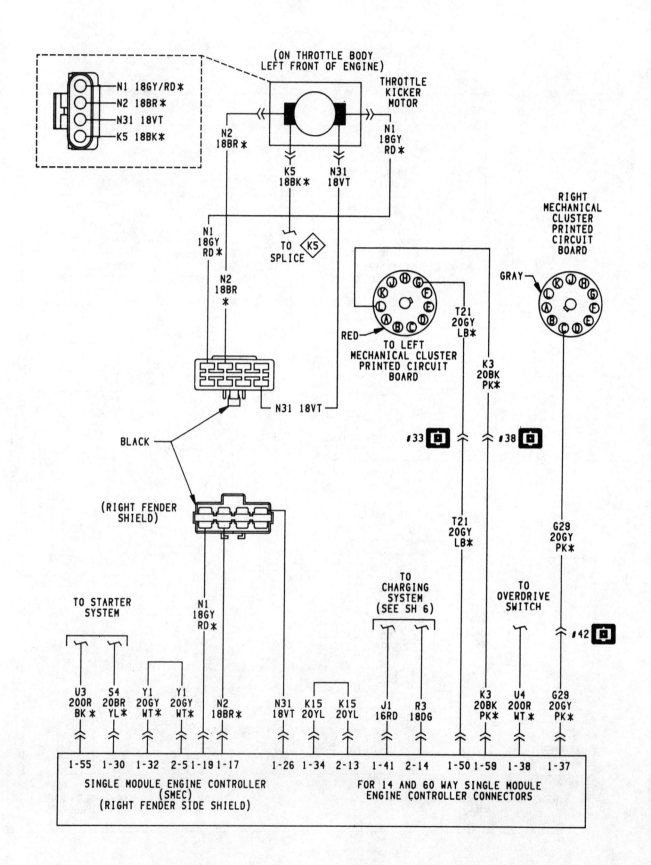

Typical V6 and V8 engine fuel injection wiring diagram – models with Throttle Body Injection (TBI) – (3 of 4)

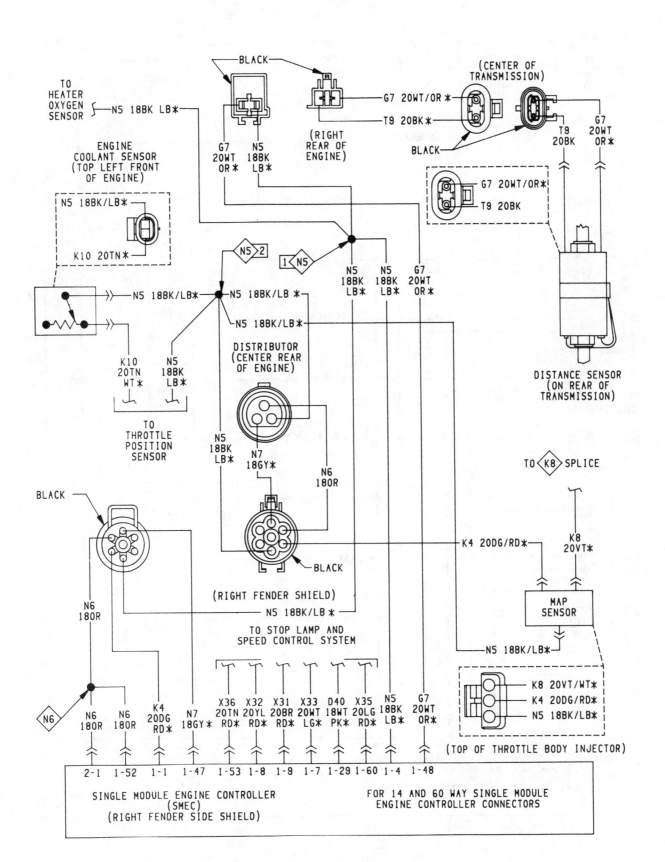

Typical V6 and V8 engine fuel injection wiring diagram – models with Throttle Body Injection (TBI) – (4 of 4)

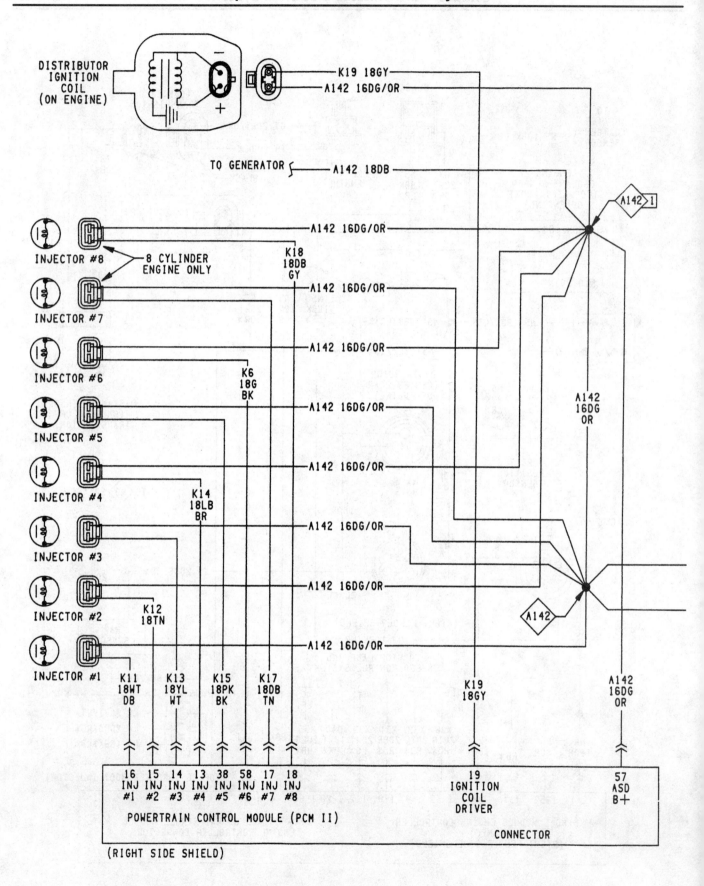

Typical V6 and V8 engine fuel injection wiring diagram – models with Multi-Port Injection (MPI) (1 of 6)

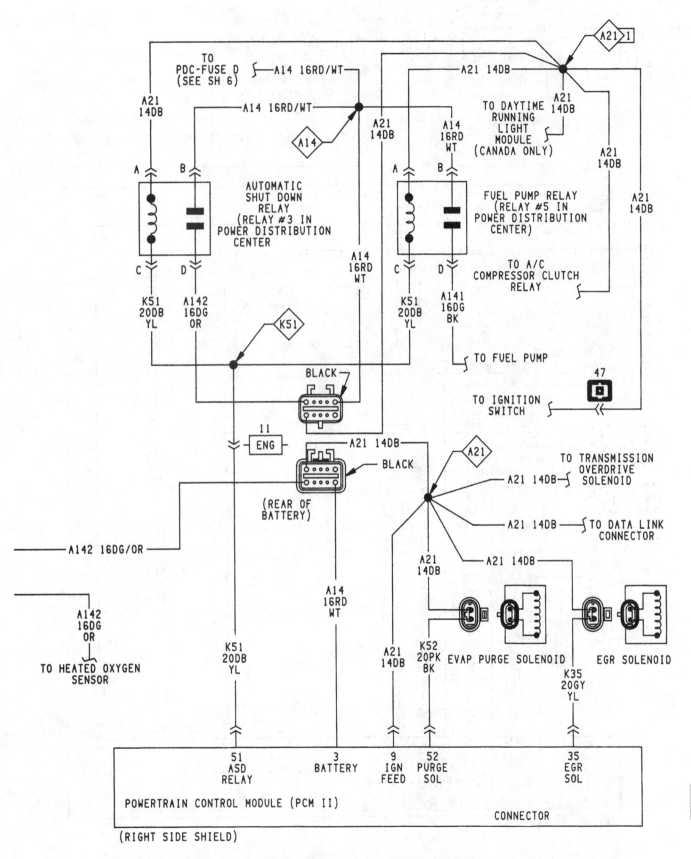

Typical V6 and V8 engine fuel injection wiring diagram – models with Multi-Port Injection (MPI) (2 of 6)

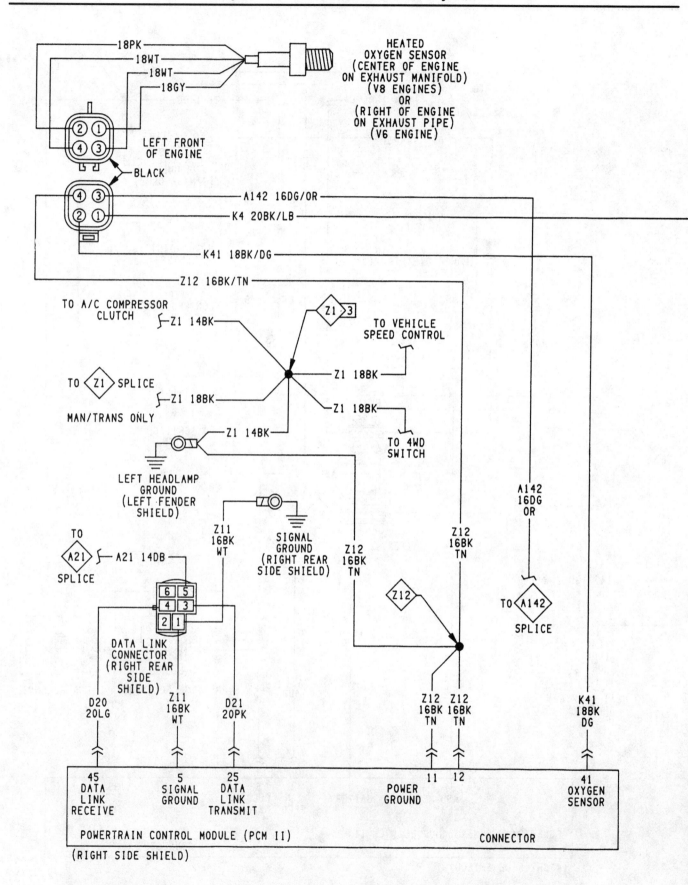

Typical V6 and V8 engine fuel injection wiring diagram – models with Multi-Port Injection (MPI) (3 of 6)

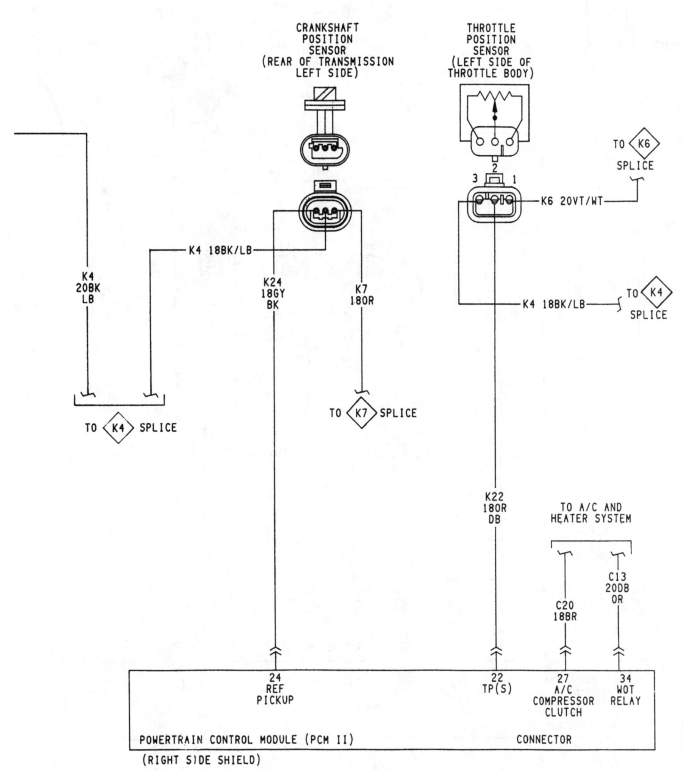

Typical V6 and V8 engine fuel injection wiring diagram – models with Multi-Port Injection (MPI) (4 of 6)

12

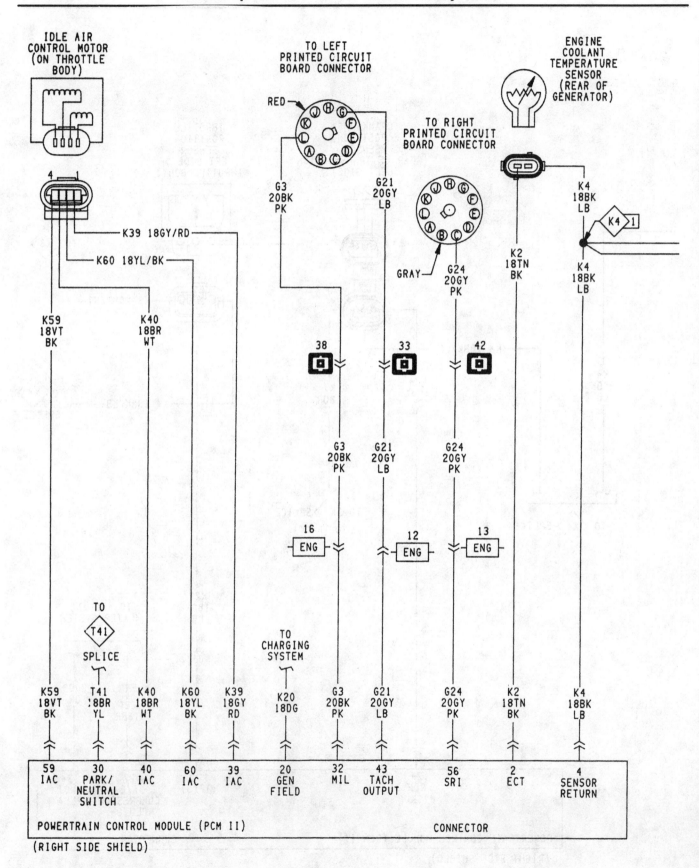

Typical V6 and V8 engine fuel injection wiring diagram – models with Multi-Port Injection (MPI) (5 of 6)

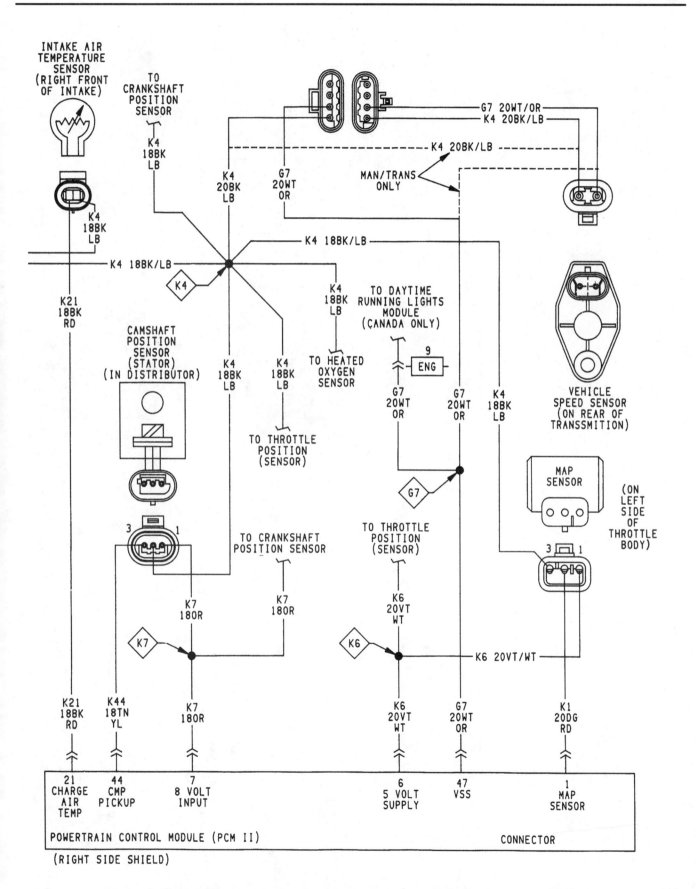

Typical V6 and V8 engine fuel injection wiring diagram – models with Multi-Port Injection (MPI) (6 of 6)

Index

HAYNES AUTOMOTIVE MANUALS

NOTE: New manuals are added to this list on a periodic basis. If you do not see a listing for your vehicle, consult your local Haynes dealer for the latest product information.

ACURA
1776	**Integra & Legend** '86 thru '90

AMC
	Jeep CJ – see JEEP (412)
694	**Mid-size models,** Concord, Hornet, Gremlin & Spirit '70 thru '83
934	**(Renault) Alliance & Encore** all models '83 thru '87

AUDI
615	**4000** all models '80 thru '87
428	**5000** all models '77 thru '83
1117	**5000** all models '84 thru '88

AUSTIN
	Healey Sprite – see MG Midget Roadster (265)

BMW
276	**320i** all 4 cyl models '75 thru '83
632	**528i & 530i** all models '75 thru '80
240	**1500 thru 2002** all models except Turbo '59 thru '77
348	**2500, 2800, 3.0 & Bavaria** '69 thru '76

BUICK
	Century (front wheel drive) – see GENERAL MOTORS A-Cars (829)
*1627	**Buick, Oldsmobile & Pontiac Full-size (Front wheel drive)** all models '85 thru '93 **Buick** Electra, LeSabre and Park Avenue; **Oldsmobile** Delta 88 Royale, Ninety Eight and Regency; **Pontiac** Bonneville
*1551	**Buick Oldsmobile & Pontiac Full-size (Rear wheel drive) Buick** Electra '70 thru '84, Estate '70 thru '90, LeSabre '70 thru '79 **Oldsmobile** Custom Cruiser '70 thru '90, Delta 88 '70 thru '85, Ninety-eight '70 thru '84 **Pontiac** Bonneville '70 thru '81, Catalina '70 thru '81, Grandville '70 thru '75, Parisienne '84 thru '86
627	**Mid-size** all rear-drive **Regal & Century** models with V6, V8 and Turbo '74 thru '87
	Regal – see GENERAL MOTORS (1671)
	Skyhawk – see GENERAL MOTORS J-Cars (766)
552	**Skylark** all X-car models '80 thru '85

CADILLAC
*751	**Cadillac Rear Wheel Drive** all gasoline models '70 thru '90
	Cimarron – see GENERAL MOTORS J-Cars (766)

CAPRI
296	**2000 MK I Coupe** all models '71 thru '75
205	**2600 & 2800 V6 Coupe** '71 thru '75
375	**2800 Mk II V6 Coupe** '75 thru '78
	Mercury Capri – see FORD Mustang (654)

CHEVROLET
*1477	**Astro & GMC Safari Mini-vans** all models '85 thru '91
554	**Camaro** V8 all models '70 thru '81
*866	**Camaro** all models '82 thru '91
	Cavalier – see GENERAL MOTORS J-Cars (766)
	Celebrity – see GENERAL MOTORS A-Cars (829)
625	**Chevelle, Malibu & El Camino** all V6 & V8 models '69 thru '87
449	**Chevette & Pontiac T1000** all models '76 thru '87
550	**Citation** all models '80 thru '85
*1628	**Corsica/Beretta** all models '87 thru '92
274	**Corvette** all V8 models '68 thru '82
*1336	**Corvette** all models '84 thru '91

704	**Full-size Sedans** Caprice, Impala, Biscayne, Bel Air & Wagons, all V6 & V8 models '69 thru '90
	Lumina – see GENERAL MOTORS (1671)
	Lumina APV – see GENERAL MOTORS (2035)
319	**Luv Pick-up** all 2WD & 4WD models '72 thru '82
626	**Monte Carlo** all V6, V8 & Turbo models '70 thru '88
241	**Nova** all V8 models '69 thru '79
*1642	**Nova and Geo Prizm** all front wheel drive models, '85 thru '90
*420	**Pick-ups '67 thru '87 – Chevrolet & GMC,** all full-size models '67 thru '87; Suburban, Blazer & Jimmy '67 thru '91
*1664	**Pick-ups '88 thru '92 – Chevrolet & GMC,** all full-size (C and K) models, '88 thru '92
*1727	**Sprint & Geo Metro** '85 thru '91
*831	**S-10 & GMC S-15 Pick-ups** all models '82 thru '92
*345	**Vans – Chevrolet & GMC,** V8 & in-line 6 cyl models '68 thru '92

CHRYSLER
*1337	**Chrysler & Plymouth Mid-size** front wheel drive '82 thru '93
	K-Cars – see DODGE Aries (723)
	Laser – see DODGE Daytona (1140)

DATSUN
402	**200SX** all models '77 thru '79
647	**200SX** all models '80 thru '83
228	**B-210** all models '73 thru '78
525	**210** all models '78 thru '82
206	**240Z, 260Z & 280Z** Coupe & 2+2 '70 thru '78
563	**280ZX** Coupe & 2+2 '79 thru '83
	300ZX – see NISSAN (1137)
679	**310** all models '78 thru '82
123	**510 & PL521 Pick-up** '68 thru '73
430	**510** all models '78 thru '81
372	**610** all models '72 thru '76
277	**620 Series Pick-up** all models '73 thru '79
	720 Series Pick-up – see NISSAN Pick-ups (771)
376	**810/Maxima** all gasoline models '77 thru '84
124	**1200** all models '70 thru '73
368	**F10** all models '76 thru '79
	Pulsar – see NISSAN (876)
	Sentra – see NISSAN (982)
	Stanza – see NISSAN (981)

DODGE
*723	**Aries & Plymouth Reliant** all models '81 thru '89
*1231	**Caravan & Plymouth Voyager Mini-Vans** all models '84 thru '91
699	**Challenger & Plymouth Saporro** all models '78 thru '83
236	**Colt** all models '71 thru '77
610	**Colt & Plymouth Champ (front wheel drive)** all models '78 thru '87
*556	**D50/Ram 50/Plymouth Arrow Pick-ups & Raider** '79 thru '91
*1668	**Dakota Pick-up** all models '87 thru '90
234	**Dart & Plymouth Valiant** all 6 cyl models '67 thru '76
*1140	**Daytona & Chrysler Laser** all models '84 thru '89
*545	**Omni & Plymouth Horizon** all models '78 thru '90
*912	**Pick-ups** all full-size models '74 thru '91
*1726	**Shadow & Plymouth Sundance** '87 thru '91
*1779	**Spirit & Plymouth Acclaim** '89 thru '92
*349	**Vans – Dodge & Plymouth** V8 & 6 cyl models '71 thru '91

FIAT
094	**124 Sport Coupe & Spider** '68 thru '78

479	**Strada** all models '79 thru '82
273	**X1/9** all models '74 thru '80

FORD
*1476	**Aerostar Mini-vans** all models '86 thru '92
788	**Bronco and Pick-ups** '73 thru '79
*880	**Bronco and Pick-ups** '80 thru '91
268	**Courier Pick-up** all models '72 thru '82
789	**Escort & Mercury Lynx** all models '81 thru '90
*2046	**Escort & Mercury Tracer** all models '91 thru '93
*2021	**Explorer & Mazda Navajo** '91 thru '92
560	**Fairmont & Mercury Zephyr** all in-line & V8 models '78 thru '83
334	**Fiesta** all models '77 thru '80
754	**Ford & Mercury Full-size,** Ford LTD & Mercury Marquis ('75 thru '82); Ford Custom 500, Country Squire, Crown Victoria & Mercury Colony Park ('75 thru '87); Ford LTD Crown Victoria & Mercury Gran Marquis ('83 thru '87)
359	**Granada & Mercury Monarch** all in-line, 6 cyl & V8 models '75 thru '80
773	**Ford & Mercury Mid-size,** Ford Thunderbird & Mercury Cougar ('75 thru '82); Ford LTD & Mercury Marquis ('83 thru '86); Ford Torino, Gran Torino, Elite, Ranchero pick-up, LTD II, Mercury Montego, Comet, XR-7 & Lincoln Versailles ('75 thru '86)
*654	**Mustang & Mercury Capri** all models including Turbo '79 thru '92
357	**Mustang V8** all models '64-1/2 thru '73
231	**Mustang II** all 4 cyl, V6 & V8 models '74 thru '78
649	**Pinto & Mercury Bobcat** all models '75 thru '80
*1670	**Probe** all models '89 thru '92
*1026	**Ranger & Bronco II** all gasoline models '83 thru '92
*1421	**Taurus & Mercury Sable** '86 thru '92
*1418	**Tempo & Mercury Topaz** all gasoline models '84 thru '91
1338	**Thunderbird & Mercury Cougar/XR7** '83 thru '88
*1725	**Thunderbird & Mercury Cougar** '89 and '90
*344	**Vans** all V8 Econoline models '69 thru '91

GENERAL MOTORS
*829	**A-Cars** – Chevrolet Celebrity, Buick Century, Pontiac 6000 & Oldsmobile Cutlass Ciera all models '82 thru '90
*766	**J-Cars** – Chevrolet Cavalier, Pontiac J-2000, Oldsmobile Firenza, Buick Skyhawk & Cadillac Cimarron all models '82 thru '92
*1420	**N-Cars** – Buick Somerset '85 thru '87; Pontiac Grand Am and Oldsmobile Calais '85 thru '91; Buick Skylark '86 thru '91
*1671	**GM: Buick Regal, Chevrolet Lumina, Oldsmobile Cutlass Supreme, Pontiac** Grand Prix, all front wheel drive models '88 thru '90
*2035	**GM: Chevrolet Lumina APV, Oldsmobile Silhouette, Pontiac Trans Sport** '90 thru '92

GEO
	Metro – see CHEVROLET Sprint (1727)
	Prizm – see CHEVROLET Nova (1642)
	Tracker – see SUZUKI Samurai (1626)

GMC
	Safari – see CHEVROLET ASTRO (1477)
	Vans & Pick-ups – see CHEVROLET (420, 831, 345, 1664)

(continued on next page)

---

* Listings shown with an asterisk (*) indicate model coverage as of this printing. These titles will be periodically updated to include later model years – consult your Haynes dealer for more information.

Haynes North America, Inc., 861 Lawrence Drive, Newbury Park, CA 91320 • (805) 498-6703

HAYNES AUTOMOTIVE MANUALS

(continued from previous page)

NOTE: New manuals are added to this list on a periodic basis. If you do not see a listing for your vehicle, consult your local Haynes dealer for the latest product information.

HONDA
- 351 **Accord CVCC** all models '76 thru '83
- *1221 **Accord** all models '84 thru '89
- 160 **Civic 1200** all models '73 thru '79
- 633 **Civic 1300 & 1500 CVCC** all models '80 thru '83
- 297 **Civic 1500 CVCC** all models '75 thru '79
- *1227 **Civic** all models '84 thru '91
- *601 **Prelude CVCC** all models '79 thru '89

HYUNDAI
- *1552 **Excel** all models '86 thru '91

ISUZU
- *1641 **Trooper & Pick-up**, all gasoline models '81 thru '91

JAGUAR
- *242 **XJ6** all 6 cyl models '68 thru '86
- *478 **XJ12 & XJS** all 12 cyl models '72 thru '85

JEEP
- *1553 **Cherokee, Comanche & Wagoneer Limited** all models '84 thru '91
- 412 **CJ** all models '49 thru '86
- *1777 **Wrangler** all models '87 thru '92

LADA
- *413 **1200, 1300, 1500 & 1600** all models including Riva '74 thru '86

MAZDA
- 648 **626 Sedan & Coupe (rear wheel drive)** all models '79 thru '82
- 1082 **626 & MX-6 (front wheel drive)** all models '83 thru '92
- 370 **GLC Hatchback (rear wheel drive)** all models '77 thru '83
- 757 **GLC (front wheel drive)** all models '81 thru '86
- *2047 **MPV** '89 thru '93
- **Navajo** – see FORD Explorer (2021)
- *267 **Pick-ups** '72 thru '92
- 460 **RX-7** all models '79 thru '85
- *1419 **RX-7** all models '86 thru '91

MERCEDES-BENZ
- *1643 **190 Series** all four-cylinder gasoline models, '84 thru '88
- 346 **230, 250 & 280 Sedan, Coupe & Roadster** all 6 cyl sohc models '68 thru '72
- 983 **280 123 Series** all gasoline models '77 thru '81
- 698 **350 & 450 Sedan, Coupe & Roadster** all models '71 thru '80
- 697 **Diesel 123 Series** 200D, 220D, 240D, 240TD, 300D, 300CD, 300TD, 4- & 5-cyl incl. Turbo '76 thru '85

MERCURY
For all PLYMOUTH titles see FORD Listing

MG
- 111 **MGB** Roadster & GT Coupe all models '62 thru '80
- 265 **MG Midget & Austin Healey Sprite** Roadster '58 thru '80

MITSUBISHI
- *1669 **Cordia, Tredia, Galant, Precis & Mirage** '83 thru '90
- *2022 **Pick-ups & Montero** '83 thru '91

MORRIS
- 074 **(Austin) Marina 1.8** all models '71 thru '80
- 024 **Minor 1000** sedan & wagon '56 thru '71

NISSAN
- 1137 **300ZX** all Turbo & non-Turbo models '84 thru '89

- *1341 **Maxima** all models '85 thru '91
- *771 **Pick-ups/Pathfinder** gas models '80 thru '91
- *876 **Pulsar** all models '83 thru '86
- *982 **Sentra** all models '82 thru '90
- *981 **Stanza** all models '82 thru '90

OLDSMOBILE
- **Custom Cruiser** – see BUICK Full-size (1551)
- 658 **Cutlass** all standard gasoline V6 & V8 models '74 thru '88
- **Cutlass Ciera** – see GENERAL MOTORS A-Cars (829)
- **Cutlass Supreme** – see GENERAL MOTORS (1671)
- **Firenza** – see GENERAL MOTORS J-Cars (766)
- **Ninety-eight** – see BUICK Full-size (1551)
- **Omega** – see PONTIAC Phoenix & Omega (551)
- **Silhouette** – see GENERAL MOTORS (2035)

PEUGEOT
- 663 **504** all diesel models '74 thru '83

PLYMOUTH
For all PLYMOUTH titles, see DODGE listing.

PONTIAC
- **T1000** – see CHEVROLET Chevette (449)
- **J-2000** – see GENERAL MOTORS J-Cars (766)
- **6000** – see GENERAL MOTORS A-Cars (829)
- 1232 **Fiero** all models '84 thru '88
- 555 **Firebird** all V8 models except Turbo '70 thru '81
- *867 **Firebird** all models '82 thru '91
- **Full-size Rear Wheel Drive** – see Buick, Oldsmobile, Pontiac Full-size (1551)
- **Grand Prix** – see GENERAL MOTORS (1671)
- 551 **Phoenix & Oldsmobile Omega** all X-car models '80 thru '84
- **Trans Sport** – see GENERAL MOTORS (2035)

PORSCHE
- *264 **911** all Coupe & Targa models except Turbo & Carrera 4 '65 thru '89
- 239 **914** all 4 cyl models '69 thru '76
- 397 **924** all models including Turbo '76 thru '82
- *1027 **944** all models including Turbo '83 thru '89

RENAULT
- 141 **5 Le Car** all models '76 thru '83
- 079 **8 & 10** all models with 58.4 cu in engines '62 thru '72
- 097 **12 Saloon & Estate** all models 1289 cc engines '70 thru '80
- 768 **15 & 17** all models '73 thru '79
- 081 **16** all models 89.7 cu in & 95.5 cu in engines '65 thru '72
- **Alliance & Encore** – see AMC (934)

SAAB
- 247 **99** all models including Turbo '69 thru '80
- *980 **900** all models including Turbo '79 thru '88

SUBARU
- 237 **1100, 1300, 1400 & 1600** all models '71 thru '79
- *681 **1600 & 1800** 2WD & 4WD all models '80 thru '89

SUZUKI
- *1626 **Samurai/Sidekick and Geo Tracker** all models '86 thru '91

TOYOTA
- *1023 **Camry** all models '83 thru '91
- 150 **Carina Sedan** all models '71 thru '74
- *2038 **Celica Front Wheel Drive** '86 thru '92
- 935 **Celica Rear Wheel Drive** '71 thru '85
- *1139 **Celica Supra** '79 thru '92
- 361 **Corolla** all models '75 thru '79
- 961 **Corolla** all models (rear wheel drive) '80 thru '87
- *1025 **Corolla** all models (front wheel drive) '84 thru '91
- *636 **Corolla Tercel** all models '80 thru '82
- 230 **Corona & MK II** all 4 cyl sohc models '69 thru '74
- 360 **Corona** all models '74 thru '82
- *532 **Cressida** all models '78 thru '82
- 313 **Land Cruiser** all models '68 thru '82
- 200 **MK II** all 6 cyl models '72 thru '76
- *1339 **MR2** all models '85 thru '87
- 304 **Pick-up** all models '69 thru '78
- *656 **Pick-up** all models '79 thru '92

TRIUMPH
- 112 **GT6 & Vitesse** all models '62 thru '74
- 113 **Spitfire** all models '62 thru '81
- 322 **TR7** all models '75 thru '81

VW
- 159 **Beetle & Karmann Ghia** all models '54 thru '79
- 238 **Dasher** all gasoline models '74 thru '81
- *884 **Rabbit, Jetta, Scirocco, & Pick-up** all gasoline models '74 thru '91 & **Convertible** '80 thru '91
- 451 **Rabbit, Jetta & Pick-up** all diesel models '77 thru '84
- 082 **Transporter 1600** all models '68 thru '79
- 226 **Transporter 1700, 1800 & 2000** all models '72 thru '79
- 084 **Type 3 1500 & 1600** all models '63 thru '73
- 1029 **Vanagon** all air-cooled models '80 thru '83

VOLVO
- 203 **120, 130 Series & 1800 Sports** '61 thru '73
- 129 **140 Series** all models '66 thru '74
- *270 **240 Series** all models '74 thru '90
- 400 **260 Series** all models '75 thru '82
- *1550 **740 & 760 Series** all models '82 thru '88

SPECIAL MANUALS
- 1479 **Automotive Body Repair & Painting Manual**
- 1654 **Automotive Electrical Manual**
- 1480 **Automotive Heating & Air Conditioning Manual**
- 1762 **Chevrolet Engine Overhaul Manual**
- 1736 **Diesel Engine Repair Manual**
- 1667 **Emission Control Manual**
- 1763 **Ford Engine Overhaul Manual**
- 482 **Fuel Injection Manual**
- 1666 **Small Engine Repair Manual**
- 299 **SU Carburetors** thru '88
- 393 **Weber Carburetors** thru '79
- 300 **Zenith/Stromberg CD Carburetors** thru '76

See your dealer for other available titles

Over 100 Haynes motorcycle manuals also available

1-93

---

* *Listings shown with an asterisk (*) indicate model coverage as of this printing. These titles will be periodically updated to include later model years – consult your Haynes dealer for more information.*

Haynes North America, Inc., 861 Lawrence Drive, Newbury Park, CA 91320 • (805) 498-6703